The Law of Ancient Athens

LAW AND SOCIETY IN THE ANCIENT WORLD

The study of law in ancient societies has a distinguished tradition in both Anglo-American and continental scholarship. Many of our fundamental ideas about ancient society were built on research into legal sources. These traditions continue to provide a foundation for newer approaches to law and society. More recent scholarship draws on a range of methodologies to analyze legal practices, including critical legal studies, sociology of law, economics, and literary criticism.

This series, distinguished by its emphasis on interdisciplinary approaches to law and society, seeks out innovative approaches to ancient legal studies that bring new perspectives to legal topics as well as to broader questions concerning the impact of law on commercial, political, and cultural practices in the ancient world.

The Law of Ancient Athens

DAVID D. PHILLIPS

The University of Michigan Press
Ann Arbor

Published in the United States of America by
The University of Michigan Press

2016 2015 2014 2013 4 3 2 1

A CIP catalog record for this book is available from the British Library.

Library of Congress Cataloging-in-Publication Data

Phillips, David D., 1971-
The law of ancient Athens / David D. Phillips.
pages cm. — (Law and society in the ancient world)
Includes bibliographical references and index.
ISBN 978-0-472-11887-8 (cloth : alk. paper) — ISBN 978-0-472-03591-5 (pbk. : alk. paper) — ISBN 978-0-472-02926-6 (e-book)
1. Law—Greece—Athens—History—To 1500. 2. Law, Greek.
I. Title.
KL4115.A75P45 2013
340.5'385—dc23

2013015598

Preface

The purpose of this book is to provide, in English translation, and for the widest possible readership, from specialists to those who come to the book with no knowledge of the subject, the principal literary and epigraphical sources that state, illustrate, and elucidate the substantive law (and, to a significant extent, the procedural law: on these terms, see below) of ancient Athens in the Archaic and Classical periods, from the first known historical Athenian trial (**1** [Trial and punishment of the Alcmaeonids for the killing of Cylon's partisans]), which occurred between 636 and 621 B.C., to the dissolution of Athenian democracy by the Macedonians in 322 B.C., with the addition of a few slightly later and particularly illustrative events. Designed to be essentially—but not completely—comprehensive, this is, to my knowledge, the first book of its type and scale to be published in English (I. Arnaoutoglou, *Ancient Greek Laws: A Sourcebook* [London and New York 1998], owing to its coverage of the ancient Greek world generally and to its more concise scale, is necessarily and intentionally quite selective as to Athenian material). As a glance at the table of contents will show, the present volume covers in considerable depth a wide range of laws and procedures, with the primary exception being what today would fall under the category of constitutional law: topics such as the selection, composition, and functions of the various political bodies and officials of the Athenian state are treated summarily in the Introduction but not in detail in the chapters that follow, except insofar as concerns jurisdiction over the legal procedures discussed therein. (The reader who is interested in the development and operation of the Athenian constitution per se is advised to begin his or her investigation with the pseudo-Aristotelian treatise titled *Constitution of the Athenians* [*Athênaiôn Politeia*, abbreviated *Ath. Pol.*: see the headnote and references under **1c** [Arist.] *Ath. Pol.* 1] and the modern scholarly works listed under **History of the Athenian Constitution** in the bibliography at the head of §1 of the Introduction [p. 1]).

Owing to the fragmentary state of the surviving evidence, our knowledge of Athenian law is far from complete (p. 17); this statement applies, in particular, to the ways in which the Athenians may have formally and systematically classified their laws. The laws written by Athens' first two lawgivers, Draco and Solon, were inscribed on numbered *axones* (see under **2** *IG* I[3] 104), but as these are long gone and the surviving sources offer only very partial (and often disputed) evidence of their contents (on very rare occasions a specific axon is cited: e.g., **2** *IG* I[3] 104; **358** Plut. *Solon* 19.4), it is impossible to reconstruct in any meaningful way the organizational principles employed by Draco (apart from the observation that homicide laws were inscribed on at least his first two *axones*) or by Solon (whose first axon contained, presumably among others, one law prohibiting the export of agricultural products other than olive oil [**322** Plut. *Solon* 24.1–2] and another regulating the grain allotment for widows and orphans [**123** Harpo. s.v. *sitos*]). Between 410 and 399 B.C.—almost two centuries after the legislation of Solon—the Athenians embarked upon a new and systematic codification of their laws (pp. 12, 13), which presumably proceeded according to some organizational logic, but again—and despite the fact that in the fourth century the state maintained an archive of laws, decrees, and other public records (p. 17)—our evidence is highly fragmentary and permits no general conclusion as to what official categorization of laws may have existed.

Questions of law, both specific and general, were topics of special interest for a number of Greek philosophers, including Plato, Aristotle, and Theophrastus, all active in Athens in the fourth century; but with regard to any systematization that may have applied to Athenian law as a whole, the value of the works authored by or associated with these philosophers is largely limited and conjectural. Plato and Theophrastus both composed treatises titled (*On*) *Laws*, but Plato's *Laws*, which records an imaginary conversation between a Cretan, a Spartan, and an Athenian who draft legislation for a new colony at Magnesia in Crete, is not a trustworthy source for Athenian law absent independent corroboration and is accordingly excluded here (as is, *a fortiori*, Plato's description of his own ideal state in the *Republic,* passages from which are cited on rare occasions as comparanda), while that of Theophrastus (**312** Theophr. *Laws* fr. 21.1 Szegedy-Maszak; see also, e.g., **29** Harpo. s.v. *hypophonia*), a comparative and apparently comprehensive study of the laws of the Greek city-states, survives in such fragmentary form that we cannot reliably tell to what degree it may have reflected or otherwise addressed the general organization of Athenian law. Aristotle, the student of Plato and teacher of Theophrastus, dealt with legal issues in a number of works including the *Rhetoric* (**47** Arist. *Rhet.* [selections]; **291** Arist. *Rhet.* 1373b38–1374a5, 1374a15–16), the *Nicomachean Ethics* (**343a** Arist. *EN* 1111a8–10), and the *Politics*, and supervised the publication of studies on the constitutions of 158 city-states, of which the sole (mostly) surviving representative is the *Ath. Pol.* (on the mode of presentation employed by the author of the *Ath. Pol.*, see the end of the next paragraph); with the exception of the *Ath. Pol.*, my inclusion of works from the Aristotelian corpus is extremely selective, since the same evidentiary principle that motivates my exclusion of Plato's *Laws* applies also to works of Aristotle such as the *Rhetoric*.

With virtually no authoritative Athenian structural principles to dictate ours, it is necessary in comprehensive books such as this one to impose a general and overarching principle of organization and focus. It is common practice to privilege, in some way and to some extent, one of two broad categories that derive from Roman law and characterize many modern legal systems, including that of the United States: substantive law (which defines what acts, committed with what state of mind and under what circumstances, are mandated, permitted, or prohibited) or procedural law (which defines how a person may or must go about asserting a right or redressing a wrong). That a formal distinction between substance and procedure is not Athenian is evident in the surviving Athenian laws themselves, which characteristically take the conditional form "if *x*, then *y*" and contain both substantive and procedural elements, often (but not always or completely) corresponding to *x* and *y* respectively (e.g., **2** *IG* I[3] 104; **35** Dem. 21.47; **64c** Aeschin. 1.28–30, 32; **176** [Dem.] 43.51; **330** [Dem.] 43.71; **361** Dem. 21.113; **373** Hyp. 4.7–8). (Observe, too, that the class of lawsuits known as *dikai emporikai* ["mercantile lawsuits": **§10.5**] and the laws that governed them [referred to as *emporikoi nomoi*, "mercantile laws": **171** [Dem.] 35.3–4] possessed distinctive features both substantive and procedural.) In the informal categorization of laws, to the extent that the distinction can be made, the Athenians appear generally to have been interested more in procedure than in substance. As is commonly observed, the preserved laws often devote more attention to the former than to the latter (the paradigmatic instance of this phenomenon is **35** Dem. 21.47, which regulates the offense of hubris without giving it a substantive definition), and in the second part of the *Ath. Pol.*, the author's regular practice is to list legal procedures under the magistrate(s) who introduce them before a court (e.g., **25** [Arist.] *Ath. Pol.* 57.2–4; **60** [Arist.] *Ath. Pol.* 59.3; **79** [Arist.] *Ath. Pol.* 59.5; **152** [Arist.] *Ath. Pol.* 56.6–7; **200** [Arist.] *Ath. Pol.* 58.3; **302** [Arist.] *Ath. Pol.* [selections]; **333** [Arist.] *Ath. Pol.* 59.2; cf., e.g., **59** Hyp. 1.12).

Yet the Athenians were equally capable of thinking about their laws in substantive terms: note especially the grouping of various procedures under the substantive rubric of theft (**288** Dem. 22.25–27, 69–73, at §§25–27) or of impiety (**349b** Dem. 22.27), and also, e.g., references to "the homicide laws" (**3e** Dem. 23.51; **5** Dem. 9.44; **22a** Dem. 21.43; cf. the survey of courts and procedures for homicide in **20** Dem. 23.65–80) and to "the laws concerning *epiklêroi*" (**164** Dem. 37.45–46). Moreover, the tendency of (some) laws to concentrate on procedure over substance is by no means universal (witness the detail afforded to substantive issues in, e.g., **373** Hyp. 4.7–8; **374** [Dem.] 46.26) and can be at least partly attributed to the fact that the Athenians possessed neither professional lawyers (p. 28) nor a true technical legal vocabulary (although the predominant significance of a given term might differ depending on its occurrence in a legal or other context; for example, *agôn*, the general word for "contest," in a legal context normally refers to a "trial" or "lawsuit," as opposed to, say, an athletic competition [p. 29; cf. pp. 28–32 generally], and the extent to which the concept of hubris has a common meaning across various genres—including law and oratory, tragedy, and philosophy—is a matter of scholarly debate). In many cases, Athenians evidently felt comfortable in assuming that the meaning of the words in laws was generally understood; and in all cases, according to the prevailing ethic of the Athenian democracy, the right to interpret the laws belonged to all adult male citizens equally, and when litigants' interpretations conflicted, the right to decide which interpretation prevailed belonged to the jury (pp. 26, 39). In general, too, the surviving speeches delivered in Athenian courts demonstrate clearly that litigants were at least as concerned with issues of substance as with issues of procedure.

Both potential approaches to the subject, the substantive and the procedural, carry their benefits and costs and are to some degree anachronistic and artificial. I have here chosen to organize the material along substantive lines, for three main reasons. First, teaching courses on Athenian law has convinced me that the substantive approach is more congenial to non-specialists. Second, in a significant number of cases we have a good understanding of the substantive matters at issue but cannot securely identify the legal procedure being used. Third, a substantive approach consistently and vividly illustrates a central and defining feature of the Athenian legal system; namely, the availability of a variety of procedures to redress a given wrongful act (p. 33). Those who prefer a procedural approach will, it is hoped, find that this book meets their needs as well, since the indices, along with the cross-references in the introductions and headnotes, permit reconstruction of the material according to legal procedure (*dikê phonou*, *graphê traumatos ek pronoias*, etc.).

The substantive organization of the book means that after the Introduction, procedure is subordinated to substance and addressed as relevant in the various chapters, rather than systematically. Most fundamentally, it must be observed that the Athenian legal system had no substantive or procedural distinction corresponding to the modern division between criminal and civil law; these terms, accordingly, do not figure in this book. However, privileging substance does involve to some degree the superimposition of alien categories on an Athenian system that did not so possess and/or formalize them. Sometimes substance and procedure coincide, as, for example, in chapter 1, devoted to the substantive category of homicide, which includes—but is not limited to—treatment of the *dikê phonou*, the dedicated private lawsuit for homicide; or in chapter 8, which treats under the substantive category of damage (*blabê*) a variety of acts that definitely or possibly were redressed by the dedicated private lawsuit for damage (the *dikê blabês*; note, however, that as one of the common uses of the *dikê blabês* was to redress breach of contract, there is also a considerable amount of relevant material in chapter 10). Often, though, an individual procedure applied to acts that crossed the substantive boundaries employed here. The indictment for hubris (*graphê hybreôs*), for example, is attested or reliably presumed in use to redress a variety of acts including aggravated battery (chapter 2) and a range of sexual offenses—itself an anachronistic category—including rape, seduction, and pandering (chapter 3). Similarly, the type of impeachment (*eisangelia*) that targeted major offenses against the Athenian state is attested in use not only against various forms of treason (chapter 12) but also against impiety (chapter 11), seduction (**§3.1**), violation of a statutory limit on prices for prostitutes (**§3.2**), and a fraudulent claim to citizenship (**390a** Hyp. 4.1–3, 14–20, 30–31, 39, at §3; cf. **§6.1**). The substantive categories themselves are not absolute; for example, while contracts are the subject of chapter 10, contracts concerning marriage and dowry are treated in chapter 5 (with additional material in chapters 6 and 7). While the divisions between categories and the resulting assignment of material to the various chapters are to some degree necessarily arbitrary, it is my belief that they are logical and comprehensible, and in some instances they correspond to procedural as well as substantive differences (to return to the example just given, treating marriage and dowry separately from other types of contract makes sense because—in addition to other aspects—the normal remedies for wrongful behavior differed: failure to abide by the terms of a dowry gave rise not to a *dikê blabês* but to a *dikê proikos* or a *dikê sitou*: see **§5.3.3**).

This book begins with an Introduction in two parts: a short history of Archaic and Classical Athens, with attention to the development of the Athenian constitution and of Athenian law (§1), and an overview of the sources for Athenian law and of the institutions and legal procedures of Athens during the age of the Attic orators, the period from the later fifth century to 322 B.C., which provides the overwhelming majority of our evidence (§2); each section is headed by a bibliography. Thereafter, I have ordered the chapters, each addressing one or more substantive topics and the procedures associated with them, so as to comprise a succession of areas of focus, from the person (chapters 1 through 4) to the family (chapters 5 through 7) to property and obligations (chapters 8 through 10) to the gods and the state (chapters 11 and 12). Again, this is not to say that the Athenians had, for example, formal categories of family or property law (although many, if not all, of the above designations would be comprehensible to an Athenian: note, e.g., the grouping of lawsuits for defamation, battery, wounding, and homicide in **33** Dem. 54.17–19; the inclusion of [at least] lawsuits for battery and hubris under the rubric of "persons" in **36** Isoc. 20.2; and the predominance and variety of matters affecting the family that fall under the competence of the eponymous archon in **152** [Arist.] *Ath. Pol.* 56.6–

7); nor should these areas be understood as corresponding to their modern equivalents. Moreover, the overlap between areas will be immediately evident, as with the law of succession upon death (chapter 7), in accordance with which the property of a decedent was normally, and in many instances mandatorily, conveyed to one or more members of his family; or with the offense of *hierosylia* ("temple-robbery"), which I have included in chapter 9 as a species of theft but could just as well have included in chapter 11 as a species of impiety.

Each chapter (in chapter 3, each section of the chapter) opens with its own introduction, headed by a bibliography. These bibliographies, along with those in the Introduction, as well as the references under the individual numbered texts that follow, are selective, and they exhibit in general an intentional—but not complete—Anglophone bias, on the presumption that all readers of this book can read English and some can read no other language. Relevant and important scholarship in other languages, as well as in English, can be found not only in the bibliographies of the cited works but also on the extraordinarily useful and comprehensive NOMOI website (NOMOI: Ancient Greek Law on the World Wide Web: http://www.sfu.ca/nomoi), maintained and updated twice annually by D. Mirhady, I. Arnaoutoglou, and M. J. Sundahl, who have also published a print version current to 2010 (M. Sundahl-D. Mirhady-I. Arnaoutoglou, *A New Working Bibliography of Ancient Greek Law [7th–4th Centuries B.C.]* [Athens 2011]). Each chapter introduction offers a summary analysis of the evidence for the topic of the chapter, with references to the relevant texts both within and outside the chapter. It must be noted at the outset that modern scholars of Athenian law can be just as contentious as ancient Athenian litigants, and a significant number of very important issues in Athenian law lack a modern interpretive consensus. Sometimes, but not always (the Athenians, for instance, did not worry about whether the word *dikastês* should be rendered "juror" or "judge" [p. 8] in a language that did not yet exist, nor, generally—and unfortunately for us—about which of the many laws they attributed to Solon were actually his work [p. 4]), ancient litigants and modern scholars argue over the same issues, although in necessarily different terms (e.g., What is the meaning of *pronoia* in the law of homicide [chapter 1] and of wounding [chapter 2]? Given the lack of a substantive legal definition, what constitutes hubris and distinguishes it from *aikeia* [chapter 2]? Do the relatives entitled to inherit from an intestate decedent end with first cousins once removed or with second cousins [chapter 7]?). I have accordingly endeavored, in the introductions and elsewhere, to alert readers to many of these scholarly debates, although the analysis presented in this book naturally inclines toward the interpretations that I favor.

After its introduction, each chapter contains a series of sequentially numbered texts in translation; some chapters are divided into sections as I have deemed advisable in order to aid in organization and comprehension of the material. Most of the texts are excerpts from speeches delivered in Athenian lawsuits and from the *Ath. Pol.*; others are excerpts from literary works of a variety of other genres or from surviving Athenian inscriptions on stone (see p. 17). I have selected and excerpted the texts with the aim of isolating and emphasizing the legal matters at issue, both substantive and procedural, and including evidence not only for the content of the laws but also for their interpretation and application (on the problems inherent in the sources, including the transmission and interpretation of laws, see §2 of the Introduction). All translations are mine; in preparing the translations and headnotes, I have consulted a number of excellent commentaries and translations—including, in particular, those listed among the references—to which my debt will be obvious. Translation is by its very nature an act of interpretation, and in this book, as commonly, Athenian legal terms tend to be translated by Anglophone ones (e.g., "indictment" for *graphê* [e.g., p. 30]; "impeachment" for *eisangelia* [see especially the introduction to chapter 12]). It may be obvious but should nonetheless be stressed that such translations do not imply anything resembling an exact correspondence between the meanings of the respective words; and it seems prudent at this point to offer the disclaimer that I do not assert expertise in any legal system other than that of ancient Athens, and I accordingly request the indulgence of experts in modern law to whom my usage may seem errant or otherwise wanting in a technicality that the Athenians did not themselves possess.

The heading for each text normally consists of its number, a full citation, a brief summary of its contents, and the relevant date(s). Where a text consists entirely of one or more directly stated or quoted laws, decrees, or oaths that are not themselves contained within a law or decree, the full citation is followed by the corresponding Latin word(s) in parentheses: *lex* ("law"), plural *leges*; *decretum* ("decree"), plural *decreta*; *iusiurandum* ("oath"), plural *iuraiuranda*. Where a text contains both one or more of the aforementioned items and statements by the author of the text in his own words, the notation "+ commentary" appears within the parentheses after the relevant Latin word(s). Significant doubt as to matters such as the accuracy of a quotation, the authenticity or ascription of a law or decree, the procedure employed in a given case, and the dates of texts and the included laws and decrees is indicated by a question mark, commonly prefixed to the relevant word(s) or date(s).

In order to compensate in part for the necessary decontextualization of the texts, I have made it standard practice to preface each text with selective references and with a headnote. The references normally include commentaries on and translations of the entire literary work or epigraphical document from which the text is excerpted; the headnotes contain introductory and explanatory material about the author, the source, and/or the passage, as well as comparanda for the matters at issue. It should be noted that the references do not systematically, or even usually, include the edition of a given text that I have translated. In general, my translations are based upon (one of) the prevailing critical edition(s) of the text in question. For the Attic orators and the *Ath. Pol.* in specific, these are the following: for Antiphon, M. Gagarin (Cambridge 1997); for Andocides 1 (*On the Mysteries*), D. M. MacDowell (Oxford 1962), and for other speeches of Andocides, the Budé edition of G. Dalmeyda (Paris 1930); for Lysias, the Oxford Classical Texts (OCT) edition of C. Carey (Oxford 2007); for Isocrates, the Teubner edition of B. G. Mandilaras (3 vols., Munich and Leipzig 2003); for Isaeus, W. Wyse (Cambridge 1904); for Demosthenes, the OCT of M. R. Dilts (4 vols., Oxford 2002–9); for Aeschines, the Teubner of M. R. Dilts (Stuttgart and Leipzig 1997); for Hypereides, the Teubner of C. Jensen (Leipzig 1917); for Lycurgus, the Teubner of N. C. Conomis (Leipzig 1970); for Deinarchus, the Teubner of N. C. Conomis (Leipzig 1975); and for the *Ath. Pol.*, the Teubner of M. Chambers (ed. corr., Stuttgart and Leipzig 1994).

The order of the texts within each chapter, or section of a chapter, is chronological, as far as can be determined, on the basis of the date of composition of the source or the date of the law(s) or event(s) described in the source. Where these dates diverge significantly, I have made a judgment call as to which date to employ in placing the text. The same chronological principle applies to the order of references in the chapter bibliographies and under the individual texts, which are cited in the order of their dates of publication. Where the references are divided into groups (as regularly in the bibliographies in the format "**Handbooks:** . . . **Studies:** . . . ," and occasionally elsewhere in the format "See especially . . . ; also . . ."), the order within each group is chronological.

In the translations, I employ the following conventions:

Square brackets [ ] enclose (1) numbers corresponding to editorial divisions of a literary text—including, as applicable, book, chapter, section, and line—or to lines of an inscription; and (2) explanatory material, including transliterated Greek words and phrases that are of especial importance and/or disputed meaning, as well as supplementary words included in a translation for the sake of clarity (an exception being phrases such as "the deme" and "the tribe," which I have regularly prefixed to the relevant proper names without using square brackets). Square brackets surrounding the name of an author in a citation indicate a spurious work: see p. 21. With regard to transliteration, I employ a more traditional—frequently Latinate—and less strict method for the names of persons, cities, demes, and the like, which are rendered in regular font; so, for example, Andocides, not Andokides (or Andokidês); Isaeus, not Isaios; Draco, not Drakon (or Drakôn); Athens, not Athenai (or Athênai); Paeania, not Paiania. I transliterate the Greek diphthong epsilon-iota as -ei-, not -i-; so, for example, Deinarchus, not Dinarchus (but I follow general scholarly practice in using the abbreviation "Din." in citations). For other words, which are rendered in italics, I transliterate more strictly; for example, *hybris* (translated, however, as "hubris"); *ephetai*, not ephetae; *dikê* and *graphê* rather than *dike* and *graphe* (*e* and *o* stand for epsilon and omicron; *ê* and *ô* for eta and omega). Readers who do not know ancient Greek should be aware that it is a highly inflected language. So, for example, the noun *dikê* ("lawsuit," among other meanings: p. 29) appears in a variety of grammatical cases (nominative *dikê*, genitive *dikês*, dative *dikêi*, accusative *dikên*; in the plural, *dikai*, *dikôn*, *dikais*, *dikas*, respectively) depending on its use in a phrase or sentence; the typical Greek verb, inflected for grammatical person, number, tense, mood, and voice, has hundreds of forms.

Angled brackets < > enclose editorial insertions, hooked brackets { } enclose editorial deletions of spurious content, and daggers † † enclose content that is clearly corrupt and defies emendation. These three notations are employed sparingly; in general, they appear only where (1) there is no editorial consensus and (2) the textual or editorial variants affect a matter of law discussed in the text. The same conditions apply to the indication of the adoption of variant manuscript readings.

Those instances in which an ellipsis (. . .) in the translation corresponds to a lacuna in the text are indicated as such in the headnotes.

Citations of ancient texts are done in accordance with standard scholarly conventions. In the cross-references that occur throughout the book (e.g., **20** Dem. 23.65–80), the names of authors and works are usually abbreviated as in H. G. Liddell-R. Scott, *A Greek-English Lexicon*, ed. 9 rev. H. S. Jones with the assistance of R. MacKenzie, with revised supplement (Oxford 1996), and/or S. Hornblower-A. Spawforth, eds., *The Oxford Classical Dictionary*, ed. 3 (Oxford 1996). Where I diverge, I have normally done so for the sake of greater clarity; for example, in order to spare nonspecialist readers some confusion, I cite the plays of Aristophanes by English rather than Latin titles; so "Ar. *Wasps*" rather than "Ar. *Vesp.*" The Attic orators, in particular, are cited by author, speech number (standardized for every orator except Hypereides, for whom, although I translate Jensen's text, I adhere to the Anglophone norm of using the speech numbers in F. G. Kenyon, *Hyperidis orationes et fragmenta* [Oxford 1906]), and section number(s); in full citations at the heads of the texts (e.g., **20. Demosthenes 23 *Against Aristocrates* 65–80**), the title of the speech appears after the speech number and before the section number(s). For fragmentary speeches (and other fragmentary literary works), editorial numbering varies, so the citation normally includes the fragment number and corresponding edition; for example, **37. Lysias fr. 178 Carey *Against Isocrates*** (= ***Suda* s.v. *hybris***). (In most cases, the abbreviations "fr." for a single fragment and "frr." for multiple fragments are employed, but for the fragments of historians collected in F. Jacoby, *Die Fragmente der griechischen Historiker* [Leiden 1957–], the standard abbreviation is "F" [plural "FF"].)

Readers who are beginning their study of Athenian law are advised to complement the present volume with an expository comprehensive introduction to

Athenian law (such as D. M. MacDowell, *The Law in Classical Athens* [Ithaca, NY 1978], or S. C. Todd, *The Shape of Athenian Law* [Oxford 1993]; also useful is M. Gagarin-D. Cohen, eds., *The Cambridge Companion to Ancient Greek Law* [Cambridge 2005]; J. H. Lipsius, *Das attische Recht und Rechtsverfahren* [Leipzig 1905–15, repr. Hildesheim 1984] and A. R. W. Harrison, *The Law of Athens* [Oxford 1968–71, repr. Indianapolis 1998], while less congenial to the non-specialist, remain indispensable on matters of detail) and with a collection of legal speeches presented in their (preserved) entirety that covers a range of offenses and procedures (good options include C. Carey, *Trials from Classical Athens*, ed. 2 [London and New York 2012]; A. Wolpert-K. Kapparis, *Legal Speeches of Democratic Athens: Sources for Athenian History* [Indianapolis 2011]; and M. Gagarin, ed., *Speeches from Athenian Law* [Austin 2011], which presents selections from the comprehensive University of Texas Press series titled *The Oratory of Classical Greece* and comprising translations of all of the Attic orators).

~ ~ ~

I am pleased to record my gratitude to those colleagues who have offered useful commentary, advice, and support in the completion of this book. For their careful reading of and commentary upon the manuscript at various stages, I thank the anonymous readers for the Indiana University Press and the University of Michigan Press, the original and present homes of the Law and Society in the Ancient World series, respectively, and Werner Riess, a scholar of exemplary generosity, collegiality, and acumen. The insights provided by these readers have improved the book considerably; the responsibility for any remaining errors is mine. I am likewise grateful to the Executive Committee of the University of Michigan Press and to the series editors for agreeing to publish this book; to Ellen Bauerle, Senior Acquiring Editor for Classical Studies, for her consummate skill, professionalism, and patience; and to the members of the copyediting and production staff for seeing the book through to publication. Finally, I wish to thank for their encouragement and counsel Edwin Carawan, Darel Engen, Bruce Frier, Adriaan Lanni, David Potter, and Rex and Melissa Stem, as well as my parents, James and Jane Phillips, and my grandmother, Bernice Bauman.

D. D. P.
Los Angeles, California
June 2012

Contents

Introduction 1
§1. Archaic and Classical Athens: A Short History 1
§2. Athens in the Age of the Orators: Sources, Institutions, and Procedures 16

Chapter 1. Homicide 44

Chapter 2. Wounding, Battery, and Hubris 85
§2.1. *Trauma ek pronoias* (Intentional Wounding) 87
§2.2. *Aikeia* (Battery) and Hubris 91

Chapter 3. Sexual Offenses 102
§3.1. *Moicheia* (Seduction) and Rape 102
§3.2. Pandering and Prostitution 116

Chapter 4. Defamation 124

Chapter 5. Marriage and Dowry 137
§5.1. Formation of Marriage 141
§5.1.1. *Engyê* (Pledge) and *Ekdosis* (Delivery) 141
§5.1.2. Husband as *Kyrios* of Wife 146
§5.1.3. Bars to Marriage 148
§5.2. Termination of Marriage 151
§5.2.1. Death of Spouse 151
§5.2.2. Divorce 153
§5.3. *Proix* (Dowry) 157
§5.3.1. Payment and Contents 157
§5.3.2. Valuation and Security 163
§5.3.3. Maintenance (*Sitos*), Restitution, and Transfer 169

Chapter 6. Children and Citizenship 174
§6.1. Legitimacy and Citizenship 179
§6.2. Adoption 189
§6.3. Guardianship 194

§6.4. *Kakôsis* (Maltreatment) 205
§6.4.1. *Kakôsis goneôn* (Maltreatment of Parents) 207
§6.4.2. *Kakôsis orphanôn* (Maltreatment of Orphans) 211
§6.4.3. *Kakôsis epiklêrou* (Maltreatment of an *Epiklêros*) 214

Chapter 7. Estates and *Epiklêroi* 216
§7.1. Contents of Estate 222
§7.1.1. Assets 222
§7.1.2. Liability for Debts 224
§7.1.3. Obligations toward Decedent 228
§7.2. Intestate Succession 230
§7.2.1. Legitimate Sons and Their Descendants 230
§7.2.2. *Epiklêroi* and Their Descendants 232
§7.2.3. Collateral Relatives 243
§7.2.4. *Nothoi* (Illegitimate Children) 249
§7.2.5. Non-citizens 250
§7.3. Succession by Will 251
§7.3.1. Testamentary Adoption and *Epiklêroi* 252
§7.3.2. Testamentary Capacity 253
§7.3.3. Conditional Wills 256
§7.3.4. Forms of Will 257
§7.3.5. Modification and Revocation of Will 262
§7.4. Asserting a Claim 264
§7.4.1. Direct Claim (*Embateusis*, Entry) 264
§7.4.2. *Dikê exoulês* (For Ejectment) 266
§7.4.3. Claim for Adjudication (*Lêxis*) 267
§7.4.4. *Epidikasia/Diadikasia* (Adjudication) and *Diamartyria* (Declaration on Oath) 269
§7.4.5. *Episkêpsis* and *Dikê pseudomartyriôn* 276
§7.4.6. New *Diadikasia* 281

Chapter 8. Damage 286

Chapter 9. Theft 332

Chapter 10. Contracts and Commerce 370
§10.1. Contracts in General 376
§10.2. Sale 380
§10.3. Loan 383
§10.4. *Prasis epi lysei* (Sale on Condition of Release) 390
§10.5. Imports, Exports, Maritime Loans, and the *Dikai emporikai* (Mercantile Lawsuits) 397

Chapter 11. Impiety 407

§11.1. Sacred Olive Trees 412

§11.2. *Probolê* (Presentation) 415

§11.3. The Scandals of the Herms and the Mysteries (415) and the Trial of Andocides (400 or 399) 421

§11.4. The Trial of Socrates (399) 437

§11.5. Other Cases 444

Chapter 12. Treason, Subversion, Bribery, and *Apatê tou dêmou* (Deceiving the People) 463

Bibliography 509

Index Locorum 523

General Index 533

Introduction

1. Archaic and Classical Athens: A Short History

General: The standard multi-volume English-language scholarly survey of the history of the ancient Mediterranean and Near Eastern world is ***The Cambridge Ancient History***; the Archaic and Classical periods of Greek history are covered in vol. 3 pt. 3 ed. 2 (*The Expansion of the Greek World, Eighth to Sixth Centuries B.C.*, ed. J. **Boardman**-N.G.L. **Hammond**, Cambridge 1982); vol. 4 ed. 2 (*Persia, Greece and the Western Mediterranean c. 525–479 B.C.*, ed. J. **Boardman** et al., Cambridge 1988); vol. 5 ed. 2 (*The Fifth Century B.C.*, ed. D. M. **Lewis** et al., Cambridge 1992); vol. 6 ed. 2 (*The Fourth Century B.C.*, ed. D. M. **Lewis** et al., Cambridge 1994). Good introductions to Archaic and/or Classical Greece include J. B. **Bury**-R. **Meiggs**, *A History of Greece to the Death of Alexander the Great*[4] (New York 1975); R. **Sealey**, *A History of the Greek City-States ca. 700–338 B.C.* (Berkeley and Los Angeles 1976); J. V. A. **Fine**, *The Ancient Greeks: A Critical History* (Cambridge, MA 1983); J. M. **Hall**, *A History of the Archaic Greek World ca. 1200–479 BCE* (Malden, MA 2007); R. **Osborne**, *Greece in the Making, 1200–479 BC*[2] (London and New York 2009); P. J. **Rhodes**, *A History of the Classical Greek World 478–323 BC*[2] (Malden, MA 2010); S. **Hornblower**, *The Greek World 479–323 BC*[4] (London and New York 2011). **History of the Athenian Constitution:** C. **Hignett**, *A History of the Athenian Constitution to the End of the Fifth Century B.C.* (Oxford 1952); P. J. **Rhodes**, *The Athenian Boule* (Oxford 1972); M. **Ostwald**, *From Popular Sovereignty to the Sovereignty of Law: Law, Society, and Politics in Fifth-Century Athens* (Berkeley and Los Angeles 1986); T. C. **Loening**, *The Reconciliation Agreement of 403/402 B.C. in Athens: Its Content and Application* (Stuttgart 1987); R. W. **Wallace**, *The Areopagos Council, to 307 B.C.* (Baltimore 1989); M. H. **Hansen**, *The Athe-*

nian Assembly in the Age of Demosthenes (Oxford 1987); ***idem***, *The Athenian Democracy in the Age of Demosthenes* (Oxford 1991); P. J. **Rhodes**, *A Commentary on the Aristotelian* Athenaion Politeia (rev. ed. Oxford 1993); J. H. **Blok**-A. P. M. H. **Lardinois**, eds., *Solon of Athens: New Historical and Philological Approaches* (Leiden 2006). See also the bibliography at the head of the next section (p. 16).

Earliest Athens, to Draco

In the beginning, the city of Athens was ruled by kings. Probably before the end of the monarchy, and definitely by the seventh century, Athens had extended its sway over the entire surrounding region of Attica (an area of approximately 1,000 square miles or 2,600 square kilometers), which thenceforth comprised a single unified city-state (*polis*; plural *poleis*); while government was centered in Athens, all citizens, wherever in Attica they lived, called themselves Athenians. During the Archaic period (776–479 B.C.), most Greek *poleis* shed themselves of their traditional monarchies, and Athens was no exception. By 683/2, the Athenian monarchy had been replaced by an aristocracy headed by one or more chief magistrates called archons (for theories on the origin of the archons see [Aristotle], *Constitution of the Athenians* [*Ath. Pol.*] 3 with P. J. Rhodes, *A Commentary on the Aristotelian* Athenaion Politeia [rev. ed. Oxford 1993]); by the late seventh century (**1b** Thuc. 1.126.3–12), the board of archons had reached its canonical number of nine, and members of the board served annual terms. The nine archons were the archon (often called the "eponymous archon" because he gave his name to the year); the *basileus* ("king"), whose title and some of whose prerogatives survived from the earlier monarchy; the polemarch ("war-leader"), whose original function was to command the army; and six *thesmothetai* ("lawgivers"; singular *thesmothetês*), whose responsibilities were primarily judicial. Until the reforms of Solon (594/3, see below), only members of the hereditary aristocracy—known collectively as the Eupatrids—were eligible for the archonships; by Solon at the latest, the Council of the Areopagus (Athens' original council of government, which took its name from the hill next to the Acropolis where it met and which probably began as a council of noble advisors to the king) comprised all living former archons, who at the end of their archonships assumed life tenure on the Areopagus.

Two other characteristic phenomena of Archaic Greece were the rise of unconventional rulers called tyrants—the word did not originally have the negative connotation it does today—and the promulgation of written codes of law. Like traditional kings, tyrants were sole rulers, but unlike traditional kings, tyrants generally seized and exercised power in extralegal and/or supralegal ways. The first unquestionably historical event in Athenian history was a failed attempt at tyranny made by a nobleman named Cylon in 636, 632, 628, or 624 (**1** [Trial and punishment of the Alcmaeonids for the killing of Cylon's partisans]); the second was the appointment of Draco to draw up Athens' first written laws in 621/0 (**6a** [Arist.] *Ath. Pol.* 4.1). Most of Draco's laws were annulled by Solon less than thirty years later (**6b** [Arist.] *Ath. Pol.* 7.1) and so have left little to no trace in our sources (see, e.g., **266** Plut. *Solon* 17.1–3), but his homicide laws (see chapter 1, especially **2** *IG* I[3] 104; **3** Dem. 23 [selections]; **4** [Dem.] 43.57; **17** [Dem.] 47.67–73; **18** Dem. 20.157–58) remained in force down to the end of the Classical period.

Solon

In 594/3, facing severe civil strife caused by endemic debt, the Athenians appointed Solon as eponymous archon with extraordinary powers to revise the constitution and the laws ([Aristotle], *Constitution of the Athenians* [*Ath. Pol.*] 5–12; Plutarch, *Solon*). By his reform known as the *seisachtheia* ("Shaking-Off of Burdens"), Solon cancelled all debts, freeing debt-slaves and restoring to them unencumbered title to their lands, and banned the practice of contracting loans on the security of the person (**313** [Solon's *seisachtheia*]). Solon's chief constitutional reform transformed Athens from an aristocracy to a timocracy, a system in which political power was based not on birth but on wealth. He assigned all Athenians to one of four classes determined by their annual income (see **181** [Dem.] 43.54): the *pentakosiomedimnoi*, whose lands produced 500 or more standard measures (these were the medimnus, equivalent to about 1.5 bushels or 53 liters [**206** Isae. 10.9–10], for dry goods such as grain, and the *metrêtês*, equivalent to about 10 gallons or 38 liters, for liquid goods such as olive oil); the *hippeis*, whose lands produced at least 300 but less than 500 measures; the *zeugitai* (at least 200 but less than 300 measures); and the *thetes* (less than 200 measures). Eligibility for political office depended on class membership; only members of the two highest classes, for example, could serve as archons, and *thetes* were not permitted to hold office but were allowed to attend and vote in the Assembly, which now—if not before—consisted of all adult male Athenian citizens. (Solon is also said to have created a new Council of 400, with 100 members from each of Athens' four tribes, but this is almost certainly a fiction invented later on the basis of Cleisthenes' Council of 500 [p. 6].)

Solon abolished all Draco's laws except those governing homicide (**6b** [Arist.] *Ath. Pol.* 7.1) and wrote a new lawcode. He gave all Athenians the right to appeal a magistrate's decision to the Assembly (called, it appears, the (*h*)*êliaia* when it met in a judicial capacity: see, e.g., **3b** Dem. 23.28) and created a new class of lawsuits that any adult male citizen, not just the individual victim—or, in the case of homicide, his relatives—was permitted to prosecute (these lawsuits were known later, if not already under Solon's reform, as *graphai*: see §2, under ***Types of procedure***). Of especially enduring importance were Solon's law banning the export of agricultural products other than olive oil (**322** Plut. *Solon* 24.1–2) and his laws on inheritance (see chapter 7, especially **176** [Dem.] 43.51; **181** [Dem.] 43.54; **201** [Dem.] 46.14). Economic concerns also motivated Solon to modify the standard Athenian system of weights. The lowest common unit of weight was the obol (approximately .025 oz/.7 g); following Solon's revision (which lightened the drachma from 1/70 to 1/100 of a mina), the larger units were as follows:

6 obols (ob.) = 1 drachma (dr.) (approximately .15 oz/4.25 g)
100 dr. = 1 mina (mn.) (approximately 15 oz/425 g)
6,000 dr. = 60 mn. = 1 talent (tal. or T.) (approximately 57 lb/26 kg)

Later in the sixth century, when coinage was introduced by the tyrant Peisistratus or his sons (see below), these became units of coinage as well as weight, with obol and drachma coins struck in silver (where a law of Solon specifies a penalty in drachmas, the reference is to weighed silver: see, e.g., **68** Plut. *Solon* 21.1–2; **314** Lys. 10.18).

Athenians of the Classical period (479–323 B.C.) venerated Solon as their lawgiver *par excellence* (and even, inaccurately, as the founder of their democracy); because of this, and because after Solon developments in Athenian law regularly occurred by the addition of new laws rather than by the amendment or repeal of old ones, in the fifth and fourth centuries Athenians commonly referred to their body of laws as "the laws of (Draco and) Solon" (e.g., **12a** Andoc. 1.83–84). By a sort of legislative fiction, any law not governing homicide—which would be attributed to Draco—could be ascribed to Solon (even when the ascription was obviously incorrect: for example, Hypereides 3.22, where Solon is credited with the law of 403/2 that granted laws primacy over decrees [p. 13]); while many of Solon's laws doubtless remained in force down through the Classical period, they are in most cases difficult to identify with certainty (see, e.g., **35** Dem. 21.47; **68** Plut. *Solon* 21.1–2; **83** [Dem.] 46.18; **288** Dem. 22.25–27, 69–73).

The Peisistratid Tyranny

Despite Solon's sweeping reforms, serious civil strife continued, with factions based in different parts of Attica vying for supremacy. The eventual victor in this regional power struggle was Peisistratus, who established himself as Athens' first tyrant. After seizing control briefly in 561/0 and again in 556/5, each time only to be driven out by his enemies after no more than a few months in power, Peisistratus finally established his tyranny on a firm footing in 546/5 and held it until his death. Later Athenians (see Herodotus 1.59; Thucydides 6.54; [Aristotle], *Constitution of the Athenians* [*Ath. Pol.*] 16) remembered Peisistratus as a good tyrant who ruled Athens by and large according to the established laws (except the law that made tyranny a capital offense: **360** [Arist.] *Ath. Pol.* 16.10). Peisistratus made an innovation in the administration of justice by his creation of the deme dicasts (*dikastai kata dêmous*), a group of magistrates that toured Attica settling minor disputes. Under Peisistratus and his sons—the family is known as the Peisistratids—Athens prospered: regional strife was ended and Attica was, perhaps for the first time, truly and securely unified, and the Attic economy improved dramatically (abetted in part by the introduction of coinage: see above, ***Solon***). Upon Peisistratus' death in 528/7, power passed without incident to his sons Hippias and Hipparchus. But after Hipparchus was assassinated in 514 (see **78** Hyp. 2.3), Hippias began a reign of terror that lasted until 510, when he was deposed by a Spartan army acting in concert with the Athenian Alcmaeonid clan (see **1** [Trial and punishment of the Alcmaeonids for the killing of Cylon's partisans]) and other enemies of the Peisistratids.

Cleisthenes and the Birth of Democracy

The ouster of Hippias occasioned a struggle for supremacy in Athens, where two rival politicians, Isagoras and Cleisthenes, emerged as the main contenders. When Isagoras was elected eponymous archon for 508/7, Cleisthenes, an Alcmaeonid, countered by promising reforms that would benefit the common people. Isagoras and his ally, the Spartan king Cleomenes, responded by expelling from Athens Cleisthenes and 700 Alcmaeonid households, citing the curse that the Alcmaeonids had incurred in the slaughter of Cylon's partisans (**1** [Trial and punishment of the Alcmaeonids for the killing of Cylon's partisans]). Next, Cleomenes and Isagoras attempted to disband the Council of the Areopagus; the Athenians rose in resistance, ejected Isagoras and the Spartans, and recalled Cleisthenes and the rest of the Alcmaeonids.

Later in the year 508/7, Cleisthenes carried the reforms that created the world's first democracy. The Greek word, *dêmokratia*, means "rule by the *dêmos* (people)"; the word *dêmos* (among other meanings, including "deme": see below) henceforth denoted both the (sovereign) people and the democratic state they constituted—including, in particular, its manifestation in the Assembly (note, for example, the standard preface to decrees passed by the democracy, which began, "Resolved by the Council [of 500: see below] and the people [*tôi dêmôi*: i.e., the Assembly]": e.g., **2** *IG* I^3 104; and the offenses of "deceiving the people" and "subversion of the people" [*apatê tou dêmou* and *katalysis tou dêmou* respectively: see chapter 12]).

Cleisthenes' first major reform was the creation of a new system of tribes and demes. Up to this point, the Athenian citizen body had been divided into four hereditary tribes (see the introduction to chapter 1); these continued to exist but were supplanted for virtually all purposes by ten new tribes created by Cleisthenes and named after famous legendary Athenians (the "Eponymous Heroes": **169** [Dem.] 43.58). Cleisthenes organized his new tribal system on the basis of geography. He divided Attica into three regions—the city of Athens, the coast, and the interior—and into approximately 140 demes, of which some were traditional villages or towns and others were new creations. To each tribe were assigned one group of demes (called a *trittys*, "third") from the city, one from the coast, and one from the interior. A man's place of residence at the time of the reform determined his deme membership and thus his tribe membership; thenceforth, however, deme and tribe membership were hereditary, so that wherever an Athenian lived, he belonged to the deme and tribe assigned to his relevant ancestor in the male line in 508/7. Deme membership was a requirement for and proof of citizenship. At the age of eighteen, boys were presented to their fathers' demes and, if approved, would be entered on the deme rolls (the *lêxiarchikon grammateion*, "register of candidates eligible for allotment to office": e.g., **76** Dem. 57.30; **133** Isae. 12.9; **136** Isae. 7.13–17, 27–28, 30); for official purposes, the full name of an adult male citizen took the form "*X* son of *Y* of the deme *D*" (e.g., **254** Dem. 39.1, 5, 7–18).

The ten tribes, in turn, formed the basis of Cleisthenes' second major reform, the creation of a new organ of government called the Council of 500. This was an annual body to which each tribe contributed fifty men chosen by lot. Both the use of sortition (allotment) to fill political offices and the principle of equal representation of tribes were defining and pervasive elements of Athenian democracy. A tenth member, with the title "secretary of the *thesmothetai*," was added to the board of archons (who nonetheless continued to be referred to as "the nine archons": e.g., **329c** Lys. 7.16–17, 19, 22, 25–26), along with the requirement that one archon had to come from each tribe; and starting in 501/0, the Assembly elected ten generals each year, one from each tribe (the generalship was the primary exception to the use of sortition). The chief function of the Council of 500 was probouleutic ("deliberating in advance" of the Assembly): no motion could be brought before the Assembly without first being approved by the Council of 500.

Each tribal delegation of the Council of 500 held the prytany (*prytaneia*, "presidency") of the Council for one-tenth of the year, with the order of tribal prytanies determined by lot (see, e.g., **384** *SEG* 12.87). The members of the delegation holding the prytany were called the *prytaneis* (e.g., **375** Xen. *Hell.* 1.7.1–16, 20–26, 34–35), and on every day of their prytany, the *prytaneis* chose by lot from among themselves a chairman (*epistatês*). This official originally served as the presiding official of the delegation, the Council of 500 as a whole, and—if it met—the Assembly; in the early fourth century, the system was changed so that allotted *proedroi* ("presiders": **332b** Dem. 21.8–11) performed the last two functions. This conciliar calendar of ten prytanies henceforth operated simultaneously with the traditional Athenian calendar of twelve months, in which the new year began at the first new moon after the summer solstice and whose months were as follows (since the Athenian calendar was lunar and ours is solar, the equivalents are variable and approximate):

1. Hecatombaeon (approximately July)
2. Metageitnion (August)
3. Boedromion (September)
4. Pyanopsion (October)
5. Maemacterion (November)
6. Poseideon (December)
7. Gamelion (January)
8. Anthesterion (February)
9. Elaphebolion (March)
10. Munychion (April)
11. Thargelion (May)
12. Scirophorion (June)

An Athenian year thus spanned the second half of one year by modern reckoning and the first half of the next, and was named after its eponymous archon. For example, the year to which Athenians referred as "the archonship of Aristaechmus," when Draco enacted his laws (**6a** [Arist.] *Ath. Pol.* 4.1), corresponds to the second half of 621 B.C. and the first half of 620 B.C. and is accordingly designated 621/0 B.C. Because their calendar was lunar rather than solar, in order to keep the new year in its proper place and the months consistent with the seasons, the Athenians would occasionally intercalate (insert into the calendar) an extra month (**345** *IG* I^3 78).

The third major reform of Cleisthenes was the institution of ostracism (see, e.g., **367** [Banishment of Themistocles for treason]), which was presumably designed to safeguard the new democracy against powerful individuals who might attempt to install themselves as tyrants. Every year, in the sixth prytany, the question was put to the Assembly whether an ostracism should be held. If the motion passed by majority vote, a second Assembly meeting was held in the eighth prytany to determine who would be ostracized. Each voter received a postherd (*ostrakon*, whence the name of the procedure) and wrote a name on it. Provided that a quorum of 6,000 votes was cast, whoever received a plurality—not necessarily a majority—of the votes was banished from Attica for ten years.

The first Athenian to be ostracized was Hipparchus son of Charmus (**365** Lyc. 1.117–18), a member of the Peisistratid family, in 488/7; for most of the remainder of the 480s, ostracism was commonly used against prominent men with ties to the Peisistratids and/or to Persia (see ***The Fifth Century***). Thereafter, the Athenians employed ostracism sporadically against leading politicians until the 410s, after which the procedure remained in existence but was not used.

The Assembly's power to ostracize was an early indication of its growth, within fifty years of Cleisthenes' reforms, into the dominant body of the Athenian state. From at least the mid-fifth century, the Assembly met on the Pnyx hill, adjacent to the Acropolis and Areopagus; by the fourth century, there were four scheduled meetings per prytany, with extraordinary meetings convened in times of emergency. Any male citizen over the age of twenty could attend, speak (although, in practice, discussion was dominated by leading citizens called *rhêtores*—literally "speakers," singular *rhêtôr*; commonly translated "politicians": e.g., **373** Hyp. 4.7–8), and vote in the Assembly, whose decisions, normally determined by majority vote, set the policy of the state. Even before Cleisthenes, the Assembly had discharged important functions: in addition to its judicial capacity as the (*h*)*êliaia* (see ***Solon***), it had probably elected magistrates, declared war and made peace, and issued laws and decrees. In practice, however, the power of the pre-Cleisthenic Assembly was severely limited, since the archonships, and consequently membership in the Council of the Areopagus, were the exclusive prerogative first of the Eupatrids, and after Solon, of the *pentakosiomedimnoi* and *hippeis*, in whose ranks the old aristocracy remained heavily represented. Cleisthenes' assignment of probouleutic power to the new democratic Council of 500 presumably came at the expense of the Areopagus, and in 462/1, Ephialtes stripped the Areopagus of many of its remaining political and juridical powers, distributing them among the Assembly, the Council of 500, and the jury-courts (*dikastêria*: see below). Thenceforth, the Areopagus served primarily as a court of law, retaining jurisdiction over cases including the intentional homicide of an Athenian citizen (chapter 1), intentional wounding (chapter 2), and offenses concerning sacred olive trees (**§11.1**).

The powers of the archons had likewise undergone considerable reduction. Between Solon's grant of appeal of their decisions to the Assembly (p. 3) and the middle of the fifth century, the archons' role in judging lawsuits had been reduced to holding preliminary hearings, assigning cases to lawcourts, and formally presiding over—but not voting in—those courts (p. 33). Probably by 462/1, the date of Ephialtes' reforms, and definitely by the 450s, when Pericles introduced jury-pay (if this had not already occurred in the late 460s: see p. 27), the Assembly's judicial functions had in virtually all cases devolved upon the *dikastêria* ("jury-courts"; singular *dikastêrion*), which were manned by volunteer citizen jurors (*dikastai*; singular *dikastês*: some prefer the translation "judges" or Anglicization as "dicasts"; on the *dikastêria* see p. 26). In 487/6, the Athenians changed their method of selecting archons from election to *klêrôsis ek prokritôn* ("sortition from pre-chosen men"), a two-stage process in which a short list was chosen by election and then the archons were determined by lottery from the short list. The prestige of the archonships correspondingly decreased, and by the middle of the fifth century, when eligibility for the archonships was extended to the *zeugitai*, the most powerful and influential magistrates in Athens were not the nine—or, rather, ten—archons but the ten generals chosen by annual election in the Assembly.

The Fifth Century

The history of Athens in the fifth century is dominated by war, first with the Persian Empire and then with the Peloponnesian League led by Sparta. At the very beginning of the century, Athens had sent twenty warships to aid the Greek cities of Ionia, on the west coast of Asia Minor (modern Turkey), in their revolt against Persia. Although the Athenians withdrew their forces after less than a year, and the Ionian rebellion was crushed in 494, the attention of Darius I, king of Persia, had been irrevocably drawn to mainland Greece. Following abortive attempts at both armed force and diplomacy, in 490 Darius assembled an expeditionary army and sent it on a mission of revenge against Eretria—which had also provided aid to the Ionian Greeks—and Athens. In the short conflict known as the First Persian War, this army, probably about 20,000 men strong, swept through the Aegean, captured Eretria, then sailed south along the Euripus strait, landing in Attica at Marathon under the guidance of the deposed Athenian tyrant Hippias, who hoped to be restored to his former position. At the Battle of Marathon (August 490), the Athenian army in its entirety (numbering at most 10,000 men), joined by the men of the nearby Boeotian city of Plataea (numbering no more than 1,000), routed the Persians; at the end of the battle, 6,400 Persians lay dead, as against 192 Athenians. The majority of the Athenian survivors then hastened to Athens in order to prevent the landing of the Persian cavalry, which had left Marathon by ship during the previous night. Finding Athens unexpectedly defended, the Persian cavalry lay at anchor until the arrival of the ships bearing their compatriots who had escaped death at Marathon; then all sailed away, ending the invasion.

A decade later, Darius' successor, Xerxes, launched the Second Persian War (480–479), a full-scale invasion of Greece by an army of perhaps 200,000 men and over a thousand ships. The year 481 saw the creation of the Hellenic League, an alliance of Greek cities determined to resist Xerxes, which included Sparta and its allies in the Peloponnesian League, as well as Athens, which thanks to the efforts of Themistocles (see **367** [Banishment of Themistocles for treason]) had transformed its navy into the finest in Greece (and had commenced the fortification of its principal harbor at Peiraeus on the Attic coast) and accordingly provided the bulk of the Hellenic League's fleet. The first clashes between the Persians and Greeks occurred simultaneously on land at Thermopylae and on the sea at Artemisium (August 480); a costly victory at Thermopylae gave Xerxes a clear path into central Greece and necessitated the withdrawal of the Greek fleet from Artemisium, where it had fought the Persians to a draw.

The Hellenic League commanders now had to decide where to take their next stand. The cities of Boeotia medized (went over to the Persian side: for the term see, e.g., **344b** D. L. 2.12–14; **367a** Thuc. 1.135.2–136.1, 138.6), and Attica was evacuated by its inhabitants and overrun by Xerxes. Thanks to a stratagem of Themistocles, the Greek and Persian navies met in the straits of Salamis (September 480). The Battle of Salamis was an overwhelming Greek victory and resulted in a change in Persian strategy: Xerxes departed for Asia with the bulk of his fleet, leaving his general Mardonius in Greece with instructions to carry on the invasion by land alone. After wintering in Thessaly, Mardonius sent an offer of alliance to Athens; when that was rejected, he returned and reoccupied Attica, whose residents again evacuated just ahead of the Persian advance, relocating to Salamis in the spring of 479. Under pressure from the Athenians, who rejected renewed overtures from Mardonius (**366** [Killing of Lycides/Cyrsilus]), the Spartans and other members of the Hellenic League marched north, confronting Mardonius and his Persians at Plataea in Boeotia (August 479). At the Battle of Plataea, the Greeks routed the Persians; Mardonius was killed in action, and the remnants of his invasion force retreated north and left Greece.

Meanwhile, the fleet of the Hellenic League, headquartered at Delos, had received a request from the Ionian Greeks to liberate them from Persian rule. Proceeding to Mycale (on the Asia Minor coast opposite Samos), where Xerxes' fleet had beached its ships under the protection of a land army, the Greeks disembarked and crushed the Persians (August 479). From Mycale they moved north, freeing the Ionian cities, until they arrived at the Hellespont and discovered that the bridges built by Xerxes for his army's crossing into Europe had been destroyed by a storm. The Spartans and Peloponnesians, satisfied that the Persians could not easily invade Greece again, decided that their mission had been accomplished and sailed home; the Athenians, however, remained behind to besiege and capture the Persian-occupied city of Sestos on the European side of the Hellespont in the winter of 479/8.

For modern scholars, the siege of Sestos marks the transition between the Archaic (776–479 B.C.) and Classical (479–323 B.C.) periods of Greek history. This apparently minor divergence in policy between Athens and Sparta quickly grew more serious. Over Spartan objections, the Athenians rebuilt their city wall (which had been destroyed by the Persians) and completed the fortification of the Peiraeus; and in 478, the Ionian Greeks, chafing under the command of the Spartan Pausanias (**367** [Banishment of Themistocles for treason]), invited the Athenians to lead them. The result was the creation of the Delian League (478/7), led by Athens and with a membership that quickly spread so as to comprise most of the Aegean islands and the Greek cities in coastal Asia Minor, as well as those of the Hellespont, Propontis (Sea of Marmara), and Bosporus, some cities on the south coast of Thrace, and most of Euboea. Established with the express purpose of avenging the Persian invasion of 480/79, the Delian League—so called because its treasury was located on Delos before being moved to Athens in 454—quickly became an Athenian Empire, with mandatory tribute assessed and exacted by Athens, revolts suppressed by force of arms, and aggressive Athenian interference in the governments and jurisdictions of allied cities.

Meanwhile, relations between Athens and Sparta steadily worsened, until in 460 the Delian and Peloponnesian Leagues went to war. During this First Peloponnesian War (460–446), which failed to alter the status quo between the belligerents, Pericles became the unofficial first citizen of Athens, a position he would occupy until his death in 429. In addition to supervising a public building program that was funded by tribute from Athens' allies and included the Parthenon, a new temple to Athena Parthenos (the Virgin) on the Acropolis (**270** Philochorus, *FGrHist* 328 F 121), Pericles sponsored a number of reforms, including the introduction of payment for jurors in the *dikastêria* at the rate of 2 obols per day; the revival in 453/2 of the deme dicasts (now numbering thirty, presumably three from each Cleisthenic tribe), who had been instituted by Peisistratus but had been abolished in the intervening time; and a law of 451/0 restricting citizenship to the children of two citizen parents (**125** [Arist.] *Ath. Pol.* 26.4).

The Second or Great Peloponnesian War—usually called simply the Peloponnesian War—which broke out in 431 proved disastrous for Athens. The first stage of the conflict (the Archidamian War, 431–421) ended in a virtual stalemate with the signing of the Peace of Nicias (421), but that peace proved to be illusory. Urged on by Alcibiades (see, e.g., **334** Thuc. 6.27–29, 53, 60–61), the Athenians attempted a large-scale invasion of Sicily (415–413), which ended in utter disaster; in 413, open hostilities resumed with the Spartan occupation of Deceleia (**369** Lyc. 1.120–21), which ushered in the final phase of the conflict (the Deceleian War, 413–404).

Of particular importance for the development of Athenian law during this period was the Revolution of 411 and its aftermath. In 411, the oligarchy of the Four Hundred (see, e.g., **370** Lyc. 1.112–15; **371** [Plut.] *Lives of the Ten Orators* 833d–834b) seized power in Athens. The Four Hundred ruled for only a few months before being replaced by the more moderate oligarchy of the Five

Thousand—also known as the Intermediate Regime—but this proved almost equally short-lived, and after little more than a year of oligarchy, the democracy was restored in 410. The Athenians now confirmed and safeguarded their democratic constitution by enacting a decree proposed by Demophantus (**372** Andoc. 1.96–98), and, moreover, decreed a complete review of their body of laws, to be supervised by two boards of officials called *syngrapheis* (Compilers) and *anagrapheis* (Recorders) (**2** *IG* I³ 104; **277** Lys. 30.21, 23–25).

Although the renewed democracy won some important victories, particularly at Arginusae in 406 (**375** Xen. *Hell.* 1.7.1–16, 20–26, 34–35), the destruction of the Athenian navy the next year at Aegospotami proved to be decisive, and the threat of starvation forced Athens to capitulate in 404. As the price of peace, the Athenians were compelled to dismantle their fortifications, surrender their empire and the bulk of their remaining navy, and accept an alliance with Sparta on terms dictated by the Spartans. To ensure Athenian cooperation, the Spartans intimidated the Athenians into installing a new oligarchy headed by thirty men, known to posterity as the Thirty Tyrants. During their eight months in power in 404/3, the Thirty were unable to conduct a thorough revision of the constitution, but they did enact some legal reforms, including the annulment of the laws of Ephialtes—and the laws of Archestratus, which defy identification—concerning the Council of the Areopagus (p. 2), which theoretically returned to the Areopagus many of its lost powers; and the repeal or amendment of some of the laws of Solon, including the removal of invalidating conditions from Solon's testamentary law (**201** [Dem.] 46.14; **203** [Arist.] *Ath. Pol.* 35.2). In order to secure their position, the Thirty installed magistrates friendly to themselves, including a Council of 500 that the tyrants stacked with their supporters and employed as a court of law in order to remove real or presumed enemies of the regime; by the end of the oligarchy, some 1,500 Athenians had been executed and 5,000 more exiled.

The organization of resistance among pro-democratic exiles soon culminated in civil war between the supporters of the Thirty and the proponents of democracy, called "the men of the city" (i.e., Athens) and "the men of the Peiraeus" after their respective bases of operations. After the oligarchs were defeated at Munychia in the Peiraeus, they deposed the survivors among the Thirty and entrusted the government to a board of Ten; hostilities continued for a brief time thereafter, until Sparta brokered a peace settlement between the oligarchs and the democrats. The terms included oaths of reconciliation to be sworn by all Athenians (**12b** Andoc. 1.90–91); an amnesty, known as the Amnesty of 403, which indemnified all Athenians other than the Thirty and their chief subordinates for almost all acts committed under the oligarchy apart from homicide committed with one's own hand (**11** [Arist.] *Ath. Pol.* 39.5–6; **12** Andoc. 1 [selections]); and the separation from the Athenian state of the town of Eleusis in western Attica, to which any supporter of the late oligarchy was permitted to migrate—a disposition that would last until 401/0, when Athens reabsorbed Eleusis. For the second time in less than a decade, the democratic constitution was restored; this time it would remain in effect, with occasional modifications, until 322, when as the price for failed resistance in the Lamian War (p. 16) the Macedonians garrisoned Athens and installed an oligarchy.

The restoration of democracy in 403 ushered in a brief period of intensive legal reform. The codification of laws by the *syngrapheis* and *anagrapheis*, which had been interrupted by the Thirty, was now resumed, and would last until 400/399. A decree authored by Teisamenus and passed in 403/2 (**12a** Andoc. 1.83–84) reinstated the laws of Draco and Solon, annulling the changes that had been made by the Thirty, and created a new legislative procedure: henceforth new laws (*nomoi*) were to be drafted by a board of *nomothetai* (Lawgivers) chosen by the Council of 500, posted in public for inspection, and passed only after scrutiny by a second board of *nomothetai* consisting of 500 men chosen by the demes, and by the Council of 500 at a meeting where any Athenian citizen who so wished might participate (the decree does not specify whether, as before, ratification by the Assembly was required). Later in 403/2, after the passage of the Teisamenus decree, laws were enacted that prohibited the use of unwritten laws—thereby annulling any law that had not undergone and passed the review process instituted in 410 and revised by the Teisamenus decree—forbade the passage of an *ad hominem* law except by secret-ballot vote of the Assembly with a quorum of 6,000, confirmed the judgments of courts and arbitrators passed under the democracy, mandated the enforcement of both traditional and new laws from 403/2 on, and established the rule that a law (*nomos*) held primacy over a decree (*psêphisma*) of the Council of 500 and the Assembly (**338h** Andoc. 1.87). The important general result of this last provision, together with the rule about *ad hominem* laws, was that *nomos* ("law"; plural *nomoi*) and *psêphisma* ("decree"; plural *psêphismata*), which since the institution of democracy by Cleisthenes had referred more or less interchangeably to measures passed by the Council of 500 and the Assembly (laws of Draco and Solon were sometimes called by the older term *thesmoi*, singular *thesmos*: e.g., **3h** Dem. 23.62; **12a** Andoc. 1.83–84; **358** Plut. *Solon* 19.4), henceforth usually designated different types of enactment: a *nomos* (which now had to undergo the review process specified in the Teisamenus decree) was intended to be general and permanent, while a *psêphisma* (which remained contingent solely upon majority vote by the Council of 500 and then by the Assembly) was a response to a specific issue (although *psêphismata* could assume more permanent status, as with the decree of Demosthenes that created the legal procedure of *apophasis*: **391k** Din. 1.61–63). Laws and decrees that conflicted with existing laws or were otherwise deemed unacceptable could be challenged by dedicated procedures; namely, the *graphê paranomôn* (indictment for illegal proposals), which applied to both laws and decrees from at least 415 on, and the *graphê nomon mê epitêdeion theinai* (indictment for enacting an unsuitable law), which applied to laws alone and probably was created in or after 403/2 (e.g., **160** Dem. 24.103, 107; **333** [Arist.] *Ath. Pol.* 59.2; **375** Xen. *Hell.* 1.7.1–16, 20–26, 34–35; **390a** Hyp. 4.1–3, 14–20, 30–31, 39). Successful prosecution by one of these procedures, which were tried in a *dikastêrion* (p. 26), resulted in the annulment of the law or decree in question and in some cases (e.g., **390a** Hyp. 4.1–3, 14–20, 30–31, 39) punishment of the man who had proposed it.

The creation of two new legal procedures rounded out the spate of reforms. Between 403/2 and the end of the century, a law written by Archinus created the procedure called *paragraphê* (counter-indictment). The original purpose of *paragraphê* was to block prosecutions mounted in breach of the Amnesty of 403 (**244** Isoc. 18.1–8, 10–13, 33, 63); by the middle of the fourth century, the procedure was commonly used to block any allegedly illegal prosecution (e.g., **323** [Dem.] 35 [selections]; **324** [Dem.] 33.1–3, 23; **326** Dem. 32.1). In a *paragraphê*, tried before a *dikastêrion*, the roles of the prosecutor and defendant were reversed: the defendant in the original action became the prosecutor in the *paragraphê*, and vice versa. If the defendant-turned-prosecutor won the *paragraphê*, the original action was quashed; if he lost, the original action might proceed. Whoever lost the *paragraphê*—at least if he had garnered less than one-fifth of the jurors' votes, and possibly regardless of his margin of defeat (**244** Isoc. 18.1–8, 10–13, 33, 63; **323b** [Dem.] 35.45–46)—had to pay the *epôbelia*, a fine of one-sixth (one obol per drachma) of the sum at issue in the original lawsuit. In 399, shortly after the creation of the *paragraphê*, the number of deme dicasts was raised to forty (four per Cleisthenic tribe); these officials, henceforth commonly called the Forty, ceased to be traveling judges and were relocated to Athens, where they supervised all lawsuits involving mandatory public arbitration (see pp. 35–36).

The Fourth Century

The end of the Peloponnesian War opened a period of Spartan hegemony in Greece, which would last until 371 B.C. The Athenians, however, quickly rebounded from their defeat, and in 395 formed a coalition with Corinth, Thebes, and Argos and declared war on Sparta. The resulting Corinthian War (395–387/6) ended on terms dictated by the king of Persia, Artaxerxes II Mnemon, that confirmed Sparta's dominant position. On the strength of their rebuilt and battle-tested navy, in 378/7 the Athenians established a new league of allies, the Second Athenian Confederacy, with the purpose of defense against

Spartan encroachment, and with policy to be determined jointly by the Athenian Assembly and a congress of representatives from the allied cities. Victory at sea over the Spartans at the Battle of Naxos in 376 gave back to Athens the Aegean maritime supremacy that it had lost at the end of the Peloponnesian War, and in 371 the Spartan hegemony on land ended with the loss of the Battle of Leuctra to Thebes. The resulting Theban hegemony lasted less than a decade, dissolving after the Battle of Mantinea in 362.

The power vacuum thus left in Greece would soon be exploited by the rising power of Macedon. Soon after assuming the Macedonian throne in 359, King Philip II began a process of aggressive expansion. In 357, Philip reneged on an agreement with the Athenians and seized the Athenian-held city of Pydna on the Macedonian coast. Athens accordingly declared war on Macedon but was prevented from mounting effective resistance in the north due to the outbreak of a mass revolt of its allies in the Second Athenian Confederacy (the Social War, 357–355), which ended with the concession of autonomy to seventy-five rebel cities. Over the course of the Third Sacred War (355–346), Philip continued to expand his power and influence in northern and central Greece. By the end of the war, Philip controlled not only the Chalcidice (taken in 348 despite Athenian assistance to the Chalcidic League) but also Thessaly and Phocis.

In 346, just before the end of the Third Sacred War, Athens concluded a separate peace with Philip, known as the Peace of Philocrates after its lead Athenian negotiator. Fragile from the outset, the peace soon became a cold war. At Athens, objections to the terms of peace and accusations of bad faith by Philip and of treasonous conduct by the Athenian ambassadors flared up immediately; by 343, when Philocrates was impeached for treason (**390b** Hyp. 4.28–30), the anti-Macedonian faction at Athens, led by Demosthenes and Hypereides (see §2, under ***The Canon of the Attic Orators***), was in the ascendant, and the Athenians were actively soliciting allies for a new war with Macedon. Rising security concerns probably also lay behind the creation, by a decree of Demosthenes ca. 344/3, of a new legal procedure, *apophasis*, whereby the Council of the Areopagus was empowered to investigate and report potential threats to the state (**391k** Din. 1.61–63). (For the other important legal innovation of this period, the creation between 355 and 342 of the *dikai emporikai* [mercantile lawsuits], see chapter 10.) Athenian-Macedonian relations steadily deteriorated until 338, when at the Battle of Chaeroneia Philip and the Macedonians defeated a coalition of Greek cities led by Athens and Thebes. In the following year, Macedonian hegemony over Greece was cemented by the creation of the League of Corinth, a federal organization under the personal command of Philip and comprising virtually the entire Greek mainland and many of the Aegean islands, which promptly declared war on Persia.

The planned invasion of Persia was delayed by the assassination of Philip in

336. His son and successor, Alexander III (the Great), after quelling resistance in Greece and elsewhere occasioned by his father's death, landed in Asia Minor in 334 and commenced the series of conquests that by his death in 323 would include the entire Persian Empire and parts of northwest India. During Alexander's absence, Athens remained largely quiescent, enjoying increased prosperity under the leadership of Lycurgus (see §2, under ***The Canon of the Attic Orators***). Yet anti-Macedonian resentment remained sufficiently strong that collusion or sympathy with Macedon could still be considered treason (e.g., **390a** Hyp. 4.1–3, 14–20, 30–31, 39); and arguably the key legal development in Athens under Alexander was the increased use of the *eisangelia* (impeachment) procedure (chapter 12) by Lycurgus and others to prosecute relatively minor offenses (see **385** Hyp. 1 [selections]; **390** Hyp. 4 [selections]). At the very end of Alexander's reign, his fugitive treasurer Harpalus fled to Athens, where the Athenians granted him asylum and deposited the money he had brought with him on the Acropolis. Soon thereafter, Harpalus fled again to avoid extradition, and the Athenians discovered that half the money was missing; the resulting investigation ended in the spring of 323 with the convictions of a number of leading Athenian politicians, including Demosthenes, for taking bribes (**391** [*Apophasis* against Demosthenes and others for receiving bribes in the Harpalus affair]).

The Harpalus affair was quickly forgotten when the news of Alexander's death, which occurred in June 323, reached Athens. Demosthenes was recalled from exile—he had been imprisoned pending payment of a fine but had managed to escape—and with Hypereides, who had been one of his prosecutors in the Harpalus affair, convinced the Assembly to revolt against Macedonian rule. The resulting conflict, known as the Lamian War, ended in 322 with the defeat of Athens and its allies. The victorious Macedonians deposed the democracy at Athens and issued arrest warrants for their leading Athenian opponents, including Demosthenes and Hypereides; the former avoided capture at the last moment by taking poison (Plutarch, *Demosthenes* 29), while the latter, according to one account ([Plutarch], *Lives of the Ten Orators* 849b), was apprehended but, when put to the torture, avoided divulging state secrets by swallowing his tongue.

2. Athens in the Age of the Orators: Sources, Institutions, and Procedures

In addition to the works listed in the bibliography at the head of the preceding section, especially those listed under **History of the Athenian Constitution**, see the following: **General:** L. **Beauchet**, *Histoire du droit privé de la république athénienne* (Paris 1897); J. H. **Lipsius**, *Das attische Recht und*

Rechtsverfahren (Leipzig 1905–15); R. J. **Bonner**-G. **Smith**, *The Administration of Justice from Homer to Aristotle* (Chicago 1930–38); D. M. **MacDowell**, *The Law in Classical Athens* (Ithaca, NY 1978); A. R. W. **Harrison**, *The Law of Athens* (Oxford 1968–71); S. C. **Todd**, *The Shape of Athenian Law* (Oxford 1993); A. L. **Boegehold**, *The Athenian Agora*, vol. XXVIII: *The Lawcourts at Athens: Sites, Buildings, Equipment, Procedure, and Testimonia* (Princeton 1995); M. **Gagarin**-D. **Cohen**, eds., *The Cambridge Companion to Ancient Greek Law* (Cambridge 2005). **Lives and Works of the Attic Orators:** A. **Schäfer**, *Demosthenes und seine Zeit* (Leipzig 1858–87); F. **Blass**, *Die attische Beredsamkeit* (Leipzig 1887–98); R. C. **Jebb**, *The Attic Orators from Antiphon to Isaeus*[2] (London 1893); K. J. **Dover**, *Lysias and the* Corpus Lysiacum (Berkeley and Los Angeles 1968); J. **Trevett**, *Apollodoros the Son of Pasion* (Oxford 1992); S. **Usher**, *Greek Oratory: Tradition and Originality* (Oxford 1999); D. M. **MacDowell**, *Demosthenes the Orator* (Oxford 2009). On **individual procedures**, see the references in the relevant subsequent chapters.

Sources and Problems

The study of Athenian law is, to a large extent, an exercise in reconstruction. Although from 410 B.C. onward all laws, including earlier laws still in effect, were inscribed on stone, and in the fourth century the Athenians maintained an archive of public records, including laws and decrees, at the Metroon in the agora—the governmental and commercial hub of Classical Athens, adjacent to the Acropolis, Areopagus, and Pnyx and containing government buildings including, in addition to the Metroon, the hall where the Council of 500 met and at least some of the *dikastêria*—very rarely has the actual text of a law survived, either on stone or by direct quotation in a literary source. Our knowledge of Athenian law relies upon a wide variety of sources, including the surviving inscriptions on stone that record laws, decrees, and transactions between individuals, which are particularly valuable (allowing for the significant problem of their state of preservation) insofar as they provide a direct contemporary witness to events; archaeological evidence (for matters such as court sites, buildings, and equipment); and literary works of all genres.

Among the literary sources, the most important and wide-ranging are the pseudo-Aristotelian treatise titled *Constitution of the Athenians* (*Athênaiôn Politeia*, abbreviated *Ath. Pol.*), composed between 332 and 322 B.C. and containing a history of the Athenian constitution down to the democratic restoration of 403 (chapters 1–41; the beginning of the work is unfortunately lost: see **1c** [Arist.] *Ath. Pol.* 1) followed by a description of the constitution in operation at the time of writing (chapters 42–69); and the works of the Attic orators, which fall into three broad categories (Aristotle, *Rhetoric* 1358a-b): deliberative speeches, which were delivered before a political body (such as the Assembly or the Council of 500); epideictic (display) speeches, including funeral orations and political tracts; and forensic speeches, which were delivered in lawsuits. Thanks largely to the *Ath. Pol.* and the Attic orators, especially the approximately 100 forensic speeches—and fragments of others—that were delivered in Athenian lawsuits between the late fifth century and 323 B.C., something approximating a comprehensive (but nowhere near complete) picture of Athenian law, which is impossible before the second half of the fifth century, can be attempted for the later fifth and (especially) the fourth century. Valuable evidence is also provided by literature belonging to genres ranging from historiography (e.g., **1a** Hdt. 5.71; **1b** Thuc. 1.126.3–12; **375** Xen. *Hell.* 1.7.1–16, 20–26, 34–35) to drama (e.g., **273** Ar. *Wasps* 836–47, 893–900, 931–35, 952–66; **89** Menander [selections]) to lexicography (e.g., **28** Harpo. s.v. *bouleuseôs;* **117** Pollux, *Onomasticon* [selections]; **49** Photius, *Lexicon* s.v. *hybris* = *Suda* s.v. *hybris*) and beyond (e.g., **1d** Plut. *Solon* 12.1–9; **340** Pl. *Ap.* [selections]; **47** Arist. *Rhet.* [selections]), with each genre, and each text, carrying its own evidentiary merits and risks: the lexicographers, for example, had access to a far larger corpus of Attic oratory than we do, and so constitute a major source of fragments of lost speeches, but deserve particular caution owing to the centuries that passed between the time of the orators and their own writings.

The Canon of the Attic Orators

Between the third and first centuries B.C., scholars at the Library of Alexandria compiled a canon of the ten best Classical Athenian orators and selected their works for preservation and transmission. To this day, we remain dependent on the Alexandrian canon, since almost no speech attributed to anyone other than the canonical ten has survived; however, the great majority of the works possessed by the Alexandrians has been lost in the intervening centuries. In their canonical—and approximately chronological—order, the Attic orators, all of whom were Athenian citizens, except Lysias, Deinarchus, and perhaps Isaeus, are the following.

Antiphon (ca. 480–411) was the first Athenian logographer (*logographos*, "speechwriter"; specifically, one who wrote speeches for others to deliver, whether in court or elsewhere). His six surviving complete works, the earliest of which may belong to the 440s, all concern homicide; three (orations 1, 5, and 6) were delivered in actual lawsuits, while the other three (the *Tetralogies*: orations 2, 3, and 4) are sets of model speeches (two for the prosecution, two for the defense) in hypothetical lawsuits. Antiphon played a leading role in establishing the oligarchy of the Four Hundred and was impeached for treason and executed following their deposition (**371** [Plut.] *Lives of the Ten Orators* 833d–834b).

Andocides (ca. 440–*post* 391) rose to notoriety in 415, when, on condition of immunity, he confessed that his oligarchic political club had been responsible for the mutilation of the herms (see **§11.3**). Soon thereafter, he was targeted by a decree of Isotimides (**337** Lys. 6 [selections]; **338** Andoc. 1 [selections]), which barred from the sanctuaries and agora of Athens any person who confessed to an act of impiety. Essentially barred from public life, Andocides withdrew into exile, returning upon the democratic restoration of 403. In 400 or 399, he was prosecuted for violating the Isotimides decree, delivered the speech *On the Mysteries* (oration 1) in his own defense, and won an acquittal. The last known detail of Andocides' life is his service on an embassy to Sparta in 392/1, following which he was accused of corruption and fled Athens.

Lysias (?459/8–*post* 380) belonged to a family of prosperous metics (see p. 23). In 404/3, he and his brother Polemarchus were targeted by the Thirty Tyrants; Lysias escaped to Megara, but Polemarchus was executed and the brothers' assets confiscated. After the democracy was restored in 403, Lysias prosecuted Eratosthenes, one of the erstwhile Thirty, for his role in Polemarchus' death; the verdict in the case is unknown. From 403 until his death, Lysias worked as a logographer; his surviving speeches deal with a wide variety of issues and are particularly important sources for the reign of the Thirty and its aftermath.

Isocrates (436–338) worked as a logographer for about a decade after the Peloponnesian War, which had greatly reduced his family's wealth; six forensic speeches from this period (orations 16–21) survive. About 390, Isocrates gave up logography—a profession he would later vilify—and turned to teaching, in which he professed to combine the art of rhetoric with the pursuit of morality; his students included the orators Isaeus, Hypereides, and Lycurgus. A proponent of oligarchy, advocate of Panhellenism, and enemy of Persia, he did not participate in politics personally but attempted to influence policy by writing and publishing letters and pamphlets, which comprise the bulk of his corpus.

Isaeus (ca. 420–*post* 344/3) was either an Athenian citizen or a metic from Chalcis; almost no details of his life survive. He studied under Isocrates and worked as a logographer and a teacher of rhetoric; his most famous student was Demosthenes. Isaeus is an especially important source for Athenian inheritance law, the subject of eleven of his twelve surviving speeches.

Demosthenes (384±1–322), commonly considered the best of the Attic orators, studied under Isaeus and delivered his first forensic speeches in 364, when he prosecuted his guardians for mismanaging his estate (orations 27–31: see, for example, **87** Dem. 27.4–5). His rise to prominence in politics began in the mid- to late 350s, when he wrote speeches for high-profile trials and also delivered his first orations before the Assembly; from 351 onward, he established himself as the foremost Athenian opponent of Philip II of Macedon. In 346, Demosthenes served on the Athenian embassies to Philip that culminated in the Peace of Philocrates (p. 15); upon his return, he accused several of his fellow ambassadors, including Aeschines, of misconduct. The rivalry between Demosthenes and Aeschines continued until 330, when Aeschines prosecuted Demosthenes' ally Ctesiphon for illegally proposing that Demosthenes be awarded a gold crown for his services to Athens. Demosthenes delivered his most celebrated speech, *On the Crown* (oration 18), in Ctesiphon's defense; Ctesiphon was acquitted by a large margin, and Aeschines moved to Rhodes. In 324/3, Demosthenes was implicated in the Harpalus affair (p. 16); convicted of receiving bribes and sentenced to pay a fine of 50 talents, he was imprisoned pending payment but managed to escape into exile. Soon thereafter, upon the death of Alexander the Great, Demosthenes was recalled to Athens, where he played a leading role in the Lamian War against Macedon; at the end of the war, facing arrest by the victorious Macedonians, he committed suicide (p. 16).

Aeschines (390–ca. 322) rose from humble beginnings as an actor to become one of Athens' leading politicians and, owing to his generally more conciliatory policy toward Macedon, the principal rival of Demosthenes. In 346, following the Peace of Philocrates, he prosecuted Demosthenes' ally Timarchus for speaking in the Assembly after prostituting himself, winning the lawsuit with his speech *Against Timarchus* (oration 1: **57** Aeschin. 1 [selections]); in 343, prosecuted by Demosthenes for receiving bribes as an ambassador to Philip three years earlier, he defended himself with the speech *On the False Embassy* (oration 2: **24** Aeschin. 2.87) and barely escaped conviction. After losing the *Crown* case to Demosthenes in 330 (in which he delivered oration 3, *Against Ctesiphon*: **27** Aeschin. 3.244), Aeschines retired to Rhodes, where he became a teacher of rhetoric.

Hypereides (390/89–322) was already influential in Athenian politics when, in the wake of the Peace of Philocrates, he allied himself with Demosthenes as a hard-line opponent of Philip of Macedon. In 343, Hypereides impeached and convicted Philocrates for treason (**390b** Hyp. 4.28–30); he remained a dedicated enemy of Macedon until, and after, the Battle of Chaeroneia (p. 15). During the 330s and 320s, Hypereides found himself repeatedly at odds with Lycurgus (see below): of the six speeches of Hypereides that survive in complete or substantial form, two (orations 1 and 4, *For Lycophron* and *For Euxenippus*: **59** Hyp. 1.12; **385** Hyp. 1 [selections]; **66** Hyp. 4.3; **390** Hyp. 4 [selections]) were delivered for the defense in trials by *eisangelia* (impeachment: see chapter 12) for which Lycurgus wrote and/or delivered speeches for the prosecution. Hypereides was one of the prosecutors in the Harpalus affair (p. 16), in which capacity he delivered oration 5, *Against Demosthenes* (**303** Hyp. 5 col. 26; **391** [*Apophasis* against Demosthenes and others for receiving bribes in the Harpalus affair]). Reconciled with Demosthenes upon the latter's recall, Hypereides helped lead the Athenian resistance in the Lamian War; at the end of the war, he was apprehended and died in Macedonian custody (p. 16).

Lycurgus (ca. 390–324) rose to prominence after the Battle of Chaeroneia (p. 15) and administered the Athenian state treasury, serving essentially as de facto head of state, from 336 until his death. A deeply pious man, Lycurgus saw himself as a moral reformer, to which end he involved himself as prosecutor and/or logographer for the prosecution in numerous lawsuits, especially *eisangeliai* (impeachments: see chapter 12). His sole surviving complete speech, *Against Leocrates* (oration 1: **26** Lyc. 1 [selections]; **387** Lyc. 1 [selections]), was delivered in an *eisangelia* for treason, which he lost by one vote.

Deinarchus (ca. 360–*post* 292/1), the last of the Attic orators, was a metic from Corinth who had a long and successful career as a logographer. His three surviving complete or nearly complete speeches were written for delivery by one of the prosecutors in the Harpalus affair (p. 16). After the fall of the democracy in 322, Deinarchus enjoyed the patronage of Demetrius of Phaleron during the latter's tenure as governor of Athens (318/7–307). When Demetrius I Poliorcetes captured Athens in 307, Deinarchus fled to Chalcis; the last known event in Deinarchus' life, his prosecution of Proxenus for damage (**264** D. H. *Din.* 3), occurred shortly after his return to Athens in 292/1.

The corpora of several of the Attic orators contain not only genuine works written by the authors to whom they are attributed but also spurious works preserved under the orator's name but in fact written by someone else—usually a contemporary orator but occasionally a later forger. By scholarly convention, spurious works are designated by the placing of square brackets around the name of the author in whose corpus they are preserved: this applies not just to the Attic orators (e.g., [Demosthenes]—read "pseudo-Demosthenes"—59, written by Apollodorus: see below) but generally (so, for example, the pseudo-Aristotelian *Constitution of the Athenians* is cited as [Aristotle], *Constitution of the Athenians*). In most cases, the actual author of a spurious work cannot be identified; the primary exceptions occur in the corpus of Demosthenes, where at least six of the spurious speeches can be reliably attributed to his contemporary **Apollodorus** (ca. 394–*post* 343: see, e.g., **21** [Dem.] 59.9–10).

Virtually all ancient sources require significant caution in their use as evidence for Athenian law (and otherwise): problems include the lapse of time (how reliable, for example, are the discussions of Solon's late sixth-century reforms in the late fourth-century pseudo-Aristotelian *Constitution of the Athenians* and in Plutarch's first- or second-century A.D. *Life of Solon*?) and the related question of the sources of our sources (apart from the *Ath. Pol.*, what sources did Plutarch use, and given the tendency of Athenians from the fourth century B.C. onward to ascribe their laws to Solon regardless of provenance [p. 4], was Plutarch able, or even necessarily inclined, to distinguish which laws were really Solon's?). Special additional difficulties attend the use of Attic oratory as evidence. First, the purpose of the authors and speakers of these works was not to offer a disinterested statement of the facts but to win an argument, whether a trial or a debate in the Assembly. Since citing a nonexistent law was punishable by death ([Demosthenes] 26.24), and since a speaker's opponent would be presumed to have the same access to the laws as the speaker himself, direct quotations of laws, and to a lesser extent paraphrases of laws, generally carry the presumption of accuracy (although they present their own problems: see below). This presumption, however, does not extend to speakers' interpretations of laws bearing on their cases or to their narrations of the facts of those cases, both of which were carefully designed to serve their own interests. In these areas, the only real constraint upon a speaker was his need to convince a large number of fellow citizens to vote in his favor: victory required plausibility, not necessarily truth. Moreover, in only a distinct minority of lawsuits do we know the verdict, and even then, owing to the nature of the Athenian legal process (see pp. 39–40), it is generally not possible to know why the jury ruled as it did.

The second particular difficulty with Attic oratory arises from the fact that, while speakers commonly cite laws, decrees, oral or written testimony by witnesses (see p. 38), and other documents—such as wills and contracts—these are usually not preserved in the texts of the speeches; the point at which the speaker had a witness testify or the court clerk read out a document is often marked simply by the word designating the testimony or type of document (e.g., **114** Dem. 41.5–7, 10 ["WITNESSES" . . . "LAW. DOCUMENTS. DEPOSITION"]; **369** Lyc. 1.120–21 ["DECREE"]; **211** Isae. 6.5–7 ["WILL"]; **328** [Dem.] 34.3–7, 33, 36–37, 42 ["CONTRACT"]). Even when the total or partial text of a document is included in the text, problems of authenticity arise: some documents—ideally when independent confirmation is available—can be accepted as genuine (as, for example, **35** Dem. 21.47, confirmed by quotation of clauses in **64a** Aeschin. 1.13–15), but others must be rejected as spurious interpolations by later editors, who sometimes composed documents by extrapolation from the text of the speech and/or other sources (e.g., **289** Dem. 24.104–5, 112–15, 120–21, 129, 146, where the terms of the alleged law inserted at §105 do not match its paraphrase; and the alleged law on hubris at Aeschines 1.16, inserted by a later editor who reconstructed the document on the basis of Aeschines 1.15). In the majority of cases, the acceptance or rejection of a document is a matter of scholarly conjecture and debate (see, e.g., **380** Dem. 24.63).

Another issue that is often raised concerns revision; namely, how faithfully does a published speech reflect what a litigant or a speaker in the Assembly actually said? There can be no general answer to this question, and frequently extemporaneous changes will have been made in response to an opponent's arguments, but most preserved speeches can be presumed to be broadly, if not in every detail, accurate: for the sake of his reputation, a politician would presumably not publish a deliberative speech that bore little resemblance to what he had said before thousands of his fellow citizens, and most preserved forensic speeches presumably originate with the authors' personal copies of speeches that they gave to litigants to memorize and deliver, or that they memorized and delivered themselves. In any case, moreover, the fidelity of the published speech to the delivered speech can be safely presumed to have little bearing on the accuracy (or lack thereof) of the published version with regard to matters of law (with the possible exception of the amount of time in which the speech was delivered: see p. 37).

Law, Government, and Society: General Principles

All residents of Attica belonged to one of three classes: citizens, metics, and slaves. Originally, the citizen status of a father sufficed to confer citizenship upon his children, but from 451/0 onward, a law of Pericles (p. 11) mandated that only the children of two citizen parents were eligible for citizenship. Women, girls, and boys of citizen birth were spoken of as citizens and received legal protection accordingly, but for all practical purposes the active exercise of civic rights—including attendance and voting in the Assembly, tenure of political office, and jury service—were the province of adult male citizens alone. Women (**21** [Dem.] 59.9–10), and perhaps children, could be prosecuted in lawsuits, but only adult male citizens—and adult male metics—could prosecute lawsuits or appear in court as witnesses. If an offense was committed against a woman or child, it had to be prosecuted by an adult male: in a private lawsuit by his or her *kyrios* (plural *kyrioi*: see the introduction to chapter 5), and in a public lawsuit (at least theoretically) by any willing adult male citizen (or, in some cases, metic; for the distinction between private and public lawsuits see ***Types of Procedure***). If a litigant wished to introduce the statement of a woman as evidence, he did so by having the woman swear an oath before trial and then having the oath read out during the trial (**131** Dem. 39–40 [selections]).

Metics were free foreign residents of Attica. A metic was required to register himself with the state, to pay a special tax (the *metoikion*, "metic tax": 12 drachmas per year for men and 6 drachmas per year for women), and to have a citizen patron (*prostatês*); failure to comply with any of these rules was punishable by enslavement. Adult male metics, like their citizen counterparts, were liable to military service and to some liturgies (see p. 25) and could participate in lawsuits as prosecutors, defendants, or witnesses (although the procedure might differ depending on whether a litigant was a citizen or a metic: see p. 33), but without a special grant by the Assembly, a metic was not allowed to own real property in Attica (see the introduction to chapter 6).

All residents of Attica who were not citizens or metics were slaves. The majority of slaves were privately owned, either by citizens or by metics. There were also public slaves owned by the Athenian state, many of whom assisted citizen officials in the functioning of government (such as the corps of Scythian archers that helped maintain public order and ensure attendance in the Assembly). As human property, slaves were simultaneously legal persons—both possessing liability for offenses and enjoying (at least theoretical) legal protection against offenses such as homicide (**10** Isoc. 18.52–54; **17** [Dem.] 47.67–73; **25** [Arist.] *Ath. Pol.* 57.2–4), hubris (**35** Dem. 21.47), and rape (**51** Lys. 10.18–19)—and legal things: like other property, they were at the disposal of their owners, and so were subject to alienation by sale, gift, or will, as well as pledge and temporary loan and hire (see, e.g., **167** Dem. 27.9–11; **262** Hyp. 3.5–11, 18, 21–22; **309** Hyp. 3.14–15; **320** [Dem.] 33.6–12). Slaves, like women and children, could be prosecuted in lawsuits (e.g., **249d** Dem. 55.31–32, 34) but—with the possible exception of the *dikai emporikai*: see chapter 10—could not prosecute lawsuits or appear in court as witnesses. If an offense was committed against a slave, a private lawsuit could be prosecuted only by the slave's owner, who was his *kyrios* (**17** [Dem.] 47.67–73); a public lawsuit could in theory be brought by any willing adult male citizen (or, in some cases, metic). If an offense was committed by a slave, either the slave or his owner—or a third party for whom the slave was working—might be prosecuted (**249** Dem. 55 [selections]; **262** Hyp. 3.5–11, 18, 21–22). Statements by slaves were admissible as evidence in lawsuits only if they had been obtained under torture conducted before trial with the consent of both litigants. A litigant who wished to torture a slave, whether the slave belonged to himself or to his opponent—or to a third party, in which case the third party's consent was required—tendered a challenge to his opponent; only if the challenge was accepted and the torture was duly carried out in accordance with the resulting agreement could the statement made by the slave be read out to the court. Challenges to torture slaves appear with considerable frequency in Attic oratory but appear seldom to have been accepted, much less carried to fruition; instead, litigants commonly use rejected or aborted challenges as evidence that they are telling the truth and their opponents are lying (e.g., **256d** Dem. 37.39–44; **317** [Dem.] 49.48–49, 51–52).

The rights of citizen and metic men were balanced by corresponding duties to the state, both personal and financial. Between the ages of eighteen and sixty, unless they were disqualified by physical incapacity, they were liable to be called up for military service ([Aristotle], *Constitution of the Athenians*

[*Ath. Pol.*] 53.4). Depending on their financial standing, they served in the land forces as cavalry (for which only the wealthiest men were eligible), hoplites (the standard heavy infantry soldiers of later Archaic and Classical Greece), or light infantry, or in the navy as officers, marines, or (in the case of the poorest men) rowers. The standard warship, the trireme (e.g., **173** *IG* II^2 1631.429–41; **366c** Dem. 18.204), was powered in battle by three superimposed banks of oars (hence its Greek name, *triêrês*, "three-fitted") and crewed by a standard complement of 170 rowers and 30 officers and marines. The ten annual generals—who like all other magistrates had to be citizens, but unlike most other magistrates were elected rather than allotted and had the possibility of unlimited iteration in office—served as staff officers in command of armies and fleets; subordinate officers were elected by the tribes to command their respective contingents of the land army.

Athenian state revenues came from both external and internal sources. During its periods of hegemony over the Delian League (478–404) and the Second Athenian Confederacy (378/7–338), Athens derived significant external revenue from its allies, in the form of mandatory annual tribute and more or less voluntary contributions respectively; other external revenues, at all times, came from sources such as the harbor duties exacted from vessels landing at the Peiraeus. Internal revenue was raised not by regular taxation of all citizens, which appears to have obtained in Athens only under the Peisistratids (p. 4), but by the exaction of contributions from the wealthiest citizens and metics in the form of liturgies and *eisphorai*. Liturgies, to which in the fourth century the wealthiest 1,200 residents of Attica were liable, were assigned annually for the performance of specific public functions. The Athenian navy was funded to a significant extent by the liturgy known as the trierarchy, performed by a man called a trierarch (**46** [Arist.] *Ath. Pol.* 52.2; **254** Dem. 39.1, 5, 7–18; **315** Lys. 19.25–26; **377** Dem. 51.8–9; **378** [Dem.] 47.41–43). Each trireme was assigned to one (or sometimes more than one: e.g., **139** Lys. 32.8–10, 19–24) trierarch, who had to be an Athenian citizen. The trierarch was responsible for the upkeep of his ship; originally, but not always in the time of the orators, a trierarch commanded his ship in battle. Other liturgies financed dramatic performances at state religious festivals; the most important festival liturgy was the *chorêgia* (choregy), discharged by a *chorêgos* (chorus-producer), either a citizen or a metic, who supervised, paid, and equipped a dramatic chorus and its director (**9** Ant. 6 [selections]; **332** Dem. 21 [selections]). Liturgies involved considerable financial burdens but also provided the men who performed them with opportunities to display their civic commitment; accordingly, speakers in the courts and Assembly frequently referred to liturgies performed by themselves or their ancestors, often with higher expenditures than necessary. A man who was assigned a liturgy but believed that someone wealthier than himself had been exempted could challenge him to an *antidosis* (exchange: **122** [Dem.] 42.27): the man challenged had the choice of accepting the liturgy or exchanging the entirety of his property for that of his challenger (who then retained the liturgy). *Eisphorai* ("war-taxes," literally "contributions"; singular *eisphora*: e.g., **254** Dem. 39.1, 5, 7–18) originated during the Peloponnesian War as emergency taxes decreed by the Assembly and were exacted with growing frequency in the fourth century from the wealthiest residents of Attica, citizen and metic alike. Other sources of internal revenue included leased public contracts (e.g., for the operation of mines: **256** Dem. 37 [selections]), the products of sacred olive trees (**331** [Arist.] *Ath. Pol.* 60.2–3), fines paid to the state (e.g., **44b** Dem. 21.45; **302a** [Arist.] *Ath. Pol.* 48.4–5, 54.2), and the metic tax (p. 23).

Athenian democratic law and government were characterized by their participatory and amateur nature. Any male citizen over twenty could attend, speak, and vote in the Assembly (p. 3); any male citizen over thirty was eligible for virtually any state office, including membership in the Council of 500 and on the boards of archons and generals, and for service as a juror in the *dikastêria*. Considered one of the cornerstones of Athenian democracy ([Aristotle], *Constitution of the Athenians* [*Ath. Pol.*] 9.1), the *dikastêria* heard the great majority of trials from at least the mid-fifth century on (p. 8; exceptions included the *dikê phonou*, the *graphê traumatos ek pronoias*, and offenses against sacred olive trees: see chapters 1, 2, and 11 respectively). At the beginning of each year, the state empaneled a pool of 6,000 volunteer jurors (*dikastai*; singular *dikastês*: p. 8), who swore on oath (the heliastic oath, named after the (*h*)*êliaia*: see p. 3) that they would vote in accordance with the laws and decrees of the Assembly and the Council of 500, would employ their "most just judgment" in matters not governed by existing law, and would serve honestly and impartially. On each day the *dikastêria* were in session, jurors who presented themselves for service were randomly allotted to trials (for the system in operation in the late fourth century see [Aristotle], *Constitution of the Athenians* [*Ath. Pol.*] 63–69; for this and previous periods see A. L. Boegehold, *The Athenian Agora*, vol. XXVIII: *The Lawcourts at Athens: Sites, Buildings, Equipment, Procedure, and Testimonia* [Princeton 1995]), with the size of the jury, usually between 201 and 501 members, determined by the type of lawsuit (see p. 37; on occasion, for major public lawsuits, juries in the thousands are attested: e.g., **391** [*Apophasis* against Demosthenes and others for receiving bribes in the Harpalus affair] with Deinarchus 1.107 [jury of 1,500]).

We have at Demosthenes 24.148–51 a problematic document that purports to contain the provisions of the heliastic oath (on documents preserved in the Attic orators see p. 22; on the heliastic oath see, for example, R. J. **Bonner**-G. **Smith**, *The Administration of Justice from Homer to Aristotle* [Chicago 1930–38] 2.152–56; A. R. W. **Harrison**, *The Law of Athens* [Oxford 1968–71] 2.48; M. H. **Hansen**, *The Athenian Democracy in the Age of Demosthenes* [Oxford 1991] 182–83). Many elements of the document are confirmed elsewhere (cf., e.g., **12b** Andoc. 1.90–91), but some provisions attested elsewhere are not present in the document, including, in particular, the clause averring that in matters concerning which no law existed, the juror would decide in accordance with his "most just judgment" (*gnômêi têi dikaiotatêi*: see, e.g., Demosthenes 20.118). The document reads as follows:

OATH OF THE HELIASTS [i.e., members of the *hêliaia*]. [149] "I shall vote in accordance with the laws and the decrees of the people of Athens and the Council of 500. I shall not vote that there be a tyranny or an oligarchy, and if a person subverts the people of Athens or makes a proposal or puts a proposal to the vote in violation of these provisions, I shall not obey. I shall not vote for a cancellation of private debts or a redistribution of the land of the Athenians or of their houses. I shall not readmit exiles or those who have been sentenced to death, nor shall I expel residents [of Attica] in violation of the established laws and the decrees of the people of Athens and the Council; I shall not do so myself nor permit anyone else to do so. [150] I shall not appoint a magistrate to hold office when he is still subject to review for another [previous] office; namely, [the offices of] the nine archons, the *hieromnêmôn* [i.e., the Athenian representative on the supervising council of the Amphictyonic League at Delphi (on which see the headnote under **2** *IG* I[3] 104)], all the [other] offices that are allotted along with the nine archons on that day, and [the offices of] herald, ambassador, and conciliar delegates. I shall not appoint the same man to the same office twice, nor shall I appoint the same man to hold two offices in the same year. I shall not myself accept bribes for my service on the *hêliaia*, nor shall another, male or female, do so for me with my knowledge, by any manner or means. [151] I am no less than thirty years old. I shall listen to the prosecutor and to the defendant, both alike, and I shall vote between them with regard only to the matter that the prosecution concerns." [The heliast] shall swear by Zeus, Poseidon, and Demeter, and shall curse himself and his house with destruction should he violate any of the aforementioned terms, while [praying that] if he remains true to his oath he shall enjoy many benefits.

Owing to their size and content, these juries were considered to represent the Athenian citizenry as a whole; hence a speaker will often tell his jury, "You did *x*," when the act was performed by some other manifestation of the citizenry, usually the Assembly or another jury in a different trial (e.g., **337b** Lys. 6.9–10; **337g** Lys. 6.54). In order to facilitate participation by poorer Athenians, daily payment for service in the *dikastêria* was instituted at the rate of 2 obols by

Pericles in the late 460s or 450s (p. 11; [Aristotle], *Constitution of the Athenians* [*Ath. Pol.*] 27; Plutarch, *Pericles* 9) and raised to 3 obols by Cleon in the 420s (Aristophanes, *Knights* 255, 797–800; [Aristotle], *Constitution of the Athenians* [*Ath. Pol.*] 62.2); similar payments were made for attendance in the Assembly (instituted in 403/2 at 3 obols per day and raised by the date of composition of the *Ath. Pol.* to 1–1.5 drachmas [6–9 obols]: [Aristotle], *Constitution of the Athenians* [*Ath. Pol.*] 41.3, 62.2) and for participation in the Council of 500 (5 obols per day, plus an extra obol for the *prytaneis*, at the date of composition of the *Ath. Pol.*: [Aristotle], *Constitution of the Athenians* [*Ath. Pol.*] 62.2), as well as for the tenure of many other magistracies.

While men who were skilled in rhetoric and knew the law well might offer their services as logographers (p. 18) and/or *synêgoroi* (see below), the Athenians recognized no class of persons possessing authority in the practice or interpretation of law (with the partial and limited exception of the *Exêgêtai* ["Interpreters"], who had special—but not legally binding—powers of interpretation in religious matters, including homicide and impiety: see chapters 1 and 11); in a word, the Athenians had no lawyers. The Athenian legal system was, rather, an amateur one that relied to a large extent on the initiative of private individuals at every stage of the administration of justice, before, during, and after trial. The fact that Athenian laws frequently fail to give substantive definitions of the offenses they govern (e.g., **35** Dem. 21.47) will have provided significant latitude to litigants, magistrates, and juries. Moreover, Athens had no standing state prosecutorial service and no police force empowered to investigate and apprehend offenders. Under some procedures (such as *apagôgê*, *endeixis*, *ephêgêsis*, *eisangelia*, *euthynai*, and *apophasis*: see ***Types of Procedure***), arrest and/or prosecution were regularly authorized and/or conducted by the appropriate magistrates—such as the Eleven, the Council of 500, or the Areopagus—or by the Assembly; but the great majority of offenses of virtually all kinds were investigated and prosecuted by private volunteers acting of their own accord. At trial—and in any preliminary proceedings—a litigant, whether prosecutor or defendant, was expected to plead his case in person (although excessive display of legal knowledge was commonly viewed with suspicion as the mark of a sycophant [see below]). Logography was an open secret: a litigant who lacked confidence in his own ability and could afford to commission a logographer might do so but would never advertise the fact. In addition to delivering his own trial speech (or speeches: see ***Stages of Procedure***), a litigant might call upon one or more *synêgoroi* ("advocates"; singular *synêgoros*), who would assist him by delivering supporting speeches (e.g., **21** [Dem.] 59.9–10; **66** Hyp. 4.3 with **390** Hyp. 4 [selections]; **147** Dem. 29.30–31; **148** Dem. 36.20, 22). *Synêgoroi* were—or at least were supposed to be—relatives or friends of the litigant who assisted him for free; paid advocacy was a prosecutable offense (**374**

[Dem.] 46.26). After trial, the enforcement of a verdict might be carried out by the state (as, for example, when the penalty was death: e.g., **341** Pl. *Phaedo* [selections]) but more often was in the hands of the winning litigant (e.g., **17** [Dem.] 47.67–73).

Types of Procedure

The general word for a "lawsuit" of any kind was *dikê* (plural *dikai*; the corresponding verb in the active voice, *dikazein*, means "to judge a lawsuit," and in the middle voice, *dikazesthai*, means "to bring or contend in a lawsuit"). *Dikê* had a broad range of meanings also including—among others—"justice" in the abstract, the "judgment" handed down by a court, and a specific type of private lawsuit. Often used as a synonym for *dikê* in the sense of "lawsuit" was the word *agôn*—a "contest" of any sort, whether judicial, athletic, or other. The two broad procedural divisions of Athenian lawsuits were, first, a division between private and public lawsuits (a distinction affecting the capacity to prosecute, discussed below) and second, a division between non-assessable and assessable lawsuits (a distinction affecting the determination of a penalty upon conviction: see under ***Stages of Procedure***).

The most basic distinction among Athenian legal procedures was that between *dikai idiai*, "private lawsuits" (singular *dikê idia*) and *dikai dêmosiai*, "public lawsuits" (singular *dikê dêmosia*). Private lawsuits could be prosecuted only by the injured party; namely, the victim himself (e.g., **42** Dem. 54 [selections]), the *kyrios* of the victim if the latter was a woman, child, or slave (e.g., **17** [Dem.] 47.67–73), or, in a *dikê phonou* for the killing of a free person, the victim's relatives (**2** *IG* I[3] 104; **17** [Dem.] 47.67–73). Most private lawsuits were of the class called *dikai* (here denoting a specific type of private action) and were named by the word *dikê* followed by the name of the offense (usually, but not always, a noun in the genitive case). The members of this class discussed in this book include the *dikê phonou* (for homicide: chapter 1), the *dikê aikeias* (for battery: chapter 2), the *dikê biaiôn* (for acts of violence: **45** Dem. 37.33; **61** Harpo. s.v. *biaiôn*), the *dikê kakêgorias* (for defamation: chapter 4), the *dikê proikos* (for a dowry: chapter 5), the *dikê sitou* (for maintenance: chapter 6), the *dikê epitropês* (for [abuse of] a guardianship: chapter 6), the *dikê exoulês* (for ejectment: chapter 7), the *dikê blabês* (for damage: chapter 8), the *dikê klopês* (for theft: chapter 9), the *dikai emporikai* (mercantile lawsuits: chapter 10), and the *dikê pseudomartyriôn* (for false witness: see p. 43, and, e.g., **170** Andoc. 1.73–79; **230** [Dem.] 44 [selections]; **§7.4.5**). The other principal type of private lawsuit was the *diadikasia* ("adjudication"; plural *diadikasiai*), which served to decide between two or more rival claimants who sought to assert a right (especially to an inheritance or an *epiklêros*: see chapter 7; but note also, e.g.,

338c Andoc. 1.27–28) or to evade a duty (such as the performance of a liturgy: e.g., **122** [Dem.] 42.27; cf. **254** Dem. 39.1, 5, 7–18; [Aristotle], *Constitution of the Athenians* [*Ath. Pol.*] 61.1). In most *diadikasiai*, there was no prosecutor and no defendant; rather, all claimants were on equal footing before the court (see, e.g., **236** [Dem.] 48.22–32).

Public lawsuits could be prosecuted by any willing adult male Athenian (and in some cases, such as *probolê* and *euthynai* [see below], by any willing adult male metic) who was not barred from taking legal action (normally by total or partial *atimia*: see p. 41). The most common type of public lawsuit was the *graphê* ("indictment" [literally "writ(ing)"]; plural *graphai*). This term probably arose from the fact that when the first *graphai* were introduced (probably by Solon: p. 3), the charge had to be submitted in writing. By the age of the orators, however, written charges were required in almost all lawsuits, and just as *dikê* and *dikazein/dikazesthai* could be used either generally, in reference to any lawsuit, or specifically, in reference to the type of private lawsuit called a *dikê*, so too *graphê* (and the corresponding verb *graphein* [active]/ *graphesthai* [middle]) could be used either in reference to the type of procedure called *graphê* or in reference to the written indictment in any type of lawsuit. Individual procedures of the type called *graphai*, like those of the type called *dikai*, are specified by the word *graphê* followed by the name of the offense; the *graphai* discussed in this book include the *graphê traumatos ek pronoias* (for intentional wounding: chapter 2), the *graphê hybreôs* (for hubris: chapter 2), the *graphê moicheias* (for seduction: chapter 3), the *graphê adikôs heirchthênai hôs moichon* (for having been unjustly detained as a seducer: chapter 3), the *graphê hetairêseôs* (for prostitution: chapter 3), the *graphê proagôgeias* (for pandering: chapter 3), the *graphê xenias* (for being a foreigner; i.e., for falsely posing as a citizen: see p. 42 and the introduction to chapter 6), the *graphê klopês* (for theft, including *dêmosiôn chrêmatôn*, for theft of public property, and *hierôn chrêmatôn*, for theft of sacred property: chapter 9), the *graphê hierosylias* (for temple-robbery: chapter 9), the *graphê asebeias* (for impiety: chapter 11), the *graphê dôrôn* (for bribery: **302a** [Arist.] *Ath. Pol.* 48.4–5, 54.2 and chapter 12), the *graphê lipotaxiou* and *graphê astrateias* (for desertion and for avoiding military service, respectively: **170** Andoc. 1.73–79; **387** Lyc. 1 [selections]), and the *graphê paranomôn* and *graphê nomon mê epitêdeion theinai* (for illegal proposals and for enacting an unsuitable law, respectively: see p. 14).

Other public lawsuits included *apagôgê, endeixis, ephêgesis, phasis, apographê, probolê, dokimasia, euthynai, eisangelia*, and *apophasis*. *Apagôgê* ("summary arrest"; literally "leading away") was an ancient procedure (**3b** Dem. 23.28) whereby any person might arrest an offender and hale him before a magistrate. Related to *apagôgê*, and probably of equal antiquity (**3e** Dem. 23.51), were *endeixis* ("denunciation"; literally "indication, pointing out") and *ephêgê-*

sis ("conducting, leading to"), which differed from *apagôgê* in that the arrest was performed by a magistrate: in *endeixis* a person denounced an offender to a magistrate, who then carried out the arrest, and in *ephêgêsis* a person led the magistrate to the offender (**288** Dem. 22.25–27, 69–73). In the age of the orators, *apagôgê*, *endeixis*, and *ephêgêsis* were available against three categories of offender; namely, (1) the class of offenders collectively known as *kakourgoi* ("malefactors"; singular *kakourgos*) and comprising killers, seducers, thieves, clothes-snatchers, cutpurses, burglars, temple-robbers, pirates, kidnappers, and traitors (e.g., **57a** Aeschin. 1.91; **283** Xen. *Mem.* 1.2.62; **288** Dem. 22.25–27, 69–73); (2) persons caught in specified public areas (such as the agora, the law-courts, and sacred precincts) from which they had been barred (e.g., **337** Lys. 6 [selections]; **338** Andoc. 1 [selections]); and (3) persons exiled by the state who violated the terms of their banishment (e.g., **3e** Dem. 23.51; **369** Lyc. 1.120–21). Any of the offenders belonging to the first and third categories—with the proviso for members of the first category, by the beginning of the fourth century, that they were caught "in the act" (*ep' autophôrôi*, etymologically "in the very act of theft": e.g., **14** Lys. 13.85–87)—could be arrested and brought before the Eleven, the board of magistrates that superintended the state prison and executions. If the offender confessed his wrongdoing, he was immediately executed; if he maintained his innocence, he went to trial before a *dikastêrion* and was punished with death if convicted (**57a** Aeschin. 1.91; **302b** [Arist.] *Ath. Pol.* 52.1). Offenders belonging to the second category were granted automatic trial before a *dikastêrion*; depending on the specific offense, a conviction might result in either a mandatory penalty of death or penal assessment by the jury (see ***Stages of Procedure***). (On the availability of *apagôgê* and *endeixis* from the mid-fourth century onward against malicious prosecutors of merchants and ship-captains, see chapter 12.)

Phasis ("declaration") and *apographê* ("registration [for confiscation]") were procedures concerned primarily with property. *Phasis* was available against a variety of offenses, including unauthorized possession of public property, mismanagement of an estate by guardians, and violation of laws on maritime commerce and loans (**150** Dem. 38.3–4, 14–15, 17, 23; **151** Harpo. s.v. *phasis*; **244** Isoc. 18.1–8, 10–13, 33, 63; **323c** [Dem.] 35.50–51; **325** [Dem.] 58.5–6, 8, 10–12). *Apographê* targeted persons in debt to the state: the prosecutor compiled an inventory of the debtor's property that was subject to confiscation so as to satisfy the debt (**40** [Dem.] 53.16; **70** Lys. 9.5–12, 15–16; **108** Lys. 19 (selections); **173** *IG* II² 1631.429–41; **281** Lys. 29.1–2, 11; **285** *SEG* 12.100.1–16; **302b** [Arist.] *Ath. Pol.* 52.1; **319** *SEG* 12.100.16–21, 23–25, 30–39; **323c** [Dem.] 35.50–51; [Aristotle], *Constitution of the Athenians* [*Ath. Pol.*] 47.2–5). *Phasis* and *apographê* were initiated before the appropriate magistrate and, if contested, went to trial in a *dikastêrion*; a prosecutor who obtained a conviction was rewarded with a portion of any fine imposed (one-half in a *phasis* and perhaps one-third in an *apographê*).

Probolê ("presentation") was available against three types of offender: from the late fifth or early fourth century against offenders at religious festivals (**§11.2**), from 405 or 404 against those who deceived the Athenian people (**375** Xen. *Hell.* 1.7.1–16, 20–26, 34–35; **386** [Arist.] *Ath. Pol.* 43.5), and from an unknown date against sycophants (**386** [Arist.] *Ath. Pol.* 43.5; on sycophants see below). Any free—not necessarily Athenian—adult male could bring a *probolê* before the Assembly, which voted either to condemn or to acquit the accused. This vote, however, was neither binding nor (other than formally) punitive; a prosecutor who wished to secure anything more than a formal sanction of the accused could, at his sole discretion and regardless of the Assembly's vote, bring the case to a *dikastêrion* for trial.

Dokimasia ("scrutiny") and *euthynai* ("review"; literally "correction[s]") were regular procedures undergone by all magistrates before the beginning and after the end of their terms in office respectively. The *dokimasia* served to ensure that a man selected for office was qualified to hold it and included, in particular, questions designed to ascertain his citizen status ([Aristotle], *Constitution of the Athenians* [*Ath. Pol.*] 45, 55, 59; **132** Dem. 57.46; **158** Xen. *Mem.* 2.2.13). Distinct from this type of *dokimasia* were the *dokimasia* that boys had to pass in order to be admitted to the ranks of adult male citizens (**134** [Arist.] *Ath. Pol.* 42.1–2) and the *dokimasia tôn rhêtorôn,* "scrutiny of [public] speakers (or 'politicians')," under which any citizen could prosecute a man who violated a law prohibiting him from speaking in the Assembly (**64c** Aeschin. 1.28–30, 32). All outgoing magistrates were required to undergo *euthynai,* which included a mandatory inspection of their financial accounts and the opportunity for any adult male citizen or metic to lodge grievances; any offenses considered to be sufficiently serious were referred to the competent magistrates for trial in a *dikastêrion* (see, e.g., **170** Andoc. 1.73–79; **289** Dem. 24.104–5, 112–15, 120–21, 129, 146; **299** [Dem.] 58.14–15; **301** Aeschin. 3.10; **302a** [Arist.] *Ath. Pol.* 48.4–5, 54.2).

Eisangelia ("impeachment") came in three distinct types, with significant procedural and penal differences (**392a** Harpo. s.v. *eisangelia*): one for major offenses against the state (chapter 12), one for maltreatment of parents, orphans, and *epiklêroi* (**§6.4**), and one for misconduct by arbitrators (on whom see ***Stages of Procedure***). *Apophasis* ("report" by the Council of the Areopagus) was created ca. 344/3 and functioned thenceforth as an alternative to *eisangelia* for the prosecution of major offenses against the state (**383** Dem. 18.132–33; **391** [*Apophasis* against Demosthenes and others for receiving bribes in the Harpalus affair]).

Besides being open to prosecution by any willing and qualified Athenian citizen, the common factor uniting almost all public lawsuits (exceptions included *eisangelia* for major offenses against the state until 333–330 [**59** Hyp. 1.12; **389** Dem. 18.250], *eisangelia* for maltreatment of an *epiklêros* [**164** Dem. 37.45–46], and presumably *apophasis*) and distinguishing them from private lawsuits was that a prosecutor in a public lawsuit who obtained less than 20 percent of the jurors' votes at trial, or who dropped his case before trial, was fined 1,000 drachmas (see, for example, **20** Dem. 23.65–80; **35** Dem. 21.47; **288** Dem. 22.25–27, 69–73) and, at least in some cases, was barred from bringing a lawsuit of the same type in the future (see, e.g., **170** Andoc. 1.73–79; this constituted a type of partial *atimia*: see p. 41). By comparison, in at least some and perhaps most *dikai*, a prosecutor who failed to receive 20 percent of the votes incurred the *epôbelia* (e.g., **41b** [Dem.] 47.64; cf. p. 14). The purpose of these penalties was to discourage sycophancy, the bringing of malicious or otherwise baseless prosecutions in the hope of harming a personal enemy and/or making money either by extorting payment for dropping charges or by securing a monetary verdict (the man who engaged in such practices was called a sycophant). To judge from the Attic orators and other contemporary sources—especially the comedies of Aristophanes—sycophancy in both public and private lawsuits was a serious problem in Classical Athens; speakers in all kinds of lawsuits accused their opponents of sycophancy as a matter of course (see, e.g., **58a** [Dem.] 59.64–70; **142** Lys. 19.8–9; **386** [Arist.] *Ath. Pol.* 43.5).

The Athenian legal system was characterized by a high degree of procedural flexibility. Many—perhaps most—unlawful acts might be prosecuted under more than one procedure, and a would-be prosecutor chose which procedure to use on the basis of a number of factors, including the risk to himself and the penalty mandatorily or potentially imposed upon conviction. Seduction, for example, could be prosecuted by a *graphê moicheias*, a *graphê hybreôs*, or even—at least in the late fourth century—*eisangelia*; if the seducer was caught in the act (*ep' autophôrôi*), he was also liable to *apagôgê* by any willing adult male Athenian and to detention for ransom, torture, or summary execution by a qualified male relative of the woman he seduced (chapter 3). Similar procedural variety is attested for theft (see **288** Dem. 22.25–27, 69–73 and chapter 9 generally), impiety (**349b** Dem. 22.27 and chapter 11 generally), and other offenses.

Stages of Procedure

A would-be prosecutor who had decided on a procedure had first to find out which magistrate(s) held initial jurisdiction over that procedure. In the second half of the fourth century, the relevant magistrates included the eponymous archon for most issues of family law—including inheritance, guardianship, maltreatment, and the protection of widows, orphans, and *epiklêroi*—among citizens, and the polemarch for corresponding matters among metics (e.g., **152** [Arist.] *Ath. Pol.* 56.6–7; **227** [Dem.] 46.22–23); the *basileus* for matters affecting religion, including the *graphê asebeias* (chapter 11) and the *dikê phonou* (chapter 1); the *thesmothetai* for a wide range of lawsuits both public and private (**35** Dem. 21.47; **58a** [Dem.] 59.64–70; **60** [Arist.] *Ath. Pol.* 59.3; **79** [Arist.] *Ath. Pol.* 59.5; **333** [Arist.] *Ath. Pol.* 59.2); the Eleven for *apagôgê*, *endeixis*, and *ephêgêsis* (**14** Lys. 13.85–87; **57a** Aeschin. 1.91; **302b** [Arist.] *Ath. Pol.* 52.1); the Council of 500 or the Assembly for *eisangelia* (see chapter 12); the Introducers (*Eisagôgeis*) for many of the *dikai emmênoi* ("monthly lawsuits": **46** [Arist.] *Ath. Pol.* 52.2; the major exception was the *dikai emporikai*, which came before the *thesmothetai*: **79** [Arist.] *Ath. Pol.* 59.5; **324** [Dem.] 33.1–3, 23); and the Forty (see below) for the majority of remaining private lawsuits (see [Aristotle], *Constitution of the Athenians* [*Ath. Pol.*] 53 and, e.g., **45** Dem. 37.33; **75** Dem. 21.79, 81, 83–84, 88). Most, but not all, procedures were governed by a statute or clause of limitations (*nomos prothesmias* or simply *prothesmia*: **150** Dem. 38.3–4, 14–15, 17, 23; **228** Isae. 3.40–50, 57–60, 62; **234** [Dem.] 43.5–16; **329c** Lys. 7.16–17, 19, 22, 25–26) mandating prosecution within five years of the alleged offense.

In most cases (with exceptions including *apagôgê*, *endeixis*, and *ephêgêsis*, where arrest took the place of summons; the *dikê phonou*, where proclamations took the place of summons [see chapter 1]; and *diadikasia*, except in cases where an inheritance or *epiklêros* had been previously adjudicated [**234** [Dem.] 43.5–16; **236** [Dem.] 48.22–32]; otherwise a proclamation in the Assembly took the place of summons [**224** [Arist.] *Ath. Pol.* 43.4; **234** [Dem.] 43.5–16]), the would-be prosecutor next had to issue an oral summons (*prosklêsis*) to the defendant, in person and in the presence of one or more summons-witnesses (*klêtêres*), to appear before the relevant magistrate(s) at a specified date and time (e.g., **241** Ar. *Wasps* 1389–1408; **285** *SEG* 12.100.1–16; **337c** Lys. 6.11–12; cf. **170** Andoc. 1.73–79).

At the resulting meeting with the magistrate, the prosecutor presented a written statement of the charge (variously called *enklêma* ["charge"], *graphê* ["writ(ing)," "(written) indictment"], or *antigraphê*: e.g., **256b** Dem. 37.22–26, 28–33; **340c** Pl. *Ap.* 26b2-d9; **340d** Pl. *Ap.* 27c5–8). If the magistrate accepted the lawsuit, he collected any required court fees from the prosecutor (or claimant in a *diadikasia*: see, for example, **60** [Arist.] *Ath. Pol.* 59.3; **185** Andoc. 1.117–21; **228** Isae. 3.40–50, 57–60, 62) and scheduled a preliminary hearing (*anakrisis*, literally "inquiry": e.g., **152** [Arist.] *Ath. Pol.* 56.6–7; **236** [Dem.] 48.22–32; in a *dikê phonou* there were three preliminary hearings, called *prodikasiai*: see chapter 1). Since the date of the *anakrisis* was determined by lot, the term for (successfully) filing a lawsuit or claim was the verb *lanchanein* (literally, "to get [a lawsuit/claim] allotted"); the corresponding noun is *lêxis*, "filing, claim" [literally "allotment"]: e.g., **189** Isae. 6.46; **254** Dem. 39.1, 5, 7–18, at §16).

At the *anakrisis*, the defendant submitted a written reply to the prosecutor's charge (the *antigraphê*, "writ in response": **390a** Hyp. 4.1–3, 14–20, 30–31, 39; compare the use of the verb *antigraphesthai* in reference to the written statements by claimants in a *diadikasia*: **236** [Dem.] 48.22–32), and each litigant swore an oath affirming that his written statement was true (the term *antômosia*, "affidavit," was used both of the oath and, by extension, of the written statement: **231** Isae. 5.6–7, 9, 12–18; **232** Isae. 3.3–7; **340b** Pl. *Ap.* 24b7-c2; **342** D. L. 2.40). The magistrate questioned the litigants and the litigants questioned each other, thus establishing, at least in broad outline, the elements of the prosecutor's and defendant's cases. In only very rare cases do we possess speeches from opposing sides in the same trial (Lysias 6 and Andocides 1; Demosthenes 19 and Aeschines 2; Demosthenes 18 and Aeschines 3; in some other cases one side is represented only by fragments: e.g., Lycurgus, fragmentary speeches X–XI Conomis and Hypereides 1), but the *anakrisis* (and especially public arbitration, where applicable: see below) gave litigants sufficient knowledge of their opponents' evidence and arguments that these could be anticipated and rebutted at trial (e.g., **71b** Lys. 10.6–9; **250** Dem. 41.7–9, 11–12; **253** Dem. 36.2–4, 12, 18–20; **304b** Hyp. 3.13). If a defendant asserted that the prosecutor's lawsuit was illegal, he announced his intent to proceed by *paragraphê*, and trial of the *paragraphê* determined whether the original lawsuit would proceed (see p. 14); in a *diadikasia* over an inheritance, a claimant might swear a *diamartyria* (declaration on oath), which likewise blocked the *diadikasia* unless and until a rival claimant successfully prosecuted a *dikê pseudomartyriôn* (see pp. 29, 43) and established that the *diamartyria* was false (see chapter 7). If there were no such legal objections, and if neither party applied for excuse from or adjournment of the case, the magistrate scheduled the case for public arbitration or for trial; if a litigant was absent from the *anakrisis*, summary judgment could be given against him (e.g., **325** [Dem.] 58.5–6, 8, 10–12).

Arbitration in Athens came in two forms: private arbitration, which was voluntary and binding, and public arbitration, which was mandatory and nonbinding. Private arbitration might be employed in virtually any dispute either in lieu of litigation or after litigation had commenced—although in public lawsuits the prosecutor who dropped his case might remain, at least in theory, liable to penalties. The disputants chose their arbitrators and the terms of arbitration, and if the process was completed as agreed, the arbitrators' verdict was binding and barred legal action on the matter. Since Attic forensic oratory by definition records cases that went to trial (with a few certain or possible exceptions, such as Demosthenes 21, *Against Meidias*: see **22** Dem. 21 [selections];

332 Dem. 21 [selections]), most accounts of private arbitration therein describe failed or contested attempts (e.g., **244** Isoc. 18.1–8, 10–13, 33, 63; **260** [Dem.] 33.19–20, 22, 32–33); descriptions of successful instances are comparatively rare (e.g., **94b** [Dem.] 59.51–53).

From 399/8 on, public arbitration was mandatory in almost all lawsuits that fell under the initial jurisdiction of the Forty (see p. 14). The Forty, allotted annually, four from each Cleisthenic tribe, were competent to judge on their own authority lawsuits involving sums of up to 10 drachmas; all other lawsuits had to be referred for public arbitration. The pool of public arbitrators (*diaitêtai*, singular *diaitêtês*: the word is used of private as well as public arbitrators) comprised all citizen men in their sixtieth year. The public arbitrator allotted to a lawsuit held one or more hearings in which the litigants presented their cases and the arbitrator attempted to reconcile them. If the arbitrator could not effect a reconciliation, he announced a date when he would issue his judgment either for the prosecutor or for the defendant. Either litigant could apply for excuse from appearance or for postponement of the arbitrator's judgment (**19b** Dem. 54.27–28; **75** Dem. 21.79, 81, 83–84, 88). If the arbitrator granted the request, judgment was delayed accordingly, but if he refused it, he would rule as scheduled even in the absence of a litigant (if the arbitrator rendered his judgment against an absent litigant, the case was referred to as a *dikê erêmê*, "lawsuit decided by default" [literally, "empty" or "deserted lawsuit"]: see, e.g., **75** Dem. 21.79, 81, 83–84, 88; **249** Dem. 55 [selections]).

The arbitrator's judgment was final only if both litigants accepted it. If either litigant was dissatisfied with the judgment, he could lodge an appeal for trial in a *dikastêrion*, which was automatically granted. The arbitrator assembled the documents presented before him by the litigants, including their written statements and those of their witnesses (see p. 38), as well as any other documents (such as laws, decrees, challenges, contracts, and wills) they had produced, and placed them in sealed jars, one for the prosecutor and one for the defendant, attaching a written statement of his judgment (see, e.g., **251** [Dem.] 49.17–20). These evidence jars were then handed over to the four members of the Forty who belonged to the defendant's tribe, who introduced and presided over the resulting trial in a *dikastêrion*; at trial no written evidence not contained in the evidence jars could be produced (the extent to which this rule also applied to cases that were not subject to public arbitration, in which case jars would be sealed at the end of the *anakrisis*, is debated).

Trial venue was determined by the type of procedure. In the fifth and fourth centuries, the great majority of procedures, both private and public (prominent exceptions include the *dikê phonou*, *graphê traumatos ek pronoias*, and lawsuits concerning sacred olive trees: p. 8), were tried in the *dikastêria*, located in or near the agora, by jurors selected at random from the number who presented themselves for jury service on a given day (see p. 26) and with the number of jurors for a particular lawsuit determined by the type and seriousness of the lawsuit and/or the amount of money or other property at issue (in the late fourth century, private lawsuits, at least those under the initial jurisdiction of the Forty, were heard by a jury of 201 if the amount at issue was 1,000 drachmas or less and a jury of 401 if it was over 1,000 drachmas: [Aristotle], *Constitution of the Athenians* [*Ath. Pol.*] 53.3; public lawsuits were normally tried by juries of 501 or more). Trials in the *dikastêria* and elsewhere were scheduled and presided over by the magistrates who held initial jurisdiction over the relevant procedure. As in preliminary hearings and arbitration, a litigant could apply for postponement of trial; the decision lay with the jury, which could either grant postponement or declare a *dikê erêmê* (see p. 36) and issue a summary verdict against the absent litigant (**236** [Dem.] 48.22–32). The latter course of action was followed automatically when a litigant failed to appear and offered no explanation (e.g., **390** Hyp. 4 [selections]; **365** Lyc. 1.117–18).

If both litigants were present, trial began with the formal introduction of the case by the presiding magistrate(s), including the reading by the court clerk of the prosecutor's charge (see, e.g., Aeschines 1.2; **273** Ar. *Wasps* 836–47, 893–900, 931–35, 952–66, at lines 894–97) and the defendant's reply (and, in the *dikê phonou* and *graphê traumatos ek pronoias*, the special oaths [*diômosiai*] by the litigants and by their witnesses [unless each witness swore his *diômosia* at the time of his testimony]: see chapters 1 and 2). Then came the speeches, first by the prosecution and then by the defense; in some lawsuits (such as the *dikê phonou*; see also, e.g., **83** [Dem.] 46.18; **87** Dem. 27.4–5) these were followed by a second round of speeches, with the prosecution again speaking first. Each side was given an equal amount of time to present its case; timing was done by a water-clock (*klepsydra*, literally "water-thief"), and the amount of time for speeches was determined by the type of procedure. All trials took place within one day or less, with public lawsuits assigned more time than private ones.

The rules obtaining in the late fourth century, as stated in [Aristotle], *Constitution of the Athenians* (*Ath. Pol.*) 67, were as follows. On any given day, a *dikastêrion* heard either one public lawsuit or four private lawsuits. In a public lawsuit, equal amounts of time (44 *choes* of water [approximately 37 gallons/140 liters: see **234** [Dem.] 43.5–16], which on one reconstruction of the rate of drainage—three minutes per *chous*—corresponds to slightly over two hours) were assigned to the prosecution, to the defense, and to the penal phase of the trial if the defendant was convicted and the lawsuit was assessable (see p. 40). The time assigned to private lawsuits depended on the amount of money or other property at issue. If the amount was over 5,000 drachmas, each side received 10 *choes* (?30 minutes) for its first speech and 3 *choes* (?9 minutes) for its second; if the amount was between 1,000 and 5,000 drachmas, 7 *choes* (?21 minutes) for the first speech and 2 *choes* (?6 minutes) for the second; if the amount was under 1,000 drachmas, 5 *choes* (?15 minutes) for the first speech and 2 *choes* for the second. In a *diadikasia*, 6 *choes* were assigned to each claimant, and there was only one round of speeches (but note *contra* **234** [Dem.] 43.5–16, delivered ca. 345, which describes a *diadikasia* over an inheritance in which each claimant was granted 1 amphora [12 *choes*, ?36 minutes] for his first speech and 3 *choes* for his second). Another way to estimate the time allotted for speeches in various types of lawsuit is to time the recitation of the relevant preserved speeches, but this method is problematic as well, owing to the possibility that a speech was one of several delivered during the allotted time and/or was revised before publication (see p. 22).

The time permitted for each side's speeches included those delivered by the litigant himself and by any *synêgoroi* speaking on his behalf. Speakers combined oral argument with the presentation of evidence, including laws, decrees, testimony by witnesses, oaths, contracts, wills, challenges, and other documents. In private lawsuits, but not in public ones ([Aristotle], *Constitution of the Athenians* [*Ath. Pol.*] 67.3), the water-clock was stopped for the reading of documents, which in all lawsuits was done by the court clerk (e.g., **256b** Dem. 37.22–26, 28–33). It was the responsibility of the litigants to provide any and all evidence, including laws, that they wished to use at trial. Witnesses (*martyres*; singular *martys*) originally testified orally and might be questioned by the litigant who called them and cross-examined by the opposing side, but in the early fourth century (around 380) the procedure was changed: thenceforth a written deposition (*martyria*, which can also refer to oral testimony) was drawn up before trial, and at trial the deposition was read out by the court clerk and simply affirmed by the witness. If the witness did not wish to affirm the deposition (which might have been composed not by the witness himself but by the litigant who wished to call him), he might either swear the oath of denial (*exômosia*: e.g., **16** Isae. 9.17–19; **251** [Dem.] 49.17–20) or simply fail to respond and, at least in some cases, risk a fine of 1,000 drachmas (Aeschines 1.45–50). Litigants might cross-examine each other but could not serve as their own witnesses ([Demosthenes] 46.9–10). Hearsay testimony by witnesses was permitted only when the original speaker was dead; if a witness was physically unable to attend a preliminary hearing and/or trial, owing to absence from Attica, illness, or disability, he gave a written deposition out of court (*ekmartyria*) in the presence of witnesses, and these witnesses affirmed the *ekmartyria* at trial ([Demosthenes] 46.6–8; Isaeus 3.18–21; [Demosthenes] 35.20, 34). Since the selection and presentation of witnesses was entirely up to the litigants, who naturally would under normal circumstances choose family, friends, and others upon whom they could rely for favorable testimony, it seems to have been understood (although there is considerable scholarly debate on the subject: see, e.g., G. Thür, "The Role of the Witness in Athenian Law," in *The Cambridge Companion to Ancient Greek Law*, ed. M. Gagarin-D. Cohen [Cambridge 2005] 146–69) that the role of the witness was not simply to tell the truth but—and potentially regardless of the truth—to support the litigant who called him. Accordingly, it was very common for the loser in a trial to retaliate against an opposing witness by means of a *dikê pseudomartyriôn* (lawsuit for false witness: see pp. 29, 43).

The role of witnesses is but one aspect of a general and lively debate as to the absolute and the relative values of various types of argument and evidence as elements affecting the decisions of Athenian juries, and correspondingly as to the nature and extent of the rule of law at Athens (see, e.g., H. Meyer-Laurin, *Gesetz und Billigkeit im attischen Prozess* [Weimar 1965]; M. Ostwald, *From Popular Sovereignty to the Sovereignty of Law: Law, Society, and Politics in Fifth-Century Athens* [Berkeley and Los Angeles 1986]; E. M. Harris, "Law and Oratory," in I. Worthington, ed., *Persuasion: Greek Rhetoric in Action* [London and New York 1994] 130–50; S. C. Todd, *The Shape of Athenian Law* [Oxford 1993], especially chapters 4 and 6; H. Yunis, "The Rhetoric of Law in Fourth Century Athens," in *The Cambridge Companion to Ancient Greek Law*, ed. M. Gagarin and D. Cohen [Cambridge 2005] 191–208; A. Lanni, *Law and Justice in the Courts of Classical Athens* [Cambridge 2006]). Laws were by definition authoritative, and jurors swore in the heliastic oath (p. 26) that they would vote in accordance with the laws and with sole regard to the matter concerned in the prosecution, but it is evident throughout the corpus of forensic oratory that speakers expect serious attention also to be paid to other considerations, including—but not limited to—appeals to equity and pity and descriptions of good or bad behavior committed in the past and/or predicted for the future. Accordingly, some scholars see laws, like other forms of evidence, primarily as tools of proof and persuasion rather than as rules that will automatically govern a jury's verdict, and accordingly tend to be skeptical about the degree to which Athenian juries actually enforced their laws; others, however, believe that jurors took the provisions of the heliastic oath seriously and are correspondingly more positive in their assessments of the Athenian administration of justice. In the end, though, since juries did not accompany their verdicts with explanations and the verdicts themselves are known in only a minority of cases (p. 22), definitive general answers are elusive, and the impacts of various considerations on a jury will have varied from case to case—and, in any given case, from juror to juror. Also worthy of note is that Athenian law had no doctrine of binding precedent, so the value of earlier similar lawsuits, commonly discussed by speakers, was purely persuasive. Moreover, although at least some courts and procedures had rules mandating that litigants confine their remarks to the specific matter at issue (e.g., **9a** Ant. 6.9; **26a** Lyc. 1.12–13), in fact litigants almost never do so: at trial, the entire lives of the litigants—and of their supporters, witnesses, family, and friends—were fair game, and so forensic speeches regularly devote significant attention to descriptions of the good services performed by the speaker and assaults on the character of his opponents.

Immediately after the speeches by the prosecution and defense, the jury voted. The jury was given no time to deliberate and no instruction as to which arguments or evidence they were or were not allowed to consider; issues of fact and of law were not treated as separate (except in a *paragraphê* [see p. 14], and even then only formally), and jurors were at their own discretion in evaluating both. Voting was done by secret ballot, with the jurors casting their ballots into voting-urns (e.g., **234** [Dem.] 43.5–16; for the procedure, which changed several times in the age of the orators, see A. L. Boegehold, *The Athenian Agora*, vol. XXVIII: *The Lawcourts at Athens: Sites, Buildings, Equipment, Procedure, and Testimonia* [Princeton 1995]). Each juror voted either for the prosecutor or for the defendant (or, in a *diadikasia*, for one of the competing parties), and the verdict was determined by simple majority (in a *diadikasia*, by plurality), with a tie going to the defendant (Antiphon 5.51; Aeschines 3.252).

If the jury voted to convict, a penalty had to be determined; it was at this point that another defining division of procedures came into play. Some procedures (e.g., the *dikê phonou* [chapter 1] and *apagôgê* against a *kakourgos* [p. 31]) carried mandatory fixed penalties specified in the laws governing those procedures; these were collectively called *agônes* (or *dikai*) *atimêtoi*, "non-assessable lawsuits" (singular *agôn*/*dikê atimêtos*; e.g., **249** Dem. 55 [selections]). Procedures lacking mandatory penalties were called *agônes timêtoi* (or *dikai timêtai*), "assessable lawsuits" (singular *agôn timêtos*/*dike timêtê*; e.g., **145** Dem. 27.34, 40, 46, 49–50, 58, 60–61, 67); a given *agôn timêtos* might feature either unlimited penal assessment (e.g., the *graphê hybreôs*: **35** Dem. 21.47) or limited penal assessment (e.g., the *dikê aikeias*, where assessment was limited to a monetary fine: **37** Lys. fr. 178 Carey). In an assessable lawsuit, the jury's vote to convict was followed immediately by assessment (*timêsis*) of the sentence (see, e.g., **340** Pl. *Ap.* [selections]). The prosecutor and the defendant each proposed a penalty (called the *timêma*, "assessment," and *antitimêma*, "counter-assessment," respectively; the prosecutor's proposal might be included in his original statement of the charge: e.g., **264** D. H. *Din.* 3; **342** D. L. 2.40) and gave (or had a *synêgoros* give) a speech in favor of his proposal; the jury then voted (again without deliberation or instruction) either for the prosecutor's proposal or for the defendant's—the jury was not allowed to determine its own penalty—with a simple majority deciding the issue (and a tie again favoring the defendant).

The penalty imposed upon a convicted defendant—in an assessable or non-assessable lawsuit—might affect his person (*sôma*: e.g., **70** Lys. 9.5–12, 15–16; **161** Isae. 11.6, 31, 35; **278** Lys. 5.1, 5; **281** Lys. 29.1–2, 11; **329c** Lys. 7.16–17, 19, 22, 25–26), his property, or both; the distinction between personal and financial penalties (e.g., **228** Isae. 3.40–50, 57–60, 62) is reflected in the standard formula designating an *agôn timêtos* without penal limit, which expressed the penalty to be determined as "whatever [the convicted defendant] must suffer or pay" (e.g., **35** Dem. 21.47; **289** Dem. 24.104–5, 112–15, 120–21, 129, 146). The two most common penalties affecting the person were death and *atimia*. Enforcement of death sentences was the duty of the Eleven (e.g., **302b** [Arist.] *Ath. Pol.* 52.1; **341b** Pl. *Phaedo* 116b7–c4, 116c8–d2, 117a4–b2, 117b6–c5, 117e4–118a8) and in the age of the orators was normally carried out by *apotympanismos* (in which the condemned person was fastened to a board [*tympanon*] and left to die: e.g., Lysias 13.56, 68) or by poisoning with hemlock (see **341b** Pl. *Phaedo* 116b7–c4, 116c8–d2, 117a4–b2, 117b6–c5, 117e4–118a8). Another method, precipitation into a pit, seems to have gone out of fashion by the beginning of the fourth century (but remained at least theoretically possible for certain offenses): see **369** Lyc. 1.120–21; **375** Xen. *Hell.* 1.7.1–16, 20–26, 34–35; **391k** Din. 1.61–63. The death penalty might be aggravated by confiscation of property and/or loss of the right to be buried in Attica (e.g., **3d** Dem. 23.44–45; **13b** Lys. 1.50; **22a** Dem. 21.43; **371** [Plut.] *Lives of the Ten Orators* 833d–834b; **375** Xen. *Hell.* 1.7.1–16, 20–26, 34–35; **385c** Hyp. 1.20; **390a** Hyp. 4.1–3, 14–20, 30–31, 39).

Atimia (fundamentally "dishonor[ing]" or "lack/loss of rights") was a complex concept whose significance varied from time to time and from case to case. Originally, *atimia* meant "outlawry": a person sentenced to *atimia* (who was called *atimos*, translated "outlaw"; plural *atimoi*) lost all rights, including the right to life, such that he might be killed with impunity (e.g., **3h** Dem. 23.62; **358** Plut. *Solon* 19.4; **360** [Arist.] *Ath. Pol.* 16.10; **368** Dem. 9.41–45). In the Classical period, however, while in rare and extreme cases *atimia* retained this original meaning (e.g., ?**371** [Plut.] *Lives of the Ten Orators* 833d-834b; **384** *SEG* 12.87), normally *atimia* involved the loss of certain important rights (but not the right to life) and is accordingly translated "disfranchisement" (an *atimos* being "disfranchised"). This sort of *atimia* could be total or partial. Total *atimia* meant that a person was deprived of an entire package of citizen rights: he could not speak or vote in the Assembly, hold any office, speak in a court of law, or serve on a jury; moreover, he was prohibited from entering the agora and all sacred sites. Partial *atimia* meant that a person was deprived of some but not all of the aforementioned rights (see especially **170** Andoc. 1.73–79, and on *atimia* generally see M. H. Hansen, Apagoge, Endeixis *and* Ephegesis *against* Kakourgoi, Atimoi *and* Pheugontes [Odense 1976]). An *atimos* who engaged in any activity from which he was prohibited by the terms of his *atimia* was liable to *endeixis* (e.g., **337** Lys. 6 [selections]; **338** Andoc. 1 [selections]) or *apagôgê* (e.g., **20** Dem. 23.65–80); in some (but not all) of these cases, unlike in the *endeixis* or *apagôgê* of a *kakourgos* or an exile, the penalty upon conviction was not necessarily death (above, p. 31).

Less common penalties affecting the person were exile, enslavement, and imprisonment. The penalties of exile and enslavement are attested in the age of the orators only for certain specified offenses. Exile was the mandatory penalty in a *dikê phonou* for the unintentional killing of a citizen or for the killing (intentional or unintentional) of a non-citizen (chapter 1), and in a *graphê traumatos ek pronoias* (where the penalty of exile was aggravated by confiscation of property: chapter 2); it could also be imposed for serious offenses against the state (chapter 12) and was regularly imposed, with or without confiscation of property, upon a defendant who absconded from trial for a capital offense (e.g., **367** [Banishment of Themistocles for treason]). A person who violated the terms of his exile could be killed with impunity or arrested by *apagôgê*, *endeixis*, or *ephêgêsis* (see above, ***Types of Procedure***).

Until Solon's *seisachtheia*, citizens could be enslaved for debt (**313** [Solon's *seisachtheia*]); in the fifth and fourth centuries, enslavement of citizens appears to have been limited to the case where a citizen was ransomed from the enemy and did not reimburse his ransomer (**316** [Dem.] 53.6–13). Non-citizens could be enslaved if they posed as citizens or otherwise disguised their status, by exercising a right reserved to citizens, residing in Athens without being registered as a metic, failing to pay the metic tax, or (after the right to marry was limited to citizens: see chapter 5) cohabiting with a citizen as his or her spouse. The dedicated remedy for usurpation of citizen rights was the *graphê xenias* (indictment for being a foreigner), which carried a mandatory penalty of enslavement (**60** [Arist.] *Ath. Pol.* 59.3; **94a** [Dem.] 59.16–17; **94b** [Dem.] 59.51–53; **376** [Dem.] 49.66–67).

Imprisonment was not normally imposed as a penalty per se, except in cases of theft, where the penalty might include five (or ten) days' detention in wooden stocks placed in a public location (**160** Dem. 24.103, 107; **267b** Lys. 10.15–17; **289** Dem. 24.104–5, 112–15, 120–21, 129, 146). The Athenian state prison, adjacent to the agora, was commonly employed for pre-trial detention in cases where a defendant was not permitted or able to post sureties (as in *apagôgê*: e.g., **20** Dem. 23.65–80; **292** Isae. 4.28–29; **302b** [Arist.] *Ath. Pol.* 52.1; for other cases see, e.g., **362** Dem. 24.144–45; cf. §**11.3**) and for post-trial detention pending execution of a sentence of death (**341** Pl. *Phaedo* [selections]) or payment of a fine (e.g., **35** Dem. 21.47; **323b** [Dem.] 35.45–46; **324** [Dem.] 33.1–3, 23).

Penalties affecting the property of a convicted person came in the form of confiscation or, more commonly, a fine payable to the state (normally in public lawsuits: e.g., **44b** Dem. 21.45), to the prosecutor who secured the conviction (normally in private lawsuits: e.g., **41b** [Dem.] 47.64), or to both (as in *phasis* and *apographê* [see ***Types of Procedure***] and the *dikê kakêgorias* [chapter 4]). Default on a judgment owed to the state resulted in registration as a state debtor and the consequent *atimia* (e.g., **170** Andoc. 1.73–79). Default on a judgment owed to a person might result in a *dikê exoulês* (lawsuit for ejectment: **§7.4.2**) brought by the creditor (or his or her *kyrios*: p. 23). If the creditor won the *dikê exoulês*, the debtor was sentenced to pay to the state a fine equal to the judgment on which he had defaulted, both the original creditor and the state were authorized to distrain on the debtor's property in the amount owed to them, and if the debt to the state went unpaid, the debtor was registered as a state debtor, as above.

The verdict and sentence of an Athenian court were final and not subject to appeal, but they might be reversed, de facto if not always de jure, by subsequent litigation or by pardon. Most commonly subsequent litigation took the form of a *dikê pseudomartyriôn* (pp. 29, 39) brought by the losing litigant against one or more of the witnesses who had given testimony for his adversary. This action was an *agôn timêtos*, and so, for example, a person who had been convicted and sentenced to pay a fine in the original lawsuit might prosecute a witness, assess the amount of his fine as the penalty for the witness, and if successful, recover from the witness the fine he had paid to his original prosecutor. In some cases, including a *diadikasia* over an estate or *epiklêros* (see chapter 7), conviction of a witness in a *dikê pseudomartyriôn* constituted automatic grounds for a new trial of the original issue (**233** Isae. 11.45–46). In cases dealing with estates and *epiklêroi*, moreover, the verdict of a court could be challenged and potentially reversed by the filing of a new lawsuit by either a previous or a new claimant within five years of the death of the first heir(s) or awardee(s) (**228** Isae. 3.40–50, 57–60, 62; **234** [Dem.] 43.5–16; **235** Isae. 4.24–25).

Pardon, retrospective or prospective, could be granted with binding force by the state (as in the Amnesty of 403: p. 12; note also the prospective immunity granted to killers of specified offenders in, e.g., **3f** Dem. 23.53; **372** Andoc. 1.96–98; and see also, e.g., **§11.3** on the immunity granted to Andocides in the affair of the herms) or by the individual victim of an offense or claimant to a right. A person who tendered an oral or written quitclaim, commonly designated "release" (*aphesis*, with the corresponding verb *aphienai*) and/or "discharge" (*apallagê*, with the corresponding verb *apallattein*) (e.g., **257b** Dem. 38.6–9; **320** [Dem.] 33.6–12; **324** [Dem.] 33.1–3, 23), thereby gave up the right to pursue legal action on the relevant matter. Pardon by the victim of a homicide likewise barred prosecution (**23** Dem. 37.59), and unanimous pardon by the qualified relatives of the victim was required for the sentence of exile to be lifted from a person convicted of unintentional homicide in a *dikê phonou* (**2** *IG* I[3] 104; **4** [Dem.] 43.57).

CHAPTER 1

Homicide

Handbooks: J. H. **Lipsius**, *Das attische Recht und Rechtsverfahren* (Leipzig 1905–15) 317–38, 600–19; A. R. W. **Harrison**, *The Law of Athens* (Oxford 1968–71) 2.36–43, 77–78, 86–87, 225–28; D. M. **MacDowell**, *The Law in Classical Athens* (Ithaca, NY 1978) 109–22; S. C. **Todd**, *The Shape of Athenian Law* (Oxford 1993) 271–76. **Studies:** G. **Glotz**, *La solidarité de la famille dans le droit criminel en Grèce* (Paris 1904); E. **Ruschenbusch**, "ΦΟΝΟΣ: Zum Recht Drakons und seiner Bedeutung für das Werden des athenischen Staates," *Historia* 9 (1960) 129–54; D. M. **MacDowell**, *Athenian Homicide Law in the Age of the Orators* (Manchester 1963); W. T. **Loomis**, "The Nature of Premeditation in Athenian Homicide Law," *JHS* 92 (1972) 86–95; R. S. **Stroud**, *Drakon's Law on Homicide* (Berkeley 1968); M. H. **Hansen**, Apagoge, Endeixis *and* Ephegesis *against* Kakourgoi, Atimoi *and* Pheugontes (Odense 1976); E. **Cantarella**, *Studi sull'omicidio in diritto greco e romano* (Milan 1976); M. **Gagarin**, "Self-Defense in Athenian Homicide Law," *GRBS* 19 (1978) 111–20; R. **Stroud**, *The Axones and Kyrbeis of Drakon and Solon* (Berkeley 1979); M. **Gagarin**, "The Prosecution of Homicide in Athens," *GRBS* 20 (1979) 301–23; M. H. **Hansen**, "The Prosecution of Homicide in Athens," *GRBS* 22 (1981) 11–30; M. **Gagarin**, *Drakon and Early Athenian Homicide Law* (New Haven 1981); R. W. **Wallace**, *The Areopagos Council, to 307 B.C.* (Baltimore 1989); S. C. **Humphreys**, "A Historical Approach to Drakon's Law on Homicide," in *Symposion 1990*, ed. M. Gagarin (Köln 1991) 17–45; A. **Tulin**, *Dike Phonou: The Right of Prosecution and Attic Homicide Procedure* (Stuttgart 1996); E. **Carawan**, *Rhetoric and the Law of Draco* (Oxford 1998); E. **Volonaki**, "'Apagoge' in Homicide Cases," *Dike* 3 (2000) 147–76; M. **Gagarin**, *Writing Greek Law* (Cambridge 2008) 93–109; D. D. **Phillips**, *Avengers of Blood: Homicide in Athenian Law and Custom from Draco to Demosthenes* (Stuttgart 2008); W. **Riess**, "Private Violence and State Control: The Prosecution of Homicide and Its Symbolic Meanings in Fourth-Century BC Athens," in *Sécurité col-*

lective et ordre public dans les sociétés anciennes, ed. P. Ducrey and C. Brelaz (Geneva 2008) 49–101.

While the Classical Athenians believed that their homicide laws and courts originated in legendary antiquity (**20**; cf. **8b**), and the Alcmaeonids were tried and exiled for acts of homicide and sacrilege (**1**), the history of Athenian homicide law in the strict sense begins with Draco, who was appointed to codify the laws of Athens in 621/0 B.C. (**6a**). Although the rest of Draco's laws were repealed by Solon in 594/3 (**6b**), his homicide law remained in force through the Classical period. Draco's homicide law is known from a late fifth-century inscription (**2**), supplemented by provisions cited by Classical orators (**3**, **4**, **5**). Draco distinguished between intentional and unintentional killing, established equal liability for killing with one's own hand and conspiracy to kill (see also **7b**, **9b**, **25**, **28**), and restricted homicide prosecutions to relatives of the victim within the degree of descendant first cousin once removed (although, in default of these, further kin may have been eligible to prosecute: see **2**). Draco also defined circumstances under which killing was lawful (**3f**, **13a**; cf. **3b**).

The legal procedure for homicide created by Draco, called the *dikê phonou* (cf. **3e**, **3i**), commenced at the funeral of the victim, where his kinsmen made a proclamation against the suspected killer announcing their intent to prosecute (**2**, **4**, **17**). In the Classical period, a second proclamation was made by the archon known as the *basileus*, who superintended the system of homicide courts (**9c-d**, **25**; cf. **18**). The proclamation by the *basileus* was followed by three preliminary hearings (*prodikasiai*; singular *prodikasia*) in successive months; the case went to trial in the fourth month (**9c**). A defendant could be prosecuted by *dikê phonou* for intentional homicide (*hekousios phonos/phonos ek pronoias*: **19b**, **20**, **22a**, **25**), unintentional homicide (*akousios phonos/phonos mê ek pronoias*: **2**, **20**, **22a**, **25**), conspiracy to commit intentional homicide (*bouleusis hekousiou phonou*: **7**; ?**19a**), or conspiracy to commit unintentional homicide (*bouleusis akousiou phonou*: **9**).

Draco and the Classical sources on Athenian homicide law employ a variety of terms to describe the volition of the killer, and modern translations of these terms vary. The positive terms are *hekôn* and *hekousios* (commonly rendered "intentional," "voluntary," or "willing") and *ek pronoias* (literally "as a result of *pronoia*," a word that is rendered "intent," "deliberation," or "premeditation"; *ek pronoias* accordingly would mean "intentional," "deliberate," or "with premeditation"). The corresponding negative terms are *akôn* and *akousios* ("unintentional," "involuntary," "unwilling") and *ou/mê ek pronoias* ("not as a result of *pronoia*," therefore "unintentional," "not deliberate," "without premeditation"). The predominant view, adopted here, holds that in the law of homicide the positive terms are all equivalent and denote the presence of intent to cause harm (not necessarily death), and the negative terms are also all equivalent and denote the absence of such intent. On this issue, and for varying scholarly opinions, see especially **Loomis**, "The Nature of Premeditation"; **Gagarin**, *Drakon* 30–37; **Carawan**, *Rhetoric* 33–41, 68–75, 223–27.

By the fifth century, the Athenians had five special homicide courts, and lawsuits were assigned to one of these courts depending on the nature and circumstances of the offense (**20**, **25**). Defendants accused of intentionally killing an Athenian citizen were tried at the Areopagus; those accused of unintentionally killing a citizen, killing a non-citizen, or conspiring to kill were tried at the Palladion (except, perhaps, for those charged with *bouleusis* of the intentional killing of a citizen, who may have been tried at the Areopagus: see **19a**, **25**, and **28**). Those who asserted a defense of lawful homicide were tried at the Delphinion; accused killers who were already in exile were tried at Phreatto in the Peiraeus; and non-human killers (animals and inanimate objects) were tried at the Prytaneion. At the Areopagus court the entire Council of the Areopagus served as the jury; a board of fifty-one *ephetai*, who cannot be identified with certainty but were probably a subcommittee of the Council of the Areopagus, served as the jury at the Palladion, Delphinion, and Phreatto courts (although we have evidence that seems to describe a regular dicastic jury serving at the Palladion: contrast **2**, **4**, and **25** with **10** and **21**). The jury at the Prytaneion consisted of the *basileus* and the four *phylobasileis* ("tribe-kings": the officials in charge of Athens' four pre-Cleisthenic tribes).

A homicide trial by *dikê phonou* opened with special oaths (*diômosiai*; singular *diômosia*) sworn by both sides (**7c**, **15**, **20**, **21**). Each side then gave two speeches, in the order prosecution, defense, prosecution, defense, as demonstrated in the *Tetralogies* of Antiphon (Antiphon 2–4); a defendant was allowed to flee into voluntary exile without hindrance at any point before beginning his second speech (**20**). After the jury rendered its verdict, which was determined by majority vote, the victorious litigant swore another *diômosia* (**24**). Upon conviction, intentional killers of Athenian citizens were punished by execution and confiscation of their property, intentional killers of non-citizens by permanent exile, and unintentional killers by exile that lasted until they were pardoned by their victims' kin (**2**, **3d**, **13b**, **20**, **22a**, **23**); in accordance with Draco's law, the penalties for conspirators were the same as those for own-hand killers. While convicted killers who obeyed the terms of their exile were protected by law (**2**, **3c**, **3d**), those who entered forbidden areas could be killed or arrested with impunity (**3b**; cf. **5**).

Important changes to Athenian homicide law occurred toward the end of the fifth century. By this time (if not earlier: see **18**), the Athenians had come to believe that unpurified killers might spread a religious pollution (*miasma*) to those around them, and hence took precautions to prevent such transmission (**5**, **8c**, **23**, **25**; cf. **18**). During the last quarter of the fifth century, the scope of the *endeixis* (denunciation) and *apagôgê* (summary arrest) procedures (p. 30), which were traditionally available against *kakourgoi* ("malefactors") such as seducers and thieves (cf. **57a** Aeschin. 1.91), was broadened so as to include suspected killers, and so these procedures became alternatives to the *dikê phonou* for the prosecution of homicide (**8a**). Unlike the *dikê phonou*, *endeixis* and/or *apagôgê* did not require the prosecutor to be related to the victim, involved no preliminary hearings, were tried in ordinary jury-courts (*dikastêria*: p. 26), and imposed a mandatory death sentence upon all convicted defendants. By the early fourth century, however, prosecutors by *apagôgê* had to declare that they had apprehended their defendants "in the act" (*ep' autophôrôi*: **14**). Another fundamental, but temporary, change to the homicide law came in the aftermath of the reign of the Thirty Tyrants in 404/3, when the Athenians passed an amnesty—the Amnesty of 403—that drastically limited liability for acts committed during the late oligarchy: only those who had killed with their own hands would be liable to prosecution for homicide, while those who had denounced people and so procured their executions were (at least by the letter of the law) immunized by the Amnesty (**11**, **12**). With this exception, the *dikê phonou* instituted by Draco and the more recent extension of *endeixis* and *apagôgê* to suspected killers remained in effect through the end of the Classical period.

See also **33** Dem. 54.17–19; **43** Dem. 23.50; **54** Lys. 1.24–33; **57a** Aeschin. 1.91; **62** Lucian, *Eunuch* 10; **71** Lys. 10 (selections); **170** Andoc. 1.73–79; **240** Dem. 23.50; **266** Plut. *Solon* 17.1–3; **339** Pl. *Euthyphro* (selections); **349a** Dem. 22.2–3; **358** Plut. *Solon* 19.4; **368** Dem. 9.41–45; **372** Andoc. 1.96–98; **384** *SEG* 12.87.

1. Trial and punishment of the Alcmaeonids for the killing of Cylon's partisans. (date of trial 636–621)

In 640, Cylon won an Olympic victory in the *diaulos* ("double-flute," roughly a 400-meter sprint: Eusebius, *Chronica* 1.33); during a subsequent Olympic festival (**1b**), but before the legislation of Draco (621/0), he attempted to establish himself as tyrant of Athens by a coup d'état (the possible dates for which are thus 636, 632, 628, and 624). He and his partisans occupied the Acropolis but promptly came under siege by the Athenians en masse, who eventually entrusted command to the nine archons (**1b-d**; Herodotus' identification in **1a** of the relevant magistrates as the "presidents of the naucraries," about whom little is known, is generally rejected), led by Megacles of the Alcmaeonid clan (*genos*, a hereditary group of related families: cf. **136** Isae. 7.13–17, 27–28, 30). After placing themselves under the protection of Athena ("the goddess" in **1b** and **1d**), who had a temple (**1b**), a cult statue (**1a**, **1d**), and an altar (**1b**) on the Acropolis, the Cylonians agreed to a conditional surrender (**1a-b**), but as they came down the Acropolis, many of them were killed, some while seeking refuge at the shrine of the Awful Goddesses (*Semnai Theai*, who came to be identified [Aeschylus, *Eumenides*] with the Furies: **1b**, **1d**). These killings and the attendant sacrilege gave rise to the earliest known historical trial in Athens (for some mythical precursors see **20** Dem. 23.65–80, at §§66, 74). The entire Alcmaeonid clan was convicted and sentenced to a religious curse (**1a-d**) and perpetual exile (**1b**, **1c**), and a Cretan named Epimenides was called in to perform a ritual purification of the city (**1c-d**). The sentence was revoked in the first half of the sixth century but briefly reinstated in 508/7 (**1a**).

a. Herodotus 5.71. (date of composition 440s-420s)

R. W. **Macan**, *Herodotus: The Fourth, Fifth, and Sixth Books*, 2 vols. (London 1895: text and commentary); W. W. **How**-J. **Wells**, *A Commentary on Herodotus*, 2 vols. (ed. corr. Oxford 1928); R. B. **Strassler**, ed., *The Landmark Herodotus* (New York 2007: translation with introduction and notes).

Herodotus of Halicarnassus, the "father of history" (Cicero, *De Legibus* 1.5), recounts in his *Histories* the conflicts between the Greeks and Persians that culminated in the Persian Wars (490, 480–479 B.C.). In this passage, he explains the origins of the curse that provided the pretext for the temporary expulsion of Cleisthenes (who upon his return would establish the Athenian democracy) and 700 Alcmaeonid households from Athens in 508/7 (cf. [Aristotle], *Constitution of the Athenians* [*Ath. Pol.*] 20).

Those of the Athenians called "the accursed" got their name in the following way. Among the Athenians there was a man named Cylon, an Olympic victor. He aspired to tyranny, and after attracting a faction of men his own age, he attempted to seize the Acropolis. When he was unable to gain control, he sat down in front of the statue as a suppliant. [2] The presidents of the naucraries, who governed Athens at that time, got [Cylon and his men] to rise and abandon sanctuary [by agreeing that they would be] liable to any penalty except death, but they were killed, and the blame fell upon the Alcmaeonids.

b. Thucydides 1.126.3–12. (date of composition 431-ca. 400)

A. W. **Gomme**-A. **Andrewes**-K. J. **Dover**, *A Historical Commentary on Thucydides*, 5 vols. (Oxford 1945–81); R. B. **Strassler**, ed., *The Landmark Thucydides* (New York 1996: translation with introduction and notes).

Thucydides, the immediate successor of Herodotus (**1a**) in the writing of history, composed a monograph on the Peloponnesian War (431–404 B.C.); he served as an Athenian general in 424 but, due to his failure to maintain control of the city of Amphipolis, was promptly exiled from Athens for the remainder of the conflict. In 432/1, on the eve of war, the Spartans attempted to revive once again the ancient curse upon the Alcmaeonids, demanding that Athens exile them (and in particular, the leading Athenian politician Pericles, who was an Alcmaeonid on his mother's side). In the following passage, Thucydides offers his version of the origin of the curse. "The god" (1.126.4) is Apollo, whose oracle at Delphi was the most important and influential religious site in ancient Greece.

There was a man of Athens named Cylon, an Olympic victor of long ago, wellborn and powerful. He had married the daughter of Theagenes the Megarian, who at that time was tyrant of Megara. [4] When Cylon consulted the oracle at Delphi, the god responded that he should seize the Acropolis of Athens during the greatest festival of Zeus. [5] Cylon obtained a troop of men from Theagenes and persuaded his friends to join him, and when the Olympic festival in the Peloponnese arrived, he seized the Acropolis with the goal of becoming tyrant; he believed that this was the greatest festival of Zeus and that it had a particular connection to him, since he had been an Olympic victor. [6] He did not consider, nor did the oracle make clear, whether the "greatest festival" that was mentioned was in Attica or somewhere else: the Athenians too have a festival of Zeus [*Diasia*], which is called "the greatest festival of Zeus the Gracious." . . . But, thinking that he understood [the oracle] correctly, he attempted the deed.

[7] The Athenians, realizing what was happening, came out of the fields in full force against [Cylon and his men], took up positions, and besieged them. [8] As time passed, the Athenians grew tired of the siege, and most of them departed, entrusting to the nine archons the guard duty and full powers to dispose of the entire matter however they decided was best (at that time the nine archons conducted the majority of political affairs). [9] Cylon and his men were faring poorly under siege due to a lack of food and water. [10] So Cylon and his brother escaped, but the rest, since they were hard-pressed and some were even dying of hunger, sat down as suppliants at the altar on the Acropolis.

[11] Those of the Athenians who had been entrusted with the guard duty,

when they saw men dying in the temple, got them to rise and abandon sanctuary by guaranteeing that they would do them no harm, but then led them away and killed them; they even did away with some who sat down at the altars of the Awful Goddesses as they passed by. From this act they and their descendants were called accursed and offenders against the goddess. [12] So the Athenians drove out these accursed ones. . . . : they drove out the living, and they took up the bones of the dead and cast them out [of Attica].

c. [Aristotle], *Constitution of the Athenians* (*Ath. Pol.*) 1. (date of composition 332–322)

J. E. **Sandys**, *Aristotle's* Constitution of Athens[2] (London 1912: text and commentary); P. J. **Rhodes**, *Aristotle:* The Athenian Constitution (London 1984: translation with introduction and notes); ***idem,*** *A Commentary on the Aristotelian* Athenaion Politeia (rev. ed. Oxford 1993: commentary).

A treatise titled *Constitution of the Athenians* (in Greek, *Athênaiôn Politeia,* whence the common scholarly abbreviation *Ath. Pol.*) was composed by a student of Aristotle—or, less probably, by Aristotle himself—between 332 and 322 B.C. This work is not an authoritative legal document—such as the U.S. Constitution—but rather an analysis of the Athenian constitution divided into two parts. The first part (chapters 1–41) surveys the history of the Athenian constitution from the aftermath of Cylon's conspiracy to the restoration of democracy at the end of the fifth century (the original beginning of the work, which dealt primarily with the Athenian monarchy, has been lost); the second part (chapters 42–69) describes the constitution in operation at the time of writing. Below is the opening passage of the (preserved) *Ath. Pol.*, which summarizes the trial and sentencing of the Alcmaeonids and the purification of the city. "By birth" indicates that the jury was drawn from the Athenian aristocracy; from the remains of an *Epitome* of the *Ath. Pol.* made by Heracleides Lembus in the second century B.C., we know that the lost beginning of the *Ath. Pol.* named Megacles as the leader of the Cylonians' killers (cf. **1d**).

. . . . with Myron [prosecuting and the jury chosen] by birth and having taken an oath over sacrificial victims. After the sentence of a curse was passed, the perpetrators themselves were exhumed and banished, and their descendants went into perpetual exile [*aeiphygian*]. On these conditions Epimenides of Crete purified the city.

d. Plutarch, *Solon* 12.1–9. (date of composition late 1st-early 2nd c. A.D.)

M. **Manfredini**-L. **Piccirilli**, *Plutarco:* La vita di Solone (Verona 1977: text, Italian translation, and commentary); R. **Waterfield**, *Plutarch: Greek Lives* (Oxford 1998: translation with introduction and notes by P. A. Stadter); on Solon generally see I. M. **Linforth**, *Solon the Athenian* (Berkeley 1919); E. **Ruschenbusch**, *ΣΟΛΩΝΟΣ ΝΟΜΟΙ: Die Fragmente des solonischen Gesetzeswerkes mit einer Text- und Überlieferungsgeschichte* (Wiesbaden 1966); J. H. **Blok**-A. P. M. H. **Lardinois**, eds., *Solon of Athens: New Historical and Philological Approaches* (Leiden 2006); E. **Ruschenbusch**, *Solon: Das Gesetzeswerk—Fragmente: Übersetzung und Kommentar* (Stuttgart 2010).

Plutarch (?40s–?120s A.D.), a Greek from Chaeroneia in Boeotia, composed biographies of famous figures in Greek and Roman history, including Solon, who as eponymous archon in 594/3 B.C. revised the Athenian constitution and wrote a comprehensive new lawcode (see **6b** [Arist.] *Ath. Pol.* 7.1, and chapters 5–12 of the *Ath. Pol.* generally, with references under **1c**). Here Plutarch gives his account of the killing of the Cylonians, the trial and sentencing of the killers, and the purification of Athens. For the selection of the jury "on the basis of birth" (12.3) cf. **1c**; Phlya (12.4) was a village (after Cleisthenes' reforms, a deme) located about five miles northeast of Athens. Plutarch's association of Solon with the trial of the Alcmaeonids and Epimenides' purification is problematic. The context of this passage indicates that Plutarch placed these events shortly before Solon's archonship, but the *Ath. Pol.* unambiguously places the trial and purification before Draco's legislation, and the most likely conclusion is that Plutarch has compressed events in favor of the subject of his biography.

By this point the Cylonian curse had been troubling the city for a long time, ever since the archon Megacles persuaded the members of Cylon's conspiracy, who were seeking sanctuary with the goddess, to come down for judgment. They had attached a spun thread to the statue and were holding on to it, but as they came down, when they were near the [sanctuary of the] Awful Goddesses, the thread spontaneously broke, and Megacles and his fellow archons rushed to arrest them, on the grounds that the goddess was refusing their supplication. Some of them they stoned to death outside [the sanctuary]; others were slaughtered after they had fled to the altars for refuge. The only ones who were spared were those who begged the archons' wives for sanctuary. [2] As a result of this act [the archons] were called accursed and were hated. . . .

[3] . . . Solon came forward to mediate along with the leaders of the Athenians, and . . . he persuaded those who were called accursed to submit to trial

and judgment before a jury of 300 chosen on the basis of birth. [4] With Myron of Phlya serving as prosecutor, the men were convicted; the living were banished, and they dug up the corpses of the dead and cast them over the borders. [5] Owing to these disturbances and the coincident attacks by the Megarians, the Athenians lost Nisaea and were again expelled from Salamis. [6] Superstitious fears and apparitions held the city in thrall, and the seers announced that curses and pollutions requiring purification were indicated by the sacrifices. [7] So they summoned Epimenides of Phaestus, who arrived from Crete. . . . [8] He came, treated Solon as a friend, and in many ways made preparations and paved the way for Solon's legislation. . . . [9] Most importantly, by means of certain propitiatory and cleansing rites and by founding temples, he instituted rituals and purified the city. . . .

2. *Inscriptiones Graecae* I[3] 104. Republication of Draco's homicide law. (409/8; law originally passed in 621/0)

D. **Lewis**, ed., ***Inscriptiones Graecae,*** vol. 1 ed. 3 fasc. 1 (Berlin and New York 1981: text and Latin notes); **MacDowell**, *AHL* (text and translation pp. 118–20; commentary *passim*); **Stroud**, *Drakon's Law* (text, translation, and commentary); **Gagarin**, *Drakon* (text, translation, and commentary); H. **van Effenterre**-F. **Ruzé**, *Nomima,* vol. 1 (Rome 1994) no. 02 (text, French translation, and commentary); **Tulin**, *Dike Phonou* 7–19 (text, translation, and commentary); **Carawan**, *Rhetoric* (text and translation pp. 33–34; commentary *passim*); **Phillips**, *Avengers of Blood* (text and translation pp. 49–50, 137, commentary *passim,* esp. pp. 35–57).

Draco's laws were originally inscribed on revolving blocks called *axones,* which were probably made of wood and do not survive (see **Stroud**, *Axones*). In 409/8, however, the Athenians decided to reinscribe Draco's homicide law on stone. The result is the following inscription, which opens with a preamble mandating the republication of Draco's law on homicide (lines 1–9) and continues with the law itself (lines 10ff.), beginning with a transcription of the first axon. Unfortunately, most of the inscribed law (considerable sections of the first axon, and all following axones) is no longer legible.

In the preamble, "the Council" is the Council of 500, and "the people" refers to the Assembly; on prytanies see p. 6; the Royal Stoa, located at the northwest corner of the agora, was the site of the office of the *basileus*; the *pôlêtai* are the "Sellers" of state contracts and confiscated property (see [Aristotle], *Constitution of the Athenians* [*Ath. Pol.*] 47.2–5; **302b** [Arist.] *Ath. Pol.* 52.1); the *Hellênotamiai* ("Treasurers of the Greeks") are assessors and administrators of the tribute paid by Athens' allies in the Delian

League/Athenian Empire (478–404: p. 11). For *pheugein* (line 11), here translated "stand trial," many scholars (e.g., **Gagarin**, *Drakon* xvi, 30–37 with p. 30 n. 1) prefer the meaning "be exiled"; "the kings" (line 12) may refer either to the *basileus* alone (plural because a new *basileus* was chosen each year) or to the *basileus* and the four *phylobasileis* (see **Stroud**, *Drakon's Law* 45–47). On conspiracy to kill (lines 12–13) cf. **12c** Andoc. 1.94; **9b** Ant. 6.15–16, 19. The provisions on pardon, prosecution, and proclamation (lines 13–22) are heavily restored on the basis of **4** [Dem.] 43.57. For "phratry members" (lines 18, 23) see chapter 6; for their selection "on the basis of birth" (line 19) cf. **1c** [Arist.] *Ath. Pol.* 1; **1d** Plut. *Solon* 12.1–9. Lines 26–29 are heavily restored on the basis of **3c** Dem. 23.37. The border-market lay on the boundary between Attica and Boeotia or the Megarid; "games" presumably refers to Panhellenic athletic festivals, including the Olympic games; "Amphictyonic rites" refers to the observances connected with the oracle of Apollo at Delphi, which was supervised by an association of city-states known as the Amphictyonic League. The phrase "the killer of an Athenian" means "the killer of an Athenian citizen in full possession of his civic rights," which a killer in exile did not enjoy. With the phrase "our land" in lines 30–31 cf. **3b** Dem. 23.28; "starting a fight unjustly" (lines 33–34) translates *archôn cheirôn adikôn*, literally "beginning unjust hands": cf. **41** [Dem.] 47.40; **43** Dem. 23.50. The clause on self-defense against robbery (lines 37–38) is restored on the basis of **3g** Dem. 23.60. Ellipses in the translation correspond to lacunae in the text for which a restoration is not generally accepted.

Diognetus of the deme Phrearrhioe was secretary; Diocles was archon [409/8].

Resolved by the Council and the people; the tribe Acamantis held the prytany, Diognetus was secretary, Euthydicus presided, . . . e . . . anes made the motion. Let the Recorders of the Laws inscribe Draco's law on homicide, having received it from the *basileus* along with the secretary of the Council, on a stone pillar; and let them place it in front of the Royal Stoa. Let the *pôlêtai* let out the contract according to the law, and let the *Hellênotamiai* provide the funds.

First Axon. Even if a person kills someone unintentionally [*mê 'k pronoias*], he shall stand trial [*pheugein*]. The kings shall judge him guilty of homicide [*phonou*] whether he killed with his own hand or conspired to kill [*bouleusanta*], and the *ephetai* shall decide the case. If father or brother or sons are alive, they shall all grant pardon; otherwise he who objects shall prevail. If these do not exist, relatives up to first cousin's son and first cousin shall grant pardon, if all are willing to pardon; otherwise he who objects shall prevail. If none of these exists and he kills unintentionally [*akôn*], and the Fifty-One, the *ephetai*, pass a verdict that he killed unintentionally, then let ten phratry members admit him, if they are willing; let the Fifty-One choose these men on the basis of birth. Let those who [20] killed previously also be bound by this law. Relatives up to first cousin's son and first cousin shall issue a proclamation to the killer in public [*en agorai*]; first cousins, sons of first cousins, fathers-in-law, sons-in-law, and phratry members shall assist in the prosecution [*syndiôkein*] . . .

. . . is guilty of homicide . . .

. . . the Fifty-One . . .

. . . convict of homicide . . .

[26] And if a person kills the killer or is responsible for his killing, when the killer has stayed away from the border-market, games, and Amphictyonic rites, he shall be bound by the same terms as the killer of an Athenian. The *ephetai* shall decide the case . . .

[30] . . . our land . . .

. . . starting a fight unjustly . . .

. . . a fight unjustly, [35] he kills . . .

. . . the *ephetai* shall decide the case . . .

. . . he is a free man. And if in immediate self-defense he kills someone carrying or leading away [his property] forcibly and without justification, the death shall be uncompensated . . .

. . .

[56] Second Axon. . . .

3. Demosthenes 23 *Against Aristocrates* (selections). (date of speech 352/1; laws attributed to Draco, 621/0, but see below)

On the laws quoted here see references under **2**; on the speech see A. **Schäfer**, *Demosthenes und seine Zeit* (Leipzig 1858–87) 1.424–47; H. **Weil**, *Les plaidoyers politiques de Démosthène*, ser. 2 (Paris 1886: text and commentary); F. **Blass**, *Die attische Beredsamkeit* (Leipzig 1887–98) 3.1.292–300; J. H. **Vince**, *Demosthenes III: Against Meidias, Androtion, Aristocrates, Timocrates, Aristogeiton: XXI–XXVI* (Cambridge, MA 1935: text and translation); S. **Usher**, *Greek Oratory: Tradition and Originality* (Oxford 1999) 204–9; D. M. **MacDowell**, *Demosthenes the Orator* (Oxford 2009) 196–206.

Demosthenes' oration *Against Aristocrates* was composed for delivery by Euthycles in a *graphê paranomôn* (p. 14) against Aristocrates for proposing an unlawful decree; among other illegalities, Aristocrates' decree allegedly violated numerous laws on homicide. While the speaker attributes all the homicide laws he cites to Draco (**3e**), in a manner consistent with the common legislative fiction whereby Athenians of the fifth and fourth centuries credited their homicide laws to Draco and the rest of their laws by default to Solon (p. 4), it is likely that **3a** and **3b** are post-Draconian (see the relevant headnotes).

a. Dem. 23.22 (*lex*). Jurisdiction of the Areopagus. (date of law ?594/3 or later)

Cf. **20** Dem. 23.65–80; **25** [Arist.] *Ath. Pol.* 57.2–4. While it is likely that Draco assigned some homicide lawsuits to the Areopagus—in addition to the argument from survival raised by fifth- and fourth-century Athenian practice (e.g., **20** Dem. 23.65–80), note especially **358** Plut. *Solon* 19.4—this law is probably Solonian or later, since it governs intentional wounding (see chapter 2) as well as homicide, and Solon is said to have annulled all Draco's laws except those on homicide (**6b** [Arist.] *Ath. Pol.* 7.1). The wording of the law is ambiguous in that the phrase "with intent" (*ek pronoias*) may qualify either wounding alone or both homicide and wounding; the latter reading is arguably supported by the fact that in the fifth and fourth centuries the homicide jurisdiction of the Areopagus encompassed only *dikai phonou* for the intentional killing (and, perhaps, for plotting the intentional killing: ?**19a** Dem. 54.25; **28** Harpo. s.v. *bouleuseôs*) of an Athenian citizen (**20** Dem. 23.65–80; **25** [Arist.] *Ath. Pol.* 57.2–4).

LAW FROM THE HOMICIDE LAWS ON THE AREOPAGUS. The Council of the Areopagus shall judge cases of homicide [*phonou*] and wounding with intent [*traumatos ek pronoias*] and arson and poisoning, if a person kills by giving poison.

b. Dem. 23.28 (*lex*). Treatment of killers. (date of law ?594/3 or later)

Reference to, and apparent modification of, a clause from "the <first> axon" (the angled brackets < > enclose an editorial supplement to the text, as also below "<before> the archons"; for the identification of the axon cf. **2** *IG* I^3 104, at lines 30–31, where the phrase "our land" appears) indicates that this provision is not part of Draco's original homicide law but a later rider specifying that arrested killers may not be tortured or held for ransom and providing a remedy in case they are. The term (*h*)*êliaia* seems originally to have designated the Athenian Assembly sitting as a court of law; by the fifth century the term was also applied to one or more of the regular jury-courts (*dikastêria*) under the supervision of the six archons known as the *thesmothetai* (*IG* I^3 40 [= R. **Meiggs**-D. **Lewis**, *A Selection of Greek Historical Inscriptions to the End of the Fifth Century BC* (rev. ed. Oxford 1988: text and commentary), no. 52 = C. W. **Fornara**, *Archaic Times to the End of the Peloponnesian War*[2] (Cambridge 1983: translation with notes), no. 103], lines 74–76; Antiphon 6.21; **380** Dem. 24.63).

Killing and arrest [*apagein*] of killers in our land shall be allowed, as it states on the <first> axon. Torture, however, shall not be allowed, nor ransom, or else he shall owe twice the amount of damage he causes. Anyone who wishes may bring the case <before> the archons for those cases which each of them judges. The *hêliaia* shall decide the case.

c. Dem. 23.37 (*lex*). Immunity of killer in exile.

Cf. **2** *IG* I[3] 104, at lines 26–29.

And if a person kills the killer or is responsible for his killing, when the killer has stayed away from the border-market, games, and Amphictyonic rites, he shall be bound by the same terms as the killer of an Athenian. The *ephetai* shall decide the case.

d. Dem. 23.44–45 (*lex* + commentary). Immunity of exiled (unintentional) killer's person and property outside Attica; confiscation of intentional killer's property.

Demosthenes understands this clause as guaranteeing specifically against the forcible repatriation of the unintentional killer (§49).

LAW. If, beyond the border, a person drives, carries, or leads [the person and/or property of] one of the killers who have left the country and whose property is unconfiscated, he shall owe the same amount as if he committed the act in our land.

. . .

[45] The law states, "If a person . . . one of the killers who have left the country and whose property is unconfiscated." It is talking about people who have moved away because of an unintentional killing [*akousiôi phonôi*]. How is this made clear? By the fact that the law says "who have left the country," not "who have been exiled"; and by the fact that it defines these people as "those whose property is unconfiscated": for the property of intentional [*ek pronoias*] killers is confiscated.

e. Dem. 23.51 (*lex* + commentary). Immunity for denunciation of killers in violation of exile.

LAW. There shall be no trials [*dikas*] for homicide [*phonou*] anywhere against those who denounce [*endeiknyntôn*] exiles, if one of them returns where he is not allowed.

This is a law of Draco, men of Athens, as are all the rest that I have cited from the homicide laws. . . .

f. Dem. 23.53 (*lex*). Lawful homicide.

These provisions specify homicides for which the killer bears no liability. "The games" here presumably refers to any established athletic competition, in Attica or elsewhere (cf. **2** *IG* I³ 104, at lines 26–29; **3c**). "Having come upon a highway robber on the road" *vel sim.* is the usual understanding of the Greek *en hodôi kathelôn*, literally "having come upon [him] on the road" (see, e.g., **MacDowell**, *AHL* 75–76; cf. Herodotus 1.41.2). In the phrase "upon his consort," "consort" translates Greek *damarti*, an archaic and poetic word for "wife" (cf. **13a** Lys. 1.30–31); *epi* "(up)on" is sometimes translated "with," although the requirement of carnal proximity is not disputed. For *pheugein*, here translated "stand trial," some scholars prefer the meaning "be exiled" (cf. **2** *IG* I³ 104, at line 11).

If a person kills unintentionally [*akôn*] in the games, or having come upon a highway robber on the road, or in war without recognizing his victim, or [finding his victim] upon his consort, mother, sister, daughter, or concubine whom he keeps for the procreation of free children, for these acts he shall not stand trial [*pheugein*] as a killer.

g. Dem. 23.60 (*lex*). Self-defense against robbery.

Cf. **2** *IG* I³ 104, at lines 37–38.

And if in immediate self-defense he kills someone carrying or leading away [his property] forcibly and without justification, the death shall be uncompensated.

h. Dem. 23.62 (*lex*). Penalty for repeal or amendment.

Any magistrate or private citizen who is responsible for abolishing this law [*thesmon*] or alters it shall be outlawed [*atimon*], as shall his children and his property.

i. Dem. 23.82 (*lex*). Seizure of hostages (*androlêpsia,* "man-taking").

> We have no instance of this procedure in action; those who may be compelled to stand trial, besides the accused killer himself, may have included his relatives or citizens of the city where he has taken refuge (see Demosthenes' comments later in the speech at §§83–85, 218).

If a person dies a violent death, on his behalf his relatives shall have the right to seize hostages [*tas androlêpsias*] until they either submit to trial for the homicide [*dikas tou phonou*] or surrender the killers. The seizure shall be of up to three people and no more.

4. [Demosthenes] 43 *Against Macartatus* 57 (*lex*). Proclamation, prosecution, and pardon. (date of speech ?ca. 345; legislation of Draco dated 621/0)

> On the law quoted here see references under **2**; on the speech see **Schäfer,** *Demosthenes* 4.229–36; **Blass,** *AB* 3.1.549–56; L. **Gernet,** *Démosthène: Plaidoyers civils, Tome II, Discours XXXIX–XLVIII* (Paris 1957: text, French translation, and notes); **Usher,** *GO* 266–67; **MacDowell,** *DO* 83–87; A. C. **Scafuro,** *Demosthenes, Speeches 39–49* (Austin 2011: translation with introduction and notes).
>
> [Demosthenes] 43 was delivered in an inheritance lawsuit (a *diadikasia*: see chapter 7) over the estate of Hagnias. The speaker, who asserts that his biological son is related to Hagnias more closely than the rival claimant, adduces provisions of Draco's homicide law as examples of the duties incumbent upon relatives of a decedent. Note that these clauses are restored in somewhat different order in **2** *IG* I^3 104, at lines 13–23.

Relatives up to first cousin's son and first cousin shall issue a proclamation to the killer in public [*en agorai*]; first cousins, sons of first cousins, fathers-in-law, sons-in-law, and phratry members shall assist in the prosecution [*syndiôkein*]. If father or brother or sons are alive, they shall all grant pardon; otherwise he who objects shall prevail. If none of these exists and he kills unintentionally [*akôn*], and the Fifty-One, the *ephetai*, pass a verdict that he killed unintentionally, then let ten phratry members admit him, if they are willing; let the Fifty-One choose these men on the basis of birth. Let those who killed previously also be bound by this law.

5. Demosthenes 9 *3 Philippic* 44 (*lex* + commentary). Lawful homicide. (341, quoting Draco's law of 621/0)

Schäfer, *Demosthenes* 2.467–80; **Blass**, *AB* 3.1.374–82; J. E. **Sandys**, *Demosthenes:* On the Peace, Second Philippic, On the Chersonesus *and* Third Philippic (repr. rev. ed. London 1962: text and commentary); **Usher**, *GO* 239–41; D. D. **Phillips**, *Athenian Political Oratory* (New York and London 2004) 165–80 (translation with introduction and notes); **MacDowell**, *DO* 349–54; J. **Trevett**, *Demosthenes, Speeches 1–17* (Austin 2011: translation with introduction and notes).

In this speech, delivered before the Athenian Assembly, Demosthenes urges his countrymen to abandon their reactive posture and mount aggressive military action against Philip II of Macedon. In comparing his contemporaries to their predecessors, the orator refers to the case of Arthmius of Zeleia, who was outlawed from the Athenian Empire in the 460s or 450s (**368** Dem. 9.41–45). He then explains the concept of outlawry by reference to Draco's homicide law. On the pollution normally occasioned by a homicide cf. **8c** Ant. 5.82–83.

. . . . it is written in the homicide laws, concerning persons in whose cases no homicide trial is granted, but whose killing is sanctioned: "and let him die an outlaw [*atimos*]." What this means is that the killer of one of these persons is free of pollution.

6. [Aristotle], *Constitution of the Athenians* (*Ath. Pol.*) (selections). (composed 332–322)

See references and headnote under **1c**. With **6b** cf. **266** Plut. *Solon* 17.1–3.

a. [Arist.] *Ath. Pol.* 4.1. Date of Draco's legislation.

Not long afterward, in the archonship of Aristaechmus [621/0], Draco enacted his laws.

b. [Arist.] *Ath. Pol.* 7.1. Draco's homicide laws survive Solon's recension (594/3).

[Solon] established a constitution and enacted other laws, and they stopped using Draco's laws except those on homicide.

7. Antiphon 1 *Against the Stepmother* (selections). *Dikê phonou* for conspiracy to commit intentional homicide (*bouleusis hekousiou phonou*) of citizen. (?440s-411)

See especially M. **Gagarin**, *Antiphon: The Speeches* (Cambridge 1997: text and commentary); M. **Gagarin**-D. M. **MacDowell**, *Antiphon and Andocides* (Austin 1998: translation with introduction and notes); also **Blass**, *AB* 1.187–94; R. C. **Jebb**, *The Attic Orators from Antiphon to Isaeus*[2] (London 1893) 1.64–67; **Usher**, *GO* 27–30.

In this case, the defendant ("the stepmother") stands accused of lethally poisoning the victim, her husband, through a slave intermediary: since she did not administer the poison herself, she is charged with conspiracy to commit intentional homicide (*bouleusis hekousiou phonou*). The prosecutor and speaker is the victim's son and the stepson of the defendant, who is represented by her sons, the speaker's half-brothers; the trial took place either at the Palladion or at the Areopagus (**25** [Arist.] *Ath. Pol.* 57.2–4; **28** Harpo. s.v. *bouleuseôs*). (Some scholars identify the action as a *dikê phonou* for own-hand killing rather than *bouleusis*, in which case trial will definitely have occurred at the Areopagus; note also Areopagite jurisdiction over lethal poisoning: **3a** Dem. 23.22.) For the dying injunction (**7a**) cf. Lysias 13.39–42. The *diômosia* (**7c**) is explained in **20** Dem. 23.65–80, at §§67–69; cf. **31a** Lys. 3.1.

a. Ant. 1.28–30. Dying injunction.

Obviously those who plot the deaths of people close to them do not conduct their machinations and preparations in the presence of witnesses; they do it as secretly as they can and so that no one knows. [29] And the victims of such plots know nothing until they are already caught in the evil and realize the doom they are facing. Then, if they are able and have time before they die, they summon their friends and relatives and call them to witness; they tell them at whose hands they are dying and enjoin them to avenge them for the wrongs they have suffered. [30] This is the injunction my father laid upon me when I was a boy, as he was suffering his miserable final illness. If, however, [the victims] lack such people, they compose documents, call on their household slaves as witnesses, and disclose at whose hands they are dying.

b. Ant. 1.26. *Bouleusis* of intentional homicide.

She killed him intentionally [*hekousiôs*] by plotting [*bouleusasa*] his death, and he died unwillingly and violently. For how did he not die violently, gentlemen?

He was about to sail out of this country, he was dining at the home of a man who was his friend; and she, by sending the drug and ordering that it be given to him to drink, killed our father.

c. Ant. 1.28. *Diômosia* for *bouleusis.*

For my part, I am amazed at my brother's audacity and mindset, to take the oath [*diomosasthai*] on his mother's behalf that he knows well that she did not do these things.

d. Ant. 1.25. Penalty for *bouleusis* of intentional homicide of citizen.

Therefore I now ask this of you: just as she killed him without mercy or pity, so too should she herself be put to death by you and by justice.

8. Antiphon 5 *On the Killing of Herodes* (selections). (427–412)

See especially M. **Gagarin**, *The Murder of Herodes* (Frankfurt am Main 1989); **Gagarin**, *Antiphon* (text and commentary); **Gagarin-MacDowell**, *Antiphon and Andocides* (translation with introduction and notes); also **Blass**, *AB* 1.174–87, 645; **Jebb**, *AO* 1.55–61; **Usher**, *GO* 34–40.

The defendant in this case, Euxitheus of Mytilene, stands accused of intentionally killing an Athenian citizen named Herodes. Herodes' kinsmen have employed *endeixis* and *apagôgê*, rather than the *dikê phonou*, to prosecute Euxitheus. Euxitheus asserts in his defense that the use of these procedures against a suspected killer is unprecedented and illegal (**8a**-**b**), and in fact this case may well represent the first use of *endeixis* and *apagôgê* against a suspected killer (cf. **14** Lys. 13.85–87; **20** Dem. 23.65–80, at §80; **57a** Aeschin. 1.91). Euxitheus further offers the evident lack of *miasma* surrounding his person as presumptive proof of his innocence (**8c**).

a. Ant. 5.9. *Endeixis* and *apagôgê* for homicide.

First, I am on trial for homicide [*phonou*] having been denounced [*endedeigmenos*] as a malefactor [*kakourgos*]—a thing that has never happened to anyone in this country. And my adversaries themselves have borne witness that I am not a malefactor, nor am I liable under the law on malefactors. For that law concerns thieves and clothes-snatchers, and they have not shown that any of those charges applies to me. So, regarding this summary arrest [*apagôgên*], they have made it completely legal and just for you to acquit me.

b. Ant. 5.14. Age and permanence of the homicide laws.

And yet I think you would all agree that the laws established for such offenses are the best and most hallowed of all laws. They are the oldest laws in this country, and furthermore, they have always been the same regarding the same things, which is the greatest sign of well-made laws . . .

c. Ant. 5.82–83. Pollution doctrine.

For I think you know that many people with unclean hands or with some other pollution [*miasma*] have boarded ship and destroyed, along with their own lives, people who were pious toward the gods. Others have not been destroyed but have risked the utmost dangers because of such people; and many men have been exposed as impure by attending sacred rites and hindering the performance of the customary sacrifices. [83] In my case, however, in all these situations the opposite occurred. All the people I sailed with enjoyed excellent voyages, and wherever I was present at sacrifices, they always turned out outstandingly. I maintain that these facts constitute powerful evidence that my adversaries are bringing a false charge against me.

9. Antiphon 6 *On the Chorister* (selections). *Dikê phonou* for conspiracy to commit unintentional homicide (*bouleusis akousiou phonou*). (419/8)

See especially E. **Heitsch**, *Recht und Argumentation in Antiphons 6. Rede* (Mainz and Wiesbaden 1980); **Gagarin**, *Antiphon* (text and commentary); **Gagarin-MacDowell**, *Antiphon and Andocides* (translation with commentary and notes); also **Blass**, *AB* 1.194–203; **Jebb**, *AO* 1.61–64; **Usher**, *GO* 30–34.

Antiphon 6 was delivered by a defendant on trial at the Palladion for conspiracy to commit unintentional homicide (*bouleusis akousiou phonou*). While the defendant was serving as chorus-producer (*chorêgos*) for his tribe, one of his choristers, a boy named Diodotus, died after drinking a drug administered by a third party. Antiphon 6 is our best source for the preliminary hearings (*prodikasiai*) mandatory in a *dikê phonou* (**9c**); Thargelion and Scirophorion are the last two months of the Attic year, corresponding roughly to our May and June (p. 7). The speaker also discusses the restrictions imposed on a homicide defendant's pretrial movements (**9d**; for further detail on "the places specified by law" see **18** Dem. 20.158) and the procedural rule observed in *dikai phonou* that litigants must limit their comments to the specific charge (**9a**; cf. **26a** Lyc. 1.12–13; Lysias 3.46). On the *diômosiai* sworn by both sides at trial (**9b**) cf. **20** Dem. 23.65–80, at §§67–69;

with the defendant's oath that he killed neither with his own hand nor by plotting cf. **2** *IG* I³ 104, at lines 11–13.

a. Ant. 6.9. Relevance rule.

. . . but in this trial, although they are prosecuting me for homicide [*phonou*] and the law holds that they must prosecute on the actual issue, they plot against me, constructing false stories and slandering my conduct toward the city.

b. Ant. 6.15–16, 19. *Bouleusis* of unintentional homicide.

[15] First, then, I will demonstrate to you that I neither ordered nor forced the boy to drink the drug, nor did I give it to him, nor was I even present when he drank it. . . . [16] . . . My adversaries swore [*diômosanto*] that I killed Diodotus by plotting [*bouleusanta*] his death, but I swore that I did not kill him, either by acting with my own hand [*cheiri ergasamenos*] or by plotting. . . .

[19] . . . the prosecutors themselves admit that the boy's death did not occur as a result of intent [*ek pronoias*] or preparation . . . .

c. Ant. 6.42. Preliminary hearings (*prodikasiai*) and the *basileus*.

After he registered the lawsuit, the *basileus* had to conduct three preliminary hearings [*prodikasias*] in three months, and he had to bring the case to court in the fourth month, just as has happened now. But there were only two months left in his term of office, Thargelion and Scirophorion. Obviously he could not bring the case to court during his own term; and it is not permitted to hand a lawsuit for homicide [*phonou dikên*] on to a successor, nor has any *basileus* ever handed one on in this country.

d. Ant. 6.35–36. Homicide defendant barred from courts before trial.

. . . but when they persuaded these men to register the lawsuit and issue the proclamation to me to keep away from the places specified by law, they believed that this would be their salvation and release from all their problems. [36] For the law states that when a person is registered as the defendant in a lawsuit for homicide [*phonou dikên*], he must keep away from the places specified by law. I would be unable to prosecute, being barred from the places specified by law, and since I who impeached them and knew their affairs could not prosecute them, they would easily secure acquittal and avoid being punished by you for their offenses.

10. Isocrates 18 *Against Callimachus* 52–54. ?Dicastic jury in *dikê phonou* at Palladion. (*post* 404/3)

Blass, *AB* 2.213–17; **Jebb**, *AO* 2.233–38; G. **Mathieu**-E. **Brémond**, *Isocrate: Discours, Tome I* (Paris 1928: text with French translation and notes); D. C. **Mirhady**-Y. L. **Too**, *Isocrates I* (Austin 2000: translation with introduction and notes); **Usher**, *GO* 119–20.

The speaker of Isocrates 18 accuses his opponent Callimachus of mounting a prosecution in violation of the Amnesty of 403 (p. 12; **11** [Arist.] *Ath. Pol.* 39.5–6; **244** Isoc. 18.1–8, 10–13, 33, 63). Here he discusses a previous lawsuit in which Callimachus and his brother-in-law accused one Cratinus of killing a slave and brought him to trial at the Palladion (since the alleged victim was a non-citizen: **25** [Arist.] *Ath. Pol.* 57.2–4). Homicide trials at the Palladion were originally heard by the 51 *ephetai,* but as the speaker mentions a jury of 700, this passage is sometimes taken as evidence that the *ephetai* were replaced by a regular dicastic jury at some point during the fourth century (cf. **21** [Dem.] 59.9–10).

Cratinus, you see, was disputing possession of a plot of land with my adversary's brother-in-law. After they were involved in a brawl, they secretly hid away a female slave and accused Cratinus of crushing her skull. Claiming that the woman had died from the wound, they filed a lawsuit for homicide [*phonou dikên*] against him at the Palladion. [53] Having learned of their plots, Cratinus kept quiet in the meantime, in order that they might not change their plan or come up with additional arguments but would be caught in the act as malefactors. But once my adversary's brother-in-law had conducted the prosecution and my adversary had testified that the woman was in fact dead, [54] they entered the house where she had been hidden, seized her by force, brought her into court, and displayed her alive to all those present. And so, in a case with seven hundred jurors, and with fourteen witnesses offering the same testimony as my adversary, he received not a single vote.

11. [Aristotle], *Constitution of the Athenians* (*Ath. Pol.*) 39.5–6. The Amnesty of 403 and Athenian homicide law. (composed 332–322)

See references under **1c**. For the relation of the Amnesty of 403 to Athenian homicide law cf. **12b** Andoc. 1.90–91; **12c** Andoc. 1.94; **14** Lys. 13.85–87; Isocrates 18.20: " . . . the terms of reconciliation explicitly absolve of responsibility those who made denunciations [*endeixantas*] or declarations [*phênantas*: see **151** Harpo. s.v. *phasis*] or did anything else of the sort." The Thirty were the heads of the oligarchic regime that held sway in Athens in

404/3 (p. 12); the Ten were their successors as heads of state in the brief time between the downfall of the Thirty and the restoration of democracy; the Eleven (superintendents of the state prison and executions, with judicial competence including *apagôgê*: p. 30; **8** Ant. 5 [selections] with additional references in headnote; **302b** [Arist.] *Ath. Pol.* 52.1) and the governors of the Peiraeus were the Thirty's chief subordinates. On *euthynai*, the review of a magistrate's conduct held at the end of his term, see p. 32. For the terms and scope of the Amnesty cf. **12b** Andoc. 1.90–91; **12c** Andoc. 1.94; **338h** Andoc. 1.87.

Lawsuits for homicide [*tas . . . dikas tou phonou*] were to take place according to ancestral custom, if a person killed someone by wounding with his own hand. [39.6] No one was to bear malice against anyone for past actions, except against the Thirty, the Ten, the Eleven, and those who governed the Peiraeus, and not even against these if they submitted to review [*euthynas*].

12. Andocides 1 *On the Mysteries* (selections). (400 or 399)

See especially D. M. **MacDowell**, *Andokides*: On the Mysteries (Oxford 1962: text and commentary); **Gagarin-MacDowell**, *Antiphon and Andocides* (translation with introduction and notes); also **Blass**, *AB* 1.311–22; **Jebb**, *AO* 1.112–25; **Usher**, *GO* 44–49.

Andocides was prosecuted by *endeixis* for illegally attending the Eleusinian Mysteries, an annual religious festival in honor of the goddesses Demeter and Persephone held at the town of Eleusis in western Attica (see **§11.3**). In the first passage below (**12a**), he cites the Teisamenus decree, which was passed by the Athenian Assembly ("the people": cf., e.g., **2** *IG* I^3 104, at line 3) and by which, among other provisions, the Athenians reaffirmed the validity of Draco's homicide law. In the decree, "the Council" *tout court* is the Council of 500, while the Council of the Areopagus is named fully; by "the Eponymous Heroes" are meant the statues of the eponymous heroes of the ten Cleisthenic tribes (p. 6), located in the Athenian agora. (Andocides explains in §85 that the wall where ratified laws were to be inscribed was located in the Royal Stoa, on which see the headnote under **2** *IG* I^3 104.) The second passage (**12b**) contains partial quotations of three oaths: the first sworn by all Athenian citizens in 403 in confirmation of the Amnesty (cf. **11** [Arist.] *Ath. Pol.* 39.5–6, whence the editorial addition [marked by angled brackets < >] of the phrase "and the Ten"; note that here the Amnesty appears to be limited to citizens), the second by each annual Council of 500, and the third by the jurors in the *dikastêria* (the heliastic oath: p. 26). In the third passage (**12c**), Andocides mentions the killing of Leon of Salamis and its results as an example of the effect of the Amnesty of 403 on prosecutions for homicide (see **11** [Arist.] *Ath. Pol.* 39.5–6). The use of the verb *apêgagen* ("arrested") indicates that Meletus employed *apagôgê* (cf. **8a** Ant. 5.9; **20** Dem. 23.65–80, at §80) against Leon; on the incident see Plato, *Apology* 32c-d. Andocides' statement that Leon "was put to death without trial" is not necessarily to be taken literally: this became a stock accusation against the Thirty (cf. Lysias 12.36, 82–83; Isocrates 20.11), who did put at least some of their victims on trial but violated the democratic standards of due process in doing so (see Lysias 13.35–38). For the equal liability borne by the own-hand killer and the plotter of a homicide cf. **2** *IG* I[3] 104, at lines 11–13; **9b** Ant. 6.15–16, 19.

a. Andoc. 1.83–84 (*decretum*). Decree of Teisamenus. (date of decree 403)

Resolved by the people; Teisamenus made the motion. The Athenians shall govern themselves according to ancestral tradition: they shall use the laws [*nomois*], measures, and weights of Solon, and they shall also use the laws [*thesmois*] of Draco that we used previously. If there is need of additional laws, the Lawgivers elected by the Council shall record them on boards and display them by the Eponymous Heroes for anyone who wishes to inspect; and they shall hand them over to the authorities during this month. [84] The laws handed over shall first be examined by the Council and the five hundred Lawgivers whom their demesmen have chosen, after they have sworn their oath. Furthermore, any willing private citizen may go before the Council and give any good advice he has regarding the laws. When the laws are enacted, the Council of the Areopagus shall oversee the laws, in order that the authorities use the established laws. Those laws that are ratified are to be inscribed on the wall where they were previously inscribed, for anyone who wishes to inspect.

b. Andoc. 1.90–91 (*iuraiuranda* + commentary). Amnesty of 403 and oaths.

Tell me, now, how do your oaths go? The one common to the entire city, which you all swore after the reconciliation, states, "And I will bear no malice against any citizen except the Thirty <and the Ten> and the Eleven, nor even against any of these who is willing to submit to review [*euthynas*] for the office he held." . . . [91] . . . And the Council in office at any given time, what does it swear? "And I will not accept a denunciation [*endeixin*] or summary arrest [*apagôgên*] for what happened in the past, except against exiles." And you, Athenians, what do you swear before serving as jurors? "And I will not bear malice or be persuaded by another [to do so], but I will vote in accordance with the established laws."

c. Andoc. 1.94. Liability for conspiracy (*bouleusis*); effect of the Amnesty of 403.

And again, this man Meletus here arrested [*apêgagen*] Leon during the regime of the Thirty, as you all know, and Leon was put to death without trial. And this law was in existence in the past and also exists now, because it is a good law, and you use it: it states that the plotter [*bouleusanta*] shall bear the same liability as the person who acts with his own hand [*têi cheiri ergasamenon*]. Leon's sons, then, cannot prosecute Meletus for homicide [*phonou*] because we must use the laws starting from the archonship of Eucleides [403/2]—since even Meletus himself does not dispute that he carried out the arrest.

13. Lysias 1 *On the Killing of Eratosthenes* (selections). (403–380)

See especially C. **Carey**, *Lysias: Selected Speeches* (Cambridge 1989: text and commentary); S. C. **Todd**, *A Commentary on Lysias, Speeches 1–11* (Oxford 2007: text, translation, and commentary); also **Blass**, *AB* 1.571–77; **Jebb**, *AO* 1.271–72; **Usher**, *GO* 55–58; S. C. **Todd**, *Lysias* (Austin 2000: translation with introduction and notes).

In this case, the speaker, Euphiletus, stands trial in a *dikê phonou* for intentionally killing his wife's lover, Eratosthenes. Euphiletus contends that the killing was lawful, since he caught Eratosthenes in bed with his wife and is therefore immunized by Draco's law (the law cited in **13a** is presumably **3f** Dem. 23.53); trial accordingly occurred at the Delphinion (**20** Dem. 23.65–80, at §74; **25** [Arist.] *Ath. Pol.* 57.2–4). Since Eratosthenes was an Athenian citizen and the killing was intentional, Euphiletus, if convicted, faces a penalty of death and confiscation of his property (**13b**; for the confiscation of an intentional killer's property cf. **3d** Dem. 23.44–45, and on the phrase "with regard to my person," which translates *peri tou sômatos*, see **70** Lys. 9.5–12, 15–16). On seduction (*moicheia*) see **§3.1**.

a. Lys. 1.30–31. Lawful homicide of seducer.

[To the court clerk:] Please also read this law from the pillar on the Areopagus.

LAW.

You hear, gentlemen, that the court of the Areopagus itself, where the judging of lawsuits for homicide [*tou phonou tas dikas*] is both an ancestral prerogative and has been assigned in our own time, is explicitly forbidden to convict of homicide [*phonon*] a man who catches a seducer [*moichon*] upon his consort and exacts this punishment. [31] And the lawgiver so strongly believed that this was just in the case of wedded wives that he even imposed the same penalty in the case of concubines, who are valued less.

b. Lys. 1.50. Penalty in *dikê phonou* for intentional homicide of Athenian citizen.

For I am now at risk with regard to my person, my property, and everything else. . . .

14. Lysias 13 *Against Agoratus* 85–87. *Apagôgê* and the *ep' autophôrôi* ("in the act") requirement. (ca. 398)

See especially C. **Bearzot**, *Lisia e la tradizione su Teramene* (Milan 1997: commentary); **Todd**, *Lysias* (translation with introduction and notes); **Phillips**, *Avengers of Blood* 185–235 (on this passage see especially pp. 186–92); also **Blass**, *AB* 1.551–62; H. **Frohberger**, *Ausgewählte Reden des Lysias* (Leipzig 1882: text and commentary); E. S. **Shuckburgh**, *Lysiae orationes XVI* (London 1892: text and commentary); **Jebb**, *AO* 1.265–71; A. P. **Dorjahn**, *Political Forgiveness in Old Athens: The Amnesty of 403 B.C.* (Evanston, IL 1946); E. M. **Harris**, "'In the Act' or 'Red-Handed'? Apagoge to the Eleven and Furtum Manifestum," in *Symposion 1993*, ed. G. Thür (Köln 1994); P. **Krentz**, *The Thirty at Athens* (Ithaca, NY 1982); T. C. **Loening**, *The Reconciliation Agreement of 403/402 B.C. in Athens* (Stuttgart 1987); **Usher**, *GO* 64–68; A. **Wolpert**, *Remembering Defeat: Civil War and Civic Memory in Ancient Athens* (Baltimore 2002); **Phillips**, *Athenian Political Oratory* (translation with introduction and notes).

During the reign of the Thirty, Agoratus served as an informer and in that capacity consigned a number of men to their deaths. One of his victims was Dionysodorus, whose brother (named Dionysius, §86) and first cousin and brother-in-law (the anonymous speaker of Lysias 13) arrested and prosecuted Agoratus by *apagôgê* (cf. **8a** Ant. 5.9; **20** Dem. 23.65–80, at §80) some five years later for his role in Dionysodorus' death. The case was brought to trial despite the Amnesty of 403 (**11** [Arist.] *Ath. Pol.* 39.5–6; **12b** Andoc. 1.90–91; **12c** Andoc. 1.94; significantly, Agoratus claimed to be an Athenian citizen, while his prosecutors vehemently asserted that he was not) and the *ep' autophôrôi* ("in the act") requirement for *apagôgê*. In this passage, the speaker attempts to explain in his favor the Eleven's insistence that the phrase *ep' autophôrôi* be added to the written indictment of Agoratus (the word *apagôgê* can be used both of the procedure of summary arrest and of the warrant authorizing the arrest) and argues that Agoratus qualifies as *ep' autophôrôi*. In §86, the "five hundred men" are the Council of 500, and "all Athenians" refers to the Assembly; Agoratus' victims "were forced to die" (§87) by self-administered hemlock (cf. **341b** Pl. *Phaedo* 116b7-c4, 116c8-d2, 117a4-b2, 117b6-c5, 117e4–118a8).

I hear that [Agoratus] will also rely on the fact that "in the act" [*ep' autophôrôi*] has been added to the arrest warrant [*apagôgêi*], which I think is the most foolish thing of all: as though, if the phrase "in the act" had not been added, he would be liable to summary arrest [*apagôgêi*], but because it has been added, he thinks he gets some relief. This looks like nothing other than an admission that he killed, but not "in the act," and a reliance on this point—as though, if he was not "in the act" but did kill, he should be acquitted for that reason. [86] But as I see it, the Eleven, who accepted this arrest warrant, did not think that they were aiding Agoratus, who even then was relying on this point, and they acted entirely correctly in compelling Dionysius, when he submitted the arrest warrant, to add the phrase "in the act." How is it that a person who denounced people first in the presence of five hundred men, and then again in the presence of all Athenians, could not be their killer and the one responsible for their deaths? [87] [To Agoratus:] Certainly you don't think that it is only "in the act" if a person strikes someone with a club or dagger and knocks him down, since then, by your reasoning, it will be clear that no one killed the men you denounced: no one struck them or cut their throats; they were forced to die by your denunciation. So, is not the man responsible for their deaths "in the act"? Who, then, is responsible other than you, who denounced them? And so how are you, their killer, not "in the act"?

15. Lysias 10 / *Against Theomnestus* 11. *Diômosiai* by prosecutor and defendant in *dikê phonou*. (384/3)

See especially M. **Hillgruber**, *Die zehnte Rede des Lysias* (Berlin 1988: text and commentary); **Todd**, *Commentary on Lysias 1–11* (text, translation, and commentary); also **Blass**, *AB* 1.601–8; **Jebb**, *AO* 1.289–92; M. **Edwards**-S. **Usher**, *Greek Orators 1: Antiphon and Lysias* (Warminster 1985: text, translation, and commentary); **Usher**, *GO* 102–6; **Todd**, *Lysias* (translation with introduction and notes).

Lysias 10 was delivered by a prosecutor in a lawsuit for defamation (*dikê kakêgorias*: see chapter 4). Much of the argument in this speech centers around the exact meanings of words and the equivalence of synonymous terms in relation to the law on defamation. As an example the speaker compares the language of the *diômosiai* employed in homicide lawsuits. "That place" is the Areopagus; "this word" is *androphonos* ("man-slayer, killer": see chapter 4).

For you all know that in that place, when they judge lawsuits for homicide [*tas tou phonou dikas*], they do not conduct the oaths [*diômosias*] using this word, but using the same word I was maligned with: the prosecutor swears that the defendant "killed" [*ekteine*], and the defendant swears that he "did not kill" [*ouk ekteinen*].

16. Isaeus 9 *On the Estate of Astyphilus* 17–19. Fratricide. (*post* 371)

See especially W. **Wyse**, *The Speeches of Isaeus* (Cambridge 1904: text and commentary); R. F. **Wevers**, *Isaeus: Chronology, Prosopography, and Social History* (The Hague 1969); M. **Edwards**, *Isaeus* (Austin 2007: translation with introduction and notes); also **Blass**, *AB* 2.560–63; **Jebb**, *AO* 2.330–33; **Usher**, *GO* 146–49.

Isaeus 9 was delivered in an inheritance lawsuit (a *diadikasia*: see chapter 7) over the estate of Astyphilus. The speaker argues that Astyphilus could not have adopted as his son and heir the rival claimant, who is the biological son of Cleon, because of a family quarrel that arose in the generation before Astyphilus when Astyphilus' father Euthycrates was killed by his brother (and Cleon's father) Thudippus. Thudippus was evidently never prosecuted for the homicide. Araphen (§18) was a deme in eastern Attica; for Euthycrates' dying injunction cf. **7a** Ant. 1.28–30; on the oath of denial (*exômosia*) see **251** [Dem.] 49.17–20. For another instance of an accusation of homicide within the family see Plato, *Euthyphro* 3e-5e.

You see, gentlemen, Thudippus, the father of my adversary Cleon here, is said to have been responsible for the death of Euthycrates, the father of Astyphilus: when a dispute arose between them during the division of their land, Thudippus assaulted Euthycrates; and Euthycrates was in such poor condition that, as a result of the blows, he fell ill and died a few days later. [18] Probably many of the men from the deme Araphen who farmed with them at the time could testify for me that these allegations are true, but I would be unable to provide you with one to testify explicitly regarding so grave a matter. And in fact Hierocles, the one who claims that the document was deposited with him, saw Euthycrates being beaten, but obviously he would not be willing to testify against the will that he himself produces. But nonetheless call Hierocles as well, so that in the presence of these men he may either testify or take the oath of denial [*exomosêtai*]. . . . [19] . . . To the fact that, as Euthycrates, the father of Astyphilus, lay dying, he enjoined his family never to allow any of Thudippus' family to visit his tomb, I will bring before you as a witness the husband of Astyphilus' aunt.

17. [Demosthenes] 47 *Against Euergus and Mnesibulus* 67–73. The *Exêgêtai* (Interpreters) and the right to prosecute a *dikê phonou*. (*post* 358/7)

Schäfer, *Demosthenes* 4.193–99; **Blass**, *AB* 3.1.543–49; **Gernet**, *Démosthène: Plaidoyers civils II* (text, French translation, and notes); **Usher**, *GO* 263–64; **MacDowell**, *DO* 136–41; **Scafuro**, *Demosthenes* 39–49 (translation with introduction and notes). On the *Exêgêtai* see J. H. **Oliver**, *The Athenian Expounders of the Sacred and Ancestral Law* (Baltimore 1950).

This speech comes from a lawsuit for false witness (*dikê pseudomartyriôn*: p. 29) in which the speaker accuses Euergus and Mnesibulus of lying in a joint statement rendered in an earlier lawsuit for battery (*dikê aikeias*: see chapter 2) that resulted in the speaker's conviction. The speaker alleges that Euergus, Mnesibulus, and the victorious litigant Theophemus plundered his farm in his absence in order to collect the fine levied against him at the *dikê aikeias*, and that during the raid they beat and mortally wounded an elderly freedwoman who had once been his wet-nurse. In the aftermath of the woman's death, the speaker consulted the *Exêgêtai* (Interpreters), a college of priests who interpreted the sacred law and had some expertise in the law of homicide owing to the religious aspects of the offense (cf. **8c** Ant. 5.82–83, and see chapter 11). The Interpreters' advice, as related by the speaker, is an important source for the funerary customs observed in the case of a homicide victim (§69), the *diômosia* sworn at *dikai phonou* (§§70, 73), and the fourth-century interpretation of Draco's law as restricting *dikai phonou* to relatives of the victim within the degree of first cousin once removed (§72; cf. **2** *IG* I³ 104, at lines 20ff.; **4** [Dem.] 43.57). A *dikê phonou* for the freedwoman's killing would have taken place at the Palladion (§70) because she was not an Athenian citizen (cf. **25** [Arist.] *Ath. Pol.* 57.2–4).

[67] Moreover, men of the jury, after I issued him a summons to provide care for the woman they had beaten and they did not care to bring in a doctor, I myself brought in a doctor whom I had used for many years. He provided care for her in her illness, and I brought in witnesses and displayed her condition. And when I heard from the doctor that the woman would not survive any longer, I again got hold of still other witnesses and displayed the woman's condition, and I issued my adversaries a summons to provide care for her. And so, five days after these men entered my house, the nurse died. . . .

[68] Now, then, after she died, I went to the Interpreters to find out what I was obliged to do about these matters. I explained to them everything that had happened: the arrival of these men, the kindly nature of the woman, how I kept her in my house, and how she died on account of the cup, because she would not let it go. After hearing these things from me, the Interpreters asked me whether they should simply give me an interpretation or counsel me as well. [69] When I answered, "Both," they told me, "Well, then, we will explain your legal obligations, and we will recommend what is in your interest. First, carry a spear at the funeral procession, and issue a proclamation over the tomb to see if the woman has a relative. Then stand guard over the tomb for three days. Now, here is our advice to you. Since you were not present yourself, but only your wife and children, and you have no other witnesses, you should not issue a proclamation to anyone by name, but rather 'to the perpetrators and killers.' And then do not file a lawsuit with the *basileus.* [70] You see, it is not your right under the law: the woman is not a member of your kin, nor is she your slave, from what you tell us; and the laws mandate that the prosecution belong to these people. So, if you take the oath [*diomei*] at the Palladion, you and your wife and children, and if you call down curses upon yourselves and your house, you will come off worse in the eyes of many, and if he wins an acquittal, you will be considered a perjurer, while if you convict him, you will be resented. Instead, you should expiate yourself and your house and bear the misfortune as lightly as you can; and if you want revenge by some other means, take it."

[71] After hearing these words from the Interpreters and inspecting the laws of Draco on the pillar, I consulted my friends as to what I should do. Since they gave me the same advice, I did what was proper for me to do on behalf of my house and what the Interpreters had explained to me; but with regard to what was no longer my concern according to the laws, I kept quiet. [72] For the law commands, men of the jury, that the relatives up to sons of first cousins conduct the prosecution (and in the oath it is defined what a relative is), and that if [the victim] is a slave, the injunctions are their prerogative. But the woman bore no relation to me as kin, except insofar as she had been my nurse, nor was she my slave: she had been let go by my father as a free woman, lived apart from us, and had a husband. [73] And I would never have dared to lie to you and take the oath—myself, my son, and my wife—not even if I had full knowledge that I would convict them; for I do not hate these men as much as I love myself.

18. Demosthenes 20 *Against Leptines* 157–58. Areopagus court; restrictions on killer; lawful homicide. (355/4)

Schäfer, *Demosthenes* 1.391–419; **Blass**, *AB* 3.1.264–76; J. E. **Sandys**, *The Speech of Demosthenes Against the Law of Leptines* (Cambridge 1890: text and commentary); **Usher**, *GO* 192–98; E. M. **Harris**, *Demosthenes, Speeches 20–22* (Austin 2008: translation with introduction and notes); **MacDowell**, *DO* 152–67; C. **Kremmydas**, *Commentary on Demosthenes* Against Leptines *with Introduction, Text, and Translation* (Oxford 2012).

In this speech, Demosthenes argues for the repeal of a law authored by Leptines that revoked exemptions from liturgies (p. 25) and other duties previously granted to Athenian citizens and others for meritorious service rendered to the state by themselves or their ancestors. Near the end of the speech, Demosthenes contrasts Leptines' law with the law on homicide, highlighting the role of the Areopagus court (cf. **20** Dem. 23.65–80, at §§67–70; **25** [Arist.] *Ath. Pol.* 57.2–4) and the restrictions imposed on the movements of a killer (cf. **9d** Ant. 6.35–36). On lawful killing and ritual pollution cf. **3f** Dem. 23.53; **8c** Ant. 5.82–83; **5** Dem. 9.44. If the provisions stated in §158 are actually Draconian, the original meaning of "the agora" (as the word would have been understood in the Classical period) will have been "(public) gathering(-place)" (cf. **2** *IG* I³ 104, at line 21; **4** [Dem.] 43.57; but note that the term can refer to a public market [**2** *IG* I³ 104, at lines 27–28, and **3c** Dem. 23.37, where "the border-market" translates *agoras ephorias*]).

Tell me, by Zeus: what would we all pray to avoid most of all, and what is the highest concern in all the laws? The prevention of homicides [*phonoi*] among ourselves, in which matters the Council of the Areopagus has been assigned as special guardian. [158] In the laws concerning these things, Draco made it a fearsome and terrible thing for a man to kill another with his own hand. He wrote that the killer was to be barred from purification by water, from libations, mixing-bowls, sanctuaries, and the agora—going through everything else by which he thought he would especially deter people from committing such an act. Nonetheless, he did not rob justice of its place but established conditions under which killing was permitted, and if a person acted thus, he defined him as free of pollution.

19. Demosthenes 54 *Against Conon* (selections). (?355/341)

Schäfer, *Demosthenes* 4.247–52; **Blass**, *AB* 3.1.456–61; J. E. **Sandys**-F. A. **Paley**, *Demosthenes: Select Private Orations* 2⁴ (Cambridge 1910: text and commentary); C. **Carey**-R. A. **Reid**, *Demosthenes: Selected Private Speeches* (Cambridge 1985: text and commentary); **Usher**, *GO* 245–47; V. **Bers**, *Demosthenes, Speeches 50–59* (Austin 2003: translation with introduction and notes); **MacDowell**, *DO* 240–45.

Demosthenes wrote this speech for a client named Ariston, who prosecuted Conon for battery in a *dikê aikeias* (see chapter 2). Ariston claims that a gang led by Conon beat him so severely that he almost died; if he had died, Conon would have been liable to a *dikê phonou* at the Areopagus for the intentional homicide of a citizen (**19b**). (On challenges for the evidentiary torture of slaves see p. 24; on hubris see chapter 2.) The first passage below (**19a**) may indicate that trials for *bouleusis* of the intentional homicide of a citizen occurred not at the Palladion (cf. **25** [Arist.] *Ath. Pol.* 57.2–4) but at the Areopagus (cf. **28** Harpo. s.v. *bouleuseôs*), but Ariston's description of the relevant case is incomplete and unclear.

a. Dem. 54.25. ?Areopagite jurisdiction over *dikê phonou* for conspiracy to commit intentional homicide (*bouleusis hekousiou phonou*) of citizen.

And in fact, if by chance something had happened to me, he would have been liable for homicide [*phonou*] and the most fearsome charges. The Council of the Areopagus, at any rate, exiled the father of the priestess from Brauron, although by all accounts he did not touch the man who died, because he urged the one who hit him to hit him—and they were right to do so.

b. Dem. 54.27–28. Investigative function and jurisdiction of the Areopagus.

But I think you must all look to the fact that my adversaries, if they were issuing a challenge for torture to occur and were trusting in that right, would not have issued the challenge when the arbitration verdict was already being given, at night, and with no excuse [*skêpseôs*] remaining. [28] Instead, in the first place, before the lawsuit was filed, when I was lying sick in bed, not knowing whether I would survive, and was disclosing to all who visited me that the defendant struck the first blow and committed most of the acts of hubris that I suffered—at that time he would have come immediately to my house with numerous witnesses, offered to hand over his slaves, and set about summoning members of the Areopagus: for if I had died, the trial would have occurred in their court.

20. Demosthenes 23 *Against Aristocrates* 65–80. Homicide courts and *apagôgê* for homicide in the mid-fourth century. (352/1)

See references and headnote under **3**. In this lengthy and valuable excursus, the speaker describes the functioning of the courts that tried *dikai phonou* (§§65–79) and the use of *apagôgê* for homicide (§80) at the time of the *graphê paranomôn* against Aristocrates (cf. especially **25** [Arist.] *Ath. Pol.* 57.2–4). For the mythical trials mentioned in §§66, 74 cf. Aeschylus, *Eumen-*

ides 566–777; Hellanicus, *FGrHist* (F. **Jacoby**, *Die Fragmente der griechischen Historiker* [Leiden 1957-]) 323a F 22; on the competence and quality of the Areopagite jury cf. **13a** Lys. 1.30–31; **26a** Lyc. 1.12–13. On the *diômosiai* sworn in *dikai phonou* (§§67–69) cf. especially **17** [Dem.] 47.67–73, at §§70–73; the characterization of the *diômosia* as unique to *dikai phonou* is inaccurate, as it was also sworn in lawsuits for intentional wounding (**31a** Lys. 3.1). In §72, the text of the phrase translated "one . . . pardons him" is corrupt: most editors read *aidesêtai tis* (adopted here) for the manuscripts' *aidesêtai tina*, but this does not resolve the evident contradiction of Draco's law, which required unanimity among the victim's kin as a condition of pardon (**2** *IG* I^3 104, at lines 13–19; cf. the plural used at §77). For lawful killings (§74) see **3f** Dem. 23.53 and cf. **13a** Lys. 1.30–31. In §77, "to come here" means to set foot on Attic soil; on the use of *apagôgê* against a suspected killer (§80) cf. **8a** Ant. 5.9; **14** Lys. 13.85–87; **57a** Aeschin. 1.91.

Among us there are many institutions such as are not found elsewhere, but the one most distinctive and revered of all is the court of the Areopagus. Concerning this court one could mention more fine traditions, both those of legend and those to which we ourselves are witnesses, than one could about any other court. But it is worthwhile to hear one or two of these by way of example. [66] Now, for one thing, in antiquity, as it has been handed down to us to hear, in this court alone did the gods see fit to give and exact recompense for homicide [*dikas phonou*] and to serve as jurors when disputes arose among them, as tradition relates: Poseidon exacted recompense from Ares in the matter of his son Halirrhothius, and the Twelve Gods served as jurors for the Furies and Orestes. Those are the ancient stories; as for later times, this is the only court that no tyrant, no oligarchy, no democracy has ever dared to deprive of homicide trials [*tas phonikas dikas*]; on the contrary, all men believe that the justice they themselves would determine in these matters would be less potent than the justice determined by this court. In addition to these facts of such great importance, here alone has no convicted defendant or defeated prosecutor ever proven that his case was decided unjustly.

[67] . . . . All of you certainly know that on the Areopagus, where the law grants and commands that homicide trials be held, first, the man who accuses someone of committing such an act swears an oath [*diomeitai*] on the destruction of himself, his kin, and his house. [68] Moreover, he is to do this in no ordinary way; rather, he swears an oath that no one swears in any other matter: he stands over pieces of a boar, a ram, and a bull, which have been slaughtered by the requisite people and on the proper days, so that with regard to both timing and participation the whole thing has been carried out as religiously as possible. And after that, the man who has sworn such a weighty oath is not believed yet;

in fact, if he is caught telling a lie, he will bring home his perjury to his children and his kin, and he will not gain a thing. [69] But if he is deemed to be bringing a just charge and convicts the perpetrator of the killing, even so he does not gain authority over the convicted man: the laws and the designated individuals have the authority to punish the offender, and the prosecutor may watch the convicted man pay the penalty assigned by law but may do nothing beyond this. That is the role of the prosecutor. As for the defendant, the elements of the oath [*diômosias*] are the same; and after delivering his first speech he may leave the country, and neither the prosecutor nor the jury nor any other person has the power to stop him. [70] Whyever, men of Athens, is this so? Because those who originally established these customs—whoever they were, whether heroes or gods—did not want to put an additional burden on the unfortunate; rather, they generously lightened their misfortunes as much as was right. . . .

[71] There is also a second lawcourt, for unintentional killings [*tôn akousiôn phonôn*] . . . , the court at the Palladion. . . . Here the prescribed order is the oath [*diômosia*] first, the speeches second, and the verdict of the court third. . . . If the perpetrator is convicted and deemed to have committed the act, neither the prosecutor nor anyone else but the law has authority over him. [72] What, then, does the law command? That a man convicted of unintentional homicide leave the country within a certain stated time by a fixed route, and that he remain in exile until one of the victim's kin pardons him. And then the law allows him to return in a certain manner, not haphazardly: the law states explicitly that he must sacrifice and be purified and do the other things that he must do—and the law is right, men of Athens, to specify all these requirements. [73] For in fact it is just to assign a lesser penalty for unintentional homicides than for intentional ones [*tôn hekousiôn*], and the provision ordering the defendant into exile only after providing him safe departure is correctly framed. And the requirement that the returning exile expiate and purify himself by certain customary procedures, and the fact that the laws have authority over all, and all these provisions, are good. . . .

[74] There is yet a third court in addition to these: the most holy and fearsome of all, [which has jurisdiction] if a person admits a killing but asserts that he acted lawfully. This is the court at the Delphinion. The men who originally defined justice in these matters seem to me, men of the jury, to have inquired first of all whether no killing should be considered lawful or there was a type of killing that should be considered lawful. Considering that Orestes admitted having killed his mother but was acquitted by a jury of gods, they thought that there was such a thing as a just killing, since gods would not render an unjust verdict. Upon reaching this conclusion, they straightaway wrote up and clearly defined the conditions under which killing is allowed. . . .

[76] There is, moreover, yet a fourth court in addition to these, the court

at the Prytaneion. If a piece of stone or wood or iron or the like falls and hits someone, and a person does not know who threw it but knows and possesses the object that committed the killing, he brings suit against such objects here. . . .

[77] There is, moreover, still a fifth court . . . , the court in Phreatto. Here, men of Athens, the law commands that people submit to trial "if a person in exile for unintentional homicide and not yet pardoned by those who exiled him is charged with another, intentional homicide." And the man who set up each of these provisions did not overlook such a person because he is not allowed to come here, nor, on the grounds that the accused had done something of the sort in the past, did he accordingly presume a similar charge against him to be credible. [78] Instead, he found a way for piety to prevail, and he did not deprive the accused of a hearing and judgment. So, what did he do? He brought the men who were to serve as jurors to a place where the accused was allowed to appear, designating a location in our land on the seashore called "in Phreatto." The accused then sails up in a boat and speaks without touching the land, and the jurors listen and decide the case on land. If the defendant is convicted, he rightly pays the penalty for intentional homicide; if he is acquitted, he is set free on the present charge but still suffers the penalty of exile for the previous killing.

[79] Why, then, is such care taken in these matters? The one who made these determinations considered it equally impious to leave a guilty man alone and to surrender an innocent man before trial. . . .

[80] Moreover, in addition to all these there is still a sixth means of punishment. . . . If a person is ignorant of everything previously mentioned, or also if the time in which he had to do each of the aforementioned things has elapsed, or if for some other reason he does not wish to prosecute in the aforementioned ways, and he sees the killer walking about in the sanctuaries and around the agora, he may arrest [*apagein*] him and take him to the prison—not to his home or wherever he wishes. . . . And after his arrest the killer will suffer absolutely no punishment before he is tried; but if convicted he will be punished with death, while if the man who arrested him fails to receive a fifth of the votes, he will incur a fine of 1,000 drachmas.

21. [Demosthenes] 59 *Against Neaera* 9–10. *Diômosia*; ?dicastic jury in *dikê phonou* at Palladion. (date of speech 343–339; date of event *post* 348)

See especially K. A. **Kapparis**, *Apollodoros*: 'Against Neaira' *[D. 59]* (Berlin 1999: text, translation, and commentary); V. **Bers**, *Demosthenes: Speeches 50–59* (Austin 2003: translation with notes); also **Schäfer**, *Demosthenes* 4.179–84; **Blass**, *AB* 3.1.535–42; J. **Trevett**, *Apollodoros the Son of Pasion*

(Oxford 1992); C. **Carey**, *Greek Orators VI: Apollodorus*: Against Neaira: *[Demosthenes] 59* (Warminster 1992: text, translation, and commentary); **Usher**, *GO* 341–43; **MacDowell**, *DO* 121–26.

Apollodorus composed this speech for delivery by the prosecution in a *graphê xenias* (for usurpation of citizen rights: see chapter 6) against a famous prostitute named Neaera. The beginning of the speech (§§1–15) was delivered by the nominal prosecutor, Theomnestus, and the rest of the speech by Apollodorus himself as *synêgoros* (p. 28). In this passage Theomnestus accuses Neaera's husband Stephanus of concocting a fraudulent *dikê phonou* against Apollodorus and bringing him to trial at the Palladion (since the alleged victim was a non-citizen: cf. **10** Isoc. 18.52–54; **25** [Arist.] *Ath. Pol.* 57.2–4). For the *diômosia* sworn by Stephanus cf. especially **20** Dem. 23.65–80, at §§67–69. According to Theomnestus, the jury numbered 500, which suggests that the case was heard by a regular dicastic jury and not by the *ephetai* (cf. **10** Isoc. 18.52–54).

[Stephanus], you see, brought a false charge against [Apollodorus], stating that once, after arriving at Aphidna in search of a runaway slave of his, he had hit a woman and she had died from the blow. [Stephanus] prepared and suborned slaves to claim that they were citizens of Cyrene, and he issued a proclamation to [Apollodorus] that he would be charged with homicide [*phonou*] at the Palladion. [10] And my adversary Stephanus here pled the case, after swearing [*diomosamenos*] that Apollodorus had killed the woman with his own hand [*autocheiriai*], calling down destruction upon himself, his kin, and his house, and alleging things that never happened and that he never saw or heard about from any person whatsoever. When he was exposed as perjuring himself and bringing a false charge, and it became obvious that he had been hired and paid money by Cephisophon and Apollophanes to get Apollodorus banished or disfranchised, he received only a few votes out of five hundred and went away having broken his oath and having gained a reputation as a scoundrel.

22. Demosthenes 21 *Against Meidias* (selections). (347/6)

See especially D. M. **MacDowell**, *Demosthenes:* Against Meidias *(Oration 21)* (Oxford 1990: text, translation, and commentary); also **Schäfer**, *Demosthenes* 4.58–63; **Blass**, *AB* 3.1.328–41; W. W. **Goodwin**, *Demosthenes:* Against Midias (Cambridge 1906: text and commentary); **Usher**, *GO* 226–30; **Harris**, *Demosthenes, Speeches 20–22* (translation with introduction and notes); **MacDowell**, *DO* 240–41, 245–56.

In this speech, which may have been circulated in writing but not delivered in court, Demosthenes accuses Meidias of committing offenses against the Greater Dionysia festival of 348, including punching Demosthenes in the face while he was serving as *chorêgos* (chorus-producer) for his tribe (see **332** Dem. 21 [selections]). The first passage (**22a**) comes from a section of the *Against Meidias* where Demosthenes contrasts the heavier penalties meted out for intentional offenses (such as Meidias' assault) with the lighter penalties for unintentional offenses; the second (**22b**) narrates the near-acquittal of Euaeon, who killed Boeotus after Boeotus hubristically struck him (on hubris see chapter 2).

a. Dem. 21.43. Penalties in *dikai phonou.*

Second, the homicide laws punish those who kill intentionally [*ek pronoias*] with death, perpetual exile, and confiscation of their property, but consider those who kill unintentionally [*akousiôs*] worthy of pardon and considerable generosity.

b. Dem. 21.71, 75. Self-defense.

Many people know that Euaeon, the brother of Leodamas, killed Boeotus at a dinner gathering of friends on account of a single blow. . . .

[75] . . . I hear that he was convicted by a margin of only one vote, and that when he had not cried or begged any of the jurors, and had made absolutely no gesture of generosity, great or small, toward the jurors. Let us, then, suppose that the jurors who voted to convict him did so not because he had defended himself but because he had done so in such a manner as to kill, while those who voted to acquit allowed even this excess of vengeance to a man whose person had been the victim of hubris.

23. Demosthenes 37 *Against Pantaenetus* 59. Pardon by relatives and by victim. (ca. 346)

See especially F. A. **Paley**-J. E. **Sandys**, *Demosthenes: Select Private Orations* 1[3] (Cambridge 1898: text and commentary); **Carey**-**Reid**, *Demosthenes: Selected Private Speeches* (text and commentary); S. **Isager**-M. H. **Hansen**, *Aspects of Athenian Society in the Fourth Century B.C.: A Historical Introduction to and Commentary on the Paragraphe-speeches and the Speech Against Dionysodorus in the Corpus Demosthenicum (XXXII–XXXVIII and LVI)* (Odense 1975); D. M. **MacDowell**, *Demosthenes, Speeches 27–38* (Austin 2004: translation with introduction and notes); ***idem,*** *DO* 266–71; also **Schäfer**, *Demosthenes* 4.200–7; **Blass**, *AB* 3.1.477–81; **Usher**, *GO* 249–50.

Demosthenes 37 was delivered in a *paragraphê* (p. 14) arising from contested mining rights. The speaker Nicobulus asserts that his opponent Pantaenetus has already released him from liability for any wrongs suffered, and invokes the comparison of the homicide law, under which pardon granted by the victim before his death, or by the relatives of the victim following an unintentional killer's conviction (cf. **2** *IG* I[3] 104, at lines 13ff.), is binding and irrevocable. The provision on binding pardon by the relatives is also cited at Demosthenes 38.22; with regard to pardon by the victim, "that word" is to be understood as *aphiêmi*, "I release." For the pollution caused by a homicide cf. **8c** Ant. 5.82–83; **5** Dem. 9.44; **18** Dem. 20.157–58.

And this right is so valid in all cases that if a person who has convicted another of unintentional homicide [*akousiou phonou*] and has clearly proven that he is not free of pollution afterward pardons and releases him, he no longer has the power to exile the same man. And if the victim himself, before he dies, releases the perpetrator from liability for his killing, none of his surviving relatives is allowed to prosecute; instead, as for those whom the laws sentence to banishment, exile, and death upon conviction, once they are released [*aphethôsin*], that word sets them free from all terrors.

24. Aeschines 2 *On the False Embassy* 87. Post-verdict *diômosia*. (343)

See especially C. **Carey**, *Aeschines* (Austin 2000: translation with introduction and notes); D. M. **MacDowell**, *Demosthenes:* On the False Embassy *(Oration 19)* (Oxford 2000) 1–22; also **Blass**, *AB* 3.2.201–8; J.-M. **Julien**-H. L. **de Péréra**, *Eschine: Discours sur l'ambassade* (Paris 1902: text and commentary); V. **Martin**-G. **de Budé**, *Eschine: Discours, Tome I* (Paris 1952: text with French translation and notes); E. M. **Harris**, *Aeschines and Athenian Politics* (Oxford 1995); **Usher**, *GO* 284–87.

In 346, Demosthenes accused Aeschines of misconduct during an Athenian embassy to Philip II of Macedon; the resulting lawsuit, in which Aeschines gave this speech in his own defense, came to trial in 343 and resulted in Aeschines' acquittal by a slim margin. Here Aeschines accuses Demosthenes of fabricating accusations against him and discusses the *diômosia* sworn by the victorious litigant in a *dikê phonou* (cf. **7c** Ant. 1.28, **15** Lys. 10.11, **17** [Dem.] 47.67–73, **20** Dem. 23.65–80, **21** [Dem.] 59.9–10 on the pretrial *diômosiai*) in order to alert his jurors to the dangers inherent in a wrongful conviction.

How was it not reasonable for our forefathers to direct that, in homicide trials [*tais phonikais dikais*] at the Palladion, as they cut up the sacrificial victims, the winner of the verdict must swear an oath (and this is still your ancestral custom today) that all those jurors who cast their votes for him voted what was true and just, and that he told no lie; and that if this is not so, he curses himself and his house with destruction, but prays for many blessings for the jurors?

25. [Aristotle], *Constitution of the Athenians* (*Ath. Pol.*) 57.2–4. Duties of the *basileus*; homicide courts. (332–322)

See references under **1c**. In this section of the *Ath. Pol.* (cf. especially **20** Dem. 23.65–80), the author describes the *basileus*' supervision over *dikai phonou*, the jurisdictions of the various dedicated homicide courts, and the restrictions on a homicide defendant's movements in the period between accusation and trial (cf. **9d** Ant. 6.35–36; **18** Dem. 20.157–58). For liability, jurisdiction, and jury composition in trials for own-hand killing and for conspiracy (*bouleusis*) to kill cf. **2** *IG* I[3] 104; **10** Isoc. 18.52–54; **19a** Dem. 54.25; **21** [Dem.] 59.9–10; **28** Harpo. s.v. *bouleuseôs*; for the law on Areopagite jurisdiction see **3a** Dem. 23.22, and for lawful homicide cf. **3f** Dem. 23.53. "At that time" (§57.4) means at the time of the accused killer's own trial; for a *dikê phonou* filed against "the perpetrator" cf. **17** Dem. 47.67–73, at §69. The angled brackets surrounding the words "as *ephetai*" and "in a sanctuary" (§57.4) indicate that these are hypothetical supplements filling lacunae in the text.

Also, all lawsuits for homicide [*phonou dikai*] are filed with him, and he is the one who issues the proclamation barring [the accused] from the things stated in the law. [57.3] Trials for homicide and wounding, if someone kills or wounds with intent [*ek pronoias*], occur on the Areopagus; also for poisoning, if he kills by giving poison, and for arson. These are the only lawsuits the Council judges. For unintentional homicides [*tôn . . . akousiôn*] and conspiracy [*bouleuseôs*], and if a person kills a slave, metic, or foreigner, the court at the Palladion [tries the lawsuit]. If a person admits a killing but claims that he acted according to the laws (for example, having caught a seducer [*moichon*], or in war without recognizing his victim, or competing in an athletic contest), they judge his case at the Delphinion. If a person who is in exile for an action for which pardon is available incurs a charge of killing or wounding someone, they judge his case in Phreatto; he offers his defense in a boat moored to shore. [57.4] Except for the trials that take place on the Areopagus, these cases are judged by the men allotted <as *ephetai*>. The *basileus* introduces the cases, and they judge them <in a sanctuary> and under the open sky; and when he judges, the *basileus* takes off his crown. In the meantime the accused is barred from the sanctuaries, and the law does not even allow him to intrude upon the agora; but at that time he enters the sanctuary and offers his defense. When someone does not know who committed the act, he files suit against "the perpetrator." The *basileus* and the tribe-kings [*phylobasileis*] also judge lawsuits against inanimate objects and animals.

26. Lycurgus 1 *Against Leocrates* (selections). (330)

See especially A. **Petrie**, *Lycurgus: The Speech Against Leocrates* (Cambridge 1922: text and commentary); F. **Durrbach**, *Lycurgue*: Contre Léocrate, *Fragments* (Paris 1932: text with French translation and notes); I. **Worthington**-C. **Cooper**-E. M. **Harris**, *Dinarchus, Hyperides, and Lycurgus* (Austin 2001: translation with introduction and notes); J. **Engels**, *Lykurg: Rede gegen Leokrates* (Darmstadt 2008: text, German translation, and commentary); also **Blass**, *AB* 3.2.111–16; S. C. **Humphreys**, "Lycurgus of Butadae: An Athenian Aristocrat," in *The Craft of the Ancient Historian: Essays in Honor of Chester G. Starr*, ed. J. W. Eadie-J. Ober (Lanham, MD 1985) 199–252; M. **Faraguna**, *Atene nell' età di Alessandro* (Rome 1992); **Usher**, *GO* 324–28.

Lycurgus prosecuted Leocrates by *eisangelia* (impeachment: see chapter 12, especially **387** Lyc. 1 [selections]), charging him with treason for leaving Attica after the Battle of Chaeroneia in 338 (p. 15). In the first passage below (**26a**) Lycurgus addresses the jury, drawing a comparison with the procedure of the Council of the Areopagus, before which litigants were compelled to restrict their comments to the case at hand (cf. **9a** Ant. 6.9). (With Lycurgus' comment on the excellence of the Areopagite court cf. **20** Dem. 23.65–80, at §66.) Since Lycurgus proposed that Leocrates receive the death penalty, in the second passage (**26b**) he expounds upon the (alleged) use of capital punishment by Athenians in times past. For the restrictions on a killer's movements cf. **9d** Ant. 6.35–36; **18** Dem. 20.157–58; for the severity that fourth-century (and later) Athenians attributed to Draco (whom Lycurgus presumably has in mind in his assertion concerning the former ubiquity of the death penalty) cf. **266** Plut. *Solon* 17.1–3. On theft, including temple-robbery, see chapter 9.

a. Lyc. 1.12–13. Reputation of the Areopagus; relevance rule.

. . . the Council of the Areopagus, which so excels the other lawcourts that even those convicted in their court admit that their verdict was just. [13] You should look to that court and not allow people to speak off the topic: that way trial will happen without slander of defendants, with the fewest false accusations by prosecutors, and with you rendering the verdict most true to your oath.

b. Lyc. 1.64–65. Use of death penalty in earlier times.

And in fact it is easy, gentlemen, to discover the truth by looking at the intent of the ancient lawgivers. [65] For they did not sentence to death a person who stole a hundred talents while imposing a lesser fine on one who stole ten drachmas, nor did they execute a person who committed temple-robbery on a large scale while punishing one who did so on a small scale with a lesser penalty, nor did they impose a monetary fine on the killer of a slave while barring a free man's killer from the things specified by law. Instead, they established death as the penalty for all violations of the law alike, even the least serious.

27. Aeschines 3 *Against Ctesiphon* 244. Homicide by inanimate objects; suicide. (330)

See especially R. B. **Richardson**, *Aeschines:* Against Ctesiphon (Boston 1889: text and commentary); W. W. **Goodwin**, *Demosthenes:* On the Crown (Cambridge 1901) 229–99, 327–32; **Harris**, *Aeschines;* **Carey**, *Aeschines* (translation with introduction and notes); H. **Yunis**, *Demosthenes:* On the Crown (Cambridge 2001) 1–17; also **Blass**, *AB* 3.2.208–21; V. **Martin**-G. **de Budé**, *Eschine: Discours, Tome II* (Paris 1928: text with French translation and notes); **Usher**, *GO* 287–93.

The *Against Ctesiphon* is Aeschines' prosecution speech from the famous *Crown* case of 330, a *graphê paranomôn* (p. 14) in which Ctesiphon was accused and acquitted of illegally proposing in 336 to award a crown to Demosthenes for his public benefactions. In contrasting Demosthenes with other leading men who have received crowns from the Athenian people, Aeschines accuses Demosthenes of abandoning fellow citizens to their deaths at the Battle of Chaeronea (338: p. 15 and headnote under **26** Lyc. 1 [selections]). He accordingly compares Ctesiphon's proposal to reward Demosthenes' culpable behavior with a crown to the treatment of inanimate objects judged responsible for a death (trial by *dikê phonou* occurred at the Prytaneion: **20** Dem. 23.65–80, at §76; **25** [Arist.] *Ath. Pol.* 57.2–4; if convicted, the object was cast over the border separating Attica from Boeotia) and of suicides.

. . . if objects of wood or rock or iron—things without speech or judgment—fall on someone and kill him, we cast them over the border; and if a person kills himself, we bury the hand that committed the act apart from the body. . . .

28. Harpocration s.v. *bouleuseôs*. *Bouleusis* (conspiracy). (Harpocration *fl.* 2nd c. A.D.; Isaeus *fl.* ca. 389–344/3; Deinarchus *fl.* 336/5–307/6)

G. **Dindorf**, *Harpocrationis lexicon in decem oratores Atticos* (1853; repr. Athens 2004: text and Latin commentary); J. J. **Keaney**, *Harpocration*: Lexeis *of the Ten Orators* (Amsterdam 1991: text).

In the second century A.D., the Alexandrian scholar Valerius Harpocration compiled a *Lexicon* designed to explain to contemporary readers recondite terms found in the works of the Attic orators. Many of his citations, as here, come from speeches now lost except in fragmentary form. In this lemma Harpocration defines *bouleusis* (conspiracy): cf. **2** *IG* I[3] 104; **7** Ant. 1 (selections); **9** Ant. 6 (selections); **12c** Andoc. 1.94; **25** [Arist.] *Ath. Pol.* 57.2–4. The references are, in order, Isaeus fr. 62 Baiter-Sauppe (cf. fragmentary speech XIV Thalheim); Deinarchus fr. XV.2 Conomis; **25** [Arist.] *Ath. Pol.* 57.2–4. For the possibility of Areopagite jurisdiction over *bouleusis* of the intentional killing of an Athenian citizen cf. **19a** Dem. 54.25.

Bouleuseôs ["for conspiracy"]: the name of a charge, assigned to two actions. One is when a person contrives the death of another by plotting, whether the victim of the plot dies or not. . . . Testimony . . . is provided by Isaeus in his speech *Against Eucleides*, who says that the trials occur at the Palladion, and by Deinarchus in his speech *Against Pistias*, who says that they occur on the Areopagus. Aristotle in the *Constitution of the Athenians* agrees with Isaeus.

29. Harpocration s.v. *hypophonia. Hypophonia* (payment to avoid prosecution for homicide). (Harpocration *fl.* 2nd c. A.D.; Deinarchus *fl.* 336/5–307/6; Theophrastus b. 372–370, d. 288–286)

See references and headnote under **28**. Here Harpocration defines *hypophonia*, the name given to the payment made by a killer to his victim's relatives in order to avert a lawsuit; whether Athenian law permitted such payments is debated. The cited orations of Deinarchus are fragmentary speeches X, XIX Conomis. Theophrastus was a philosopher and author who succeeded Aristotle as head of the Lyceum; for the surviving fragments of his treatise titled (*On*) *Laws* (cf. **312** Theophr. *Laws* fr. 21.1 Szegedy-Maszak) see A. **Szegedy-Maszak**, *The* Nomoi *of Theophrastus* (New York 1981). A similar definition of *hypophonia* is given at *Suda* (see references and headnote under **49**) s.v. *hypophonia*; for an allegation of the receipt of *hypophonia* see [Demosthenes] 58.28–29.

Hypophonia: the money paid for a homicide [*phonôi*] to the relatives of the person killed so that they do not prosecute: Deinarchus in his speeches *Against Callisthenes* and *Against Phormisius*; Theophrastus, *Laws*, book 16.

CHAPTER 2

Wounding, Battery, and Hubris

Handbooks: J. H. **Lipsius**, *Das attische Recht und Rechtsverfahren* (Leipzig 1905–15) 123, 420–29, 605–7, 643–46, 826–27; A. R. W. **Harrison**, *The Law of Athens* (Oxford 1968–71) 2.9, 21–23, 75–76, 93–94; D. M. **MacDowell**, *The Law in Classical Athens* (Ithaca, NY 1978) 123–24, 126, 129–32; S. C. **Todd**, *The Shape of Athenian Law* (Oxford 1993) 269–73. **Studies:** L. **Gernet**, *Recherches sur le développement de la pensée juridique et morale en Grèce* (Paris 1917); E. **Ruschenbusch**, "*Hybreos graphe*: ein Fremdkörper im athenischen Recht des 4. Jahrhunderts v. Chr.," *ZSS* 82 (1965) 302–9; W. T. **Loomis**, "The Nature of Premeditation in Athenian Homicide Law," *JHS* 92 (1972) 86–95; M. **Gagarin**, "The Athenian Law Against Hybris," in *Arktouros: Hellenic Studies Presented to Bernard M. Knox*, ed. G. W. Bowersock, W. Burkert, and M. C. J. Putnam (Berlin 1979) 229–36; M. H. **Hansen**, "*Graphe* or *dike traumatos*?," *GRBS* 24 (1983) 307–20; D. M. **MacDowell**, *Demosthenes*: Against Meidias (*Oration 21*) (Oxford 1990); O. **Murray**, "The Solonian Law of *hubris*," in *Nomos*, ed. P. Cartledge, P. Millett, and S. Todd (Cambridge 1990) 139–45; N. R. E. **Fisher**, "The Law of *hubris* in Athens," in *Nomos*, ed. P. Cartledge, P. Millett, and S. Todd (Cambridge 1990) 123–38; ***idem,*** *Hybris* (Warminster 1992), esp. ch. 2; D. D. **Phillips**, "*Trauma ek pronoias* in Athenian Law," *JHS* 127 (2007) 74–105.

Classical Athenian law had three principal actions for non-homicidal physical assaults: the *graphê traumatos ek pronoias*, for intentional wounding; the *dikê aikeias*, for battery; and the *graphê hybreôs*, for hubris (aggravated battery).

Trauma ek pronoias, literally "wounding as a result of intent," had a physical and a mental requirement. In physical terms, *trauma* required the use of a weapon. Athenian litigants assume that normal weapons are the sword (or knife), rock, and club (**32a**, **33**; cf. **20** Dem. 23.65–80, at §76; Antiphon 4 β 2; Aeschines 3.244), but in the two best-attested surviving *trauma* cases (Lysias

3 and 4) the defendant stands accused of wounding his prosecutor with a potsherd (**31b**, **32a**). The mental requirement for *trauma ek pronoias* was *pronoia* (intent). *Trauma* defendants argue that *pronoia* indicates an intent to kill (**31d**, **32a**), and accordingly some modern scholars treat *trauma ek pronoias* as attempted homicide. Yet the law on *trauma* (unfortunately lost) evidently did not specify an intent to kill, since defendants do not cite the law in support of their interpretation of *pronoia*. In the phrase *trauma ek pronoias*, therefore, *pronoia* probably designated an intent to wound, not (necessarily) an intent to kill; establishing intent to kill would prove intent to wound *a fortiori* but was not legally necessary (see **31d**; on varying interpretations of the term *ek pronoias* see the introduction to chapter 1).

The action for *trauma* was a *graphê* (**33**, **34**) and therefore could be mounted by any willing Athenian citizen regardless of his relationship to the victim (p. 30). *Trauma* lawsuits were heard by the Council of the Areopagus (**31a**, **34**; **3a** Dem. 23.22; **25** [Arist.] *Ath. Pol.* 57.2–4); litigants swore the *diômosia* (**31a**), as in a *dikê phonou* (see chapter 1); and the penalty upon conviction was lifelong exile from Attica with confiscation of property (**31d**, **32c**; cf. **30**).

Physical assaults that did not involve a weapon and did not result in death were classified as either *aikeia* or hubris. The law of *aikeia* required that an offender start a fight without justification: *aikeia* was defined as *archein cheirôn adikôn*, literally "beginning unjust hands" (**41a**, **43**). Hubris is a more difficult concept. Since the surviving hubris statute (**35**) fails to define the offense, and speakers in the Athenian courts—including, but not limited to, *aikeia* prosecutors—commonly allege that their adversaries have committed hubris (e.g., **42a-b**), the aggravating factor that distinguished hubris from *aikeia* has been the subject of much scholarly debate. From the descriptions of actual or hypothetical hubristic assaults in Attic oratory (**38**, **39**, **40**, **42a-b**, **44a**) and the definitions of hubris given by Aristotle (**47**) and by Photius and the *Suda* (**49**), it appears that hubris, as a term of law, designated a physical assault with an added mental aspect; namely, the perpetrator's intent to aggrandize himself and/or humiliate his victim. (For sexual offenses as hubris see chapter 3.)

Aikeia was the subject of a *dikê* (**33**, **42a**, **48**), and thus had to be prosecuted by the victim (see p. 29). *Dikai aikeias* were tried in the *dikastêria* and were supervised by the Forty in the mid-fourth century (**45**), but later by the Introducers (*Eisagôgeis*: **46**). The *dikê aikeias* was assessable (*timêtos*: p. 40), and the penalty was limited to a monetary fine (**37**, **41b**; cf. **48**): upon conviction the prosecutor and defendant each proposed an amount and the jury chose one of the proposals. The action for hubris, however, was a *graphê* (**35**, **36**, **42a**, **44a-b**). *Graphai hybreôs* were superintended by the *thesmothetai* (**35**, **45**); originally heard by the (*h*)*êliaia* (**35**), by the fourth century they were tried in the *dikastêria*. The *graphê hybreôs* was assessable without penal limit, and so a prosecutor could propose capital punishment (**35**, **37**, **42a**); by the middle of the fourth century, any fine levied was paid not to the victim but to the state (**44b**).

2.1. *Trauma ek pronoias* (Intentional Wounding)

See also **3a** Dem. 23.22; **25** [Arist.] *Ath. Pol.* 57.2–4.

30. Lysias 6 *Against Andocides* 15. Penalty of exile from victim's city. (400 or 399)

See especially S. C. **Todd**, *A Commentary on Lysias, Speeches 1–11* (Oxford 2007: text, translation, and commentary); also F. **Blass**, *Die attische Beredsamkeit* (Leipzig 1887–98) 1.562–70; R. C. **Jebb**, *The Attic Orators from Antiphon to Isaeus*[2] (London 1893) 1.277–82; D. M. **MacDowell**, *Andokides*: On the Mysteries (Oxford 1962) 14–15; S. **Usher**, *Greek Oratory: Tradition and Originality* (Oxford 1999) 113–14; S. C. **Todd**, *Lysias* (Austin 2000: translation with introduction and notes).

Lysias 6 was delivered by one of Andocides' prosecutors in the *Mysteries* case of 400 or 399 (see the headnote under **12** and **§11.3**). Here the speaker compares the *endeixis* (denunciation: p. **30**) of Andocides to the *endeixis* available against a person convicted of *trauma* who violates his exile. Presumably "the laws of the Areopagus" mentioned here date from the period of the Delian League/Athenian Empire (478/7–404: p. 11) and applied the preexisting penalty of exile for *trauma* within Attica to instances of wounding involving Athenian cleruchs (Athenian citizens settled on conquered territory) and inhabitants of allied cities. For similar Athenian interference with the jurisdictions of allies, including the mandatory referral to Athens of all lawsuits involving penalties of death, exile, or disfranchisement, see (e.g.) *IG* I[3] 10 = R. **Meiggs**-D. **Lewis**, *A Selection of Greek Historical Inscriptions to the End of the Fifth Century B.C.* (rev. ed. Oxford 1988: text and commentary), no. 31 = C. W. **Fornara**, *Archaic Times to the End of the Peloponnesian War*[2] (Cambridge 1983: translation with notes), no. 68; *IG* I[3] 40 = Meiggs-Lewis, no. 52 = Fornara, no. 103.

. . . if a person wounds a man's body, the head, face, hands, or feet, in accordance with the laws of the Areopagus he will be exiled from the victim's city, and if he returns, he will be denounced [*endeichtheis*] and punished with death. . . .

31. Lysias 3 *Against Simon* (selections). (*post* 394)

See especially C. **Carey**, *Lysias: Selected Speeches* (Cambridge 1989: text and commentary); **Todd**, *Commentary on Lysias 1–11* (text, translation, and commentary); also **Blass**, *AB* 1.577–82; **Jebb**, *AO* 1.272–74; **Usher**, *GO* 91–93; **Todd**, *Lysias* (translation with introduction and notes).

Lysias 3 is a defense speech from a *graphê traumatos ek pronoias*. The prosecutor, Simon, alleges that the unnamed speaker and the speaker's lover Theodotus broke into his home armed with potsherds, and that the speaker gave him a severe beating. The speaker, however, asserts that Simon has a history of violence and that the incident in question began when Simon and his friends ambushed him and Theodotus, and culminated in a public brawl in which every participant received a head wound. In addition to the standard defense argument equating *pronoia* with intent to kill (**31b**, **31d**; cf. **32a**), this speech provides evidence for several features of the *graphê traumatos ek pronoias*, including the weapon requirement (**31b**), the jurisdiction of the Council of the Areopagus (**31a**; cf. **3a** Dem. 23.22; **25** [Arist.] *Ath. Pol.* 57.2–4; Lysias 4.1), the *diômosia* (**31a**; see also Lysias 4.4), and the penalty upon conviction (**31c**, **31d**).

a. Lys. 3.1. Jurisdiction of Areopagus; *diômosia*.

Although I know many terrible things about Simon, councillors, I never thought he would reach such a level of audacity as to bring a charge as the wronged party for acts for which he ought to pay the penalty, and to come before you having sworn [*diomosamenon*] such a great and solemn oath.

b. Lys. 3.28. Weapon requirement; definition of *pronoia* (intent).

He says that we came to his house with a potsherd and that I threatened to kill him, and that this constitutes intent [*pronoia*].

c. Lys. 3.38. Penalty: exile and confiscation of property.

. . . I have become involved in a lawsuit so serious that I am at risk with regard to my homeland and all my property . . .

d. Lys. 3.41–43. Definition of *pronoia*; penalty.

[41] Moreover, I also thought that there was no intent [*pronoian*] to wound if a person wounded without intending to kill. For who is so stupid that he would plan far in advance for one of his enemies to receive a wound? [42] Obviously

the men who established the laws here did not see fit to exile from their homeland men who happened to break each other's heads open in a fight (or else they would have exiled many men indeed); rather, they established such severe penalties for those who plotted to kill people and inflicted wounds but were unable to kill them. They did so in the belief that these men should pay the penalty for what they plotted and intended; if they failed to achieve their goal, the deed was no less done on their part. [43] And you have often in the past decided the question of intent in this way.

32. Lysias 4 *On an Intentional Wounding* (selections). (403–380)

See especially **Todd**, *Commentary on Lysias 1–11* (text, translation, and commentary); also **Blass**, *AB* 1.583–87; **Jebb**, *AO* 1.274–76; **Usher**, *GO* 112–13; **Todd**, *Lysias* (translation with introduction and notes).

Lysias 4, like Lysias 3, is a defense speech from a *graphê traumatos ek pronoias*. The speaker and his prosecutor had been involved in a long-standing dispute over the ownership of a slave ("the woman" in **32a-b**); the speaker asserts that the two men agreed to joint ownership, while the prosecutor alleges sole ownership and denies the speaker's claim. According to the prosecutor, the speaker broke into his house and assaulted him with a potsherd; the speaker admits only that he gave the prosecutor a black eye and implies that he did so in self-defense (**32b**: the phrase translated "he started the fight" is *êrche cheirôn adikôn*, literally "he began unjust hands": see the introduction to this chapter and cf. **2** *IG* I³ 104, at lines 33–35; **41a** [Dem.] 47.40). As the speaker contests both the physical and the mental element of the charged offense, Lysias 4 provides evidence for the weapon requirement for *trauma* as well as the defendant's interpretation of *pronoia* (**32a**); the speaker also alludes to the penalty he faces if convicted (**32c**; cf. **31c** Lys. 3.38; **31d** Lys. 3.41–43). On the evidentiary torture of slaves (**32b**) see p. 24.

a. Lys. 4.5–9. Weapon requirement; definition of *pronoia* (intent) and *trauma* (wound).

So I came to kill him, as he claims, and I entered his house by force. Well, why didn't I kill him, then, since I had his person under my control and had so overpowered him as to actually take the woman? Let him explain that to you. But he has nothing to say. [6] And in fact all of you know that he would have died faster if he were struck with a dagger than if he were punched with a fist. And even he clearly does not allege that we came armed with anything of the sort: he claims that he was struck with a potsherd. Moreover, it is already clear from the things he has said that there was no intent [*pronoia*]. [7] If there had been, we would not have come as we did, since it was unclear whether we would find in his house a potsherd or something to kill him with; instead, we would have brought it from home. As it is, though, we admit that we had gone to see boys and flute-girls and had been drinking. So how is that intent? In no way, as I see it.

[8] . . . Then, spurred on by the woman, he gets too quick with his fists and becomes a violent drunk, and a person has to defend himself . . . [9] . . . But he has reached such a level of churlishness that he feels no shame at calling a black eye a "wound" [*trauma*] and being carried around in a litter and pretending to be in terrible shape, all on account of a prostitute. . . .

b. Lys. 4.10–11. Self-defense as defense.

[10] He claims that he was the victim of a terrible plot and disputes all these facts with us; but, although we could have put it to the test by torturing the woman, he refused. And she would have stated . . . whether we came by invitation or without anyone summoning us, and whether he started the fight or I hit him first.

c. Lys. 4.13. Penalty.

. . . but in the case of personal enemies this cannot happen, since they do not desire to take money but make it their job to expel a person from his homeland.

33. Demosthenes 54 *Against Conon* 17–19. Escalating offenses; weapon requirement for *trauma*; *dikê kakêgorias*, *dikê aikeias*, and *graphê traumatos ek pronoias*. (?355/341)

See references and headnote under **19**. Here Demosthenes has his client Ariston interpret the various actions for defamation (*kakêgoria*: see chapter 4), battery (*aikeia*), wounding, and homicide (see chapter 1) as attempts to curtail the escalation of disputes (cf. Isocrates 20.7–8). Note that the use of a weapon distinguishes wounding, which is justiciable by a *graphê*, from *aikeia*; Ariston does not mention hubris.

For the laws . . . have made provision so that pleas of necessity do not become more serious. For example . . . there are lawsuits [*dikai*] for defamation [*kakêgorias*]. [18] They say that these exist so that people exchanging insults are not induced to hit each other. And then there are lawsuits for battery [*aikeias*]. And I hear that these lawsuits [*dikas*] exist so that a person finding himself in a weaker position should not defend himself with a rock or something similar, but instead should await the justice provided by the law. And again, there are indictments [*graphai*] for wounding [*traumatos*], so that, when people are being wounded, homicides [*phonous*] do not occur. [19] As I see it, the least of these actions, the one for verbal abuse, has in view the last and most terrible, with the goal that killing not occur and that people not be led on little by little from insults to blows, from blows to wounds [*traumata*], and from wounds to death. The goal, rather, was that a lawsuit for each of these acts be present in the laws, and that these matters not be judged by the anger or will of a random individual.

34. Aeschines 2 *On the False Embassy* 93. *Graphê traumatos ek pronoias*; fine for non-prosecution. (343)

See references and headnote under **24**. Demosthenes has alleged in his prosecution that Aeschines received bribes from Philip II; Aeschines here accuses Demosthenes of inflicting a wound upon himself and then filing a *graphê traumatos ek pronoias* against his cousin Demomeles which he subsequently dropped. For the fine for non-prosecution of an initiated *graphê* cf. **35** Dem. 21.47. On the incident alleged here cf. Aeschines 3.51, 212; for a similar accusation see [Demosthenes] 40.32.

And now you bring an accusation of receiving bribes, you who once received a fine from the Council of the Areopagus because you did not prosecute the indictment for wounding [*têi tou traumatos graphêi*] that you brought against Demomeles of the deme Paeania, your cousin, after you cut your own head?

2.2. *Aikeia* (Battery) and Hubris

See also **19** Dem. 54 (selections); **33** Dem. 54.17–19; **56** Dem. 45.3–4; **59** Hyp. 1.12; **64a** Aeschin. 1.13–15; **67** Din. 1.23; **228** Isae. 3.40–50, 57–60, 62; **255** Dem. 21 (selections); **256** Dem. 37 (selections); **260** [Dem.] 33.19–20, 22, 32–33; **291** Arist. *Rhet.* 1373b38–1374a5, 1374a15–16; **332d** Dem. 21.25, 28; **332e** Dem. 21.51, 55–56; **348** *IG* II^2 1635.134–40; **378** [Dem.] 47.41–43.

35. Demosthenes 21 *Against Meidias* 47 (*lex*). Law on hubris. (date of speech 347/6; law ?enacted by Solon, 594/3)

See references and headnote under **22**. Here Demosthenes cites the statute (whose authenticity is supported by quotation in **64a** Aeschin. 1.13–

15) defining the legal procedure and penalty for hubris. Since the *graphê* procedure was probably invented by Solon ([Aristotle], *Constitution of the Athenians* [*Ath. Pol.*] 9.1; p. 4) and the law contains some Archaic features (including perhaps the role of the (*h*)*êliaia*: see **3b** Dem. 23.28), it is possible that this law dates to Solon's archonship (594/3). Notably, the law fails to define hubris, instead assuming (as often in Athenian legislation: p. 28) that the significance of the term is understood. For the availability of the *graphê hybreôs* in the case of both free and slave victims cf. Hypereides fr. 120 Jensen. The penalty of 1,000 dr. levied upon a prosecutor who received less than 20 percent of the jurors' votes was a standard feature of *graphai* (p. 33); for the similar penalty for non-prosecution after the filing of a *graphê* cf. **34** Aeschin. 2.93.

If a person commits hubris against another, whether a child or a woman or a man, free or slave, or does anything unlawful to any of these, any willing Athenian to whom it is permitted shall file an indictment [*graphesthô*] with the *thesmothetai*. The *thesmothetai* shall bring the case before the *hêliaia* within thirty days after the filing [*graphê*], unless some public business prevents it; otherwise, at the first opportunity. Whomever the *hêliaia* convicts, it shall punish him immediately with whatever it decides he deserves to suffer or pay. As for those who file an indictment in accordance with this law, if a person does not prosecute, or prosecutes but does not receive one-fifth of the votes, he shall pay 1,000 drachmas to the public treasury. If [the defendant] is punished with a fine for his hubris, he shall be imprisoned, if he committed hubris against a free person, until he pays the fine.

36. Isocrates 20 *Against Lochites* 2. Variety of legal actions for offenses against the person; exemption from court deposit; *graphê hybreôs*: prosecution and jurisdiction. (*post* 404/3)

See especially G. **Mathieu**-E. **Brémond**, *Isocrate: Discours, Tome I* (Paris 1928: text, French translation, and notes); D. C. **Mirhady**-Y. L. **Too**, *Isocrates I* (Austin 2000: translation with introduction and notes); D. G. **Spatharas**, *Ἰσοκράτης· Κατὰ Λοχίτου* (Athens 2009: text, Modern Greek translation, and commentary); also **Blass**, *AB* 2.217–19; **Jebb**, *AO* 2.215–17; **Usher**, *GO* 125.

This speech was delivered by the prosecutor in a *dikê aikeias* not long after the restoration of democracy in 403. In introducing his case to the jury, the speaker asserts the importance of redress for physical assault in Athenian law and discusses several key aspects of the *dikê aikeias* and *graphê hybreôs*.

You will also find that the men who established our laws were especially concerned with persons. First of all, you see, for this offense alone they created both [private] lawsuits [*dikas*] and indictments [*graphas*] without a deposit [*parakatabolês*], so that each of us might be able to punish his wrongdoers however he is able and willing. Moreover, for other charges the perpetrator is subject to prosecution only by the victim himself, but in the case of hubris, because the problem is a public one, any willing citizen may file an indictment [*grapsamenôi*] with the *thesmothetai* and come before you.

37. Lysias fr. 178 Carey *Against Isocrates* (= *Suda* s.v. *hybris*). Penalties for *aikeia* and hubris. (403–380)

L. **Gernet**-M. **Bizos**, *Lysias: Discours*, 2 vols. (Paris 1989: text, French translation, and notes).

This fragment comes from Lysias' speech *Against Isocrates*, which was delivered in a *dikê aikeias*. In it the speaker contrasts the assessable penalty for *aikeia*, which was limited to a fine, with that for hubris, which might result in execution.

And yet who among you does not know that battery [*aikian*] can be punished only with a fine, while you are permitted to punish men convicted of hubris with death?

38. Lysias fr. 279 Carey *Against Teisis* (= Dionysius of Halicarnassus, *Demosthenes* 11). Case of *aikeia*? hubris? (403–380)

See especially **Gernet-Bizos**, *Lysias* (text, French translation, and notes); **Todd**, *Lysias* (translation with introduction and notes); also **Blass**, *AB* 1.623; **Jebb**, *AO* 1.308.

The speech *Against Teisis*, from which this significant fragment survives, was delivered by the prosecution in either a *dikê aikeias* or a *graphê hybreôs*. The word *dikên* (§1) may indicate a *dikê aikeias*, but it is possible that the word is used in the general sense (p. 29) and that the case was a *graphê hybreôs:* compare §4 with the characterization of confinement and physical abuse as hubris in **39** Isae. 8.40–41 and **40** [Dem.] 53.16, and note that Dionysius of Halicarnassus introduces the passage as containing "a narrative dealing with hubris" (*diêgêsin tina . . . hybristikên*). The speaker alleges that a quarrel between the defendant Teisis and the victim Archippus culminated in a vicious and humiliating assault by the former upon the latter (cf. especially **33** Dem. 54.17–19 for the escalation of disputes from words to blows, and for a narrative similar to that given here see Aeschines 1.58–64). The

Deigma (§6) was a place in the Peiraeus where vendors displayed foodstuffs (scholion to D. H. *Dem.* 11).

[1] You see, Athenians, Archippus here exercised at the same wrestling school as Teisis, the defendant in this lawsuit [*dikên*]. A dispute arose, and they became involved in insults and argument and enmity and verbal abuse. Now, Pytheas is the young man's lover—for the whole truth will be told before you—and his guardian, left by his father. [2] When Teisis recounted to him the abuse in the wrestling school, Pytheas, wishing to win his favor and to seem a clever schemer, instructed him (as we have perceived from what happened and have learned from those in the know) to reconcile with Archippus for the present, but to look for some way to catch him alone.

[3] Teisis obeyed these instructions, reconciled with Archippus, associated with him, and pretended to be his friend. Then, being the sort of person that he is, he reached such a pitch of insanity that, as the Anaceia horse race was going on, catching sight of Archippus passing by his door with me (they happen to be neighbors), he first invited Archippus to dine with him, and when Archippus declined, he asked him to come to a party, saying that Archippus should drink with him and his slaves. [4] So, after we ate dinner, when it was already getting dark, we came and knocked on his door, and they told us to enter. But when we got inside, they threw me out of the house and grabbed Archippus here and tied him to a column, and Teisis took a whip, struck him numerous blows, and confined him in a room. And it was not enough for Teisis to commit only these offenses, but, imitating the most depraved youths in the city, having recently obtained his patrimony and affecting the role of a wealthy young man, he ordered his slaves, after day had already broken, again to tie Archippus to the column and whip him.

[5] With Archippus' body now in such awful condition, Teisis sent for Antimachus and told him nothing of what had happened, saying instead that he had happened to be dining when Archippus showed up drunk, broke open the door, entered, and insulted him, Antimachus, and their wives. Antimachus was angry at them for the serious offenses they had committed; nonetheless he summoned witnesses and asked Archippus how he got in, and Archippus said, "At the invitation of Teisis and his friends." [6] Since the newcomers advised them to untie Archippus as quickly as possible and considered what had happened to be terrible, they returned Archippus to his brothers. Since he was unable to walk, they carried him to the Deigma on a litter, displaying him to a number of Athenians, and to many foreigners as well, in such a condition that the spectators not only were furious at the perpetrators but even denounced the city for not publicly and immediately punishing such offenders.

39. Isaeus 8 *On the Estate of Ciron* 40–41. False imprisonment as hubris. (?383–363)

See especially W. **Wyse**, *The Speeches of Isaeus* (Cambridge 1904: text and commentary); R. F. **Wevers**, *Isaeus: Chronology, Prosopography, and Social History* (The Hague 1969); M. **Edwards**, *Isaeus* (Austin 2007: translation with introduction and notes); also **Blass**, *AB* 2.555–60; **Jebb**, *AO* 2.327–30; **Usher**, *GO* 140–45.

Isaeus 8 was delivered by a claimant in an inheritance lawsuit (a *diadikasia*: see chapter 7) concerning the estate of Ciron. The claim of the speaker's opponent is supported by Diocles of the deme Phlya, whose character the speaker impugns by means of the following anecdote. "The sisters" are Diocles' uterine half-sisters; for improper confinement as grounds for a charge of hubris cf. **40** [Dem.] 53.16, and possibly **38** Lys. fr. 279 Carey and **67** Din. 1.23. Isaeus also composed a speech for the prosecution in Diocles' hubris trial, but only small fragments survive (Isaeus fr. 5 Thalheim).

If you are familiar with Diocles' shamelessness and with the kind of person he is in other respects, you would not doubt anything I have said. . . . [41] When an attempt to recover the money belonging to two of the sisters was being made by their husbands, he confined the elder sister's husband in his house and got him disfranchised by means of a plot. Diocles was brought up on an indictment for hubris [*graphên hybreôs*] but has not yet paid the penalty for his actions. . . .

40. [Demosthenes] 53 *Against Nicostratus* 16. Confinement and beating as hubris. (*post* 368/7)

J. E. **Sandys**-F. A. **Paley**, *Demosthenes: Select Private Orations* 2[4] (Cambridge 1910: text and commentary); V. **Bers**, *Demosthenes, Speeches 50–59* (Austin 2003: translation with introduction and notes); D. M. **MacDowell**, *Demosthenes the Orator* (Oxford 2009) 106–9.

This oration was delivered by Apollodorus in an *apographê*, an action in which the prosecutor sought to confiscate property belonging to the defendant in order to pay a debt owed by the defendant to the state. Here Apollodorus alleges that the defendant Nicostratus and his brother Arethusius, with whom he had been involved in a previous dispute, attempted to entrap him into committing hubris by treating a citizen boy as though he were a slave.

In addition to these things, in daytime they sent in a little citizen boy (because we were neighbors and my land bordered theirs) and told him to pluck flowers from my rose garden, which was in bloom, so that if I caught him and bound or beat him in the belief that he was a slave, they could bring an indictment for hubris [*graphên hybreôs*] against me.

41. [Demosthenes] 47 *Against Euergus and Mnesibulus* (selections). (*post* 358/7)

See references and headnote under **17**. In discussing his allegedly wrongful conviction by Theophemus in a *dikê aikeias* (related in §§45–46), the speaker defines *aikeia* (**41a**; similar language occurs in §§7, 8, 15, 35, 39, 47; cf. **2** *IG* I[3] 104, at lines 33–35) and relates to his jury the total amount he was fined (**41b**). "The woman" in **41a** is a slave; on challenges for the evidentiary torture of slaves see p. 24. The *epôbelia* (**41b**) was an additional fine, amounting to 1 obol per drachma of the principal fine, assessed against a prosecutor in at least some (perhaps most) *dikai* who received less than 20 percent of the jurors' votes.

a. [Dem.] 47.40. Definition of *aikeia*.

So, since they refuse to hand over the woman, for whom they themselves claimed to have issued a challenge, I wish to bring before you the witnesses who saw me struck first by Theophemus (and this is [the definition of] battery [*aikeia*]: whoever starts a fight unjustly [*arxêi cheirôn adikôn*] first). . . .

b. [Dem.] 47.64. Example of fine for *aikeia*.

When I paid Theophemus, to whom I had lost the lawsuit—when I paid out, in the presence of numerous witnesses, the fine of 1,100 drachmas, the *epôbelia* of 183 drachmas 2 obols, and the court fees of 30 drachmas . . . , he received from me at the bank the entire sum, 1,313 drachmas 2 obols. . . .

42. Demosthenes 54 *Against Conon* (selections). (?355/341)

See references and headnote under **19**. According to the speaker, Ariston, the life-threatening and humiliating assault perpetrated upon him by a gang led by Conon (**42b**) meets the standard for a *graphê hybreôs* and deserves the death penalty; however, after consulting his family and friends, Ariston decided to bring a lesser *dikê aikeias* (**42a**). On *apagôgê* (summary arrest) see p. 30 and (e.g.) **57a** Aeschin. 1.91; for the distinction between *dikai idiai* (private lawsuits, including the *dikê aikeias*) and *dikai dêmosiai* (public lawsuits, including *apagôgê* and the *graphê hybreôs*), see p. 29.

a. Dem. 54.1. *Dikê aikeias* and *graphê hybreôs*; possibility of death penalty for hubris.

I was the victim of hubris, men of the jury, and I suffered such treatment at the hands of the defendant Conon here that for a very long time neither my family nor any of my doctors expected me to survive; but I unexpectedly got well and lived, and I filed against him this lawsuit for battery [*dikên . . . aikeias*]. All my friends and family whom I consulted asserted that, on the basis of what had happened, he was liable both to summary arrest [*apagôgêi*] as a clothes-snatcher and to indictments for hubris [*tais tês hybreôs graphais*]. But they advised and recommended that I not bring upon myself bigger problems than I could handle, and that I not be seen as bringing a charge for the things I had suffered that was inappropriate to my age. So I acted accordingly and on their account filed a private lawsuit [*idian . . . dikên*]—although, men of Athens, I would most gladly condemn the defendant here to death.

b. Dem. 54.8–9. Details of the charge.

We happened to be turning back from the sanctuary of Persephone and walking back right near the Leocorion, and we ran into them. When we mixed it up, one of them, some unknown person, fell upon Phanostratus and held him down; Conon here, his son, and the son of Andromenes fell upon me. First they stripped me; then they tripped me and pushed me into the mud, and put me in such a condition by jumping on me and treating me with hubris that my lip was cut through and my eyes were swollen shut. They left me in such bad shape that I could neither stand nor speak. As I lay there, I heard them say many awful things. [9] The rest of it involved blasphemy and I would hesitate to quote some of it in your presence, but I will give you an indication of the defendant's hubris and proof that the whole thing happened at his bidding: he crowed in imitation of victorious roosters, and the others encouraged him to flap his elbows against his sides like wings. And after that I was carried away unclothed by bystanders, and they left, taking my cloak.

43. Demosthenes 23 *Against Aristocrates* 50 (*lex* + commentary). Definition of *aikeia*; right of self-defense. (352/1)

See references and headnote under **3**. Here the speaker argues that the right of self-defense is a constant in Athenian law and not limited to the law of homicide (cf. **2** *IG* I³ 104, at lines 33–35). The language quoted by the speaker may be the opening clause of the law on *aikeia*; for "starting a fight unjustly" cf. **41a** [Dem.] 47.40.

For you see that in all the laws, not just the homicide laws, this is the case. "If a person strikes someone," it states, "starting a fight unjustly" [*archôn cheirôn adikôn*]—since, if he defended himself, he does no wrong.

44. Demosthenes 21 *Against Meidias* (selections). (347/6)

See references and headnotes under **22** and **35**, and **332** Dem. 21 (selections). In the first passage below (**44a**), Demosthenes argues that Meidias' assault upon him constitutes hubris in part because he was exercising an official function as chorus-producer (*chorêgos*) at the Greater Dionysia when Meidias struck him, and therefore Meidias committed an offense not just against Demosthenes but against the city as a whole. On defamation see chapter 4. In the second passage (**44b**), we see that by the date of this speech, when a person convicted in a *graphê hybreôs* was penalized with a fine, the money was paid to the state rather than to the victim; note that this detail is absent from the surviving law on hubris (**35** Dem. 21.47).

a. Dem. 21.31–33. Hubris and defamation against public officials.

For on that day [Meidias] did not brutalize me as Demosthenes alone, but as your chorus-producer; and you may realize how important this is from the following. [32] You know, obviously, that "*thesmothetês*" is not the name of any of these *thesmothetai*, but each has whatever name he has. If, then, a person commits hubris against or speaks ill of one of them in his capacity as a private citizen, he will be prosecuted by an indictment for hubris [*graphên hybreôs*] or a private lawsuit for defamation [*dikên kakêgorias idian*]; but if it occurs in his capacity as *thesmothetês*, [the offender] will be disfranchised permanently [*atimos kathapax*]. Why? Because in that situation the man who commits this act also commits hubris against the laws, against your public crown, and against the name of the city: for *thesmothetês* is a name belonging to no man, but to the city. [33] And again, the same applies for the archon: if a person strikes or speaks ill of him while he is wearing his crown, that person is disfranchised; but if it occurs in his capacity as a private citizen, [the offender] is liable to a private lawsuit. And these provisions hold not only for the aforementioned individuals but for everyone to whom the city grants any immunity, crown, or honor.

b. Dem. 21.45. Qualification to prosecute *graphê hybreôs*; fine payable to the state.

For this very reason the lawgiver granted indictments [*graphas*] for hubris [*hybreôs*] to every willing person and made the fine entirely public property. He believed, you see, that a man who sets out to commit hubris wrongs the city, not just his victim; and that for the victim vengeance is sufficient recompense and he should not receive money for himself for such matters.

45. Demosthenes 37 *Against Pantaenetus* 33. Jurisdiction over *aikeia* and hubris. (ca. 346)

See references and headnote under **23**. In this passage, the speaker alleges that his adversary Pantaenetus has employed an improper procedure to bring multiple accusations against him; in explaining the correct procedures for each of Pantaenetus' allegations he mentions the officials who superintend the relevant lawsuits, including the *dikê aikeias* and the *graphê hybreôs*. For "acts of violence" (*biaia*) see **61** Harpo. s.v. *biaiôn*; on *epiklêroi* see chapters 6 and 7. On the Forty see [Aristotle], *Constitution of the Athenians (Ath. Pol.)* 53; cf. *contra* **46** [Arist.] *Ath. Pol.* 52.2, where *aikeia* cases come before the Introducers (*Eisagôgeis*): evidently there was a change in jurisdiction between the delivery of this speech and the composition of the *Ath. Pol.* (332–322).

Here he charges me with many terrible things at the same time: battery [*aikeian*], hubris [*hybrin*], acts of violence [*biaiôn*], and offenses against *epiklêroi*. There are separate lawsuits for each of these offenses, and they neither come before the same magistrate nor involve the same penalties: battery and acts of violence come before the Forty, hubris lawsuits come before the *thesmothetai*, and all offenses against *epiklêroi* come before the archon.

46. [Aristotle], *Constitution of the Athenians (Ath. Pol.)* 52.2. Jurisdiction over *dikai emmênoi*, including *dikê aikeias*. (332–322)

See references under **1c**; on the "monthly lawsuits" (*dikai emmênoi*) cf. **§10.5** and see especially E. E. **Cohen**, *Ancient Athenian Maritime Courts* (Princeton 1973); P. J. **Rhodes**, *A Commentary on the Aristotelian* Athenaion Politeia (Oxford 1993) 582–86, 664–65; also **Lipsius**, *ARR* 901; **Harrison**, *LA* 2.16; C. **Carey**-R. A. **Reid**, *Demosthenes: Selected Private Speeches* (Cambridge 1985) 119–20; **MacDowell**, *Demosthenes:* Against Meidias 266–67. By the date of composition of the *Ath. Pol.*, *dikai aikeias* had been classified as "monthly lawsuits," and jurisdiction over them had been transferred from the Forty (**45** Dem. 37.33) to the Introducers (*Eisagôgeis*). On dowries see chapter 5; on *eranoi* ("joint loans": interest-free loans provided by groups of contributors) see chapter 10; on the trierarchy see p. 25. "At the rate of 1 drachma": i.e., at an interest rate of 1 drachma per mina per month (= 1 percent monthly = 12 percent annually).

They also allot five men as Introducers [*Eisagôgeas*], who introduce the monthly lawsuits [*emmênous . . . dikas*], each Introducer for two tribes. The monthly lawsuits are: for a dowry [*proikos*], if a person who owes a dowry does not pay it; if a person borrows at the rate of 1 drachma and defaults; if a person wishing to conduct business in the agora borrows start-up capital from someone [and defaults]; and also for battery [*aikeias*], joint loans [*eranikas*], corporations, slaves, draft animals, trierarchies, and banks.

47. Aristotle, *Rhetoric* (selections). Aristotle's definition of hubris. (?350s-322)

E. M. **Cope**-J. E. **Sandys**, *The* Rhetoric *of Aristotle*, 3 vols. (Cambridge 1877: text and commentary); W. D. **Ross**, ed., *The Works of Aristotle*, vol. 11 (Oxford 1924: translation with notes by W. R. Roberts); **Fisher**, *Hybris* ch. 1.

While not a definitive source for Athenian law, Aristotle's *Rhetoric* provides valuable information regarding contemporary Athenian values and moral precepts. Aristotle defines hubris as an action that brings pleasure to the perpetrator and shame to the victim. This mental component is presumably the aggravating factor that distinguished hubris from *aikeia* in Athenian law: cf. the descriptions of the assaults in **38** Lys. fr. 279 Carey, **39** Isae. 8.40–41, **40** [Dem.] 53.16, and **42** Dem. 54 (selections), and see also **49** Photius s.v. *hybris* = *Suda* s.v. *hybris*. Note that in the second passage below (**47b**) Aristotle borrows Athenian legal terminology: for "starting a fight unjustly" cf. **41a** [Dem.] 47.40; **2** *IG* I³ 104, at lines 33–35. For other Aristotelian formulations concerning hubris, see *Rhetoric* 1373b38–1374a15, 1379a30–34, 1382b34–1383a3, 1384a15–18, 1385b19–23, 1390b32–34, 1391a14–19; *Nicomachean Ethics* 1149b20–23.

a. Arist. *Rhet.* 1378b14–30.

There are three types of contempt: scorn, spite, and hubris. . . . A man who commits hubris also exhibits contempt; for hubris is doing and saying things that involve shame for the victim, not in order that anything accrue to the perpetrator other than what happened, but so that he may feel pleasure. Those who retaliate, you see, do not commit hubris but get vengeance. The cause of pleasure for those who commit hubris is their belief that, by doing others ill, they themselves excel more; this is why the young and the rich are perpetrators of hubris: they think they excel by committing hubris. Dishonor is an element of hubris, and he who dishonors exhibits contempt. . . .

b. Arist. *Rhet.* 1402a1–3.

Or if someone were to say that striking free men is hubris: for it is not so in all cases, but only when one starts a fight unjustly [*archêi cheirôn adikôn*].

48. Harpocration s.v. *aikias*. *Dikê aikeias*; assessment of fine. (Harpocration *fl.* 2nd c.A.D.)

See references and headnote under **28**. In this lemma Harpocration defines the *dikê aikeias*; "adds in writing" means that the prosecutor included his assessment of the penalty in his written statement of the charge (cf., e.g., **264** D. H. *Din.* 3; **342** D. L. 2.40).

For battery [*aikias*]: a type of private lawsuit [*dikês . . . idiôtikês*] filed for blows [*plêgais*]. For this lawsuit the penalty is not fixed in the laws; instead, the prosecutor adds in writing as a penalty however much he thinks the offense is worth, and the jurors decide.

49. Photius, *Lexicon* s.v. *hybris* = *Suda* s.v. *hybris*. Definitions of hubris and *aikeia*. (Photius *fl.* late 9th c.A.D.; *Suda* composed late 10th c. A.D.)

C. **Theodoridis**, *Photii Patriarchae lexicon* (Berlin 1982-: text); A. **Adler**, *Suidae lexicon* (Leipzig 1928–38: text).

In the ninth century, Photius (patriarch of Constantinople 858–867, 878–886) compiled from earlier lexica his own *Lexicon* of terms found in Classical and later Greek authors; this in turn was one of many sources used by the author of the *Suda*, a lexicon compiled in the late tenth century. With the definition of hubris given here cf. **47** Arist. *Rhet.* (selections).

Hubris: battery [*aikia*] accompanied by humiliation and spite; battery [*aikia*] is blows [*plêgai*] alone.

CHAPTER 3

Sexual Offenses

3.1. *Moicheia* (Seduction) and Rape

Handbooks: J. H. **Lipsius**, *Das attische Recht und Rechtsverfahren* (Leipzig 1905–15) 429–35, 482, 636–39, 710; A. R. W. **Harrison**, *The Law of Athens* (Oxford 1968–71) 1.13–15, 19, 32–39; 2.15, 78, 81–82, 167–68; D. M. **MacDowell**, *The Law in Classical Athens* (Ithaca, NY 1978) 124–26; S. C. **Todd**, *The Shape of Athenian Law* (Oxford 1993) 276–79; E. **Cantarella**, "Gender, Sexuality, and Law," in *The Cambridge Companion to Ancient Greek Law*, ed. M. Gagarin-D. Cohen (Cambridge 2005) 236–53. **Studies:** S. G. **Cole**, "Greek Sanctions against Sexual Assault," *CP* 79 (1984) 97–113; E. M. **Harris**, "Did the Athenians Regard Seduction As a Worse Crime Than Rape?," *CQ* 40 (1990) 370–77; D. **Cohen**, *Law, Sexuality, and Society: The Enforcement of Morals in Classical Athens* (Cambridge 1991); ***idem***, *Law, Violence, and Community in Classical Athens* (Cambridge 1995) 143–62; C. **Carey**, "Rape and Adultery in Athenian Law," *CQ* 45 (1995) 407–17; K. **Kapparis**, "When Were the Athenian Adultery Laws Introduced?," *RIDA* ser. 3 vol. 42 (1995) 97–122; ***idem***, "Humiliating the Adulterer: The Law and the Practice in Classical Athens," *RIDA* ser. 3 vol. 43 (1996) 63–77; D. **Ogden**, "Rape, Adultery and the Protection of Bloodlines in Classical Athens," in *Rape in Antiquity*, ed. S. Deacy-K. F. Pierce (London 1997) 25–41; A. C. **Scafuro**, *The Forensic Stage: Settling Disputes in Graeco-Roman New Comedy* (Cambridge 1997) 193–216, 229–31, 474–79; W. **Schmitz**, "Der nomos moicheias—Das athenische Gesetz über den Ehebruch," *ZSS* 114 (1997) 45–140; C. B. **Patterson**, *The Family in Greek History* (Cambridge, MA 1998) 70–179; R. **Omitowoju**, *Rape and the Politics of Consent in Classical Athens* (Cambridge 2002); D. D. **Phillips**, "Why Was Lycophron Prosecuted by *Eisangelia*?," *GRBS* 46 (2006) 375–94.

The earliest surviving Athenian law that deals (indirectly) with seduction and rape is the clause in Draco's homicide law concerning lawful killings (**3f** Dem. 23.53; cf. **54**), which permits the killing of a man discovered in the act of intercourse with the killer's wife, mother, sister, daughter, or concubine kept for the procreation of free children; these provisions do not distinguish between consensual intercourse and rape.

> The lost beginning of the pseudo-Aristotelian *Constitution of the Athenians* (*Ath. Pol.*: see references and headnote under **1c**) contained an anecdote in which the Athenian king (or archon) Hippomenes (?late eighth century B.C.), after catching a seducer with his daughter Leimone, killed the former by dragging him behind a chariot and the latter by locking her up with a horse (Heraclides Lembus, *Epitome of the Ath. Pol.* 1). In all probability, the only factual element of the story is that one of the last Athenian kings was named Hippomenes, and the rest was invented later to explain the fall of the monarchy: see P. J. **Rhodes**, *A Commentary on the Aristotelian* Athenaion Politeia (Oxford 1993) 78–79; N. R. E. **Fisher**, *Aeschines*: Against Timarchos (Oxford 2001) 331–34. The inventions presumably arose from the fact that the name Hippomenes means "horse-strength" (in addition to the fates of Leimone and her seducer, note that Leimone's name means "meadow"). The story, therefore, has no value for the treatment of seduction in Athenian law, except insofar as a speaker might employ it as evidence (cf., e.g., Aeschines 1.182) for the antiquity of the Draconian rule.

According to Plutarch (**50**), Solon penalized the rape of a free woman with a fine of 100 drachmas. The bulk of our evidence for seduction and rape, however, comes from the late fifth and fourth centuries, at which time multiple remedies were available for each offense (as commonly in Athenian law: see p. 33). However, we are comparatively ill-informed about the treatment of seduction and rape in the time of the Attic orators: in general, we have better evidence for the existence of various legal procedures than for their application.

With regard to sex, Athenians had differing sociolegal expectations of men and women. Citizen women were expected to have sex only within the marital bond, while men, regardless of their marital status, were permitted to have sex with both male and female partners, provided that they obeyed social and legal strictures (for example, punitive sanctions applied to a man who had sex with a citizen woman who was not his wife, and social stigma attached to an adult man who took the passive role in homosexual intercourse). The term *moicheia* (seduction) embraced illicit consensual sex between a man and a woman. The man was seen as the primary offender (the *moichos*, seducer), the woman as the object of or party to seduction. Although most allegations of *moicheia* involve a married woman (e.g., **54**), there is one clear instance of an unmarried woman's being party to *moicheia* (**58a**), and therefore the term is understood by most scholars as being broader than "adultery."

In the late fifth and fourth centuries, a variety of legal and customary remedies was available against the seducer. (1) A dedicated action for seduction, the *graphê moicheias*, could be brought before the *thesmothetai* (**60**; cf. **59**) by any willing citizen (p. 30). The penalty upon conviction is not attested; scholars have proposed that the penalty was an automatic death sentence, or that the action was assessable (an *agôn timêtos*: p. 40) either with or without penal limit (in the latter case a penalty of death will have been possible: cf. **55**). (2) It is commonly assumed, on the basis of the frequency of hubris language in descriptions of seduction (e.g., **54**), that the *graphê hybreôs* (see chapter 2) was available against the seducer (see **56**, **59**). (3) At least once, in the late fourth century, impeachment (*eisangelia*: see chapter 12) was employed to prosecute an accused seducer (**59**). If the seducer was caught in the act, additional remedies were available. (4) The seducer might be executed on the spot by a qualified relative of the female party (**3f** Dem. 23.53; **54**). (5) The seducer was liable to *apagôgê* (summary arrest: p. 30) as a *kakourgos* (malefactor) (**57a**). (6) The seducer might be subjected to painful and humiliating punishment at the hands of his captor, including the insertion of a large radish into the anus and the removal of pubic hair with the aid of hot ash (**52**; cf. **53**). (7) The seducer might be held for ransom (**58a**; cf. **54**); in this case a man who had been held wrongfully—for instance, because the woman in question was a known prostitute (**58a**; cf. **50**, **51**)—had available to him against his captor a *graphê adikôs heirchthênai hôs moichon* (for having been unjustly detained as a seducer) (**58a**).

Penalties also attached to the female party to *moicheia*: if she was married, divorce was mandatory (**58b**), and regardless of her marital status, she was forbidden to wear jewelry or attend public religious rites, on pain of beating and humiliation (**57b**, **58b**). According to Plutarch, Solon permitted a man to sell his unmarried daughter or sister into slavery if she was caught with a seducer (**50**), but we have no evidence of this penalty being employed in the time of the orators.

Rape was also subject to numerous remedies, some of which applied to seduction as well: it is generally assumed that the *graphê hybreôs* (number 2 above) was available for rape, and a rapist caught in the act could be killed by a qualified relative of the victim (**3f** Dem. 23.53; number 4 above) and may also have been subject to detention and self-help punishment (number 6 above) and/or extortion of ransom (number 7 above) by his captor. Additionally, a general lawsuit for acts of violence, the *dikê biaiôn*, applied in cases of rape (**61**). Legal penalties for rape attested in the orators vary. The law of Solon that fixed the penalty for the rape of a free woman at 100 drachmas (**50**) seems to have become obsolete, and available penalties depended upon the procedure chosen by the prosecutor. Under the *graphê hybreôs*, a prosecutor could propose any penalty, up to and including death, but under the *dikê biaiôn* only a (presumably assessable) fine was available: double damages for the rape of a free person, with equal amounts paid to the prosecutor and to the state (**61**; cf. **54**), and possibly simple damages for the rape of a slave (**51**). Since slaves were property, the rape of a slave may have been justiciable by the *dikê blabês* (see chapter 8) rather than, or as an alternative to, the *dikê biaiôn*.

See also **3f** Dem. 23.53; **13a** Lys. 1.30–31; **25** [Arist.] *Ath. Pol.* 57.2–4; **45** Dem. 37.33; **291** Arist. *Rhet.* 1373b38–1374a5, 1374a15–16; **294** Dem. 21.44–45; **385** Hyp. 1 (selections); **392b** Pollux, *Onomasticon* 8.51–53.

50. Plutarch, *Solon* 23.1–2. Solon's penalties for sexual offenses. (date of composition late 1st-early 2nd c.A.D.; laws attributed to Solon, 594/3 B.C.)

See references and headnote under **1d**. In this passage, Plutarch discusses laws attributed to Solon regarding seduction, rape, and prostitution. The provision permitting the self-help killing of a seducer probably refers to Draco's law (**3f** Dem. 23.53), which remained in force after Solon revised the laws of Athens (**6b** [Arist.] *Ath. Pol.* 7.1). For the 100 dr. penalty for rape of a free woman cf. **54** Lys. 1.24–33, at §§31–33; for the exemption from liability for pandering in the case of known prostitutes cf. **51** Lys. 10.18–19; **58a** [Dem.] 59.64–70, at §67.

[Solon] allowed the man who caught a seducer [*moichon*] to kill him; but if a person seized a free woman and raped her, he imposed a penalty of 100 drachmas, and if a person prostituted someone, he imposed a penalty of 20 drachmas, except in the case of women who go about in public [*pephasmenôs pôlountai*]; that is, courtesans. . . . [23.2] Moreover, he did not allow a person to sell his daughters or sisters unless he caught one of them who was unmarried having had sex with a man.

51. Lysias 10 / *Against Theomnestus* 18–19 (*lex* + commentary). Prostitution; ?rape of slave. (384/3; laws attributed to Solon, 594/3)

See references and headnote under **15**. Here the speaker quotes from a law that he ascribes to Solon (§15) and that deals with prostitution and (probably) rape (cf. **54** Lys. 1.24–33, at §§31–33; **58a** [Dem.] 59.64–70, at §67). If the law regulated a specific procedure, it was probably the *dikê biaiôn* or the *dikê blabês* (see the introduction to this section). The clause "let it be permitted to owe the damage of a male or female slave" is problematic: "of a male or female slave" might mean either "caused by a male or female slave" or "inflicted upon a male or female slave"; the latter interpretation seems more likely, since this law evidently addressed sexual offenses (cf. the similar language in **50** Plut. *Solon* 23.1–2). Some editors insert the word *diplên*, "double"; the clause would then be translated "let it be permitted to owe (or simply 'let him owe') double the damage of a male or female slave."

[To the court clerk:] Read as well the end of this law.

<LAW.>

[19] "Women who go about in public [*pephasmenôs pôlountai*]," and "let it be permitted to owe the damage of a male [*oikeôs*] or female slave." Pay attention: *pephasmenôs* means "in public," *pôleisthai* means "go about," and *oikeôs* means "of a [male] servant."

52. Aristophanes (selections). Self-help punishment of seducer.

K. J. **Dover**, *Aristophanes:* Clouds (Oxford 1968: text and commentary); A. H. **Sommerstein**, *Aristophanes:* Clouds (Warminster 1982: text, translation, and commentary); ***idem***, *Aristophanes:* Wealth (Warminster 2001: text, translation, and commentary).

In the following passages, characters in the plays of Aristophanes, the master of Athenian Old Comedy, refer to traditional self-help remedies against a seducer caught in the act, including "radishing" (**52a**), depilation of pubic hair by means of hot ash (**52a-b**; cf. Aristophanes, *Thesmophoriazusae* 536–38), and extortion of ransom (**52b**). In the latter passage, "you" is Wealth; the point is that a rich man caught in the act of seduction can bribe his captor so as to escape with only a plucking, as opposed to more severe punishment.

a. Ar. *Clouds* 1083–84. (original version 424/3; partially revised *ante* 416)

BETTER ARGUMENT. And what if he listens to you and gets radished and plucked with ash? Will he have any grounds for saying that he doesn't have a gaping asshole?

b. Ar. *Wealth* 168. (388)

CHREMYLUS. And this one, caught as a seducer [*moichos*], on account of you gets plucked.

53. Xenophon, *Memorabilia* 2.1.5. Punishment of seducer. (early 4th c.)

J. R. **Smith**, *Xenophon:* Memorabilia (Boston 1903: text and commentary); E. C. **Marchant**, *Xenophon:* Memorabilia *and* Oeconomicus (Cambridge, MA 1959: text, translation, and notes); H. **Tredennick**-R. **Waterfield**, *Xenophon: Conversations of Socrates* (London 1990: translation with introduction and notes).

Xenophon's *Memorabilia* contains the author's recollections of and comments upon conversations featuring his teacher Socrates. This passage quotes Socrates in a conversation with the philosopher Aristippus of Cyrene. "Hubris" here (cf. chapter 2) refers to the painful and humiliating punishments mentioned in **52** Ar. (selections).

"For instance, seducers [*moichoi*] go into women's quarters knowing that for a seducer [*tôi moicheuonti*] there is the danger of suffering what the law threatens, and of being entrapped, caught, and subjected to hubris. . . ."

54. Lysias 1 *On the Killing of Eratosthenes* 24–33. Seduction; rape of free person. (403–380)

See references and headnote under **13**. Here Euphiletus describes his apprehension and killing of Eratosthenes, which he justifies by reference to three laws. The context of the first law (§28) suggests that it dealt with seduction and/or *apagôgê* (cf. **57a** Aeschin. 1.91). The paraphrase that follows the second law (§30) shows that it is to be identified as **3f** Dem. 23.53; for the application of these provisions to seducers caught in the act cf. Xenarchus fr. 4 Kassel-Austin; Pausanias 9.36.8. From the paraphrase that follows the third law (§31) we may infer that it addressed the rape of a free person; it may have regulated the *dikê biaiôn* (note the phrase "shames by violence," and cf. **61** Harpo. s.v. *biaiôn*). On Euphiletus' argument that Athenian law considered seduction a more serious offense than rape see especially **Harris**, "Did the Athenians Regard Seduction as a Worse Crime Than Rape?" and **Carey**, "Rape and Adultery in Athenian Law"; scholars on both sides of the issue concur that Euphiletus presents an incomplete and distorted picture of the procedural and penal options available for these offenses.

Pushing open the door to the bedroom, the first of us to enter saw him still lying next to my wife, and those who came in later saw him standing naked on the bed. [25] And I, gentlemen, hit him and knocked him down, and after pulling his hands behind his back and tying them, I asked why he was committing hubris against my house by entering it. And he admitted that he did wrong but begged and pleaded with me not to kill him but to exact money from him.

[26] But I said, "It is not I who will kill you but the law of the city, which you by your transgression have valued less than your pleasures; you chose to commit an offense of such magnitude against my wife and my children rather than to obey the laws and behave yourself." [27] Thus, gentlemen, he met with the treatment that the laws command for people who do such things. He had not been snatched in off the street, nor had he fled for refuge to the hearth, as my adversaries say. How could he have? He was struck in the bedroom and immediately fell down, and I pulled his hands behind him, and there were so many people in the house that he could not escape, since he had no implement of iron or wood or anything else with which he could have defended himself against those coming in. [28] Gentlemen, I think you know that those who commit unjust acts do not admit that their enemies are telling the truth; instead, by lying and similar contrivances they incite in their hearers anger against those who act justly. [To the court clerk:] So, then, first read out the law.

LAW.

[29] He did not dispute it, gentlemen, but admitted doing wrong, and he begged and pleaded not to be put to death, and he was ready to pay money as recompense. I, however, did not agree with his assessment of the penalty but considered the law of the city to be more authoritative, and I exacted the penalty that you, believing it most just, have imposed on those who commit such practices. Would the witnesses to these things please come forth.

WITNESSES.

[30] [To the court clerk:] Please also read this law from the pillar on the Areopagus.

LAW.

You hear, gentlemen, that the court of the Areopagus itself, where the judging of lawsuits for homicide is both an ancestral prerogative and has been assigned in our own time, is explicitly forbidden to convict of homicide a man who catches a seducer [*moichon*] upon his consort and exacts this punishment. [31] And the lawgiver so strongly believed that this was just in the case of wedded wives that he even imposed the same penalty in the case of concubines, who are valued less. Clearly, then, if he had had at his disposal any greater punishment than this, he would have imposed it in the case of wives. But as it was, since he was unable to find any penalty more severe than this for their case, he saw fit that the same penalty apply as in the case of concubines. [To the court clerk:] Please also read this law.

LAW.

[32] You hear, gentlemen, that it commands that if a person shames by violence [*biai*] a free adult or child, he is to owe double the damage; and if the victim is a woman of the categories where killing is permitted, he is bound by the same terms. Thus, gentlemen, [the lawgiver] believed that those who

use force deserve a lesser penalty than those who use persuasion: the latter he condemned to death, [33] while for the former he imposed a penalty of double the damage, in the belief that those who get their way by force are hated by the victims of that force, while those who use persuasion so corrupt their victims' souls that they make other men's wives more intimately connected to themselves than to their husbands, the entire house falls under their control, and it is unclear whose the children actually are, the husbands' or the seducers'. In response to these things, the man who enacted the law imposed death as the penalty for seducers.

55. Lysias 13 *Against Agoratus* 66. Death penalty for seduction. (ca. 398)

See references and headnote under **14**. In this part of Lysias 13, the speaker attacks Agoratus' character by describing his servile origins and his prior and habitual acts of sycophancy (p. 33) and—in the brief excerpt that follows—seduction. Note that, as in **54** Lys. 1.24–33, Lysias greatly oversimplifies—and thus distorts—the treatment of seduction under Athenian law: death was not the automatic penalty for seduction (and obviously was not enforced upon Agoratus, who was still alive to defend himself in the present trial).

Moreover, although [Agoratus] is a person of this sort, he endeavored to seduce [*moicheuein*] citizens' wives and to corrupt free women, and he was caught as a seducer [*moichos*]; and the penalty for that is death.

56. Demosthenes 45 *I Against Stephanus* 3–4. *Graphê hybreôs* for seduction and/or improper marriage. (?349)

A. **Schäfer**, *Demosthenes und seine Zeit* (Leipzig 1858–87) 4.170–79; F. **Blass**, *Die attische Beredsamkeit* (Leipzig 1887–98) 3.1.467–73; J. E. **Sandys**-F. A. **Paley**, *Demosthenes: Select Private Orations* 2[4] (Cambridge 1910: text and commentary); L. **Gernet**, *Démosthène: Plaidoyers civils, Tome II, Discours XXXIX–XLVIII* (Paris 1957: text, French translation, and notes); J. **Trevett**, *Apollodoros the Son of Pasion* (Oxford 1992) 26–27, 50–76, 183–84; S. **Usher**, *Greek Oratory: Tradition and Originality* (Oxford 1999) 257–59; D. M. **MacDowell**, *Demosthenes the Orator* (Oxford 2009) 99–100, 115–20; A. C. **Scafuro**, *Demosthenes, Speeches 39–49* (Austin 2011: translation with introduction and notes).

This speech, composed by Demosthenes, was delivered by Apollodorus in his prosecution of Stephanus by *dikê pseudomartyriôn* (p. 29). The will of

Apollodorus' father Pasion (d. 370/69) provided for the remarriage of his wife (and Apollodorus' mother) Archippe to his freedman Phormion (see **92** Dem. 45.27–28, 30). Here Apollodorus describes a *graphê hybreôs* that he initiated against Phormion and then dropped. Apollodorus may have maintained that the cohabitation of Phormion and Archippe was humiliating in that Phormion was a former slave (although, notably, Pasion was as well, but he had been naturalized as an Athenian citizen before his death); the act might be characterized as hubris by rough analogy with cases in which a citizen is treated like a slave (**38** Lys. fr. 279 Carey; **39** Isae. 8.40–41; **40** [Dem.] 53.16). Later in the speech (§84), moreover, Apollodorus suggests that his younger brother Pasicles is not Pasion's son but Phormion's. Since Pasicles was born eight years before Pasion died, Apollodorus may have accused Phormion of hubris for seducing Archippe (cf. **55** Lys. 13.66; **59** Hyp. 1.12). Nonetheless, in comparison to the other attested uses of the *graphê hybreôs*, this is an abnormal case (though arguably admissible due to the latitude of the statute on hubris: **35** Dem. 21.47). Apollodorus appears to acknowledge this fact in his repeated statement that private lawsuits (*dikai* in the strict sense: p. 29) were unavailable (on account of war with Thebes in the years between 371 and 362), and the irregularity may have contributed to his dropping the lawsuit. For the jurisdiction of the *thesmothetai* cf. **35** Dem. 21.47; **36** Isoc. 20.2; on the trierarchy (§3) see p. 25.

Men of the jury, my father left me a lot of property. Phormion was in possession of it, and on top of that, he even married my mother while I was abroad on public business serving as your trierarch (how he did so is probably not right for a son to discuss in detail about his mother). When I sailed home, found out, and saw what had been done, I was very angry and took it hard. [4] I was unable to file a private [*idian*] lawsuit [*dikên*] (since at that time there were no private lawsuits: you postponed them on account of the war), so I indicted him for hubris [*graphên hybreôs graphomai*] before the *thesmothetai*. Time passed, the indictment kept getting adjourned and there were no private lawsuits, and children were born to my mother by Phormion. After that . . . , many conciliatory words and pleas on behalf of this man Phormion here came from my mother, and many temperate and humble words came from the man himself.

57. Aeschines 1 *Against Timarchus* (selections). (346/5)

See especially C. **Carey**, *Aeschines* (Austin 2000: translation with introduction and notes); N. R. E. **Fisher**, *Aeschines*: Against Timarchos (Oxford 2001: translation and commentary); also **Blass**, *AB* 3.2.192–201; **Usher**, *GO*

280–84. On *apagôgê* (summary arrest: p. 30) and related procedures see especially M. H. **Hansen**, Apagoge, Endeixis *and* Ephegesis *against* Kakourgoi, Atimoi *and* Pheugontes (Odense 1976).

In 346/5, Aeschines prosecuted Timarchus by the procedure titled *dokimasia tôn rhêtorôn* (scrutiny of public speakers), alleging that Timarchus had been a prostitute and was therefore debarred from addressing the Assembly (see §**3.2**, and especially **64b** Aeschin. 1.19–20). Timarchus was convicted and sentenced to the automatic statutory penalty of total *atimia* (disfranchisement: p. 41). Aeschines' successful prosecution speech is our best source for the *dokimasia tôn rhêtorôn* and for Athenian laws dealing with pandering and (especially male) prostitution generally. The first passage below (**57a**) mentions seducers as a category of offender subject to *apagôgê* (note, however, that not all scholars accept this interpretation of the passage, and that it does not list all categories of liable offender: see p. 31). For the use of *apagôgê* for homicide cf. **8a** Ant. 5.9; **14** Lys. 13.85–87 (including the "in the act" requirement); **20** Dem. 23.65–80, at §80; for the use of *apagôgê* for "clothes-snatching" and other types of theft see chapter 9. The second passage (**57b**) discusses the penalties incurred by the woman who is caught with a seducer; cf. **58b** [Dem.] 59.87.

a. Aeschin. 1.91. Offenders subject to *apagôgê*.

For what clothes-snatcher [*tôn lôpodytôn*] or thief [*tôn kleptôn*] or seducer [*tôn moichôn*] or killer [*tôn androphonôn*] or person who commits the most serious offenses but does so in secret will be punished? For in fact, of these people, those who are caught in the act [*ep' autophôrôi*], if they confess, are immediately punished with death, while those who escape detection and deny it are tried in the jury-courts [*dikastêriois*], and the truth is discovered on the basis of probabilities.

b. Aeschin. 1.183. Penalties for woman caught with seducer.

And Solon, the most venerated of lawgivers, has written in ancient and solemn fashion regarding the proper conduct of women. He does not permit the woman with whom a seducer [*moichos*] is caught to adorn herself or to attend public sacred rites, in order that she not mingle with and corrupt blameless women. And if she does attend or adorn herself, he commands anyone who encounters her to tear her clothing, remove her adornment, and beat her, with the restriction that he not kill or maim her. Thereby Solon inflicts dishonor upon such a woman and makes her life unliveable.

58. [Demosthenes] 59 *Against Neaera* (selections). (date of speech 343–339)

See references and headnote under **21**. In the first passage below (**58a**), the speaker describes Stephanus' detention of Epaenetus of Andros as an alleged seducer and Epaenetus' consequent filing of a *graphê adikôs heirchthênai hôs moichon* (for having been unjustly detained as a seducer). "These people" (§64) are Stephanus and Neaera; the daughter of Neaera in question, named Phano, was unmarried at the time of the events described (Phrastor, mentioned in §69, was her first husband, who had divorced her). For the clause permitting a man who catches a seducer to "do with him whatever he wishes" (§66) cf. Lysias 1.49; with the absence of liability for seduction in the case of known prostitutes (§67) cf. **50** Plut. *Solon* 23.1–2; **51** Lys. 10.18–19; on sycophancy (§68) see p. 33. The second passage (**58b**) quotes a law on seduction. The verbs "to catch" (*hairein*) and "to be caught" (*haliskesthai*) can also mean "to convict" and "to be convicted"; some scholars accordingly believe that the law refers to the conviction of a seducer in court. On *atimia* (disfranchisement) see p. 41; for the penalties imposed upon the woman caught with a seducer cf. **57b** Aeschin. 1.183.

a. [Dem.] 59.64–70. Seizure of alleged seducer; *graphê adikôs heirchthênai hôs moichon.*

And consider too the shameless greed and wickedness of my adversary Stephanus here, so that from this too you may know that the defendant Neaera is not a citizen. Epaenetus of Andros was an old lover of Neaera here; he had spent a lot of money on her, and on account of his friendship with Neaera he stayed with these people whenever he was in Athens. [65] My adversary Stephanus here plotted against him, summoned him to the country on the pretense that he was conducting a sacrifice, and caught him as a seducer [*moichon*] with the daughter of Neaera here. By putting him in a state of terror, he exacted 30 minae, and after securing as sureties for the money Aristomachus the former *thesmothetês* and Nausiphilus the son of Nausinicus the former archon, he let Epaenetus go so that Epaenetus could pay him the money he owed. [66] But once Epaenetus got out and regained control of himself, he filed with the *thesmothetai* an indictment [*graphên*] against Stephanus here, stating that he had been unjustly detained [*adikôs heirchthênai*] by him, in accordance with the law that commands that if a person unjustly detains someone as a seducer, [the victim] may file with the *thesmothetai* an indictment for having been unjustly detained, and that if he convicts the one who detained him and is deemed to have been the victim of an unjust plot, he is to be set free and his sureties released from their pledge. If, however, he is deemed to be a seducer, the law commands that his sureties hand him over to the man who caught him, and that that man, in the jury-court [*dikastêriou*], do with him whatever he wishes without using a dagger, since he is a seducer.

[67] In accordance with this very law, Epaenetus indicted Stephanus; he admitted having sex with the woman but denied that he was a seducer, since she was not Stephanus' daughter but Neaera's, and her mother knew that she was consorting with him, and he had spent a lot of money on them, and he supported the whole household whenever he was in town. In addition, he cited the law that does not permit the seizure of [a man as] a seducer in the company of those women who are located in a brothel or go about in public [*pôlôntai apopephasmenôs*], asserting that Stephanus' house was a brothel, and this was their business, and from these activities they were very well off. [68] When Epaenetus made this argument and had brought his indictment, Stephanus here, realizing that he would be exposed as a pimp and a sycophant, offered to entrust his dispute with Epaenetus to arbitration by the very same sureties, with the terms that the sureties would be released from their pledge and Epaenetus would drop the indictment.

[69] On these terms Epaenetus was persuaded and dropped the indictment he was prosecuting against Stephanus. They held a meeting, with the sureties sitting as arbitrators, and Stephanus had no just argument to make, but he pressed Epaenetus to contribute to the dowering of Neaera's daughter, citing his own poverty and her previous bad luck with Phrastor, and the fact that she had lost her dowry and he could not dower her again. [70] "You have enjoyed the woman," he said, "and you ought to do something good for her," and he used other coaxing words that a person needing to get out of shameful troubles would say. The arbitrators heard from both of them and reconciled them; they persuaded Epaenetus to contribute 1,000 drachmas to the dowering of Neaera's daughter.

b. [Dem.] 59.87 (*lex*). Law on seduction: mandatory divorce; penalties for husband who fails to divorce and for woman caught with seducer.

LAW ON SEDUCTION [*moicheias*]. And after he catches [*helêi*] the seducer [*moichon*], the one who caught [*tôi helonti*] the seducer shall not be permitted to cohabit with his wife; if he does cohabit with her, he shall be disfranchised [*atimos*]. And the woman with whom a seducer is caught [*halôi*] shall not be permitted to attend public sacred rites; if she does attend, she shall suffer with impunity whatever she suffers, except death.

59. Hypereides 1 *For Lycophron* 12. *Eisangelia* (impeachment) and other remedies for seduction. (333–330)

See especially D. **Whitehead**, *Hypereides: The Forensic Speeches* (Oxford 2000: translation and commentary); D. D. **Phillips**, *Athenian Political Oratory: 16 Key Speeches* (New York and London 2004: translation with introduction and notes); ***idem***, "Why Was Lycophron Prosecuted by *Eisangelia*?"; also **Blass**, *AB* 3.2.66–72; **Usher**, *GO* 329–30; I. **Worthington**-C. **Cooper**-E. M. **Harris**, *Dinarchus, Hyperides, and Lycurgus* (Austin 2001: translation with introduction and notes).

Hypereides 1 is a defense speech delivered by Lycophron, who was prosecuted by *eisangelia* (impeachment: see chapter 12) for seducing the sister of the Olympic victor Dioxippus. Here Lycophron complains that the prosecution has abused the *eisangelia* procedure and should have proceeded against him by a *graphê*. For the *graphê moicheias* see **60** [Arist.] *Ath. Pol.* 59.3; Lycophron may also be referring to the *graphê hybreôs*, which also came before the *thesmothetai* (**35** Dem. 21.47).

And you accuse me in your impeachment [*eisangeliai*] of subverting the people by violating the laws; but you yourself have taken a flying leap over all the laws and handed in an impeachment concerning matters for which there are indictments [*graphai*] before the *thesmothetai* provided by the laws. You did this, first, so that you could go to trial without risk, and second, so that you could write into the impeachment tragedies of the sort you have now written: you accuse me of making numerous women grow old, unmarried, in their houses, and of making numerous others cohabit with unsuitable men in violation of the laws.

60. [Aristotle], *Constitution of the Athenians (Ath. Pol.)* 59.3. *Graphai* (including *graphê moicheias*) under the jurisdiction of the *thesmothetai*. (332–322)

See references and headnote under **1c**. Here the author discusses the duties of the *thesmothetai*. On the *graphê xenias* (for falsely claiming Athenian citizenship) see chapter 6; on the *graphê dôrôn* and bribery see chapter 12. The *graphê bouleuseôs* lay against those who fraudulently kept on the register of state debtors those who had discharged their debts.

There also come before them indictments [*graphai*] for which a [prosecutor's] deposit [*parastasis*] is paid; namely, for being a foreigner [*xenias*] and for bribery on behalf of a foreigner [*dôroxenias*], if a person by giving bribes gets acquitted of being a foreigner; and for sycophancy [*sykophantias*], bribery [*dôrôn*], false registration of a state debtor [*pseudengraphês*], false witness to a summons [*pseudoklêteias*], conspiracy [*bouleuseôs*], failure to register a state debtor [*agraphiou*], and seduction [*moicheias*].

61. Harpocration s.v. *biaiôn. Dikê biaiôn* (lawsuit for acts of violence, including rape). (Harpocration *fl.* 2nd c. A.D.)

See references and headnote under **28**. In this lemma Harpocration defines the *dikê biaiôn,* a lawsuit for acts of violence that applied in cases of rape (cf. **54** Lys. 1.24–33, at §§31–33). For the first reference see **294** Dem. 21.44–45. For speeches of Lysias delivered in *dikai biaiôn* see Lysias, fragments 31, 299–302 Carey. On the *dikê biaiôn* and "the corruption of virgins" cf. Lucian, *Hermotimus* 81; for other acts that might give rise to a *dikê biaiôn* see, for example, Lysias 23.12.

For acts of violence [*biaiôn*]: the name of a lawsuit [*dikês*] available against those who do anything whatsoever by violence [*biai*]. He who is convicted pays to the public treasury the same amount he pays to the one who convicts him. Demosthenes, *Against Meidias*; there are also speeches concerning acts of violence preserved among the works of Lysias. And it is clear that both the term and the lawsuit were applied not only to the corruption of virgins but to other cases as well.

62. Lucian, *Eunuch* 10 (*?lex* + commentary). ?Quotation from law on seduction and/or homicide. (2nd c. A.D.)

A. M. **Harmon**, *Lucian*, vol. 5 (Cambridge, MA 1936: text and translation).

Lucian of Samosata (ca. A.D. 120-*post* A.D. 180) was an Atticizing prose author of the Second Sophistic, trained in rhetoric and philosophy, who wrote predominantly comic and satirical works. The *Eunuch* is a satirical dialogue set in Athens; here Lucian's character Lycinus, relating the speech of a third party, may be quoting an otherwise unattested clause from an axon (cf., e.g., **2** *IG* I^3 104; **322** Plut. *Solon* 24.1–2) of the laws of Draco or Solon, or else Lucian may be engaging in authorial license.

"And unless the people who talk about him are lying, he was even once caught as a seducer, 'with limbs entwined in limbs' [*arthra en arthrois echôn*], as the axon says."

3.2. Pandering and Prostitution

Handbooks: J. H. **Lipsius**, *Das attische Recht und Rechtsverfahren* (Leipzig 1905–15) 278–82, 435–37; A. R. W. **Harrison**, *The Law of Athens* (Oxford 1968–71) 1.37–38; 2.15, 82, 171–72, 204–5; D. M. **MacDowell**, *The Law in Classical Athens* (Ithaca, NY 1978) 125–26; S. C. **Todd**, *The Shape of Athenian Law* (Oxford 1993) 107, 110–11, 116; E. **Cantarella**, "Gender, Sexuality, and Law," in *The Cambridge Companion to Ancient Greek Law*, ed. M. Gagarin-D. Cohen (Cambridge 2005) 236–53, esp. 250–52. **Studies:** S. B. **Pomeroy**, *Goddesses, Whores, Wives, and Slaves* (New York 1975) 88–92; R. **Just**, *Women in Athenian Law and Life* (London 1989) 137–45; K. J. **Dover**, *Greek Homosexuality*[2] (Cambridge, MA 1989); D. **Cohen**, *Law, Sexuality, and Society: The Enforcement of Morals in Classical Athens* (Cambridge 1991), esp. ch. 7; C. **Carey**, *Greek Orators VI: Apollodorus:* Against Neaira: *[Demosthenes] 59* (Warminster 1992); K. J. **Dover**, *Greek Popular Morality in the Time of Plato and Aristotle*, ed. corr. (Indianapolis 1994) 205–16; R. W. **Wallace**, "On Not Legislating Sexual Conduct in Fourth-Century Athens," in *Symposion 1995*, ed. G. Thür and J. Vélissaropoulos-Karakostas (Köln 1997) 151–66; K. A. **Kapparis**, *Apollodoros:* 'Against Neaira' *[D. 59]* (Berlin 1999); D. M. **MacDowell**, "Athenian Laws about Homosexuality," *RIDA* ser. 3 vol. 47 (2000) 13–27; E. E. **Cohen**, "Whoring under Contract: The Legal Context of Prostitution in Fourth-Century Athens," in *Law and Social Status in Classical Athens*, ed. V. Hunter-J. Edmondson (Oxford 2000) 113–47; N. **Fisher**, *Aeschines:* Against Timarchos (Oxford 2001), esp. 36–53; E. E. **Cohen**, "Free and Unfree Sexual Work: An Economic Analysis of Athenian Prostitution"; A. **Glazebrook**, "The Bad Girls of Athens: The Image and Function of *Hetairai* in Judicial Oratory"; and S. **Lape**, "The Psychology of Prostitution in Aeschines' Speech against Timarchus," in *Prostitutes and Courtesans in the Ancient World*, ed. C. A. Faraone-L. K. McClure (Madison 2006) 95–124, 125–38, 139–60.

In Athens, prostitution per se was legal and regulated by the state (e.g., **64e**, **65**, **66**), but a number of laws restricted who could be prostituted and by whom, governed the conduct of current and former prostitutes, and penalized violations of these rules. As is characteristic of Athenian law (p. 33), in the areas of pandering (providing a person for sexual use by a third party) and prostitution there were multiple procedures that might apply to a given case, with potentially differing penalties and conflicting definitions of illegal behavior.

In Athenian parlance a distinction was commonly, but not always consistently, drawn between the type of prostitute called *pornos* (masculine)/*pornê* (feminine) and that called *hetairos* (masculine)/*hetaira* (feminine): see, e.g., **64c**. Frequently the former terms designate a short-term assignation, and the latter (often translated "courtesan" or "escort") a longer-term and potentially exclusive arrangement, which might be determined by contract (see, e.g., Aeschines 1.51–52, 160, 165; Lysias 3.22). There is no evidence that this distinction had any relevance in Athenian law.

Plutarch quotes a law ascribed to Solon (**50**) that established a fixed penalty of 20 drachmas for pandering, except in the case of "women who go about in public" (*hosai pephasmenôs pôlountai*; i.e., known prostitutes; cf. **51**, **58a**). Later Athenians also believed that Solon had established state-operated brothels (e.g., Philemon fr. 4 Kassel-Austin = Athenaeus, *Deipnosophistae* 13.569d-e; Harpocration s.v. *pandêmos Aphroditê*). Whether or not the specific attributions to Solon are correct—and the comparatively low fine, along with the fact that Lysias (**51**) quotes the phrase "women who go about in public" as an instance of archaic legal language, suggests that the law predates the fifth century—these passages indicate that prostitution, at least within certain limits, was a traditional and licit activity.

In the time of the orators, there appear to have been three general legal procedures available for pandering and/or prostitution; all were *graphai* and hence could be prosecuted by any willing Athenian citizen (p. 30). (1) The *graphê hetairêseôs* (for prostitution), which was filed before the *thesmothetai* (**63a**), lay, under various conditions, against adult citizen men who were or had been prostitutes (**64b**) and—if the same procedure is described in **64a**, which is arguably likely but not certain—against both the person who pandered and the person who hired a free boy. Under this procedure the death penalty was probably available (**64d**, if it refers to the *graphê hetairêseôs* rather than, or in addition to, the *graphê proagôgeias*) but not mandatory (note the provision in **64a** excusing a boy grown to manhood from supporting the father who had pandered him, which would be superfluous if all such offenders were executed); therefore the procedure was probably assessable (*timêtos*: p. 40) without penal limit. (2) The *graphê proagôgeias* (for pandering) was available against the pimp who prostituted a free woman or child; the death penalty was at least available, if not mandatory (**64a**, **64f**). (3) The *graphê hybreôs* might likewise be employed as a legal remedy against the panderer of a free woman or child (**64a**; this procedure may also be a referent in **64d** and in one or more of the cases listed in **67**); the penalty was assessable and unlimited (see chapter 2 and §3.1). The restriction in the scope of protected categories of free persons (women and children but not adult men) corresponds to a distinction in legal status: free adult men were legally independent and therefore (in theory) could not be prostituted without their consent, while free adult women and children were under the legal control of a *kyrios* (see **64a** and chapters 5–7, especially the introduction to chapter 5).

While the written terms of these laws (with a possible exception in **64d**, which Aeschines paraphrases as referring to citizens) seem to have defined the protected categories as "free" women and children (the law on hubris certainly did so, and added slaves: **35** Dem. 21.47), it seems clear from the descriptions of prostitution in Attic oratory (see especially [Demosthenes] 59 *Against Neaera*), and from the few attested prosecutions relating to prostitution, that in practice Athenians were primarily concerned with the prostitution of Athenian citizens, and particularly of boys and men. The great majority of prostitutes of both sexes were slaves or free non-citizens, whether metics (p. 23) or visiting foreigners; as property, slaves were by definition at the disposal of their owners, and free non-citizen prostitution too was viewed as unproblematic, except, perhaps, when a person was pandered under duress (**67**).

Citizen prostitution, while culturally frowned upon and in principle legally actionable, was also probably largely tolerated, but men who had been prostitutes were barred from assuming an active role in politics. This special case came under the purview of the procedure titled *dokimasia tôn rhêtorôn* (scrutiny of public speakers). The law governing this procedure (**64c**) included current and former prostitutes among the categories of men prohibited from addressing the Athenian people in a deliberative capacity (i.e., in the Council of 500 or the Assembly). The procedure could be initiated by proclamation by any Athenian citizen, who then prosecuted the accused in a regular jury-court (*dikastêrion*); the penalty upon conviction was total *atimia* (disfranchisement: p. 41; cf. **63c**). The ban on prostitutes' addressing the Council or Assembly also appears in the law governing the *graphê hetairêseôs*, which moreover explicitly bars the prostitute from holding any political office whatsoever (**63a-b**, **64b**); and it has been argued that, as a matter of common practice if not actual statutory language, the *graphê hetairêseôs* applied against current or former male prostitutes only when they assumed political roles. (For additional references to the disfranchisement of male prostitutes, with no legal procedure specified, see Aristophanes, *Knights* 875–80; Andocides 1.100.)

See also **50** Plut. *Solon* 23.1–2; **51** Lys. 10.18–19; **57a** Aeschin. 1.91; **58a** [Dem.] 59.64–70; **162** Aeschin. 1.158; **295** Aeschin. 1.110–13; **390a** Hyp. 4.1–3, 14–20, 30–31, 39.

63. Demosthenes 22 *Against Androtion* (selections). (355/4)

A. **Schäfer**, *Demosthenes und seine Zeit* (Leipzig 1858–87) 1.350–64; W. **Wayte**, *Demosthenes:* Against Androtion *and* Against Timocrates (Cambridge 1882: text and commentary); H. **Weil**, *Les plaidoyers politiques de Démosthène*, ser. 2 (Paris 1886: text and French commentary); F. **Blass**, *Die attische Beredsamkeit* (Leipzig 1887–98) 3.1.258–64; S. **Usher**, *Greek Oratory: Tradition and Originality* (Oxford 1999) 198–201; E. M. **Harris**, *Demosthenes,*

Orations 20–22 (Austin 2008: translation with introduction and notes); D. M. **MacDowell**, *Demosthenes the Orator* (Oxford 2009) 167–81.

Demosthenes composed this speech for delivery by Diodorus in a prosecution of the prominent politician Androtion (J. K. **Davies**, *Athenian Propertied Families 600–300 B.C.* [Oxford 1971], no. 913) for proposing unconstitutional legislation (a *graphê paranomôn*: **63a**; see p. 14). In these passages Diodorus alleges that Androtion, as a former prostitute, is barred from political activity and liable to a *graphê hetairêseôs*. The 1,000-drachma fine for malicious prosecution (**63a**) indicates that the procedure alluded to is a *graphê*: see p. 33 and cf. **64b** Aeschin. 1.19–20.

a. Dem. 22.21, 23–24. Law on prostitution (*hetairêsis*); *graphê hetairêseôs* before the *thesmothetai*; legal restrictions on prostitutes.

Furthermore, with regard to the law on prostitution [*hetairêseôs*], he attempts to argue that we are treating him with hubris and making improper and slanderous allegations against him. And he says that if we actually believed these accusations were true, we should confront him before the *thesmothetai*, so that there we would risk 1,000 drachmas if we were clearly lying about these things. . . . [23] . . . And when he says that we should have denounced him to the *thesmothetai*, give him this reply: that we are going to do so, and that we are now acting properly in speaking about the law. [24] [To Androtion:] For if we were making these accusations when you were defending yourself in another sort of lawsuit, you would be right to be indignant. [To the jury:] But given that the present lawsuit is for an illegal proposal [*paranomôn*], and the laws do not permit those who have lived as he has to make even a legal proposal, and if we demonstrate that he has not only made an illegal proposal but has lived his life illegally, then how is it not proper to discuss the very law by which these things are proven?

b. Dem. 22.30. Legal restrictions on prostitutes.

Moreover, it is worthwhile, men of Athens, also to examine Solon, the man who enacted the law, and to see how much care he exercised in all the laws that he enacted. . . . One could see this in many places, and not least in this law, which states that those who have been prostitutes are not permitted to make speeches or proposals.

c. Dem. 22.73. Prostitutes barred from sacred rites.

And the name of this man, whose body the laws do not permit to attend sacred rites because he has prostituted himself, is written on bowls in the sanctuaries.

64. Aeschines 1 *Against Timarchus* (selections). (346/5)

See references and headnote under **57**. In the following passages, Aeschines discusses multiple laws and procedures relevant to pandering and/or prostitution; namely, a law or laws on pandering and hiring prostitutes (**64a**; cf. **64d**), at least the former of which was the subject of a *graphê proagôgeias* (**64f**); the *graphê hybreôs* (**64a**); the *graphê hetairêseôs* (**64b**); an unnamed *graphê* (**64a**), which may also refer to the *graphê hetairêseôs*, since the immediate context mentions both the *graphê proagôgeias* and the *graphê hybreôs* and there are no other named *graphai* attested for these offenses; and the *dokimasia tôn rhêtorôn* (**64c**). The speech also provides evidence for state regulation of prostitution in the form of the *pornikon telos* (tax on prostitutes: **64e**). In **64a**, for the *kyrios* see the introduction to chapter 5 and chapters 5–7 *passim*; the law on hubris paraphrased and cited at §15 is **35** Dem. 21.47. "The Council" (**64b**, **64e**) is the Council of 500.

a. Aeschin. 1.13–15. Law on pandering and hiring boy prostitute (*graphê ?hetairêseôs*); law on pandering (*proagôgeia*) of free boy or woman; *graphê hybreôs* for pandering.

Now, the law states this explicitly: if a father, brother, uncle, guardian, or in general any *kyrios* hires a boy out for prostitution, the law does not permit there to be an indictment [*graphên*] against the boy himself, but rather against the one who hired him out and the one who paid for him: against the former because he hired him out, and against the latter because, it says, he paid for him. And the law has made the penalties the same for each of them and has ordained that it not be required for the boy who has been hired out for prostitution, when he reaches adulthood, to support his father or provide lodging for him; but when the father dies, the boy must bury him and conduct the other customary rituals.

[14] . . . . And what other law did the lawgiver establish as guardian of your boys? The law on pandering [*proagôgeias*], in which he included the most severe penalties, if a person prostitutes a free boy or woman.

[15] And what other law? The law on hubris [*hybreôs*], . . . in which it is explicitly written: if a person commits hubris against a boy (and obviously the one who hires a boy commits hubris) or a man or a woman, free or slave, or does anything unlawful to any of these, the law has established that there be indictments for hubris [*graphas hybreôs*] and has imposed as a penalty whatever [the convicted defendant] must suffer or pay. [To the court clerk:] Read the law.

LAW.

b. Aeschin. 1.19–20 (*lex* + commentary). *Graphê hetairêseôs*; legal restrictions on prostitutes.

And what does the lawgiver say? "If any Athenian," he says, "prostitutes himself, he shall not be permitted to become one of the nine archons . . . or to serve in a priesthood . . . or to serve as an advocate for the state, or to hold," he says, "any office at any time, either domestic or foreign, either allotted or elected; [20] and he shall not serve as herald or ambassador . . . or express an opinion at any time either in the Council or in the Assembly. . . ." And if a person acts in violation of these provisions, the lawgiver has created indictments for prostitution [*graphas hetairêseôs*] and has imposed the most severe penalties.

c. Aeschin. 1.28–30, 32 (*lex* + commentary). Law concerning *dokimasia tôn rhêtorôn* (scrutiny of public speakers).

And who did the lawgiver think should not speak? Those who have lived shameful lives: these he does not permit to address the people. And where does he make this clear? "Scrutiny," he says, "of public speakers. If a person speaks in the Assembly who beats his father or mother or does not support them or does not provide them with lodging . . . . , [29] . . . . or has not served on the military campaigns to which he has been assigned, or has thrown away his shield . . . , or has been a prostitute [*peporneumenos*] or an escort [*hêtairêkôs*] . . . [30] or has devoured his patrimony or whatever he is heir to . . . , [32] . . . any willing Athenian to whom it is permitted shall proclaim a scrutiny." Thereupon the lawgiver commands you to decide these matters in a jury-court [*dikastêriôi*]; and in accordance with this law I have now come before you.

d. Aeschin. 1.87. Death penalty for person who hires citizen prostitute and for willing citizen prostitute.

. . . when the penalty provided by the law for each is death, just as it is in this case, if a person hires an Athenian for hubris, or again, if any Athenian willingly takes pay for the shaming of his body.

e. Aeschin. 1.119. Tax on prostitutes (*pornikon telos*).

For [Demosthenes] expresses utter astonishment if you do not all remember that every year the Council farms out the tax on prostitutes [*pornikon telos*], and that those who buy the tax contract do not guess but know exactly who engages in this business. So, then, when I have had the audacity to bring a counter-charge that Timarchus, since he has prostituted himself, is not permitted to address the people, Demosthenes claims that the practice itself requires not the accusation of a prosecutor but the testimony of a tax-collector who collected this tax from Timarchus.

f. Aeschin. 1.184. *Graphê proagôgeias* against pimp; death penalty.

And [Solon] commands that female and male pimps [*proagôgous*] be indicted [*graphesthai*] and, if convicted, punished with death. . . .

65. [Aristotle], *Constitution of the Athenians* (*Ath. Pol.*) 50.1–2. Limit on fees for prostitutes. (332–322)

See references under **1c**. Here the author discusses the duty of the *astynomoi* (City Magistrates) to regulate the fees charged for female flute-, harp-, and lyre-players, who commonly provided sexual as well as musical services. The figure of 2 drachmas is a daily rate (cf. **66** Hyp. 4.3).

And there are ten *astynomoi*; [50.2] of these five hold office in the Peiraeus and five in the city. They see to it that female flute-players, harpists, and lyre-players are not hired out for more than 2 drachmas, and if several people desire to obtain the same one, they hold a lottery and hire her out to the winner.

66. Hypereides 4 *For Euxenippus* 3. *Eisangelia* (impeachment) for violating limit on prostitutes' fees. (330–324)

See especially D. **Whitehead**, *Hypereides: The Forensic Speeches* (Oxford 2000: translation and commentary); D. D. **Phillips**, *Athenian Political Oratory: 16 Key Speeches* (New York and London 2004: translation with introduction and notes); also **Blass**, *AB* 3.2.61–66; **Usher**, *GO* 333–35; I. **Worthington**-C. **Cooper**-E. M. **Harris**, *Dinarchus, Hyperides, and Lycurgus* (Austin 2001: translation with introduction and notes).

Hypereides wrote and delivered this speech in defense of Euxenippus, who at some point between 330 and 324 was tried by *eisangelia* (impeachment: see chapter 12) for giving to the Assembly a false report of a dream he had while incubating in the temple of Amphiaraus at Oropus (see **390** Hyp. 4 [selections]). At some point not long before Euxenippus' trial, the *eisangelia* procedure had been used to prosecute two pimps for violating the fee limit for female flute-players stated in **65** [Arist.] *Ath. Pol.* 50.1–2; the passage below suggests that using *eisangelia* for this purpose was a novelty.

Now, though, what is going on in the city is utterly ridiculous. Diognides and Antidorus the metic are impeached [*eisangellontai*] for hiring out female flute-players for more than the law ordains. . . .

67. Deinarchus 1 *Against Demosthenes* 23. Death penalty for pandering. (324/3)

See especially I. **Worthington**, *A Historical Commentary on Dinarchus* (Ann Arbor 1992: translation and commentary); ***idem,*** *Greek Orators II: Dinarchus and Hyperides* (Warminster 1999: text, translation, and commentary); also **Blass**, *AB* 3.2.309–14; **Usher**, *GO* 344–46; **Worthington-Cooper-Harris**, *Dinarchus, Hyperides, and Lycurgus* (translation with introduction and notes).

In the summer or fall of 324, a scandal erupted in Athens when it was discovered that, of the 700 talents (p. 4) that had been brought to Athens by Harpalus, Alexander the Great's fugitive former royal treasurer, and had been deposited on the Acropolis for safekeeping, half had disappeared. After a six-month investigation by the Council of the Areopagus, a number of Athenian politicians were charged with receiving bribes from Harpalus; the defendants included Demosthenes, who was convicted. Deinarchus composed this speech for delivery by one of the ten special prosecutors appointed to the case. See **391** (*Apophasis* against Demosthenes and others for receiving bribes in the Harpalus affair).

In this passage, the speaker cites (apparently well-known) instances in which individuals were sentenced to death for offenses that, he argues, are less serious than Demosthenes'. The mention of the deme Pellene suggests that the boy in the first case was a citizen; mill work was stereotypical and undesirable slave labor. The lawsuit may have been a *graphê hybreôs*: cf. **38** Lys. fr. 279 Carey; **39** Isae. 8.40–41; **40** [Dem.] 53.16. The second case may also have been a *graphê hybreôs*, but the identification is not definite since the verb *hybrizein* ("to commit hubris") alone does not reliably indicate that the charge was hubris (see, e.g., **42a** Dem. 54.1; **54** Lys. 1.24–33, at §25). The Eleusinia was the annual festival in honor of the goddesses Demeter and Persephone celebrated at the town of Eleusis in western Attica. The procedure employed in the third case is even less certain: in addition to the dedicated remedies for pandering and prostitution, this case may have been a *graphê hybreôs* or an *apagôgê* for kidnapping (see **283** Xen. *Mem.* 1.2.62 with additional references in headnote; ?cf. Lysias 13.67). Olynthus was a city in the Chalcidice destroyed by Philip II of Macedon in 348.

You executed Menon the miller because he kept a free boy from Pellene in his mill; and you punished with death Themistius of the deme Aphidna because he committed hubris against the female cithara-player from Rhodes at the Eleusinia, and also Euthymachus, because he put the girl from Olynthus in a brothel.

CHAPTER 4

Defamation

Handbooks: J. H. **Lipsius**, *Das attische Recht und Rechtsverfahren* (Leipzig 1905–15) 646–51; D. M. **MacDowell**, *The Law in Classical Athens* (Ithaca, NY 1978) 126–29; S. C. **Todd**, *The Shape of Athenian Law* (Oxford 1993) 258–62; R. W. **Wallace**, "Law, Attic Comedy, and the Regulation of Comic Speech," in *The Cambridge Companion to Ancient Greek Law*, ed. M. Gagarin-D. Cohen (Cambridge 2005) 357–73. **Studies:** L. **Gernet**, *Recherches sur le développement de la pensée juridique et morale en Grèce* (1917, repr. Paris 2001) 238–44; E. **Ruschenbusch**, *Untersuchungen zur Geschichte des athenischen Strafrechts* (Köln 1968) 24–27; M. **Hillgruber**, *Die zehnte Rede des Lysias* (Berlin 1988); S. **Halliwell**, "Comic Satire and Freedom of Speech in Classical Athens," *JHS* 111 (1991) 48–70; R. W. **Wallace**, "The Athenian Laws against Slander," in *Symposion 1993*, ed. G. Thür (Köln 1994) 109–24; A. H. **Sommerstein**, "Comedy and the Unspeakable," in *Law, Rhetoric, and Comedy in Classical Athens: Essays in Honour of Douglas M. MacDowell*, ed. D. L. Cairns-R. A. Knox (Swansea 2004) 205–22.

Although the Classical Athenians prided themselves on the freedom of speech (*parrhêsia*) that they considered characteristic of their city (e.g., Demosthenes 9.3), Athenian law placed restrictions on the defamation of persons. According to Plutarch (**68**), the code of laws that Solon promulgated during his archonship (594/3: **6b** [Arist.] *Ath. Pol.* 7.1) included provisions against defaming the dead and against defaming the living in specified locations. The penalty for the latter was a fine of 5 drachmas, of which 3 were paid to the victim and 2 to the state; the penalty for the former may have totaled 10 drachmas (see below).

Plutarch does not explain what constituted illegal defamatory speech under the laws he cites, but it is probable that at least some items in the category mentioned by the orators under the rubric *ta aporrhêta* ("the unmentionables" or "the forbidden words") were already prohibited in the Archaic period. In the time of the orators, there was a dedicated private lawsuit for defamation, the *dikê kakêgorias* (**33** Dem. 54.17–19; **75**, **79**, **81**), which applied against a person who used against another, whether living (**71**, **77**) or dead (**72**, **74**), any of the terms prohibited by law; these were sufficiently familiar to Athenians that speakers could refer to "the forbidden words" in passing and without explanation (**69**, **77**, **80**). Lysias 10, our most informative source for the Classical *dikê kakêgorias* (**71**), yields a list of "dirty words" that includes the nouns *androphonos* ("killer"), *patraloias* ("father-beater"), and *mêtraloias* ("mother-beater") and the verb *apobeblêkenai* (with stated or understood object *tên aspida*: "to have thrown away" one's shield, this being the archetype of cowardice in battle: cf. **64c** Aeschin. 1.28–30, 32). The truth of the matter asserted served as an affirmative defense against a charge of defamation arising from the use of these words (**71d**, **73**). By the middle of the fourth century the *dikê kakêgorias* also lay against one who reproached a citizen for working in the agora (**76**); it is generally assumed that in this case the accuracy of the allegation was irrelevant.

In the fourth century, the *dikê kakêgorias* normally came under the supervision of the Forty, who in the first instance assigned the case to a public arbitrator (**75**; p. 36). (When a slave was accused of defaming a free person, the case came before the *thesmothetai*: **79**.) If either litigant contested the arbitrator's finding, the case went to trial in a regular jury-court (*dikastêrion*: p. 26). The penalty imposed upon a convicted defendant was a monetary fine that was fixed by statute. Several sources state the penalty as 500 drachmas (**69**, **71c**; cf. **81**), but when Meidias lost a *dikê kakêgorias* to Demosthenes he had to pay 1,000 drachmas (**75**), and according to a lost oration of Hypereides the fine was 500 drachmas for defamation of the living and 1,000 drachmas for defamation of the dead (**81**). One reasonable and popular reconstruction of the history of penalties for defamation holds that, between the promulgation of the allegedly Solonian laws cited by Plutarch and the time of the orators, all the fine amounts were multiplied by 100: thus, in the Classical period, the total fine for defaming a living person was 500 drachmas (of which, if the ratio given in **68** continued to apply, 300 were awarded to the victim and 200 to the state), and in the Archaic period the penalty for defaming a dead person was 10 drachmas (extrapolated from the figure of 1,000 drachmas given in **81**; the ratio of awards is unattested but was possibly also 3:2).

Besides the general remedy for defamation provided by the *dikê kakêgorias*, there were specific remedies available in the cases of certain individuals by virtue of their special relationship to the Athenian state. One or more laws punished the person who verbally abused a magistrate acting in his official capacity; according to Demosthenes (**44a** Dem. 21.31–33) the penalty was total *atimia* (disfranchisement: p. 41), while in Lysias 9 (**70**) the offended officials attempted to impose a summary fine. These laws apparently did not limit punishable speech to the "forbidden words" that activated a *dikê kakêgorias*; note that, in contrast to the sources that refer to the *dikê kakêgorias*, which commonly use the noun *kakêgoria* "defamation" and the verbal phrases *kakôs agoreuein/legein* "to speak ill of" and *kakôs akouein* "to be spoken ill of," Lysias 9 features the verb *loidorein* "to insult." Another, *ad hominem* law, in force in the late fourth century (**78**), forbade the maligning of Harmodius and Aristogeiton (d. 514), who in the Classical period were (inaccurately) honored as martyrs of the nascent democracy; the penalty for violating this law is not attested. Finally, at some periods during the second half of the fifth century the satirizing of individuals in comedies performed at state-sponsored dramatic festivals was regulated by decree (**82**).

See also **15** Lys. 10.11; **33** Dem. 54.17–19; **44a** Dem. 21.31–33; **64c** Aeschin. 1.28–30, 32; **170** Andoc. 1.73–79; **357** D. L. 2.116.

68. Plutarch, *Solon* 21.1–2. Solon's laws on defamation. (date of composition late 1st-early 2nd c. A.D.; laws attributed to Solon, 594/3)

See references and headnote under **1d**. Here Plutarch discusses laws attributed to Solon regarding defamation of living and dead persons. The low fine given for defamation of the living (cf., for the Classical period, **69** Isoc. 20.3; **71c** Lys. 10.12; **75** Dem. 21.79, 81, 83–84, 88; **81** *Lex. Cantab.* s.v. *kakêgorias dikê*) indicates that the relevant law, even if not Solonian, must predate the fifth century; if the law is Solonian, the drachma refers to weighed rather than coined silver (see **314** Lys. 10.18). For "government offices" cf. **70** Lys. 9.9–10.

Also praised is Solon's law prohibiting speaking ill of [*kakôs agoreuein*] a dead person. . . . [21.2] And he prohibited speaking ill of [*kakôs legein*] a living person in the vicinity of sanctuaries, lawcourts, and government offices [*archeiois*], and during the viewing of public competitions; he assigned as a penalty the payment of three drachmas to the individual [victim] and two more to the public treasury.

69. Isocrates 20 *Against Lochites* 3. Law on defamation; penalty. (*post* 404/3)

See references and headnote under **36**. Here the speaker summarizes a law on defamation that governed the *dikê kakêgorias* in the late fifth and fourth centuries (cf. **33** Dem. 54.17–19; **71–77**, **79–81**).

And [the lawgivers] considered it so terrible for people to hit one another that they even enacted a law concerning defamation [*kakêgorias*], which commands those who say any of the forbidden words [*tôn aporrhêtôn*] to pay a fine of 500 drachmas.

70. Lysias 9 *For the Soldier* 5–12, 15–16. Law against insulting magistrate in session. (?395–386)

See especially D. M. **MacDowell**, "The Case of the Rude Soldier (Lysias 9)," in *Symposion 1993*, ed. G. Thür (Köln 1994) 153–64; S. C. **Todd**, *A Commentary on Lysias, Speeches 1–11* (Oxford 2007: text, translation, and commentary); also F. **Blass**, *Die attische Beredsamkeit* (Leipzig 1887–98) 1.596–601; R. C. **Jebb**, *The Attic Orators from Antiphon to Isaeus*[2] (London 1893) 1.227–30; S. **Usher**, *Greek Oratory: Tradition and Originality* (Oxford 1999) 114; S. C. **Todd**, *Lysias* (Austin 2000: translation with introduction and notes).

Lysias 9 is a defense speech delivered by a man named Polyaenus, who stood trial under the *apographê* procedure (for the collection of a debt owed to the state: cf. **40** [Dem.] 53.16; **108** Lys. 19 [selections]; **173** *IG* II^2 1631.429–41). Polyaenus had been issued a summary fine (*epibolê*) by the board of generals, who alleged that he had insulted them; Polyaenus had not paid the fine, and in the following excerpts he alleges that he is not liable under a law (apparently distinct from that governing the *dikê kakêgorias*) that prohibits insulting a magistrate acting in his official capacity (cf. **44a** Dem. 21.31–33). In §6, the phrase translated "in session" (i.e., when a magistrate is performing the duties of his office) may also mean "in a government building/office" (cf. **68** Plut. *Solon* 21.1–2). The duties of "the treasurers" (§§6–7; cf. **170** Andoc. 1.73–79, where the relevant officials are named as the Exactors [*praktores*], the Treasurers of the Goddess [i.e., Athena] and of the Other Gods, and the *basileus*) included the collection of debts owed to the state. In §7, "to be registered" means to be registered as state debtors; the risk referred to is that of a trial under the *euthynai* procedure (end-of-term review of a magistrate's conduct in office: p. 32; **302a** [Arist.] *Ath. Pol.* 48.4–5, 54.2). At the end of §7, the angled brackets < > around the word "Witnesses" indicate that this is an editorial supplement to the text (that witnesses were called is certain from §9). The phrase *peri tou sômatos* (§15), translated "on a capital charge" (literally, "concerning my person": cf., e.g., **13b** Lys. 1.50), refers to a charge carrying a possible penalty of death, exile, or disfranchisement.

And the aforementioned conversation of mine had been held at Philius' bank; [6] but Ctesicles the magistrate and his supporters, when somebody reported that I was insulting [*loidoroimi*] them—and although what the law forbids is if a person insults [*loidorêi*] a magistrate [*archên*] in session [*en synedriôi*]—saw fit to fine me in violation of the law. They imposed the fine but did not attempt to exact it; instead, as their term of office was expiring, they wrote it up on a board and handed it over to the treasurers. [7] That is what these men did; the treasurers, however, did not share their opinion at all: they summoned those who had handed over the document and investigated the stated reason for the charge. After hearing what had happened, considering what I had suffered, they first tried to persuade them to let the matter drop by informing them that it was not fair for citizens to be registered on account of private enmities. Being unable to make them change their minds, they took upon themselves the risk at your hands and ruled the fine invalid.

<WITNESSES.>

[8] So, then, you know that I was let off by the treasurers. Although I believe that I ought to stand acquitted of the charge just on the basis of this demonstration, I will provide still more laws and other justifications. [To the court clerk:] Please take this law.

LAW.

[9] You have heard the law, which explicitly orders the fining of those who insult [*loidorountas*] in a magistrate's session [*en tôi synedriôi*]. But I have provided witnesses to the fact that I did not enter the government office [*archeion*], and since I was fined unjustly, I neither owe the fine nor deserve to pay it. [10] And if it is evident that I did not enter the government office, and the law orders those who offend inside it to owe the fine, then clearly I have not committed any offense. . . . [11] And they themselves knew that they had done wrong, for they neither underwent a review of conduct [*euthynas*] nor went into court and ratified their actions by vote. Now, if these men had fined me properly and had ratified the summary fine [*epibolên*] before you, then, once the treasurers let me off, I would reasonably stand acquitted of the charge. [12] For if they did not have the authority to exact or dismiss the fine, if I had been legally fined, I would rightly owe it. But if they are empowered to dismiss the fine, and they give an account of the affairs they have administered, then, if they have done anything wrong, they will easily receive the proper penalty. . . .

[15] . . . So, then, after swearing that they would enroll those who had not served on campaign, they violated their oaths, and they brought my case to the people to decide on a capital charge [*peri tou sômatos*] [16] after fining me on the allegation that I was insulting [*loidorounta*] their office [*tên archên*]. . . .

71. Lysias 10 / *Against Theomnestus* (selections). (384/3)

See references and headnote under **15**. The following passages provide vital evidence for the law on defamation governing the *dikê kakêgorias* under which the speaker stands trial; the terms of the law discussed by the speaker include a (perhaps incomplete) list of "the forbidden words" (*ta aporrhêta*) specified in the statute (**71a-c**), the penalty upon conviction (**71c**), and the exception for truthful use of the *aporrhêta* (**71d**; cf. **73** Dem. 23.50).

a. Lys. 10.1–2. Grounds for charge against defendant; "the forbidden words" (*ta aporrhêta*).

During that lawsuit [Theomnestus] said that I had killed my own father. [2] Now, if he had accused me of killing his father, I would have pardoned him for what he said, since I considered him trivial and worthless; nor would I have prosecuted him if I had been called any other of the forbidden words [*tôn aporrhêtôn*], since I consider prosecuting for defamation [*kakêgorias*] to be undignified and excessively litigious.

b. Lys. 10.6–9. Wording of defamation law; "the forbidden words."

And yet perhaps, men of the jury, he will make no defense concerning these issues but will say before you what he had the audacity to say before the arbitrator; namely, that it is not among the forbidden words [*tôn aporrhêtôn*] if a person says that someone killed his father [*ton patera apektonenai*], since the law does not forbid that but prohibits saying "killer" [*androphonon*]. [7] But I think, men of the jury, that we are arguing not about words but about their meaning; and I think everybody knows that all those who have killed [*apektonasi*] people are killers [*androphonoi*], and all those who are killers [*androphonoi*] have killed [*apektonasi*] people. It would have been a lot of work for the lawgiver to write down all the words that have the same meaning; instead, by mentioning one he made clear his position on all of them. [8] Obviously it is not the case, Theomnestus, that if a person were to call you "father-beater" [*patraloian*] or "mother-beater" [*mêtraloian*], you would think he should lose a lawsuit to you, but if a person were to say that you struck the woman who gave birth to you or the man who produced you, you would think that he ought to go unpunished since he had not spoken any of the forbidden words. [9] I would be happy to learn this from you . . . : if a person said that you had cast aside [*rhipsai*] your shield, but it is stated in the law "if a person says that someone has thrown away [his shield] [*apobeblêkenai*], he shall be liable," would you not prosecute him but be content with having cast aside [*errhiphenai*] your shield, claiming that it was no concern of yours, since "casting aside" [*rhipsai*] and "having thrown away" [*apobeblêkenai*] are not the same thing?

c. Lys. 10.12. Wording of defamation law; penalty.

[To Theomnestus:] And you yourself prosecuted Theon for defamation [*kakêgorias*] because he said that you had cast aside [*errhiphenai*] your shield. And yet in the law nothing is said about "casting aside" [*rhipsai*]; but if a person says that someone has thrown away his shield [*apobeblêkenai tên aspida*], it commands that he be fined 500 drachmas.

d. Lys. 10.30. Truth as affirmative defense.

But bear in mind, men of the jury, that the lawgiver grants no pardon to anger but punishes the speaker unless he demonstrates that what he said is true.

72. Demosthenes 20 *Against Leptines* 104. Law on defamation of dead person. (355/4)

See references and headnote under **18**. Here Demosthenes mentions a law, which he attributes to Solon, that prohibits speaking ill of the dead (cf. **68** Plut. *Solon* 21.1–2).

Moreover, another of the well-regarded laws of Solon is the one that forbids speaking ill of [*legein kakôs*] a dead man, even if a person is himself spoken ill of by the dead man's children.

73. Demosthenes 23 *Against Aristocrates* 50 (*lex* + commentary). Law on defamation; truth as affirmative defense. (352/1)

See references and headnote under **3**, and for the context cf. **43** Dem. 23.50. Here the speaker cites a law (presumably that governing the *dikê kakêgorias*: note the quoted verbal phrase *kakôs agoreuei*) containing a requirement that a defamatory statement be false in order to be actionable (cf. **71d** Lys. 10.30; also Lysias 10.26: "So, then, do not pity Theomnestus for having been spoken ill of fittingly . . .").

For you see that in all the laws, not just the homicide laws, this is the case. . . . "If a person speaks ill [*kakôs agoreuêi*]": "falsely [*ta pseudê*]," the law adds, since if he tells the truth, it is fitting.

74. [Demosthenes] 40 2 *Against Boeotus* 49. Law(s) on defamation of dead person. (date of speech *post* 348/7)

See especially F. A. **Paley**-J. E. **Sandys**, *Demosthenes: Select Private Orations* 1[3] (Cambridge 1898: text and commentary); C. **Carey**-R. A. **Reid**, *Demosthenes: Selected Private Speeches* (Cambridge 1985: text of and commentary on Dem. 39); J. K. **Davies**, *Athenian Propertied Families 600–300 B.C.* (Oxford 1971), no. 9667; D. M. **MacDowell**, *Demosthenes the Orator* (Oxford 2009) 66–79; A. C. **Scafuro**, *Demosthenes, Speeches 39–49* (Austin 2011:

translation with introduction and notes); also A. **Schäfer**, *Demosthenes und seine Zeit* (Leipzig 1858–87) 4.211–26; **Blass**, *AB* 3.1.473–77, 509–13; L. **Gernet**, *Démosthène: Plaidoyers civils, Tome II, Discours XXXIX–XLVIII* (Paris 1957: text, French translation, and notes); **Usher**, *GO* 259–61.

Two orations in the corpus of Demosthenes, speeches 39 (genuine) and 40 (spurious), were written for a man named Mantitheus to deliver in lawsuits against his paternal half-brother, whom he calls Boeotus. In the first lawsuit (Dem. 39), which was probably a *dikê blabês* (see chapter 8, especially **254** Dem. 39.1, 5, 7–18), Mantitheus argued that Boeotus had no right to the name Mantitheus (which he was also using) and lost. In the second lawsuit ([Dem.] 40), which cannot be securely identified but may have been a *dikê proikos* (see chapter 5), Mantitheus and Boeotus/Mantitheus both claimed the dowry of their respective mothers from their father's estate (at **121a** [Dem.] 40.14 this is stated as 1 talent each [cf. **88** [Dem.] 40.6–7]; at **111** [Dem.] 40.19–20, 25, Boeotus/Mantitheus' claim is stated as "more than 100 minae"). Here, in criticizing Boeotus/Mantitheus' conduct toward their father, Mantitheus refers to a law against defamation of the dead (cf. **68** Plut. *Solon* 21.1–2; **72** Dem. 20.104).

But my adversary feels no shame at disparaging in your presence the man whom he compelled to become his father; rather, he has reached such a level of boorishness that, when the laws forbid speaking ill of [*kakôs legein*] even others' fathers once they are dead, he is going to insult [*loidorêsei*] the man whose son he claims to be. . . .

75. Demosthenes 21 *Against Meidias* 79, 81, 83–84, 88. Demosthenes' conviction of Meidias in a *dikê kakêgorias*; procedure, including public arbitration; penalty. (347/6)

See **22**, **35**, and especially **44a** and **332** with references and headnotes. Here Demosthenes recounts an incident in which he and his family were verbally abused by Meidias and others; Demosthenes prosecuted Meidias by a *dikê kakêgorias* and won by default. The reference to public arbitration (§§83ff.; p. 36) indicates that the *dikê kakêgorias* came under the supervision of the Forty (see [Aristotle], *Constitution of the Athenians* [*Ath. Pol.*] 53). Meidias may have been fined 1,000 drachmas (§88) for defaming two living people or one dead person (presumably Demosthenes' father), or for using two of the "forbidden words" (cf. **69** Isoc. 20.3; **71c** Lys. 10.12; **81** *Lex. Cantab.* s.v. *kakêgorias dikê*). In §84, for the *paragraphê* (counter-indictment) see p. 14 and, e.g., **244** Isoc. 18.1–8, 10–13, 33, 63; Demosthenes "would not consent" to postponing the arbitration hearing.

First they burst open the doors of the rooms . . . ; then, in the presence of my sister, who was still at home then and was a young girl, they uttered the sort of profanities that men of that kind would utter (I could not be induced to say before you any of the things that were said at that time), and they called my mother and me and all of us both utterable and unutterable [*arrhêta*] bad things. . . . [81] I later filed a lawsuit [*dikên*] against [Meidias] for his defamation [*kakêgorias*] and won it by default [*erêmên*], since he did not appear. . . .

[83] . . . For the lawsuit—I am talking about the one in which I convicted [Meidias]—my arbitrator was Straton of the deme Phaleron. . . . [84] This Straton, serving as our arbitrator, when the day for his verdict finally arrived and everything permitted by the laws—postponements [*hypômosiai*] and counter-indictments [*paragraphai*]—had at that point expired and nothing more was left, ... finally, since I would not consent and my adversary did not appear, and it was getting late in the day, issued the arbitration verdict against him. . . .

[88] . . . . But the fine was only 1,000 drachmas.

76. Demosthenes 57 *Against Eubulides* 30. Reproaching citizen for working in the agora as defamation. (ca. 345/4)

Schäfer, *Demosthenes* 4.257–66; **Blass**, *AB* 3.1.486–92; L. **Gernet**, *Démosthène: Plaidoyers civils, Tome IV, Discours LVII–LIX* (Paris 1960: text, French translation, and notes); **Usher**, *GO* 261–63; V. **Bers**, *Demosthenes, Speeches 50–59* (Austin 2003: translation with introduction and notes); **MacDowell**, *DO* 288–93.

In 346/5, the Athenian Assembly ordered each deme to conduct a *diapsêphisis*, a revision of its list of members (*lêxiarchikon grammateion*: cf. **133** Isae. 12.9; **136** Isae. 7.13–17, 27–28, 30), in order to remove those with improper claims to citizenship. One of the casualties of this process, named Euxitheus, lodged an appeal in order to have his deme membership and citizen status restored, and in the consequent lawsuit against Eubulides and other officials of his deme delivered Demosthenes 57. In the following passage, Euxitheus refers to legislation that made the *dikê kakêgorias* available against a person who maligned an Athenian citizen for working in the agora.

Furthermore, men of Athens, Eubulides maligned us concerning the agora not only in violation of the decree but also in violation of the laws that ordain that a person who reproaches [*oneidizonta*] any male or female citizen for working in the agora shall be liable for defamation [*kakêgoriai*].

77. [Demosthenes] 58 *Against Theocrines* 40. "The forbidden words." (ca. 340)

Schäfer, *Demosthenes* 4.266–80; **Blass**, *AB* 3.1.498–504; M. H. **Hansen**, Apagoge, Endeixis *and* Ephegesis *against* Kakourgoi, Atimoi *and* Pheugontes (Odense 1976), esp. 137–38; **Gernet**, *Démosthène: Plaidoyers civils IV* (text, French translation, and notes); **Usher**, *GO* 264–65; **Bers**, *Demosthenes, Speeches 50–59* (translation with introduction and notes); **MacDowell**, *DO* 293–98.

This speech was delivered in an *endeixis* (p. 30) against Theocrines, who was charged with prosecuting lawsuits while owing a debt to the state. Here the speaker, Epichares, mentions the category of "forbidden words" (cf. **71a-b** Lys. 10.1–2, 6–9; **75** Dem. 21.79, 81, 83–84, 88; **80** Dem. 18.123). "The speaker's platform" is that in the Assembly; on "the tenth day" see the introduction to chapter 6 and **131** Dem. 39–40 (selections).

For you have often seen them in the lawcourts and on the speaker's platform claiming to be each other's enemies, but in private cooperating and sharing the income, and at one time insulting [*loidoroumenous*] and abusing each other with the forbidden words [*taporrhēta*], but a little later celebrating the tenth day and sharing in the same sacred rites with the very same people.

78. Hypereides 2 *Against Philippides* 3. Law forbidding defamation of Harmodius and Aristogeiton. (338–336)

See especially D. **Whitehead**, *Hypereides: The Forensic Speeches* (Oxford 2000: translation and commentary); also **Blass**, *AB* 3.2.76–81; **Usher**, *GO* 330–31; I. **Worthington**-C. **Cooper**-E. M. **Harris**, *Dinarchus, Hyperides, and Lycurgus* (Austin 2001: translation with introduction and notes).

This speech was delivered by a prosecutor (perhaps Hypereides himself) against Philippides in a *graphê paranomôn* (for proposing an illegal decree: p. 14). Here the speaker mentions a law that specifically prohibits defamatory speech or song about Harmodius and Aristogeiton. In 514, these two, motivated by a private grudge, led a plot to assassinate the tyrants Hippias and Hipparchus; Hipparchus was killed (as were Harmodius and Aristogeiton), but Hippias survived (see Herodotus 5.55; Thucydides 6.53–59; [Aristotle], *Constitution of the Athenians* [*Ath. Pol.*] 18–19). Nonetheless, the tyrant-slayers came to be venerated as heroes of the democracy (which was instituted by Cleisthenes in 508/7), and drinking-songs (*skolia*) honoring them were popular in Athens: see D. L. **Page**, *Lyrica Graeca Selecta* (ed. corr. Oxford 1973), nos. 447–50 = C. W. **Fornara**, *Archaic Times to the End* *of the Peloponnesian War*[2] (Cambridge 1983), no. 39a. That such songs were current by the late fifth century is evident from several allusions in Aristophanes (e.g., *Lysistrata* 632–33).

Second, because the people, by writing it in a law, has forbidden anyone to have the right to speak ill of [*legein . . . kakôs*] Harmodius and Aristogeiton or to sing about them in a disparaging manner.

79. [Aristotle], *Constitution of the Athenians* (*Ath. Pol.*) 59.5. Defamation of free person by slave. (332–322)

See references and headnote under **1c**. Here the author discusses the duties of the *thesmothetai* (cf. **35** Dem. 21.47; **45** Dem. 37.33; **59** Hyp. 1.12; **60** [Arist.] *Ath. Pol.* 59.3; **63a** Dem. 22.21, 23–24), which include the supervision of *dikai kakêgorias* in the special case where the accused is a slave and the victim is free (in the default case these lawsuits came before the Forty: see **75** Dem. 21.79, 81, 83–84, 88). On the *dikai emporikai* (mercantile lawsuits) see chapter 10.

And they also introduce private lawsuits [*dikas idias*] concerning commerce [*emporikas*], mines [*metallikas*], and slaves, if a slave speaks ill of [*kakôs legêi*] a free person.

80. Demosthenes 18 *On the Crown* 123. "The forbidden words." (330)

See especially W. W. **Goodwin**, *Demosthenes*: On the Crown (Cambridge 1901: text and commentary); H. **Yunis**, *Demosthenes*: On the Crown (Cambridge 2001: text and commentary); ***idem***, *Demosthenes, Speeches 18 and 19* (Austin 2005: translation with introduction and notes); **MacDowell**, *DO* 382–97; also **Schäfer**, *Demosthenes*, esp. 3.221–92; **Blass**, *AB* 3.1.419–38; **Usher**, *GO* 270–76.

This speech was delivered by Demosthenes in defense of Ctesiphon in the *Crown* case (see headnote under **27**). Here Demosthenes mentions the category of forbidden words (*ta aporrhêta*) in discussing Aeschines' conduct toward him.

I believe that insult [*loidorian*] differs from accusation in this respect: accusation encompasses offenses for which there are penalties in the laws, while insult encompasses profanities that personal enemies by their very nature say about each other. And I suppose that our ancestors built these very jury-courts [*dikastêria*] not so that, having brought you together in them, we might call each other the forbidden words [*ta aporrhêta*] for our own private reasons, but so that we might convict a person who has committed an offense against the city.

81. *Lexicon Cantabrigiense* s.v. *kakêgorias dikê* (= Hypereides fr. 100 Jensen). *Dikê kakêgorias*; defamation of living and dead; penalties. (*Lexicon* of unknown Byzantine date; Hypereides d. 322 B.C.)

E. O. **Houtsma**, *Lexicon rhetoricum Cantabrigiense* (Leiden 1870, repr. in K. **Latte**-H. **Erbse**, *Lexica Graeca minora*, Hildesheim 1965: text with Latin notes); C. **Jensen**, *Hyperidis orationes sex cum ceterarum fragmentis* (Leipzig 1917: text); **Lipsius**, *ARR* 650–51 n. 54.

The *Lexicon* (*Rhetoricum*) *Cantabrigiense* consists of glosses in the margins of a text of Harpocration (cf. headnote under **28**) now located in Cambridge. In this lemma the (anonymous) author defines the *dikê kakêgorias*. Angled brackets (< >) enclose the emendations adopted by Lipsius. On defamation of the dead cf. **68** Plut. *Solon* 21.1–2; **72** Dem. 20.104; **74** [Dem.] 40.49; for the total fine of 500 dr. cf. **69** Isoc. 20.3; **71c** Lys. 10.12; **75** Dem. 21.79, 81, 83–84, 88, at §88, with headnote. The emendations (200 dr. paid to the state, 300 dr. to the prosecutor) result from the assumption that at some point before the time of the orators all the figures given in **68** (5 dr. total: 2 to the state, 3 to the prosecutor) were multiplied by 100 (see the introduction to this chapter).

Lawsuit for defamation [*kakêgorias dikê*]: if a person spoke ill of [*kakôs eipêi*] one of the dead, even if he was spoken ill of by the dead man's children, upon conviction he was fined 500 drachmas<: 200> paid to the public treasury and 30<0> to the individual [prosecutor]. Hypereides in his speech *Against Dorotheus* says that the fine is 1,000 drachmas <if [a person speaks ill of]> the dead and 500 <if [a person speaks ill of]> the living.

82. Scholia to Aristophanes (selections). (Byzantine; date unknown)

F. **Dübner**, *Scholia Graeca in Aristophanem* (Paris 1842: text); W. J. W. **Koster** et al., *Scholia in Aristophanem*, fasc. IB ed. N. G. **Wilson**, *Scholia in Aristophanis Acharnenses* (Groningen 1975: text); for translations and discussions see the following headnote.

These scholia provide evidence for two decrees that specifically regulated defamatory speech in comic plays. The first scholion mentions a decree passed in the archonship of Morychides (440/39) and annulled in the archonship of Euthymenes (437/6); its specific terms are unknown. The second scholion mentions a decree, probably authored by a politician named Syracosius, that prohibited the satirizing of individuals by name; "those around the speaker's platform" (cf. 77 [Dem.] 58.40) are politicians, and in the final sentence "they" refers to comic playwrights. Both Aristophanes' *Birds* and Phrynichus' *Monotropos* were produced in 414; this year is thus the *terminus ante quem* of both the passage of the decree and of its annulment (since Syracosius is targeted by name in both plays). On the (disputed) interpretation of both scholia and the legal issue of defamation in Attic comedy see especially **Halliwell**, "Comic Satire"; **Wallace**, "The Athenian Laws against Slander" and "Law, Attic Comedy, and the Regulation of Comic Speech"; **Sommerstein**, "Comedy and the Unspeakable"; E. **Csapo**-W. J. **Slater**, *The Context of Ancient Drama* (Ann Arbor 1995) 165–85.

a. Scholion to Ar. *Acharnians* 67. Decree restricting speech in comedy. (decree enacted 440/39, annulled 437/6)

"In the archonship of Euthymenes": This is the archon during whose term the decree about not satirizing, written during the archonship of Morychides, was annulled. It was in effect for that year and the two succeeding years, the archonships of Glaucinus and Theodorus, after which, during the archonship of Euthymenes, it was annulled.

b. Scholion to Ar. *Birds* 1297. Decree prohibiting satirizing person by name in comedy. (decree enacted and annulled before 414)

"And [the name given] to Syracosius [is] 'Jaybird'": This was one of those around the speaker's platform. Eupolis ridicules him as a babbler in *Poleis* [fr. 220 Kassel-Austin]: "Whenever Syracosius speaks, he looks like the puppies on top of the walls: he mounts the platform, runs around, and barks." He also seems to have enacted a decree prohibiting a person's being satirized by name, as Phrynichus says in *Monotropos* [fr. 27 Kassel-Austin]: "May the itch take Syracosius. . . ." For he took away the right to satirize those whom they wanted to, on which account they attack him especially bitterly.

CHAPTER 5

Marriage and Dowry

Handbooks: J. H. **Lipsius**, *Das attische Recht und Rechtsverfahren* (Leipzig 1905–15) 468–99; A. R. W. **Harrison**, *The Law of Athens* (Oxford 1968–71) 1.1–60, 296–303; D. M. **MacDowell**, *The Law in Classical Athens* (Ithaca, NY 1978) 84–89; S. C. **Todd**, *The Shape of Athenian Law* (Oxford 1993) 204–16; E. **Cantarella**, "Gender, Sexuality, and Law," and A. **Maffi**, "Family and Property Law," in *The Cambridge Companion to Ancient Greek Law*, ed. M. Gagarin-D. Cohen (Cambridge 2005) 236–53, 254–66. **Studies:** L. **Beauchet**, *Histoire du droit privé de la république athénienne* (Paris 1897) 1.1–398; H. J. **Wolff**, "Marriage Law and Family Organisation in Ancient Athens," *Traditio* 2 (1944) 43–95; ***idem,*** "Προίξ," in *Paulys Realencyclopädie der classischen Altertumswissenschaft*, vol. XXIII, 1 (Stuttgart 1957) coll. 133–70; W. K. **Lacey**, *The Family in Classical Greece* (Ithaca, NY 1968) 100–113; S. B. **Pomeroy**, *Goddesses, Whores, Wives, and Slaves* (New York 1975) 62–68; J. E. **Karnezis**, "The Law of *Engye* in Demosthenes XLVI. 18, 20, 22," *Apollinaris* 49 (1976) 278–85; D. M. **Schaps**, *Economic Rights of Women in Ancient Greece* (Edinburgh 1979); J. M. **Modrzejewski**, "La structure juridique du mariage grec," in *Symposion 1979*, ed. P. Dimakis (Köln 1983) 37–71; V. J. **Rosivach**, "*Aphairesis* and *Apoleipsis*: A Study of the Sources," *RIDA* ser. 3 vol. 31 (1984) 193–230; D. M. **MacDowell**, "The *Oikos* in Athenian Law," *CQ* 39 (1989) 10–21; L. **Foxhall**, "Household, Gender and Property in Classical Athens," *CQ* 39 (1989) 22–44; R. **Just**, *Women in Athenian Law and Life* (London 1989) 40–75; R. **Sealey**, *Women and Law in Classical Greece* (Chapel Hill 1990) 12–49; E. M. **Harris**, "*Apotimema*: Athenian Terminology for Real Security in Leases and Dowry Arrangements," *CQ* 43 (1993) 73–95 (republished with addenda in ***idem,*** *Democracy and the Rule of Law in Classical Athens: Essays on Law, Society, and Politics* [Cambridge 2006] 207–39); L. **Cohn-Haft**, "Divorce in Classical Athens," *JHS* 115 (1995) 1–14; C. B. **Patterson**, *The Family in Greek History* (Cambridge, MA 1998) 107–14;

R. V. **Cudjoe**, *The Social and Legal Position of Widows and Orphans in Classical Athens* (Athens 2010).

The basic social unit of the Athenian *polis* was the *oikos* (household), which, at least in its ideal form, corresponded approximately to the modern nuclear family and was headed by an adult male *kyrios* ("lord, master, [man in] authority"; plural *kyrioi*). (The word *oikos* can also designate the "estate" of a decedent, on which see chapter 7.) The *kyrios* exercised legal control and guardianship over his dependents, typically his wife, minor sons, and unmarried daughters. When a son reached adulthood, he became his own *kyrios*, and when he married, he became *kyrios* of his wife, of the new *oikos* formed by the marriage, and of any children it produced. Women, however, were never legally independent persons but were always subject to a *kyrios*. From birth to marriage, a woman's *kyrios* was her father. If he died, a guardian had to be appointed to serve as her *kyrios*; normally this would be the father's heir, in the first instance his son and her brother (e.g., **83**, **88**). The *kyrios* of a married woman was her husband (e.g., **90–92**), but even when a woman was married, her *kyrios* in the natal line retained some vestigial authority, as seen in his right to compel a divorce (**101**, **102**). When divorce occurred, the *kyrios* in the natal line resumed control over the woman (e.g., **101**); when a husband died leaving a wife and a son—or, possibly, a daughter—the wife might either return to her natal household, and thus to her *kyrios* in the natal line, or come under the power of a new *kyrios* (see below).

In Classical Athens—and in Archaic Athens, at least from the time of Solon—marriage was achieved in one of two ways: by *engyê* and *ekdosis* (pledge and delivery: the subject of this chapter) or by *epidikasia* (adjudication: treated in chapter 7, in connection with the law of succession). In the context of marriage, *engyê* (etymologically "a thing placed in the hand," hence "a pledge," marital or other) was a contract of betrothal between the *kyrios* of the bride—the consent of the bride herself was not legally relevant—and the groom. For the marriage to be complete and valid, *ekdosis* (lit., "giving out"; i.e., "giving in marriage") had to take place: this was the delivery of the bride by her *kyrios* to her husband. *Engyê* thus corresponds very roughly to modern marital "engagement" (note that "gage" in "engagement" likewise means "pledge"), but it was by no means standard for any significant delay to intervene between *engyê* and *ekdosis*: while *engyê* could be performed years before the intended marriage (**87**), frequently *engyê* and *ekdosis* were simultaneous (e.g., **85**, **87**). *Engyê* was usually accompanied by an agreement as to the dowry of the bride (e.g., **92**), and all three elements (*engyê*, *ekdosis*, and dowry) were customarily witnessed (e.g., **85**, **86**) and performed using standard (but not legally mandated) verbal formulae (**89**).

With regard to *engyê*, the corresponding Greek verb is used in the active voice (*engyan*) of the pledgor (here the *kyrios* who gives the bride in pledge), in the middle voice (*engyasthai*) of the pledgee (the groom who takes the bride in pledge), and in the passive voice (*engyasthai*) of the pledged object (the bride). With regard to *ekdosis*, the corresponding verb is used in the active voice (*ekdidonai*) of the *kyrios* who gives the bride in marriage and in the passive voice (*ekdidosthai*) of the bride given in marriage. Other verbs frequently used to denote marriage are *synoikein* (used in the active voice of both husband and wife), "to cohabit, live together as married," and *gamein* (active, of the husband)/*gameisthai* (passive, of the wife), "to marry." The usual age of first marriage was in the mid-teens for women and around thirty for men.

Upon marriage, the husband became *kyrios* of his wife and of her dowry (**91**, **92**, **115**); this gave him significant but not absolute rights as to their disposal. As *kyrios* of the dowry, he enjoyed the usufruct of it; that is, the right to use it as capital and to keep any profits from it. As *kyrios* of his wife, he functioned as her legal representative (**90**) and had the power to marry her off to another man, either while he was still living (**103**) or by testament upon his death (**87**). Marriages within families were common, although marriage between uterine siblings (siblings by the same mother) was forbidden by law (**93**, **95**). Moreover, while in the Archaic and early Classical periods (until Pericles' citizenship law of 451/0: see chapter 6) marriages between Athenians (usually Athenian men) and foreigners were not uncommon, at some point between the revival of Pericles' law in 403/2 (**127** [Reenactment of Pericles' citizenship law]) and the delivery of [Demosthenes] 59 *Against Neaera* (343–339), marriages between a citizen and a non-citizen became illegal (**94**).

Marriage was terminated either by the death of a spouse (**87**, **88**, **96**, **97**) or by divorce. When a husband died without making provisions for the remarriage of his wife (as, e.g., **87**, **92**), and the union had produced (or might produce) a child—a son certainly, a daughter possibly—the widow could either remain in her husband's *oikos* (e.g., **121**, **122**)—in which case her son (if he was an adult) or his guardian (if he was a minor: see chapter 6) became her new *kyrios*—or return to the *oikos*, and to the power, of her *kyrios* in the natal line (e.g., **88**). Divorce was required by law when a wife was caught with a seducer (**58b** [Dem.] 59.87) or (by the date of the *Against Neaera*) when a citizen was found to be cohabiting with a non-citizen (**94**). Divorce might occur by the mutual consent of the spouses (**103**) or at the instance of the husband (**94b**, **99**) or of the wife and/or her *kyrios* in the natal line (**98**, **100–102**). When divorce proceeded from one party or the other, the husband had simply to dismiss his wife from his house (**94b**, **99**), while the wife had to file a written notice of divorce with the eponymous archon (**98, 100, 102**). There was no required delay between the termination of one marriage (by death or divorce) and the formation of another (**87, 92, 101, 103**).

> The standard vocabulary of divorce depended upon whether the husband, the wife, or the wife's *kyrios* in the natal line was spoken of as the party initiating the divorce. For the husband the usual terms are the verbs *ekpempein* "to send out" and *apopempein* "to send away"; for the wife, the noun *apoleipsis* "leaving" and the verb *apoleipein* "to leave"; for the wife's *kyrios* in the natal line, the verb *aphairein* "to take away."

A dowry (*proix*) was paid with virtually all Athenian brides. While it was possible for marriage to be contracted without a dowry (**107, 108a, 111**), normally the *kyrios* of a bride provided her dowry (e.g., **88, 105, 107**), sometimes with the aid of a third party (**58a** [Dem.] 59.64–70; **108b**). (On the mandatory dowering of *epiklêroi* who belonged to the thetic class see chapter 7.) Dowry was normally paid in full at or shortly after the *engyê* (e.g., **87**) but could be paid in installments (**114, 115**) and could involve supplemental conditions (**98a**). Dowries were usually paid in cash (e.g., **106, 109**) but could include other valuables, such as real property (**92**), furniture (**110**), and slaves (**92**). The dowry was valuated (e.g., **113, 116, 117b**) as distinct from the clothing and jewelry that a bride brought with her as her trousseau (*phernê*) (**92, 103, 104, 106, 119**) and from any gifts her husband might give her (**92, 106, 109**), and securities could be offered by the bride's *kyrios* for its payment and by her husband for its repayment in the event of divorce or death (**112, 114–117**).

The status of a dowry upon the termination of a marriage followed a complex set of rules. When a couple divorced, the husband had to repay the dowry to the wife's *kyrios* in the natal line (**97, 100, 113**); the same was true when a man failed to marry his pledged bride (**119**), when a husband died without producing a son—or, possibly, a daughter—and the wife returned to the household of her *kyrios* in the natal line (**100, 118**), and when a wife died without producing a son, or, possibly, a daughter (**113**). But dowry was not repayable if the wife died after producing a son (**121**), or if the husband died leaving a son and the wife remained in the marital household; in the latter case, a minor son was supported by the proceeds of the dowry, and an adult son assumed control of the dowry and was required to provide maintenance (*sitos*) to his mother from the proceeds (**121, 122**). A decedent husband who married his wife to a new husband by will had to forward her dowry to the new husband (**92, 103**). When the payment or restitution of a dowry was delayed, the payable amount accrued interest at an annual rate of 18 percent (**94b, 119**), and the creditor had two legal remedies available to him: the *dikê proikos* (lawsuit for a dowry), for the full amount of the dowry (**46** [Arist.] *Ath. Pol.* 52.2; **94b**, **100**), and the *dikê sitou* (lawsuit for maintenance), for interest owed on the dowry (**94b**, **100**, **123**, **124**); the *dikê sitou* also lay when a man pledged himself to marry and received a dowry but failed to maintain his pledged bride in the time between the payment of the dowry and the consummation of marriage by *ekdosis* (**119**, **120**).

See also chapters 6 and 7 *passim*.

5.1. Formation of Marriage

5.1.1. *ENGYÊ* (PLEDGE) AND *EKDOSIS* (DELIVERY)

See also **91** Dem. 27.55; **92** Dem. 45.27–28, 30; **94** [Dem.] 59 (selections); **97** Isae. 3.8–10; **100** Isae. 3.77–78; **101** Dem. 41.3–4; **103** Isae. 2.7–9; **105** Lys. (selections); **107** Isae. 3.28–29; **108** Lys. 19 (selections); **109** Dem. 41.26–28; **111** [Dem.] 40.19–20, 25; **113** Isae. 3.35–37; **114** Dem. 41.5–7, 10; **115** Dem. 30–31 (selections); **117** Pollux, *Onomasticon* (selections); **118** Isae. 8.7–8; **125** [Arist.] *Ath. Pol.* 26.4; **127** (Reenactment of Pericles' citizenship law); **128** *IG* II² 1237.9–125; **130** Isae. 8.18–20; **134** [Arist.] *Ath. Pol.* 42.1–2; **135** Isae. 2.13–17, 19; **137** [Dem.] 44 (selections); **139** Lys. 32.8–10, 19–24; **146** Dem. 28.15–16; **181** [Dem.] 43.54; **186** Isae. 3 (selections); **188** Isae. 10.4–5; **192** Harpo. s.v. *epidikos* etc.; **193** Pollux, *Onomasticon* 3.33; **214** Dem. 41.16; **217** D. L. 5.11–16; **228** Isae. 3.40–50, 57–60, 62; **376** [Dem.] 49.66–67.

83. [Demosthenes] 46 *2 Against Stephanus* 18 (*lex* + commentary). Capacity to pledge; legitimacy of children; marriage of *epiklêros*; *kyrios* of unmarried woman. (date of speech ?349; law probably authored by Solon, 594/3)

A. **Schäfer**, *Demosthenes und seine Zeit* (Leipzig 1858–87) 4.170–79; F. **Blass**, *Die attische Beredsamkeit* (Leipzig 1887–98) 3.1.531–34; W. **Wyse**, *The Speeches of Isaeus* (Cambridge 1904) 285–86; J. E. **Sandys**-F. A. **Paley**, *Demosthenes: Select Private Orations* 2⁴ (Cambridge 1910: text and commentary); L. **Gernet**, *Démosthène: Plaidoyers civils, Tome II, Discours XXXIX–XLVIII* (Paris 1957: text, French translation, and notes); J. **Trevett**, *Apollodoros the Son of Pasion* (Oxford 1992); S. **Usher**, *Greek Oratory: Tradition and Originality* (Oxford 1999) 244, 338; D. M. **MacDowell**, *Demosthenes the Orator* (Oxford 2009) 115–20; A. C. **Scafuro**, *Demosthenes, Speeches 39–49* (Austin 2011: translation with introduction and notes).

This speech, written by Apollodorus, comes from the same lawsuit as

Demosthenes 45 (see **56** Dem. 45.3–4) and was delivered by Apollodorus as his second speech, in response to a defense speech by Stephanus. The law here cited lists relatives who have the capacity to pledge a woman as a bride; the list is commonly interpreted as presenting an order of succession, with each named relative having the power to pledge in default of the previous named relative (i.e., if the father is not living, the brother pledges; if no brother is living, the paternal grandfather pledges). The subject of the clause "whoever he entrusts her to" is presumably to be understood as the woman's previous, and now deceased, *kyrios*. The use of the word *damar* "consort" indicates the antiquity of the law (cf. **3f** Dem. 23.53; **54** Lys. 1.24–33, at §30). On the legitimacy of children see chapter 6; on the *epiklêros* see chapter 7.

Moreover, consider also by whom the laws command that pledges [*engyas*] be made. . . .

LAW. Anyone whom either her father or her brother by the same father or her grandfather on the father's side pledges [*engyêsêi*] on just terms to be a consort [*damarta*], the children born from her shall be legitimate [*gnêsious*]. And if none of these exists, if she is an *epiklêros*, her *kyrios* shall have her [as his wife], and if she is not [an *epiklêros*], whoever he entrusts her to shall be her *kyrios*.

84. Herodotus 6.130.2. *Engyê* and marriage of Agariste. (date of composition 440s-420s; date of event described 575 or 571)

See references and headnote under **1a**. After winning the Olympic four-horse chariot race in either 576 or 572, Cleisthenes, tyrant of Sicyon, held a year-long competition for the hand of his daughter Agariste (Herodotus 6.126–30). When the favorite in the competition, an Athenian named Hippocleides, disqualified himself by becoming drunk and dancing on a table (and then reacted with the famous retort *ou phrontis Hippokleidêi*, "Hippocleides doesn't care"), Cleisthenes awarded Agariste to another Athenian, Megacles. The passage below begins with Cleisthenes' announcing the winner. As Harrison (*LA* 1.5) observes, "[t]his may not be very good evidence for Athenian practice in the sixth century, when the marriage of Agariste actually took place; but it is good evidence for Athenian practice in the middle of the fifth century, the latest date at which one can imagine the story Herodotos is using first became current." Note also the evidence of the passage that *engyê* alone does not form a marriage.

" . . . and to Megacles son of Alcmeon I pledge [*engyô*] my daughter Agariste according to the laws of the Athenians." And when Megacles consented to take her in pledge [*engyasthai*], the marriage [*gamos*] was ratified [*ekekyrôto*] by Cleisthenes.

85. Isaeus 3 *On the Estate of Pyrrhus* 70. Witnessed *engyê* and *ekdosis*. (?ca. 389)

See especially W. **Wyse**, *The Speeches of Isaeus* (Cambridge 1904: text and commentary); R. F. **Wevers**, *Isaeus: Chronology, Prosopography, and Social History* (The Hague 1969); M. **Edwards**, *Isaeus* (Austin 2007: translation with introduction and notes); also **Blass**, *AB* 2.536–40; R. C. **Jebb**, *The Attic Orators from Antiphon to Isaeus*[2] (London 1893) 2.340–43; **Usher**, *GO* 163–67.

This speech was delivered in a *dikê pseudomartyriôn* (p. 29) arising from a dispute over the estate of Pyrrhus. Here the speaker describes the processes of two marriages: (1) the marriage of Phile, pledged by her adoptive brother Endius, to Xenocles; and (2) the marriage of an unnamed woman to Pyrrhus. The uncles mentioned as witnesses are the brothers of Pyrrhus' (unnamed) mother; on the tenth-day ceremony (*dekatê*) see the introduction to chapter 6 and **131** Dem. 39–40 (selections).

But when Endius pledged [*êngya*] the woman and gave her in marriage [*exedidou*], did you, his uncles, allow the daughter of your own nephew to be pledged [*engyasthai*] to [Xenocles] as if she were the daughter of a prostitute, especially given that you claim to have been present when your nephew took her mother in pledge [*êngyato*] to have her as his wife according to the laws, and moreover to have been invited to and joined in celebrating her tenth-day ceremony?

86. Isaeus 8 *On the Estate of Ciron* 14, 28–29. Witnessed *engyê* and *ekdosis*. (?383–363)

See references and headnote under **39**. Here the speaker, who claims to be Ciron's grandson and heir, responds to his adversaries' assertion that his mother was not the legitimate daughter of Ciron. According to this account, the speaker's mother was pledged and given in marriage twice by Ciron: first to Nausimenes and then to the speaker's (unnamed) father. On the evidentiary torture of slaves see p. 24.

[14] . . . . And who must know the details about the giving in marriage [*ekdosin*] of my mother? The men who took her in pledge [*engyêsamenous*] and the men who were present with them when they took her in pledge [*êngyônto*]. So, then, the relatives of Nausimenes and those of my father have testified as witnesses.

. . .

[28] . . . So how could one demonstrate that my mother was a legitimate [*gnêsian*] daughter of Ciron more clearly than by demonstrating it in this way: [29] by providing the hearsay reports of the original witnesses and, among

those still living, those who know about each of these matters, who have full knowledge that she was raised in his house, acknowledged as his daughter, twice given in marriage [*ekdotheisan*], twice pledged [*engyêtheisan*]; and by demonstrating moreover that, on all these topics, my adversaries have evaded [getting evidence by] torture from the slaves who knew all these things? By the Olympian gods, I certainly could not state proofs stronger than these. . . .

87. Demosthenes 27 / *Against Aphobus* 4–5. Testamentary disposition of dependent relatives, including *engyê* with immediate *ekdosis*, *engyê* with delayed *ekdosis*, and dowries. (364/3)

Schäfer, *Demosthenes* 1.261–302; **Blass**, *AB* 3.1.225–31; L. **Pearson**, *Demosthenes: Six Private Speeches* (Norman, OK 1972: text and commentary); **Usher**, *GO* 171–76; D. M. **MacDowell**, *Demosthenes, Speeches 27–38* (Austin 2004: translation with introduction and notes); ***idem***, *DO* 30–58.

This oration is the first of Demosthenes' "guardian-speeches" (Demosthenes 27–31), which the orator delivered, beginning at the age of twenty, in lawsuits against his erstwhile guardians, whom he accused of mismanaging the estate left by his father, Demosthenes senior (d. 377/6). Demosthenes 27 and 28 (*1* and *2 Against Aphobus*) were delivered in a successful *dikê epitropês* (see **115a** Dem. 30.7–11, at §8, and chapter 6) against Aphobus, one of the guardians (and Demosthenes' first cousin), in 364/3. This passage (with which compare the versions at Dem. 28.15–16 and 29.43–45) describes Demosthenes senior's disposition of his estate, including provisions for the remarriage of his wife Cleobule and the marriage of his daughter (cf. **91** Dem. 27.55). The figure of 50 mn. (§4) represents the value of the dowry with which Cleobule was given to Demosthenes senior. Therippides is granted the right to use 70 mn. of Demosthenes' inheritance until Demosthenes comes of age and passes his *dokimasia* (see the introduction to chapter 6); at that point, Therippides must restore the money to Demosthenes (on guardianship see chapter 6). The 2 tal. dowry of Demosthenes' sister is payable immediately; when she reaches marriageable age Demophon must marry her or dower her with the same sum to marry another.

My father Demosthenes, men of the jury, left behind an estate worth approximately 14 talents, as well as myself, aged seven years, and my sister, aged five, and also our mother, who had brought 50 minae into the household. When he was about to die, he took precautions concerning us and entrusted all these matters to the defendant Aphobus here and Demophon son of Demon, who were his nephews, the latter his brother's son and the former his sister's, and also to Therippides of the deme Paeania, who was not related to him but was his friend since childhood. [5] To Therippides he gave the usufruct of 70 minae from my share for the time until I passed scrutiny as a man, so that Therippides would not manage any of my affairs worse than he should out of a desire for money; to Demophon he gave my sister and two talents to have immediately; and to Aphobus here he gave our mother and a dowry of 80 minae, and the right to live in the house and use my furniture. . . .

88. [Demosthenes] 40 *2 Against Boeotus* 6–7. *Ekdosis* by father and joint *ekdosis* by brothers of bride, with dowry. (*post* 348/7)

See references and headnote under **74**. Here the speaker relates the marriages of his mother: the first *ekdosis* was performed by her father; the second, after his death, by her two adult brothers (Periander, the third brother, was still a minor). For additional examples of *ekdosis* by brothers see Isaeus 2.3–5; [Demosthenes] 44.9, 17.

My mother, men of the jury, was the daughter of Polyaratus of the deme Cholargus and the sister of Menexenus, Bathyllus, and Periander. Her father gave her in marriage [*ekdontos*] to Cleomedon son of Cleon and paid with her a dowry of a talent, and she was married to him first. She had three daughters and one son, Cleon, and after that, when her husband died, she left his household, taking the dowry. [7] Then her brothers Menexenus and Bathyllus gave her in marriage [*ekdontôn*] again (Periander was still a boy) and paid the talent as a dowry, and she married my father.

89. Menander (selections). Formulae for *engyê*, *ekdosis*, and dowry.

See especially A. W. **Gomme**-F. H. **Sandbach**, *Menander: A Commentary* (Oxford 1973); W. G. **Arnott**, *Menander*, 2 vols. (Cambridge, MA 1979–97: text and translation); also E. **Capps**, *Four Plays of Menander*: The Hero, Epitrepontes, Periceiromene, *and* Samia (Boston 1910: text and commentary); D. M. **Bain**, *Menander:* Samia (Warminster 1983: text, translation, and commentary); N. **Miller**, *Menander: Plays and Fragments* (London 1987: translation with notes); S. **Ireland**, *Menander*: The Bad-Tempered Man (ΔΥΣΚΟΛΟΣ) (Warminster 1995: text, translation, and commentary); A. C. **Scafuro**, *The Forensic Stage: Settling Disputes in Graeco-Roman New Comedy* (Cambridge 1997).

The following are scenes of marriage arrangement in the Athenian New Comic poet Menander (?344/3–292/1). The formulae uttered by the brides' fathers—Pataecus, Callippides, and Niceratus—and the responses of the grooms, Polemon and Moschion, probably do not deviate significantly from the customary formulae actually in use; the phrase "for the procreation [a metaphorical use of *arotos*, "plowing, crop": cf. Euripides, *Medea* 1280–81, *Hypsipyle* fragment I iii lines 25–26; Plato, *Cratylus* 406b4–5] of legitimate children" is found also at Lucian, *Timon* 17.

a. Menander, *Periceiromene* 1013–15 Gomme-Sandbach (= 435–37 Koerte). (*post* 325)

PATAECUS. I give this woman to you for the procreation of legitimate children.

POLEMON. I accept.

PATAECUS. And a dowry of three talents.

POLEMON. Bravo!

b. Menander, *Dyscolus* 841–44. (316)

SOSTRATUS. . . . it's left for us to pledge her [*engyan*].

CALLIPPIDES. Well, then, I now pledge [*engyô*] my daughter to you, young man, for the procreation of legitimate children, and with her I give a dowry of three talents.

c. Menander, *Samia* 726–29. (ca. 310)

NICERATUS. In the presence of witnesses I give you this woman to have for the procreation of legitimate children, and as a dowry I give you all that is mine when I die; may that never happen, but let me live forever.

MOSCHION. I take her to wife, I accept her, I cherish her.

5.1.2. HUSBAND AS *KYRIOS* OF WIFE

See also **56** Dem. 45.3–4; **83** [Dem.] 46.18; **87** Dem. 27.4–5; **92** Dem. 45.27–28, 30; **103** Isae. 2.7–9; **106** Lys. 32.6; **115** Dem. 30–31 (selections); **179** Dem. 36.8–9, 11, 34; **232** Isae. 3.3–7.

90. Isaeus 3 *On the Estate of Pyrrhus* 2. Husband acting as *kyrios* of wife. (?ca. 389)

See references and headnote under **85**. Here the speaker discusses a claim to the estate of Pyrrhus filed on behalf of Phile (who claims to be Pyrrhus' legitimate daughter) by her husband Xenocles in his capacity as her *kyrios*.

But with my brother having died last year, Phile has come forward, passing over the last heir and claiming to be the legitimate daughter of our uncle; and her *kyrios* Xenocles of the deme Coprus has seen fit to file a claim to the estate of Pyrrhus, who has been dead for more than twenty years, stating the value of the estate as three talents.

91. Demosthenes 27 / *Against Aphobus* 55. Husband becomes *kyrios* of wife and dowry upon marriage. (364/3)

See **87** with references and headnote. This passage demonstrates that Aphobus, had he married Cleobule, would thereby have become her *kyrios*. Note that Demosthenes senior, as *kyrios* of his wife Cleobule, has the legal power to transfer her by will to another husband and *kyrios* (cf. **92** Dem. 45.27–28, 30).

For if my father distrusted these men, obviously he would not have entrusted the rest of his estate to them, nor, if he had left this money as they claim, would he have told them. . . . Nor would he have given this money to my mother to safeguard while giving her herself to my adversary [Aphobus], one of the guardians, to be his wife. For it makes no sense to endeavor to keep the money safe by means of my mother while making one of the men he distrusted *kyrios* of both her and the money.

92. Demosthenes 45 / *Against Stephanus* 27–28, 30. Husband disposes of wife by will; distinction between dowry and gifts; husband as *kyrios* of dowry. (?349)

See references and headnote under **56**. With the will of Pasion (d. 370/69) cited below compare the will of Demosthenes senior (**87** Dem. 27.4–5; **91** Dem. 27.55); the marriage of Phormion to Archippe in accordance with the will is mentioned also at [Demosthenes] 36.8. The questions of the authenticity of the will (attacked by Apollodorus) and of the document as preserved in the speech (questioned by some scholars, but guaranteed at least in part by the subsequent quotation by Apollodorus) have no bearing on the matters of law illustrated here; namely, that a decedent husband had the power to marry his wife to another man by will, and that the new husband automatically succeeded the old as *kyrios* of both the woman and her dowry. Note, however, the problematic terminology in the will: it is unclear exactly which items are being given as dowry (the objects of *epididômi*) and which are being given as gifts (the objects of *didômi*). Either the language is inexact, or perhaps *epididômi* governs everything through "the apartment house worth 100 minae" (or "the female slaves and the gold"), and *didômi* governs what follows. Peparethos is a small island northeast of Euboea; "here" refers to Athens. For an apartment house as content of a dowry cf. Isaeus 5.26–27.

So, then, in order that you may know for how significant and how many purposes the fabrication of the will occurred, listen to me briefly. The first purpose, men of Athens, was this: that [Phormion] not pay the penalty for having corrupted a woman whom it is not right for me to name . . . ; the second was that he gain control of all my father's money that was in my mother's possession; and in addition to these things, that he become *kyrios* of all our other property as well. That this is the case you will recognize when you hear the actual will. . . . [28] [To the court clerk:] Read them the actual will, to which my adversaries have borne witness. . . .

WILL. The following is the will of Pasion of the deme Acharnae. I give my wife Archippe to Phormion, and with Archippe I give [*epididômi*] as a dowry one talent from Peparethos, one talent from here, the apartment house worth 100 minae, the female slaves and the gold, and everything else she has in the house: all these items I give [*didômi*] to Archippe.

You have heard, men of Athens, the size of the dowry: "a talent from Peparethos, a talent from here, the apartment house worth 100 minae, the female slaves and the gold, and everything else," it states, "that she has, I give [*didômi*]". . . .

. . .

[30] [Phormion] made himself *kyrios* of the property in the house, as it had been given [*dothentôn*] as dowry with [*epi*] my mother by means of the will. . . .

5.1.3. BARS TO MARRIAGE

93. Aristophanes, *Clouds* 1371–72 and scholion. Marriage to non-uterine sister permitted; marriage to uterine sister forbidden. (original version of play 424/3, partially revised *ante* 416; scholion of unknown Byzantine date)

See references and headnote under **52**; also F. **Dübner**, *Scholia Graeca in Aristophanem* (Paris 1842: text of scholion).

The quotation from *Clouds* below comes from a passage in which the character Strepsiades is relating an altercation with his son Pheidippides; the fact that he adds "by the same mother" indicates that there must have been something particularly repellent about a brother's sleeping with his uterine sister. ("God save us" translates *ô 'lexikake*, literally "O averter of evil"—an epithet of Heracles.) The explanation given in the scholion is supported by a fourth-century B.C. source (**95** Dem. 57.20–21) and by later authors who discuss the Archaic and Classical periods (Nepos, *Cimon* 1.2; Philo, *On Special Laws* 3.22; Plutarch, *Themistocles* 32.2).

a. Ar. *Clouds* 1371–72.

STREPSIADES. And straightaway he quoted a speech from Euripides about a brother, God save us, screwing his sister by the same mother!

b. Scholion to Ar. *Clouds* 1371.

"About a brother screwing": . . . Euripides wrote a play called *Aeolus*, in which he represented Macareus, the son of Aeolus, as having corrupted his sister Canache. Since among the Athenians it is permitted to marry sisters born of the same father, [Aristophanes] added "by the same mother" in order to magnify the offense.

94. [Demosthenes] 59 *Against Neaera* (selections). (date of speech 343–339; date of laws prohibiting marriage of citizen to foreigner and fraudulent *ekdosis* of foreign bride 403/2–343/339)

See references and headnote under **21**. In the following passages, Apollodorus asserts that Stephanus and Neaera are in violation of a law prohibiting cohabitation as a married couple by an Athenian citizen and a foreigner (**94a**) and that Stephanus illegally represented Neaera's daughter Phano as his own when he gave her in marriage to Phrastor, an Athenian citizen (**94b**). "To be sold" (§17) means to be sold as a slave. The figure of 9 ob. (§52) means 9 obols per mina per month (= 1.5 percent per month = 18 percent per year); the Odeion (of Pericles) was located below the southeastern corner of the Acropolis. For disfranchisement (*atimia*) see p. 41; for the *graphê xenias* (against a foreigner for usurping citizen status) see **60** [Arist.] *Ath. Pol.* 59.3 and the introduction to chapter 6.

a. [Dem.] 59.16–17 (*lex* + commentary). Law prohibiting marriage of citizen to foreigner and providing *graphê xenias.*

. . . I want to demonstrate clearly to you that Neaera is a foreigner [*xenê*] and is cohabiting with [*synoikei*] Stephanus in violation of the laws. First, then, [the court clerk] will read to you the law in accordance with which Theomnestus filed this indictment [*graphên*] and this trial has come before you.

LAW. If a foreign man [*xenos*] cohabits with [*synoikêi*] a citizen woman [*astêi*] in any way or manner whatsoever, let any willing Athenian to whom it is permitted file an indictment [*graphesthô*] with the *thesmothetai*. If he is convicted, he shall be sold, himself and his property, and a share of one-third shall belong to the man who convicted him. The same shall also apply if a foreign woman [*xenê*] cohabits with a citizen man [*astôi*]; and the man cohabiting with the convicted foreign woman shall be fined 1,000 drachmas.

[17] Well, now, men of the jury, you have heard the law, which forbids a foreign woman's cohabiting with a citizen man and a citizen woman's cohabiting with a foreign man and their procreation of children in any way or manner; and if a person acts in violation of these provisions, the law has made it so that there is an indictment [*graphên*] against them before the *thesmothetai*, both against the foreign man and against the foreign woman, and if convicted, the law orders the defendant to be sold.

b. [Dem.] 59.51–53 (*lex* + commentary). Phrastor's divorce of Phano; law on return of dowry upon divorce; *dikê sitou*; law prohibiting fraudulent *ekdosis* of foreign bride to citizen.

And Phrastor saw that [Phano] was neither behaving herself nor willing to listen to him, and at the same time he had by this point obtained clear knowledge that she was not Stephanus' daughter but Neaera's; at first he had been deceived when he took her in pledge [*êngyato*] on the understanding that he was marrying Stephanus' daughter and not Neaera's, that she was Stephanus' daughter by a citizen woman from before Stephanus started cohabiting with [*synoikêsai*] Neaera here. He got angry at all this, and considering himself the victim of hubris and deception, he threw the woman out [*ekballei*], after cohabiting with her for about a year and with her being pregnant, and he would not return the dowry. [52] And when Stephanus filed a lawsuit for maintenance [*dikên sitou*] against him at the Odeion—in accordance with the law that commands that if a man divorces [*apopempêi*] his wife, he must return the dowry, and if he does not, the dowry collects interest at the rate of nine obols, and the woman's *kyrios* has the right to bring a lawsuit [*dikasasthai*] for maintenance [*sitou*] on her behalf at the Odeion—then Phrastor filed [*graphetai*] an indictment [*graphên*] against Stephanus here with the *thesmothetai*, charging that Stephanus had pledged [*engyêsai*] the daughter of a foreign woman [*xenês*] to him, an Athenian, on the pretext that she was Stephanus' own relative. Phrastor did so in accordance with this law here; [To the court clerk:] please read it.

LAW. If a person gives in marriage [*ekdôi*] a foreign [*xenên*] woman to an Athenian man on the pretext that she is his own relative, he shall be disfranchised [*atimos*], and his property shall be confiscated, and a share of one-third shall belong to the man who convicted him. Those to whom it is permitted shall file indictments [*graphesthôn*] with the *thesmothetai*, just as with a charge of being a foreigner [*xenias*].

[53] So, then, [the court clerk] has read to you the law in accordance with which my adversary Stephanus here was indicted [*egraphê*] by Phrastor before the *thesmothetai*. Stephanus realized that he was about to risk being exposed as having pledged [*êngyêkenai*] the daughter of a foreign woman and incurring the most severe penalties, so he reconciled with Phrastor and gave up his claim to the dowry. He withdrew his lawsuit for Phano's maintenance [*tên dikên tou sitou*], and Phrastor withdrew his indictment [*graphên*] from the *thesmothetai*.

95. Demosthenes 57 *Against Eubulides* 20–21. Marriage to non-uterine sister permitted. (ca. 345/4)

See references and headnote under **76**. In this passage, Euxitheus calls relatives as witnesses in support of his claim to citizen ancestry; the fact that he openly represents his paternal grandparents as half-siblings on the father's side indicates that such a marriage was considered proper, and implies by contrast that marriage between uterine siblings was not; cf. **93** Ar. *Clouds* 1371–72 and scholion.

Please call first Thucritides and Charisiades: their father Charisius was the brother of my grandfather Thucritides and my grandmother Lysarete (my grandfather married his sister who was not from the same mother) and the uncle of my father. [21] Then call Niciades: his father Lysanias was the brother of Thucritides and Lysarete and the uncle of my father. Then call Nicostratus: his father Niciades was the nephew of my grandfather and grandmother and first cousin to my father.

5.2. Termination of Marriage

5.2.1. DEATH OF SPOUSE

See also **87** Dem. 27.4–5; **88** [Dem.] 40.6–7; **91** Dem. 27.55; **92** Dem. 45.27–28, 30; **100** Isae. 3.77–78; **106** Lys. 32.6; **111** [Dem.] 40.19–20, 25; **118** Isae. 8.7–8; **179** Dem. 36.8–9, 11, 34.

96. [Demosthenes] 43 *Against Macartatus* 75 (*lex*). Law on abuse of orphans, *epiklêroi*, vacant households, and pregnant widows. (date of speech ?ca. 345; law of Archaic date, probably authored by Solon, 594/3)

See references and headnote under **4**. By specifying the (eponymous) archon's protection of widows who elect to remain in their deceased husbands' houses in the case of pregnancy, this law shows that a woman had the legal power to leave her husband's house upon his death, and that the death dissolved the marriage. The use of the term (*h*)*êliaia* (see **3b** Dem. 23.28) may suggest an Archaic date for the law, and Solon is known to have legislated regarding these topics (e.g., **123** Harpo. s.v. *sitos*). For orphans and *epiklêroi* see chapters 6 and 7; on vacant households see **136** Isae. 7.13–17, 27–28, 30, at §30. Cf. **152** [Arist.] *Ath. Pol.* 56.6–7.

The archon shall oversee orphans, *epiklêroi*, households that have been left vacant, and women who remain in the households of their deceased husbands claiming to be pregnant. He shall oversee these and shall not allow anyone to commit hubris concerning them. If a person commits hubris or does anything contrary to law, [the archon] shall have the authority to impose a fine up to the limit [of his power of office]. If [the accused] is deemed to be deserving of a more severe penalty, [the archon] shall issue a summons five days in advance, add in writing whatever penalty seems fit to him, and introduce the lawsuit before the *hêliaia*. If [the accused] is convicted, the *hêliaia* shall determine for the person convicted what penalty he must suffer or pay.

97. Isaeus 3 *On the Estate of Pyrrhus* 8–10. Marriage terminated by divorce or by death of spouse; *dikê sitou* and *dikê proikos*; remarriage. (?ca. 389)

See references and headnote under **85**. The speaker's comments here demonstrate that the marriage of the woman under discussion would have been terminated either by divorce or upon the death of her husband, and that once the marriage was terminated she would have been eligible to remarry; the speaker's sarcasm at §§9–10 relies on the fact that remarriage was possible, however unlikely the speaker finds it in this case.

Now, I want to learn first what dowry [Nicodemus] paid when he gave his sister in marriage [*ekdounai*], given his testimony that he gave her in marriage to the possessor of an estate worth three talents; second, whether this wedded wife left [*apelipe*] her husband while he was living or left his household after he died, and from whom my adversary recovered his sister's dowry—since the man to whom he has testified he pledged [*engyêsai*] her had died—[9] or if he did not recover it, what lawsuit [*dikên*] for maintenance [*sitou*] or for her dowry [*proikos*] he has seen fit to prosecute in twenty years against the holder of the estate. . . . So, with regard to these matters, I would be glad to learn what in the world was the reason that none of these things happened concerning this wedded (as my adversary has testified) wife, [10] and, moreover, whether anyone else has taken my adversary's sister as his wedded wife, either among those who had relations with her before our uncle knew her or among those who consorted with her when he did know her or among those who consorted with her later, after his death. . . .

5.2.2. DIVORCE

See also **58b** [Dem.] 59.87; **94** [Dem.] 59 (selections); **97** Isae. 3.8–10; **107** Isae. 3.28–29; **113** Isae. 3.35–37; **115** Dem. 30–31 (selections); **124** Photius, *Lexicon* s.v. *sitou dikê* = *Suda* s.v. *sitou dikê*; **186a** Isae. 3.64.

98. Attempted divorce proceeding from wife; notice of divorce before eponymous archon; dowry with conditional clause. (date of event described *ante* 413)

The following passages describe the dowry arrangements for the marriage of Hipparete, sister of Callias and daughter of Hipponicus, to the prominent Athenian politician Alcibiades (J. K. **Davies**, *Athenian Propertied Families 600–300 BC* [Oxford 1971], no. 600: the father of Alcibiades the younger [see **99** Lys. 14.28]), and Hipparete's subsequent unsuccessful attempt to divorce Alcibiades. When divorce proceeded from the wife, a filing had to be made in writing with the eponymous archon (cf. **100** Isae. 3.77–78).

a. [Andocides] 4 *Against Alcibiades* 13–14. (composed 4th c. B.C. or later)

M. **Edwards**, *Greek Orators IV: Andocides* (Warminster 1995: text, translation, and notes); M. **Gagarin**-D. M. **MacDowell**, *Antiphon and Andocides* (Austin 1998: translation with introduction and notes).

[Andocides] 4, which purports to be a speech delivered in connection with an ostracism between 417 and 415 B.C., is in fact a rhetorical exercise that significantly postdates the events described (see Edwards, pp. 131–36; Gagarin-MacDowell, pp. 159–61).

He married the sister of Callias with a dowry of 10 talents, and then, when Hipponicus died while serving as general at Delium, he exacted another sum of equal size, claiming that Hipponicus had agreed to add that amount if and when a child was born to Alcibiades from his daughter. [14] And after receiving a larger dowry than any other Greek, he behaved with such hubris—bringing prostitutes, both slave and free, into the same house with them—that he compelled his wife, a most temperate woman, to file for divorce [*apolipein*], by going to the archon in accordance with the law. In this instance he displayed his power most especially: he called upon his associates and went dragging his wife out of the agora by force, demonstrating to everyone his contempt for the archons, the laws, and the rest of his fellow citizens.

b. Plutarch, *Alcibiades* 8.4–6. (composed late 1st-early 2nd c. A.D.)

R. **Flacelière**-E. **Chambry**, *Plutarque: Vies, Tome III* (Paris 1964: text, French translation, and notes); R. **Waterfield**, *Plutarch: Greek Lives* (Oxford 1998: translation with introduction and notes). On Plutarch see the headnote under **1d**.

Hipparete was a well-behaved woman and loved her husband, but she was aggrieved by his conduct in their marriage, by his associating with foreign and citizen prostitutes, so she left the house and went to her brother's. [8.5] Since Alcibiades paid no mind but kept making a mockery of her, she had to file the document for the divorce [*apoleipseôs*] with the archon—not through others, but appearing in person. So when she arrived to do this in accordance with the law, Alcibiades went out after her, snatched her up, and went carrying her back home through the agora, with no one daring to oppose him or rescue her. [8.6] And so she remained with him until her death; she died not long afterward, when Alcibiades had set sail for Ephesus.

99. Lysias 14 / *Against Alcibiades* 28. Divorce proceeding from husband. (395/4)

See especially C. **Carey**, *Lysias: Selected Speeches* (Cambridge 1989: text and commentary); S. C. **Todd**, *Lysias* (Austin 2000: translation with introduction and notes); also **Blass**, *AB* 1.486–95; **Jebb**, *AO* 1.251–56; **Davies**, *APF* no. 600; **Usher**, *GO* 85–87.

This speech was composed for delivery by a prosecutor of the younger Alcibiades (son of the prominent politician of the same name: see **98** [Andoc.] 4.13–14, Plut. *Alcib.* 8.4–6) in a *graphê lipotaxiou* or a *graphê astrateias* (for desertion and for avoidance of military service respectively: see

387 Lyc. 1 [selections]). Here the speaker narrates the divorce of Hipponicus from the defendant's sister. Witnesses were not required in the case of a divorce; in this instance Hipponicus used them presumably in an effort to humiliate Alcibiades and his sister publicly.

Hipponicus, though, called many men to witness and cast out [*exepempse*] his own wife, claiming that my adversary had been coming into his house not as her brother but as her husband.

100. Isaeus 3 *On the Estate of Pyrrhus* 77–78. Divorce proceeding from wife; notice of divorce or of separation from household of decedent husband before eponymous archon; *dikê sitou* and *dikê proikos*. (?ca. 389)

See references and headnote under **85** and headnote under **97**; for the procedure before the eponymous archon cf. **98** [Andoc.] 4.13–14, Plut. *Alcib.* 8.4–6.

But you, I think, will not believe it unless he proves to you . . . [78] first, with what dowry he pledged [*engyêsai*] his sister to Pyrrhus, as he claims; second, with what archon this wedded wife filed her separation from [*apelipe*] her husband or his household; and third, from whom he recovered her dowry, since the man to whom he claims to have pledged her was dead—or, if he demanded the dowry back but was unable to recover it for twenty years, what lawsuit [*dikên*] for maintenance [*sitou*] or for her dowry [*proikos*] he prosecuted on behalf of this wedded wife against the holder of Pyrrhus' estate.

101. Demosthenes 41 *Against Spudias* 3–4. Divorce at the instigation of wife's *kyrios* in the natal line (father) and remarriage. (*post* 364/3)

Schäfer, *Demosthenes* 4.227–28; **Blass**, *AB* 3.1.249–53; **Gernet**, *Démosthène: Plaidoyers civils II* (text, French translation, and notes); **Usher**, *GO* 184–86; **MacDowell**, *DO* 60–63; **Scafuro**, *Demosthenes 39–49* (translation with introduction and notes).

Demosthenes composed this oration for delivery by an unnamed man in a prosecution of Spudias (possibly by *dikê blabês*: see **250** Dem. 41.7–9, 11–12) to recover alleged debts, including 10 minae owed on the dowry of the speaker's wife, the elder daughter of Polyeuctus. Here the speaker describes Polyeuctus' compelling his younger daughter to divorce one husband (Leocrates) and marry another (the defendant Spudias).

There was a certain Polyeuctus of the deme Teithras, whom some of you probably know. This Polyeuctus, since he had no male children, adopted Leocrates, his wife's brother. Of the two daughters he had by Leocrates' sister, he gave the elder in marriage to me with a dowry of 40 minae, and the younger to Leocrates. [4] This being the situation, when a quarrel arose between Polyeuctus and Leocrates, . . . Polyeuctus took away [*aphelomenos*] his daughter and gave her to my adversary Spudias here. Leocrates then became angry and filed lawsuits against Polyeuctus and Spudias here, and they were compelled to account for everything. In the end they were reconciled; the terms were that Leocrates would recover all that he had contributed to the estate and would bear no malice toward Polyeuctus, and that they would abandon all charges against each other.

102. Demosthenes 30 / *Against Onetor* 15–17. Divorce at the instigation of wife's *kyrios* in the natal line (brother). (362–360)

Schäfer, *Demosthenes* 1.297–302; **Blass**, *AB* 3.1.238–42; **Pearson**, *Demosthenes* (text and commentary); **Usher**, *GO* 180–82; **MacDowell**, *Demosthenes 27–38* (translation with introduction and notes); ***idem***, *DO* 30–58.

Demosthenes composed two speeches (30 and 31, *1* and *2 Against Onetor*) for use in his prosecution of Onetor by *dikê exoulês* (see §**7.4.2**). Demosthenes' conviction of Aphobus (see headnote under **87**) had resulted in Aphobus' owing him 10 tal.; Demosthenes had attempted to seize a farm in satisfaction of the debt, but Onetor, the brother of Aphobus' wife, had refused to vacate the farm on the grounds that it was not Aphobus' property but his own. Here Demosthenes maintains that Onetor's sister was still married to Aphobus when he initiated the present lawsuit (cf. Dem. 30.26, 31, 33). Scirophorion in the archonship of Polyzelus is approximately June 367/6; Poseideon in the archonship of Timocrates is approximately December 364/3 (for the Athenian calendar see p. 7). The divorce was registered by Onetor (§31), perhaps (if the plurals here are significant rather than generalizing) jointly with other natal relatives of his sister; for the requirement of a written filing (before the eponymous archon) cf. **98** [Andoc.] 4.13–14, Plut. *Alcib.* 8.4–6; **100** Isae. 3.77–78.

There are two years between the time the woman got married and the time when my adversaries claim to have carried out the divorce [*apoleipsin*]: she got married in the month of Scirophorion in the archonship of Polyzelus, and the divorce [*apoleipsis*] was registered in writing [*egraphê*] in the month of Poseideon in the archonship of Timocrates. . . . [17] And to prove that the woman got married at the time I state, and that we had already become involved as opponents in litigation in the meantime, and that these men registered the divorce [*apoleipsin*] with the archon after I filed the lawsuit—[To the court clerk:] as to each of these matters please take these depositions.

103. Isaeus 2 *On the Estate of Menecles* 7–9. Divorce by mutual consent and remarriage; transfer of dowry; distinction between dowry and bridal paraphernalia. (ca. 354/3)

See especially **Wyse**, *Isaeus* (text and commentary); **Wevers**, *Isaeus*; **Edwards**, *Isaeus* (translation with introduction and notes); also **Jebb**, *AO* 2.336–39; **Blass**, *AB* 2.532–36; **Usher**, *GO* 157–59.

This speech was delivered in a *dikê pseudomartyriôn* (p. 29) arising from a dispute over the estate of Menecles. Here the speaker describes his sister's amicable divorce from Menecles.

A month or two later, [Menecles], who praised our sister greatly, had a conversation with us and said that he was concerned about his old age and childlessness; this, he said, was not the reward she should get for her kindness, to grow old with him in a state of childlessness—he himself, he said, was sufficiently unlucky. [8] So he asked us to do him this favor: to give her in marriage [*ekdounai*] to another with his approval. And we urged him to persuade her of these things; whatever she consented to, we said that we would do. [9] At first she would not put up with this proposal of his, but as time went on, and with difficulty, she was persuaded. And so we gave her in marriage [*ekdidomen*] to Eleius of the deme Sphettus; Menecles returned her dowry . . . and gave to her the clothes with which she had come into his household and the gold jewelry that she had.

5.3. *Proix* (Dowry)

5.3.1. PAYMENT AND CONTENTS

See also **46** [Arist.] *Ath. Pol.* 52.2; **58a** [Dem.] 59.64–70; **87** Dem. 27.4–5; **88** [Dem.] 40.6–7; **89** Menander (selections); **91** Dem. 27.55; **92** Dem. 45.27–28, 30; **98a** [Andoc.] 4.13–14; **100** Isae. 3.77–78; **101** Dem. 41.3–4; **102** Isae. 2.7–9; **114** Dem. 41.5–7, 10; **116** Harpo. (selections); **118** Isae. 8.7–8; **119** Dem. 27.15–17; **120** Dem. 29.33; **139** Lys. 32.8–10, 19–24; **145** Dem. 27.34, 40, 46, 49–50, 58, 60–61, 67; **146** Dem. 28.15–16; **147** Dem. 29.30–31; **181** [Dem.] 43.54; **191** Menander, *Aspis* 250–73; **192** Harpo. s.v. *epidikos* etc.; **214** Dem. 41.16; **228** Isae. 3.40–50, 57–60, 62.

104. Plutarch, *Solon* 20.6. Limit on bridal paraphernalia (*phernê*). (composed late 1st-early 2nd c. A.D.; law attributed to Solon, 594/3 B.C.)

See references and headnote under **1d**. Here Plutarch mentions a law of Solon concerning marriages not involving *epiklêroi* ("other" means "other than those involving *epiklêroi*," on whom see chapter 7). This provision seems to refer not to dowry but to items brought with the bride into the household of her husband as her personal property (cf. **92** Dem. 45.27–28, 30; **103** Isae. 2.7–9; **106** Lys. 32.6; **109** Dem. 41.26–28; for the difference between *proix* [dowry] and *phernê* [bridal paraphernalia, trousseau] see **Wolff**, "Marriage Law" and "Προίξ"), although it is not clear whether Plutarch understands it as such.

From other marriages [Solon] took away the bridal paraphernalia [*phernas*], commanding that the bride bring with her three cloaks and accoutrements of little value and nothing else.

105. Lysias (selections). Customary obligation of *kyrios* to dower bride.

For Lysias 13 see references and headnote under **14**; for Lysias 12 and 16, in addition to the references under **14**, see especially C. D. **Adams**, *Lysias: Selected Speeches* (New York 1905, repr. Norman, OK 1970: text and commentary); **Todd**, *Lysias* (translation with introduction and notes); D. D. **Phillips**, *Athenian Political Oratory* (New York and London 2004: translation with introduction and notes); also **Blass**, *AB* 1.540–51, 517–22; **Jebb**, *AO* 1.256–64, 240–43; M. J. **Edwards**, *Lysias: Five Speeches: Speeches 1, 12, 19, 22, 30* (London 1999: text and commentary); **Usher**, *GO* 58–64, 93–94.

These passages all reveal the expectation that the *kyrios* of a bride (her father in the first passage, her brother in the second and third) provide her with a dowry, and discuss the obstacles to performing this function that were caused by the executions and confiscations carried out by the Thirty Tyrants during their brief rule in Athens (404/3: p. 12).

a. Lysias 12 *Against Eratosthenes* 21. (403/2)

These men, you see, drove many citizens into the hands of the enemy, and they killed many without just cause and denied them burial; many who possessed citizen rights they deprived of those rights, and they prevented many men's daughters from being given in marriage [*ekdidosthai*] as intended.

b. Lysias 13 *Against Agoratus* 45. (ca. 398)

These men, who had done no harm to the city, were forced to die the most shameful and dishonorable death. Some of them left behind elderly parents who expected that their children would support them in their old age and bury them when they ended their lives; others left behind unmarried [*anekdotous*] sisters. . . .

c. Lysias 16 *For Mantitheus* 10. (394–389/8)

First of all, although not much property was left to me on account of the disasters that befell both my father and the city, I gave two sisters in marriage [*exedôka*], paying a dowry of 30 minae with each. . . .

106. Lysias 32 *Against Diogeiton* 6. Dowry as distinct from bridal paraphernalia and gifts. (ca. 400)

Blass, *AB* 1.608–15; **Jebb**, *AO* 1.293–96; **Adams**, *Lysias* (text and commentary); **Carey**, *Lysias* (text and commentary); **Todd**, *Lysias* (translation with introduction and notes); **Usher**, *GO* 80–82.

Lysias 32 is a prosecution speech from a *dikê epitropês* (see chapter 6; cf. headnote under **87**) delivered on behalf of a young man (the nominal prosecutor) whose inheritance has allegedly been mismanaged by his former guardian Diogeiton. Here the speaker relates the contents of the will of Diodotus, brother of the defendant Diogeiton and father of the nominal prosecutor, including provisions made by Diodotus for his wife and daughter in the case of his death. For the distinction between dowry and gifts cf. **92** Dem. 45.27–28, 30; **103** Isae. 2.7–9; **109** Dem. 41.26–28.

And he enjoined [Diogeiton], if anything should happen to him, to provide a dowry [*epidounai*] of one talent for his wife and to give [*dounai*] her what was in the bedroom, and to provide a dowry of one talent for his daughter.

107. Isaeus 3 *On the Estate of Pyrrhus* 28–29. Possibility of undowered bride; customary witnessing of *engyê* and dowry. (?ca. 389)

See references and headnote under **85**; here the speaker discusses the disputed details of the marriage of the sister of the defendant Nicodemus ("the giver" at the start of the passage) to Pyrrhus ("the receiver" at the start of the passage), whose estate is at issue. On this episode cf. **113** Isae. 3.35–37; for a witnessed *engyê* with dowry cf. Demosthenes 41.6.

Moreover, I am also amazed at the assertion that neither the giver nor the receiver agreed to have a dowry with the woman. For one thing, if he gave a dowry, presumably the dowry given would be testified to by those who claim to have been present; and for another thing, if our uncle had pledged himself [*tên engyên epoieito*] to such a woman out of desire, obviously the man who pledged her [*ho engyôn*] would have agreed that he have much more money as dowry with the woman, so that he would not be able to divorce [*apallattesthai*] the woman easily whenever he wished. [29] And presumably the man who was pledging [*engyônta*] such a woman would invite many more witnesses than the one who was taking her in pledge [*engyômenon*], since you all know that few things of this sort tend to last. However, the man who claims to have pledged [*engyêsai*] his sister says he pledged her in the presence of a single witness and without an agreement as to the dowry to [the holder of] an estate worth three talents; and the uncles have testified that they were present when their nephew took such a woman in pledge [*engyômenôi*] without a dowry.

108. Lysias 19 *On the Property of Aristophanes* (selections). (387/6)

Blass, *AB* 1.530–39; **Jebb**, *AO* 1.230–34; **Adams**, *Lysias* (text and commentary); **Edwards**, *Lysias* (text and commentary); **Todd**, *Lysias* (translation with introduction and notes); **Usher**, *GO* 94–98.

Lysias 19 was composed for delivery in a lawsuit concerning the former estate of an Athenian politician named Aristophanes (not to be confused with the comic playwright of the same name). Aristophanes had been executed, and his estate confiscated, ca. 390. His wife's father was subsequently accused of sequestering some of the property; upon his death this will have passed to his son (Aristophanes' brother-in-law), the speaker of Lysias 19, who was probably tried by the action for confiscation called *apographê* (cf. **70** Lys. 9.5–12, 15–16 with additional references in headnote). In the first passage below (**108a**), the speaker discusses his father's conduct regarding his own marriage and those of his daughters; in the second passage (**108b**), he relates his father's assistance to needy Athenians in the form of third-party contributions to dowries, for which cf. **58a** [Dem.] 59.64–70; Plutarch, *Pericles* 24.8; Hypereides 1.13.

a. Lys. 19.14–15. Undowered and dowered brides.

You see, when he was in his youth, although he could have married some other woman with a lot of money, he took in marriage my mother, even though she brought no dowry, because she was the daughter of Xenophon son of Euripides, who not only was considered a good man in his private life but was deemed fit by you to serve as general, as I am told. [15] Now, although some very rich men were willing to take my sisters in marriage without dowries, my father declined, since they seemed to be too low-born. Instead, he gave one of them to Philomelus of the deme Paeania, whom most consider more honorable than rich, and the other to Phaedrus of the deme Myrrhinus, his nephew, who had become poor not on account of bad character, paying a dowry of 40 minae; later he paid the same dowry to Aristophanes.

b. Lys. 19.59. Third-party contributions to dowries.

Moreover, he also, at his own expense, cooperated in giving in marriage [*synexedôke*] the daughters and sisters of some destitute citizens. . . . .

109. Demosthenes 41 *Against Spudias* 26–28. Money as component of dowry; relation of dowry to bridal paraphernalia and gifts; dowry valuation. (*post* 364/3)

See **101** with references and headnote. Of the two daughters of Polyeuctus, the elder married the speaker; the younger married first Leocrates, then Spudias. In this passage (whose precise interpretation is difficult at several points: see, e.g., Gernet *ad loc.*) the speaker contests Spudias' allegations regarding the relative sizes of their wives' dowries. In the phrase translated "for which Polyeuctus had made an additional payment [*prosapeteisen*] to Leocrates of more than 1,000 drachmas" (§27), some manuscripts read *prosapetimêse* in place of *prosapeteisen*; the resulting translation would be "the value of which Polyeuctus had set in addition [*prosapetimêse*] for Leocrates at more than 1,000 drachmas." Later in §27, "included in the dowry valuation as" may alternatively be rendered "received as security for."

And in fact, even if all these things really did happen, it is obviously not right that I should not receive the agreed-upon dowry—if, that is, the laws are of any use—or that Polyeuctus, if he wanted to give a smaller dowry with one of his daughters and a larger dowry with the other, should now be prevented from doing so. [To Spudias:] You see, Spudias, you yourself had the power not to take her, if the thousand drachmas were not added as they were for me. But in fact you got no less than I did, as I will demonstrate. [To the court clerk:] First, then, please take the deposition regarding the terms on which she was given in marriage [*exedoto*] to my adversary.

DEPOSITION.

[27] So how does he have no less than I, you will ask, if the gold and the

clothing, valued at 1,000 drachmas, was included [*enetimato*] in the 40 minae in his case, while in my case the 10 minae were paid separately and in addition [*chôris prosapedidonto*]? That is exactly what I am about to tell you. Spudias, men of the jury, received his wife from Leocrates along with the gold and the clothing, for which Polyeuctus had made an additional payment [*prosapeteisen*] to Leocrates of more than 1,000 drachmas. But as for me, if you compare what [Polyeuctus] sent to me apart from the dowry—which is all I have—with what was given to my adversary [Spudias], you will find their values equivalent, without reckoning in the items that were included in the dowry valuation [*apotimêthentôn*] as part of the 1,000 drachmas. [28] So it was reasonable that these items be included in the 40 minae, since [Polyeuctus] had paid Leocrates for them and they were more than what I had been given.

110. [Demosthenes] 47 *Against Euergus and Mnesibulus* 56–57. Home furnishings as component of dowry; dowry valuation. (*post* 358/7)

See references and headnote under **17**. Here the speaker describes the plundering of his farm by the defendants and Theophemus.

. . . but they removed the furnishings from the rest of the house, [57] even though my wife ordered them not to touch them and told them that they were hers, included in her dowry valuation [*en têi proiki tetimêmena*]. . . .

111. [Demosthenes] 40 *2 Against Boeotus* 19–20, 25. Law on dowries; restitution of dowry upon death of husband; possibility of undowered bride. (date of speech *post* 348/7)

See references and headnote under **74**, and **88** with headnote. Here the speaker contests his adversary's assertion that his mother was married without a dowry. The content of the law on dowries cited at §19 cannot be determined on the basis of the surrounding text. On Cleon, who defeated the Spartans at Pylos and Sphacteria in 425 (Thucydides 4.3–41), see **Davies**, *APF* no. 8674.

[To the court clerk:] Come take as well this law about dowries.

LAW.

[20] So, then, this being the law, I think that my adversary here, Boeotus or Mantitheus or whatever else he enjoys being called, will have no just or truthful response to give; instead, trusting in his audacity and overconfidence, he will attempt to transfer their own misfortunes onto me . . . by claiming that after

the confiscation of the estate of Pamphilus, who was the father of Plangon, my father took the remaining money from the Council Hall. In this way he will try to prove that his mother brought a dowry of more than 100 minae, while claiming that my mother got married [*synoikêsai*] without a dowry.

. . .

[25] Moreover, it is evident that my mother was given in marriage [*ekdotheisa*] first to Cleomedon, whose father Cleon, they say, served as general among your ancestors, captured alive many Spartans at Pylos, and was the most celebrated man in the city. So it was not fitting that that man's son marry her without a dowry, nor is it likely that Menexenus and Bathyllus, who themselves possessed considerable estates and who recovered the dowry upon Cleomedon's death, would have deprived their sister. Rather, they would have added to the dowry themselves when they gave her in marriage [*ekdounai*] to my father; and this is exactly what they and the other witnesses have testified before you.

5.3.2. VALUATION AND SECURITY

See also **109** Dem. 41.26–28; **110** [Dem.] 47.56–57; **214** Dem. 41.16; **321a** Finley, *SLC* no. 146; **321c** Finley, *SLC* no. 49.

112. Boundary-markers (*horoi*) designating real property pledged as security (*apotimêmata*) for dowries.

I. **Kirchner**, ed., ***Inscriptiones Graecae*** II[2] (ed. min. Berlin 1913–40: text with Latin notes); J. V. A. **Fine**, *Horoi: Studies in Mortgage, Real Security and Land Tenure in Ancient Athens* (Baltimore 1951); M. I. **Finley**, *Studies in Land and Credit in Ancient Athens, 500–200 B.C.: The* Horos *Inscriptions* (repr. with introduction by P. Millett, New Brunswick 1985); **Harrison**, *LA* 1.296–303; **Harris**, "*Apotimema*."

When real property was pledged as security for a dowry, inscribed stone pillars called *horoi* were customarily set up to mark the boundaries of the pledged house and/or land. The inscriptions tend to be formulaic; for additional examples, and for varying interpretations of the transactions recorded, see the works of Fine, Finley, Harrison, and Harris cited above. See also **321** (Boundary-markers [*horoi*] designating encumbrances on real property, including *prasis epi lysei*).

a. Finley, *SLC* no. 133. (?4th or 3rd c. B.C.)

IG II[2] 2659; **Finley**, *SLC* no. 133.

Boundary [*horos*] of land and house. Security [*apotimêma*] for the dowry of Archippe, 1 talent 2,000 drachmas.

b. Finley, *SLC* no. 134. (?4th or 3rd c. B.C.)

IG II² 2662; **Finley**, *SLC* no. 134.

Boundary [*horos*] of land and house. Security [*apotimêma*] for the dowry of Timodice daughter of Philippus of the deme Anagyrus, 4,500 drachmas.

113. Isaeus 3 *On the Estate of Pyrrhus* 35–37. Dowry valuation; restitution of dowry upon divorce; possibility of undowered bride. (?ca. 389)

See references and headnote under **85**, and **107** with headnote. Here the speaker mentions laws that limited restitution of dowry in the case of divorce to items included in the dowry valuation, and that mandated the restitution of dowry to the wife's *kyrios* in the natal line—here, her brother—in the case where the wife dies childless.

If a person gives something not included in the valuation [*atimêton*], then as far as the law is concerned, if the wife leaves [*apolipêi*] the husband or the husband dismisses [*ekpempsêi*] the wife, the giver may not recover anything that he gave without including it in the dowry valuation [*mê en proiki timêsas*]. So surely anyone who says that he pledged [*engyêsai*] his sister without an agreement as to a dowry is clearly exposed as shameless. [36] For what use would the pledge [*engyês*] be to him, if the man who took the woman in pledge [*tôi engyêsamenôi*] were able to divorce [*ekpempsai*] her whenever he wished? And he would be able to do so, gentlemen, obviously, if he had not agreed that he would receive a dowry with her. So would Nicodemus have pledged [*êngyêse*] his sister to our uncle on these terms, knowing as he did that she had been childless for her entire life, and when the agreed-upon dowry by law accrued to him if anything happened to the woman before children were born to her? [37] Does any of you believe that Nicodemus is so careless when it comes to money that any of these facts would have escaped him? I think not.

114. Demosthenes 41 *Against Spudias* 5–7, 10. Partially delayed payment of dowry; security for dowry; law on securities. (*post* 364/3)

See **101** and **109** with references and headnotes. Here the speaker describes his receiving a house as security for part of his wife's dowry and Spudias' infringement on his rights as holder of the security.

Why, then, men of the jury, have I told you these things? Because I have not received the entire dowry: 1,000 drachmas remain, which it was agreed I would receive when Polyeuctus died. As long as Leocrates was Polyeuctus' heir, the contract was between me and him; but when Leocrates had left the family and Polyeuctus was in poor condition, at that point, men of the jury, I got this house as security [*apotimômai*] for the 10 minae, from which Spudias is preventing me from collecting the rents. [6] So, then, first I will bring before you as witnesses the men who were present when Polyeuctus pledged [*êngya*] his daughter to me with a dowry of 40 minae; I will then show that I recovered 1,000 drachmas less [than that amount], and furthermore, that Polyeuctus always admitted owing a debt to me, and that he made Leocrates guarantor, and that when he was dying he provided in his will for the erection of boundary-markers [*horous*] on the house for the 1,000 drachmas owed to me on the dowry. [To the court clerk:] Please call the witnesses.

WITNESSES.

[7] That, then, men of the jury, is one of the charges I am bringing against Spudias. On this matter, what greater or more powerful support could I come to you with than the law that explicitly denies lawsuits [*dikas*] over whatever a person has pledged as security [*apetimêsen*] both to the pledgors themselves and to their heirs? . . .

. . .

[10] . . . [To the court clerk:] Please first take the law that denies any further lawsuit [*dikên*] over things pledged as security [*tôn apotimêthentôn*] against their holders, and then the documents that were left behind and Aristogenes' deposition.

LAW. DOCUMENTS. DEPOSITION.

115. Demosthenes 30–31 *1–2 Against Onetor* (selections). Delayed payment of dowry; husband as *kyrios* of dowry; restitution of dowry upon divorce; witnesses to payment of dowry; security for dowry. (362–360)

See references and headnote under **102**. In these passages Demosthenes contests the defendant Onetor's account of the dowry arrangements for the marriage of his sister to Aphobus. In **115a** note that the first mention of security (§7) is connected with guardianship (see chapter 6), the second (§8) with a dowry (cf. **115c**); with the interest rate in §7 of 5 obols (per mina per month = 0.833% per month = 10% per year) cf. **94b** [Dem.] 59.51–53.

a. Dem. 30.7–11.

Onetor wanted to give his sister in marriage to Aphobus, seeing that Aphobus had become *kyrios* of both his own ancestral estates and mine, which was not insignificant. But he did not have the confidence to let go of the dowry, as though he thought that guardians' property functioned as security [*apotimêma*] [that could be forfeited] to their wards. Nonetheless, he gave him his sister, and Timocrates, to whom the woman was previously married, agreed to owe him the dowry at an interest rate of 5 obols.

[8] When Aphobus lost the lawsuit [*dikên*] over his guardianship [*epitropês*] to me and was unwilling to do what was right, Onetor made no attempt to reconcile us; although he had not returned the dowry but was still *kyrios* of it himself, on the pretext that his sister had gotten divorced [*apoleleipyias*] and he had paid the dowry but was unable to recover it, he claimed that he had received the land as security [*apotimêsasthai*] and had the audacity to eject me from it: so great was his contempt of me and you and the established laws. [9] . . . As witnesses I will provide first Timocrates himself, to testify that he agreed to owe the dowry and that he paid the interest on the dowry to Aphobus in accordance with the contract, and then that Aphobus himself admitted receiving the interest from Timocrates. . . .

[10] From the beginning, then, it is agreed that the dowry was not paid and Aphobus did not become *kyrios* of it. And it is obvious on the basis of probabilities that it was on account of the things I have mentioned that they chose to owe the dowry rather than combining it in Aphobus' estate, which was about to face such serious risk. For one cannot say that it was on account of lack of means that they did not pay the dowry immediately—Timocrates has an estate worth more than ten talents, and Onetor's is worth more than thirty, so that can't be why they didn't pay immediately—[11] nor was it that they had properties but no available money and the woman was husbandless, and that was why they were pressed to do this without simultaneously paying the dowry. You see, they lend considerable sums of money to other people, and they took her from Timocrates and gave her in marriage [*exedosan*] when she was still married and not husbandless, so you could not reasonably accept that excuse from them either.

b. Dem. 30.19–22.

Men of the jury, I asked each of them in the presence of numerous witnesses: Onetor and Timocrates, whether there were any witnesses before whom they had paid the dowry; and Aphobus himself, whether there were any when he received it. [20] And they all answered, each of them, that no witness had been present, but that Aphobus had collected the dowry from them, receiving payment at whatever rate he asked. And yet who among you is going to believe that, with the dowry being a talent, Onetor and Timocrates transferred so much money to Aphobus without witnesses? Aphobus is a person whom no one would have the confidence to pay haphazardly, not only in this way but even with numerous witnesses, so that if some dispute arose, he might easily recover his money in your court. [21] And not only is this the case with regard to Aphobus, being the sort of person that he is, but even with another man no one would have acted without witnesses when performing any transaction like this. This, in fact, is why we conduct wedding ceremonies and invite our closest friends and relatives: because we are entrusting no casual affair but the lives of our sisters and daughters. . . . [22] So presumably my adversary too would have settled his debt with Aphobus in the presence of the very same witnesses before whom he had agreed that he owed the debt and would pay the interest—if, that is, he actually did pay him the dowry.

c. Dem. 31.2–4.

And what does [Onetor] do? [3] He removes the boundary-markers [*horous*] from the house and claims that the dowry is only a talent, for which the land had been given as security [*apotetimêsthai*]. . . . [4] . . . And to prove that my statements are true—that even now he claims that the land was given as security [*apotetimêsthai*] for one talent, and that he had additional boundary-markers put on [*prosôrisato*] the house for 2,000 drachmas and then removed those boundary-markers [*horous*] after the lawsuit occurred—I will bring before you as witnesses those who know these things.

d. Dem. 31.11.

For what person is stupid enough to pay so much money and then receive as security [*apotimêsin*] a single piece of disputed land, and then, on top of what he had already lost, also to stand surety for the offender (as though he would do what was right!) for the fine he owed from the lawsuit? No one, I think. . . . From these very actions it is clear that he did not pay the dowry but, being a friend of Aphobus, took these things as security [*apetimato*] in exchange for a lot of property that belonged to me: he wanted to make his sister, together with Aphobus, heir to what was mine.

116. Harpocration (selections). Vocabulary of dotal and other securities. (Harpocration *fl.* 2nd c. A.D.)

See references and headnote under **28**. In the following lemmata, Harpocration defines *apotimêma* and related terms (**116a**) and distinguishes between the verbs *apotimasthai* (to obtain as security) and *entimasthai* (to get a thing included in a valuation) (**116b**). In **116a**, for the citation of Demosthenes cf.

115c-d Dem. 31.2–4, 11; for the citation of Lysias see C. **Carey**, *Lysiae orationes cum fragmentis* (Oxford 2007), fragmentary speech XXXIX = frr. 89–94. For the citation in **116b** see **109** Dem. 41.26–28.

a. Harpo. s.v. *apotimêtai* etc.

Apotimêtai, *apotimêma*, *apotiman*, and words derived from them: Those who leased the households of orphans from the archon provided securities [*enechyra*] for the lease, and the archon had to send out men to make a valuation of [*apotimêsomenous*] the securities. The valuated securities were called *apotimêmata*, the men sent to conduct the valuation were called *apotimêtai*, and the act [of valuation] was called *apotiman* ["to valuate, valuating"]. Also the people of that time, if the relatives paid a dowry for a woman who was getting married, used to demand from the husband as security [*enechyron*] something of equivalent value to the dowry, such as a house or a plot of land. The one who gave the security [*apotimêma*] was said to "give security" [*apotiman*] in the active voice; the one who received the security was said to "get security given" [*apotimasthai*]. The same language also applied to other debts. Demosthenes in his *Second Speech against Onetor*; Lysias in his speech *Against Diogenes on the Rent of a Household*, if genuine.

b. Harpo. s.v. *enetimato*.

Enetimato ["got included in the valuation"]: Demosthenes in his speech *Against Spudias*. The word *apetimato* ["got as security"] differs from the word *enetimato* ["got included in the valuation"]: when a person obtains something as security [*apotimêma*] for whatever amount of money, he is said to "get it as security" [*apotimasthai*]; when a person reckons some part of the money [as consisting] in certain goods, it is said that he "got" this "included in the valuation" [*enetimêsato*].

117. Pollux, *Onomasticon* (selections). Vocabulary of marriage, dowry, and dotal securities. (late 2nd c. A.D.)

E. **Bethe**, *Lexicographi Graeci* vol. IX: *Pollucis Onomasticon*, 2 vols. (Stuttgart 1910–31: text); **Φιλολογική Ομάδα Κάκτου**, *Πολυδεύκης· 'Ονομαστικόν*, 2 vols. (Athens 2004: text).

Julius Pollux (Polydeuces), a native of Naucratis in Egypt, was a professor of rhetoric in Athens. His *Onomasticon*, dedicated to the Roman emperor Commodus (r. A.D. 180–192), is a combination dictionary and thesaurus arranged by subject.

a. Pollux, *Onomasticon* 3.35–36.

The wife's relative [*pentheros*] "pledges" [*engya*] . . . and "gives in marriage" [*ekdidôsi*]; the act is called "giving in marriage" [*ekdosis*] . . . , and contributing money for the *ekdosis* is called "cooperating in the *ekdosis*" [*synekdounai*]. . . . You may call what is given from the wife "dowry" [*proika*] and "bridal paraphernalia" [*phernên*]. . . . [36] The pledges [*hypothêkai*] for the dowry are called "securities" [*apotimêmata*].

b. Pollux, *Onomasticon* 8.142.

"Including in a dowry valuation" [*entimêsasthai*] is when a person giving a dowry reckons how much it is to be valued at. A "security" [*apotimêma*] is a type of pledge [*hypothêkê*], properly applied to dowries but actually to leases as well. The verb is "to get security given" [*apotimêsasthai*]. "To put down [*theinai*] a house" is to give it in pledge; "to get a house put down [*thesthai*]" is to take it in pledge. . . .

5.3.3. MAINTENANCE (*SITOS*), RESTITUTION, AND TRANSFER

See also **46** [Arist.] *Ath. Pol.* 52.2; **87** Dem. 27.4–5; **88** [Dem.] 40.6–7; **92** Dem. 45.27–28, 30; **94** [Dem.] 59 (selections); **96** [Dem.] 43.75; **97** Isae. 3.8–10; **100** Isae. 3.77–78; **103** Isae. 2.7–9; **108** Lys. 19 (selections); **109** Dem. 41.26–28; **111** [Dem.] 40.19–20, 25; **113** Isae. 3.35–37; **115** Dem. 30–31 (selections); **139** Lys. 32.8–10, 19–24; **145** Dem. 27.34, 40, 46, 49–50, 58, 60–61, 67; **146** Dem. 28.15–16; **147** Dem. 29.30–31; **182** [Dem.] 46.19–20.

118. Isaeus 8 *On the Estate of Ciron* 7–8. Restitution of dowry upon death of husband without issue; dowry as distinct from bridal paraphernalia. (?383–363)

See references and headnotes under **39** and **86**. Here the speaker explains why his mother's dowry for her second marriage was less than that for her first marriage. 1,000 drachmas (= 10 mn.) amounts to 40 percent of 25 minae (= 2,500 dr.); note the distinction between dowry and bridal paraphernalia (clothes and gold jewelry) in connection with the first marriage, to Nausimenes (cf., e.g., **106** Lys. 32.6; **109** Dem. 41.26–28).

And [Ciron] raised her in the company of his wife and together with the children he had by her, [8] and while they were still living, when she was old enough to marry [*synoikein*], he gave her in marriage [*ekdidôsin*] to Nausimenes of the deme Cholargus, with her clothes and gold jewelry and a dowry of 25 minae. Three or four years afterward, Nausimenes became ill and died, before any children were born to him by our mother; our grandfather took her back and—since on account of Nausimenes' lack of means he did not recover all of the dowry he had given—gave her in marriage again, to my father, and gave with her a dowry of 1,000 drachmas.

119. Demosthenes 27 / *Against Aphobus* 15–17. Restitution of dowry by man who fails to marry pledged bride; relation of dowry to bridal paraphernalia; statutory interest rate on delinquent dowry. (364/3)

See references and headnote under **87**. Here Demosthenes describes Aphobus' failure to marry his mother, to provide her with maintenance (*sitos*) from her dowry, or to return the dowry with interest as prescribed by law (cf. Demosthenes 28.11). For the statutory interest rate (9 obols per mina per month = 1.5 percent monthly = 18 percent annually) see **94b** [Dem.] 59.51–53; the interest rate offered by Demosthenes is two-thirds the statutory rate (1 dr. = 6 ob.: p. 4).

For since [Aphobus] would not provide maintenance [*siton*] to my mother—even though he had the dowry—and was unwilling to lease the estate, but saw fit to manage it along with the other guardians, Demochares had a conversation with him about these matters. Aphobus listened and did not dispute having the dowry or complain about not having received it, but admitted [that he had it] and said that he was still involved in a small dispute with my mother about her gold jewelry. So when he got this sorted out, he said, he would manage my sustenance [*trophês*] and the rest so that everything would be fine for me.

[16] Now, if it is clear that he admitted these things to Demochares and the others who were present, and that he received the prices of the slaves from Demophon and Therippides as part of the dowry, and that he stated in writing to his fellow guardians that he had the dowry, and that he has inhabited the house ever since my father died, then, since the matter is agreed upon by all, how will it not be concluded that he obviously possesses the dowry, all 80 minae, and is most shameless when he denies receiving it? [17] [To the court clerk:] And to prove that I am telling the truth, take these depositions and read them.

DEPOSITIONS.

So in this manner he got and kept the dowry. And since he did not marry my mother, the law commands that he owe the dowry at an interest rate of 9 obols; I, however, reckon it at only a drachma.

120. Demosthenes 29 *3 Against Aphobus* 33. Maintenance (*sitos*) due to pledged and dowered but unmarried woman by prospective husband. (?362/1)

Schäfer, *Demosthenes* 4.82–89; **Blass**, *AB* 3.1.232–38; L. **Gernet**, *Démosthène: Plaidoyers civils, Tome I, Discours XXVII–XXXVIII* (Paris 1954: text, French translation, and notes); **Usher**, *GO* 178–80; **MacDowell**, *Demosthenes 27–38* (translation with introduction and notes); ***idem***, *DO* 30–58.

For the episode described here cf. **87** Dem. 27.4–5; **119** Dem. 27.15–17; for the speech see **147** Dem. 29.30–31 with headnote.

First, [Aphobus'] fellow guardian Therippides testified that he paid him the dowry; second, his uncle Demon and those others who were present testified that [Aphobus] agreed to provide maintenance [*siton*] to my mother, since he had the dowry.

121. [Demosthenes] 40 *2 Against Boeotus* (selections). Rights of minor son and of adult son as to dowry of widowed mother who remains in her husband's household. (*post* 348/7)

See references and headnote under **74**, and **88** with headnote. In these passages, the speaker describes the cross-claims lodged by himself and his homopatric half-brothers to the dowries of their respective mothers, and attests to his childhood maintenance from his mother's dowry.

a. [Dem.] 40.14.

And . . . when we were dividing our patrimony and I demanded to receive my mother's dowry, my adversaries lodged a counter-claim, asserting that the same amount of dowry was owed to their mother as well.

b. [Dem.] 40.50.

But you must remember that my mother died leaving me a child, and so the interest on her dowry sufficed for my sustenance [*trephesthai*] and education. . . . .

c. [Dem.] 40.59.

And who among you could believe that, especially when I am here in court now . . . concerning the dowry which, since my mother brought it into the household, the laws command that I recover?

122. [Demosthenes] 42 *Against Phaenippus* 27. Rights of adult son as to dowry of widowed mother who remains in her husband's household. (330–323)

Schäfer, *Demosthenes* 4.280–85; **Blass**, *AB* 3.1.505–9; **Gernet**, *Démosthène: Plaidoyers civils II* (text, French translation, and notes); **Usher**, *GO* 267–68; **MacDowell**, *DO* 147–51; K. E. **Apostolakis**, *[Δημοσθένους]* Πρὸς Φαίνιππον περὶ ἀντιδόσεως (Athens 2009: text, Modern Greek translation, and commentary); **Scafuro**, *Demosthenes 39–49* (translation with introduction and notes).

[Demosthenes] 42 was delivered in a *diadikasia* over an *antidosis* (exchange of property: p. 26). At this time, the 1,200 wealthiest Athenians, who were liable to the *eisphora* (p. 26), were organized in groups; the richest 300 among the 1,200 were the heads of the groups and had to pay the *eisphora* for their groups in advance (the advance payment was called *proeisphora*) and then reimburse themselves from the group members. The speaker had proposed that Phaenippus either replace him on the catalogue of the 300 or exchange the whole of his property with him. The two men accordingly agreed to compile inventories of their respective estates; now, however, the speaker contends that Phaenippus has failed to disclose assets. In the passage below the speaker contests his adversary's representation of the status of his mother's dowry; the inventory to which he refers is a written list of assets proffered by Phaenippus in support of his claims (cf. **304c** [Dem.] 42.12).

This Aristonoe, men of the jury, is the daughter of Philostratus and the mother of my adversary here. Phaenippus claims that her dowry, of which the laws make him *kyrios*, is owed to her as a debt; but he is lying and not acting justly in his use of the inventory. Since my mother remains in the household and is still living and brought a dowry with her, why is it, Phaenippus, that I don't list her dowry as a debt to her and mislead the jurors, but instead allow my mother to share in what is mine, whether I possess Phaenippus' property or my own? Because that is what the laws command, my good man, whereas you do everything in violation of the laws.

123. Harpocration s.v. *sitos*. *Sitos* (maintenance) for widows and orphans. (Harpocration *fl.* 2nd c. A.D.)

See references and headnote under **28**. In this entry Harpocration defines *sitos*. For the citations see, in order, **119** Dem. 27.15–17; **96** [Dem.] 43.75 (cf. **182** [Dem.] 46.19–20); **152** [Arist.] *Ath. Pol.* 56.6–7.

Sitos [maintenance]: Demosthenes, *First Oration against Aphobus*. *Sitos* is the name for the revenue paid for the sustenance [*trophên*] of wives and orphans, as can be learned from other sources and in particular from Solon's first axon and from Aristotle's *Constitution of the Athenians*.

124. Photius, *Lexicon* s.v. *sitou dikê* = *Suda* s.v. *sitou dikê*. *Dikê sitou* (lawsuit for maintenance). (Photius *fl.* late 9th c. A.D.; *Suda* composed late 10th c. A.D.)

See references and headnote under **49**. Below is the entry defining the *dikê sitou* in both the *Lexicon* of Photius and the *Suda*. The phrase translated "against him" (referring to the ex-husband) may also mean "before him" (referring to the eponymous archon).

Sitou dikê [lawsuit for maintenance]: When a woman who has divorced herself [*apodikein poiêsamenê*] from her husband through the archon or who has been divorced [*ekpemphtheisa*] by her husband does not receive her dowry back, and time passes, and she brings a lawsuit against him [*pros auton*] and demands her dowry and sustenance [*trophas*] from the date when she separated [from him], this [lawsuit] is called a *dikê sitou*.

CHAPTER 6

Children and Citizenship

Handbooks: J. H. **Lipsius**, *Das attische Recht und Rechtsverfahren* (Leipzig 1905–15) 342–53, 412–20, 468–76, 499–537; A. R. W. **Harrison**, *The Law of Athens* (Oxford 1968–71) 1.61–121, 163–99; 2.15, 23–25, 86; D. M. **MacDowell**, *The Law in Classical Athens* (Ithaca, NY 1978) 67–86, 91–101; S. C. **Todd**, *The Shape of Athenian Law* (Oxford 1993) 109, 111, 139, 174–84, 208, 221–31; A. **Maffi**, "Family and Property Law," and C. **Patterson**, "Athenian Citizenship Law," in *The Cambridge Companion to Ancient Greek Law*, ed. M. Gagarin-D. Cohen (Cambridge 2005) 254–66, 267–89. **Studies:** A. **Philippi**, *Beiträge zu einer Geschichte des attischen Bürgerrechtes* (Berlin 1870); O. **Schulthess**, *Vormundschaft nach attischem Recht* (Freiburg 1886); L. **Beauchet**, *Histoire du droit privé de la république athénienne* (Paris 1897) 1.488–535; 2.1–72, 74–392; H. J. **Wolff**, "Marriage Law and Family Organisation in Ancient Athens," *Traditio* 2 (1944) 43–95; W. K. **Lacey**, *The Family in Classical Greece* (Ithaca, NY 1968) 84–85, 90–96, 100–5, 110–13, 116–18, 145–46; D. M. **MacDowell**, "Bastards as Athenian Citizens," *CQ* 26 (1976) 88–91; P. J. **Rhodes**, "Bastards as Athenian Citizens," *CQ* 28 (1978) 89–92; C. **Patterson**, *Pericles' Citizenship Law of 451–50 B.C.* (New York 1981); M. J. **Osborne**, *Naturalization in Athens* (Brussels 1981–83); A. **Maffi**, "Matrimonio, concubinato, e filiazione illegittima nell'Atene degli oratori," in *Symposion 1985*, ed. G. Thür (Köln 1989) 177–214; D. M. **MacDowell**, "The *Oikos* in Athenian Law," *CQ* 39 (1989) 10–21; R. **Just**, *Women in Athenian Law and Life* (London 1989) 55–68; C. B. **Patterson**, "Those Athenian Bastards," *ClAnt* 9 (1990) 40–73; L. **Rubinstein**, *Adoption in IV. Century Athens* (Copenhagen 1993); D. **Ogden**, *Greek Bastardy in the Classical and Hellenistic Periods* (Oxford 1996); E. **Cantarella**, "Filiazione e cittadinanza ad Atene," in *Symposion 1995*, ed. G. Thür-J. Vélissaropoulos-Karakostas (Köln 1997) 97–111; S. **Lape**, "Solon and the Institution of the 'Democratic' Family Form," *CJ* 98 (2002–3) 117–39; E. **Carawan**, "Pericles the Younger and the Citizenship Law," *CJ* 103 (2008)

383–406; J. H. **Blok**, "Pericles' Citizenship Law: A New Perspective," *Historia* 58 (2009) 141–70; R. V. **Cudjoe**, *The Social and Legal Position of Widows and Orphans in Classical Athens* (Athens 2010).

From Solon (**83** [Dem.] 46.18) onward, Athenian law defined a legitimate (masculine *gnêsios*, plural *gnêsioi*; feminine *gnêsia*) child as the product of a marriage either by *engyê* and *ekdosis* (see chapter 5) or by *epidikasia* (the judicial award of an *epiklêros* to her father's nearest living male relative: see chapter 7). All other children were illegitimate (masculine *nothos*, plural *nothoi*; feminine *nothê*). In the time of the orators, an Athenian father would customarily assert the legitimacy of a child by a series of actions. Nine days after a child's birth, the father hosted a naming ceremony called the *dekatê* (since it occurred on the "tenth day" by inclusive reckoning, with the day of birth counted as day 1: **131**). Then, at some point during childhood, a son was presented to his father's phratry—a large hereditary association to one of which most, if not all, citizen males belonged—and, if approved, was enrolled as a member (**128**, **130–132**, **135–137**; cf. **126**); a daughter might be presented to her father's phratry (**129**) but was not enrolled. Finally, if a son was eligible for citizenship (see below), when he was eighteen years old, his father would present him for enrollment in his deme (p. 6), and if the son was admitted to the deme and then passed scrutiny (*dokimasia*) before the Council of 500, he obtained the rights of an adult male citizen (**131**, **132**, **134–137**). No comparable procedure existed for daughters.

The status of a child determined its rights of inheritance (see chapter 7); the relationship between legitimacy and citizenship (**§6.1**: **125–134**) is more complex and less certain. Debate over this relationship centers around three pieces of legislation. (1) The aforementioned law of Solon (**83** [Dem.] 46.18), passed in 594/3, required that the parents of a child be married in order for the child to be legitimate. (2) A law of Pericles (**125**), passed in 451/0, required that both parents be citizens in order for their child to be a citizen. (3) A decree passed in 403/2 (**127**) reenacted Pericles' citizenship law, which had ceased to be enforced at some point after 414, and may have imposed additional restrictions on the rights of illegitimate children.

It is clear that, between Solon and Pericles, the citizen status of the father alone sufficed to confer citizen status on his children (see headnote under **125**). However, whether illegitimate children (of an Athenian father before Pericles' law, and of two Athenian parents thereafter) qualified for citizenship is an open question. Scholars who argue for an affirmative answer rely upon the fact that the description of Pericles' law in the pseudo-Aristotelian *Constitution of the Athenians* (*Ath. Pol.*), our best source for it, does not mention the marital status of the parents; and they warn against the assumption that the restrictions on the familial rights of an illegitimate child—with regard to admission to hereditary groups (**126**, **128–132**, **134**) as well as inheritance (chapter 7)—automatically applied to the issue of citizenship. Those who favor a negative answer observe that the version of Pericles' law given in the *Ath. Pol.* may not be complete, and adduce the statements made in fourth-century trials that explicitly connect legitimacy, as proven by membership in hereditary groups, with citizenship (**131a**, **132**, **133**).

Citizenship carried, for adult males, a package of highly important and exclusive rights, including participation in the Assembly, eligibility for political office and for jury service, and the right to own real property in Attica (*enktêsis gês kai oikias*, "acquisition of land and house," which might be extended by decree to specially privileged metics: e.g., D. Lewis, ed., *Inscriptiones Graecae*, vol. 1 ed. 3 fasc. 1 [Berlin and New York 1981], no. 102 = R. Meiggs-D. Lewis, eds., *A Selection of Greek Historical Inscriptions to the End of the Fifth Century BC* [rev. ed. Oxford 1988], no. 85). In the time of the orators, the Athenians guarded their citizenship jealously; if a person was not born of citizen stock, it was highly unlikely that he or she would ever become a citizen. Naturalization, done by decree of the Assembly (see, e.g., *IG* I^3 102 = Meiggs-Lewis no. 85; [Demosthenes] 59.89–93; and the headnote under **370** Lyc. 1.112–15), was very rare and was conferred as a reward for conspicuous service to the Athenian state. Slaves freed by their masters became metics (see, e.g., **17** [Dem.] 47.67–73), not citizens. False assertion of citizenship was subject to severe punishment: the dedicated legal remedy, the *graphê xenias* ("for being a foreigner"), which could be prosecuted by any willing and qualified citizen (p. 30), provided that a convicted defendant be sold into slavery (**94a** [Dem.] 59.16–17; **94b** [Dem.] 59.51–53; see also **60** [Arist.] *Ath. Pol.* 59.3; **376** [Dem.] 49.66–67; Demosthenes 24.131 with scholia; Demosthenes, *Letters* 3.29).

Athenian men who lacked legitimate sons were permitted to adopt. Since adoption was seen primarily as a way to ensure the maintenance of the adopter in his old age and the preservation of the adopter's *oikos* (see the introduction to chapter 5) after his death, the adoptee was usually male and could be either a child or an adult. Adoption occurred in one of three ways: during the lifetime of the adopter (adoption *inter vivos*, Latin for "between living people": **135**, **136**), upon the death of the adopter in accordance with his will (testamentary adoption: **135**, **136**), or after the death of the adopter at the instance of a family member (posthumous adoption: **137**). Since the adoptee became heir to his adopter, adoption was governed by the terms of Solon's law on wills (**201** [Dem.] 46.14): a man could not adopt if he had a legitimate son; if his mental capacity was impaired by insanity, senility, drugs, disease, or female influence; if he was under mental or physical duress; or if he himself had been adopted *inter vivos* (whether men adopted by will or posthumously could adopt is a matter of debate: see **196** [Dem.] 44.24–26, 32–34; **221** [Dem.] 44.64).

After the passage of Pericles' citizenship law, only the children of two (possibly married: see above) Athenian parents were eligible to be adopted. Adoption required the consent of the adoptee if he was an adult male and that of the adoptee's *kyrios* (see the introduction to chapter 5) in all other cases. A legally adopted child lost all legal relationship to his or her biological father and became the legitimate child of the adopter; accordingly, an adopted son was enrolled in his adoptive father's phratry and deme (**135–137**). Once a son was adopted, he was allowed to annul the adoption and return to his natal *oikos* only if he left behind a legitimate son of his own to take his place in the *oikos* of his adopter (**138**; see also chapter 7). The material on adoption presented in this chapter (**§6.2**: **135–138**) addresses the adopted son's entry into (and possible departure from) his adoptive family; for sources that deal primarily with the inheritance rights of adoptees see chapter 7.

If a father died leaving a minor child, the law classified the child as an orphan (*orphanos*) and mandated the appointment of a guardian (*epitropos*) (**§6.3**: **139–151**). (Whether the child's mother was still living was irrelevant.) Multiple guardians could be appointed, and a guardian had to be an adult male, but did not have to be related to his ward (**145**, **146**; cf. **87** Dem. 27.4–5: Therippides was unrelated to his ward Demosthenes). As with adoption, the appointment of a guardian could occur *inter vivos*, by will, or posthumously. The first two methods were at the discretion of the father, who could specify the conditions of the guardianship (**145**, **146**, **149**), and a guardianship established *inter vivos* to take effect upon the father's death might be confirmed in his will (**145**, **146**; cf. **87** Dem. 27.4–5). If a father had failed to name a guardian either *inter vivos* or by will, one had to be appointed posthumously. In at least some cases, the appointment of a guardian was confirmed by the eponymous archon (**144**); scholars generally assume that that official's general mandate to oversee orphans (**144**, **151**, **152**) included the power to select a guardian from among competing applicants and to assign a guardian if no applicant came forward, but we have no secure instance of either of these procedures (for possible cases see **141–143**).

The guardian assumed the father's capacity as *kyrios* of the child (**141**). As such, he was responsible for the child's physical and financial well-being. The former, for which the standard—and generally interchangeable—terms are *sitos* and *trophê* (here usually translated "maintenance" and "sustenance" respectively; cf. **§5.3.3**), included food, housing, clothing, and (for boys, at least in cases where the father's estate was sufficient to pay for it) education (**139**, **141**, **145**); failure to provide such maintenance could give rise to a *dikê sitou* (private lawsuit for maintenance: **123** Harpo. s.v. *sitos*; **152**). The latter involved supervision of the ward's property. The guardian was *kyrios* of the property as well as of his ward (**146**, **148**), but his control of the property was limited. He had to obey any mandates left by the ward's father regarding the maintenance of his estate (**145**, **146**, **149**), including the leasing of the estate (*misthôsis oikou*: **139**, **144–146**, **150**, **151**), which was regulated by the eponymous archon and might be compelled, even when the father had not so directed, by a procedure called *phasis* (declaration: **150**, **151**). The guardianship of a male ward ended when he reached manhood at the age of 18 (**139**, **148**); that of a female ward ended when she was married, at which point her husband became her *kyrios* (see chapter 5). At the termination of guardianship, the guardian had to turn over the property to the ward, along with an account statement (*logos*, *logismos*) detailing the amount of property left by the ward's father, income accrued on it during the guardianship, and expenditures made for the maintenance of the ward (**139**, **145**, **148**, **150**). If a ward contended that his guardian had not surrendered all the property due to him, he could proceed against his guardian by a *dikê epitropês* (private lawsuit over a guardianship) within five years of the termination of the guardianship (**139**, **145–147**, **150**).

The status of certain individuals within the family granted them legal protection against maltreatment (*kakôsis*: **§6.4**: **152–165**). The protected classes were parents (and perhaps further direct ascendants), who were protected against maltreatment by their children (and perhaps further direct descendants: **159**), and orphans and *epiklêroi*, who were protected against maltreatment by anyone. Maltreatment of parents (*kakôsis goneôn*: **152**, **154**; **§6.4.1**: **155–160**) might consist in beating them (**157**), failing to provide them with housing and sustenance (**155**, **157–160**), or failing to perform their funerary rites (**158**, **160**). Maltreatment of orphans (*kakôsis orphanôn*: **152**, **154**; **§6.4.2**: **161–163**) and *epiklêroi* (*kakôsis epiklêrou*: **152**, **154**; **§6.4.3**: **164–165**) embraced any wrongdoing against them, including infringement upon the rights of the orphan or *epiklêros* as to the property left by his or her father (**161**, **163**; see also chapter 7); maltreatment of the estate of an orphan (*kakôsis oikou orphanikou*) is mentioned as a separate category in the *Ath. Pol.* (**152**) but is not confirmed elsewhere.

Although some sources (**152–154**, **163**) use the generalizing terms *graphê* (indictment) or *dikê* (in the broad sense, designating any lawsuit: see p. 29), it appears that (in the fourth century, at any rate) the action for maltreatment of a parent, orphan, or *epiklêros* was an *eisangelia* (impeachment: **161**, **164**, **165**; note the distinction between this type of *eisangelia* and *eisangelia* for major offenses against the state, on which see chapter 12). These impeachments fell under the supervision of the eponymous archon (**152**, **162–164**) and could be brought by any willing citizen; there was no time limit for speakers (**154**), and the fine of 1,000 drachmas levied against a prosecutor who received less than 20 percent of the jurors' votes, a standard feature of public lawsuits, did not apply (**152**, **164**). For *kakôsis goneôn* the penalty was *atimia* (disfranchisement: p. 41) (**155**, **158**, **160**; contrast **157**); the action for maltreatment of an *epiklêros* definitely (**164**), and that for maltreatment of an orphan almost certainly (**161**), was an assessable lawsuit (*agôn timêtos*: p. 40) without penal limit, and a guardian convicted of maltreating his ward was removed from the guardianship (**161**).

See also chapters 5 and 7 *passim*.

6.1. Legitimacy and Citizenship

See also **3f** Dem. 23.53; **60** [Arist.] *Ath. Pol.* 59.3; **74** [Dem.] 40.49; **77** [Dem.] 58.40; **83** [Dem.] 46.18; **85** Isae. 3.70; **86** Isae. 8.14, 28–29; **87** Dem. 27.4–5; **89** Menander (selections); **90** Isae. 3.2; **94** [Dem.] 59 (selections); **135** Isae. 2.13–17, 19; **136** Isae. 7.13–17, 27–28, 30; **137** [Dem.] 44 (selections); **138** Harpo. s.v. *hoti hoi poiêtoi* etc.; **139** Lys. 32.8–10, 19–24; **156** Plut. *Solon* 22.1, 4; **176** [Dem.] 43.51; **178** Isae. 6.25, 28, 63; **184** Ar. *Birds* 1641–70; **186b** Isae. 3.72–74; **§7.2.4**; **204** Isae. 3.67–69; **206** Isae. 10.9–10; **210** [Dem.] 46.24; **221** [Dem.] 44.64; **228** Isae. 3.40–50, 57–60, 62; **229** Isae. 6.3–4, 43–44, 52; **230** [Dem.] 44 (selections); **231** Isae. 5.6–7, 9, 12–18; **232** Isae. 3.3–7; **234** [Dem.] 43.5–16; **254** Dem. 39.1, 5, 7–18; **274** Ar. *Birds* 493–98; **371** [Plut.] *Lives of the Ten Orators* 833d-834b; **376** [Dem.] 49.66–67; **383** Dem. 18.132–33; **390a** Hyp. 4.1–3, 14–20, 30–31, 39.

125. [Aristotle], *Constitution of the Athenians (Ath. Pol.)* 26.4. Pericles' citizenship law. (date of composition 332–322; date of law 451/0)

See references and headnote under **1c**. Here the author mentions the law on citizenship authored by the prominent fifth-century politician Pericles (J. K. **Davies**, *Athenian Propertied Families 600–300 B.C.* [Oxford 1971], no. 11811). For additional references to this law see **184** Ar. *Birds* 1641–70, which suggests that the law was still being enforced in 414 (cf. **127** Dem. 57.30, schol. Aeschin. 1.39, Athenaeus 577b-c); Plutarch, *Pericles* 37.2–5 (which mentions an exception granted in the case of Pericles junior, Pericles' son by Aspasia of Corinth); Aelian, *Varia Historia* 13.24; *Suda* s.v. *dêmopoiêtos*. Before this law was passed, a child qualified for citizen status if his father was an Athenian citizen. Examples of men with Athenian fathers and foreign mothers' prominently exercising citizen rights before 451/0 include Cleisthenes, the father of Athenian democracy, whose father, Megacles, was an Athenian citizen and whose mother was Agariste, the daughter of Cleisthenes tyrant of Sicyon (cf. **84** Hdt. 6.130.2); and Cimon (**Davies**, *APF* no. 8429), the son of the Athenian Miltiades and the Thracian princess Hegesipyle, who was elected and served as a general after the passage of Pericles' citizenship law—a fact that demonstrates that the law was not retroactive.

Two years later, in the archonship of Antidotus [451/0], due to the large number of citizens, they decided, on the proposal of Pericles, that anyone who was not born from two citizen parents [*astoin*] should have no share in the city [*mê metechein tês poleôs*].

126. Harpocration s.v. *nautodikai* (*decretum* + commentary). Decree providing for lawsuit for participation in phratry by son of two foreign parents. (Harpocration *fl.* 2nd c. A.D.; Craterus *fl.* 3rd c. B.C.; Aristophanes' *Banqueters* produced 428/7 B.C.)

For Harpocration see references and headnote under **28**. For Aristophanes see headnote under **52**; on his *Banqueters* (now fragmentary) see D. M. **MacDowell**, *Aristophanes and Athens* (Oxford 1995) 27–29, 34–40. For Craterus, the author of a *Collection of Decrees*, most of which dated to the fifth century, see F. **Jacoby**, *Die Fragmente der griechischen Historiker* (Leiden 1957-) no. 342 (text and German commentary; the quotation below is *FGrHist* 342 F 4). The (poorly-attested) *nautodikai* were primarily, as their name indicates, "Judges of Sailors" (see the introduction to chapter 10); the decree quoted from Craterus probably postdates Pericles' citizenship law (**125** [Arist.] *Ath. Pol.* 26.4) and may date to the 430s.

The *nautodikai* were a body of magistrates at Athens: Craterus in the fourth book of his *Decrees* states, "If a person born from two foreign parents [*xenoin*] participates in a phratry, any willing Athenian to whom lawsuits [*dikai*] are available may prosecute, and he shall file the lawsuit with the *nautodikai* on the last day of the month." Aristophanes, *Banqueters*: "I want to give a bloody nose to [*bapsas*] a foreigner [*xenon*] and instantaneously [?denounce him] to the *nautodikai*."

127. Reenactment of Pericles' citizenship law. (403/2)

For Demosthenes 57 see references and headnote under **76**; for the scholion to Aeschines see M. R. **Dilts**, *Scholia in Aeschinem* (Stuttgart 1992: text). For Athenaeus' *Deipnosophistae*, a fictional account of a long symposium attended by numerous learned men, see S. D. **Olson**, *Athenaeus*: The Learned Banqueters, 7 vols. (Cambridge, MA 2006–11: text and translation); the quotation below comes from a part of the work in which the symposiasts are discussing famous prostitutes and their clients.

At some point between 414 (**184** Ar. *Birds* 1641–70) and the end of the Peloponnesian War (404), Pericles' citizenship law (**125** [Arist.] *Ath. Pol.* 26.4) ceased to be enforced, but in 403/2 (the archonship of Eucleides) it was reenacted (although note that the sources disagree on the identification of the proposer), again with no retroactive provision (**127a-b**). At the same time, it appears, *nothoi* were denied all rights of intestate succession: see the final sentence (a rider dated to 403/2) of **176** [Dem.] 43.51. These provisions remained in force down to the end of the Classical period (**134** [Arist.] *Ath. Pol.* 42.1–2).

a. Demosthenes 57 *Against Eubulides* 30. (ca. 345/4)

Moreover, it is evident that he was born at such a time that, even if he were of citizen birth [*astos*] on only one side, he was entitled to be a citizen [*politên*]: he was born, you see, before the archonship of Eucleides.

b. Scholion to Aeschines 1 *Against Timarchus* 39 (= Eumelus, *FGrHist* 77 F 2). (Eumelus *fl.* ?3rd c. B.C.; scholion of uncertain Byzantine date)

Eumelus the Peripatetic, in the third book of his *On Old Comedy*, states that one Nicomenes enacted a decree providing that no one born after Eucleides was archon should have a share in the city [*metechein tês poleôs*] unless he could demonstrate that both his parents were citizens [*astous*], but that those born before Eucleides should be left alone without examination.

c. Athenaeus, *Deipnosophistae* 577b-c. (Athenaeus *fl.* ca. A.D. 200; Carystius *fl.* ?late 2nd c. B.C.)

And the politician Aristophon, who proposed the law in the archonship of Eucleides providing that anyone not born from a citizen woman [*astês*] should be illegitimate [*nothon*], was himself proven by Calliades the comic playwright to have had a child by the prostitute [*hetairas*] Choregis, as . . . Carystius relates in the third book of his *Commentaries.*

128. *Inscriptiones Graecae* II[2] 1237.9–125 (*decreta*). Decrees of the phratry Demotionidae. (396/5 to mid-4th c.)

See references and headnote under **112**; also C. W. **Hedrick**, *The Decrees of the Demotionidai* (Atlanta 1990); S. D. **Lambert**, *The Phratries of Attica*[2] (Ann Arbor 1998) 95–141, 285–93 (text, translation, and commentary).

This inscription contains three decrees of the phratry Demotionidae, proposed by Hierocles (lines 9–68), Nicodemus (lines 68–113), and Menexenus (lines 114–126), and regulating the admission of members. The first decree is dated to 396/5, the second was passed sometime after the first, and the third appears to belong to the middle of the fourth century. The phratriarch was an official in charge of a phratry, and "the treasury" here refers to the treasury of the phratry. About the "(house of the) Deceleians" nothing certain can be said except that they formed a subgroup of the Demotionidae; for conjectures see Hedrick and Lambert. The *koureion* was a sacrifice offered by the father of a child; Koureotis was the name of one of the three days of the Apaturia (see **131** Dem. 39–40 [selections]). A *thiasos* was a religious association devoted to the worship of a particular god or hero (e.g., Heracles: Isaeus 9.30).

The following was resolved by the phratry members in [10] the archonship of Phormion at Athens [396/5] and in the phratriarchy of Pantacles of the deme Oeon. Hierocles made the motion. All those who have not yet undergone scrutiny [*diedikasthêsan*] in accordance with the law of the Demotionidae shall undergo scrutiny by the phratry members immediately. . . . If anyone is found to have been introduced when he is not a member of the phratry, the priest [20] and the phratriarch shall erase his name from the register kept by the Demotionidae and from the copy, and the one who introduced the rejected person shall be fined 100 drachmas, which shall be consecrated to Zeus of the Phratries; the priest and the phratriarch shall exact this money or else owe it themselves.

In the future the scrutiny shall occur the year after [the introducer of a candidate] sacrifices the *koureion*, on Koureotis during the Apaturia. . . . [30] If any of those rejected wishes to appeal to the Demotionidae, he may; in these cases the house of the Deceleians shall choose five men over thirty years of age as advocates [*synêgorous*], and the phratriarch and the priest shall bind them by oath to advocate in the most just manner and not to permit anyone who is not a phratry member to participate in the phratry. Any appellant whom the Demotionidae reject shall be fined 1,000 drachmas, [40] which shall be consecrated to Zeus of the Phratries; the priest of the house of the Deceleians shall exact this money or else owe it himself, and any other willing phratry member may exact the money for the treasury. These provisions shall apply from the archonship of Phormion on.

The phratriarch shall put to the vote all cases requiring scrutiny each year. If he does not put them to the vote, he shall be fined 500 drachmas, which shall be consecrated to Zeus [50] of the Phratries. The priest and any other willing person shall exact this money for the treasury.

. . .

[68] Nicodemus made the motion. In other respects [the phratry shall con-

duct itself] in accordance with the previous decrees established regarding the introduction of children and the scrutiny. But as to the three aforementioned witnesses, [the introducer] shall provide them at the preliminary hearing [*anakrisei*] from among the members of his own *thiasos*, to testify as to the questions asked and to swear by Zeus of the Phratries. . . . When the scrutiny takes place, the phratriarch shall not [80] put the vote regarding the children to the entire phratry before the members of the *thiasos* of the introducer himself have voted in secret, carrying their votes from the altar. The phratriarch shall count their votes in the presence of all members of the phratry present at the meeting and shall announce which way they have voted. If the members of the *thiasos* vote that [a candidate] should be a member of the phratry but the other [90] phratry members reject him, the members of the *thiasos*, except for those who accused or opposed [the candidate] during the scrutiny, shall be fined 100 drachmas, which shall be consecrated to Zeus of the Phratries. If the members of the *thiasos* reject [the candidate] and the introducer appeals to the entire phratry, and the entire phratry decides that [the candidate] should be a member, he shall be enrolled on the common registers; but if the entire phratry rejects him, [the introducer] shall be fined 100 drachmas, [100] which shall be consecrated to Zeus of the Phratries. And if the members of the *thiasos* reject [the candidate] and [the introducer] does not appeal to the entire phratry, the rejection by the members of the *thiasos* shall be binding. The members of the *thiasos* shall not cast their votes along with the rest of the phratry members concerning the children of members of their own *thiasos*.

. . .

The oath sworn by witnesses at the introduction of children [shall be]: "I attest that the boy whom [the introducer] is introducing [110] is his own legitimate [*gnêsion*] son by a wedded wife [*gametês*]. This is the truth, by Zeus of the Phratries. If my oath is truthful, may I enjoy many good things; but if my oath should be false, [may] the opposite [occur]."

[114] Menexenus made the motion. Be it resolved by the phratry members, concerning the introduction of children, in other respects [to act] in accordance with the previous decrees; however, in order that the phratry members may know who is going to be introduced, the name [of each candidate] with his father's name and deme and his mother's name and her father's name and deme shall be reported in writing to the phratriarch in the [child's] first year or in the year when [the introducer] conducts the *koureion*. Once the names have been reported in writing, the phratriarch shall inscribe and display them wherever the Deceleians frequent, and the priest shall also inscribe them on a white board and display them in the Temple of Leto.

129. Isaeus 3 *On the Estate of Pyrrhus* 75–76. Marital status of parents; presentation of daughter to father's phratry. (?ca. 389)

See references and headnotes under **85** and **90**. Here the speaker offers as proof of the illegitimacy of Phile (cf. **232** Isae. 3.3–7) the failure of her father (and the speaker's uncle) Pyrrhus to formalize his union with her mother and to present Phile to the members of his phratry. The *gamêlia* (marriage contribution) was a gift of money by a bridegroom to his phratry (cf. Isaeus 3.79; **130** Isae. 8.18–20; Demosthenes 57.43, 69) that was used to finance a celebratory feast and/or sacrifice. For the "law" (in our terms, the by-law) of a phratry cf. **128** *IG* II² 1237.9–125.

So, by introducing the daughter to his phratry and not adopting my brother as his son, that is what he would have accomplished; but by adopting him and not introducing her, he rendered her illegitimate [*nothên*], as was his right, and deprived her of his estate, and left him behind as heir to his property. [76] In fact, to prove that our uncle neither made the marriage contribution [*gamêlian*] nor saw fit to introduce to his phratry the daughter who my adversaries claim is his legitimate [*gnêsian*] child, although they have a law [on the topic], [the court clerk] will read to you the deposition of our uncle's fellow phratry members.

130. Isaeus 8 *On the Estate of Ciron* 18–20. Marital and citizenship status of parents; enrollment of sons in father's phratry. (?383–363)

See references and headnote under **39**. Here, in reply to his adversaries' attack on the citizen status of his mother, the speaker cites the facts that his father publicized the marriage and enrolled his sons in his phratry (contrast **129** Isae. 3.75–76) without objection. The Thesmophoria was a festival in honor of the goddess Demeter celebrated by women. For the oath sworn by the sponsor of a candidate for phratry membership—normally the candidate's father, if living—attesting that the candidate was the son of a married citizen woman, cf. **128** *IG* II² 1237.9–125.

It is clear, then, that our mother was the legitimate [*gnêsia*] daughter of Ciron not only from these things but also from our father's actions and from the decisions that the wives of his demesmen made about her. You see, when our father married her, he gave a wedding feast and invited three of his friends along with his relatives, and he made the marriage contribution to his phratry according to their laws. [19] The wives of his demesmen later selected her, along with the wife of Diocles of the deme Pithus, to preside at the Thesmophoria and conduct the customary rites with her. And when we were born, our father introduced us to his phratry, swearing in accordance with the established laws that he was introducing children by a citizen [*astês*] wedded [*engyêtês*] wife. None of the phratry members objected or claimed that these things were not true—and there are many members and they investigate such matters strictly. [20] Now, do not think that if our mother were of the sort that our adversaries claim, our father would have given a wedding feast and made a marriage contribution; instead, he would have concealed it all. Nor would the wives of his fellow demesmen have chosen her to join in conducting sacred rites with Diocles' wife and put her in charge of sacred things; instead, they would have entrusted these affairs to someone else. Nor would the members of the phratry have admitted us; instead, they would have brought accusations and put us to the test, if it were not agreed on all sides that our mother was the legitimate [*gnêsian*] daughter of Ciron.

131. Demosthenes 39-[Demosthenes] 40 *1–2 Against Boeotus* (selections). Naming ceremony (*dekatê*); enrollment of sons in father's phratry (and deme). (Mantias d. ca. 358; Dem. 39 delivered ?349/8; [Dem.] 40 delivered *post* 348/7)

See references and headnote under **74**. In these passages, Mantitheus describes how his father, Mantias, was compelled to acknowledge paternity of Boeotus and Pamphilus (a process that Mantitheus refers to as adoption: cf. **166** Dem. 39.35) and then to enroll them in his phratry; Mantias died before the next stage, enrollment in his deme, could be carried out. The phrase "being deprived of his country" (**131a**) is equivalent to "being deprived of his citizenship." The Apaturia (**131a**) was a religious festival held annually in the latter half of the month Pyanopsion (roughly October: p. 7). For the *dekatê* (**131b**, **131e**) cf. **77** [Dem.] 58.40; for the Delphinion (**131d**) see the introduction to chapter 1 and **20** Dem. 23.65–80, at §74. We have little solid evidence for the procedure and effects of *apokêryxis* ("renunciation" of a child: **131c**): see Harrison, *LA* 1.75–77.

a. Dem. 39.2–4.

Now, if my adversary were claiming to be the son of some other father rather than mine, I would reasonably be considered meddlesome for caring about what he wants to call himself. But as it is, he filed a lawsuit against my father . . . and commenced legal proceedings, claiming that he was his son by the daughter of Pamphilus, and that he was being treated terribly and being deprived of his country. [3] My father . . . was afraid to go to court [*dikastêrion*] . . . and was deceived by my adversary's mother. She had sworn that if he tendered her an oath concerning these matters, she would refuse to swear it, and once that was done they would have no further dealings. She got a sum of money deposited with a third party, and on those conditions he tendered the oath. [4] But she accepted it, and she swore that not only my adversary but his brother, the other one, as well, was a son of my father. Once she did that, it was necessary to introduce these two to the phratry; no argument remained. He introduced them, he adopted them; to cut short the intervening events, at the Apaturia he enrolled them in his phratry: my adversary here under the name Boeotus, and the other one under the name Pamphilus; I had already been enrolled under the name Mantitheus.

b. Dem. 39.20–21.

And in order that you may know not only that my father conducted the enrollment in the phratry as the witnesses have testified, but also that this is the name he gave me when he performed my tenth-day ceremony [*dekatên*], [To the court clerk:] please take this deposition.

DEPOSITION.

[21] You hear, men of Athens, that I have been in possession of this name for my entire life, while my father enrolled my adversary in his phratry, when he was forced to do so, under the name Boeotus. So I would happily ask him in front of you: if my father had not died, what in the world would you have done in the presence of the demesmen? Would you have refused to allow him to enroll you as Boeotus? . . . And yet if you allowed him, he would have enrolled you in the deme just as he did in the phratry.

c. Dem. 39.39.

Now, if my adversary is able to point out a law that gives children authority over their own names, you could correctly vote for what he is now proposing. But if the law, which you all know as well as I do, gives parents the authority not only to give the name in the beginning but even to erase it and renounce the child [*apokêryxai*] if they so desire, and if I have demonstrated that my father, who was entitled by the law, gave my adversary the name Boeotus and me the name Mantitheus, then how is it possible for you to vote for anything other than what I propose?

d. [Dem.] 40.10–11.

A lot of meetings over these matters took place, and my father kept asserting that he could not be convinced that these two were his sons. But finally Plangon, men of the jury (for the whole truth will be told before you), along with Menecles, set a trap for my father and deceived him with an oath that is considered by all men to be the greatest and most fearful: she agreed, upon receipt of 30 minae, that she would get these two adopted as sons of her brothers, and that she herself, if my father challenged her before the arbitrator to swear that the children were his, would not accept the challenge; that way these two would neither be deprived of their city nor be able to cause further problems for my father, since their mother did not accept the oath. [11] But after this agreement was made—why should I make it a long story? When she appeared before the arbitrator, Plangon violated all the terms of the agreement: she accepted the challenge and swore at the Delphinion a different oath, the opposite of the previous one, as most of you know, since the deed became famous. Thus, owing to his own challenge, my father was forced to abide by the arbitrator's decision, but he was indignant at what had happened and took it hard; despite the decision he did not see fit to accept these two into his house, but he was forced to introduce them to his phratry. He enrolled this one under the name Boeotus and the other one under the name Pamphilus.

e. [Dem.] 40.28.

And yet my adversary has reached such a level of audacity that he claims that my father celebrated the tenth-day ceremony [*dekatên*] for him.

132. Demosthenes 57 *Against Eubulides* 46. Descent from two citizen parents; enrollment of son in father's phratry and deme. (ca. 345/4)

See references and headnote under **76**. Here the speaker supports his claim to citizenship by citing the citizen status of his father and mother, his enrollment in his father's phratry and deme, and his tenure of religious and political offices, which were restricted to citizens. For the type of *dokimasia* mentioned here (scrutiny of candidates selected for public office, which included questions designed to ascertain the citizenship of both the candidate's parents), see [Aristotle], *Constitution of the Athenians* (*Ath. Pol.*) 45, 55, 59.

So, then, that I am a citizen [*astos*] both on my mother's side and on my father's you have all learned, in part from the testimony just given and in part from that given earlier about my father. It remains for me to say to you about myself what, in my opinion, is the simplest and most just statement of all; namely, that since I am the son of citizens [*astôn*] on both sides and have inherited both the property and the kinship [*genos*], I am a citizen [*politên*]. All the same, I will provide witnesses and prove all the relevant facts: that I was introduced to the phratry, that I was enrolled in the deme, that I was selected by those same men to draw lots among men of the highest birth for the priesthood of Heracles, and that I have held offices after passing scrutiny [*dokimastheis*].

133. Isaeus 12 *For Euphiletus* 9. Citizenship and marital status of parents. (344/3)

See especially W. **Wyse**, *The Speeches of Isaeus* (Cambridge 1904: text and commentary); R. F. **Wevers**, *Isaeus: Chronology, Prosopography, and Social History* (The Hague 1969); M. **Edwards**, *Isaeus* (Austin 2007: translation with introduction and notes); also F. **Blass**, *Die attische Beredsamkeit* (Leipzig 1887–98) 2.570–73; R. C. **Jebb**, *The Attic Orators from Antiphon to Isaeus*[2] (London 1893) 2.360–63; S. **Usher**, *Greek Oratory: Tradition and Originality* (Oxford 1999) 167–69.

This speech originates in the same review of the rolls of the demes as Demosthenes 57 (see headnote under **76**). In this case the members of Euphiletus' deme, Erchia, had struck him from their register (*lêxiarchikon grammateion*: **76** Dem. 57.30; **136** Isae. 7.13–17, 27–28, 30) on the grounds of improper birth; Euphiletus appealed the deme's decision, and Isaeus 12 was delivered by his paternal half-brother in the resulting trial, which took place in a regular jury-court (*dikastêrion*: p. 26; the type of action cannot be identified with certainty). Here the speaker offers as proof of Euphiletus' citizenship the willingness of Euphiletus' father and mother to swear to their parentage and to their citizenship and marriage status. For the Delphinion see **131** Dem. 39–40 (selections) with references.

And in addition to the depositions, men of the jury, first of all, Euphiletus' mother, who my adversaries admit is a citizen [*astên*], was willing to swear an oath in the presence of the arbitrator at the Delphinion that this man Euphiletus here is the son of herself and of our father. And who should know that better than she herself? Second, men of the jury, our father, who presumably, after Euphiletus' mother, best recognizes his own son, was willing both then and now to swear that this man Euphiletus here is his son by a citizen [*astês*] wedded [*gametês*] wife.

134. [Aristotle], *Constitution of the Athenians (Ath. Pol.)* 42.1–2. Citizenship (?and marital) status of parents; enrollment of son in father's deme and appeal in case of rejection; *dokimasia* by Council of 500. (332–322)

See references and headnote under **1c**. Here the author describes the requirements for citizen status. (1) A man must have two citizen parents; whether the parents must be married is a point of scholarly contention (see the introduction to this chapter). The phrase "was born in accordance with the laws" certainly refers to Pericles' citizenship law (**125** [Arist.] *Ath. Pol.* 26.4) and its reenactment (**127** Dem. 57.30, schol. Aeschin. 1.39, Athenaeus 577b-c); if either of these contained a marriage requirement, and/or if the phrase refers also to Solon's law on legitimacy (**83** [Dem.] 46.18), then citizenship was restricted to the children of married citizen parents (cf. **128** *IG* II^2 1237.9–125; **130** Isae. 8.18–20). (2) At the age of eighteen, he must be admitted to his father's deme and then pass a scrutiny (*dokimasia*) before the Council of 500. Note that this type of *dokimasia*—the examination for admission to the ranks of adult male citizens—is distinct from the scrutiny of candidates for public office (see **132** Dem. 57.46) and from the *dokimasia tôn rhêtorôn* (**64c** Aeschin. 1.28–30, 32).

The present state of the constitution is as follows. Those who are born from two citizen parents [*astôn*] have a share in the state; they are enrolled in their demes when they are eighteen years old. When they are being enrolled, the demesmen swear an oath and vote regarding them: first, whether they appear to be the age required by law, and if they do not, they go back to the [category of] boys; and second, whether one is a free person and was born in accordance with the laws. Then, if they vote to reject him on the grounds that he is not a free person, he has an appeal to the jury-court [*dikastêrion*], and the demesmen choose five men from among themselves as prosecutors; if he is found not to have the right to be enrolled, the city sells him [as a slave], while if he wins, the demesmen must enroll him. [42.2] After that the Council scrutinizes [*dokimazei*] those who have been enrolled, and if one is found to be younger than eighteen years, the Council fines the demesmen who enrolled him.

6.2. Adoption

See also **101** Dem. 41.3–4; **114** Dem. 41.5–7, 10; **129** Isae. 3.75–76; **131** Dem. 39–40 (selections); **144** Isae. 6.35–37; **163** [Dem.] 58.30–32; **166** Dem. 39.35; **186b** Isae. 3.72–74; **188** Isae. 10.4–5; **194** Isae. 11.1–5, 8–12, 17–18, 29–30; **195** Isae. 7.5–7; **196** [Dem.] 44.24–26, 32–34; **201** [Dem.] 46.14; **204** Isae. 3.67–69; **206** Isae. 10.9–10; **208** Aeschin. 3.21; **209** [Dem.] 44.67–68; **211** Isae. 6.5–7; **213** Isae. 9.7–12; **220** Isae. 9.3; **221** [Dem.] 44.64; **228** Isae. 3.40–50, 57–60, 62; **229** Isae. 6.3–4, 43–44, 52; **230** [Dem.] 44 (selections); **231** Isae. 5.6–7, 9, 12–18; **234** [Dem.] 43.5–16; **235** Isae. 4.24–25; **371** [Plut.] *Lives of the Ten Orators* 833d-834b.

135. Isaeus 2 *On the Estate of Menecles* 13–17, 19. Adoption, *inter vivos* and testamentary; capacity to adopt; introduction of son adopted *inter vivos* to phratry, religious brotherhood, and deme. (ca. 354/3)

See references under **103**. This speech was delivered in a *dikê pseudomartyriôn* (p. 29) arising from a dispute over the estate of Menecles. Here the speaker justifies his adoption *inter vivos* by Menecles by reference to Solon's testamentary law (**201** [Dem.] 46.14), which regulated adoption as well as wills (see the introduction to this chapter), and cites his unobstructed admission into Menecles' phratry, religious brotherhood, and deme.

Now, then, I will explain to you how the adoption occurred in accordance with the laws. [To the court clerk:] Please read the law itself, which commands that a person shall be permitted to dispose of his property however he wishes if there are no legitimate male children. [To the jury:] You see, gentlemen, the lawgiver enacted the law in this form for this reason: he saw that for childless men the only refuge from solitude and consolation in life was the ability to adopt whomever they wished. [14] So, since the laws allowed him to adopt on account of his childlessness, he adopted me: not by writing it in a will, gentlemen, when he was about to die, as some other citizens do, and not while he was ill; rather, while he was healthy, of sound mind, and of good intent, he adopted me and introduced me to the members of his phratry in the presence of my adversaries, and he enrolled me among his demesmen and among the members of his religious brotherhood [*orgeônas*]. [15] And at that time my adversaries made no objection on the grounds that he was not of sound mind. . . . You see, he lived not for one or two years but for twenty-three years after the adoption, and in all that length of time he did not regret any of his actions, since everyone agreed that he had made the right decision. [16] To prove that my statements are true, I will provide to you as witnesses to the adoption the members of his phratry, his religious brotherhood, and his deme; and to prove that he had the power to adopt, [the court clerk] will read you the actual law under which the adoption occurred. [To the court clerk:] Please read these depositions and the law.

DEPOSITIONS.

LAW.

[17] So the law itself makes it clear that Menecles had the power to adopt as his son whomever he wished, and the members of his phratry, his deme, and his religious brotherhood have testified to you that he did adopt. . . .

[19] And you can easily recognize from the following that Menecles made the adoption not when he was out of his mind or under the influence of a woman, but when he was of sound mind. First of all, his sister, concerning whom my

adversary has made the majority of his argument, to the effect that Menecles was under her influence when he adopted me, was given in marriage [*ên ekdedomenê*] long before the adoption occurred. So if he were adopting a son under her influence, he would have adopted one of her sons; she has two.

136. Isaeus 7 *On the Estate of Apollodorus* 13–17, 27–28, 30. Adoption, *inter vivos* and testamentary: enrollment of adopted son in father's *genos* (clan), phratry, and deme; vacant households. (350s)

See especially **Wyse**, *Isaeus* (text and commentary); **Wevers**, *Isaeus*; **Edwards**, *Isaeus* (translation with introduction and notes); also **Blass**, *AB* 2.551–55; **Jebb**, *AO* 2.325–27; **Usher**, *GO* 160–63.

This speech was delivered by Apollodorus' adopted son (the biological son of his uterine half-sister) in a *diadikasia* (see chapter 7) over Apollodorus' estate. Here the speaker describes the process of the adoption, including his admission into Apollodorus' clan (*genos*, here denoting a hereditary group of related families: cf. **1** [Trial and punishment of the Alcmaeonids for the killing of Cylon's partisans]), phratry, and deme. Maemacterion (§14) corresponds roughly to November on our calendar; the Thargelia (§15) was an annual religious festival celebrated in Thargelion (roughly May: p. 7); the Pythaid (§27) was another festival, held at Delphi shortly after the Thargelia. For the register of deme members (*lêxiarchikon grammateion*, §27) see **133** Isae. 12.9 with additional references in headnote; for the process before the phratry (§§16–17), including the terms of the oath sworn by the sponsor of a candidate for admission, cf. **128** *IG* II^2 1237.9–125; **130** Isae. 8.18–20. On the eponymous archon's role with regard to vacant households (§30) cf. **96** [Dem.] 43.75.

As to the fact that he personally, while he was alive, adopted me as his son, made me *kyrios* of his property, and enrolled me among the members of his clan [*gennêtas*] and his phratry, please pay attention to the following, gentlemen. [14] Apollodorus had a son, whom he brought up and treated attentively, as was fitting. While the son was alive, he expected to make him successor to his estate; but when the son died of illness last year during the month of Maemacterion, he became despondent at his circumstances and deplored his old age, but he did not forget who had treated him well from the beginning. He went to my mother, his sister, whom he valued most of all, and he asked to take me as his son, begged her permission, and got it. [15] He was so convinced that this should be done quickly that he immediately took me and brought me into his house and handed over the administration of all his affairs, saying that he was no longer able to conduct any of them and I would be able to do everything. And when the Thargelia occurred, he brought me before the altars in the presence of the members of his clan and phratry. [16] They have the same law whether a person introduces a biological or an adopted son: he must swear a pledge over the sacred offerings that he is introducing a child who is the offspring of a citizen woman [*astês*] and has been born properly, whether it is a biological or an adopted son. Even after the introducer does this, the others nonetheless must take a vote, and if the child is approved, then, and not before, they enroll him in the public register: such is the strictness that their regulations involve. [17] That being the law, and since the members of the phratry and clan neither disbelieved him nor were ignorant of the fact that I was his sister's son, they enrolled me in the public register by unanimous vote, after he swore his pledge over the sacred offerings. In that way I was adopted by him while he was alive, and I was enrolled in the public register as Thrasyllus son of Apollodorus, since he had adopted me in the aforementioned manner and the laws granted it to him.

. . .

[27] Before I came back from the Pythaid, Apollodorus told his demesmen that he had adopted me as his son, enrolled me among the members of his clan and phratry, and handed over his estate; and he directed them, if anything should happen to him before I arrived, to enroll me in the register of candidates for office [*lêxiarchikon grammateion*] as Thrasyllus son of Apollodorus and not to do otherwise. [28] They listened to this, and although at the elections my adversaries accused me and alleged that he had not adopted me as his son, on the basis of what they had been told and what they knew, they swore the oath over the sacred offerings and enrolled me, just as he had instructed. . . .

. . .

[30] You see, all those who are about to die take precautions for themselves so that they do not render their households [*oikous*] vacant, but rather that there be someone to offer the funerary sacrifices and conduct all the customary rites for them. This is why, even if they die childless, they at least adopt children and leave them behind. And not only do they make this decision privately, but the government of the city has made the same decision publicly as well: by law it assigns to the archon the oversight of households so that they do not become vacant.

137. [Demosthenes] 44 *Against Leochares* (selections). Posthumous adoption; enrollment of adopted son in father's phratry and deme; annulment of adoption. (?320s)

A. **Schäfer**, *Demosthenes und seine Zeit* (Leipzig 1858–87) 4.241–47; **Blass**, *AB* 3.1.568–72; L. **Gernet**, *Démosthène: Plaidoyers civils, Tome II, Discours*

XXXIX–XLVIII (Paris 1957: text, French translation, and notes); **Usher**, *GO* 268–70; D. M. **MacDowell**, *Demosthenes the Orator* (Oxford 2009) 92–98; A. C. **Scafuro**, *Demosthenes, Speeches 39–49* (Austin 2011: translation with introduction and notes).

This speech was delivered in a *dikê pseudomartyriôn* (p. 29) arising from a dispute over the estate of Archiades of the deme Otryne, whose adoptive history the speaker describes here. All the adopted sons were natal members of the deme Eleusis. The first of them, Leocrates I (the biological grand-nephew of Archiades), was adopted either by will or posthumously (contrast the language regarding his adoption in **137a** and **137c**); he later returned to his natal household, leaving behind his son Leostratus II in his place as Archiades' posthumous adoptee. Leostratus II later did the same, leaving behind his son Leocrates II in his place as Archiades' posthumous adoptee. Following the death of Leocrates II, Leostratus II attempted to reassert his previous standing as Archiades' adopted son, and when that failed, got his other son, Leochares, adopted as Archiades' son. For the rule of return for adopted sons cf. **138** Harpo. s.v. *hoti hoi poiêtoi* etc.; on claims to an estate, including *embateusis* (direct entry into possession of an estate: **137a**) and *diamartyria* (declaration on oath: **137c**), see chapter 7.

a. [Dem.] 44.17–19.

To start from the beginning, men of the jury, Meidylides and Archiades gave their sister in marriage [*ekdidoasin*] to Leostratus [I] of the deme Eleusis. Later, from the daughter of this married sister of theirs was born Leocrates [I], the father of this man Leostratus [II] here. . . . [18] . . . Not long afterward . . . Archiades fell ill and died unmarried. . . . [19] At that moment, Leocrates [I], the father of this man Leostratus [II] here, using his family connection through women as a pretext, adopted himself as Archiades' son and entered into possession [*enebateusen*] of the estate as though he had been adopted by Archiades while Archiades was still alive. When Meidylides arrived, he was furious at what had happened and ready to prosecute Leocrates [I]. But his relatives urged and begged him to let Leocrates [I] remain in Archiades' household [*oikôi*] as his adopted son, so Meidylides consented—not because he had been defeated in court [*dikastêriôi*], but because he had been utterly deceived by these men, and moreover, he was being swayed by his relatives as well.

b. [Dem.] 44.41.

When Leostratus [II] failed to get himself enrolled, he introduced his son Leochares as the adopted son of Archiades, in violation of all the laws, before the deme's scrutiny [*dokimasian*] occurred: he had not yet brought Leochares before the members of Archiades' phratry; instead, after Leochares was enrolled, he then persuaded a certain one of the phratry members and so got him enrolled in the phratry register.

c. [Dem.] 44.46–47.

The aforementioned Archiades . . . adopted as his son the grandfather of the man who has now made a declaration on oath [*diamemartyrêkotos*]; and that grandfather, after leaving behind in [the household of Archiades] a legitimate [*gnêsion*] son—this man's father Leostratus [II]—returned to the deme of Eleusis. [47] Later this Leostratus [II] himself did the same: after leaving behind a son [in the household of Archiades], he left and went back to his ancestral household [*oikon*].

138. Harpocration s.v. *hoti hoi poiêtoi* etc. Annulment of adoption. (Harpocration *fl.* 2nd c. A.D.; Antiphon d. 411 B.C.; date of Solon's laws 594/3 B.C.)

See references and headnote under **28**. In this entry Harpocration cites sources for the condition under which an adoption could be annulled. This citation is the only evidence for Antiphon's *Against Callistratus* (cf. Antiphon fr. 5 Thalheim); quotation from a specific axon (see, e.g., **2** *IG* I³ 104) indicates that the law attributed to Solon is genuine. For the rule of return cf. **196** [Dem.] 44.24–26, 32–34; **209** [Dem.] 44.67–68; **221** [Dem.] 44.64.

That adopted sons did not have the power to return to their ancestral household [*oikon*] unless they left behind legitimate [*gnêsious*] sons in the household of the adopter [is stated by] Antiphon in his speech *Against Callistratus Concerning a Guardianship* and Solon on the twenty-first [axon] of his laws.

6.3. Guardianship

See also **38** Lys. fr. 279 Carey; **64a** Aeschin. 1.13–15; **87** Dem. 27.4–5; **91** Dem. 27.55; **96** [Dem.] 43.75; **106** Lys. 32.6; **115** Dem. 30–31 (selections); **116** Harpo. (selections); **119** Dem. 27.15–17; **120** Dem. 29.33; **123** Harpo. s.v. *sitos*; **152** [Arist.] *Ath. Pol.* 56.6–7; **154** Harpo. s.v. *kakôseôs*; **161** Isae. 11.6, 31, 35; **167** Dem. 27.9–11; **173** *IG* II² 1631.429–41; **179** Dem. 36.8–9, 11, 34; **195** Isae. 7.5–7; **212** Lys. 32.5, 7; **217** D. L. 5.11–16; **234** [Dem.] 43.5–16; **253** Dem. 36.2–4, 12, 18–20; **257** Dem. 38 (selections); **293** Dem. 45.80–81; **321d** Finley, *SLC* no. 57.

139. Lysias 32 *Against Diogeiton* 8–10, 19–24. *Dikê epitropês*; allegations of guardian's malfeasance; termination of guardianship upon male ward's majority; account of guardianship; lease of estate (*misthôsis oikou*). (ca. 400)

See references and headnote under **106**. Here the speaker describes Diogeiton's conduct as guardian of the children of his brother Diodotus. For the type of *dokimasia* mentioned in §§9, 24 see **134** [Arist.] *Ath. Pol.* 42.1–2; for the value of the stater (§9) see **205** Lys. 19.39–40. "The Dionysia" (§21) refers to one of the two annual religious festivals in honor of the god Dionysus: the City Dionysia, celebrated in Elaphebolion (approximately March), and the Rural Dionysia, celebrated in Poseideon (approximately December: p. 7). On the trierarchy (§24) see p. 25.

When in time he had made Diodotus' death known to them and they had conducted the customary rites, for the first year they kept living in Peiraeus, since all the necessities had been left there. But when the necessities started running out, he sent the children up to the city [of Athens] and gave their mother in marriage [*ekdidôsin*] with a dowry of 5,000 drachmas, a thousand less than her husband had provided.

[9] Seven years later, when the elder of the two boys passed scrutiny [*dokimasthentos*], Diogeiton summoned them and told them that their father had left them 20 minae in cash and 30 staters. "So I," he said, "have spent a lot of my own money on your sustenance [*trophên*]. While I had it, it made no difference to me, but now I myself am in need. So you, since you have passed scrutiny and become a man, now see to it yourself where you will get your necessities from." [10] When they heard that, they were terrified, and they went to their mother in tears; then, taking her along, they came to me. They were in pitiful condition owing to their suffering and had been cast out in wretched fashion, and they cried and begged me not to allow them to be robbed of their patrimony and reduced to poverty, suffering hubris at the hands of those who should least act in such a manner, but instead to help them for their sister's sake and their own.

. . .

[19] Now I ask, men of the jury, that you pay attention to the account statement [*logismôi*], so that you may pity the boys for the magnitude of their sufferings and consider my adversary deserving of all citizens' anger. You see, Diogeiton has made all mankind so suspicious of one another that neither the living nor the dead have any more faith in their closest relatives than in their worst enemies. [20] He had the gall to deny receiving part of the money, and, after finally admitting that he possesses the rest, to report as receipt and expenditure on two boys and their sister 7 talents 4,000 drachmas in cash over a period of eight years. And he has reached such a level of shamelessness that,

having nowhere to assign the money, he charged to the account 5 obols a day for food for two boys and their sister; and as for shoes, the fuller's shop, and the barbershop, he has not recorded monthly or even yearly expenses but a total amount for the entire period of more than a talent in cash. [21] Although he did not spend 25 minae of [the stated] 5,000 drachmas for their father's tomb, he puts down half [the cost] under his own name and has charged the other half to them. And for the Dionysia . . . he reported that he bought a lamb for 16 drachmas and charged eight drachmas of that to the children. . . . [22] And for the other festivals and sacrifices he charged them with more than 4,000 drachmas in expenditures, as well as an enormous amount of other items that he collected and reckoned into the total amount—as if he had been left behind as the children's guardian [*epitropos*] so that he could show them documents instead of money, prove that they were penniless instead of wealthy, and so that, if they had any enemy inherited from their father, they could forget about him and make war on their guardian for depriving them of their patrimony.

[23] And yet if he were willing to do the right thing by the children, he could, in accordance with the laws that apply in the case of orphans to both incapable and capable guardians, have leased the estate [*misthôsai ton oikon*] and rid himself of a lot of problems; or he could have purchased land and supported the children from the proceeds. . . . [24] And here is the most terrible thing of all, men of the jury. He claims that when he was serving as joint trierarch with Alexis son of Aristodicus, he paid him a contribution of 48 minae, and he has charged half of it to these orphans, whom the city not only has made exempt while they are children but has released from all liturgies for a year after they pass scrutiny [*dokimasthôsin*].

140. Lysias fr. 428 Carey (= *Suda* s.v. *engeion*). Limit on guardians' freedom to invest property of their wards. (Lysias *fl.* 403-ca. 380; *Suda* composed late 10th c.A.D.)

For the *Suda* see references and headnote under **49**; in this portion of the entry under *engeion* ("on/in land"), the author quotes a short passage from an unidentified speech of Lysias. For a specific allegation of a maritime venture financed by the property of orphans see Lysias 32.25.

. . . whereas the law commands that guardians [*epitropous*] invest the property of orphans in land, this man declares that we are involved in maritime ventures.

141. Isaeus 5 *On the Estate of Dicaeogenes* 10–11. Guardian as *kyrios* of ward; next of kin as guardian (posthumous appointment?); allegations of guardian's malfeasance. (ca. 389)

See especially **Wyse**, *Isaeus* (text and commentary); **Wevers**, *Isaeus*; **Edwards**, *Isaeus* (translation with introduction and notes); also **Blass**, *AB* 2.543–48; **Jebb**, *AO* 2.349–55; **Usher**, *GO* 133–37.

For the persons and matters involved in this lawsuit see the headnote under **231** Isae. 5.6–7, 9, 12–18. Here the speaker describes the conduct of Dicaeogenes III as guardian of the children of Theopompus. The description of Dicaeogenes III as his wards' next of kin may indicate that he assumed guardianship on those grounds by posthumous appointment rather than as Theopompus' (*inter vivos* and/or testamentary) designee. On the disposition of an estate "before judgment" (*pro dikês*, §10) see **225** D. H. *Isaeus* 15.1.

In fact, he was their guardian [*epitropos*], *kyrios*, and opponent in litigation all at the same time, and they received no pity from him even in the slightest degree on account of their family relationship; instead, they became orphans, unprotected and without means, and they lacked everything, even daily necessities. This is how Dicaeogenes [III] here, their next of kin, acted as their guardian: Dicaeogenes [III], who handed over to their enemies what their father Theopompus had left them, and who himself robbed them, before judgment [*pro dikês*], of what their maternal uncle and their grandfather had given them. [11] And, most terrible of all, while they were children, he bought their ancestral house, tore it down, and made it into a garden next to his own house in the city. And although he was receiving 80 minae in revenue from the property of our uncle Dicaeogenes [II], he sent Dicaeogenes' [II] nephew Cephisodotus to accompany his own brother Harmodius to Corinth in the place of a servant; that is the level of hubris and brutality that he reached.

142. Lysias 19 *On the Property of Aristophanes* 8–9. ?Compulsory guardianship. (387/6)

See references and headnote under **108**. Here the speaker mentions his guardianship of Aristophanes' children (Aristophanes' widow is the speaker's sister). How the speaker was appointed guardian is not known; his statement that he has been "forced to support" the children may refer to legal and/or moral compulsion. On sycophancy (malicious prosecution) see p. 33.

Much more pitiable, it seems to me, are Aristophanes' children: although they have wronged no one either privately or publicly, not only have they lost their patrimony, in contravention of your laws, but what was their last remaining hope—to be brought up on the proceeds of their grandfather's estate—has been placed in such serious danger. And we, moreover, having been deprived of our relatives by marriage, having been deprived of the dowry, and having been forced to support three little children, are on top of that being maliciously prosecuted [*sykophantoumetha*] and risk losing what our ancestors acquired by just means and left to us.

143. Isaeus 8 *On the Estate of Ciron* 41–42. ?Posthumous appointment of guardian; allegations of guardian's malfeasance. (?383–363)

See references and headnote under **39**; here the speaker continues his attack on the character of Diocles of Phlya. Since the homicide victim—the husband of one of Diocles' uterine half-sisters—had been attempting to recover his wife's patrimony from Diocles (**39** Isae. 8.40–41), he probably did not designate Diocles as guardian, either *inter vivos* or by will; on this assumption, Diocles would have obtained the guardianship by appointment after the victim's death.

And he ordered a slave to kill the husband of the younger sister and then sent the slave abroad and turned the blame onto his sister; [42] and on top of that, by terrifying her with his abominable actions, he robbed her son of his property, having become his guardian [*epitropeusas*]: he occupies the farmland and has given the son the rocky ground.

144. Isaeus 6 *On the Estate of Philoctemon* 35–37. Eponymous archon's oversight of orphans: registration of guardians; procedure for lease of estate (*misthôsis oikou*). (365–363)

See especially **Wyse**, *Isaeus* (text and commentary); **Wevers**, *Isaeus;* **Edwards**, *Isaeus* (translation with introduction and notes); also **Blass**, *AB* 2.548–51; **Jebb**, *AO* 2.343–48; **Usher**, *GO* 149–54.

Isaeus 6 is a prosecution speech from a *dikê pseudomartyriôn* (p. 29) arising from a dispute over the estate of Philoctemon (and/or that of his father Euctemon: the speaker is intentionally confusing on this point). Here the speaker describes the actions of his adversaries Androcles and Antidorus. The adoption of the two boys—who the speaker claims are the biological sons of a freedman named Dion and a prostitute named Alce, and his adversaries claim are the biological sons of Euctemon and his second wife, Callippe—was either testamentary or posthumous. For securities (*apotimêmata*) cf. §5.3.2, especially **116a** Harpo. s.v. *apotimêtai* etc.

Seeing that Euctemon was utterly incapacitated by old age and not even able to get out of bed, they started looking for a way that, once he died, his property would be under their control. [36] And what did they do? They registered these two boys with the archon as adopted children of Euctemon's deceased sons, recording themselves as the guardians, and they instructed the archon to lease [*misthoun*] their estates [*oikous*] on the grounds that they were orphans. They did this so that part of the property would be leased in their names, part would constitute securities [*apotimêmata*] with boundary-markers [*horoi*] placed on them while Euctemon was still alive, and they themselves would become the lessees and receive the revenues. [37] And as soon as the jury-courts [*dikastêria*] convened, the archon made the proclamation [*proekêrytten*] and they bid on the lease. But some of the people in attendance reported the plot to the relatives, and the relatives came and explained the matter to the jurors, so the jurors voted not to lease the estates.

145. Demosthenes 27 / *Against Aphobus* 34, 40, 46, 49–50, 58, 60–61, 67. *Dikê epitropês*, including penal assessment (*timêma*) upon conviction and *epôbelia* (penalty for malicious prosecution); account of guardianship; allegations of guardians' malfeasance; testamentary appointment of guardians with stated conditions; lease of estate (*misthôsis oikou*). (364/3)

See references and headnote under **87**, and cf. **146** Dem. 28.15–16. Here Demosthenes details the mismanagement of his estate by his former guardians Aphobus, Demophon, and Therippides. In §67, we see that the *dikê epitropês* was an assessable lawsuit (*agôn timêtos*: p. 40). The potential *epôbelia* (see **41b** [Dem.] 47.64) of 100 mn. indicates that Demosthenes' proposed—and successful—*timêma* (penal assessment) was 10 tal.; the *timêma* proposed by the defendant Aphobus was 1 tal. (Demosthenes 30.32). For Demosthenes' reference to potential *atimia* consequent on his failure to pay the *epôbelia* cf. **170** Andoc. 1.73–79.

Moreover, men of the jury, in accordance with the account statement [*logon*] that they have produced, I will demonstrate to you from what they themselves admit to having received that the three of them are in possession of more than eight talents of my property, and that out of this Aphobus has personally received 3 talents 1,000 drachmas. . . .

. . .

[40] And you would understand this even more precisely if my adversaries had been willing to hand over to me the will that my father left. For in that will was written, as my mother says, everything that my father left, and from what sources my adversaries were to take what they were given, and in what manner they were to lease [*misthôsousi*] the estate [*ton oikon*].

. . .

[46] Moreover, my adversary himself had taken the female slaves in addition to the dowry, and was living in the house, and now that he has to give an accounting [*logon*] of these things, he claims that it is his own business. And he has reached such a level of shameful greed that he has even deprived my teachers of their fees and failed to pay some of the war-taxes [*eisphoras*], but charges these things to me anyway.

. . .

[49] And then he had the gall to say before the arbitrator that out of the money he had paid enormous debts on my behalf to Demophon and Therippides, his fellow guardians [*synepitropois*], and that they had received a lot of my money. But he could not prove either of these claims: he did not show in the documents that my father had left me in debt, nor has he provided as witnesses the people to whom he claims to have paid this money, nor again did he ascribe to his fellow guardians the same amount of money that he himself evidently received, but rather a lot less. [50] When he was questioned by the arbitrator about each of these things, as well as whether he had been managing his own property from the profits or by spending the principal, and whether if he were under guardianship he would have accepted this account statement [*logon*] from his guardians or would demand to recover the principal along with the interest accrued, he gave no answer to these questions. . . .

. . .

[58] My adversary could have had none of these problems if he had leased the estate in accordance with these laws here. [To the court clerk:] Take the laws and read them.

LAWS.

In accordance with these laws, Antidorus, from [an estate of] 3 talents 3,000 drachmas, received payment in six years of six talents and more from its being leased; and some of you saw it, since Theogenes of the deme Probalinthus, the lessee of his estate, counted out the money in the agora.

. . .

[60] So, then, since the estate that was left to me was of such a size as you heard in the beginning, and produced 50 minae as income from one-third of it, my adversaries, extraordinarily greedy for money as they are, even if they did

not want to lease the estate [*misthoun ton oikon*], could have, from those proceeds, leaving things in place as they were, supported [*trephein*] us and managed affairs with the city, and could have saved what remained from that. [61] And if they had made the rest of the estate, which was twice that amount, productive [*energon*], if they were after money, they could have taken a moderate amount from that for themselves, and in addition to [maintaining] the principal, they could have increased the estate for me from the income. But they did none of these things. . . .

. . .

[67] And now, by seeking to recover what is my own, I have placed myself in the greatest danger. You see, if my adversary gets acquitted—which heaven forbid—I will be fined 100 minae as an *epôbelia*. For my adversary, if you convict him, the penalty is assessable [*timêton*], and he will make the payment not out of his own money but out of mine; for me, though, the penalty is not assessable [*atimêton*], and so I will be not only deprived of my patrimony but also disfranchised [*êtimômenos*] as well, unless you take pity on me now.

146. Demosthenes 28 *2 Against Aphobus* 15–16. *Dikê epitropês*; appointment of guardians *inter vivos* with stated conditions, including leasing of estate (*misthôsis oikou*); guardian as *kyrios* of ward's property. (364/3)

See references and headnote under **87**. Here Demosthenes narrates the deathbed provisions made by his father, Demosthenes senior (cf. **87** Dem. 27.4–5). Demosthenes senior's instructions to his children's guardians-to-be were confirmed in his will (Demosthenes 27.41–43).

For my father, men of the jury, when he realized that he would not escape from his illness, summoned these three, sat his brother Demon down beside them, and placed our persons in their hands, calling us a trust. He gave my sister to Demophon, along with a dowry of two talents payable immediately, and pledged [*engyôn*] her to be his wife; he placed me, together with his property, in the trust of all of them jointly, and enjoined them to lease the estate [*misthôsai . . . ton oikon*] and to assist me in preserving the estate; [16] and at the same time he gave Therippides the 70 minae, pledged my mother to Aphobus with a dowry of 80 minae, and placed me upon Aphobus' knees. But Aphobus, the most unholy of all men, paid no attention to these things after he became *kyrios* of my property on these conditions; instead, having deprived me of all the money in concert with his fellow guardians [*synepitropôn*], he will now ask to receive your pity. . . .

147. Demosthenes 29 *3 Against Aphobus* 30–31. *Dikê epitropês*, including written statement of charge and penal assessment upon conviction (*timêma*). (?362/1)

See references under **120**. About two years after Demosthenes won his *dikê epitropês* against Aphobus (see **87** Dem. 27.4–5; **102** Dem. 30.15–17), Aphobus prosecuted Phanus, one of Demosthenes' witnesses, by *dikê pseudomartyriôn* (p. 29) for having given false testimony. Demosthenes delivered this speech as *synêgoros* (advocate: p. 28) for Phanus; here he discusses the *dikê epitropês* in which he convicted Aphobus (see **145** Dem. 27.34, 40, 46, 49–50, 58, 60–61, 67 with references).

Men of the jury, when I filed the lawsuit [*dikên*] over my guardianship [*epitropês*] against my adversary, I did not just compile a single assessment [*timêma*], as a person would do if he were endeavoring to mount a malicious lawsuit [*sykophantein*]; instead, I wrote in each item: where he got it from, how much the amount was, and who he got it from. . . . [31] Here, then, is the beginning of the charge: "Demosthenes charges Aphobus as follows: Aphobus has money belonging to me, held as the result of a guardianship [*epitropês*]: 80 minae, which he received as my mother's dowry in accordance with my father's will." This is the first of the sums of money of which I state that I have been deprived.

148. Demosthenes 36 *For Phormion* 20, 22. Termination of guardianship upon male ward's majority; account of guardianship; guardian as *kyrios* of ward's property. (?350/49)

Schäfer, *Demosthenes* 4.164–70; **Blass**, *AB* 3.1.461–67; J. E. **Sandys**-F. A. **Paley**, *Demosthenes: Select Private Orations* 2[4] (Cambridge 1910: text and commentary); L. **Pearson**, *Demosthenes: Six Private Speeches* (Norman, OK 1972: text and commentary); S. **Isager**-M. H. **Hansen**, *Aspects of Athenian Society in the Fourth Century B.C.: A Historical Introduction to and Commentary on the Paragraphe-speeches and the Speech Against Dionysodorus in the Corpus Demosthenicum (XXXII–XXXVIII and LVI)* (Odense 1975); **Usher**, *GO* 247–49; **MacDowell**, *Demosthenes 27–38* (translation with introduction and notes); ***idem***, *DO* 109–15.

This speech was delivered by a *synêgoros* (p. 28) of Phormion in Phormion's *paragraphê* (counter-indictment: p. 14) against a lawsuit initiated by Apollodorus, the elder son of Pasion and his wife Archippe, over a debt he claimed Phormion owed him. Here the speaker describes Phormion's conduct as guardian of Pasicles, the younger son of Pasion and Archippe (cf. **149** Dem. 45.37 with headnote).

Second, when Pasicles, having become a man, was receiving the account statement of his guardianship [*ton logon tês epitropês*], who, if on his own he hesitated to accuse his mother of destroying the documents, would not have indicated this to Pasicles, so that it could be investigated through him? . . .

[22] So, then, men of Athens, I think that, of the many significant facts from which it can be seen that Phormion here is not guilty of wrongdoing, the most significant of all is the fact that Pasicles, the brother of my adversary Apollodorus here, has not filed a lawsuit and is not bringing any of the charges that Apollodorus is. [To Apollodorus:] And yet obviously it cannot be that Phormion would have refrained from wronging the boy who had been left behind by his father and of whose property he was *kyrios*, having been left as his guardian, but would have wronged you, who were left behind a man, twenty-four years old, and who could easily secure your rights on your own behalf straightaway if you were somehow wronged.

149. Demosthenes 45 / *Against Stephanus* 37. Testamentary appointment of guardian with stated conditions. (?349)

See references and headnote under **56**. For the will of Pasion and the guardianship of his minor son Pasicles cf. **92** Dem. 45.27–28, 30; **148** Dem. 36.20, 22; **179** Dem. 36.8–9, 11, 34; for the appointment of a guardian on stated conditions cf. **146** Dem. 28.15–16.

And then [Phormion] goes around saying that Nicocles has testified that he acted as guardian [*epitropeusai*] in accordance with the will, and that Pasicles has testified that his guardianship was conducted [*epitropeuthênai*] in accordance with the will.

150. Demosthenes 38 *Against Nausimachus and Xenopeithes* 3–4, 14–15, 17, 23. *Dikê epitropês*, including time limit (*prothesmia*); account of guardianship; lease of estate (*misthôsis oikou*) and related *phasis* (declaration). (?ca. 346)

Schäfer, *Demosthenes* 4.207–11; **Blass**, *AB* 3.1.482–85; **Gernet**, *Démosthène: Plaidoyers civils I* (text, French translation, and notes); **Isager-Hansen**, *Paragraphe-speeches*; **Usher**, *GO* 250–51; **MacDowell**, *Demosthenes 27–38* (translation with introduction and notes); ***idem,*** *DO* 79–83.

Nausimachus and Xenopeithes, the sons of Nausicrates, claimed that the sons of Aristaechmus owed them debts, and had commenced *dikai blabês* (see chapter 8, especially **257** Dem. 38 [selections]), but Aristaechmus' sons entered a *paragraphê* (counter-indictment: p. 14) to block those lawsuits (technically, this *paragraphê* was brought against only one of the *dikai blabês*, but as all the *dikai blabês* were founded on the same allegations, the *paragraphê*, if successful, would have compromised the viability of the other *dikai blabês* as well). Demosthenes composed this speech for delivery by one of Aristaechmus' sons in the *paragraphê*; here the speaker describes the *dikai epitropês* against his father that were initiated and then dropped by his adversaries. For the time limit (*prothesmia*) of five years (i.e., five years after the ward reaches his majority) for a *dikê epitropês* (§17) cf., e.g., **234** [Dem.] 43.5–16 (*diadikasia* over previously adjudicated estate or *epiklêros*); **228** Isae. 3.40–50, 57–60, 62 (claim to estate). For *phasis* (declaration, §23) in connection with the estate of an orphan cf. **151** Harpo. s.v. *phasis*.

First, [the court clerk] will read to you the depositions stating that they released our father from the charges they brought in the matter of their guardianship [*epitropên*]. . . . [4] So, then, men of the jury, you have heard the depositions stating that they filed lawsuits [*dikas*] over their guardianship [*epitropês*] and dropped them, and that they have the money that was agreed upon.

. . .

[14] . . . My adversaries have written into the charge [*enklêma*] that they are now prosecuting that we owe them the money because our father recovered it and handed over this debt to them as still owing in his account of the guardianship [*tôi logôi tês epitropês*]. [To the court clerk:] Please take the actual charge and read it.

CHARGE.

[15] You hear written in the charge: "Aristaechmus having handed over the debt to me in his account of the guardianship." And yet when they were filing against my father for his guardianship, they wrote the opposite of this: at that time they were clearly charging that he had not rendered an account.

. . .

[17] Moreover, men of the jury, so that you may know that they are not only not being done wrong now but in fact are prosecuting us in violation of all the laws, I want to cite to you this law too, which explicitly states that if five years pass and they do not prosecute, no further lawsuit [*dikên*] shall be available to orphans concerning charges arising from their guardianship [*epitropês*]. [The court clerk] will now read you the law.

LAW.

. . .

[23] "They didn't lease [*emisthôsan*] our estate [*oikon*]," they'll probably say. [To Nausimachus and Xenopeithes:] No, because your uncle Xenopeithes didn't want to, and when Nicides brought a declaration [*phênantos*], he convinced the jurors to allow him to manage it. Everybody knows that.

151. Harpocration s.v. *phasis*. Definition of *phasis* (declaration). (Harpocration *fl.* 2nd c. A.D.; Lysias *fl.* 403-ca. 380 B.C.)

See references and headnote under **28**. In this entry Harpocration defines *phasis* as the name of two legal procedures; "the archon" is the eponymous archon, for whose oversight of orphans cf., e.g., **144** Isae. 6.35–37; **152** [Arist.] *Ath. Pol.* 56.6–7. This is our only evidence for the cited speech of Lysias (Lysias fr. 262 Carey); for *phasis* in the context of an orphan's estate cf. **150** Dem. 38.3–4, 14–15, 17, 23.

Phasis [declaration]: The word is used both of a public charge, when a person reports someone in possession of public property that he has not purchased, and it is used in reference to orphans' estates [*orphanikôn oikôn*]. When guardians [*epitropoi*] failed to lease the estate of their wards, any willing person would declare [*ephainen*] it to the archon so that it would be leased; he would also make a declaration if it had been leased for less than its value. For the first meaning one can find evidence in the works of Deinarchus and Demosthenes; for the [type of] declaration concerning orphans' estates, in Lysias' speech *Against the Declaration of the Orphan's Estate*.

6.4. *Kakôsis* (Maltreatment)

See also **224** [Arist.] *Ath. Pol.* 43.4; **392a** Harpo. s.v. *eisangelia*.

152. [Aristotle], *Constitution of the Athenians* (*Ath. Pol.*) 56.6–7. Lawsuits under supervision of eponymous archon, including lawsuits for maltreatment: preliminary hearing (*anakrisis*); trial in *dikastêrion*; oversight of orphans, including *epiklêroi*; lease of estate (*misthôsis oikou*). (332–322)

See references and headnote under **1c**. Here the author discusses the duties of the eponymous archon (cf. **45** Dem. 37.33; **98** [Andoc.] 4.13–14, Plut. *Alcib.* 8.4–6; **100** Isae. 3.77–78). "Without risking a fine" means that the standard fine of 1,000 drachmas for prosecutors in public lawsuits who received less than 20 percent of the jurors' votes (p. 33; cf., e.g., **59** Hyp. 1.12) did not apply; while the author attributes the lack of such a fine specifically to actions for *kakôsis goneôn*, it is known also to have been absent from actions for *kakôsis epiklêrou* (**164** Dem. 37.45–46; **228** Isae. 3.40–50, 57–60, 62) and probably was absent from all actions for *kakôsis*. For the archon's oversight of widows and orphans cf. **96** [Dem.] 43.75 and **§6.3**. For "production in plain sight" (*emphanôn katastasis*) cf. **218** Isae. 6.29–32; **225** D. H. *Isaeus* 15.1. On *epiklêroi* see chapter 7; the fact that the archon oversees the leasing of estates conveyed with minor *epiklêroi* until they turn fourteen indicates that they were normally married at that age (cf. the introduction to chapter 5). On securities (*apotimêmata*) cf. **144** Isae. 6.35–37 and **§5.3.2**.

[The following] indictments [*graphai*] and private lawsuits [*dikai*] are assigned to him, for which he conducts preliminary hearings [*anakrinas*] before bringing them to a jury-court [*dikastêrion*]: for maltreatment of parents [*goneôn kakôseôs*]—these anyone who wishes may prosecute without risking a fine [*azêmioi*]; for maltreatment of orphans [*orphanôn kakôseôs*]—these are available against their guardians; for maltreatment of an *epiklêros* [*epiklêrou kakôseôs*]—these are available against their guardians and against their husbands; for maltreatment of the estate of an orphan [*oikou orphanikou kakôseôs*]—these also are available against their guardians; for insanity [*paranoias*], if a person accuses someone of squandering his patrimony due to insanity; for the selection of distributors [*eis datêtôn hairesin*], if a person is unwilling to divide property held in common; for the establishment of a guardianship [*eis epitropês katastasin*]; for the adjudication of a guardianship [*eis epitropês diadikasian*]; for production in plain sight [*eis emphanôn katastasin*]; for a man's registering himself as a guardian [*epitropon hauton engrapsai*]; and awards [*epidikasiai*] of estates and *epiklêroi*.

[56.7] He also oversees orphans, *epiklêroi*, and women who claim to be pregnant upon the death of their husbands; and he has the authority to impose a fine on the offenders or to bring the matter to a jury-court [*dikastêrion*]. Also, he leases out the estates [*oikous*] of orphans, and of *epiklêroi* until they turn fourteen, and receives the securities [*apotimêmata*]; and if guardians fail to provide the children with their maintenance [*siton*], he is the one who exacts it.

153. Menander fr. 279 (328) Koerte-Thierfelder. ?*Graphê* (or *eisangelia*) *kakôseôs*. (324–292/1)

For Menander see references and headnote under **89**; for his play *Misogynês* (*The Misogynist*) see A. **Koerte**-A. **Thierfelder**, *Menandri quae supersunt*, vol. 2 (Leipzig 1959: text with Latin notes); A. W. **Gomme**-F. H. **Sandbach**, *Menander: A Commentary* (Oxford 1973) 700–701. In this fragment, the protagonist's wife may be threatening him.

I swear to you by Helios, I will bring an indictment for maltreatment [*graphên kakôseôs*] against you.

154. Harpocration s.v. *kakôseôs*. Lawsuits for maltreatment (*kakôsis*). (Harpocration *fl.* 2nd c.A.D.; Demosthenes 24 delivered 353/2 B.C.; Lysias *fl.* 403-ca. 380 B.C.; Hypereides d. 322 B.C.)

See references and headnote under **28**. Here Harpocration discusses the various lawsuits for maltreatment. For the references see, in order, **160** Dem. 24.103, 107; Lysias frr. 125–27 Carey (*On the Estate of Hegesander*; the lacuna after "*On Behalf of*" precludes identification of the second speech of Lysias); Hypereides fr. 160 Jensen (which replicates this entry); Lysias frr. 299–302 Carey, including fr. 302 = **61** Harpo. s.v. *biaiôn*. "Without a water-clock" (see p. 37) means that speakers in these lawsuits had no time limit.

Kakôseôs [for maltreatment]: the name of a lawsuit [*dikês*] granted to *epiklêroi* against those who have married them, to parents [*goneusi*] against their children, and to those who prosecute on behalf of orphans against their guardians: Demosthenes, *Against Timocrates*; Lysias in his speech *On the Estate of Hegesander* and in his speech *On Behalf of*. . . ; and Hypereides, *On the Estate of Pyrrhander*. That any willing person could bring an indictment [*graphesthai*] for maltreatment of parents [*kakôseôs goneôn*] and could assist *epiklêroi* is evidenced in the aforementioned speech of Hypereides and in Lysias' speech *Against Philonides for Acts of Violence*, if genuine. [The lawsuit] was also without a water-clock [*aneu hydatos*].

6.4.1. *KAKÔSIS GONEÔN* (MALTREATMENT OF PARENTS)

See also **64a** Aeschin. 1.13–15; **64c** Aeschin. 1.28–30, 32; **71** Lys. 10 (selections); **105b** Lys. 13.45; **170** Andoc. 1.73–79; **387f** Lyc. 1.147.

155. Diogenes Laertius 1.55 (?*lex* + commentary). Solonian law on maltreatment of parents. (date of composition 2nd-3rd c.A.D.; law attributed to Solon, 594/3 B.C.)

R. D. **Hicks**, *Diogenes Laertius: Lives of Eminent Philosophers*, 2 vols. (Cambridge, MA 1958–59: text and translation).

Diogenes Laertius' work, commonly titled in English *Lives of the Philosophers*, discusses the lives and teachings of ancient philosophers down to the second century A.D. This excerpt from his section on Solon (1.45–67) appears to contain a direct quotation of a law on *kakôsis goneôn*, or at least an accurate paraphrase: the penalty of *atimia* is attested elsewhere (see headnote under **157** Lys. 13.91) for the Classical period (although the meaning may have changed by then: see p. 41), and the simplicity of the language would be consistent with an Archaic law.

Solon is also considered to have made excellent legislation: "if a person does not support [*trephêi*] his parents [*goneas*], let him be disfranchised [*atimos*]," and similarly for the person who has devoured his patrimony.

156. Plutarch, *Solon* 22.1, 4. Solonian exceptions to mandatory support of parents. (date of composition late 1st-early 2nd c. A.D.; laws attributed to Solon, 594/3 B.C.; Heracleides of Pontus *fl.* 4th c. B.C.)

See references and headnote under **1d**. The first of these laws (§22.1) is mentioned also by Galen, *Protrepticus* 15 (late second or early third century A.D.), which does not add any information. Heracleides of Pontus, a philosopher of the fourth century B.C., was a student of Plato and Aristotle who composed—among other works—a treatise *On Laws*, which is the presumptive source of Plutarch's second law (§22.4): see F. **Wehrli**, *Die Schule des Aristoteles*, vol. 7 (Basel 1969: text and German commentary) 44–45, 109–10. For another exception to the mandatory support of a father see **64a** Aeschin. 1.13–15.

. . . and [Solon] wrote a law providing that it should not be compulsory for a son to support [*trephein*] a father who had not taught him a craft.

. . .

[22.4] Even more severe was the provision that it should not be compulsory for children born of a prostitute to support [*trephein*] their fathers, as Heracleides of Pontus has related.

157. Lysias 13 *Against Agoratus* 91. Acts constituting *kakôsis goneôn*; ?death penalty for *kakôsis goneôn*. (ca. 398)

See references and headnote under **14**. Here the speaker responds to Agoratus' claim to be a naturalized Athenian citizen by alleging that, if so, Agoratus has maltreated his "adoptive father" (i.e., the Athenian state) as well as his biological father. The death penalty for *kakôsis goneôn* is not otherwise attested; our other sources (**64c** Aeschin. 1.28–30, 32; **155** D. L. 1.55; **158** Xen. *Mem.* 2.2.13; **160** Dem. 24.103, 107; **170** Andoc. 1.73–79) state a penalty of *atimia*.

In every way, it seems to me, he deserves not just one death. He claims to have been adopted by the people, but he clearly maltreated [*kakôsas*] the people, whom he claims as his father, by compromising and betraying everything by which the people was becoming greater and stronger. So since he beat his biological father and furnished him with none of the necessities, and robbed his adoptive father of all the good things he had, how is it that on that account too, in accordance with the law on maltreatment [*kakôseôs*], he does not deserve to be punished with death?

158. Xenophon, *Memorabilia* 2.2.13. Acts constituting *kakôsis goneôn*; person convicted of *kakôsis goneôn* barred from holding office. (early 4th c.)

See references and headnote under **53**; here Socrates, addressing Aristippus, refers to forms and consequences of *kakôsis goneôn*. The bar on office-holding was a standard element of *atimia* (cf., e.g., **64c** Aeschin. 1.28–30, 32: those convicted of *kakôsis goneôn* could not address the Assembly and therefore *a fortiori* could not hold office). For the type of *dokimasia* (scrutiny) mentioned here cf. **132** Dem. 57.46; among the mandatory questions posed to the candidate were "Do you have a family tomb, and where is it?" and "Do you treat your parents well?" ([Aristotle], *Constitution of the Athenians* [*Ath. Pol.*] 55.3).

"So, then, you are prepared to look after these people, but you do not think you must take care of your mother, who loves you most of all? Don't you know that the city . . . , if a person fails to take care of his parents [*goneas*], imposes punishment on him and rejects him at his scrutiny [*apodokimazousa*] and forbids him to hold office [*archein*] . . . ? And, by Zeus, if a person fails to adorn the graves of his deceased parents, the city investigates that too during the scrutinies [*dokimasiais*] of magistrates [*archontôn*]."

159. Isaeus 8 *On the Estate of Ciron* 32. Acts constituting *kakôsis goneôn*; ?definition of *goneis* ("parents"). (?383–363)

See references and headnote under **39**. Here the speaker contends that he would be liable for *kakôsis goneôn* if he failed to support his parents, grandparents, or great-grandparents; the relevant law, which is paraphrased but not quoted, may not have specified who qualified as *goneis* (cf. **155** D. L. 1.55).

And this is clear not only from this law but also from the law on maltreatment [*kakôseôs*]. You see, if my grandfather were alive and lacked the necessities, it is not my adversary but we who would be liable for maltreatment. The law commands people to support [*trephein*] their parents, and parents [*goneis*] are one's mother and father and grandfather and grandmother and their mother and father, if they are still living: they are the origin of the family [*genous*], and their property is handed down to their descendants, and for that reason it is necessary to support them, even if they leave nothing behind.

160. Demosthenes 24 *Against Timocrates* 103, 107. Acts constituting *kakôsis goneôn*; law providing that person convicted of *kakôsis goneôn* be barred from agora on pain of imprisonment; law on theft. (353/2)

Schäfer, *Demosthenes* 1.369–90, 4.63–65; W. **Wayte**, *Demosthenes*: Against Androtion *and* Against Timocrates (Cambridge 1882: text and commentary); H. **Weil**, *Les plaidoyers politiques de Démosthène*, ser. 2 (Paris 1886: text and French commentary); **Blass**, *AB* 3.1.280–88; J. H. **Vince**, *Demosthenes III: Against Meidias, Androtion, Aristocrates, Timocrates, Aristogeiton: XXI–XXVI* (Cambridge, MA 1935: text and translation); **Usher**, *GO* 201–4; **MacDowell**, *DO* 181–96.

Demosthenes wrote this speech for delivery by Diodorus in a prosecution of Timocrates by *graphê paranomôn* or *graphê nomon mê epitêdeion theinai* (for proposing illegal or unsuitable legislation: p. 14). Here Diodorus compares Timocrates' proposal to laws that he attributes, perhaps correctly, to Solon. (At §104 Diodorus has laws, including one on *kakôsis goneôn*, read out to the jury; unfortunately, the purported text of the laws that follows in §105 is clearly spurious.) On theft see chapter 9. For the *atimia* (disfranchisement) incurred by a man convicted of maltreating his parents—which, as we see here, included a prohibition against his entering the agora—cf., e.g., **170** Andoc. 1.73–79; the "helpers of old age" in §107 are the laws mentioned in §103.

The laws that Solon . . . established state that if a person is convicted of theft [*klopês*] and not sentenced to death, the additional punishment of imprisonment shall be inflicted upon him, and that if a person convicted of maltreatment of his parents [*kakôseôs tôn goneôn*] intrudes upon the agora, he shall be imprisoned. . . .

. . .

[107] [To Timocrates:] What sufficient penalty could you pay, or by what suffering could you suffer what you should—you who (to ignore the rest) defile the helpers of old age, which both compel us to support [*trephein*] our parents [*goneas*] while they are alive and ensure that they obtain the customary rites when they die?

6.4.2. *KAKÔSIS ORPHANÔN* (MALTREATMENT OF ORPHANS)

See also **96** [Dem.] 43.75.

161. Isaeus 11 *On the Estate of Hagnias* 6, 31, 35. *Eisangelia kakôseôs orphanôn*: penalty and removal of convicted person from guardianship of victim. (*post* 361/0)

See especially **Wyse**, *Isaeus* (text and commentary); **Wevers**, *Isaeus*; W. E. **Thompson**, De Hagniae Hereditate: *An Athenian Inheritance Case* (Leiden 1976); **MacDowell**, *LCA* 103–108; **Edwards**, *Isaeus* (translation with introduction and notes); also **Blass**, *AB* 2.565–70; **Jebb**, *AO* 2.355–60; **Usher**, *GO* 154–57.

This speech concerns the same estate as [Demosthenes] 43 (see references and headnote under **4**); it was delivered in an *eisangelia kakôseôs orphanôn* that preceded the *diadikasia* attested by [Dem.] 43 by about fifteen years. The defendant and speaker, Theopompus, stands accused of maltreating his ward, the orphaned son of his brother Stratocles, by depriving him of half of the estate of Hagnias, the speaker's patrilateral second cousin (§§8, 18) and the patrilateral second cousin once removed of Stratocles' son (see **194** Isae. 11.1–5, 8–12, 17–18, 29–30). The prosecutor is another of the boy's guardians. Note that Theopompus uses the specific term *eisangelia* (§6) and the general term *graphê* (§§31, 35) interchangeably to refer to the procedure by which he is being prosecuted; cf. **392a** Harpo. s.v. *eisangelia*. For the meaning of the phrase *peri tou sômatos* (§35) see **70** Lys. 9.5–12, 15–16.

You hear that he is unable to state the degree of kinship [*anchisteian*] but instead gives every answer other than the one you need to know. And yet a person who is acting justly should not be at a loss but should answer immediately, and he should not only do that but also swear an oath and provide witnesses to the degree of kinship [*genous*], so that you would find him more credible. But as it is, in matters where he has given no answer, provided no witnesses, sworn no oath, and read out no law, he thinks that you, who have sworn an oath to vote in accordance with the laws, should believe him and convict me in this impeachment [*eisangelian*] in violation of the laws: that's how wicked and shameless a man he is.

. . .

[31] These, then, are the reasons that he did not file a claim, not because he was obstructed by me or the laws; these are the excuses he has made for arriving at these malicious allegations [*sykophantias*], on the basis of which, by bringing

an indictment [*graphên*] and slandering me, he hopes to get money and remove me from the guardianship [*epitropês*].

. . .

[35] This is what the laws command—not, by Zeus, that I defend myself in indictments [*graphas*] concerning matters for which they have provided private lawsuits [*dikas idias*], nor that I be at risk concerning my person [*peri tou sômatos*] because I do not share with the boy what I received by vote from you, by defeating those who were in possession. Now, if I possessed anything that admittedly belonged to the boy, and had managed it badly such that he was being maltreated [*kakousthai*], then it would be proper for me to be prosecuted by means of this indictment [*graphên*]—but not, by Zeus, in the case of my own property.

162. Aeschines 1 *Against Timarchus* 158. ?Acts constituting *kakôsis orphanôn*; ?arrest of person accused of *kakôsis orphanôn*. (346/5)

See references and headnote under **57**. Here Aeschines refers to an allegedly well-known case in which an orphan accused a customer ("this service" refers to prostitution) of failing to pay his fee and brought a charge before the eponymous archon. In Athenian legal contexts, the verb *apagein* (*apêgagen*, "haled") regularly refers to the procedure of summary arrest (*apagôgê*: cf., e.g., **12b** Andoc. 1.90–91; **12c** Andoc. 1.94; **20** Dem. 23.65–80, at §80; **57a** Aeschin. 1.91; **302b** [Arist.] *Ath. Pol.* 52.1), which is nowhere else attested as a remedy for *kakôsis*. If Aeschines is using the verb in this technical sense, and if his account of the event is accurate—both of which propositions are dubious—then it is possible that the arrest followed the filing of an *eisangelia kakôseôs orphanôn*: see M. H. **Hansen**, Apagoge, Endeixis *and* Ephegesis *against* Kakourgoi, Atimoi *and* Pheugontes (Odense 1976) 29; N. **Fisher**, *Aeschines*: Against Timarchos (Oxford 2001) 302–305.

Now, as for those who are of the same habits as Timarchus, in an attempt to avoid enmities I will mention those who least concern me. Who among you does not know of Diophantus, the one called "the orphan," who haled [*apêgagen*] the foreigner before the archon whose assistant was [*parêdreuen*] Aristophon of the deme Azenia, making the accusation that he had been deprived of 4 drachmas for this service and citing the laws that command the archon to oversee orphans. . . ?

163. [Demosthenes] 58 *Against Theocrines* 30–32. Acts constituting *kakôsis orphanôn*; ?*graphê* (or *eisangelia*) *kakôseôs orphanôn*. (ca. 340)

See references and headnote under **77**. Here the speaker describes Theocrines' initiating and then dropping a prosecution (probably an *eisangelia*, although the speaker uses the generalizing term *graphê*: cf. **160** Isae. 11.6, 31, 35) against Polyeuctus for maltreatment of the orphan Charidemus. The decree proposed by the speaker's father (§30) provided for the perpetual maintenance (*sitêsis*) of Charidemus at state expense at the Prytaneion (on which cf. **20** Dem. 23.65–80); "the archon" (§32) is the eponymous archon. The speaker's assertion in §31 that no adopted son has ever forfeited property held by virtue of the adoption is itself almost certainly a lie: cf. **196** [Dem.] 44.24–26, 32–34.

When [Theocrines] was prosecuting my father, . . . he said that the boy concerning whom the decree had been written was the victim of a plot. In that decree my father had proposed maintenance [*sitêsin*] for Charidemus son of Ischomachus, [31] and Theocrines asserted that if the boy returned to his ancestral household [*oikon*], he would lose all the property that Aeschylus, who had adopted him as his son, had left him. But this was a lie, since that, men of the jury, has never happened to any adopted son. He also said that Polyeuctus, the husband of the boy's mother, had been responsible for all this, since he wanted to possess the boy's property himself. The jurors became angry at these statements, and they thought that the actual decree and the gift were in accordance with the laws, and that in fact the boy was about to be robbed of his property. So they fined my father 10 talents on the grounds that he was cooperating with Polyeuctus in the matter, and they believed that my adversary had actually helped the boy.

[32] . . . When, however, this worthy individual realized that people were angry and that he had gained trust as not being completely unholy, he issued a summons to Polyeuctus, brought an indictment [*graphên*] for maltreatment [*kakôseôs*] against him with the archon, and submitted the claim [*lêxin*] to Mnesarchides, the [archon's] assistant [*paredrôi*]. But upon receiving 200 drachmas from Polyeuctus and selling for a small profit these terrible accusations for which he had gotten my father fined 10 talents, he dropped the lawsuit and revoked the indictment, betraying the orphan.

6.4.3. *KAKÔSIS EPIKLÊROU* (MALTREATMENT OF AN *EPIKLÊROS*)

See also **45** Dem. 37.33; **96** [Dem.] 43.75; **180** Plut. *Solon* 20.2–4; **181** [Dem.] 43.54; **228** Isae. 3.40–50, 57–60, 62.

164. Demosthenes 37 *Against Pantaenetus* 45–46. Acts constituting *kakôsis epiklêrou*; *eisangelia kakôseôs epiklêrou*, including penalty upon conviction and lack of penalty for malicious prosecution. (ca. 346)

See references and headnote under **23**. In a previous trial, probably a private lawsuit over mining rights, Pantaenetus had accused Euergus of violating the seclusion of *epiklêroi* under Pantaenetus' charge; as evidence against the accusation the speaker cites Pantaenetus' failure to bring an *eisangelia* for maltreatment of *epiklêroi*. (The relation of the *epiklêroi* to Pantaenetus is uncertain: they may be his own daughters, although in that case they would not technically be *epiklêroi* until his death; if they are not his daughters, he is presumably their guardian.) The seclusion of respectable women and girls from unrelated men, whatever its extent in practice, is regarded in Attic oratory as paramount (cf., e.g., **75** Dem. 21.79, 81, 83–84, 88). For the penal formula "whatever he must suffer or pay," which indicates an *agôn timêtos* (assessable lawsuit: p. 40) without penal limit, see **96** [Dem.] 43.75, and cf., e.g., **35** Dem. 21.47. For the absence of a fine for malicious prosecution cf. **152** [Arist.] *Ath. Pol.* 56.6–7.

My adversary accused Euergus, in addition to everything else, of going to his house in the country and intruding upon his *epiklêroi* and his mother, and he arrived in the jury-court [*dikastêrion*] with the laws concerning *epiklêroi*. [46] To this day he has never had the matter examined before the archon, whom the laws command to oversee such affairs and in whose court the risk to the wrongdoer is whatever [it is decided that] he must suffer or pay, while the remedy involves no fine for the prosecutor; nor has he impeached [*eisêngeilen*] either me or Euergus as wrongdoers, but he made these accusations in the jury-court and secured a judgment [*dikên*] of 2 talents.

165. Pollux, *Onomasticon* 8.53 = Demosthenes fr. 7 Baiter-Sauppe. *Eisangelia* for improper cohabitation with *epiklêros*. (date of composition late 2nd c. A.D.; Demosthenes d. 322 B.C.)

For Pollux see references and headnote under **117**. The sentence below appears as Demosthenes fr. 7 in J. G. **Baiter**-H. **Sauppe**, *Oratores Attici*, vol. 2 (Zürich 1850) and as Demosthenes fr. IV.1 in R. **Clavaud**, *Démosthène:*

Lettres et fragments (Paris 1987); the date of the *Against Medon* is unknown. Improper cohabitation with an *epiklêros* may refer to a man's living as the husband of an *epiklêros* when he is not her father's closest male relative and therefore lacks the right to do so (see chapter 7), or to the failure of an *epiklêros*' husband to perform his spousal duties (**180** Plut. *Solon* 20.2–4).

Demosthenes in his speech *Against Medon* says that impeachments [*eisangelias*] also occurred against those who improperly cohabited with an *epiklêros.*

CHAPTER 7

Estates and *Epiklêroi*

Handbooks: J. H. **Lipsius**, *Das attische Recht und Rechtsverfahren* (Leipzig 1905–15) 537–88; A. R. W. **Harrison**, *The Law of Athens* (Oxford 1968–71) 1.122–62, 2.124–31; D. M. **MacDowell**, *The Law in Classical Athens* (Ithaca, NY 1978) 92–108; S. C. **Todd**, *The Shape of Athenian Law* (Oxford 1993) 216–31. **Studies:** E. **Caillemer**, *Le droit de succession légitime à Athènes* (Paris 1879); L. **Beauchet**, *Histoire du droit privé de la république athénienne* (Paris 1897) 1.398–535, 2.1–72, 3.423–709; W. **Wyse**, *The Speeches of Isaeus* (Cambridge 1904); L. **Gernet**, "Sur l'épiclérat," *REG* 34 (1921) 337–79; U. E. **Paoli**, "L'ἀγχιστεία nel diritto successorio attico," *SDHI* 2 (1936) 77–119; J. C. **Miles**, "The Attic Law of Intestate Succession (Demosthenes, *Contra Macart.* 51)," *Hermathena* 75 (1950) 69–77; L. **Gernet**, *Droit et société dans la Grèce ancienne* (Paris 1955) 83–102, 121–49; E. **Ruschenbusch**, "ΔΙΑΤΙΘΕΣΘΑΙ ΤΑ ΕΑΥΤΟΥ. Ein Beitrag zum sogenannten Testamentsgesetz des Solon," *ZSS* 79 (1962) 307–11; W. K. **Lacey**, *The Family in Classical Greece* (Ithaca, NY 1968) 125–50; D. M. **Schaps**, *Economic Rights of Women in Ancient Greece* (Edinburgh 1979); S. C. **Humphreys**, "Kinship Patterns in the Athenian Courts," *GRBS* 27 (1986) 57–92; R. **Just**, *Women in Athenian Law and Life* (London 1989) 83–104; D. M. **MacDowell**, "The *Oikos* in Athenian Law," *CQ* 39 (1989) 10–21; L. **Foxhall**, "Household, Gender and Property in Classical Athens," *CQ* 39 (1989) 22–44; E. **Karabelias**, "La succession *ab intestat* en droit attique," *JJP* 20 (1990) 55–74; L. **Rubinstein**, *Adoption in IV. Century Athens* (Copenhagen 1993); D. **Cohen**, *Law, Violence and Community in Classical Athens* (Cambridge 1995) 163–180; C. B. **Patterson**, *The Family in Greek History* (Cambridge, MA 1998) 83–91, 97–101, 212–15; E. **Karabelias**, *L'épiclérat attique* (Athens 2002); L. **Gagliardi**, "Per un'interpretazione della legge di Solone in materia successoria," *Dike* 5 (2002) 5–59; R. V. **Cudjoe**, "The Purpose of the 'Epidikasia' for an 'Epikleros' in Classical Athens," *Dike* 8 (2005) 55–88; D. D. **Phillips**, *Avengers of Blood: Homicide in Athenian Law* *and Custom from Draco to Demosthenes* (Stuttgart 2008) 91–104; R. V. **Cudjoe**, *The Social and Legal Position of Widows and Orphans in Classical Athens* (Athens 2010).

"The law of estates and *epiklêroi*" ([Aristotle], *Constitution of the Athenians* [*Ath. Pol.*] 9.2)—in our terms, the law of succession upon death—is the best documented and most complex area of Athenian law. The estate (**§7.1**: **166–175**) left by a decedent (who is also called the *de cuius*, an abbreviation of the Latin *de cuius hereditate agitur*, "the person whose estate is at issue": e.g., Justinian, *Institutes* 3.1.15) comprised "matters sacred and profane" (*hiera kai hosia*: **166**, **176**). The latter category included assets (**§7.1.1**: **167–168**) and liability for debts, both private and public (**§7.1.2**: **169–173**); the former category consisted of membership in the religious life of the family, including in particular obligations to the funerary cult of the decedent (**§7.1.3**: **174–175**).

When a man died without a will (**§7.2**: **176–200**), the disposition of his estate was regulated by Solon's law on intestate succession (**176**, **184**), which defined the members of the decedent's *anchisteia* (close kin) and the order in which they succeeded to the estate. The list below gives the order of succession, with each numbered category precluding those that follow. Note that, as the law states (cf. **190**), precedence is given to males and children of males, if they are descended from the same people (hence a son precedes a daughter, a brother by the same father precedes a sister by the same father, and so on), even if they are further removed from the decedent in terms of generations (hence a son's son precedes a daughter, a son of a brother by the same father precedes a sister by the same father, and so on).

1. *Legitimate sons, both biological and adopted, and their direct descendants* (**§7.2.1**: **177–179**). The line of direct descent from sons may have extended theoretically to infinity (**177**), but it will have been rare for a descendant beyond a grandson to exercise his right of succession—this will have required a decedent to leave behind a living great-grandson whose father and grandfather were both dead. If more than one person existed within this category, the estate was divided according to branches of descent (*per stirpes*, to use the Latin technical term). Assume, for example, that a decedent has two sons, *A* and *B*. If both *A* and *B* are living, each inherits half the estate. If *A* is living and *B* is dead, but *B* has one or more living sons, *A* still inherits half the estate, while the half that would have gone to *B* is shared equally among his living sons.
2. *Legitimate daughters, both biological and adopted, and their direct descendants* (**§7.2.2**: **180–193**). If a decedent left no legitimate son or direct descendant of a legitimate son, but had a living legitimate daughter, she became

his *epiklêros* (plural *epiklêroi*). This term is often translated "heiress," but the translation is misleading, since the *epiklêros* did not inherit the estate but rather was transferred "with (*epi*) the estate (*klêros*)." That is, the *epiklêros* was subject to adjudication to her father's closest male relative, who could claim her hand in marriage (dissolving any preexisting marriage: **186a**) and would then manage the estate until a son born to him and the *epiklêros* survived two years past puberty, at which point the son inherited the estate (**182**, **187**, **188**; cf. **191**). To encourage the production of a son (and prevent the *epiklêros*' husband from hoarding the estate), a law of Solon required the husband to have intercourse with the *epiklêros* three times per month (**180**). The order of claim to an *epiklêros* (**185**, **186b**, **187**, **188**) was the same as the order of succession to an estate (from category 3 onward, and restricted to males; that is, starting with the decedent's brother, the paternal uncle of the *epiklêros*); if there were multiple males of equal standing in the *anchisteia*, the eldest had the first claim (**191**). If the decedent left more than one legitimate daughter, all were *epiklêroi* and the estate was divisible *per stirpes*. So, if a decedent has two daughters, *C* and *D*, and both are living, each daughter becomes *epiklêros* to half the estate; if *C* is living and *D* is dead but has at least one living son, *C* still becomes *epiklêros* to half the estate, while the other half is shared equally among *D*'s living sons, who inherit in their own right (**190**). Special requirements applied when an *epiklêros* belonged to the thetic class, the lowest of the four annual income classes instituted by Solon (p. 3): the closest male relative of a thetic *epiklêros* was compelled either to marry her or to dower her on a sliding scale according to his own class status (**181**).

If the decedent left no direct descendants, collateral relatives (**§7.2.3**: **194–196**) stood to inherit, as follows:

3. *Brothers by the same father, including full brothers, and their direct descendants* (**194**, **195**). The law of intestate succession (**176**) mentions no descendant of a brother beyond his son, but it is usually assumed that in theory the line of direct descent here (as in category 1) extended to infinity. The estate was divisible *per stirpes*.
4. *Sisters by the same father, including full sisters, and their direct descendants* (**190**, **194**), with the same rules applying as in category 3.
5. *Paternal uncles and their children and grandchildren* (**194**), with the estate divisible *per stirpes*. A child of the decedent's paternal uncle is the decedent's first cousin; that person's children are the decedent's first cousins once removed (the "children of first cousins" in the law of intestate succession: **176**; but see **194**).
6. *Paternal aunts and their children and grandchildren* (**194**), with the estate divisible *per stirpes*. The degrees of relation stated in category 5 also apply

here. This category exhausts the decedent's paternal *anchisteia.* The members of his maternal *anchisteia* then follow, beginning with brothers by the same mother, so that categories 7 through 10 (maternal collaterals) mirror categories 3 through 6 (paternal collaterals).

7. *Brothers by the same mother and their direct descendants* (**194**), with the same rules applying as in category 3.
8. *Sisters by the same mother and their direct descendants* (**194**), with the same rules applying as in category 3.
9. *Maternal uncles and their children and grandchildren* (**194**), with the same rules and degrees of relation applying as in category 5.
10. *Maternal aunts and their children and grandchildren* (**194**), with the same rules and degrees of relation applying as in category 5.

Before 403/2, illegitimate children (*nothoi,* §**7.2.4**: **197–198**; on legitimacy see §**6.1**) were excluded from the *anchisteia* if there were legitimate children; if there were no legitimate children, illegitimate children shared the estate—on unknown terms—with the decedent's closest collateral kin (**184**). From 403/2 on, *nothoi* were excluded from the *anchisteia* absolutely (**176**). A decedent could, however, will a limited bequest to an illegitimate child (**184**, **197**, **198**). As for non-citizens (§**7.2.5**: **199** **200**), there is some slight evidence that a former owner may have had rights as to the estate of his freedman (**199**); this and other issues involving the estate of a metic (p. 23) came under the supervision of the polemarch (**200**; p. 34).

Before the legislation of Solon, it is probable that Athenians were not allowed to make wills, and that a decedent's estate was inherited by his son(s), if he had any, and in all events remained within the decedent's family (**202**). Solon's testamentary law (**201**), however, gave an Athenian the capacity to make a will (*diathêkê*; the plural *diathêkai* is used both of a single document and of multiple documents, and the corresponding verb "to make a will, dispose of one's property by will" is *diatithesthai*) if he had no legitimate son and if he had not been adopted *inter vivos* (cf. **209** and see chapter 6); such a will was valid unless the testator made it while insane, senile, drugged, ill, under female influence, or under constraint by duress or detention (cf. §**7.3.2**: **205–209**). This remained the foundation of Athenian testamentary law down through the Classical period, except during the brief reign of the Thirty Tyrants (404/3: p. 12), who annulled the invalidating conditions specified by Solon (**203**). Solon or a later Archaic legislator further permitted men with legitimate sons to make wills whose validity was conditional on the death of any and all such sons before they were two years past puberty (§**7.3.3**: **210–211**).

A man without a legitimate son could adopt a child during his lifetime (*inter vivos*) or by will; adoption could also be effected posthumously on his behalf (see chapter 6). As seen in the order of intestate succession above, adopted sons became heirs to their adopter on equal footing with any legitimate biological sons (with a partial exception regarding the process of claiming their inheritance: see below). Adoption by will (testamentary adoption) seems to have been the most common method (§7.3.1: **204**; for an instance of the testamentary adoption of a daughter see **194**). If a decedent left an *epiklêros*, he could not dispose of his property without her (cf. **176**), and therefore any will had to specify an adopted son who would marry her or else forfeit the adoption. In the fourth century, it was common even for men with adult and/or minor legitimate sons to make wills, and for these wills to be treated as valid despite Solon's law (e.g., **205**). Women and children appear to have been excluded by law from making wills (**206**), although we have at least one apparent instance of a woman's will being treated as valid (**207**). A specific provision prevented magistrates who had not undergone their *euthynai* (p. 32) from making valid wills (**208**). No law regulated the form of a will (§7.3.4: **212–217**); a will could therefore be oral (**214**), but the standard procedure was to make a will in writing, in the presence of witnesses, and then to seal the document and deposit it either with a private individual or with a magistrate (**212**, **213**, **215–217**). A testator had the power to modify or revoke his will at his discretion (§7.3.5: **218–219**).

The procedure for claiming an inheritance (§7.4: **220–236**) depended upon the heir's relation to the decedent. Biological direct descendants of the decedent and children adopted by the decedent *inter vivos* were entitled to assert their claims directly by simply assuming possession of the estate or their due portion of it (§7.4.1: **220–221**; also **228**, **230**). The technical term for this direct claim was the verb *embateuein* (originally "to walk upon," hence "to enter into possession"); the noun *embateusis*, used here and commonly in modern scholarship, is post-Classical. Anyone who physically obstructed a direct heir's *embateusis* became liable to a *dikê exoulês*, a private lawsuit for ejectment instituted by Solon, and if convicted, had to restore the property to the aggrieved party and pay its cash value to the state (§7.4.2: **222–223**; also **228**).

All heirs other than direct heirs—that is, all who were not the decedent's biological direct descendants or children adopted *inter vivos*—had to claim an estate or *epiklêros* by the process of adjudication (*epidikasia*/*diadikasia*: §7.4.3–6: **224–236**).

The noun *epidikasia* and the verb *epidikazein* are used of both the act of claiming by adjudication done by a claimant and the adjudication award performed by a magistrate and/or a jury-court; the adjective *epidikos* refers to an estate or *epiklêros* that is subject to adjudication; the noun *diadikasia* is the name of the lawsuit for adjudication of an estate or *epiklêros* between two or more claimants (see below).

Members of this category had first to register a claim for adjudication (*lêxis*, plural *lêxeis*; the term is used of the filing of any claim or lawsuit: p. 35) in writing (§7.4.3: **224–226**; also **189**, **228–233**, **236**) with the relevant magistrate: the eponymous archon for citizens and the polemarch for metics. A herald made a proclamation inviting claims (**234**), and public notice of the resulting claims was given at the next chief meeting of the Assembly (*kyria ekklêsia*: **224**). Then, if there was only one claim, or multiple non-competing claims (for example, if the decedent's brothers *A* and *B* each claimed half the decedent's estate, or if, with *B* deceased, *A* claimed half the estate and each of *B*'s sons *C* and *D* claimed a quarter), the magistrate awarded the estate or *epiklêros* accordingly (**185**, **227**, **228**).

Claims for adjudication could be contested in one of two ways (§7.4.4: **227–230**). (1) A person might enter a *diamartyria* (declaration on oath: **228–230**; also **192**, **231**, **232**) asserting that adjudication was illegal owing to the existence of a direct heir. In an attempt to deter fraudulent claims, the law required the person making the *diamartyria* to pay a cash deposit (*parakatabolê*) equivalent to 10 percent of the value of the claimed property (**196**, **226**, **230d**, **234**). Once a *diamartyria* was lodged, if the person seeking adjudication wished to maintain his claim, he had to respond by filing a denunciation (*episkêpsis*) and then prosecuting the person who made the *diamartyria* by a lawsuit for false witness (*dikê pseudomartyriôn*) (§7.4.5: **231–233**; also **230**). If this lawsuit resulted in an acquittal, the direct heir named in the *diamartyria* retained the estate; if the lawsuit resulted in a conviction, the defendant forfeited his deposit and the estate became open to claim. (2) If no one entered a *diamartyria* but competing claims for adjudication arose, all claimants contended against each other in a *diadikasia* (lawsuit for adjudication: **227**, **229**, **230**; also **183**, **185**). (When a direct heir elected to proceed in this manner rather than by interposing a *diamartyria*, the *diadikasia* was said to take place by "direct trial," *euthydikia*: **229**.) The relevant magistrate held a preliminary hearing (*anakrisis*) and then submitted the case for trial by a regular jury-court (*dikastêrion*); whichever claimant received a plurality of the jurors' votes was awarded the disputed estate or *epiklêros*. As with the person who swore a *diamartyria*, a witness for the winning party in a *diadikasia* could be prosecuted by *dikê pseudomartyriôn*, and his conviction would lay the estate or *epiklêros* open to claim once again (**233**).

None of the outcomes described above necessarily represented a permanent disposition of the estate or *epiklêros* in question. Claims could be lodged by previous or new claimants, on previous or new grounds, at any time within five years of the death of the first heir(s) or awardee(s) (**228**; cf. **234**, **235**). In cases where an estate or *epiklêros* had been awarded by adjudication, a claimant wishing to contest the adjudication had to pay a *parakatabolê* and summon the possessor to appear before the eponymous archon; if the possessor wished to maintain his claim, a new *diadikasia* resulted (§7.4.6: **234–236**).

See also chapters 5 and 6 *passim*.

7.1. Contents of Estate

See also **87** Dem. 27.4–5; **92** Dem. 45.27–28, 30; **105b** Lys. 13.45; **106** Lys. 32.6; **114** Dem. 41.5–7, 10; **136** Isae. 7.13–17, 27–28, 30; **145** Dem. 27.34, 40, 46, 49–50, 58, 60–61, 67; **146** Dem. 28.15–16; **147** Dem. 29.30–31; **158** Xen. *Mem.* 2.2.13; **160** Dem. 24.103, 107; **196** [Dem.] 44.24–26, 32–34; **213** Isae. 9.7–12; **364** Hdt. 6.136.

166. Demosthenes 39 / *Against Boeotus* 35. Decedent's estate as comprising "matters sacred and profane" (*hiera kai hosia*). (?349/8)

See references and headnote under **74**. Here the speaker, Mantitheus, summarizes the contents of his father's estate as "matters sacred and profane" (cf. **176** [Dem.] 43.51; Isaeus 9.13). On the paternity of the speaker and his opponent see **131** Dem. 39–40 (selections).

So for as long as he did not adopt you, I didn't consider you a relative either; but since he adopted you, I recognize you as well. What is the proof of this? You have your share of the patrimony after my father's death: you share in matters sacred and profane [*hierôn, hosiôn*], and no one expels you from them.

7.1.1. ASSETS

167. Demosthenes 27 / *Against Aphobus* 9–11. Itemized account of estate assets. (364/3)

See **87** with references and headnote. Here Demosthenes gives a detailed inventory of the estate assets left by his father, Demosthenes senior. These assets include real estate, businesses, slaves, outstanding loans (including maritime loans, on which see **§10.5**), raw and finished materials, home furnishings and utensils, jewelry, and clothing; cf. the will of Pasion (**92** Dem. 45.27–28, 30). The interest rate stated in §9 is 1 drachma per mina per month (= 1 percent monthly = 12 percent annually); this was the usual interest rate for cash loans. Cf. **46** [Arist.] *Ath. Pol.* 52.2; **94b** [Dem.] 59.51–53; **119** Dem. 27.15–17 (18 percent statutory annual interest rate on dowry). The exact total value of the estate (estimated in §11 as 14 tal.) is 13 tal. 46 mn.

You will gain even more precise understanding by hearing about the actual estate. You see, men of the jury, my father left two workshops, each of them of no small trade. In one he had thirty cutlers, two or three worth five or six minae each and the rest no less than three minae, from whom he received a net income of 30 minae per year. In the other he had bed-makers, twenty in number, who were pledged as security for a loan of 40 minae and who yielded him 12 minae net income. He also left about a talent in cash lent out at an interest rate of 1 drachma, the interest on which each year came to more than 7 minae. [10] That is the productive capital [*energa*] that he left, as even my adversaries themselves will admit. Its total principal comes to 4 talents 5,000 drachmas, and the proceeds from it 50 minae per year. Apart from this, he left ivory and iron that they used in the workshops and wood for beds, worth about 80 minae; oak-gall dye and copper that had been bought for 70 minae; and moreover a house worth 3,000 drachmas, and furnishings and cups and gold jewelry and clothing—my mother's adornments—all of these worth about 10,000 drachmas, and 80 minae in cash in the house. [11] All this he left at home. As for maritime loans [*nautika*], he left 70 minae as a loan with Xuthus, 2,400 drachmas at Pasion's bank, 600 drachmas at Pylades', 1,600 drachmas with Demomeles son of Demon, and about a talent altogether lent out to various people in sums of two to three hundred drachmas each. Of these sums of money the total comes to more than 8 talents 50 minae. And you will find upon examination that the total value of everything together is about 14 talents.

168. [Demosthenes] 49 *Against Timotheus* 1–2, 42–43, 69. Outstanding debts to decedent as estate assets. (362)

A. **Schäfer**, *Demosthenes und seine Zeit* (Leipzig 1858–87) 4.137–43; F. **Blass**, *Die attische Beredsamkeit* (Leipzig 1887–98) 3.1.522–26; L. **Gernet**, *Démosthène: Plaidoyers civils, Tome III, Discours XLIX–LVI* (Paris 1959: text, French translation, and notes); J. **Trevett**, *Apollodoros the Son of Pasion* (Oxford 1992) 11, 25–26, 93–96, 127–28; S. **Usher**, *Greek Oratory: Tradition and Originality* (Oxford 1999) 338, 340; D. M. **MacDowell**, *Demosthenes the Orator* (Oxford 2009) 102–6; A. C. **Scafuro**, *Demosthenes, Speeches 39–49* (Austin 2011: translation with introduction and notes).

Apollodorus wrote this speech and delivered it in his prosecution of Timotheus son of Conon (J. K. **Davies**, *Athenian Propertied Families 600–300 B.C.* [Oxford 1971], no. 13700), probably by *dikê blabês* (see chapter 8). Here Apollodorus contends that, as a son and heir of Pasion (cf. **92** Dem. 45.27–28, 30), he is entitled to collect a debt that Timotheus owed to Pasion.

Let it not be incredible to any of you, men of the jury, that Timotheus owes a debt of money to my father and is now being prosecuted by me in this lawsuit [*dikên*]. Rather, when I recount to you the time when the contract was formed, and what happened to my adversary during that time and in what difficulty he found himself, you will then conclude that my father behaved most honorably toward Timotheus, while Timotheus was not only the most ungrateful but the most unjust of all men. [2] He got from my father everything he asked for, and after receiving money from the bank when he was in great distress and involved in the most serious dangers to his life, he not only failed to repay the favor but is in fact depriving me of what he was given.

. . .

[42] . . . My father, men of the jury, not only left behind the debts owed to him in writing for me, but even told me when he was sick each individual debt that was owed to him, and who had the money, and for what purpose the money had been received. He also told my brother. To prove that my statements are true, [To the court clerk:] please read out my brother's deposition.

DEPOSITION.

[43] So, then, that Timotheus was left by my father owing us this money, for which I am prosecuting him and part of which belongs to me, my brother has testified for me. . . .

. . .

[69] So, then, men of the jury, witnesses have testified for me as to everything I could provide you with witnesses to, and in addition I have also demonstrated to you by means of proofs that Timotheus owes this money to my father. I therefore ask you to join me in recovering what my father left me from the people who owe it.

7.1.2. LIABILITY FOR DEBTS

169. [Demosthenes] 43 *Against Macartatus* 58 (*lex*). Heir liable for public debt owed by decedent. (date of speech ?ca. 345; law enacted in or after 508/7)

See references and headnote under **4**. The law quoted here imposes *atimia* (disfranchisement: p. 41; **170** Andoc. 1.73–79) upon men who owe a specific type of debt to the Athenian state. "The goddess" is Athena, patron deity of Athens; the Eponymous Heroes are the ten mythical figures after whom Cleisthenes, as a part of his democratic reforms in 508/7, named the ten Athenian tribes. By the late fourth century ([Aristotle], *Constitution of the Athenians* [*Ath. Pol.*] 47.4) leases of sanctuaries, with a duration of ten years, were overseen by the *basileus*.

Those who do not pay the rents on the precincts of the goddess or of the other gods or of the Eponymous Heroes shall be disfranchised [*atimous*], themselves and their descendants and their heirs, until they pay.

170. Andocides 1 *On the Mysteries* 73–79 (*decretum* + commentary). *Atimia* (disfranchisement). (date of speech 400 or 399; date of decree 405/4)

See references and headnote under **12**. Here, in discussing and citing the decree of Patrocleides (passed during the final months of the Peloponnesian War, after the Spartans had defeated the Athenians at the battle of Aegospotami and had placed Athens under siege), Andocides explains various types of *atimia* (disfranchisement: p. 41), including that incurred by public debtors. For elements of the *atimia* incumbent upon such debtors and their heirs see **172** Dem. 24.200–1; **299** [Dem.] 58.14–15; Demosthenes 22.34. "The Council" (§§75, 77, 79) is the Council of 500. "The Goddess" (§77) is Athena (cf. **169** [Dem.] 43.58). The Four Hundred (§78; they are also "the tyrants" in §75) were the members of the oligarchic regime that had ruled Athens briefly in 411/10 (p. 11). For the Areopagus, *ephetai*, Prytaneion, Delphinion, and *basileis* see chapter 1; for "slaughterers" (§78) cf. **358** Plut. *Solon* 19.4, which served as the model for this part of Patrocleides' decree.

When the ships were destroyed and the siege occurred, you deliberated on the topic of unity, and you decided to restore citizen rights to the disfranchised [*atimous*], and Patrocleides made the motion. Who were the disfranchised, and in what way was each group disfranchised? I will explain it to you. Those who owed money to the public treasury—all those who were convicted at their reviews [*euthynas*] after holding public offices, or who had lost ejectment lawsuits [*exoulas*] or indictments [*graphas*] or had been sentenced to pay fines, or who had purchased tax contracts from the public treasury but had not deposited the money, or who had given security [*engyas*] to the public treasury (the payment for these was in the ninth prytany, and if they did not pay, they were to owe twice the amount and their property was to be sold); [74] and again, all those who had been convicted of theft [*klopês*] or of bribery [*dôrôn*] (both they themselves and their descendants had to be disfranchised).

This, then, was one type of disfranchisement [*atimias*]. Another type was that of those whose persons were disfranchised but who kept and held their property. These were the people who had abandoned their post [*lipoien tên taxin*] or had been convicted of failure to serve in the army [*astrateias*] or cowardice [*deilias*] or failure to serve in the navy [*anaumachiou*] or had thrown away their shield [*tên aspida apobaloien*], or had been convicted three times of false witness [*pseudomartyriôn*] or three times of false witness to a summons [*pseudoklêteias*], or had mistreated their parents. All these were disfranchised with respect to their persons but kept their property.

[75] Still others were disfranchised according to specifications; these were

not disfranchised completely but only with respect to some part of their personal rights: for example, the soldiers who, because they had remained in the city under the tyrants, in other respects had the same rights as the rest of the citizens, but were not permitted to speak in the Assembly or serve on the Council. As to these things they were disfranchised: this was the specification for them. [76] Others were not permitted to prosecute indictments [*graphesthai*], and some were not permitted to bring denunciations [*endeixai*]. For some the specification was that they could not sail to the Hellespont, for others that they could not sail to Ionia, and for others that they could not enter the agora.

So, then, you voted to erase all these decrees, both the originals and any copy anywhere, and to give each other a pledge of unity on the Acropolis. [To the court clerk:] Please read the decree of Patrocleides in accordance with which these things occurred.

[77] DECREE. Patrocleides made the motion: whereas the Athenians have voted that there be permission to make and put to the vote proposals concerning the disfranchised and debtors, the Assembly shall vote the same decree as it did when the Persian Wars were occurring [480–479] and it came about to the benefit of the Athenians. Concerning those who have been registered with the Exactors [*praktoras*], the Treasurers of the Goddess or of the Other Gods, or the *basileus*—or if a person has not had his name recorded—down to the time when the Council in whose term Callias was archon [406/5] left office, [78] all those who were disfranchised or debtors, and all who have been convicted at reviews [*euthynai*] in the Auditors' Offices [*logistêriois*] by the Reviewers [*euthynôn*] and Assessors [*paredrôn*] or whose indictments [*graphai*] concerning their reviews have not yet been brought to a jury-court [*dikastêrion*], or who have been sentenced to some specifications or to pay back securities, up to this same time, and all the names of any of the Four Hundred that have been registered, or anything else that is written anywhere concerning things done under the oligarchy—except for the names inscribed on pillars of those who did not remain here or who, having been convicted by the Areopagus, the *ephetai*, the Prytaneion, or the Delphinion under the supervision of the *basileis*, either are in some [type of] exile for homicide or have been sentenced to death either as slaughterers [*sphageusin*] or as tyrants—[79] all the rest shall be erased by the Exactors and the Council; the *thesmothetai* and the other magistrates shall produce the aforementioned items from wherever an item is located in public, as well as any copy anywhere. They shall do these things within three days of the date when the Assembly passes its resolution. The items aforementioned shall be erased, and no one shall be permitted to possess them privately or to bear malice at any time—otherwise the person who violates these provisions shall be liable to the same penalties as those who are in exile as a result of trial at the Areopagus—in order that the Athenians both now and in the future may have as trusting relations as possible.

171. [Demosthenes] 35 *Against Lacritus* 3–4. Heir liable for private debt owed by decedent. (355–338)

Schäfer, *Demosthenes* 4.286–91; **Blass**, *AB* 3.1.562–68; F. A. **Paley**-J. E. **Sandys**, *Select Private Orations of Demosthenes* 1³ (Cambridge 1898: text and commentary); L. **Gernet**, *Démosthène: Plaidoyers civils, Tome I, Discours XXVII–XXXVIII* (Paris 1954: text, French translation, and notes); S. **Isager**-M. H. **Hansen**, *Aspects of Athenian Society in the Fourth Century B.C.: A Historical Introduction to and Commentary on the Paragraphe-speeches and the Speech Against Dionysodorus in the Corpus Demosthenicum (XXXII–XXXVIII and LVI)* (Odense 1975); **Usher**, *GO* 253–55; **MacDowell**, *Demosthenes 27–38* (translation with introduction and notes); ***idem,*** *DO* 257–66.

Androcles had commenced prosecution of Lacritus by a *dikê emporikê* (mercantile lawsuit: see chapter 10, especially **323** [Dem.] 35 [selections]) when Lacritus responded with a *paragraphê* (counter-indictment: p. 14) alleging improper procedure. This speech was delivered by Androcles in the *paragraphê*; here he argues that his *dikê emporikê* is in fact the proper procedure for collecting a debt owed to him originally by Artemon and now by Artemon's brother and heir Lacritus. On liability for private debts cf., e.g., Lysias 17.2–3.

I, men of the jury, lent money to Artemon, the brother of my adversary, in accordance with the mercantile laws [*tous emporikous nomous*], for a voyage to the Black Sea and back to Athens. Since he died before paying me back the money, I filed this lawsuit against Lacritus here in accordance with the same laws under which I had made the contract, [4] since he is Artemon's brother and possesses all of Artemon's property—everything he left here and everything he had in Phaselis—and is the heir to his entire estate. And my adversary could not point out any law that gives him the power to hold his brother's property and to have managed it as he saw fit, but to refuse to pay back money belonging to others, and instead to claim now that he is not the heir but has surrendered his claim to his brother's estate.

172. Demosthenes 24 *Against Timocrates* 200–1. Heir liable for public debt owed by decedent. (353/2)

See references and headnote under **160**. Here Diodorus states that since Timocrates' father is a state debtor, upon his death Timocrates will inherit the debt and the attendant *atimia* (cf. **169** [Dem.] 43.58; **170** Andoc. 1.73–79).

My adversary's father, men of the jury, owes a debt to the public treasury—I say this not to criticize him but because I am compelled—and this worthy individual allows the debt to remain. [201] Now, given that he is going to inherit the disfranchisement [*atimias*] if anything happens to his father, and yet he thinks that he should not pay the debt but rather sees fit to enjoy the benefit of the money as long as his father is alive, what do you think he would refrain from doing?

173. *Inscriptiones Graecae* II² 1631.429–41. Record of public debt paid by heirs of decedent. (date of inscription 323/2; date of event described 324/3)

I. **Kirchner**, ed., ***Inscriptiones Graecae*** II² (ed. min. Berlin 1913–40: text with Latin notes).

This inscription contains the annual report of the outgoing board of Superintendents of the Dockyards (*epimelêtai tôn neôriôn*) of 323/2 to their successors in office; on this category of inscriptions see P. J. **Rhodes**-R. **Osborne**, *Greek Historical Inscriptions 404–323 BC* (Oxford 2003), no. 100. On the trierarchy (p. 25) of Stesileides cf. *IG* II² 1623.200ff. (= E. S. **Roberts**-E. A. **Gardner**, *An Introduction to Greek Epigraphy, Part II: The Inscriptions of Attica* [Cambridge 1905] no. 119, Ba 41ff., Bb 23ff.). The trireme, a vessel with three superimposed banks of oars, each oar pulled by a single rower, was the standard warship of Classical Greece; the quadrireme was a newer type, probably with two banks of oars and two rowers per oar. "The Council" is the Council of 500; on *apographê* (confiscation) cf., e.g., **40** [Dem.] 53.16; for the *pôlêtai* see **2** *IG* I³ 104. The reference to the guardian Leodicus (on guardianship see chapter 6) indicates that Stesileides' heirs were still minors.

The following exacted items we have received: from Leodicus of Siphnos, guardian of the heirs of Stesileides of Siphnos, [fine owed] on the trireme—amount doubled by the Council—named *Euphrainousa* [*Joyful*], built by Archeneus, and for the equipment that Stesileides owed on the quadrireme *Petomenê* [*Flier*], built by Aristocrates; paid as a result of the [action for] confiscation [*apographês*] prosecuted by Hermodorus of the deme Acharnae: 2 talents 117 drachmas 2 obols. This was paid to the *pôlêtai* in the archonship of Hegesias [324/3].

7.1.3. OBLIGATIONS TOWARD DECEDENT

174. [Demosthenes] 43 *Against Macartatus* 57–58 (*lex*). Law on retrieval and burial of neglected corpses. (date of speech ?ca. 345; law enacted in or after 508/7)

See references and headnote under **4**. This law immediately follows **4** [Dem.] 43.57 and immediately precedes **169** [Dem.] 43.58 in a series of laws cited by the speaker; the reference to the demarch (the annually allotted magistrate in charge of each deme) presupposes Cleisthenes' establishment of the demes of Attica (p. 6).

In the case of those who die in the demes and whom no one retrieves for burial, the demarch shall make a proclamation to the relatives to retrieve and bury and to purify the deme on the day when each of them dies. [58] He shall make the proclamation in the case of slaves to the master, and in the case of free persons to those who possess the property. If the decedent has no property, he shall make the proclamation to the relatives of the decedent. If after the demarch's proclamation the relatives do not retrieve, the demarch shall let out the contract for retrieval and burial and purification of the deme that very day at the lowest possible price. If he does not let out the contract, he shall owe 1,000 drachmas to the public treasury. Whatever he spends, he shall exact twice that amount from those who owe it; and if he does not exact it, he himself shall owe it to the demesmen.

175. Isaeus 8 *On the Estate of Ciron* 21–24. Connection between succession and funerary obligation. (?383–363)

See references and headnote under **39**. Here the speaker describes the negotiations between himself and Diocles, the brother-in-law of Ciron, over the conduct of Ciron's funeral, a duty that lay with the putative heir (cf. Isaeus 2.36, 46–47; 4.19, 26; 9.13; [Demosthenes] 43.65).

Moreover, gentlemen, even from what Diocles did when our grandfather died it is easy to recognize that we are acknowledged to be Ciron's maternal grandsons. You see, I arrived to take him, in order to conduct the burial from my house. . . . [22] But when my grandfather's wife requested that I conduct his burial from her house, saying that she would like to help prepare and adorn his body along with us, and when she begged and wept for these things, I consented, gentlemen, and in the presence of witnesses I approached Diocles and said that I would conduct the burial from there, since his sister had asked me to do so. [23] Diocles, when he heard this, made no objection. Instead, claiming that he had purchased some of the things for the funeral and had paid a deposit [*arrhabôna*] for the rest, he asked to recover the money from me, and he agreed to receive the price of the things that had been bought and, as for the things he claimed to have paid a deposit for, to present the people who received it. And straightaway he casually added that Ciron had not left a single thing, even though I had made no mention of his property at all. [24] Now, if I were not Ciron's maternal grandson, he would not have made this agreement; instead, he would have spoken these words: "Who are you? What right do you have to bury him? I don't know you; you shall not enter the house." That is what he should have said, and what he has now persuaded others to say. As it happened, though, he said no such thing but told me to bring the money in the morning.

7.2. Intestate Succession

176. [Demosthenes] 43 *Against Macartatus* 51 (*lex*). Law of intestate succession. (date of speech ?ca. 345; date of law 594/3, except for final sentence of law, dated 403/2)

See references and headnote under **4**. The following passage is a law of Solon governing intestate succession, with the exception of the final sentence, which is a rider dated to 403/2; for the status of illegitimate children before 403/2 see **184** Ar. *Birds* 1641–70. Solon omitted as obvious legitimate sons and their descendants, who stood first in the order of intestate succession (see §§**7.2.1**, **7.3**). The phrase "sisters by the same father and the children born," enclosed in angled brackets, is one editorial supplement that has been proposed to fill the acknowledged lacuna in the text between "If there are no brothers or children of brothers" and "from them shall share"; that this is the correct missing phrase is indicated by **194** Isae. 11.1–5, 8–12, 17–18, 29–30.

If a man dies without making a will [*mê diathemenos*], if he leaves female children, [his property shall go] with them [*syn tautêisin*]; otherwise, the following shall be *kyrioi* of his property. If there are brothers by the same father, [they shall be *kyrioi*,] and if there are legitimate children of brothers, they shall receive their father's share. If there are no brothers or children of brothers, <sisters by the same father and the children born> from them shall share according to the same principles. Males and children of males shall have precedence, if they are descended from the same people, even if they are further removed. If there are no relatives on the father's side down to children of first cousins, the relatives on the mother's side shall be *kyrioi* according to the same principles. If there are no relatives on either side within this degree, the closest relative on the father's side shall be *kyrios*. There shall be no right of kinship [*anchisteian*] in matters either sacred or profane [*mêth' hierôn mêth' hosiôn*] for an illegitimate male [*nothôi*] or an illegitimate female [*nothêi*] from the archonship of Eucleides [403/2] on.

7.2.1. LEGITIMATE SONS AND THEIR DESCENDANTS

See also **121a** [Dem.] 40.14; **125** [Arist.] *Ath. Pol.* 26.4; **127** (Reenactment of Pericles' citizenship law); **129** Isae. 3.75–76; **134** [Arist.] *Ath. Pol.* 42.1–2;

152 [Arist.] *Ath. Pol.* 56.6–7; **166** Dem. 39.35; **176** [Dem.] 43.51; **184** Ar. *Birds* 1641–70; **188** Isae. 10.4–5; **189** Isae. 6.46; **192** Harpo. s.v. *epidikos* etc.; **195** Isae. 7.5–7; **201** [Dem.] 46.14; **202** Plut. *Solon* 21.3–4; **204** Isae. 3.67–69; **205** Lys. 19.39–40; **206** Isae. 10.9–10; **210** [Dem.] 46.24.

177. Isaeus 8 *On the Estate of Ciron* 34. Inheritance rights of legitimate sons and their descendants. (?383–363)

See references and headnote under **39**. Here the speaker discusses the inheritance status of (legitimate) sons and their direct male descendants (perhaps, in theory, *ad infinitum*).

But I fear lest you think I am bothering you by mentioning things that are all too well agreed-upon; for all of you are heirs to the property of your fathers and grandfathers and even further relatives, having received your right of kinship [*anchisteian*] without adjudication [*anepidikon*] on the basis of descent [*genous*].

178. Isaeus 6 *On the Estate of Philoctemon* 25, 28, 63. Inheritance rights of legitimate sons (biological and adopted): estate divisible equally among legitimate sons; existence of legitimate son bars will. (365–363)

See references and headnote under **144**. The speaker's opponents, Androcles and Antidorus, had lodged a *diamartyria* (declaration on oath) asserting that the disputed estate was not subject to adjudication (*anepidikos*), since Philoctemon had a surviving sister and brothers (for the sequence of legal procedures see the introduction to this chapter and §7.4). These passages discuss the inheritance rights of legitimate sons, both biological and adopted: cf. Demosthenes 39.6 with [Demosthenes] 40.2.

Why did Euctemon need to get married, Androcles, if in fact these children had been born from him and a citizen wife, as you have testified? For if they were legitimate, who could have prevented them from being introduced [into the family]? Or why did he introduce him on specified terms, when the law commands that all legitimate sons get an equal share of their father's property?

. . .

[28] . . . no one ever records in a will any bequest to his biological sons, since the law itself grants to the son the property of his father and does not even permit a man who has legitimate children to make a will.

. . .

[63] . . . How, then, was Philoctemon childless, when he left behind his own nephew as his adopted son, and the law gives him his inheritance on equal

terms with the sons born from Philoctemon? In fact, it is explicitly written in the law that if sons are born to a man who has already adopted, each takes his share of the estate and both groups inherit equally.

179. Demosthenes 36 *For Phormion* 8–9, 11, 34. Will made by decedent with legitimate sons; division of estate; *presbeia* (privilege of seniority). (?350/49)

See references and headnote under **148**. Pasion died in 370/69 leaving two living legitimate sons by his wife Archippe, the adult Apollodorus and the minor Pasicles. Pasion nonetheless wrote a will (see **92** Dem. 45.27–28, 30), which was treated as valid. Here the speaker describes the division of Pasion's estate between his sons; Apollodorus got his choice of share presumably because he was the elder son, and in §34 an apartment house (presumably different from the one dowered with Archippe in **92**) is specifically designated as his *presbeia* (privilege of seniority).

So when Pasion had died after making this will, this man Phormion here took his wife in accordance with the will and assumed guardianship of the boy. And when my adversary seized much of the property, which was held jointly, and thought he should spend it, the guardians calculated with each other that if it were necessary under the will that they take out everything my adversary spent from the jointly-held property and split the rest between the two of them in equal shares, there would be absolutely nothing left; so they decided to split the property for the boy's sake. [9] So they split the rest of the estate, apart from what Phormion here had leased, of which they gave half the income to my adversary. . . .

. . .

[11] So, men of Athens, immediately after they released Phormion here from liability for the lease, they split the bank and the shield business, and Apollodorus, who got the choice, chose the shield business over the bank.

. . .

[34] . . . When he denies the authenticity of the will, ask him how he got and owns the apartment house as a privilege of seniority [*presbeia*] according to the will.

7.2.2. *EPIKLÊROI* AND THEIR DESCENDANTS

See also **45** Dem. 37.33; **83** [Dem.] 46.18; **90** Isae. 3.2; **96** [Dem.] 43.75; **125** [Arist.] *Ath. Pol.* 26.4; **127** (Reenactment of Pericles' citizenship law); **152**

[Arist.] *Ath. Pol.* 56.6–7; **154** Harpo. s.v. *kakôseôs*; **§6.4.3**; **176** [Dem.] 43.51; **194** Isae. 11.1–5, 8–12, 17–18, 29–30; **198** *Suda* s.v. *epiklêros*; **200** [Arist.] *Ath. Pol.* 58.3; **204** Isae. 3.67–69; **227** [Dem.] 46.22–23; **228** Isae. 3.40–50, 57–60, 62; **232** Isae. 3.3–7; **234** [Dem.] 43.5–16.

180. Plutarch, *Solon* 20.2–4. Solonian laws regarding *epiklêroi*. (date of composition late 1st-early 2nd c.A.D.; laws attributed to Solon, 594/3 B.C.)

See references and headnote under **1d**. Here Plutarch discusses two Solonian regulations regarding *epiklêroi*. The meaning of *opyesthai* at §20.2 is variously interpreted as "to have sex (with)" or "to marry"; from the comments at §20.3, it is clear that Plutarch understood the verb in the former sense.

Also appearing strange and ridiculous is the law that allows an *epiklêros*, if the man who under the law has power over her and is her *kyrios* is himself unable to engage in intercourse with her, to have sex [*opyesthai*] with her husband's closest relatives. Some say that this is rightly directed toward men who are unable to have intercourse but marry *epiklêroi* for the sake of money and so use the law to violate nature. [20.3] For if they see the *epiklêros* having intercourse with whomever she wants, they will either abandon the marriage or keep her along with the accompanying shame, thereby paying the penalty for their avarice and hubris. And it is also good that the *epiklêros* consort not with everyone but only with the relative of her husband of her choosing, so that the child who is born is kin and a part of the family. [20.4] Also contributing to this goal are the provisions that the bride eat a quince before being shut up [in the bridal chamber] with her groom, and that the man who marries an *epiklêros* by all means must sleep with her three times per month.

181. [Demosthenes] 43 *Against Macartatus* 54 (*lex*). Law on thetic *epiklêroi*. (date of speech ?ca. 345; law authored by Solon, 594/3)

See references and headnote under **4**. The law quoted here (for whose attribution to Solon cf. **193** Pollux, *Onomasticon* 3.33) governs *epiklêroi* who belong to the class of thetes, the lowest of the four income classes established by Solon. The classes were the *pentakosiomedimnoi* (singular *pentakosiomedimnos*), whose lands produced annually 500 standard measures of dry and/or wet goods; the *hippeis* (singular *hippeus*: 300 measures); the *zeugitai* (singular *zeugitês*: 200 measures); and the thetes (less than 200 measures). "The archon" means the eponymous archon; note that the law does not make provision for the case where the closest male relative of the *epiklêros* is himself a member of the thetic class. For the requirement that the closest male relative of a thetic *epiklêros* either marry or dower her cf. Isaeus 1.39. Later sources (**192** Harpo. s.v. *epidikos* etc.; Terence, *Phormio* 407–412; Diodorus 12.18.2–3; Harpocration s.v. *thêtes kai thêtikon*; *Suda* s.v. *thêtta*) appear to treat 500 dr. as the set dowry for all thetic *epiklêroi*, regardless of the class of the dowerer; either these sources paraphrase the law incompletely or at some point after the law's passage a dowry of 500 dr. became mandatory in all cases.

With regard to all *epiklêroi* who belong to the thetic class, if the closest relative is not willing to marry her, he shall give her in marriage [*ekdidotô*]: a *pentakosiomedimnos* with a dowry of 500 drachmas, a *hippeus* with a dowry of 300 drachmas, a *zeugitês* with a dowry of 150 drachmas, in addition to her property. If there is more than one person in the same degree of relation [*genei*], each shall provide dowry for the *epiklêros* proportionally. If there is more than one woman, one man shall not be required to give in marriage more than one woman; rather, the closest relative in succession shall give her in marriage or marry her himself. If the closest relative does not marry her or give her in marriage, the archon shall compel him either to marry her himself or to give her in marriage. If the archon does not compel this, he shall be fined 1,000 drachmas, which shall be consecrated to Hera. Let anyone who wishes denounce [*apographetô*] before the archon a person who does not do the aforementioned things.

182. [Demosthenes] 46 *2 Against Stephanus* 19–20 (*lex* + commentary). Rights and duties of son of *epiklêros*. (date of speech ?349; law of Archaic date, probably authored by Solon, 594/3)

See references and headnote under **83**. Here the speaker cites a law granting the son of an *epiklêros* control of the estate of her father and of the *epiklêros* herself (which includes a duty of maintenance: cf. **123** Harpo. s.v. *sitos*; **152** [Arist.] *Ath. Pol.* 56.6–7) once the son is two years past puberty (cf. **187** Isae. 8.31, 33; **188** Isae. 10.4–5; Isaeus fr. 25 Thalheim; Harpocration s.v. *epi dietes hêbêsai*). In this Archaic law, which uses the verb *metrein* "to measure (out)" rather than a verb meaning "give, pay, grant, provide," *sitos* is to be taken literally, as "[an allowance of] grain"; in the Classical period, payment could be made either in kind or in cash, and "two years past puberty" was equated with the age of 18, when males attained their legal majority.

Now, then, observe whom the laws command to be *kyrioi* of an *epiklêros*. [20] [To the court clerk:] Read the law.

LAW. And if a child is born from an *epiklêros*, as soon as he is two years past puberty, he shall control the property and shall measure out the [allowance of] grain [*siton*] for his mother.

So the law commands that children who are past puberty be *kyrioi* of their mother and measure out the [allowance of] grain for their mother.

183. Aristophanes, *Wasps* 583–86. Testamentary adoption of son to marry *epiklêros*; *diadikasia* over *epiklêros*. (423/2)

For Aristophanes see the headnote under **52**; for his *Wasps* see D. M. **MacDowell**, *Aristophanes:* Wasps (Oxford 1971: text and commentary); A. H. **Sommerstein**, *Aristophanes:* Wasps (ed. corr. Warminster 1996: text, translation, and commentary).

Aristophanes' *Wasps* satirizes the politician Cleon and the volunteer members of the Athenian jury pool who, according to the play, are his staunch supporters. In this passage, Philocleon explains to his son Bdelycleon the benefits of jury service. In the situation presumed below, a decedent has adopted by will a son who is to marry the decedent's daughter (cf. **§7.3.1**), but the will has been contested and a *diadikasia* over the *epiklêros* has resulted. The "shell" is a covering used to preserve the seal on the will.

PHILOCLEON. And if a father dies and leaves a girl as *epiklêros* and gives her to someone, we tell the will and the shell that so pompously sits over the seals to go to hell [*klaiein . . . makra tên kephalên*], and we give the girl to whoever begs and persuades us.

184. Aristophanes, *Birds* 1641–70. Decedent's daughter as *epiklêros* in default of legitimate son; bequest to illegitimate child (*notheia*); inheritance rights of illegitimate child. (414)

For Aristophanes see the headnote under **52**; for his *Birds* see A. H. **Sommerstein**, *Aristophanes:* Birds (Wiltshire 1987: text, translation, and commentary); N. **Dunbar**, *Aristophanes:* Birds (Oxford 1995: text and commentary).

On the quotation from Solon's law and the difficulties in its interpretation see **Harrison**, *LA* 1.66–68; in 403/2 the quoted clause was replaced by language denying the right of kinship to illegitimate children under any circumstances (**176** [Dem.] 43.51). From the point of view of the gods (equated here with Athenian citizens), Heracles' mother Alcmene, as a mortal, is a foreigner. On *notheia* see **197** Harpo. s.v. *notheia*; **198** *Suda* s.v. *epiklêros*. On the introduction of a legitimate son to his father's phratry, and on the status of children born to a citizen father and a foreign mother, see chapter 6.

POSEIDON. [To Heracles:] What, you wretch? Don't you know that you've been deceived for a long time? You're hurting yourself, you know. For if Zeus dies handing down his tyranny to these birds, you'll have to work for a living. You see, all the property Zeus leaves behind when he dies becomes yours.

PEISTHETAERUS. [To Heracles:] Oh dear, how he's tricking you. Come here to me so I can tell you something. Your uncle is misleading you, you poor fellow. According to the laws you get no share at all of your father's estate, since you're illegitimate [*nothos*] and not legitimate [*gnêsios*].

HERACLES. Me, illegitimate? What are you saying?

PEISTHETAERUS. You certainly are, by Zeus, since you're the son of a foreign [*xenês*] woman. Otherwise how do you think Athena, his daughter, could be an *epiklêros*, if she had legitimate brothers?

HERACLES. Well, what if my father gives me his property as an illegitimate child's portion [*nothei'*] when he dies?

PEISTHETAERUS. The law doesn't allow him to do that. Poseidon here, who is getting your hopes up now, will be the first to fight you for your father's property, by claiming that he is Zeus' legitimate brother. In fact, I shall quote Solon's law to you: "There shall be no right of kinship [*anchisteian*] for an illegitimate son [*nothôi*] when there are legitimate children. If there are no legitimate children, the closest relatives shall share in the property."

HERACLES. So I get no share of my father's property?

PEISTHETAERUS. Absolutely none, by Zeus. Tell me, has your father ever introduced you to the members of his phratry?

HERACLES. Not me, and in fact I've been wondering about that for a long time.

185. Andocides 1 *On the Mysteries* 117–21. Multiple *epiklêroi*; *epidikasia*/*diadikasia* over *epiklêros*. (400 or 399)

See references and headnote under **12**, and **§11.3**. Here Andocides describes the situation following the death of Epilycus, who died leaving two daughters, both *epiklêroi*. Andocides and Leagrus were sons of sisters of Epilycus. *Phanera ousia* or *phanera* (*chrêmata*), "visible property," and its antonym *aphanês ousia* or *aphanê* (*chrêmata*), "invisible property," are terms of significant flexibility and permeability (see especially **Wyse**, *Isaeus* 516–17; **Harrison**, *LA* 1.230–32). The former is applied to items whose ownership is manifest, including in particular real property, and sometimes slaves, livestock, and home furnishings and equipment; the latter is applied to items whose ownership or existence might be concealed, including often—but not always—money (especially in the form of outstanding loans).

Epilycus son of Teisander was my uncle, my mother's brother. He died in Sicily without male children, but leaving two daughters, who were coming to me and Leagrus. [118] His affairs at home were in poor condition: he left behind visible property [*phaneran ousian*] worth less than 2 talents, and his debts were more than 5 talents. Nonetheless I called upon Leagrus and told him in the presence of our family and friends that it was the duty of good men in such circumstances to show their family loyalties to each other. [119] "For," I said, "it is not right for us to choose other people's property or a successful man and so to scorn Epilycus' daughters. For if Epilycus were alive, or had died leaving a lot of property, we would demand, as the closest relatives, to marry his daughters. So, whereas that would have happened on account of Epilycus or on account of his property, as it is now it will happen on account of our moral virtue. So you claim [*epidikazou*] one of them and I will claim the other."

[120] He agreed with me, gentlemen. We both laid claim [*epedikasametha*] according to our agreement. As for the one I claimed, the girl fell victim to fortune, became ill, and died; but the other one is still alive. As for her, Callias, by promising Leagrus money, tried to persuade him to let him take her. But as soon as I heard, I paid the court fee [*parastasin*] and filed a claim [*elachon*], telling Leagrus first, "If you want to maintain your claim, have her, and good luck to you; but if not, I'm going to claim her." [121] When Callias realized this, he filed a claim to the *epiklêros* on behalf of his son on the tenth of the month; and to keep me from making my claim, during the twenties of the month, during the Mysteries, he paid Cephisius 1,000 drachmas and so denounced [*endeiknysi*] me and involved me in this trial. And when he saw me remaining to face trial, he placed the suppliant-branch, in order to get me executed without trial or exiled, while he, having persuaded Leagrus with money, would marry Epilycus' daughter.

186. Isaeus 3 *On the Estate of Pyrrhus* (selections). (?ca. 389)

See references and headnote under **85**. In the first passage below the speaker mentions a law under which a married woman who becomes an *epiklêros* upon her father's death can be compelled to divorce her husband and marry her father's closest male relative. The speaker treats this as a common phenomenon, although qualified relatives might fail to claim such women (**185** Andoc. 1.117–21; Isaeus 10.11–13, 19), and some scholars have expressed doubts as to the scope of the law—in particular, whether it applied to a woman who had borne children before her father's death. The second passage provides evidence for the order of claim to, and the procedure for claiming, the hand of an *epiklêros* (for the full order of claim see the introduction to this chapter). If Pyrrhus (the uncle of the speaker and of the speaker's brother, whom

Pyrrhus adopted by will) had acknowledged his daughter as legitimate, then by law the speaker's brother could not have accepted the adoption without marrying the daughter (**176** [Dem.] 43.51; **204** Isae. 3.67–69).

a. Isae. 3.64. Possibility of compulsory divorce and remarriage of *epiklêros*.

In the case of women who have been given in marriage [*ekdotheisas*] by their fathers and who are living with husbands . . . —even in the case of women given in this way, if their father dies without leaving them legitimate brothers, the law commands that they be subject to adjudication [*epidikous*] to their closest male relatives; and in the past many married men have had their own wives taken away.

b. Isae. 3.72–74. Adoption by will; order of claim to *epiklêros* (decedent's brother, brother's son, sister's son, maternal uncle); posthumous adoption; claim to *epiklêros*.

Why, if there were a legitimate daughter left behind by our uncle, did our uncle adopt my brother and leave him behind as his son? Is it because there were other relatives more closely related to him than we were, and he adopted my brother as his son because he wanted to deprive them of their claim [*epidikasian*] to his daughter? No: there never was, and is not now—since he had no legitimate sons—a single relative closer than we are: he had no brother or brother's children, and we are his sister's sons.

[73] But, you might respond, he could have adopted some other relative of his and given him both the estate and his daughter to have. And why was it necessary for him openly to incur the enmity of any member of his family, when, if he had taken in pledge [*ên êngyêmenos*] the sister of Nicodemus, he could have introduced the daughter who has been represented as hers to the members of his phratry as his own legitimate daughter, left her behind subject to adjudication [*epidikon*] with the entire estate, and enjoined that one of the children born from the daughter be introduced as his adopted son? [74] For obviously, if he left behind an *epiklêros*, he would have known full well that one of two things would be the case for her: either one of us, the closest relatives, would claim her [*epidikasamenon*] and take her to wife, or, if none of us was willing to take her, one of these uncles who are now testifying would do so, and if they did not, one of the other collateral relatives [*syngenôn*] in the same way would claim her with the entire estate and take her to wife in accordance with the laws.

187. Isaeus 8 *On the Estate of Ciron* 31, 33. Brother of decedent first in order of claim to *epiklêros*; sons of *epiklêros* become *kyrioi* of estate two years after puberty; (offspring of) *epiklêros* precedes brother (and offspring) in order of succession to estate. (?383–363)

See references and headnote under **39**. In these passages, the speaker alludes to the rule that an *epiklêros* is subject to adjudication to her father's closest male relative (with the father's brother first in order); refers to the order of intestate succession (**176** [Dem.] 43.51), in which (the child of) an *epiklêros* precedes the *de cuius*' brother (and his offspring); and mentions the law mandating that children of an *epiklêros* assume control of the estate two years after they reach puberty (**182** [Dem.] 46.19–20).

If my mother, Ciron's daughter, were alive, and he died without making a will, and this man were his brother rather than his nephew, he would be entitled [*kyrios*] to marry the widow; but it is not he who would be *kyrios* of the property but the children born to him and her, two years after they reached puberty: this is what the laws command. So, then, if even with the woman living he would not become *kyrios* of her property but the children would, obviously since she is dead and has left children—namely, us—it is not our adversaries but we who have the right to inherit the property.

. . .

[33] . . . Is Ciron's daughter or his brother more closely related to him? Obviously his daughter: she was born from him, his brother was born with him. His daughter's children or his brother? The children, obviously, since they are descendants [*genos*], not collateral relatives [*syngeneia*]. And if we come before a brother by that much, then surely we come well before this person, who is a nephew.

188. Isaeus 10 *On the Estate of Aristarchus* 4–5. Order of claim to *epiklêros*; qualified relatives fail to claim *epiklêros*. (?378–371)

See especially **Wyse**, *Isaeus* (text and commentary); **Wevers**, *Isaeus*; **Edwards**, *Isaeus* (translation with introduction and notes); also **Blass**, *AB* 2.563–65; **Jebb**, *AO* 2.333–36; **Usher**, *GO* 138–40.

This oration was delivered in a *diadikasia* over the estate of the younger Aristarchus (Aristarchus II), the adopted son of the elder Aristarchus (Aristarchus I); the speaker claims the estate on behalf of his mother, a daughter of Aristarchus I. In these passages the speaker notes the failure of Aristomenes (brother of Aristarchus I) and his son Apollodorus to marry the speaker's mother. Since Aristarchus I was survived by a legitimate son (Demochares), his daughter (the speaker's mother) succeeded to her brother, not to her father, and therefore was not an *epiklêros*. Here, though, she is discussed as though she were *epiklêros* to her father, in order to magnify the alleged offenses of the speaker's adversaries. For the rule that an estate must go with the *epiklêros* cf. **176** [Dem.] 43.51; for the provision that sons of an *epiklêros* obtain control of the estate two years past puberty cf. **182** [Dem.] 46.19–20.

Aristarchus [I], gentlemen, was from the deme Sypalettus. He married the daughter of Xenaenetus of the deme Acharnae, and from her were born Cyronides, Demochares, my mother, and their other sister. Now, Cyronides . . . was adopted out into another family [*oikon*], and so he no longer has any right to the property; and when Aristarchus [I], their father, died, his son Demochares became heir to his estate. But when he died as a child, as did the other sister, my mother became *epiklêros* to the entire estate [*epi panti tôi oikôi*]. [5] . . . Although the closest relative had the right to marry her, with the property, she suffers most terribly, gentlemen. You see, Aristomenes, the brother of the aforementioned Aristarchus [I], who has a son and a daughter, neglected either to marry her himself or to claim [*epidikasasthai*] her along with the estate for his son. He did neither of these things, but instead gave his daughter in marriage [*exedôken*] to Cyronides, with my mother's property as a dowry, and from that daughter were born my adversary Xenaenetus and the decedent Aristarchus [II].

189. Isaeus 6 *On the Estate of Philoctemon* 46. Claim for adjudication (*lêxis*) of *epiklêros* and of estate (on behalf of *epiklêros*); legitimate son excludes *epiklêros*. (365–363)

See references and headnotes under **144** and **178**. Here the speaker alleges that Androcles' testimony to the existence of a legitimate son of Euctemon is proved false by Androcles' having filed claims to the hand of one of Euctemon's daughters (on the grounds that she was an *epiklêros*) and to Euctemon's estate (on behalf of the daughter).

Moreover, note the gall and shamelessness of this witness: he filed a claim to Euctemon's daughter on his own behalf on the grounds that she was an *epiklêros*, and to Euctemon's actual estate on the grounds that it was subject to adjudication [*epidikou*]; but he has testified that Euctemon had a legitimate son! Now how is it that he has not openly exposed himself as having given false testimony? For obviously, if Euctemon had a legitimate son, his daughter would not be an *epiklêros*, and his estate would not be subject to adjudication. And to prove that he filed [*elache*] these claims [*lêxeis*], [the court clerk] will read to you these depositions.

190. Isaeus 7 *On the Estate of Apollodorus* 18–20. Equal shares of estate for *epiklêros* and son of her deceased sister. (350s)

See references and headnote under **136**. This speech was delivered by Apollodorus' adopted son (the biological son of his uterine half-sister) in a *diadikasia* (by direct trial, *euthydikia*) over Apollodorus' estate. The rival claimant, the daughter of Eupolis and wife of Pronapes (§18), is Apollodorus' first cousin. The quotation in §20 comes nearly verbatim from **176** [Dem.] 43.51.

Eupolis, you see, left two daughters: this one who is now making a claim and is married to Pronapes, and another, who was married to Aeschines of the deme Lusia and is deceased, having left behind a son, Thrasybulus, who is now an adult. [19] And there is a law that, if a brother by the same father dies childless and without a will, makes his sister and any nephew born of another sister equal sharers in the property. . . . [20] So, then, the law grants that they get equal shares of their father's and of their brother's property. But with regard to a cousin's property, or that of anyone outside this group of relatives [*syngeneias*], they do not get equal shares; instead, the law has given the right of kinship [*anchisteian*] to males before females. For it states, "Males and children of males shall have precedence, if they are descended from the same people, even if they are further removed."

191. Menander, *Aspis* 250–73. Order of claim to *epiklêros* (eldest brother first in order); possibility of qualified relative's failing to claim *epiklêros*; right of child of *epiklêros*. (324–292/1)

See references and headnote under **89**. At the beginning of Menander's *Aspis* (*The Shield*), Cleostratus is reported killed in action; his only sibling is a sister, who is now treated as *epiklêros* to the estate of their (deceased) father (cf. **188** Isae. 10.4–5). She has two paternal uncles, Smicrines and Chaerestratus; Smicrines, the elder of the two, intends to assert his right to claim her hand in marriage. For the right of a child of the *epiklêros* to inherit the estate cf. **182** [Dem.] 46.19–20.

SMICRINES. Well, then. What do you have to say to me now, Chaerestratus?

CHAERESTRATUS. First of all, my good man, we must deal with the arrangements for burial.

SMICRINES. Consider them dealt with. As for what comes next, promise the maiden to no one: this is not your business but mine. I am the elder; you have a wife and daughter at home, and she should be mine.

CHAERESTRATUS. Smicrines, don't you care at all about moderation?

SMICRINES. What for, boy?

CHAERESTRATUS. You intend, at your age, to marry a child?

SMICRINES. At what age?

CHAERESTRATUS. You certainly look like an old man to me.

SMICRINES. And I'm the only older man who has ever married?

CHAERESTRATUS. By the gods, Smicrines, deal with the matter humanely. Chaereas here was brought up with the girl and intends to marry her. So what am I proposing? You suffer no loss: you take all the property that there is and be *kyrios* of it; we give it to you. But let the girl get a husband appropriate to her age, on her own: I will pay with her a dowry of 2 talents out of my own property.

SMICRINES. . . . What are you saying? I should take the estate but let him have the girl, so that, if a child is born, I go on trial for possessing what belongs to it?

192. Harpocration s.v. *epidikos* etc. Definition of *epiklêros* and related terms. (Harpocration *fl.* 2nd c. A.D.; Isaeus *fl.* ca. 389–344/3; Deinarchus *fl.* 336/5–307/6)

See references and headnote under **28**. In this entry Harpocration defines the terms *epidikos*, *epiklêros* (or *epiklêritis*), and *epiproikos*. This is the only evidence for Isaeus' *Against Satyrus*; for his *Against Lysibius* see fragmentary speech XXVI Thalheim; for the remnants of the cited speech of Deinarchus see fragmentary speech LX Conomis. For the dowry of "destitute" *epiklêroi* see **181** [Dem.] 43.54.

Epidikos, epiklêros, epiproikos, and *epiklêritis*: An *epiklêros* is a female orphan left with an entire estate [*epi panti tôi klêrôi*] since she has no brother (the same is also called *epiklêritis*). One who is left with a portion of the estate to have as her dowry, since she has brothers, is called *epiproikos*. *Epidikos* [subject to adjudication] is the word used of an *epiklêros* when there is a dispute over whom she should be married to. These things are shown by Isaeus in his speech *Against Satyrus Concerning an* Epiklêros and by Deinarchus in his speech titled Diamartyria *Concerning the Daughter of Aristophon's Not Being Subject to Adjudication* [*epidikon*], in which speech it is also shown that destitute girls were given in marriage [*exedidosan*] by their closest relatives with a dowry of 5 minae. Isaeus in his speech *Against Lysibius* calls the *epiklêros* "*epiklêritis*."

193. Pollux, *Onomasticon* 3.33. Definition of *epiklêros* and related terms. (late 2nd c. A.D.)

See references and headnote under **117**. Here Pollux defines the terms *epiklêros* (or *epiklêritis*, a form apparently found in the laws of Solon);

anchisteus (as relating to an *epiklêros*); *epidikos* and its antonym *anepidikos*; and *thêssa* (on thetic *epiklêroi* see **181** [Dem.] 43.54).

A daughter who grows up with an entire estate [*epi panti tôi klêrôi*] is called *epiklêros*, both when her father is alive and after he dies. Some also called her *patrouchos*; Isaeus also called her *epiklêritis*, as did Solon. Her relative by kinship is called *anchisteus*. An *epiklêros* is *epidikos* [subject to adjudication] when persons engage in dispute with each other over her on the grounds that the right of kinship [*anchisteias*] applies more to themselves [than to their adversaries]; she is *anepidikos* [not subject to adjudication] when they do not engage in dispute over her. The one who has no paternal estate is called *thêssa*; her *anchisteus* gives her in marriage [*ekdidôsin*] if he is married to another woman, or by all means marries her.

7.2.3. COLLATERAL RELATIVES

See also **161** Isae. 11.6, 31, 35; **171** [Dem.] 35.3–4; **176** [Dem.] 43.51; **184** Ar. *Birds* 1641–70; **186b** Isae. 3.72–74; **187** Isae. 8.31, 33; **190** Isae. 7.18–20; **230** [Dem.] 44 (selections); **231** Isae. 5.6–7, 9, 12–18; **235** Isae. 4.24–25; **236** [Dem.] 48.22–32; **259** [Dem.] 48 (selections).

194. Isaeus 11 *On the Estate of Hagnias* 1–5, 8–12, 17–18, 29–30. Order of intestate succession; limit of *anchisteia* (decedent's first cousin once removed or second cousin?); claims to estate; rule giving precedence to males. (*post* 361/0)

See references and headnote under **161**. "The boy" (§§1, 5, 11) is the son of Stratocles, the deceased brother of the speaker Theopompus; in §8, the phrase *ek patradelphôn* is variously interpreted as "the sons of brothers by the same father" (cf. [Demosthenes] 44.13) or as "the sons of [each other's] paternal uncles" (see Pollux, *Onomasticon* 3.22). In previous litigation over the disputed estate, Theopompus had prevailed over Phylomache (the daughter of Eubulides), Hagnias' patrilateral first cousin once removed (§§9–10, 17–18), and over Hagnias' mother, who "belonged to the qualified kin of her own son" (§29) not as his mother but as his second cousin (§§17–18). Theopompus' victories in both that lawsuit and this one have led to scholarly debate over the definition of "children of first cousins" in the law of intestate succession (**176** [Dem.] 43.51). The lawgiver does not specify whether (1) he uses the term solely from the point of view of the decedent (as is clearly done elsewhere in the law), in which case the "children of [the decedent's] first cousins" are the decedent's first cousins once removed, or (2) the term is used reciprocally, as Theopompus argues here: Theopompus and the decedent are the "children of first cousins," and so Theopompus, second cousin to the decedent, is entitled to inherit under the law (while Stratocles' son, second cousin once removed to the decedent, is not). This vague wording allowed Theopompus to argue (successfully) that second cousins were included in the *anchisteia*, and allowed the speaker of [Demosthenes] 43 to argue that the *anchisteia* ended with first cousins once removed (the verdict in that lawsuit is unknown). The document included in §11 and enclosed in hooked brackets {} is a spurious addition to the text; it is a close paraphrase (but not an exact quotation) of the relevant clause of **176** [Dem.] 43.51.

LAWS.

I had the laws read out to you because [my adversary] insists that, according to the first of them, the boy has a right to half the estate; but he is not telling the truth. Hagnias, you see, was not our brother, but concerning the property of a brother the law grants the inheritance first to brothers and children of brothers, if they have the same father: this degree of kinship [*genos*] is closest to the decedent. [2] If these do not exist, in the second place the law calls upon sisters by the same father and their children. If they do not exist, the law gives the right of kinship [*anchisteian*] to a third degree of relation [*genei*]: cousins on the father's side down to sons of first cousins [*anepsiôn paidôn*]. And if this degree of kinship too is lacking, it goes back again and makes the decedent's relatives on the mother's side *kyrioi* of his property, according to the same principles by which it gave the inheritance to the relatives on the father's side at the beginning.

[3] These are the only rights of kinship [*anchisteias*] the lawgiver creates, with more concise wording than my explanation, but all the same in this way he makes plain his intent as to what he wishes. . . . [4] [To the court clerk:] You, read.

LAWS.

[5] Stop. [To the prosecutor:] I am going to question you. Is the boy Hagnias' brother, or his nephew, born from his brother or his sister, or his first cousin [*anepsios*], or the son of his first cousin on the mother's or the father's side? Which of these titles, to whom the law gives the right of kinship [*anchisteian*]? And be sure you don't say that he's my nephew. The discussion now is not about my estate; I'm still alive. If I had died childless and he were claiming my property, he could properly give that answer under questioning.

. . .

[8] Hagnias and I, gentlemen, and Eubulides and Stratocles and Stratius, the brother of Hagnias' mother, are the sons of first cousins [*anepsiôn*]: our fathers were first cousins, the sons of brothers by the same father [*ek patradelphôn*].

Now, Hagnias, when he was preparing to sail out to serve as ambassador . . . , did not leave his property in the hands of us, his closest relatives, in case anything happened to him, but instead adopted his niece as his daughter; and if anything happened to her, he gave his property to Glaucon, his brother by the same mother; these provisions he wrote in a will.

[9] Time passed, and then Eubulides died, as did the daughter whom Hagnias adopted, and Glaucon received the estate in accordance with the will. We never saw fit to contest Hagnias' will, but thought that his decision regarding his own property should be binding and abided by it. But Eubulides' daughter, along with her associates, laid claim to [*lanchanei*] the estate and took it, defeating those who laid claim in accordance with the will. She was outside the qualified kin [*anchisteias*] but hoped (as it seems) that we would not go to court against her, since we had not contested the will. [10] But we—Stratius and Stratocles and I—when the estate became subject to adjudication [*epidikos*] to the closest relatives, all began preparations to lay claim [*lanchanein*]. Before we filed our lawsuits, though, Stratius died, as did Stratocles, and so I am left as the only first cousin's son on the father's side; under the laws, the inheritance belonged to me alone, since now all the others who belonged to the qualified kin [*anchisteiai*] in the same degree as I were gone.

[11] And how will you know that the right of kinship [*anchisteia*] belonged to me and not to their children, including this boy? The law itself will make it clear. Everyone agrees, you see, that the right of kinship belongs to cousins on the father's side down to children of first cousins [*anepsiôn paidôn*]; now we have to see whether it gives the right to our children after us. [To the court clerk:] So take the law and read it to them.

LAW. {If there is no relative on the father's side down to children of first cousins, the relatives on the mother's side shall be *kyrioi* according to the same principles.}

[12] You hear, gentlemen, that the lawgiver did not say that if there is no relative on the father's side down to children of first cousins, the children of children of first cousins shall be *kyrioi*. Instead, if we do not exist, he then gave the inheritance to the decedent's relatives on the mother's side—brothers and sisters and their children and so on—according to the same principles stated at the beginning; our children, though, he placed outside the qualified kin [*anchisteias*].

. . .

[17] They were at such a loss, though, as to what they should write in response concerning the right of kinship [*anchisteias*] that when the woman who possessed the estate and those who cited her degree of kinship [*genos*] told lies, they were easily exposed by me at the time as having had the audacity to write something that was not true. But the ones who argued on behalf of

Hagnias' mother, who is related by the same degree [*genei*] as I am, since she was Stratius' sister, but is excluded by the law, which commands that males take precedence, ignored this and, intending to gain the advantage over me, wrote that she was the mother of the decedent: this was the closest of all relations by nature, but by universal consent it does not fall within the qualified degrees of kin [*anchisteiais*].

[18] I then wrote that I was the son of a first cousin [*anepsiou*], and I proved that those women do not fall within the qualified degrees of kin, and so I got the estate awarded to me [*epedikasamên*] by you. None of their arguments prevailed, either for the woman who possessed the estate that she had previously defeated those who laid claim in accordance with the will, or for the other woman that she was the mother of the person who left the estate; the men serving on the jury in that instance considered justice and their oaths so important that they cast their votes for me, the one who laid claim according to the laws.

. . .

[29] . . . For as I said earlier, the law does not give the right of kinship [*anchisteian*] in any way to our children after us, but gives it to the decedent's relatives on the mother's side. [30] So, in the first place, Glaucon, the brother of Hagnias, would have come for the property, and they not only would have had no better degree of kinship [*genos*] to cite in response but would obviously have been outside the qualified kin [*anchisteias*]. Then, if he were unwilling, his and Hagnias' mother would have come, since she too belonged to the qualified kin of her own son, and so when she went to court against people who were not related to him at all, she clearly would have received half the estate from you, since justice and the laws would have given it to her.

195. Isaeus 7 *On the Estate of Apollodorus* 5–7. Division of estate among legitimate sons; brothers and children of deceased brothers share *per stirpes*. (350s)

See references and headnotes under **136** and **190**. Eupolis, Thrasyllus, and Mneson were the sons and heirs of Apollodorus the elder (Apollodorus I); here the speaker explains that, following the deaths of Mneson and Thrasyllus, Mneson's estate was disputed between Eupolis and Thrasyllus' son Apollodorus the younger (Apollodorus II), who succeeded in claiming his half of the estate (and later adopted the speaker). Under the law of intestate succession (**176** [Dem.] 43.51), if Thrasyllus predeceased Mneson—which is unknown (note the vague language in §5)—then half of Mneson's estate was due to his surviving brother Eupolis, and the other half to Apollodorus II, the son of his deceased brother Thrasyllus. On the trierarchy and other liturgies see p. 25; on guardianship see chapter 6.

Eupolis, Thrasyllus, and Mneson, men of the jury, were brothers by the same mother and father. Their father left them an estate large enough for each of them to be deemed fit by you to perform liturgies. The three of them divided the estate among themselves. Two of them died about the same time: Mneson died here, unmarried and childless, and Thrasyllus died after being enrolled among the trierarchs in Sicily, leaving behind a son, Apollodorus [II], who has now adopted me. [6] So Eupolis, the only one of them left, did not see fit to enjoy a small part of the property but obtained for himself Mneson's estate—half of which belonged to Apollodorus [II]—in its entirety, claiming that his brother had given it to him; and as for Apollodorus [II] himself, Eupolis managed his affairs so poorly as guardian that he lost a lawsuit for 3 talents to him. [7] You see, my grandfather Archedamus, who was married to Apollodorus' [II] mother, my grandmother, seeing Apollodorus [II] being deprived of all his property, raised him when he was a boy, having taken him into his and Apollodorus' [II] mother's home. And when Apollodorus [II] became a man, he supported him in his lawsuits and recovered his half of the estate that Mneson had left, as well as everything he had been deprived of as a result of his guardianship, by winning two lawsuits, and he caused Apollodorus [II] to recover his estate in its entirety.

196. [Demosthenes] 44 *Against Leochares* 24–26, 32–34. Claim to estate by collateral relative (grandnephew/first cousin once removed); rule of return for adopted son; rule prohibiting adopted son from adopting; vacant estate; filing for estate with eponymous archon; ?father's right to inherit from son. (?320s)

See references and headnote under **137**. Upon the death without issue of Leocrates II, the biological son of Leostratus II and the third in a series of adopted sons of Archiades, Leostratus II has endeavored to have first himself, and then his other biological son, Leochares, adopted as Archiades' son and heir. The speaker contends that this is illegal and claims Archiades' estate on behalf of his father, Aristodemus, on the grounds that Aristodemus is the closest surviving natal kinsman of Archiades (specifically, a grandnephew: Archiades' brother's daughter's son) and of Leostratus II (first cousin once removed, by virtue of the adoption of Leostratus II as Archiades' son). On adoption see chapter 6; on the rule of return for adopted sons see **138** Harpo. s.v. *hoti hoi poiêtoi* etc. For the deposit (*parakatabolê*) cf. **226** Pollux, *Onomasticon* 8.32; **230d** [Dem.] 44.57–59; **234** [Dem.] 43.5–16. This passage is occasionally adduced as evidence for a father's right to inherit from his intestate son; perhaps a father had this right as the closest surviving relative in default of the named members of the *anchisteia* (**176** [Dem.] 43.51), but in this case Leostratus II's claim is tenuous, since he had returned to his natal household and Leocrates II had not.

But all the same, even with this being the situation, we put up with everything, as I have said. Until when? Until Leocrates [II], the son who had been left by Leostratus [II] in the household [*oikôi*] of Archiades, died childless. Since he died childless, we demand, as Archiades' closest relatives, that we inherit the estate and that a son not be introduced [into the family] as the adopted son of the decedent, who was himself adopted, in order to rob us of what is ours. [25] For if Leocrates [II] had adopted a son while he was living, even though that act is against the law, we would not have objected; but since he had no son by birth and did not adopt one while alive, and the law grants inheritances to the closest relatives, how do we not have the right on both grounds not to be deprived of these things? [26] For, you see, we are the closest relatives of both Archiades, to whom the estate originally belonged, and Leocrates [II], his adopted son: his father has returned to the deme of Eleusis and thus left himself no further legal family relationship, while we, in whose family he used to be, maintained the closest kinship [*tên anankaiotatên syngeneian*], as his first cousins once removed [*anepsiadoi*]. So, if you like, we demand to inherit as relatives of Archiades, or, if you like, as relatives of Leocrates [II]: for since he died childless, no one is more closely related than we are.

. . .

[32] For when Leocrates [II] had died and his burial had taken place, and we went to [take possession of] his property, since the man had died childless and unmarried, my adversary Leostratus [II] here ejected us, claiming that it was his. Now, since he was Leocrates' [II] father, the fact that he prevented us from conducting any of the customary rites for the deceased perhaps makes sense, although his act was against the law: it is reasonable that management of the burial be entrusted to the biological father, but also, in the second place, to us, the kinsmen, to whom the deceased was related by virtue of his adoption.

[33] But after the customary rites took place, what law will have empowered him, when the household [*oikou*] was vacant, to eject us, the closest relatives, from the estate? The fact, he will say, that he was the father of the deceased. But he had returned to his ancestral household and was no longer *kyrios* of the estate he had left his son in charge of! Otherwise, what use are the laws? [34] So when the ejection occurred—to make a long story short—we filed a claim [*elachomen*] to the estate with the archon, on the grounds that the deceased had, as I have said, no son by birth and no son who had been adopted according to the laws. But then my adversary Leostratus [II] here paid a deposit [*parakataballei*], as the son of the aforementioned Archiades, having considered neither the fact that he had returned to the deme of Eleusis nor the fact that adopted sons are made so not by themselves but by those who adopt them.

7.2.4. *NOTHOI* (ILLEGITIMATE CHILDREN)

See also **125** [Arist.] *Ath. Pol.* 26.4; **127** (Reenactment of Pericles' citizenship law); **176** [Dem.] 43.51; **184** Ar. *Birds* 1641–70.

197. Harpocration s.v. *notheia*. Bequest to illegitimate child. (Harpocration *fl.* 2nd c.A.D.)

See references and headnote under **28**. In this entry Harpocration defines *notheia*; with the 1,000-dr. limit attested here contrast **198** *Suda* s.v. *epiklêros*. For the citations see, in order, Lysias, fragmentary speech LXXIII Carey (on the *graphê xenias* see chapter 6); Isaeus, fragmentary speech XXVI Thalheim (cf. **192** Harpo. s.v. *epidikos* etc.); **184** Ar. *Birds* 1641–70; Hypereides, fragmentary speeches V–VI Jensen; Demosthenes 23.213. The Cynosarges was a gymnasium for *nothoi* located southeast of Athens and dedicated to Heracles (cf. **184** Ar. *Birds* 1641–70).

Notheia: Bequests [*ta didomena*] to illegitimate children [*nothois*] out of their fathers' estates are called by this name and were of up to 1,000 drachmas: Lysias in his speech *Against Calliphanes for Being a Foreigner* [*xenias*], if genuine; Isaeus, *Against Lysibius Concerning an* Epiklêros; Aristophanes, *Birds*: "Well, what if my father gives me his property as an illegitimate child's portion [*nothei'*] when he dies?" "The law doesn't allow him to do that." The things that illegitimate children were not permitted to share in are clarified by Hypereides in his *Second Oration against Aristagora*. Demosthenes in his speech *Against Aristocrates* states that they belonged to the Cynosarges.

198. *Suda* s.v. *epiklêros*. Legitimate daughter (as *epiklêros*) excludes illegitimate son; *notheia* (bequest to illegitimate child). (late 10th c.A.D.)

See references and headnote under **49**. Here, in the entry defining *epiklêros*, the author discusses the inheritance status of illegitimate children, including *notheia*, for which the limit stated here is 5 mn. = 500 dr. (cf. **197** Harpo. s.v. *notheia*: 1,000 dr.). A scholion to Aristophanes, *Birds* 1656 (cf. **184** Ar. *Birds* 1641–70) replicates this entry (among other comments) nearly verbatim. The two limits can be reconciled on the hypothesis that a decedent might bequeath 500 dr. to each of up to two illegitimate children.

The Athenians had a law providing that, where there was a legitimate [*gnêsias*] daughter and an illegitimate [*nothou*] son, the illegitimate son did not inherit his father's estate. . . . Since illegitimate children [*nothois*] were not permitted to inherit, they used to give them the money directly [*dia cheiros*]. There was an Athenian law providing that people could leave to illegitimate children up to 5 minae.

7.2.5. NON-CITIZENS

See also **125** [Arist.] *Ath. Pol.* 26.4; **127** (Reenactment of Pericles' citizenship law).

199. Isaeus 4 *On the Estate of Nicostratus* 9. ?Right of former master to estate of freedman. (?ca. 350)

See especially **Wyse**, *Isaeus* (text and commentary); **Wevers**, *Isaeus*; **Edwards**, *Isaeus* (translation with introduction and notes); also **Blass**, *AB* 2.541–43; **Jebb**, *AO* 2.322–24; **Usher**, *GO* 145–46.

This speech was delivered on behalf of the brothers Hagnon and Hagnotheus, first cousins of Nicostratus, in a *diadikasia* over Nicostratus' estate. The rival claimant, Chariades, claims to be Nicostratus' adopted son and heir. Here the speaker relates a claim made to Nicostratus' estate by two men who alleged that they were Nicostratus' former masters. No law expressly governing the rights of inheritance from freedmen is preserved, but in at least some instances (e.g., when a manumission contract so stipulated) former masters were the heirs of their freedmen. In Athens, freed slaves assumed metic status upon their manumission; naturalization as citizens was extremely rare (see the introduction to chapter 6).

Pyrrhus of the deme Lamptrae said that the money had been dedicated by Nicostratus to Athena but had been given to him by Nicostratus himself. Ctesias of the deme Besa and Cranaus first said that they had secured a judgment of a talent against Nicostratus, and when they were unable to prove it, they pretended he was their freedman, and even so did not prove what they were asserting.

200. [Aristotle], *Constitution of the Athenians (Ath. Pol.)* 58.3. Polemarch's supervision of *dikê apostasiou*, *dikê aprostasiou*, and lawsuits between metics over estates and *epiklêroi*. (332–322)

See references and headnote under **1c**. Here the author discusses the duties of the polemarch (p. 2). For the polemarch's role in lawsuits between metics (including freedmen: see headnote under **199** Isae. 4.9) concerning estates and *epiklêroi* cf. **227** [Dem.] 46.22–23; on the requirement that a metic have a citizen patron (*prostatês*) see p. 23.

And he introduces lawsuits [*dikas*] for deserting a patron [*apostasiou*] and for not having a patron [*aprostasiou*], and those concerning estates and *epiklêroi* involving metics.

7.3. Succession by Will

See also **87** Dem. 27.4–5; **91** Dem. 27.55; **92** Dem. 45.27–28, 30; **106** Lys. 32.6; **114** Dem. 41.5–7, 10; **135** Isae. 2.13–17, 19; **139** Lys. 32.8–10, 19–24; **145** Dem. 27.34, 40, 46, 49–50, 58, 60–61, 67; **146** Dem. 28.15–16; **147** Dem. 29.30–31; **148** Dem. 36.20, 22; **149** Dem. 45.37; **178** Isae. 6.25, 28, 63; §**7.2.4**; **229** Isae. 6.3–4, 43–44, 52.

201. [Demosthenes] 46 *2 Against Stephanus* 14 (*lex*). Solon's testamentary law. (date of speech ?349; date of law 594/3)

See references and headnote under **83**. Here the speaker cites the law of Solon that gave a decedent the power to dispose of his estate by will. It is sometimes hypothesized that this law was designed solely to grant a decedent the power to adopt a son, who would inherit the decedent's estate in its entirety or, if the decedent left a daughter, would have to marry her. Note, however, that these limitations are not stated, and in the fourth century the law was interpreted as granting significant latitude in wills. On the interpretation of the clause of the law dealing with adoptees (strictly, *inter vivos* adoptees: by the fourth century, at least, testamentary adoptees could refuse the adoption and did have to claim the estate by *epidikasia*) cf. **209** [Dem.] 44.67–68.

Everyone, except those who had been adopted such that they neither could renounce [*apeipein*] nor had to claim an inheritance [*epidikasasthai*], as of the date when Solon entered office, shall be permitted to dispose of [*diathesthai*] his own property however he wishes, if there are no legitimate male children, unless [he disposes] on account of insanity, senility, drugs, or illness, or under the influence of a woman, and is out of his mind due to one of the preceding, or [he disposes] while under constraint by duress [*anankês*] or detention [*desmou*].

202. Plutarch, *Solon* 21.3–4. Solon's testamentary law and prior law governing estates. (date of composition late 1st-early 2nd c.A.D.; date of law 594/3)

See references and headnote under **1d**. Here Plutarch discusses and paraphrases Solon's law on wills (**201** [Dem.] 46.14). Plutarch's statement concerning the disposition of estates before Solon is plausible but not directly attested by any Archaic source.

He was also famous for his law concerning wills. Before this it was not permitted [to make a will]; rather, the property and the estate of the deceased had to remain in his family [*genei*]. But Solon allowed a person, if he had no sons, to give his property to whomever he wished. . . . [21.4] However, he did not permit these bequests [*doseis*] without restraint or qualification, but only if [a person did] not [act] on account of illness, drugs, or detention, or while constrained by duress or under the influence of a woman. . . .

203. [Aristotle], *Constitution of the Athenians (Ath. Pol.)* 35.2. Amendment of Solon's testamentary law by the Thirty Tyrants. (date of composition 332–322; law authored 594/3, amended 404/3, amendment repealed 403)

See references and headnote under **1c**. On the Thirty Tyrants see p. 12. Here the author describes the Thirty's annulment of the conditions that invalidated a will under Solon's law (**201** [Dem.] 46.14); upon the restoration of democracy in 403 this amendment was repealed (see **12a** Andoc. 1.83–84). On sycophants see p. 33.

. . . and they annulled those of Solon's laws that gave room for disputes, and the power that was in the hands of juries, with the justification that they were correcting the constitution and rendering it indisputable. For example, they made a person entitled [*kyrion*] to give his property to whomever he wished without qualification [*kathapax*] and removed the additional obstacles—"unless he is insane or senile or under the influence of a woman"—so that sycophants would have no means of attack.

7.3.1. TESTAMENTARY ADOPTION AND *EPIKLÊROI*

See also **83** [Dem.] 46.18; **96** [Dem.] 43.75; **152** [Arist.] *Ath. Pol.* 56.6–7; **154** Harpo. s.v. *kakôseôs*; **§6.4.3**; **183** Ar. *Wasps* 583–86; **186b** Isae. 3.72–74; **194**

Isae. 11.1–5, 8–12, 17–18, 29–30; **201** [Dem.] 46.14; **206** Isae. 10.9–10; **211** Isae. 6.5–7; **213** Isae. 9.7–12; **220** Isae. 9.3; **228** Isae. 3.40–50, 57–60, 62; **229** Isae. 6.3–4, 43–44, 52; **231** Isae. 5.6–7, 9, 12–18; **235** Isae. 4.24–25.

204. Isaeus 3 *On the Estate of Pyrrhus* 67–69. Solon's testamentary law and the *epiklêros*. (?ca. 389)

See references and headnote under **85**, and cf. **186** Isae. 3 (selections). Here the speaker summarizes Solon's testamentary law (**201** [Dem.] 46.14) and paraphrases the first sentence of the law on intestate succession, which provides that the estate of an intestate decedent who leaves one or more *epiklêroi* must be transferred with them (**176** [Dem.] 43.51). Accordingly, if Pyrrhus adopted Endius by will and Pyrrhus' daughter Phile was legitimate, the will and adoption were valid only if Endius was required to marry Phile. For additional partial or complete paraphrases of Solon's testamentary law see **135** Isae. 2.13–17, 19; **202** Plut. *Solon* 21.3–4; **203** [Arist.] *Ath. Pol.* 35.2; **209** [Dem.] 44.67–68; Lysias fr. 283 Carey; Isaeus 4.16; 6.8–9; Hypereides 3.17; Demosthenes 20.102; [Demosthenes] 46.16; 48.56.

The fact that the woman was subject to adjudication [*epidikos*], if in fact she was left behind as a legitimate daughter, can be seen most clearly from the laws. For the law explicitly states that a man is permitted to dispose of his property however he wishes, if he leaves behind no legitimate male children; and if he leaves behind females, [the property must go] with these. Therefore, it is permitted to bequeath [*dounai*] and dispose of one's property with one's daughters, but without the legitimate daughters one may not adopt [a son] or bequeath any of his property to anyone. [69] So if Pyrrhus adopted Endius as his son without the legitimate daughter, his adoption would be invalid according to the law; but if he did give him his daughter and left him behind as his adopted son on that condition, how could you, Pyrrhus' uncles, have permitted Endius to lay claim to [*epidikazesthai*] Pyrrhus' estate without the legitimate daughter—if Pyrrhus had one—especially given that you have testified that your nephew enjoined you to take care of this child?

7.3.2. TESTAMENTARY CAPACITY

See also **135** Isae. 2.13–17, 19; **178** Isae. 6.25, 28, 63; **179** Dem. 36.8–9, 11, 34; **201** [Dem.] 46.14; **210** [Dem.] 46.24; **229** Isae. 6.3–4, 43–44, 52.

205. Lysias 19 *On the Property of Aristophanes* 39–40. Father of legitimate son disposing of property by will. (387/6)

See references and headnote under **108**. Here the speaker describes the will of Conon, a leading Athenian politician and general of the late fifth and early fourth century. Note that this will was treated as valid despite the existence of a legitimate son, Timotheus, to whom Conon bequeathed less than half of his estate. For additional examples of wills composed by the fathers of legitimate sons see **87** Dem. 27.4–5 (cf. **91** Dem. 27.55; also Demosthenes 27.41–43); **92** Dem. 45.27–28, 30; **106** Lys. 32.6 with **212** Lys. 32.5, 7. On the careers of Conon and Timotheus see J. K. **Davies**, *Athenian Propertied Families 600–300 B.C.* (Oxford 1971), no. 13700. The stater was a gold coin equivalent to 20 drachmas; hence the exact total value of the estate (as itemized here) was 38 tal. 2,000 dr.

Conon's death and the will that he made on Cyprus showed clearly that his property was a small fraction of what you were expecting. To Athena and to Apollo at Delphi he dedicated as offerings 5,000 staters; to his own nephew, who safeguarded and managed all his property on Cyprus, he gave about 10,000 drachmas, and to his brother he gave 3 talents. The remainder he left to his son: 17 talents. The sum of these figures comes to about 40 talents.

206. Isaeus 10 *On the Estate of Aristarchus* 9–10. Testamentary capacity of child, woman, and father of legitimate son. (?378–371)

See references and headnote under **188**. In §9, the speaker alludes to Solon's testamentary law (**201** [Dem.] 46.14). With regard to the minor Demochares, the speaker appears to make an argument from analogy: the law paraphrased in §10, which must be of Archaic date since the limit is stated in kind rather than in currency, appears to govern contracts rather than wills, but the Athenians may well have enforced it as also governing wills. Note also that some interpret this clause as meaning "the law explicitly forbids the power to make a contract to a child [absolutely], or to a woman [in a case involving a value] greater than a medimnus of barley." 1 medimnus equals about 1.5 bushels (53 liters); for the corresponding currency value during the Archaic and Classical periods (from perhaps 1 dr. in Solon's time to a normal price of 3–6 dr. in the fourth century) see **Wyse**, *Isaeus* 659.

I think you all know, gentlemen, that introductions of adopted children occur by will, when men bequeath [*didontôn*] their property and adopt sons, but otherwise they are not permitted. So if someone is going to say that Aristarchus [I] himself made a will, he will not be telling the truth: since he had a legitimate son, Demochares, he neither would have wanted to do that nor would have been permitted to bequeath his property to someone else. And if someone is going to say that when Aristarchus [I] died, Demochares adopted [Aristarchus II], that will be a lie too. [10] A child, you see, is not permitted to have a will: the law explicitly forbids to a child or a woman the power to make a contract [involving a value] greater than a medimnus of barley. Now, there has been testimony that Aristarchus [I] died before his son Demochares, and that Demochares died after his father; so even if they had made wills, under their wills [Aristarchus II] had no right to inherit this property. [To the court clerk:] Read the laws according to which neither of them was permitted to make a will.

LAWS.

207. Demosthenes 36 *For Phormion* 14. Woman disposing of property by will. (?350/49)

See references and headnote under **148**. In this passage, Archippe, the mother of Apollodorus, is apparently described as having made a will that was treated as valid; note that Archippe had multiple legitimate sons (**148** Dem. 36.20, 22), and contrast **206** Isae. 10.9–10.

As long as his mother, who had exact knowledge of all these things, was alive, Apollodorus never brought a single charge against Phormion here. But when she died, he brought a frivolous lawsuit, demanding 3,000 drachmas in cash, in addition to the 2,000 she had given to Phormion's children, and some piece of clothing and a female slave.

208. Aeschines 3 *Against Ctesiphon* 21. Magistrate who has not undergone *euthynai* prohibited from making will. (330)

See references and headnote under **27**. Here Aeschines lists actions that are forbidden to a magistrate who has not yet undergone the review of his conduct in office (*euthynai*: p. 32; **302a** [Arist.] *Ath. Pol.* 48.4–5, 54.2).

And again, the lawgiver does not permit a magistrate who has not undergone his review of conduct [*hypeuthynon*] to dedicate his property to a god, or to set up an offering, or to be adopted out of his household, or to dispose of his property by will, or to do many other things; in a word, the lawgiver takes the property of unreviewed magistrates in pledge until they render an account to the city.

209. [Demosthenes] 44 *Against Leochares* 67–68. Interpretation of adoption clause in Solon's testamentary law; rule that adopted son may not dispose of estate by will. (?320s)

See references and headnotes under **137** and **196**. Here the speaker interprets the exception for adopted sons in Solon's testamentary law (**201** [Dem.] 46.14; cf. **196** [Dem.] 44.24–26, 32–34; **221** [Dem.] 44.64) as barring adopted sons from disposing by will of an estate held by virtue of adoption. (On the rule of return for adopted sons cf. **138** Harpo. s.v. *hoti hoi poiêtoi* etc.; **196** [Dem.] 44.24–26, 32–34.) Note that the speaker's quotation of the adoption clause is incomplete: he omits the part of the clause specifying *inter vivos* adoptees.

And here is the most important point of all and the one best known to you: Solon's law does not permit an adopted son to dispose of the property of the household [*oikôi*] into which he was adopted. Rightly so, in my opinion: a son adopted by law into the estate of another should not think of it as if it were his own property but should act in accordance with the laws, as the law states in each written detail. [68] "All those who had not been adopted," it states, "as of the date when Solon entered office shall be permitted to dispose however they wish." That is, adopted sons are not permitted to dispose; instead, they must either return while living [to their original households], leaving behind a legitimate son in [the adoptive household], or, when they die, restore the inheritance to the original relatives of the adopter.

7.3.3. CONDITIONAL WILLS

See also **194** Isae. 11.1–5, 8–12, 17–18, 29–30; **201** [Dem.] 46.14.

210. [Demosthenes] 46 *2 Against Stephanus* 24 (*lex*). Law permitting will conditional on death of minor son(s). (date of speech ?349; law of Archaic date, possibly authored by Solon, 594/3)

See references and headnote under **83**. Here the speaker cites a law granting the father of a legitimate son the capacity to make a will, which becomes valid only if no legitimate son survives two years past puberty; for this age requirement cf. **182** [Dem.] 46.19–20.

Whatever will a father makes when there are legitimate sons, if the sons die before they are two years past puberty, the father's will shall be valid.

211. Isaeus 6 *On the Estate of Philoctemon* 5–7. Will specifying conditional adoption and inheritance. (365–363)

See references and headnotes under **144** and **178**. Here the speaker describes Philoctemon's will, which provided for the adoption of Chaerestratus, in default of a legitimate biological son, as son and heir to the entire estate.

Since Philoctemon had no child by the woman to whom he was married, . . . he decided to dispose of his property by will, so that he would not leave his household [*oikon*] vacant in case something should happen to him. [6] Both of the brothers that he once had had died childless. One of his sisters, who was married to Chaereas, had no male child, nor had ever had one, despite being married for many years. But there were two sons born from the other sister, who was married to Phanostratus here. Of these he adopted the elder, Chaerestratus here, as his son; [7] and accordingly he wrote in a will that if he should not have a child by his wife, Chaerestratus should inherit his estate. He deposited the will with his brother-in-law Chaereas, who was married to his other sister. And now the will itself will be read to you, and those who were present will testify. [To the court clerk:] Please read.

WILL.

WITNESSES.

7.3.4. FORMS OF WILL

See also **16** Isae. 9.17–19; **183** Ar. *Wasps* 583–86; **194** Isae. 11.1–5, 8–12, 17–18, 29–30; **201** [Dem.] 46.14; **211** Isae. 6.5–7; **219** Isae. 1 (selections).

212. Lysias 32 *Against Diogeiton* 5, 7. Sealing and deposit of written will. (ca. 400)

See **106** and **139** with references and headnotes. Here the speaker describes Diodotus' making and sealing a will and depositing it with his brother (and father-in-law) Diogeiton (cf. **106** Lys. 32.6; **139** Lys. 32.8–10, 19–24). For the sealing and/or deposit of a written will cf. **183** Ar. *Wasps* 583–86; **211** Isae. 6.5–7; **215** Isae. 4.13; Isaeus 7.1.

Later, when Diodotus was called up among the hoplites under Thrasyllus, he summoned his wife, who was his niece, and her father, who was his father-in-law and brother and the grandfather and uncle of the children. In the belief that due to these family connections no one should behave more justly toward his children, he gave this man his will, along with 5 talents in cash as a deposit to be held in trust [*parakatathêkên*]. . . . [7] After doing these things and leaving a copy at home, he went off to serve with Thrasyllus. But when he died in Ephesus, Diogeiton concealed from his daughter the death of her husband and seized the documents that he had left under seal. . . .

213. Isaeus 9 *On the Estate of Astyphilus* 7–12. Customary use of witnesses to written will; testamentary adoption. (*post* 371)

> See references and headnote under **16**. Here, in contrast to **215** Isae. 4.13, the speaker implies that it was normal procedure for a testator to summon witnesses to the creation and the contents of a will.

Since, gentlemen, none of his relatives was present when my brother died, and even I was not in Athens when his bones were brought back here, I am compelled to prove that this will is false on the sole basis of what my adversaries say. Presumably he not only desired to adopt and leave behind a son but also saw to it that the terms of his will would be completely valid, and that whoever he adopted would possess his estate, would visit his ancestral altars, and would conduct the customary rites for him when he died and for his ancestors. [8] And he would have most secure knowledge that all this would happen if he made his will not in the absence of his relatives, but instead after inviting first his relatives, then his phratry members and demesmen, and then as many of his other intimates as he could: that way, if someone made a claim either by right of kinship or according to the will, that person would easily be exposed as a liar.

[9] Apparently, though, Astyphilus did nothing of the sort and did not even call any of these people to witness when he made the will my adversaries claim he made—unless someone has actually been convinced by my adversaries to agree that he was present. But I myself will bring before you all these people as witnesses.

WITNESSES.

[10] Now, my adversary Cleon here will probably say that it is not reasonable for you to use these witnesses as proof, since they testify that they have no knowledge of Astyphilus' making this will. In my opinion, though, since this dispute concerns a will and Astyphilus' having adopted a son, the testimony of his relatives who say that they were not present at a matter of greatest importance is far more reliable for us than the testimony of people with no relation to him who claim that they were present.

[11] And Cleon himself, gentlemen, if he did not want to look like an idiot, when Astyphilus was adopting his son and leaving behind his will, should have

invited any relative he knew of who was in town, as well as the others—in short, whomever he knew Astyphilus associated with. For no one could have prevented Astyphilus from giving his property to whomever he wished, and the fact that Astyphilus did not make this will in secret would have been strong evidence for Cleon. [12] Moreover, gentlemen, if Astyphilus wanted no one to know that he was adopting Cleon's son or that he had left a will, presumably he would have recorded no one else in the document as a witness. But if he apparently made a will in the presence of witnesses, but these are not the people he most associated with but random individuals, how is there any likelihood that the will is authentic?

214. Demosthenes 41 *Against Spudias* 16. Witnessed oral will. (*post* 364/3)

See **101**, **109**, and **114** with references and headnotes. Here the speaker describes the oral will made by Polyeuctus. For another oral will (made under extraordinary circumstances, with the testator in prison awaiting execution) see Lysias 13.41–42.

Concerning the house, if he claims that it was at my persuasion that Polyeuctus ordered the erection of the boundary-markers for the 1,000 drachmas, I certainly did not also persuade the witnesses, Spudias, to give false testimony for me: the ones who were present when he pledged his daughter [*êngya*] to me, the ones who know that I received less [than the agreed-upon amount], . . . and finally the ones who were present at his will.

215. Isaeus 4 *On the Estate of Nicostratus* 13. Customary use of witnesses to written will. (?ca. 350)

See references and headnote under **199**. Here the speaker contends that testators normally employ witnesses merely to the existence of a will, not to its contents; contrast **213** Isae. 9.7–12.

Moreover, gentlemen, the majority of men making wills do not even tell those present what they are writing in the will; they summon witnesses only to the very fact of leaving behind a will, and it is up to chance whether a document gets altered and the opposite of the dispositions of the decedent gets written in, since the witnesses will know no better whether the will that they were summoned to witness is the one actually being produced.

216. Diogenes Laertius 3.41–43. Purported written will of Plato. (Diogenes Laertius *fl.* 2nd-3rd c.A.D.; Plato d. 348/7 B.C.)

See references and headnote under **155**; also **Davies**, *APF* no. 8792.X. Diogenes includes in his work the purported wills of six of his subjects (Plato; Aristotle and his Peripatetic successors Theophrastus, Straton, and Lycon; and Epicurus). Below is the will ascribed to Plato, who was an Athenian citizen. Adeimantus (§41) is probably Plato's grandnephew (the grandson of Plato's brother Adeimantus); the Cephisus is a river in Attica; for the drachma and obol as units of weight as well as coinage see p. 4.

Plato has left behind and disposed of by will the following:

The plot of land [*chôrion*] in the deme Iphistiadae, which is bounded on the north by the road from the temple in the deme Cephisia, on the south by the temple of Heracles in the deme Iphistiadae, on the east by [the property of] Archestratus of the deme Phrearrhioe, and on the west by [the property of] Philippus of the deme Cholleidae. No one shall be permitted to sell or alienate this, but it shall be the property of the boy Adeimantus insofar as this is possible.

[42] Also the plot of land [*chôrion*] in the deme Eiresidae, which I purchased from Callimachus, which is bounded on the north by [the property of] Eurymedon of the deme Myrrhinus, on the south by [the property of] Demostratus of the deme Xypete, on the east by [the property of] Eurymedon of the deme Myrrhinus, and on the west by the Cephisus; 3 minae in cash; a silver bowl weighing 165 drachmas; a cup weighing 45 drachmas; a gold ring and a gold earring, together weighing 4 drachmas 3 obols. Eucleides the stonecutter owes me 3 minae. I set Artemis free. As slaves I leave behind Tychon, Bicta, Apollonides, and Dionysius. [43] Furniture: the items listed in writing, of which Demetrius has a copy. I owe no one anything. Executors: Leosthenes, Speusippus, Demetrius, Hegias, Eurymedon, Callimachus, and Thrasippus.

217. Diogenes Laertius 5.11–16. Purported written will of Aristotle. (Diogenes Laertius *fl.* 2nd-3rd c.A.D.; Aristotle d. 322 B.C.)

See references and headnotes under **155** and **216**. This document is the will ascribed to Aristotle, who was a metic (p. 23) born in the town of Stageira in Macedonia (§§14, 16); it includes provisions concerning his de facto wife Herpyllis (under Athenian law, presumably his "concubine kept for the procreation of free children" [**3f** Dem. 23.53; **54** Lys. 1.24–33], since neither Aristotle nor Herpyllis was an Athenian citizen [see chapters 5 and 6]), his son Nicomachus, and his daughter (unnamed).

All will be well; but in case something happens, Aristotle has made the following will:

Antipater shall be executor of all affairs and of the whole together; [12] but until Nicanor arrives, Aristomenes, Timarchus, Hipparchus, Dioteles, and Theophrastus (if he wishes and it is possible for him) shall oversee the children, Herpyllis, and the property that is left behind. When the girl is of age, she shall be given in marriage [*ekdosthai*] to Nicanor; but if something happens to the girl—which heaven forbid, and will not happen—before she gets married or when she is married but there are not yet children, Nicanor shall be *kyrios* to manage affairs concerning both the girl and the other matters in a manner worthy of both himself and us. Let Nicanor oversee both the girl and the boy, Nicomachus, however he sees fit concerning them, as both a father and a brother.

But if something happens to Nicanor—which heaven forbid—either before he marries the girl or when he is married but there are not yet children, any disposition he makes shall be binding. [13] And if Theophrastus wishes to be with the girl, the same shall apply as for Nicanor. Otherwise the executors, in consultation with Antipater, shall manage affairs concerning both the girl and the boy however it seems best to them. The executors and Nicanor, in memory of me and of the fact that Herpyllis was devoted to me, shall also oversee her in other respects and, in particular, if she wishes to take a husband, shall see to it that she is given in marriage [*dothêi*] in a manner not unworthy of us. They shall give her, in addition to the gifts given previously, 1 talent in cash from the property that is left behind, and three female slaves, if she wishes, and the slave girl she has and the slave Pyrrhaeus. [14] And if she wishes to live in Chalcis, [they shall give her] the guest-house next to the garden; if [she wishes to live] in Stageira, [they shall give her] the ancestral house. Whichever of these she chooses, the executors shall equip it with whatever items of furniture seem good to them and sufficient to Herpyllis.

Let Nicanor also oversee the boy Myrmex, such that he is conveyed to his own people, in a manner worthy of us, along with the property belonging to him that we have received. Ambracis is to be free, and when my daughter is given in marriage [*ekdothêi*], she shall be given 500 drachmas and the slave girl whom she has. Thale shall be given, in addition to the slave girl whom she has, the one who was purchased, 1,000 drachmas and a slave girl. [15] Simon, apart from the money that was given to him previously for another slave, shall either have a slave purchased for him or be given additional money. Tychon shall be free when my daughter is given in marriage, as shall Philon and Olympius and his son. None of the slaves who served me shall be sold; rather, they shall remain employed, and when they reach adulthood they shall be set free according to their merit.

[The executors] shall also oversee the statues that have been hired out to Gryllion, such that after their completion they shall be set up: the statue of Nicanor, that of Proxenus, which I intended to hire out, and that of Nicanor's mother. They shall set up the statue of Arimnestus, which has been completed, so that it may be a monument for him, since he died childless. [16] They shall set up the statue of my mother as a dedication to Demeter at Nemea or wherever they think best. Wherever they conduct my burial, they shall also take up the bones of Pythias and place them there, as she herself prescribed. They shall also set up, on account of Nicanor's safe return, in accordance with the vow I made on his behalf, stone animals 4 cubits tall as dedications to Zeus the Savior and Athena the Savior in Stageira.

7.3.5. MODIFICATION AND REVOCATION OF WILL

See also **201** [Dem.] 46.14.

218. Isaeus 6 *On the Estate of Philoctemon* 29–32. Revocation of will. (365–363)

See references and headnotes under **144** and **178**. Here the speaker describes Euctemon's revocation of his will in the presence of the eponymous archon. For "visible property" (*phanera ousia*) see **185** Andoc. 1.117–21; for the *dikê eis emphanôn katastasin* (for production in plain sight) cf. **152** [Arist.] *Ath. Pol.* 56.6–7; **225** D. H. *Isaeus* 15.1. Pythodorus' request, seconded by the archon, that the *kyrios* of Chaereas' daughter (Chaereas himself was dead) be present for the revocation may indicate that the document in question was, at least in part, contractual in nature, since in the case of a will the testator's intent to revoke should have sufficed: see, e.g., **Edwards**, *Isaeus* 107 n. 25.

When the document had been on deposit for almost two years and Chaereas had died, these people, who had fallen under the woman's power and now saw that the estate was going to ruin and that Euctemon's old age and idiocy were sufficient occasion for them, went on the attack together. [30] First they persuaded Euctemon to revoke his will on the grounds that it was not beneficial to the boys, since upon Euctemon's death there would be no one entitled to his visible property [*phaneras ousias*] other than his daughters and their offspring, but if he sold part of his property and left behind cash, they would have secure possession of that. [31] Euctemon listened and immediately demanded his document back from Pythodorus, and he served him with a summons for production in plain sight [*eis emphanôn katastasin*]. And when Pythodorus presented himself before the archon, Euctemon said that he wanted to take back his will. [32] Pythodorus was willing to agree with him and with Phanostratus, who was present, to its revocation; but since his fellow depositor Chaereas had an only daughter, he requested that it be revoked only when her *kyrios* had presented himself, and the archon expressed the same opinion. Euctemon agreed to this in the presence of the archon and his assistants, and after securing numerous witnesses to the fact that his will was no longer on deposit, he left.

219. Isaeus 1 *On the Estate of Cleonymus* (selections). Modification and revocation of will. (?ca. 355)

See especially **Wyse**, *Isaeus* (text and commentary); **Wevers**, *Isaeus*; **Edwards**, *Isaeus* (translation with introduction and notes); also **Blass**, *AB* 2.528–32; **Jebb**, *AO* 2.319–21; **Usher**, *GO* 129–33.

Isaeus 1 was delivered in a *diadikasia* over the estate of Cleonymus by one of his sister's sons; the speaker contests Cleonymus' will and claims the estate jointly with one or more brothers by right of kinship (*anchisteia*). The speaker and his opponents apparently concur that Cleonymus was dissatisfied with his will but disagree as to whether Cleonymus intended to revoke the will (the contention of the speaker) or merely to revise it (the contention of the speaker's opponents). The presence of witnesses—one of the *astynomoi* (City Magistrates: cf. **65** [Arist.] *Ath. Pol.* 50.1–2) here, and the eponymous archon in **218** Isae. 6.29–32—to the modification or revocation of a will, if not mandated by law, will have helped to ensure that an earlier will was not enforced against the decedent's later wishes.

a. Isae. 1.14–15.

When he was already sick with the illness from which he died, he wanted to revoke this will and told Poseidippus to bring in the magistrate. But Poseidippus not only didn't bring one in but actually sent away the magistrate who came to the door. Cleonymus got angry with him and then told Diocles in turn to call the magistrates to appear the next day. And although he was not in such bad condition—on the contrary, there was still a lot of hope—suddenly, that night, he died. [15] Now, then, I will present to you the witnesses to the facts, first, that he made this will not because he bore a grievance against us but because he was in a state of hostilities with Deinias; second, that after Deinias died he took care of all our affairs and brought us up, taking us into his own house; and additionally, that he sent Poseidippus to get the City Magistrate [*astynomon*], but Poseidippus not only did not call him in but actually sent him away when he came to the door.

b. Isae. 1.18–19.

They rely on the will, claiming that Cleonymus sent for the magistrate wishing not to annul it but to correct it and confirm the bequest [*dôrean*] to them. But you should consider, regarding the will that was made in anger, whether it is likely that Cleonymus wished to revoke it now that he had become friendly toward us, or to see to it that he would deprive us of his property with even greater certainty. [19] You see, other people later regret the wrongs they have done to their relatives in anger; but my adversaries represent Cleonymus, when he was most friendly toward us, as wishing instead to confirm the will that he had made in anger.

c. Isae. 1.24–25.

For if in fact, gentlemen, as my adversaries claim, he gave them his estate in the will as it is now written, I cannot help wondering by what correction he would have thought he could make the will more valid: for other people, gentlemen, this is the consummate form of bequest [*dôreôn*]. [25] And moreover, if he wanted to add something to what he had written, why didn't he write it in another document and leave it behind, since he couldn't get his document from the magistrates? You see, gentlemen, he could not revoke any document other than the one on deposit with the magistrate, but he could write whatever he wanted in another document and thus prevent us from disputing this issue.

d. Isae. 1.43.

Moreover, bear in mind that Cleonymus was of sound mind when he annulled the will and was angry and not thinking correctly when he made it, so it would be the most terrible thing of all if you were to render his anger more valid than his rational thought.

7.4. Asserting a Claim

7.4.1. DIRECT CLAIM (*EMBATEUSIS*, ENTRY)

See also **177** Isae. 8.34; **223** Harpo. s.v. *exoulês*; **228** Isae. 3.40–50, 57–60, 62; **230** [Dem.] 44 (selections).

220. Isaeus 9 *On the Estate of Astyphilus* 3. Improper *embateusis* on behalf of son adopted by will. (*post* 371)

See references and headnote under **16**. Here the speaker states that Cleon claimed the estate of Astyphilus by *embateusis* on behalf of his biological minor son, whom Astyphilus had allegedly adopted by will. This act would have been illegal, since only biological direct descendants (**177** Isae. 8.34; **228** Isae. 3.40–50, 57–60, 62) and sons adopted *inter vivos* (**230a** [Dem.] 44.15–16; **137a** [Dem.] 44.17–19) were empowered to claim by *embateusis*.

And so strongly did Cleon here believe, both then and now, that no one other than himself would have the estate that, as soon as Astyphilus' death was reported, while my father was ill and I was not in Attica but away on campaign, he entered into possession [*enebateuse*] of the land [*chôrion*] and claimed that everything else Astyphilus had left belonged to his son—before you decided anything by vote.

221. [Demosthenes] 44 *Against Leochares* 64. *Embateusis*; rule barring adopted son from adopting. (?320s)

See references and headnotes under **137** and **196**. Here the speaker characterizes Leostratus II's introduction of his biological son Leochares as the adopted son of Archiades as tantamount to a direct claim by *embateusis* to Archiades' estate; among adopted sons, only those adopted *inter vivos* were permitted to claim by *embateusis* (cf. **220** Isae. 9.3). On the rule of return for adopted sons cf. **138** Harpo. s.v. *hoti hoi poiêtoi* etc.; **196** [Dem.] 44.24–26, 32–34; **209** [Dem.] 44.67–68.

The lawgiver took precautions against this and forbade a person who was himself adopted from creating an adopted son. How did he make his determination concerning these things? When he states, "A person may return [to his original household] after leaving behind in [the adoptive household] a legitimate [*gnêsion*] son," he certainly makes it manifestly clear that adoption is forbidden, since it is impossible to leave behind a legitimate son unless one has a son born by birth. But you, Leostratus [II], demand to introduce into the estate an adopted son of the deceased, who was himself adopted into our family [*genos*]; and you do so by entering into possession [*badizôn*] as though the property were your own and not property to be granted to the qualified relative [*tôi prosêkonti*] in accordance with the law.

7.4.2. *DIKÊ EXOULÊS* (FOR EJECTMENT)

See also **102** Dem. 30.15–17; **115** Dem. 30–31 (selections); **170** Andoc. 1.73–79; **228** Isae. 3.40–50, 57–60, 62.

222. *Oxyrhynchus Papyri*, no. 221, col. 14, lines 9–16 (*lex* + commentary). Solonian *dikê exoulês*. (date of papyrus 2nd c. A.D.; Crates *fl.* mid-2nd c. B.C.; date of law 594/3 B.C.)

B. P. **Grenfell**-A. S. **Hunt**, *The Oxyrhynchus Papyri, Part II* (London 1899: text with notes).

This papyrus, discovered at Oxyrhynchus, Egypt, contains scholia on the twenty-first book of Homer's *Iliad*. This excerpt comes from a note on the word *erchthent'* ("shut up, enclosed") at *Iliad* 21.282; Crates was a scholar active in Pergamum (in northern Asia Minor) in the second century B.C. The interpretation of the law's opening condition is controversial (see, e.g., **Harrison**, *LA* 1.312), but quotation from a specific axon securely indicates Solonian authorship. On the penal terms of the law cf. **223** Harpo. s.v. *exoulês*; Demosthenes 21.44.

Crates [reads] *eilthenta* ["hemmed in, shut up"] in place of *erchthenta* ["shut up, enclosed"] and thereupon [discusses?] the lawsuit for ejectment [*exoulês dikên*]. He also sets forth Solon's law from the fifth axon on ejectment: "If a person ejects someone from anything over which he has won a lawsuit, he shall owe to the public treasury whatever it is worth, and to each individual [victim] an equal amount."

223. Harpocration s.v. *exoulês*. *Dikê exoulês*. (Harpocration *fl.* 2nd c. A.D.)

See references and headnote under **28**. In this entry Harpocration defines the *dikê exoulês*. Caecilius of Caleacte (in Sicily) was a rhetorician of the first century B.C.; Phrynichus was an Athenian comic playwright of the later fifth century B.C. whose work survives in only fragmentary form. "Everyone who is ejected from his own property" includes direct heirs claiming by *embateusis*; for an instance of the *dikê exoulês* used to prosecute resistance to the recovery of "a fine arising from a conviction" see **102** Dem. 30.15–17.

For ejectment [*exoulês*]: the name of a lawsuit [*dikês*] brought by those claiming to have been barred from their own property against those who bar them. . . . Also, those who do not receive the fines they have been awarded within the proper period of time prosecute for ejectment when the fines are overdue. Those convicted of ejectment both gave their prosecutors what they had deprived them of and paid a fine of equivalent amount to the public treasury. . . . That the term applies in the case of everyone who is ejected from his own property and not, as Caecilius believes, only in the case of those who owe a fine arising from a conviction, is made clear also by Phrynichus in the *Gardeners*.

7.4.3. CLAIM FOR ADJUDICATION (*LÊXIS*)

See also **90** Isae. 3.2; **185** Andoc. 1.117–21; **189** Isae. 6.46; **194** Isae. 11.1–5, 8–12, 17–18, 29–30; **196** [Dem.] 44.24–26, 32–34; **227** [Dem.] 46.22–23; **228** Isae. 3.40–50, 57–60, 62; **229** Isae. 6.3–4, 43–44, 52; **230** [Dem.] 44 (selections); **231** Isae. 5.6–7, 9, 12–18; **232** Isae. 3.3–7; **233** Isae. 11.45–46; **234** [Dem.] 43.5–16; **236** [Dem.] 48.22–32; **259** [Dem.] 48 (selections).

224. [Aristotle], *Constitution of the Athenians* (*Ath. Pol.*) 43.4. Publication of claims (*lêxeis*) to estates and *epiklêroi*. (332–322)

See references and headnote under **1c**. Here the author describes the duties of the tribal delegation of the Council of 500 that holds the prytany (see p. 6). That *lêxeis* to an estate were filed in written form is confirmed by Isaeus 3.30; 4.2. On *eisangelia* (impeachment) of various kinds see §**6.4** and chapter 12.

They also post notice of Assembly meetings: one chief meeting [*kyrian*], at which the Assembly must give a vote of confidence in the magistrates, if they are deemed to be performing well in office, and must conduct business regarding the grain supply and the defense of the country. It is also on that day that those who wish must conduct their impeachments [*eisangelias*] and registers of property being confiscated must be read out, as well as claims to estates and *epiklêroi* [*lêxeis tôn klêrôn kai tôn epiklêrôn*], so that nothing may escape anyone's notice and lie vacant.

225. Dionysius of Halicarnassus, *Isaeus* 15.1. Claim for adjudication (*lêxis*) of estate; *dikê eis emphanôn katastasin*; *paragraphê*. (date of composition late 1st c. B.C.- early 1st c. A.D.; date of speech discussed early to mid-4th c. B.C.)

S. **Usher**, *Dionysius of Halicarnassus: The Critical Essays*, 2 vols. (Cambridge, MA 1974–85: text and translation); G. **Aujac** et al., *Denys d'Halicarnasse:*

Opuscules rhétoriques, 5 vols. (Paris 1978-: text, French translation, and notes).

The works of Dionysius of Halicarnassus (late 1st c. B.C.-early 1st c. A.D.) include essays on the literary style of Lysias, Isocrates, Isaeus, Demosthenes, and Deinarchus. For the meager remnants of Isaeus' *Against Aristogeiton and Archippus* see Isaeus frr. 1–2 Thalheim. On "invisible property" see the headnote under **185** Andoc. 1.117–21; for "production in plain sight" (*emphanôn katastasis*) cf. **152** [Arist.] *Ath. Pol.* 56.6–7; **218** Isae. 6.29–32; for *paragraphê* (counter-indictment) see p. 14. For the law prohibiting control of an estate before requisite adjudication see **227** [Dem.] 46.22–23, and cf. **141** Isae. 5.10–11.

. . . as Isaeus is found to have done in the [matter of the] claim [*lêxei*] against Aristogeiton and Archippus, in which a person laying claim to an estate, who is the brother of the decedent, issues a summons to the possessor of the invisible property [*taphanê chrêmata*] for its production in plain sight [*eis emphanôn katastasin*], and the one in control of the estate enters a counter-indictment [*paragraphetai*] against the summons, stating that the property was given to him by will. The dispute lay on two grounds: first, on the issue of whether a will had been made or not, and second, given that the will was now in dispute, who should control the estate. Isaeus first sets forth his argument concerning the laws and demonstrates in this section that it is not permitted to exercise control of an estate that is subject to adjudication [*epidikon*] before judgment [*dikês*] [is given]; he then proceeds to the narrative, in which he shows that the will was not made by the deceased.

226. Pollux, *Onomasticon* 8.32. Claim for adjudication (*lêxis*) and deposit (*parakatabolê*). (late 2nd c. A.D.)

See references and headnote under **117**. Here Pollux defines the term *parakatabolê*. The requirement of a deposit applied at least to *diamartyria* (**230b** [Dem.] 44.42–43) and to claims to a previously adjudicated estate (**234** [Dem.] 43.5–16); how far it applied to other inheritance actions is a matter of scholarly debate.

Parakatabolê [deposit] occurred when a person made a counter-claim that he himself had a better right to the estate on the basis of kinship [*anchisteias*] or a will; he would deposit one-tenth of the [value of the] estate to serve as an advance fee in case he lost.

7.4.4. *EPIDIKASIA/DIADIKASIA* (ADJUDICATION) AND *DIAMARTYRIA* (DECLARATION ON OATH)

See also **137** [Dem.] 44 (selections); **152** [Arist.] *Ath. Pol.* 56.6–7; **178** Isae. 6.25, 28, 63; **183** Ar. *Wasps* 583–86; **185** Andoc. 1.117–21; **186** Isae. 3 (selections); **187** Isae. 8.31, 33; **188** Isae. 10.4–5; **190** Isae. 7.18–20; **192** Harpo. s.v. *epidikos* etc.; **193** Pollux, *Onomasticon* 3.33; **194** Isae. 11.1–5, 8–12, 17–18, 29–30; **200** [Arist.] *Ath. Pol.* 58.3; **201** [Dem.] 46.14; **204** Isae. 3.67–69; **219** Isae. 1 (selections); **225** D. H. *Isaeus* 15.1; **226** Pollux, *Onomasticon* 8.32; **231** Isae. 5.6–7, 9, 12–18; **234** [Dem.] 43.5–16; **235** Isae. 4.24–25; **236** [Dem.] 48.22–32.

227. [Demosthenes] 46 *2 Against Stephanus* 22–23 (*lex* + commentary). Adjudication (*epidikasia/diadikasia*) of estates and *epiklêroi*: law, procedure, and jurisdiction. (date of speech ?349; date of law unknown but presumably 6th or 5th c.)

See references and headnote under **83**. Here the speaker cites and discusses a law (possibly authored by Solon) mandating the adjudication (*epidikasia*) of estates and *epiklêroi*; "the archon" is the eponymous archon, and Scirophorion was the last month of the Athenian year, corresponding roughly to June on our calendar (p. 7). Cf. **152** [Arist.] *Ath. Pol.* 56.6–7; **200** [Arist.] *Ath. Pol.* 58.3. Note the distinctions between the stated terms of the law, the speaker's paraphrase (separating the jurisdictions of the eponymous archon and the polemarch: see **234** [Dem.] 43.5–16), and contemporary procedure (not all estates were subject to adjudication: see, e.g., **230c** [Dem.] 44.45–50 with **137a** [Dem.] 44.17–19; Isaeus 2.2; 7.3).

[To the court clerk:] Read in addition the law that orders that there be adjudication [*epidikasian*] of all *epiklêroi*, both foreign and citizen; and that in the case of citizens the archon shall introduce and oversee [the lawsuit], and in the case of metics the polemarch; and that it shall not be permitted to possess an estate or an *epiklêros* without adjudication [*anepidikon*].

LAW. The archon shall allot lawsuits concerning estates and *epiklêroi* every month except Scirophorion. No one shall possess an estate without adjudication [*anepidikon*].

[23] So, if he wanted to proceed correctly, he should have filed a claim [*lachein*] to the *epiklêros*, whether he had a right to her by bequest or by kinship, with the archon if he claimed her as a citizen and with the polemarch if he claimed her as a foreigner. And only then, if he had any just argument to make, should he have become *kyrios* of her, after persuading those of you allotted to the jury, with the aid of the laws and of your vote. . . .

228. Isaeus 3 *On the Estate of Pyrrhus* 40–50, 57–60, 62. Laws on estates and *epiklêroi*; disqualification of illegitimate daughter; uncontested adjudication (*epidikasia*) of estate; claim for adjudication (*lêxis*) of estate; *diamartyria*; *eisangelia kakôseôs epiklêrou*; right of child of *epiklêros*; time limit for lawsuit over estate; *embateusis*; *dikê exoulês*. (?ca. 389)

See references and headnotes under **85** and **204**. Here the speaker argues that Nicodemus' failure to contest the adjudication (*epidikasia*) of Pyrrhus' estate to the speaker's brother Endius (whom Pyrrhus adopted by will) demonstrates that Nicodemus acknowledged Pyrrhus' daughter Phile to be illegitimate, and therefore not an *epiklêros* (cf. **232** Isae. 3.3–7). For the rule that an estate must go with an *epiklêros* cf. **176** [Dem.] 43.51; for impeachment for maltreatment of an *epiklêros* (*eisangelia kakôseôs epiklêrou*) see **§6.4.3**. For the rule that biological children and adoptees *inter vivos* may claim an estate by *embateusis*, while all others (including collateral relatives and testamentary adoptees) must file a claim (*lêxis*) with the eponymous archon and await adjudication (*epidikasia*/*diadikasia*), see **§§7.4.1, 7.4.3**. Metageitnion (§57) corresponds roughly to August on our calendar (p. 7). In §62, "private lawsuits" refers certainly to the *dikê exoulês* (see **§7.4.2**) and possibly also to the *dikê aikeias* (see chapter 2); the "public lawsuit" is the *eisangelia kakôseôs epiklêrou*.

Tell me now, Nicodemus: if you had pledged [*êstha êngyêkôs*] your sister to Pyrrhus and you knew that he was leaving behind a legitimate daughter by her, [41] how did you permit our brother to get the estate adjudicated to him [*epidikasasthai*] without the legitimate daughter who you claim was left by our uncle? Didn't you know that in the adjudication of the estate [*têi epidikasiai tou klêrou*] your own niece was being made illegitimate [*nothên*]? For when he was getting the estate adjudicated to him [*epedikazeto tou klêrou*], he was making the daughter of the man who left the estate illegitimate [*nothên*]. [42] And even earlier Pyrrhus, who adopted my brother as his son, did the same, since no one is permitted to make a will or to make a bequest of any of his property to anyone without his daughters, if he dies leaving legitimate daughters. [To the jury:] You will realize this when you hear the actual laws read out. [To the court clerk:] Read these laws to them.

LAWS.

[43] Do you think that the man who has testified that he pledged her [*engyêsai*] would have permitted any of these things to happen, rather than laying a claim on behalf of his own niece at the time of the claim to the estate [*tou klêrou têi lêxei*] that Endius filed to get the award, and declaring on oath [*diamar-*

tyrêsai] that her father's estate was not subject to adjudication [*epidikon*] to Endius? But in fact, to prove that our brother did get the estate adjudicated to him [*epedikasato*] and no one disputed his claim, [To the court clerk:] read the deposition.

DEPOSITION.

[44] So when this award was made, Nicodemus did not dare to dispute the estate or to declare on oath [*diamartyrêsai*] that his own niece had been left behind as a legitimate daughter of Pyrrhus.

[45] Now, concerning the award, someone might offer you a false excuse: my adversary might pretend that it escaped their notice, or even accuse us of lying. Let's let that be. But when Endius pledged [*êngya*] your niece to Xenocles, Nicodemus, did you allow Pyrrhus' daughter born from his wedded wife to be pledged as though she were his daughter by a prostitute? [46] And did you not bring an impeachment [*eisêngeilas*] before the archon on the grounds that the *epiklêros* was being maltreated [*kakousthai*] by the adopted son, since she was being treated with such hubris and deprived of her father's estate—especially given that these lawsuits [*dikôn*] alone are risk-free for their prosecutors, and anyone who wishes may come to the aid of *epiklêroi*? [47] For in impeachments [*eisangeliais*] before the archon there is no fine [*epitimion*] even if the prosecutors do not get a single vote, nor is any court-fee [*prytaneia*] or deposit [*parastasis*] paid for impeachments. Rather, impeachment is available without risk to the prosecutors, to anyone who wishes, while for the people convicted the most severe penalties result from impeachments.

[48] If, then, his niece had been born to our uncle by a wedded wife, would Nicodemus have allowed her to be pledged as though she were the offspring of a prostitute? And if that happened, would he not have brought an impeachment before the archon on the grounds that the *epiklêros* was being treated with hubris by the man who pledged her as such? [To Nicodemus:] If the things that you have just now had the gall to testify to were true, you would have immediately, on the spot, right then, have punished the offender. Or are you going to pretend that this too escaped your notice? [49] So, then, did you not even realize it on the basis of the dowry that was given with her? Certainly you should have become indignant and impeached Endius for the very reason that he was demanding to possess a three-talent estate [*oikon*] as his right, while seeing fit to give in marriage [*ekdounai*] this legitimate daughter to another man with a dowry of 1,000 drachmas.

[To the jury:] So, wouldn't my adversary have been indignant and impeached Endius on these grounds? Yes, by Zeus, he would have, if the thing were true. [50] But I don't believe at all that he or any adopted son would be so stupid, or so negligent concerning the established laws, that when the man who left the estate had a legitimate daughter, he would give her to another over himself. For he would have known full well that the children born from a legitimate daughter receive by right the inheritance of all their grandfather's property.

. . .

[57] Pyrrhus, you see, has been dead more than twenty years now, and Endius died last year during the month of Metageitnion, in which month, two days later, my adversaries immediately filed their claim [*lêxin*] to the estate. [58] Now, the law commands that lawsuits over estates occur within five years after the heir dies. So the woman should have done one of two things: either she should have laid claim to her patrimony while Endius was alive, or, after the adopted son was dead, she should have seen fit to get the adjudication [*epidikasian*] of her brother's estate made to her—especially if, as my adversaries claim, he had pledged [*êngyêkei*] her to Xenocles as his legitimate sister. [59] For we all know full well that the award of siblings' estates is available to all of us, whereas if a person has legitimate children born to him by birth, none of them needs to have his patrimony adjudicated to him [*epidikazesthai*]. No argument need be made on these points, since everybody—both you and the rest of the citizens—holds his own patrimony as not subject to adjudication [*anepidika*].

[60] My adversaries, however, have reached such a level of audacity that they denied that an adopted son needed to get his bequest adjudicated to him [*epidikasasthai*], but have seen fit to file their claim on behalf of Phile—who they say was left behind as a legitimate daughter of Pyrrhus—to her father's estate. And yet, as I said earlier, when people leave behind legitimate children born from themselves, there is no need for the children to get their patrimony adjudicated to them [*epidikasasthai*]; but when people adopt children by will, those children do need to claim their bequests by adjudication. . . . [62] So let none of you believe that if Xenocles thought his wife was legitimate, he would file this claim [*lêxin*] to her father's estate on her behalf. Instead, the legitimate daughter would enter into possession [*ebadizen*] of her patrimony; and if anyone tried to deprive her of it or force her out, he would be ejecting her from her patrimony, and not only would the person who used force be prosecuted by private lawsuits [*idias . . . dikas*], but he would also be impeached [*eisangeltheis*] in a public lawsuit [*dêmosiai*] before the archon and would be at risk concerning both his person and the entirety of his property.

229. Isaeus 6 *On the Estate of Philoctemon* 3–4, 43–44, 52. Claim for adjudication (*lêxis*) of estate by son adopted by will and consequent *diadikasia* (by direct trial, *euthydikia*) or *diamartyria*; possibility of future claim. (365–363)

See references and headnotes under **144** and **178**. Here the speaker describes the sequence of claims and litigation following the death of Philoctemon, a son of Euctemon. Chaerestratus, adopted by Philoctemon in his will, filed a claim to the estate with the eponymous archon. Androcles blocked that claim by a *diamartyria* asserting that the estate was not subject to adjudication since Philoctemon had surviving siblings who were legitimate children of Euctemon; the speaker criticizes Androcles' choice of *diamartyria* over *diadikasia* (by direct trial, *euthydikia*). On the choice between these procedures cf. Isaeus 2.2; 7.3.

Philoctemon of the deme Cephisia was a friend of this man Chaerestratus here; he died leaving him his property and adopting him as his son. Chaerestratus filed a claim [*lachontos*] to the estate [*klêrou*] in accordance with the law; but then, it being permitted to any willing Athenian to lodge a claim, come before you by direct trial [*euthydikiai*], and take the estate if he clearly made a more just argument, [4] Androcles here declared on oath [*diemartyrêsen*] that the estate was not subject to adjudication [*epidikon*], thus depriving Chaerestratus of his claim and you of your authority over whom to establish as heir to Philoctemon's estate. And he intends, by a single vote and a single trial, to establish as brothers to the decedent men who have no relation to him, to hold the estate himself as not subject to adjudication [*anepidikon*], to become the *kyrios* of the decedent's sister, and to render the will invalid.

. . .

[43] . . . And they have reached such a level of shamelessness that they did not dare to come to court by direct trial [*euthydikiai*] but instead made a declaration on oath [*diemartyroun*], claiming to act on behalf of legitimate children, that was both false and contrary to what they themselves had done: [44] they registered the boys before the archon stating that one was Philoctemon's son and the other was Ergamenes', but now they have declared on oath that the boys are Euctemon's.

. . .

[52] . . . This is the purpose of their declaration on oath [*diamartyria*]: to place the risk in these matters on their opponents, while they themselves, even if they lose this trial and the estate is found to be subject to adjudication [*epidikos*], may file a counter-claim [*antigrapsamenoi*] and litigate twice over the same matters. And yet, if Philoctemon made a will when he was not permitted to, this is exactly what they should have declared on oath [*diamartyrein*]: that he was not entitled to adopt this man as his son. But if it is permitted to make a will and someone is making a claim on the grounds that the decedent made no bequest or will, then he should not block proceedings by a declaration on oath but should come to court by direct trial [*euthydikiai*].

230. [Demosthenes] 44 *Against Leochares* (selections). *Embateusis*; claim for adjudication (*lêxis*) of estate; *diamartyria* with deposit (*parakatabolê*). (?320s)

See references and headnotes under **137** and **196**. According to the speaker, Leocrates I, the first adopted son of Archiades, had claimed Archiades' estate by *embateusis*; although non-*inter vivos* adoptees were not permitted to proceed in this manner (cf. **220** Isae. 9.3; **221** [Dem.] 44.64), the family had let the matter stand (**137a** [Dem.] 44.17–19). Later, following the death of Leocrates II (Archiades' third adopted son), his biological father Leostratus II (who had been Archiades' second adopted son but had returned to his natal family: **137c** [Dem.] 44.46–47), likewise claimed Archiades' estate by *embateusis* on behalf of himself and/or his biological son Leochares (**230a**); both Leostratus II and Leochares claimed as adopted sons of Archiades. The speaker responded by lodging a rival claim (*lêxis*: **230a**, **230c**) on behalf of his father, to which Leostratus II and Leochares in turn responded with a *diamartyria* (declaration on oath) asserting that the estate was not subject to adjudication since Leochares was the legitimate son of Archiades (**230a–d**). The speaker now prosecutes Leochares by *dikê pseudomartyriôn* for giving a false *diamartyria*. On the deposit (*parakatabolê*: **230b**) paid by Leostratus II, to which the speaker alludes in discussing the risk inherent in *diamartyria* (**230d**), cf. **226** Pollux, *Onomasticon* 8.32. In **230c**, the law cited at §49 is **83** [Dem.] 46.18; note that in §§49–50 the speaker misinterprets the law (the legimitacy of biological children does not imply the illegitimacy of adopted children).

a. [Dem.] 44.15–16.

So, then, men of the jury, those are the details concerning our adversaries' kinship [*genos*] and our own; and so those who have proven on the basis of the actual depositions that they are more closely related should receive the inheritance, and the insanity of the person who made the declaration on oath [*diamartyrêsantos*] should not prevail over your laws. For in fact, if they rely on the adoption—and we will show how that occurred—then, since the person who was adopted has obviously died childless and the household [*oikou*] has been vacant until our claim [*lêxeôs*], how is it not proper that those who are most closely related should receive the inheritance . . . ?

[16] Now, if we could simply demonstrate the details of the kinship and of the actual declaration on oath [*diamartyrias*] and then step down, with no need for any further argument, we would not bother you further, since essentially the most important matters would have been discussed. But since our adversaries

rely not on the laws but upon the fact that they have already gotten a head start in these matters and have entered into possession of the estate [*embebateukenai eis tên ousian*], and will use these facts as evidence for their claim to inherit, it is probably necessary to discuss these issues as well and to show that our adversaries are the worst violators of all mankind.

b. [Dem.] 44.42–43.

After that, at his declaration on oath [*diamartyriai*] before the archon, [Leostratus II] entered Leochares as being the legitimate [*gnêsion*] son of Archiades, who had been dead for many years, although he had been enrolled just the other day! The result is that both of them are laying claim to the inheritance: Leostratus [II] here paid his deposit [*parakatebale*] for the estate on the grounds that he is a legitimate son of Archiades; and Leochares, over here, has declared on oath [*diamemartyrêken*] that he is a legitimate son of the same father. [43] Each of them, though, makes himself the adopted son not of a living man but of a dead one.

c. [Dem.] 44.45–50.

Now, then, you have heard about all matters, men of the jury, both those that happened in the beginning concerning this estate and those that resulted later, as soon as we filed our claim [*lêxin*]. It remains to discuss the actual declaration on oath [*diamartyrias*] and the laws in accordance with which we demand to receive the inheritance. . . . First, let [the court clerk] read out the declaration on oath. . . .

DECLARATION ON OATH.

[46] So obviously my adversary has declared on oath [*diamemartyrêken*], as you heard, that "the estate of Archiades is not subject to adjudication [*epidikon*], since he has legitimate children in a valid manner in accordance with the law." . . .

[47] . . . The son left behind by [Leostratus II], the last of all the adopted sons, has died childless, and so the household is vacant and the inheritance has returned again to the original closest relatives. [48] . . . My adversary, however, has declared on oath that nonexistent sons exist, and has written in his declaration on oath "since he has children," claiming that he himself is one of them. [49] But in fact when he says the children are "legitimate" and "in a valid manner in accordance with the law," he is making a misrepresentation in violation of the laws. "Legitimate" means when a child is born by birth; the law testifies to this when it states, "Anyone whom her father or brother or grandfather pledges, the children born from her shall be legitimate." As for "in a valid manner," the

lawgiver took that as referring to adoptions, considering that when a person who was childless and *kyrios* of his property adopted a son, that ought to be valid. My adversary, however, claims that no son was born to Archiades by birth but has declared on oath "since he has legitimate children," thus making a declaration on oath that is contrary to the fact of the matter.

[50] He admits that he is adopted, but it is obvious that he was not adopted by the deceased himself, [To Leochares:] so how can these provisions be "valid" for you "according to the law"? [To the jury:] Because, he will respond, he was enrolled as Archiades' son. Right, because my adversaries forced their way in just the other day, when the lawsuit for adjudication of the estate [*tês tou klêrou diadikasias*] was already pending; it's certainly not right to regard that wrongdoing as evidence.

d. [Dem.] 44.57–59.

In the first place, [these trials] come about not by necessity, as others do, but rather from the deliberate choice and will of the person who proceeds by declaration on oath [*tou diamartyrountos*]. If, when matters are in dispute, it is not possible to obtain justice by any means other than declaration on oath, perhaps it is necessary to proceed by declaration on oath. [58] But if it is possible even without a declaration on oath [*diamartyrias*] not to be deprived of a hearing before all the tribunals [*synedriois*], how is it not a sign of rashness and the greatest insanity to proceed by declaration on oath? You see, the lawgiver did not make this necessary for litigants; rather, if they wanted to proceed by declaration on oath, he granted it, as though he were making a test of each of our characters, to see how we would be disposed toward rash action. [59] Moreover, if it were up to those who proceed by declaration on oath, jury-courts [*dikastêria*] would not exist and trials would not take place: the category of declarations on oath blocks all these things and excludes each matter from being brought into the jury-court, at least as far as the will of the person making the declaration on oath is concerned. This is why, in my opinion, such people should be considered common enemies of all and should never receive pardon when they litigate in your court: each of them comes into court having chosen the risk attendant upon declaration on oath, not under compulsion.

7.4.5. *EPISKÊPSIS* AND *DIKÊ PSEUDOMARTYRIÔN*

231. Isaeus 5 *On the Estate of Dicaeogenes* 6–7, 9, 12–18.

Testamentary adoption; claim for adjudication (*lêxis*) of estate on behalf of sisters of decedent; *epidikasia*; *diamartyria*; *episkêpsis* and *dikê pseudomartyriôn*. (ca. 389)

See references under **141**. Dicaeogenes the elder (Dicaeogenes I) had two grandsons of the same name, his son's son Dicaeogenes II and his daughter's son Dicaeogenes III. Upon the death of Dicaeogenes II, Proxenus, the father of Dicaeogenes III, produced a will naming Dicaeogenes III as the adopted son of Dicaeogenes II and heir to one-third of the estate, with the remainder to be split between Dicaeogenes II's sisters. Twelve years later, Dicaeogenes III produced a new will that named him sole heir and accordingly claimed the entire estate. This claim was upheld in court; the speaker's father died before he could follow up his *episkêpsis* against Dicaeogenes III's witnesses with a *dikê pseudomartyriôn*. At some point within the next decade, though, Lycon, one of Dicaeogenes III's witnesses, was convicted in a *dikê pseudomartyriôn*. Consequently, in the absence of a valid will (cf. **233** Isae. 11.45–46), the estate of Dicaeogenes II was claimed by three of his nephews, including the speaker and the successful prosecutor of Lycon, on behalf of their mothers (the sisters of Dicaeogenes II). Their claims were blocked by a *diamartyria* sworn by Leochares to the effect that the estate was not subject to adjudication since Dicaeogenes III was the legitimate son of Dicaeogenes II; the nephews responded by lodging an *episkêpsis* against Leochares and then prosecuting him by *dikê pseudomartyriôn* for having given a false *diamartyria*. To prevent Leochares from being convicted, Dicaeogenes III agreed to surrender two-thirds of the estate to Dicaeogenes II's sisters, and Leochares and Mnesiptolemus stood surety for him. This speech was subsequently delivered by one of the nephews of Dicaeogenes II in a prosecution of Leochares by *dikê engyês*, an action to compel a surety to discharge his obligation. On the trierarchy (§6) see p. 25; *Paralus* (*Seashore*) was the name of Dicaeogenes II's ship. The affidavits (*antômosiai*: see **232** Isae. 3.3–7 with additional references in headnote) mentioned in §16 were tendered by the nephews in support of the claims they filed on behalf of their mothers.

Dicaeogenes [II], having sailed out as trierarch of the *Paralus*, died in battle at Cnidus. He died childless, and Proxenus, the father of Dicaeogenes [III] here, produced a will, in compliance with which our fathers split the estate. Dicaeogenes [III] here became the adopted son of our uncle, Dicaeogenes [II] son of Menexenus, and heir to one-third of the estate; each of Menexenus' daughters got awarded [*epedikasato*] her share of the remainder. . . .

[7] After they split the estate, swearing oaths that they would not violate their agreement, each of them held what he had been allotted for twelve years; and in all that time, although lawsuits were available, none of them saw fit to assert that what had been done was unjust—until, after the city suffered disaster and civil strife occurred, Dicaeogenes [III] here . . . made a claim against us for the entire estate, claiming that he had been adopted by our uncle as his son and heir to the whole thing . . . [9] We fell victim to false testimony and lost

our property: our father, you see, died not long after the lawsuit [*dikên*], before he could prosecute the witnesses whom he had denounced [*epeskêpsato*], and Dicaeogenes [III], having made his case against us as he wished, that same day expelled from her share the daughter of Cephisophon of the deme Paeania, who was the niece of Dicaeogenes [II], who had left behind the property; robbed the woman who had been Democles' wife of what her brother Dicaeogenes [II] had given her; and robbed Cephisodotus' mother and Cephisodotus himself of everything.

. . .

[12] . . . Menexenus, the son of Cephisophon and first cousin to Cephisodotus here and to me, since he had a right to a share of the estate equal to mine, prosecuted the men who had given false testimony against us and him. He convicted Lycon, whom he brought to the jury-court [*dikastêrion*] first, and who had testified that Dicaeogenes [III]—the one now living—had been adopted by our uncle as his son and heir to his entire estate. For giving this testimony Lycon was convicted of false witness [*pseudomartyriôn*]. [13] Since Dicaeogenes [III] could no longer deceive you, gentlemen, he persuaded Menexenus . . . to recover the part of the estate that was coming to him, but to betray us, on whose behalf he was acting, and let off the witnesses who had not yet been convicted. . . .

[14] But Menexenus suffered a fate worthy of his character and was deceived by Dicaeogenes [III]: after letting the witnesses off and betraying us, he didn't recover the property for which he had done this. So, having been wronged by Dicaeogenes [III], he cooperated with us again. We, in the belief that Dicaeogenes [III] had no further right to possess any part of the property from the estate, since his witnesses had been convicted, laid claim against him for the entire estate by right of kinship [*anchisteian*]. And I can easily explain to you that our decision was correct and Dicaeogenes [III] has no further right to the estate. [15] Two wills were produced: one a long time ago and the other much later. According to the old will, which was produced by Proxenus, the father of Dicaeogenes [III] here, Dicaeogenes [III] was adopted by our uncle as his son and heir to one-third of his estate; but according to the will that Dicaeogenes [III] himself produced, he was adopted as heir to the entire estate [*oikôi*]. Of these two wills, Dicaeogenes [III] persuaded the jurors that the one Proxenus produced was not genuine; as for the one Dicaeogenes [III] produced, the men who testified that our uncle made that will were convicted of false witness [*pseudomartyriôn*].

[16] Since both wills were invalid and it was agreed that no other existed, no one had a right to the estate by bequest [*dosin*], and by right of kinship [*anchisteian*] it belonged to the sisters of the decedent Dicaeogenes [II], including our mothers. For this reason we decided to file a claim [*lachein*] to the

estate on the grounds of kinship [*anchisteian*], and each of us filed a claim to his portion [of the estate]. But when we were about to swear our affidavits [*antomnysthai*], Leochares here declared on oath [*diemartyrêse*] that the estate was not subject to adjudication [*epidikon*] to us.

[17] When we then lodged a denunciation [*episkêpsamenôn*], the claim to the estate [*lêxis tou klêrou*] was struck from [the register of pending lawsuits] [*diegraphê*] and the lawsuit for false witness [*pseudomartyriôn dikê*] was entered in. In the jury-court [*dikastêriôi*], we said everything we are saying now, Leochares responded with a lengthy defense, and the jurors found that Leochares had given false testimony. When this became apparent upon the ballots' being poured out—well, I see no need to discuss what Leochares begged of us and the jurors, or the size of the victory we could have achieved at that moment; but listen to the agreement we made. [18] We agreed with the archon not to count up but to mix up the ballots, and Dicaeogenes [III] dropped his claim to two-thirds of the estate in favor of Dicaeogenes' [II] sisters and agreed to hand over those portions to us without dispute. Leochares here offered himself as surety that Dicaeogenes [III] would in fact do this—and Leochares was not alone: Mnesiptolemus of the deme Plotheia did likewise.

232. Isaeus 3 *On the Estate of Pyrrhus* 3–7. Claim for adjudication (*lêxis*) of estate; *diamartyria*; *episkêpsis*; *dikê pseudomartyriôn*. (?ca. 389)

See references and headnotes under **85**, **90**, **129**, **204**, and **228**. In this case, Xenocles had entered a claim (*lêxis*) to the estate of Pyrrhus on behalf of his wife Phile, on the grounds that she was Pyrrhus' legitimate daughter (cf. **90** Isae. 3.2; **204** Isae. 3.67–69; **228** Isae. 3.40–50, 57–60, 62). The speaker's mother entered a rival claim to the estate, to which Xenocles responded with a *diamartyria* asserting that the estate was not subject to adjudication since Phile was Pyrrhus' legitimate daughter. The speaker then entered a denunciation (*episkêpsis*) and accordingly prosecuted and convicted Xenocles in a *dikê pseudomartyriôn* for having given a false *diamartyria*. The term *antômosiai* (singular *antômosia*: lit. "counter-oath"; here translated "affidavit") referred both to the oaths sworn by litigants at an *anakrisis* (preliminary hearing) and by extension to the documents submitted and sworn to by the litigants at the *anakrisis*; in this instance (§§6–7) the speaker refers to the affidavit he tendered at the *anakrisis* before the *dikê pseudomartyriôn* in which he convicted Xenocles (cf. **231** Isae. 5.6–7, 9, 12–18; **340b** Pl. *Ap.* 24b7-c2; **342** D. L. 2.40). The speaker is now prosecuting Nicodemus by *dikê pseudomartyriôn* for having given false testimony at Xenocles' *dikê pseudomartyriôn*.

And when our mother, Pyrrhus' sister, tried to advance her claim, the *kyrios* of the woman who had already filed a claim to the estate had the audacity to declare on oath [*diamartyrêsai*] that her brother's estate was not subject to adjudication [*epidikon*] to our mother, since there was a legitimate daughter of Pyrrhus, to whom the estate originally belonged. We then lodged a denunciation [*episkêpsamenoi*], brought before you the man who had had the audacity to make this declaration on oath, [4] exposed him as flagrantly having given false testimony, and won the lawsuit for false witness [*pseudomartyriôn dikên*] in your court. . . .

[5] . . . If Nicodemus were not found to have given false testimony on that occasion, obviously Xenocles would have left court with an acquittal as to the declaration on oath, and the woman declared on oath to be a legitimate daughter, rather than our mother, would have been established as heir to our uncle's estate. [6] But since the witness was convicted and the woman who claimed to be a legitimate daughter of Pyrrhus dropped her claim to the estate, the conclusion is inescapable that Nicodemus' testimony stands condemned at the very same time, since the man who made the declaration on oath conducted his defense in the lawsuit for false witness on this very issue; namely, whether the woman claiming the estate was our uncle's daughter by a wedded wife or by a prostitute. And you will realize this yourselves by listening to our affidavit [*antômosias*], Nicodemus' testimony, and the declaration on oath that was defeated in court. [7] [To the court clerk:] Take these and read them to them.

AFFIDAVIT.

TESTIMONY.

DECLARATION ON OATH.

233. Isaeus 11 *On the Estate of Hagnias* 45–46. Claim for adjudication (*lêxis*) of estate; *dikê pseudomartyriôn* and result if witness is convicted. (*post* 361/0)

See references and headnotes under **161** and **194**. The statement of law given here has been challenged by some scholars, but cf. **231** Isae. 5.6–7, 9, 12–18: as a result of the conviction of one of Dicaeogenes III's witnesses by *dikê pseudomartyriôn*, the will to which that witness had testified was (at least de facto) invalidated, and claims to the estate began anew.

As for the estate that Hagnias left to me, that is not yet secure: lawsuits for false witness [*dikai . . . pseudomartyriôn*] are pending, [46] and the law commands that if a person is convicted of false witness, the relevant claims [*lêxeis*] must start again from the beginning.

7.4.6. NEW *DIADIKASIA*

See also **194** Isae. 11.1–5, 8–12, 17–18, 29–30; **226** Pollux, *Onomasticon* 8.32; **231** Isae. 5.6–7, 9, 12–18; **233** Isae. 11.45–46.

234. [Demosthenes] 43 *Against Macartatus* 5–16 (*lex* + commentary). Announcement by herald inviting claims to estate; law on procedure in *diadikasia* over previously adjudicated estate or *epiklêros*, including summons and deposit (*parakatabolê*). (date of speech ?ca. 345; date of law unknown but presumably 6th or 5th c.)

See references and headnote under **4**. Here the speaker discusses previous and current litigation over the estate of Hagnias (for the sequence of lawsuits see the introduction to this chapter), and cites a law that renders a previously adjudicated estate or *epiklêros* liable to a new lawsuit for adjudication (*diadikasia*). The terms of the law require the claimant to pay a deposit (*parakatabolê*) and to issue to the party in possession a summons to appear before the eponymous archon; for the time limit (*prothesmia*) see **228** Isae. 3.40–50, 57–60, 62. The amphora and *chous* (pl. *choes*) (§8) are units of liquid capacity (1 amphora = 12 *choes* = approximately 10 gallons/38 liters) and refer to the amount of water in the *klepsydra* (water-clock: p. 37) allotted to the speakers. In §10 one voting-urn is assigned to each claimant.

At that time Theopompus, the father of my adversary Macartatus here, was in Athens, and when the herald made his announcement to see whether anyone wished to lay claim to or pay a deposit for [*parakataballein*] the estate of Hagnias either by right of kinship [*kata genos*] or in accordance with a will, he did not dare pay the deposit but instead adjudged for himself that he had no right to Hagnias' estate on any basis. [6] But now that the mother of this boy here held the estate, since she had defeated in the jury-court [*dikastêriôi*] all those who contested it with her, my adversaries are so repulsive that they think they should not obey your laws or the verdict given in the jury-court; instead, they tried by all means to steal back from the woman the estate that you awarded to her. [7] After swearing an oath together and drawing up a contract with one another, which they deposited with Medeius of the deme Hagnus, Theopompus, the father of my adversary Macartatus here, and Glaucon and Glaucus, who lost the earlier lawsuit, and another of their associates whom they took on as a fourth man—Eupolemus was his name—all these men together hatched a plot and summoned the woman to appear before the archon for a lawsuit for adjudication [*diadikasian*] of Hagnias' estate, claiming that the law commands that summons be made of the one who has been awarded and possesses the estate, if anyone wishes to dispute it.

[8] When the archon brought the lawsuit to the jury-court [*dikastêrion*] and it was time to litigate, they had arranged in their favor everything else for the trial, and in particular they got four times the water that we did to conduct their side. By necessity, you see, men of the jury, the archon had to pour in an amphora for each of the disputants, and three *choes* for the second speech. [9] And so the result was that I, who was litigating on behalf of the woman, not only could not explain to the jurors as I wished the family relationships and the other things I should have, but could not even offer a defense against even a small fraction of the lies they told about us. . . . [10] That is how they had plotted and cooperated with each other against us, with four urns put in place according to the law, and so predictably, I think, the jurors were deceived and argued with each other and, led astray by the plot, each voted whatever he voted. And only a few more votes—three or four—went in Theopompus' urn than in the woman's.

[11] . . . And when this boy was born and it seemed to be the right time, . . . I introduced this boy, who was born from Eubulides' daughter, to the members of Hagnias' phratry as the adopted son of Eubulides, in order that his household not be rendered vacant. [12] For that Eubulides, men of the jury, who was Hagnias' closest relative, used to pray most fervently to the gods that a son be born to him, just as his daughter, the mother of this boy, had been born to him. But when he did not get his wish and not a single male child was born to him, he then endeavored that a son from his daughter be adopted as his son into his and Hagnias' household [*oikon*] and be introduced into Hagnias' phratry . . . [13] And I did this service for him, since I was married to Eubulides' daughter, having claimed [*epidikasamenos*] her as the closest relative. . . .

[14] . . . And the phratry members . . . made the right vote, men of the jury; namely, that this boy be correctly and properly introduced, as the adopted son of Eubulides, into the household of Hagnias. [15] After this vote was cast by the members of the phratry of my adversary Macartatus here, this boy, as the son of Eubulides, summoned Macartatus to a lawsuit for adjudication [*diadikasian*] of the estate of Hagnias, and he filed the lawsuit [*elache*] with the archon, listing his brother as his *kyrios*: I could no longer be listed as *kyrios*, men of the jury, since I had gotten the boy adopted into the household of Eubulides. And the summons on this boy's behalf took place in accordance with the very same law under which my adversaries had summoned his mother, who had prevailed in the jury-court [*dikastêriôi*] previously and was in possession of Hagnias' estate. [16] [To the court clerk:] Please read the law that provides for summons of the person in possession of the estate.

LAW. If a person lays claim to an adjudicated [*epidedikasmenou*] estate or *epiklêros*, let him summon before the archon the one to whom adjudication has been made [*ton epidedikasmenon*], just as in other lawsuits [*dikôn*]. The person laying the claim shall make deposits [*parakatabolas*]. If he wins the adjudication [*epidikasêtai*] without issuing a summons, the adjudication [*epidikasia*] of the estate shall be void. If the one to whom the estate was adjudicated is not living, let him issue a summons according to the same rules, provided that the time limit [*prothesmia*] has not run out. The claim shall be against the possessor regarding the grounds on which the person whose property he possesses had it adjudged to him.

235. Isaeus 4 *On the Estate of Nicostratus* 24–25. *Diadikasia* over estate and possibility of future claim. (?ca. 350)

See references and headnote under **199**. Here the brothers Hagnon and Hagnotheus are contending against Chariades in a *diadikasia* over the estate of Nicostratus; the brothers claim by right of kinship (*genos*; i.e., their standing in Nicostratus' *anchisteia*) as first cousins to the decedent, while Chariades asserts that Nicostratus adopted him by will. The speaker, who supports Hagnon and Hagnotheus, states that future claims will remain available if the brothers win the present lawsuit but will be effectively precluded if Chariades wins. The latter statement, however, is not necessarily true, since further challenges to the will would remain possible: note, e.g., the invalidating conditions in **201** [Dem.] 46.14 and the challenge to the purported will of Astyphilus in Isaeus 9 (**213** Isae. 9.7–12).

And in fact, even from what my adversaries themselves say, it is in the interest of the relatives themselves for these men, rather than Chariades, to have Nicostratus' estate adjudicated to them [*epidikasasthai*]. [25] For in the future, if these men, claiming by right of kinship [*genos*], take the estate, my adversaries will be able, whenever they wish, to file a claim by right of kinship and demonstrate to you that they were more closely related to Nicostratus, and that he was the son of Smicrus, not of Thrasymachus. But if Chariades inherits the estate, no relative will be allowed to go after Nicostratus' property, since if the possessor got the estate adjudicated to him [*epidedikasmenou*] on the basis of a bequest [*dosin*], what are people claiming by right of kinship going to argue?

236. [Demosthenes] 48 *Against Olympiodorus* 22–32. Claim for adjudication (*lêxis*) of estate; original and subsequent *diadikasia* over estate; *anakrisis* before eponymous archon and trial in *dikastêrion*. (ca. 341)

Schäfer, *Demosthenes* 4.236–41; **Blass**, *AB* 3.1.557–62; L. **Gernet**, *Démosthène: Plaidoyers civils, Tome II* (Paris 1957: text, French translation, and notes); **Usher**, *GO* 265–66; **MacDowell**, *DO* 88–92; **Scafuro**, *Demosthenes 39–49* (translation with introduction and notes).

This speech was delivered by Callistratus in his prosecution of Olympiodorus by *dikê blabês* (see chapter 8, especially **259** [Dem.] 48 [selections]). When their relative Comon died childless and intestate, Callistratus and Olympiodorus made a contract specifying that they would split Comon's estate equally between themselves and cooperate in opposing any rival claims (including that of Callistratus' patrilateral half-brother Callippus, whose standing in Comon's *anchisteia* was the same as Callistratus'). Callistratus now accuses Olympiodorus of failing to abide by the contract, and here he describes the deal he made with Olympiodorus and its consequences in two successive *diadikasiai* over Comon's estate. The person Olympiodorus is said to have tortured (§§27, 32) was a slave who had belonged to Comon. For the law mentioned at §30 see **234** [Dem.] 43.5–16.

We decided, men of the jury, that my adversary Olympiodorus here would lay claim to the estate in its entirety and that I would lay claim to half the estate, since Callippus, my brother, was only laying claim to half the estate. [23] And when all the claims had undergone a preliminary hearing [*anekrithêsan*] before the archon and it was time to go to trial in the jury-court [*dikastêriôi*], my adversary Olympiodorus and I were utterly unprepared for trial at that point, since numerous claimants had suddenly fallen upon us. Owing to the situation, we looked together to see whether some adjournment [*anabolê*] might be effected for the present, so that we might prepare for the trial at our leisure. [24] And by some stroke of divine luck, you were persuaded by the politicians to dispatch troops to Acarnania, and my adversary Olympiodorus here had to serve, and he went off to serve with the rest. What had come to pass, we thought, was in fact excellent grounds for adjournment, since he was abroad on public business serving as a soldier.

[25] When the archon called all the claimants into the jury-court in accordance with the law, we swore the affidavit for adjournment [*hypômosametha*], stating that my adversary Olympiodorus here was away on public business serving as a soldier. After that affidavit was sworn, our opponents put in a counter-affidavit [*anthypômosanto*]; by slandering Olympiodorus here, speaking after us, they persuaded the jurors to vote that Olympiodorus was away on account of the trial and not on public business. [26] After the jurors rendered this vote, the archon Pythodotus, in accordance with the law, struck out Olympiodorus' claim. With that claim struck out, by necessity I too had to abandon my claim to half the estate; and when that happened, the archon awarded [*epedikasen*] Comon's estate to our opponents; that is what the laws forced him to do.

[27] After they won the adjudication [*epedikasanto*], they immediately went to Peiraeus and began seizing everything that each of us possessed as assigned

to his share. I myself was in town and handed it over in person (it was necessary to obey the laws), but as for Olympiodorus' share, since he was abroad, they took it all and left, except for the money he had from the person he had tortured: they had no way to get hold of that money.

[28] That was what happened while Olympiodorus was abroad, and that was the benefit I got from my partnership [*koinônias*] with him. When he and the other troops came back to Athens, Olympiodorus here was furious at what had happened, men of the jury, and thought that he had suffered terribly. When he had had his fill of fury, we again looked for and planned together—my adversary Olympiodorus and I—how we would get some of this property back. [29] We decided in our deliberations to issue a summons, in accordance with the law, to those who had won the adjudication [*epidedikasmenous*]; and owing to the situation, we decided that the safest course was not for both of us as a unit to run the risk against our rival claimants, but instead for each of us to act separately, with Olympiodorus here filing [*lachein*] for the whole estate, as previously, and litigating on his own, and with me filing for half the estate, since Callippus, my brother, was claiming only half the estate. [30] Our purpose was that if Olympiodorus here won at trial, I, in accordance with our contract and our oaths, would get back my share from him, while if he lost and the jurors voted the other way, he would recover his share from me in good and just fashion, as we had sworn to each other and agreed. So after we made this plan, as it seemed safest to both me and Olympiodorus, all those in possession of Comon's estate were summoned in accordance with the law. [To the court clerk:] Please read the law in accordance with which the summons occurred.

LAW.

[31] In accordance with this law, men of the jury, the summons occurred, and we filed our cross-claims [*tas amphisbêtêseis antegrapsametha*] in the way that seemed best to my adversary Olympiodorus. Then the archon held a preliminary hearing [*anekrine*] for all of us claimants, and after holding the preliminary hearing he brought the lawsuit to a jury-court [*dikastêrion*]. Olympiodorus here pled his case first, said whatever he wanted, and provided the witness testimony that seemed best to him; and I, men of the jury, sat in silence on the other platform. The trial having been rigged in this way, Olympiodorus won easily. [32] But after he won and we exacted everything we wanted in court, and he recovered from the previous awardees [*epidikasamenôn*] everything that they had taken from us—although he possesses all this property and the money he got from the person who was tortured, he has not been willing to perform any of his duties toward me. Instead, he keeps it all himself, after he swore oaths and made a contract with me that we would share it equally. Even now this contract is on deposit with Androcleides, and Androcleides has given his testimony to you.

CHAPTER 8

Damage

Handbooks: J. H. **Lipsius**, *Das attische Recht und Rechtsverfahren* (Leipzig 1905–15) 652–64; A. R. W. **Harrison**, *The Law of Athens* (1968–71) *passim*; D. M. **MacDowell**, *The Law in Classical Athens* (Ithaca, NY 1978) 149–53; S. C. **Todd**, *The Shape of Athenian Law* (Oxford 1993) 266–67, 279–83. **Studies**: L. **Beauchet**, *Histoire du droit privé de la république athénienne* (Paris 1897) 4.386–405; T. **Thalheim**, "Βλάβης δίκη," in *Paulys Realencyclopädie der classichen Altertumswissenschaft*, vol. III, 1 (Stuttgart 1897) coll. 552–54; R. J. **Bonner**-G. **Smith**, *The Administration of Justice from Homer to Aristotle* (Chicago 1930–38), vol. 2 *passim*; H. J. **Wolff**, "The ΔΙΚΗ ΒΛΑΒΗΣ in Demosthenes, *Or.*, LV," *AJP* 64 (1943) 316–24; F. **Pringsheim**, *The Greek Law of Sale* (Weimar 1950) 51–54; L. **Gernet**, "Le droit de la vente et la notion du contrat en Grèce," in ***idem***, *Droit et société dans la Grèce ancienne* (Paris 1955) 201–24; H. J. **Wolff**, "Die Grundlagen des griechischen Vertragsrechts," *ZSS* 74 (1957) 26–72; ***idem***, *Die attische Paragraphe* (Weimar 1966) *passim*; H. **Mummenthey**, *Zur Geschichte des Begriffs Βλάβη im attischen Recht* (diss. Freiburg 1971).

The evidence for a legal category of *blabê* (damage) before the Classical period is scant: we have one law attributed to Solon that appears to prescribe payment of either the simple value or twice the value of damage done to a slave (**51** Lys. 10.18–19), another on damage or injury caused by animals (**237**, **238**), and Solonian zoning regulations that may, when violated, have formed the basis for lawsuits in cases where one piece of landed property caused damage to or on another (**238**, **239**). The law on damage partially quoted in Demosthenes 23 (**240**), which distinguishes intentional from unintentional damage, is probably Archaic as well.

In the time of the orators, there was a dedicated—and amply-attested—

private lawsuit for damage, the *dikê blabês*. (For the proposal and evaluation of the alternative hypothesis that *dikê blabês* was not the name of a lawsuit but a general term for a group of specific lawsuits that addressed different types of damage, see the works of Wolff [1943], Pringsheim, Mummenthey, and Todd cited above.) The *dikê blabês* was employed to redress a wide variety of forms of wrongful financial loss, including losses consisting in or arising from physical damage to, destruction of, or disappearance of property (**241**, **249**, **255a**, **264**, and possibly **243**); withholding property (**242**, **245–247**, **256**, **261**); confiscation of property (**244**); debt (**250**, **253**, **257**, and probably **251** and **260**); failure to appear as a witness (**251**); exposing a person to prosecution in a *dikê pseudomartyriôn* (lawsuit for false witness: **252**); causing a person to become a debtor to the state (**256**); interference with mining rights (**256**); breach of contract (**256**, **259**, **263**); theft of a contract document (**261**); and contractual fraud (**262**). The *dikê blabês* could also apply in cases where financial loss was prospective rather than actual and/or where such loss could be defined in only broad or vague terms. Such cases included attempted breach of contract (**258**), usurpation of a name (**254**, if the identification of the lawsuit as a *dikê blabês* is correct), and interference with a festival chorus (**255a**: if "all the spiteful abuse concerning the chorus" represents grounds for a *dikê blabês* distinct from, rather than as a generalizing supplement to, the physical damage to the chorus' accoutrements, presumably the lawsuit would have been predicated upon the expenses Demosthenes had incurred in financing the chorus).

A person could be liable to a *dikê blabês* not only for damage he personally caused but also for damage caused, with or without his knowledge or consent, by property that he owned. The latter type of liability, called noxal liability (from Latin *noxa*, "harm, damage"), is attested or reliably presumed for slaves (**248**, **249**, **256**, **262**), animals (**237**, **238**, and possibly **243**), and land (**249**, and possibly **238** and **239**).

While we have one instance of a *dikê blabês* in which the penalty was evidently fixed by law (**249**; ?cf. **265a**), as a rule the *dikê blabês* was an assessable (*timêtos*) lawsuit (p. 40), with the penal assessment limited to a monetary fine. In his written statement of the charge (*enklêma*: **245**, **256b**, **264**), the prosecutor assessed the value of the damage he had suffered and proposed a penal assessment (*timêma*: **244**, **245**, **256a**, **257a**, **264**), which amounted to twice the value of the damage ("double damages" in modern legal parlance) if he accused the defendant of acting intentionally (designated by the adjective *hekôn*, "intentional(ly)": **240**, **255c**, and/or the verb *epibouleuein*, "to plot against": **246**, **256b**, **262**, **264**) and the simple amount of the damage ("simple damages") if he accused the defendant of acting unintentionally (*akôn*, **255c**; compare the use of the terms *hekôn* and *akôn* to indicate the presence and absence of intent with regard to homicide [see the introduction to chapter 1]). A contract document might contain language specifically mandating that intentional breach be redressed by double damages (**263**).

The *enklêma* in a *dikê blabês* followed a standard formula that began with the phrase *eblapse me* [name of defendant] ("[Name of defendant] caused me damage"), then specified the type and value of damage alleged and the *timêma*. However, not every *enklêma* featuring the *eblapse me* formula can be automatically ascribed to a *dikê blabês*; note, for example, Isaeus fr. 16 Thalheim (= Harpocration s.v. *agei*), which appears to come from a dedicated lawsuit for the assertion of the free status of an alleged slave (*aphairesis eis eleutherian*: cf. **298** [Dem.] 59.45–46). The same caution applies to the use of the noun *blabê* and the verb (*kata*)*blaptein* "to damage, to cause damage" (passive "to be damaged, to suffer damage"): see, e.g., **3b** Dem. 23.28.

In cases where noxal liability obtained, a convicted defendant who was unwilling or unable to pay his fine was compelled to hand over the damaging piece of property to his prosecutor (an act called noxal surrender: **237**, **238**, **249**, and possibly **243**). In at least one case, that of a vicious dog (**237**, **238**), it appears that noxal surrender was mandatory.

The magistrate(s) with whom a *dikê blabês* was filed depended on the facts alleged and the litigants involved. In the fourth century, in the default case, the competent magistrates will have been the Forty (p. 14; [Aristotle], *Constitution of the Athenians* [*Ath. Pol.*] 53), as indicated by the mention of public arbitration (p. 36) in **247**, **249**, **250**, and **253**. A *dikê blabês* for damage to merchandise for sale in the agora was filed with the *agoranomoi* (**241**). When a *dikê blabês* was brought as a *dikê metallikê* (mining lawsuit), as probably in **256**, or as a *dikê emporikê* (mercantile lawsuit: see chapter 10), as in **263** and probably in **260** and **261**, it came before the *thesmothetai* (**79** [Arist.] *Ath. Pol.* 59.5; Demosthenes 37.34). Regardless of the introducing magistrate(s), all *dikai blabês* came to trial before a regular jury-court (*dikastêrion*: p. 26).

See also **46** [Arist.] *Ath. Pol.* 52.2; **51** Lys. 10.18–19; **131** Dem. 39–40 (selections); **168** [Dem.] 49.1–2, 42–43, 69; **236** [Dem.] 48.22–32; chapter 10 *passim*; **332d** Dem. 21.25, 28.

237. Xenophon, *Hellenica* 2.4.41. Noxal surrender of vicious dog. (date of publication *post* 362; law ascribed elsewhere to Solon, 594/3)

E. C. **Marchant**-G. E. **Underhill**, *Xenophon*: Hellenica (Oxford 1906: text and commentary); P. **Krentz**, *Xenophon*: Hellenika *II.3.11-IV.2.8* (Warminster 1995: text, translation, and commentary); R. B. **Strassler**, ed., *The Landmark Xenophon's* Hellenika, tr. J. Marincola (New York 2009: translation with introduction and notes).

In this passage from his *Hellenica*, a history of Greece from 411 to 362, Xenophon describes a speech delivered by Thrasybulus, a leader of the democratic resistance that overthrew the Thirty Tyrants in 403 (see p. 12), at a meeting of the Assembly held upon the triumphant return of the democrats. Thrasybulus' questions quoted here are directed at the defeated oligarchs. On the noxal surrender of a vicious dog and the relevant "piece of wood" cf. **238** Plut. *Solon* 23.7–8, 24.3.

"Well, then, is it upon the Spartans that you think you should base your arrogance? How is that, when, just as people tie biting dogs to a piece of wood [*kloiôi*] and hand them over [*paradidoasin*], they have handed you over to the wronged party [*tôi êdikêmenôi*], this people [*dêmôi*], and have gone away and left?"

238. Plutarch, *Solon* 23.7–8, 24.3. Solonian agricultural zoning laws and law on damage caused by animals (*blabê tetrapodôn*), including noxal surrender of vicious dog. (date of composition late 1st–early 2nd c.A.D.; laws ascribed to Solon, 594/3 B.C.)

See references and headnote under **1d**. Here Plutarch describes laws on agricultural zoning and vicious dogs that he attributes, probably correctly, to Solon. With the zoning regulations detailed here cf. **239** *D.* 10.1.13; **249** Dem. 55 (selections). In the law on damage caused by animals (*tetrapoda*, "four-footed [creatures]"), which was in effect by the late fifth century at the latest (cf. **237** Xen. *Hell.* 2.4.41), the provision mandating that a vicious dog be "handed over" (to the wronged party: **237** Xen. *Hell.* 2.4.41) indicates noxal surrender (see the introduction to this chapter); the potential noxal surrender of slaves and land, other types of property that could cause harm, is indicated in **249** Dem. 55 (selections) (for slaves cf. **262** Hyp. 3.5–11, 18, 21–22, at §§21–22). The word *kloios*, here translated "piece of wood," can also mean "collar"; here we should presume a piece of wood attached to a collar (since a three-cubit collar on its own would have been ineffective). A cubit corresponded theoretically to the distance between a man's elbow and the tip of his middle finger; one cubit equaled 1.5 Greek feet (approximately 17.5 in/44.5 cm). Note that, as seen in the introduction to this chapter, in the Classical period (at least) the *dikê blabês* addressed damage to property, not injury to persons as such; a dog bite therefore could give rise to a *dikê blabês* only if the bite was suffered by a slave or other piece of property and not by a free person. See also **46** [Arist.] *Ath. Pol.* 52.2 regarding monthly lawsuits (*dikai emmênoi*) concerning slaves and draft animals (*hypozygia*), which presumably included cases in which they committed or suffered damage.

[Solon] also fixed the distances between planted trees with great expertise, ordering that people planting a tree in a field must remain five feet from their neighbor's property in other cases and nine feet in the case of a fig or olive tree. . . . [23.8] With regard to pits and ditches, he ordered that a person wishing to dig one must keep a distance away from the property of another equal to the depth he dug; he also ordered that a person setting up beehives must remain 300 feet from any beehives put in place previously by someone else.

. . .

[24.3] He also wrote a law on damage by animals [*blabês tetrapodôn*], in which he commands that a biting dog must be handed over [*paradounai*] with a three-cubit-long piece of wood [*kloiôi*] tied to it: a clever device for safety.

239. *Digest* 10.1.13 (*lex* + commentary). Solonian zoning laws. (*Digest* promulgated A.D. 533; law ascribed to Solon, 594/3 B.C.)

T. **Mommsen**-P. **Krueger**-A. **Watson**, eds., *The Digest of Justinian*, 4 vols. (Philadelphia 1985: text and translation).

In A.D. 533, as part of his codification of Roman law, the Roman emperor Justinian promulgated the *Digest*, a collection of excerpts from the works of prominent earlier jurists; the fragment below was excerpted from the fourth book of Gaius' second-century A.D. treatise *On the Law of the Twelve Tables*. *Taphon* ("grave") perhaps should read *taphron* ("ditch"): cf. **238** Plut. *Solon* 23.7–8, 24.3. A fathom corresponded theoretically to the distance between the tips of the middle fingers of a man with his arms outstretched; one fathom equaled 6 Greek feet (approximately 5 ft 10 in/1.78 m).

One should bear in mind, in an action on regulation of boundaries, the observance of that rule which has been written more or less on the example of the law that Solon is said to have enacted at Athens. In that law the rule is as follows: "If a person builds a dry stone wall [*haimasian*] along another's plot of land, he must not cross the boundary. If he builds a wall [*teichion*], he must keep a distance of a foot, and if he builds a building, two feet. If he digs a grave [*taphon*] or pit, he must keep a distance equal to the depth, and if he digs a well, he must keep a distance of a fathom. An olive or fig tree must be planted nine feet from another's property, and other trees five feet."

240. Demosthenes 23 *Against Aristocrates* 50 (*lex* + commentary). Law on damage; intentional and unintentional damage. (date of speech 352/1; law probably of Archaic date and possibly authored by Solon, 594/3)

See references and headnote under **3**, and for the context see **43** Dem. 23.50 and **73** Dem. 23.50. Here Demosthenes quotes directly from a law on damage; the quoted text ("If a person causes damage to another intentionally and wrongfully") is probably the opening condition of the law (cf., e.g., **35** Dem. 21.47).

For you see that in all the laws, not just the homicide laws, this is the case. . . . "If a person kills": "intentionally [*ek pronoias*]," the law adds, since if he kills unintentionally [*akôn*], it's not the same. "If a person causes damage [*katablapsêi*] to another": "intentionally [*hekôn*] and wrongfully [*adikôs*]."

241. Aristophanes, *Wasps* 1389–1408. *Dikê blabês* for damage to merchandise, under jurisdiction of *agoranomoi*; summons. (423/2)

See references and headnote under **183**. On the obol and other Athenian units of currency see p. 4. "The Two Goddesses" are Demeter and Persephone; their invocation is particularly apt in this context since Demeter was the goddess of the harvest. On the *agoranomoi* (Market Commissioners), who superintended sales in the agora of Athens and that of the Peiraeus, see **311** [Arist.] *Ath. Pol.* 51.1–3.

BREAD-SELLER. [To Chaerephon:] Come stand by me, I beg you by the gods. This man here is the one who ruined me by hitting me with his torch and knocked out of [my basket] here ten obols' worth of loaves and four more loaves in addition.

BDELYCLEON. [To Philocleon:] You see what you've done? Once again there have to be problems and lawsuits [*dikas*] because of your drinking.

PHILOCLEON. Not at all; clever arguments will settle these affairs, so I know I'll reach a settlement with this woman.

BREAD-SELLER. No way, by the Two Goddesses, will you escape unpunished from Myrtia daughter of Ancylion and Sostrate after ruining my merchandise like this!

PHILOCLEON. Listen up, woman. I want to tell you a clever story.

BREAD-SELLER. By Zeus, not to me you don't, buddy.

PHILOCLEON. Aesop was walking home from dinner one evening when an insolent, drunken bitch started barking at him. Then he said, "Bitch, bitch, if, by Zeus, you sold your evil tongue and bought some wheat somewhere, I think you'd have some sense."

BREAD-SELLER. Now you're laughing at me? I summon you, whoever you are, before the Market Commissioners [*agoranomous*] for damage to my merchandise [*blabês tôn phortiôn*], with Chaerephon here as my summons-witness.

242. Isocrates 21 *Against Euthynus* 2–3. ?*Dikê blabês* for withholding property. (403–402)

F. **Blass**, *Die attische Beredsamkeit* (Leipzig 1887–98) 2.219–23; R. C. **Jebb**, *The Attic Orators from Antiphon to Isaeus*[2] (London 1893) 2.221–23; G. **Mathieu**-E. **Brémond**, *Isocrate: Discours, Tome I* (Paris 1928: text, French translation, and notes); S. **Usher**, *Greek Oratory: Tradition and Originality* (Oxford 1999) 118–19; D. C. **Mirhady**-Y. L. **Too**, *Isocrates I* (Austin 2000: translation with introduction and notes).

This speech was delivered by a *synêgoros* (p. 28) of Nicias in the latter's prosecution of Euthynus; Nicias accused Euthynus of failing to return the total sum of 3 talents deposited with him. The legal action employed is frequently understood to have been a *dikê parakatathêkês* (lawsuit for [recovery of] a deposit), but the existence of such a procedure is not securely attested, and the lawsuit may instead have been a *dikê blabês* (the same issue applies to Isocrates 17: see **246** Isoc. 17.2–9, 11–16). In this instance Nicias made the deposit with a private individual, his cousin Euthynus, rather than with a bank (as in **246**); this distinction had no substantive bearing in law. Lysander was the Spartan admiral who cooperated in the installment of the Thirty Tyrants (p. 12); the nature of his catalogue (mentioned only here) is a matter of conjecture. "Those with a share in the state" are the 3,000 men to whom the Thirty granted full citizen rights (note the similar phrases in **245** Isoc. 16.1, 43–44, 46–47, at §46, and **125** [Arist.] *Ath. Pol.* 26.4, both describing rights of citizenship under the democracy).

So, then, I will explain to you as briefly as I can how the agreement between [Nicias] and Euthynus came into being. When the Thirty came to power, and his enemies were trying to erase him from among those with a share in the state and enroll him in the catalogue kept by Lysander, this man Nicias here, in fear of the current circumstances, . . . gave Euthynus three talents in cash for safekeeping. . . . [3] Not long afterward, wishing to sail away [from Attica], he demanded the money back; Euthynus, though, paid back two talents but denied having the third.

243. Lysias fr. 206 Carey *Defense Speech Concerning the Dog* (= Harpocration s.v. *karkinos*). ?*Dikê blabês* involving damage done by dog(s). (403–380)

J. G. **Baiter**-H. **Sauppe**, *Oratores Attici*, vol. 2 (Zürich 1850) p. 194 (Lysias, fragmentary speech LXXXI: text and Latin notes); **Blass**, *AB* 1.369; C. **Carey**, *Lysiae orationes cum fragmentis* (Oxford 2007: text and Latin notes).

This fragment, the sole surviving direct quotation from the speech in question, has given rise to several hypotheses regarding the matter at issue. Most probably "the dog" in the title of the speech belonged to the speaker and attacked and damaged (possibly killed) one or more of "the dogs" accused in the fragment of damaging the speaker's crop. If this is so, the prosecutor may be demanding, and the speaker may be resisting, the noxal surrender of the speaker's dog, as provided under Solon's law (cf. **237** Xen. *Hell.* 2.4.41; **238** Plut. *Solon* 23.7–8, 24.3).

For the dogs kept coming in and ruining my crop.

244. Isocrates 18 *Against Callimachus* 1–8, 10–13, 33, 63. *Paragraphê* against ?*dikê blabês* for confiscation of property. (*post* 404/3)

See references and headnote under **10**; also H. J. **Wolff**, *Die attische Paragraphe* (Weimar 1966). According to the speaker, this case represents the first use (§1) of the *paragraphê* (counter-indictment: p. 14) procedure, which was instituted in the wake of the democratic restoration of 403 on the proposal of the politician Archinus. The speaker contends (§§2–4) that Callimachus' lawsuit against him is rendered inadmissible by the terms of the Amnesty of 403 (p. 12; **11** [Arist.] *Ath. Pol.* 39.5–6; **12** Andoc. 1 [selections]) and is further barred by the existence of a binding private arbitration agreement (§4; on arbitration see p. 35). Callimachus charged that the speaker bore responsibility for the confiscation of property from him and sought damages in the amount of 10,000 dr. (§§5–8, 10, 13). The lawsuit brought by Callimachus was presumably (but not definitely) a *dikê blabês*: note its description as a private lawsuit and the reference to penal assessment (*timêma*) in §33, and the phrase "to be plotting against [*epibouleuein*] other people's money" in §63 (cf., e.g., **264** D. H. *Din.* 3). On sycophancy (malicious litigation: e.g., §§2, 10) see p. 33. In §3, for the *epôbelia* cf., e.g., **41b** [Dem.] 47.64; **263a** [Dem.] 56.3–6; the "30 drachmas" are the court fees (*prytaneia*) mentioned in §12 (cf. **256d** Dem. 37.39–44). On the Ten (§5) see **11** [Arist.] *Ath. Pol.* 39.5–6. In §6, for the procedure titled *phasis* (declaration) see **151** Harpo. s.v. *phasis*; "the Council" is the Council of 500. The angled brackets surrounding "Rhinon" in §8 indicate an editorial supplement to the text; in §63 "these people" are those who have "spen[t] money on the city" (by performing liturgies, on which see p. 25).

If there were any other men who had previously contended in a counter-indictment [*paragraphên*] such as this, I would begin my speech with the matter at issue. But as things are, I must first speak about the law in accordance with which we have come to court, in order that you cast your vote with knowledge of what we are disputing, and so that none of you is surprised that I, the defendant in the lawsuit [*dikên*], am speaking before the prosecutor. [2] When, after you returned from Peiraeus, you saw that some of the citizens had started behaving as sycophants [*sykophantein*] and were attempting to violate the treaty, you wanted to stop them and demonstrate to the rest that you had made the treaty not under compulsion but because you believed it was beneficial to the city. So, on the motion of Archinus, you passed a law providing that if a person litigated in violation of the oaths, the defendant could lodge a counter-indictment [*paragrapsasthai*], and the magistrates would introduce this matter first; the person lodging the counter-indictment would speak first, [3] and whichever litigant lost would be fined the *epôbelia*, so that those who had the audacity to bear malice would not just be exposed as perjurers and await vengeance from the gods, but would incur an immediate penalty as well. So I considered it a terrible thing if, when the laws provide in this fashion, I were to allow this sycophant to risk only 30 drachmas while I myself went on trial for the entirety of my property.

[4] I will prove that Callimachus is not only litigating in violation of the treaty but also lying with regard to his charges, and furthermore that we have already undergone arbitration concerning these matters. . . .

[5] The Ten who came to power after the Thirty were in office; I had a friend, Patrocles, who at that time was *basileus*, and I happened to be walking with him. Patrocles was an enemy of Callimachus, who is prosecuting me in the present lawsuit; he happened upon Callimachus while Callimachus was carrying some money. He took hold of him and said that Amphilus had left the money behind, and so it was to become public property, since Amphilus was one of the men in Peiraeus. [6] My adversary disputed this, they exchanged abusive words, and a lot of other people came running up—and, by chance, Rhinon, one of the Ten, arrived. So immediately Patrocles made the declaration [*phasin*] of the money to Rhinon. Rhinon brought both of them before his colleagues in office; they referred the matter to the Council, and when judgment was rendered, it was decided that the money was public property.

[7] Later, when the exiles returned from Peiraeus, [Callimachus] brought charges against Patrocles and filed lawsuits [*dikas*], claiming that Patrocles had

been responsible for his misfortune. Then, after reaching a settlement with him and exacting from him 10 talents in cash, he began his malicious prosecution of [*esykophantei*] Lysimachus; and after getting 200 drachmas from him as well, he started causing problems for me. At first he brought charges stating that I cooperated with those men, but in the end he reached such a level of shamelessness that he held me responsible for everything that had happened; probably he will have the audacity to bring the same accusations now as well. [8] I shall provide to you as witnesses first the men who were present at the beginning, to prove that I neither laid hold of Callimachus nor touched the money; then <Rhinon> and his colleagues in office, to prove that it was not I but Patrocles who made the declaration to them; and also the members of the Council, to prove that Patrocles was the one who brought the accusation.

. . .

[10] . . . In the end, at any rate, I was persuaded . . . to pay my adversary 200 drachmas. But, so that he would not be able to engage in malicious prosecution [*sykophantein*] again, we submitted the matter for arbitration on stated terms to Nicomachus of the deme Bate. . . . [11] At first he abided by the agreement, but later . . . he filed a lawsuit [*dikên*] against me for 10,000 drachmas. When I then put forward a witness to the fact that the lawsuit was not admissible since arbitration had occurred, he didn't prosecute the witness, [12] . . . but persuaded the magistrate and got the same lawsuit registered again, in the belief that he would be risking only the court fees [*prytaneiois*]. Being at a loss as to how I should deal with my troubles, I thought it best to put the risk on equal footing for both of us and come before you. And that's what happened.

[13] But I hear that Callimachus not only intends to tell lies with regard to his charges but is even going to deny that arbitration occurred: he has prepared arguments to deliver to the effect that he would never have entrusted arbitration of the matter to Nicomachus . . . and that it is not probable that he would have been willing to take 200 drachmas instead of ten thousand.

. . .

[33] And let no one suppose that I am being excessive or making too great claims because I have made these statements as the defendant in a private lawsuit [*dikên idian*]. For, you see, this trial is not just about the money listed [as a penalty] in the charge. That is what it's about for me, but for you it's about the things that were discussed a little earlier, concerning which no one could either speak in a worthy manner or list a sufficient penalty [*timêma*] in a charge.

. . .

[63] I myself, it will be clear, have been one of these people, and I would be the most unfortunate of all if, after spending much of my own money on the city, I should then be deemed to be plotting against [*epibouleuein*] other people's money. . . .

245. Isocrates 16 *On the Team of Horses* 1, 43–44, 46–47. *Dikê blabês* for withholding property. (398/7–395/4)

Blass, *AB* 2.224–29; **Jebb**, *AO* 2.228–33; **Mathieu-Brémond**, *Isocrate: Discours I* (text, French translation, and notes); **Usher**, *GO* 120–22; **Mirhady-Too**, *Isocrates I* (translation with introduction and notes).

This speech was delivered by the younger Alcibiades (see **99** Lys. 14.28) as defendant in a *dikê blabês*. The prosecutor, Teisias, charged the younger Alcibiades with withholding from him a team of four horses with which the elder Alcibiades (see **98** [Andoc.] 4.13–14, Plut. *Alcib.* 8.4–6) had competed in the Olympic games of 416. Teisias assessed the penalty at 5 tal. (§46). With the reference to the Amnesty of 403 in §43 cf., e.g., **244** Isoc. 18.1–8, 10–13, 33, 63, at §§1–3. In §46, for the phrase "have a share in the city"; that is, (in this case, continue to) "be a citizen," cf. **125** [Arist.] *Ath. Pol.* 26.4.

Now, then, as to the team of horses: that my father got it not by robbing Teisias but by purchase from the city of Argos, you have heard in the testimony of the ambassadors who have come from there and of the others who know about it.

. . .

[43] [To Teisias:] And then you . . . have the gall to bear malice [*mnêsikakein*] against others, and you feel no shame at violating the treaty . . . ? [44] Certainly they aren't going to exact punishment from me for what my father did but grant pardon to you for the offenses you yourself committed.

. . .

[46] Having already suffered so many misfortunes, and having twice lost my property, now I am the defendant in a lawsuit [*dikên*] for 5 talents. And the charge [*enklêm'*] concerns money, but I am on trial as to whether I should have a share in the city. [47] The same penalties' [*timêmatôn*] being listed in the charge does not present the same danger to all men: those who have money risk a fine, while those who lack means, such as myself, risk disfranchisement [*atimias*]. . . .

246. Isocrates 17 *Trapeziticus* 2–9, 11–16. ?*Dikê blabês* for withholding property; evidentiary torture of slave. (393–391)

Blass, *AB* 2.229–34; **Jebb**, *AO* 2.223–27; **Mathieu-Brémond**, *Isocrate: Discours I* (text, French translation, and notes); **Usher**, *GO* 122–23; **Mirhady-Too**, *Isocrates I* (translation with introduction and notes).

Isocrates' *Trapeziticus*, or "speech about the bank (*trapeza*)," was delivered by the prosecutor in a lawsuit identified as either a *dikê parakatathêkês* or a *dikê blabês* (cf. **242** Isoc. 21.2–3); a *dikê blabês* may be indicated by the speaker's assertion that Pasion was "plotting against [*epibouleuonta*] my property" (§8; cf., e.g., **264** D. H. *Din.* 3; **256b** Dem. 37.22–26, 28–33). The prosecutor, a citizen of the kingdom of Cimmerian Bosporus—the modern Crimea, not to be confused with the strait of Bosporus that connects the Black Sea to the Propontis—ruled by Satyrus, charges the defendant Pasion (on whom cf., e.g., **92** Dem. 45.27–28, 30) with failing to return a deposit left at his bank. (The amount of the claimed deposit is not stated but was evidently considerable: at §44 the speaker claims that Pasion stood surety for him for the sum of 7 tal., "in the belief that he possessed a sufficient guarantee in the gold that was on deposit with him.") On "visible" property (*phanera*, §7) see **185** Andoc. 1.117–21; on the evidentiary torture of slaves see p. 24 and cf. **256d** Dem. 37.39–44.

. . . I believe I will make it clear to all that I am being deprived of my money by Pasion.

[3] Now, then, I will explain to you what has happened from the beginning to the best of my ability. My father, men of the jury, is Sopaeus, who all who sail to the Black Sea know is on such close terms with Satyrus as to rule over a large territory and superintend his entire army. [4] And when I heard about this city and the rest of Greece, I desired to go abroad. So my father loaded two ships with grain, gave me money, and sent me out for the purpose of both trade and sightseeing; and after Pythodorus the Phoenician introduced me to Pasion, I used his bank. [5] Later, when a slanderous accusation was made to Satyrus that my father was plotting against his empire and I was associating with the fugitives, he arrested my father and sent letters to those from the Black Sea who were residing here, instructing them to seize the money from me and order me to sail back, and if I did neither of these things, to demand my extradition from you.

[6] In the face of such serious troubles, men of the jury, I told Pasion of my misfortunes. . . . [7] So in our consultations we decided it was best to agree to do everything Satyrus was ordering, and to hand over the money that was visible [*phanera*], but as for the money that was on deposit with Pasion, not only to deny its existence but in fact to have me appear as owing money with interest to both Pasion and others, and to take all measures by which they would best be convinced that I had no money.

[8] At that time, men of the jury, I believed that Pasion was giving me all this advice out of goodwill; but after I took care of business with the men sent by Satyrus, I realized that Pasion was plotting against [*epibouleuonta*] my property. For when I wanted to recover what was mine and sail to Byzantium, my adversary thought that an excellent opportunity had befallen him: the money that was on deposit with him was a large amount and worth shameless behav-

ior, while I, in front of many listeners, had denied owning anything, and it was apparent to all that money was being demanded as due from me and that I was admitting owing money to other people as well. [9] . . . Taking these things into account, he conceived his plan to rob me of my money. To me he pretended that he lacked means at present and would not be able to pay me back; but when . . . I sent Philomelus and Menexenus to him to demand payment, he denied to them that he had anything of mine. . . .

[11] After that, men of the jury, men came to me reporting that my father had been set free. . . . When he learned this, Pasion . . . made the slave who knew about my money disappear. [12] And when I approached him and demanded the production of the slave, in the belief that that would be the clearest test as to the charges I was making, Pasion made the most horrendous allegation of all: that Menexenus and I had corrupted and persuaded the slave, who was working at the bank, and had taken six talents in cash from him. And, so that no test or torture could occur concerning these matters, he claimed that we had made the slave disappear and were now counter-charging him and demanding the production of the very slave whom we ourselves had made disappear. Making these statements and expressing indignation and crying, he dragged me before the polemarch, demanding sureties, and he did not set me free until I had appointed sureties for him for six talents. . . .

[13] . . . I went in person to the Peloponnese to conduct a search. But Menexenus found the slave here; he seized him and demanded that he be tortured both concerning the deposit [*parakatathêkês*] and concerning the accusations my adversary was making against us. [14] Pasion, however, . . . had him released [*aphêireit'*] on the grounds that he was a free man [*hôs eleutheron onta*] . . . and felt no shame or fear at . . . preventing his being tortured. . . .

[15] And yet, after doing these things, . . . he approached us, saying that he was ready to hand over the slave for torture. We chose torturers and met at the Hephaesteion. I demanded that they whip and rack the surrendered man until they deemed him to be telling the truth, but my adversary Pasion here said that we had not chosen them as executioners, and instead instructed them to conduct verbally whatever inquiry they wanted of the slave. [16] As we were arguing, the torturers themselves refused to conduct the torture and decided that Pasion should hand over the slave to me. But my adversary wanted so badly to evade the torture that he refused to obey them as to the surrender, but was prepared to pay the money if they convicted him.

247. [Demosthenes] 52 *Against Callippus* 3–10, 12–15. *Dikê argyriou*; *dikê blabês* for withholding property. (369/8)

A. **Schäfer**, *Demosthenes und seine Zeit* (Leipzig 1858–87) 4.134–37; **Blass**, *AB* 3.1.514–18; L. **Gernet**, *Démosthène: Plaidoyers civils, Tome III, Discours*

XLIX–LVI (Paris 1959: text, French translation, and notes); **Usher**, *GO* 338–39; V. **Bers**, *Demosthenes, Speeches 50–59* (Austin 2003: translation with introduction and notes); D. M. **MacDowell**, *Demosthenes the Orator* (Oxford 2009) 100–2.

Apollodorus wrote this speech and delivered it in his own defense in a *dikê argyriou* (lawsuit for money due: §14; cf. Demosthenes 39.25; [Demosthenes] 48.45). The prosecutor, Callippus, charged that Apollodorus owed him 1,640 dr. (= 16 mn. 40 dr.: see p. 4) in accordance with the terms of a deposit made at the bank of Apollodorus' father Pasion (cf. **246** Isoc. 17.2–9, 11–16). Callippus had originally initiated a *dikê blabês* against Pasion, but the case was removed from public arbitration (see p. 36 and the introduction to this chapter) and referred to private arbitration (cf. **244** Isoc. 18.1–8, 10–13, 33, 63), and Pasion died before the private arbitrator could render a decision (§§14–15). Callippus' motive for the change in legal procedure is not clear; a contributing factor may have been his contention that the damaging act was intentional on the part of Pasion (on which charge a successful *dikê blabês* would result in payment of double damages: **255c** Dem. 21.43) but unintentional on the part of Pasion's son and heir Apollodorus (it appears that a successful *dikê argyriou* resulted in payment of the simple amount due, but the same was true of a successful *dikê blabês* for unintentional damage). A *proxenos* (§§5, 9–10) was a citizen (here Callippus of Athens and Strammenus of Argos) assigned to represent the interests of a foreign power—in both cases, the city of Heracleia, which cannot be identified securely since there were several cities by that name—in his city. On Phormion (§§5–7) cf. **92** Dem. 45.27–28, 30; **148** Dem. 36.20, 22; **179** Dem. 36.8–9, 11, 34; **207** Dem. 36.14. Sciron (§9) was a district in Attica just northwest of Athens.

Lycon of Heracleia . . . , when he was about to sail out to Libya, balanced his account with my father in the presence of Archebiades and Phrasias, and instructed him to pay to Cephisiades the money that he was leaving on deposit (this amounted to 16 minae 40 drachmas, as I will demonstrate to you with total precision), stating that this Cephisiades was his partner. . . . [4] He instructed Archebiades and Phrasias to point [Cephisiades] out and introduce him to my father when he returned from his voyage abroad. . . .

[5] But misfortune befell this man Lycon such that right away, as he was sailing out around the Argolic Gulf, he was forced by pirate ships to put in with his goods at Argos, and he himself was struck by an arrow and died. My adversary Callippus here then immediately came to the bank asking if they knew Lycon of Heracleia. When Phormion here answered that they did, he asked, "Did he use your bank?" Phormion said he did, "but why do you ask?" "I will tell you why," said Callippus. "He is dead, and I am *proxenos* of the Heracleotes. I therefore insist that you show me the documents, so that I may know whether he has

left any money behind; by necessity I must take care of all Heracleotes." [6] . . . When Phormion showed him the account statement, . . . and he saw written in it, "Lycon of Heracleia, 1,640 drachmas, to be paid to Cephisiades; Archebiades of the deme Lamptrae will point out Cephisiades," he went away in silence, and he made no mention of it for more than five months. [7] After this, Cephisiades returned to Athens, came to the bank, and demanded the money—in the presence, men of the jury, of Archebiades and Phrasias . . . and others—so Phormion here counted out the 16 minae 40 drachmas and paid him. . . .

[8] . . . A considerable time later, my adversary Callippus here came up to my father in the city and asked him whether Cephisiades . . . had returned to Athens yet. . . . [9] . . . "You can," he said, "do well by me and suffer no harm [*blabênai*] yourself. You see, I am *proxenos* of the Heracleotes, and as I see it, you might want me to receive the money rather than that metic who lives in Sciron and is worthless. What has happened is more or less this. Lycon is childless and has left no heir at home, as I understand. [10] Moreover, when he put in at Argos, having been wounded, he gave the Argive *proxenos* of the Heracleotes, Strammenus, the goods that arrived in port with him. So I too have the right to demand personal receipt of the property here. . . . You, then, if [Cephisiades] has not received it, tell Cephisiades, if he comes, that I am asserting a claim to it; if he has received it, tell him that I, with witnesses, demanded the production in plain sight [*emphanê katastêsai*] of the property or the one who received it. . . ." . . .

[12] That, men of the jury, is what my adversary told my father and my father then told Archebiades and Cephisiades at my adversary's request and as a favor to him; and from that, little by little, this lawsuit has been concocted. . . . [13] My adversary . . . let three years pass after my father first conversed with Archebiades and the other friends of Cephisiades and they told him to pay no attention to Callippus or what he was saying. [14] But when he heard that my father was in a disabled condition and could barely walk up to the city and his eyesight was betraying him, he filed a lawsuit [*dikên*] against him—not, by Zeus, for money due [*argyriou*], as in this case, but for damage [*blabês*], charging that my father caused him damage [*blaptein*] by paying Cephisiades the money that Lycon of Heracleia had left on deposit with him, when my father had agreed not to pay it without his consent. After filing the lawsuit, he withdrew the charge from the [public] arbitrator [*diaitêtou*] and challenged my father to submit the matter for arbitration to Lysitheides, a close friend of himself and Isocrates and Aphareus and an acquaintance of my father. [15] My father consented to the arbitration, and for as long as my father lived, even though he was on friendly terms with these men, all the same Lysitheides did not dare to do us any wrong.

248. [Demosthenes] 53 *Against Nicostratus* 19–20. Liability for harm caused by slave. (*post* 368/7)

See references and headnote under **40**. Here Apollodorus adduces as one proof of Arethusius' ownership of Cerdon the fact that Arethusius has assumed liability for harm caused by Cerdon. Cf. **262** Hyp. 3.5–11, 18, 21–22, at §§21–22; **249d** Dem. 55.31–32, 34.

I will now prove to you that these slaves belong to Arethusius and are part of his estate, as I have listed [*apegrapsa*] them. He raised Cerdon ever since Cerdon was a tiny little boy, and to prove that he belonged to Arethusius, I will bring before you as witnesses the men who know this.

WITNESSES.

[20] Moreover, to prove that whenever Cerdon worked for anyone, Arethusius received the payments for him, and that Arethusius, as his master, received compensation [*dikas*] and paid it whenever Cerdon caused any harm, I will bring before you as witnesses the men who know these things.

WITNESSES.

249. Demosthenes 55 *Against Callicles* (selections). *Dikê blabês* (?*atimêtos*) for damage to property; ?noxal surrender of land; ?noxal surrender of slave. (?364/3–350s)

See especially J. E. **Sandys**-F. A. **Paley**, *Demosthenes: Select Private Orations* 2[4] (Cambridge 1910: text and commentary); **Wolff**, "ΔΙΚΗ ΒΛΑΒΗΣ"; **Bers**, *Demosthenes 50–59* (translation with introduction and notes); **MacDowell**, *DO* 63–66; also **Schäfer**, *Demosthenes* 4.252–57; **Blass**, *AB* 3.1.253–57; **Gernet**, *Démosthène: Plaidoyers civils III* (text, French translation, and notes); **Usher**, *GO* 186–89.

This case presents an apparent exception to the general rule that the *dikê blabês* was an assessable (*timêtos*) lawsuit. The prosecutor, Callicles, charges the (unnamed) defendant with damage caused to his real and other property by floodwaters that were diverted onto his land by a wall separating the plots of the two men (compare the Solonian zoning regulations: **238** Plut. *Solon* 23.7–8, 24.3; **239** *D.* 10.1.13). By the speaker's account, although the damage was minor (**249c**; elsewhere, at §28, he estimates its total value at less than 50 dr.), he now stands trial in a fixed-penalty (*atimêtos*, "unassessable") lawsuit for 1,000 dr. (**249a**, **249c**). Of the various theories as to why this lawsuit was unassessable, the most influential has been that of Wolff, who proposed that a specific law on property damage caused by water mandated that a person who diverted a natural watercourse so as to cause damage to another's property either surrender the land that contained the source of the damage (in this case, the wall built by the speaker's father) or pay a fixed penalty of 1,000 dr.: note especially the speaker's concern that an arbitrator might award his property to his adversaries (**249d**, §32). On this theory, noxal liability could attach to land just as it could to animals (**237** Xen. *Hell.* 2.4.41; **238** Plut. *Solon* 23.7–8, 24.3) and slaves (see below). Three additional *dikai blabês* have been brought over the same matter: one by Callicles' brother Callicrates against the speaker (**249a**), a second by Callicles against the speaker's slave Callarus (**249d**), and a third by Callicrates against Callarus (**249d**). In §34 (**249d**), the speaker's comment that the lawsuits against Callarus are efforts "to spite me because I consider the man valuable" points to the possibility of noxal surrender (on liability for harm caused by slaves cf. **248** [Dem.] 53.19–20; **262** Hyp. 3.5–11, 18, 21–22, at §§21–22); the angled brackets surrounding "Callicrates" indicate that this is an editorial addition to the text. For the medimnus (**249c**) see **206** Isae. 10.9–10.

a. Dem. 55.1–5.

Really, men of Athens, there is nothing more difficult than encountering a wicked and covetous neighbor, which is exactly what has happened to me now. You see, because of his lusting after my property, Callicles has put me in such a position by his malicious prosecutions [*sykophantôn*] that he first suborned his cousin to dispute ownership of the property with me [2] and then, after he was openly proven wrong and I defeated their fabricated claim, got two lawsuits [*dikas*] decided in arbitration against me by default [*erêmous*]: one that he brought in his own name for 1,000 drachmas, and another that he convinced his brother Callicrates here to bring. . . .

[3] Now, then, men of Athens, in reply to all my adversaries' arguments I have one simple justification in my favor. My father built a wall around the plot of land in question shortly before I was born; at that time Callippides, the father of my adversaries, was still living and occupying the neighboring property—and he obviously had more precise knowledge [of the matter] than my adversaries—and Callicles was already a grown man and was living in Athens. [4] And in all those years no one ever came bringing a charge or complaint (although obviously rain often happened back then too), nor did anyone obstruct [the building of the wall] in the beginning, as would have happened if in fact my father was wronging anyone by building the wall around our property. But no one forbade or protested, although my father lived on for more than fifteen years and my adversaries' father Callippides lived on for no less a period.

[5] Now, Callicles, obviously back then, when you all saw the water-course being walled off, you could have immediately come and expressed your irrita-

tion and told my father, "Teisias, why are you doing this? You're walling off the water-course? Then the water will invade our property!"

b. Dem. 55.20–21.

And here's the most terrible thing of all. After the water invaded the property, Callicles brings in enormous boulders and walls it off, but because my father built a wall around his property when the same thing happened to him, he accuses my father of wrongdoing and has filed a lawsuit [*dikên*] for damage [*blabês*] against me! Now, if all those who suffered badly due to the water flowing in this area are going to file lawsuits against me, even if I had many times the property I have, it wouldn't be sufficient [to pay them]. [21] But here's the great difference between my adversaries and the rest of them: although many people have suffered great and considerable damage, my adversaries, who have suffered nothing (as I will presently prove clearly to you), are the only ones who have had the gall to go to law against me.

c. Dem. 55.23–25.

I will now endeavor to demonstrate to you that [Callicles] has filed a lawsuit [*dikên*] of such severity against me despite the fact that he has lost nothing and suffered no damage [*katabeblammenos*] worthy of mention. . . . [24] My mother went to see my adversaries' mother, and their mother was bitterly lamenting and pointing out what had happened. This is how we learned about the whole thing, men of the jury. I am telling you exactly what I heard from my mother. . . . She said that she in fact saw and heard from my adversaries' mother that not even three medimni of barley had gotten soaked—and she saw it drying—and maybe half a medimnus of wheat flour; my adversaries' mother also said that a jar of olive oil had been knocked over but had suffered no harm. [25] That, men of the jury, is the extent of what happened to my adversaries, for which I am on trial in an unassessable lawsuit [*dikên atimêton*] for 1,000 drachmas.

d. Dem. 55.31–32, 34.

. . . and now [Callicles] himself has gotten another lawsuit [*dikên*] of the same type decided in arbitration against me by default [*erêmên*], having listed the name of Callarus, one of my slaves. You see, in addition to the rest of their evil acts, they have come up with this clever trick as well: they are bringing the same lawsuit against Callarus. [32] Now, I ask you, what slave would build a wall around his master's property unless his master gave him the order? But since they cannot charge Callarus with anything else, they are prosecuting him for my father's having fenced off his property more than fifteen years before he died. And if I relinquish my claim to the property, by selling it to them or exchanging it for other plots of land, Callarus is guilty of nothing; but if I am not willing to surrender to them what belongs to me, they are suffering all kinds of horrible treatment at Callarus' hands, and they go looking for an arbitrator who will find against me and award the property to them, and for the sort of settlements by which they will get the property.

. . .

[34] And so that you may know that previously, in plotting [*epibouleuôn*] against my property, [Callicles] suborned his cousin, and that now he has gotten another lawsuit of the same type decided in arbitration against Callarus—in an effort to spite me because I consider the man valuable—and that <Callicrates> has again filed another lawsuit against Callarus, [the court clerk] will read to you the depositions regarding all these matters.

250. Demosthenes 41 *Against Spudias* 7–9, 11–12. ?*Dikê blabês* for debt. (*post* 364/3)

See references and headnote under **101**. Here the speaker itemizes the debts that he claims are owed to him by Spudias (for the details of the speaker's first charge against Spudias, mentioned at §7, see **114** Dem. 41.5–7, 10). The legal procedure employed by the speaker is not certain but may have been a *dikê blabês*; the language employed in §12 indicates that Spudias' countersuit against the speaker there mentioned was likely a *dikê blabês*. The Nemeseia (§11) was presumably a festival in honor of Nemesis, the goddess of vengeance.

That, then, men of the jury, is one of the charges I am bringing against Spudias. . . . [8] Another, men of the jury, concerns 2 minae, which Aristogenes has testified that Polyeuctus, as he was dying, charged as owed to him by Spudias, along with the interest on it (that is, the price of a slave whom my adversary purchased from Polyeuctus, a price that he neither paid to Polyeuctus nor has now brought into the common fund); and also 1,800 drachmas, about which even I don't know what just argument [Spudias] will be able to make. [9] You see, he had borrowed this money from Polyeuctus' wife. . . .

. . .

[11] Now, then, men of the jury, I wish also to instruct you as to the other charges I am bringing, one by one. There is the bowl that they took from Polyeuctus' wife and deposited as security [*enechyra*] along with some gold jewelry: although they have recovered it, they have not brought it into [the common fund], as Demophilus, the depositary, will testify to you. There is the tent that

they possess and which they also, despite having received it, refuse to bring into [the common fund]. And how many other such things are there? Lastly, my wife contributed to the Nemeseia on her father's behalf a mina in cash as an advance expenditure, and yet [Spudias] does not even see fit to contribute his part of this sum. . . .

[12] Probably, men of the jury, Spudias will have no response to give to these facts . . . but will blame Polyeuctus and his wife, claiming that they did all these things as favors at my behest, and that he, by Zeus, is suffering damage [*blaptesthai*] in many other considerable ways and has filed a lawsuit [*dikên*] against me; that, you see, is what he endeavored to argue before the arbitrator.

251. [Demosthenes] 49 *Against Timotheus* 17–20. *Dikê blabês* for failure to appear as witness; ?*dikê blabês* for debt. (362)

See references and headnote under **168**; also **Harrison**, *LA* 2.139–45. In this passage from his speech against Timotheus, which was delivered in a lawsuit (probably a *dikê blabês*) over alleged debt (cf. **168** [Dem.] 49.1–2, 42–43, 69; **250** Dem. 41.7–9, 11–12), Apollodorus describes the events that culminated in his lodging a separate *dikê blabês* against Antiphanes for failing to fulfill a promise to testify on his behalf. On the placement of witnesses' depositions in jars during public arbitration see [Aristotle], *Constitution of the Athenians* (*Ath. Pol.*) 53.2; the "day appointed for judgment" was that on which the arbitrator was scheduled to render his decision. Harrison (pp. 141–42) proposes that "the drachma" (§19) was "a court fee for bringing the charge of *lipomartyriou* against the witness, and that it was at the discretion of the arbitrator to pronounce the fine against the witness." For the oath of denial (*exômosia*, §20), by which a man asserted that he had no knowledge of the matter to which he was being called to testify, cf. **16** Isae. 9.17–19. Calaureia (§18) is an island off the coast of the Argolid peninsula, opposite Troezen.

. . . [Timotheus] approached my father and asked him to discharge his debt to Philippus and to lend him the thousand drachmas to pay Philippus. My father . . . instructed Phormion, the clerk at the bank, to pay Philippus 1,000 drachmas and to record Timotheus as owing the money. [18] . . . And I shall also call before you Antiphanes, who lent my adversary the money, the thousand drachmas, in Calaureia, and who was present when Philippus received the money from my father here [in Athens]. [19] By deception he prevented me from putting his deposition into [the jar] before the arbitrator, always telling me that he would testify for me on the day appointed for judgment. But when the arbitration hearing took place, although I summoned him from his house (since he was nowhere to be seen), he failed to appear as a witness, having been persuaded by my adversary. Although I then, in accordance with the law, deposited the drachma against him for his failure to appear as a witness [*lipomartyriou*], the arbitrator did not give judgment against my adversary but decided the arbitration hearing in his favor and then left, since it was already evening. [20] I have now filed a private lawsuit [*idian dikên*] for damage [*blabês*] against Antiphanes, since he neither testified for me nor swore the oath of denial [*exômosato*] in accordance with the law.

252. Demosthenes 29 *3 Against Aphobus* 15–16. *Dikê blabês* for exposing a person to prosecution by *dikê pseudomartyriôn* (for false witness). (?362/1)

See references and headnotes under **120** and **147**. According to Aphobus, Phanus had falsely testified that Aphobus had admitted that a man named Milyas was not a slave but had been manumitted by Demosthenes' father. Demosthenes here alleges that Aphobus' brother Aesius also testified to Milyas' free status, a fact that Aesius denies. The "immediate judgment" mentioned in §15 would have resulted if Aesius had refused either to testify or to swear the oath of denial (*exômosia*: cf. **251** [Dem.] 49.17–20). On the *dikê pseudomartyriôn* and the attendant risk of partial disfranchisement (*atimia*) see **170** Andoc. 1.73–79.

Moreover, men of the jury, Aesius, the brother of my adversary, was the first to give this testimony. Now he denies it, since he is supporting my adversary in this lawsuit, but at the time he testified to these things along with the others, since he did not want to perjure himself or become liable to an immediate judgment [*dikên*] on the spot. Obviously, if I were suborning false testimony, I would not have listed him among my witnesses, seeing that he associates with Aphobus most of all mankind and knowing that he would assist Aphobus in pleading his case and was still my opponent in litigation: it makes no sense to list as a witness one's own enemy and the brother of one's adversary if his testimony is not true. [16] Now, there are a lot of witnesses to these facts, and the evidence is no less abundant than the witnesses. First, if in fact he really did not testify to these things, he would not be denying it only now; instead, he would have denied it right then, on the spot, in the jury-court [*dikastêriou*], while his deposition was being read out, when it would have done him more good than it does now. Second, he would not have kept quiet but would have filed a lawsuit [*dikên*] for damage [*blabês*] against me, if I were improperly rendering him liable for false witness [*pseudomartyriôn*] against his brother, an action in which people risk both money and disfranchisement [*atimias*].

253. Demosthenes 36 *For Phormion* 2–4, 12, 18–20. *Dikê blabês* for debt. (?350/49)

See references and headnote under **148**. The hypothesis (introduction) to this speech authored in the fourth century A.D. by Libanius, an eminent professor of rhetoric, calls the lawsuit brought by Apollodorus against Phormion a *dikê aphormês* (for [repayment of] capital: cf. §12). But since such a procedure is poorly attested, its existence is open to serious doubt, and probably the lawsuit was a *dikê blabês*. The description (§20) of Apollodorus' writing charge statements (*enklêmata*) in the form used in the *dikê blabês* (cf. **264** D. H. *Din.* 3; **256b** Dem. 37.22–26, 28–33) indicates that Apollodorus brought *dikai blabês* for debt against others, even if not against Phormion in the instant case. For the intervening argument at §20 omitted here, see **148** Dem. 36.20, 22.

. . . and although [Phormion] has done many good services to my adversary Apollodorus here, [3] having duly paid and handed over all of Apollodorus' property of which he had been left as *kyrios*, and although after that he was granted release from all charges, nonetheless, as you see, . . . Apollodorus has filed and is maliciously prosecuting [*sykophantei*] this lawsuit for 20 talents against him. . . .

[4] First, then, [the court clerk] will read to you the contract [*synthêkas*] in accordance with which Pasion leased the bank and the shield business to Phormion.

. . .

Now you must hear and learn in what way Pasion came to owe the additional 11 talents on the bank. . . .

. . .

[12] Now, one could mention and point out numerous indications that my adversary is engaging in malicious prosecution when he makes his charge about a sum of capital [*aphormên*]. In my opinion, the strongest proof of all that Phormion here received no capital for these things is the fact that, in the lease, Pasion was listed as owing additional money on the bank, not as having given capital to Phormion; second, the fact that Apollodorus clearly brought no charge during the division; and third, the fact that when [Apollodorus] later leased the very same property to others for the same price, he did not, as will be clear, lease personal capital in addition.

. . .

[18] . . . I suppose that my adversary Apollodorus here, since he has no just argument to make concerning the charges he is bringing, will say the same things he had the gall to say before the arbitrator; namely, that his mother made

the documents disappear at Phormion's behest, and that since these documents are lost, he has no way to examine these matters with precision. [19] Now, as to these matters and this accusation, consider what weighty proofs one could state to demonstrate that he is lying. First, men of Athens, who would have let his patrimony be divided without receiving documents from which he would know the [size of the] estate that had been left behind? No one, obviously. [To Apollodorus:] And yet it is now eighteen years since you let it be divided, and you could not demonstrate that you ever brought charges concerning the documents. [20] . . . Third, on the basis of what documents did you file your lawsuits? [To the jury:] You see, my adversary has filed lawsuits [*dikas*] against a lot of citizens and exacted a lot of money, writing in his charges [*enklêmata*], "So-and-so caused me damage [*eblapse*] by not paying me back the money that my father listed him as owing in the documents he left."

254. Demosthenes 39 / *Against Boeotus* 1, 5, 7–18. ?*Dikê blabês* for usurpation of name. (?349/8)

See references and headnote under **74**. The following passages support the likely identification of Mantitheus' lawsuit against Boeotus as a *dikê blabês* (note also [Demosthenes] 40.35, referring to this lawsuit: Boeotus "forced me to file a lawsuit against him concerning my name, not so that I might get money from him . . . but so that if you decided that I was being treated terribly and suffering considerable damage [*blaptesthai*], he would be called Boeotus, the name our father gave him"). The novelty of prosecuting for usurpation of a name, admitted by Mantitheus in §1, may have contributed to his losing the lawsuit. The lawsuit that Boeotus brought against Mantias to compel him to acknowledge his paternity (§§2–5: for the omitted material in §§2–4 see **131a** Dem. 39.2–4) may also have been a *dikê blabês*. On liturgies (§§7–9) see p. 25. The duties of a producer, gymnasiarch, and banquet host all concerned state religious festivals (such as the Dionysia, §16: see **139** Lys. 32.8–10, 19–24): a producer (*chorêgos*) financed the performance of a chorus (cf. **255** Dem. 21 [selections]), a gymnasiarch financed his tribe's torch-race team, and a banquet host financed a feast for his tribe. On the trierarchy see p. 25. Symmories were the groups into which Athens' wealthiest citizens were organized for payment of war-taxes (*eisphorai*, §15: see p. 26) and for financing trierarchies. The Commissioners of the Games (*athlothetai*) were responsible for organizing the Panathenaic festival (**331** [Arist.] *Ath. Pol.* 60.2–3). "The Council" (§10) is the Council of 500. In §14, for the legal procedure of *phasis* (declaration) see **151** Harpo. s.v. *phasis*, and cf. **244** Isoc. 18.1–8, 10–13, 33, 63; on *apagôgê* (summary arrest: p. 30) see, e.g., **57a** Aeschin. 1.91; **288** Dem. 22.25–27, 69–73; on *endeixis* (denunciation: p. 30) see, e.g., **8a** Ant. 5.9; **289** Dem. 24.104–5, 112–15, 120–21, 129, 146; **337** Lys. 6 (selections). The Choes ("Pitchers," §16) was the name of the second day of the religious festival called the Anthesteria.

By the gods, men of the jury, it is not out of any fondness for causing problems that I have filed this lawsuit [*dikên*] against Boeotus; nor was I unaware that many would consider it strange for me to file a lawsuit because someone thinks he should have the same name as I do. Rather, it was necessary to submit to judgment in your court because of what will result if I do not correct this situation.

. . .

[5] . . . How much damage he causes [*blaptei*] by this action—first to me, and then to you as well—I will demonstrate. . . .

. . .

[7] First of all—on the assumption that one should discuss public affairs before private ones—in what manner will the city impose upon us whatever we are required to do? Our tribesmen, by Zeus, will nominate us in the same way as the rest. So they will nominate "Mantitheus son of Mantias of the deme Thoricus" if they are nominating a producer or gymnasiarch or banquet host or some other official. How, then, will it be clear whether they are nominating you or me? You'll say it's me; I'll say it's you. [8] Suppose that the archon or whoever has jurisdiction over the lawsuit then issues a summons. We don't answer; we don't perform the liturgy. Which of us will be liable to the penalties provided by the laws? In what manner will the generals enroll us if they are enrolling men in a symmory or appointing a trierarch? Or, if there is a military expedition, how will it be clear which of us has been called up? [9] And again, if some other magistrate is appointing liturgies (for example, the archon or *basileus* or Commissioners of the Games), what will indicate which of us they are appointing? . . .

[10] . . . By Zeus, if the city is allotting any office whatsoever, such as member of the Council, *thesmothetês*, or the rest, how will it be clear which of us has been allotted? . . . He, then, will say he's the one who has been allotted; I'll say it's me. [11] Then we go to the jury-court [*dikastêrion*]. So, then, in each of these cases the city is going to convene a jury-court for us. . . . [12] And again, if, hypothetically, . . . one of us persuades the other, if he is allotted, to hand over the office to him, and the allotment goes that way, what else is that but one man drawing lots with two tablets? . . .

[13] All right, then. Those are the ways in which the city suffers damage [*blaptetai*]. How do I suffer damage personally? . . .

[14] If, then, as time passes, [Boeotus] endeavors to employ some of the same practices as these men (these are indictments [*graphai*], declarations

[*phaseis*], denunciations [*endeixeis*], and summary arrests [*apagôgai*]), and then in one of these matters . . . incurs a debt to the public treasury, how is he going to get registered [as a state debtor] rather than I? . . . [15] . . . And what if he doesn't pay some war-taxes [*eisphoras*]? [16] And again, what if some other filing of a lawsuit [*lêxis dikês*] or unpleasant reputation in general gets attached to the name? . . . Tell me, what if he should be the defendant in a lawsuit for failure to perform military service [*dikên astrateias*] and should be serving as a chorister when he is supposed to be on campaign? As a matter of fact, just now, when the other troops went to Tamynae, he stayed here celebrating the Choes and remained behind to serve as chorister at the Dionysia. . . . [17] And when the soldiers returned from Euboea, he received a summons for desertion [*lipotaxiou*], and I, who was serving as taxiarch of my tribe, was compelled to receive the complaint, which was filed against my name and patronymic; and if pay had been available for the jury-courts [*dikastêriois*], I, obviously, would have introduced the lawsuit!

. . .

[18] . . . Do you believe it is only minor damage [*blabên*], men of Athens, to be associated for one's entire life with the reputation and deeds of my adversary?

255. Demosthenes 21 *Against Meidias* (selections). *Dikê blabês* for destruction of and damage to property and for interference with festival chorus; law(s) on damage; intentional and unintentional damage, with penalties. (347/6)

See references and headnote under **22**, and **332** with headnote. In these passages, Demosthenes discusses the *dikê blabês* that he could have brought against Meidias (**255a-b**) and the laws of damage generally (**255c**). For "the crowned archon" (**255a**) cf. **44a** Dem. 21.31–33; **25** [Arist.] *Ath. Pol.* 57.2–4; on chorus-producers cf. **254** Dem. 39.1, 5, 7–18. On battery and hubris (**255b**) see chapter 2; "this very god" is Dionysus, the namesake and honorand of the City Dionysia; the "sacred month" was that in which the festival was held (Elaphebolion: p. 7).

a. Dem. 21.16–17, 25.

[Meidias] plotted, men of Athens, to destroy the sacred clothing (I consider all the clothing that a person has prepared for the festival to be sacred until it is used) and the gold crowns that I had had made as adornment for my chorus, by breaking into the goldsmith's house at night. And destroy he did, but not all of it, since he was unable to. . . . [17] And that wasn't enough for him; he also corrupted the director of my chorus, men of Athens. And if Telephanes the flute-player had not then behaved as the finest of men toward me and had not, upon realizing what was happening, driven that person away and seen fit to organize and direct the chorus himself, we wouldn't even have competed, men of Athens: the chorus would have entered [the theater] without training, and we would have suffered the most shameful fortunes. And [Meidias] didn't even stop his hubris there. He had so much of it left that he corrupted the crowned archon and got the producers to conspire against me; by shouting, making threats, standing next to the judges while they swore their oaths, blocking and nailing up the side-scenes—a private citizen doing this to public property!—he continually caused me harm and indescribable problems.

. . .

[25] Now, the first thing that he is obviously going to say (on the basis of what he was reported to me as having discussed with certain people in private) is that if I really had suffered the things I claim, I should have filed private lawsuits [*dikas idias*] against him: a lawsuit for damage [*blabês*], for the destruction of the clothes and the gold crowns and all the spiteful abuse concerning the chorus. . . .

b. Dem. 21.35.

Your law of damage [*blabês*] has existed for a long time, as has your law of battery [*aikeias*] and your law of hubris [*hybreôs*]. Now, if it were sufficient for people who did any of these things at the Dionysia to be punished in accordance with those laws, there would be no need for this law as well. But it was not sufficient. Here's the evidence: you established a sacred law for this very god concerning the sacred month. So if a person is liable under both those previously existing laws and this law, which was enacted after them, and all the rest of the laws too, should such a person not be punished on that account, or would he rightly pay an even greater penalty? I think he should pay a greater penalty.

c. Dem. 21.43.

First of all, all these laws concerning damage [*blabês*], to start with these, command that if a person commits damage [*blapsêi*] intentionally [*hekôn*], he shall pay double the damage done [*blabos*], and if he does so unintentionally [*akôn*], he shall pay the simple damage done. And reasonably so: the victim in all cases has a right to receive aid, but for the perpetrator the law has not prescribed the same amount of anger whether he acted intentionally or unintentionally.

256. Demosthenes 37 *Against Pantaenetus* (selections). ?*Dikê metallikê blabês* for intentional infliction of various forms of financial loss, including public debt, interference with mining rights, withholding property, and breach of contract. (ca. 346)

See references and headnote under **23**. Here the speaker, Nicobulus, addresses the lawsuit initiated against him by Pantaenetus (to which he responds with the instant *paragraphê*), which appears to have been a *dikê blabês* (note the form of the written complaint, and cf. **264** D. H. *Din.* 3; **253** Dem. 36.2–4, 12, 18–20, at §20) brought under the procedural category of *dikai metallikai* (mining lawsuits: **256c**). That Pantaenetus charged Nicobulus with intentional damage is indicated by the phrase "plotting against [*epibouleusas*] me and my property" in the written charge (*enklêma*: **256b**). Nicobulus also discusses an earlier lawsuit of the same type, in which Pantaenetus convicted Euergus. In **256b**, on *atimia* (disfranchisement) as the consequence of defaulting on a debt to the state (§24) see **§7.1.2**; at §33 cf. **45** Dem. 37.33. In **256c**, on ejectment (§35) see **§7.4.2**; "another person" refers to Euergus. Digging "inside the boundaries" (§36) refers to mining trespass (i.e., crossing outside the boundary of one's own mine and inside that of a neighboring mine). In **256d**, on the evidentiary torture of slaves see p. 24 and cf. (e.g.) **246** Isoc. 17.2–9, 11–16; note that Mnesicles' function included appraising the slave's value with an eye to any damage done to the slave in the course of torture (cf. **51** Lys. 10.18–19; **46** [Arist.] *Ath. Pol.* 52.2). Pantaenetus' "deposit" (§41; cf. **36** Isoc. 20.2) is the court fees (*prytaneia*: cf., e.g., **244** Isoc. 18.1–8, 10–13, 33, 63) he paid upon filing the first lawsuit (§39). In **256e**, for the omitted material in §§45–46 see **164** Dem. 37.45–46; on liability for slaves (§§50–51) cf. **262** Hyp. 3.5–11, 18, 21–22, at §§21–22; **248** [Dem.] 53.19–20; **249** Dem. 55 (selections). On the nature of the various contractual transactions described in these passages see chapter 10.

a. Dem. 37.4–8.

Euergus and I, men of the jury, lent [*edaneisamen*] 105 minae to my adversary Pantaenetus here, on the security of a workshop at the mines in Maroneia and thirty slaves. Forty-five minae of this loan [*daneismatos*] were mine, and a talent was Euergus'. Now, it happened that my adversary owed a talent to Mnesicles of the deme Collytus and 45 minae to Phileas of the deme Eleusis and Pleistor. [5] Mnesicles was the seller [*pratêr*] of the workshop and the slaves to us (he had bought [*eônêto*] these things for my adversary from Telemachus, the previous owner), and my adversary leased [*misthoutai*] them from us for the interest [*tokou*] accruing on the money, 105 drachmas per month. And we made a contract [*synthêkas*], in which the lease [*misthôsis*] was stated in writing, as well as my adversary's right of release [*lysis*] from us within a stated period.

[6] These events transpired during the month of Elaphebolion in the archonship of Theophilus [348/7], and then I immediately left, sailing to the Black Sea, while my adversary and Euergus remained here. I cannot speak to what happened between the two of them while I was abroad. They don't always agree, nor, in fact, does my adversary always agree with himself: sometimes he says that he was forcibly ejected from the lease by Euergus in violation of the contract, sometimes he says that Euergus was responsible for his registration with the state treasury, sometimes he says whatever else he wants to. [7] Euergus says simply that since he did not receive the interest payments and my adversary did not do any of the other things contained in the contract, he went and took possession of what belonged to him, with my adversary's consent. After that, he says, my adversary left and then returned, bringing the men who were going to make competing claims, but he did not yield to them and in no way obstructed Pantaenetus from continuing to possess everything he had leased, provided that he do what had been agreed upon.

These are the accounts I hear from them. [8] But I know for a fact that if my adversary is telling the truth and has suffered terrible things, as he claims, at Euergus' hands, he has as compensation [*dikên*] the assessment that he himself made [*etimêsat'*]: he came before you and convicted Euergus, and certainly he does not have the right to receive compensation for the same matters both from the perpetrator and from me, who was not even in Athens!

b. Dem. 37.22–26, 28–33.

[To the court clerk:] Read the actual charge [*enklêma*] on which he is prosecuting me.

CHARGE. Nicobulus caused me damage [*eblapse*], plotting against [*epibouleusas*] me and my property, by ordering his slave Antigenes to seize from my slave the money that he was conveying as a payment to the city for the mine that I had purchased [*epriamên*] for 90 minae, and by being responsible for my registration with the state treasury for double that amount.

[23] Stop. [To the jury:] All of these charges that he has now brought against me he brought earlier against Euergus when he convicted him.... Nowhere has he written that I did any of these things; instead, having charged me with "plotting against him and his property," he states that I ordered my slave to do these things, and he is lying. How did I give the order, when, at the time I was sailing out, I obviously had no knowledge at all of anything that was going to happen here? [24] And then—what stupidity!—he claims that I plotted to disfranchise [*atimôsai*] him and bring about the most extreme penalties, but he has written

that I gave to a slave an order that even a citizen could not carry out against his fellow citizen? . . . [25] [To the court clerk:] Read what follows.

CHARGE. And when I became a debtor to the state treasury, [Nicobulus caused me damage] by placing Antigenes, his slave, in charge of my workshop at Thrasymus as *kyrios* of my property, despite my prohibition.

Stop. [To the jury:] Again he will stand exposed as lying about all these things by the fact itself. He has written that I placed Antigenes in charge and he prohibited it. This could not have been done by a person who was not present. . . . [26] . . . [To the court clerk:] Read what comes next.

CHARGE. And then [Nicodemus caused me damage] by persuading my slaves to sit down at the ore-grinding station [*kenchreôna*], to my detriment [*blabêi*].

. . .

[28] . . . [To the court clerk:] Read the next part.

CHARGE. And [Nicodemus caused me damage] by refining the silver ore that my slaves had produced, and by keeping the silver that came from that silver ore.

[To Pantaenetus:] Again, how can I have done this when I was not present, and when you have convicted Euergus of doing it? [29] [To the court clerk:] Read the actual charge.

CHARGE. And [Nicodemus caused me damage] by selling my workshop and the slaves in violation of the contract that he made with me.

Stop. [To the jury:] This here goes far beyond all the rest. First of all, he says, "in violation of the contract that he made with me." What contract? We leased our property to him for the accruing interest, and nothing else. Mnesicles had become seller to us in his presence and at his urging. [30] After that, we sold [*apedometha*] it to others in the same manner, on the same terms as we ourselves had bought it, and he was not just urging us anymore but begging us [to do so], since no one was willing to accept him as seller. [To Pantaenetus:] So what is your point about the lease contract here?

. . .

[31] And you testify to this yourself: what we sold for 105 minae you later sold [*apedou*] for 3 talents 2,600 drachmas! And yet who would have paid you a single drachma with you as the outright seller [*kathapax pratêra*]?

. . .

[32] . . . [To the jury:] And the rest of his charges are even more horrible. [To the court clerk:] Please now read the rest of the charge.

CHARGE.

[33] Here he charges me with many terrible things at the same time: battery [*aikeian*], hubris [*hybrin*], acts of violence [*biaiôn*], and offenses against *epiklêroi*.

c. Dem. 37.35–36.

[To the court clerk:] Now take the mining law: I think I can show on the basis of this law that [Pantaenetus'] lawsuit [*dikên*] is inadmissible. . . . Read it.

LAW.

[To the jury:] This is how clearly the law has defined the offenses for which mining lawsuits [*dikas . . . metallikas*] are properly available. So, then, the law makes a person liable if he ejects [*exillêi*] someone from his works. I, however, not only am not ejecting him myself but have placed him in control over and handed over to him things that another person was depriving him of. . . . [36] "Yes," he says, "but also if a person commits some other offense concerning the mines, lawsuits are available for those matters too." Right, Pantaenetus, but what are those matters? If a person causes smoke; if he makes an armed attack; if he digs inside the boundaries.

d. Dem. 37.39–44.

. . . last month, men of Athens, when I was about to enter the court for trial and the jury-courts [*dikastêriôn*] had already been allotted, [Pantaenetus] approached me, having surrounded himself with his men—that gang of conspirators—and did a completely outrageous thing. [40] He read out to me a long challenge [*proklêsin*], demanding that the slave who he claimed had knowledge of these allegations be tortured, and that if the allegations were truthful, I should lose the judgment [*dikên*] to him without assessment [*atimêton*], while if they were false, the torturer, Mnesicles, should be appraiser of the value of the slave. He exacted sureties for these things from me, and after I sealed the challenge—not because it was a fair one: [41] where is the fairness in either losing 2 talents or having the person engaging in sycophancy suffer no loss, depending on the body and life of a slave? At any rate, I agreed, because I wanted to have a great advantage in fairness on my side. After that, he summoned me again to appear in the lawsuit, as soon as he had recovered his deposit [*parakatabolas*]: that's how immediately it became obvious that he was not abiding even by the terms that he himself had defined! [42] And when we appeared before the torturer, instead of opening the challenge, showing its written terms, and doing in accordance with them whatever was decided—on account of the attendant tumult and the fact that the lawsuit was about to be called [into court], the challenge went like this: "I challenge you to the following." "I accept." "Let's have your ring." "Take it." "Who is surety?" "This man here"; and I had no copy [of the challenge] or anything similar made—instead of doing these things in the way I have described, he appeared with another challenge, demanding that he torture the man himself, and he grabbed hold of him and tried to drag him off, leaving no form of brutality undone. [43] . . . Anyway, to prove that I was compelled, in opposition to what I thought was fair, to issue a counter-challenge [*antipro-kaleisthai*], and that I offered to hand over the slave, and that what I say is true, [To the court clerk:] read the challenge.

CHALLENGE.

[44] [To the jury:] Now, then, since [Pantaenetus] evaded this challenge, as well as the challenge that he himself issued in the first instance, I for my part wonder what in the world he is going to say to you.

e. Dem. 37.45, 47, 50–51.

Now, I want to recount to you also by what means [Pantaenetus] deceived the previous jury and convicted Euergus, so that you may know that now too he will lose no opportunity for shamelessness or lying.

. . .

[47] In my opinion, if, in accordance with the laws, [Euergus] had known in advance the charge on which he was being tried, it would have been easy for him to demonstrate what was true and just and get acquitted; but in a mining lawsuit [*metallikêi dikêi*] it was difficult for him to be able on the spot to refute the calumny over accusations that he could never have expected to be brought against him.

. . .

[50] [To Pantaenetus:] I lent [*daneisas*] 40 minae and am on trial in this lawsuit for 2 talents. And you, it appears, have been wronged in the amount of 4 talents with regard to property on the security of which you were never able to borrow [*daneisasthai*] more than 100 minae, and which you have sold outright [*peprakas kathapax*] for 3 talents 2,000 drachmas! At whose hands did you suffer this wrong? My slave's, you'll respond. [To the jury:] Now, what citizen would give up his property to a slave? And who would say that my slave should be liable for offenses for which my adversary has already filed a lawsuit against and convicted Euergus? [51] And apart from this, my adversary himself has already granted [Antigenes] release from all such charges. You see, he shouldn't be mentioning them now . . . ; instead, he should have filed his lawsuit against [Antigenes] and prosecuted his *kyrios*; namely, me. As it is, though, he has filed against me and is accusing him. The laws do not allow this; who has ever filed a lawsuit against the master and accused the slave of the matters in question as though he were *kyrios*?

257. Demosthenes 38 *Against Nausimachus and Xenopeithes* (selections). *Dikê blabês* for debt. (?ca. 346)

See **150** with references and headnote. For the penal assessment (*timêma*, **257a**) in a *dikê blabês* cf., e.g., **264** D. H. *Din.* 3; "the two of them" are Nausimachus and Xenopeithes, and "us" refers to the sons of Aristaechmus. On visible property (*phanera* [*scil. ousia*], **257b**) see **185** Andoc. 1.117–21.

a. Dem. 38.2.

The assessment [*timêm'*] that you heard attached to the lawsuit [*dikêi*] is 30 minae, but the money for which we are on trial is 4 talents. You see, the two of them have filed four lawsuits against us, all of the lawsuits for the same sum of money, each lawsuit for 3,000 drachmas, for damage [*blabês*].

b. Dem. 38.6–9.

. . . with fourteen years having passed since they granted a release to our father, . . . and with our father, with whom their reconciliation occurred, now dead, as well as the guardians [*epitropôn*] who became *kyrioi* of our property after his death, . . . they have filed these lawsuits against us, and they do not have the confidence to make any just or reasonable argument. [7] They claim, you see, that they did not sell their patrimony for the money they received, and did not relinquish their claim to the property, but instead that all the debts, furnishings, and property in general that was left to them belongs to them. But I know from hearing about it that Xenopeithes and Nausicrates left their estate entirely in the form of debts and owned only a small amount of visible property [*phaneran*]. After the debts were collected and some of the furnishings sold, along with some slaves, the guardians bought both the land and the apartment buildings, which my adversaries received from them. [8] Now, then, if nothing about these matters had been disputed before and the issue of their improper management had not come to judgment, it would be another story. But since my adversaries brought charges concerning the entirety of their guardianship, filed lawsuits, and exacted money, release as to all these matters was granted at that time. . . .

[9] So, then, I think that you have all sufficiently learned from the laws themselves and from the [aforementioned] release that my adversaries, since they granted a discharge for the debts that my father collected before the discharge and for the money in general that he received as a result of the guardianship [*epitropês*], have no grounds for a lawsuit against us on any charge. Now I wish to demonstrate that the recovery of the money in question cannot have

occurred after the discharge (this, you see, is what my adversaries are making up in an attempt to mislead you).

258. *Inscriptiones Graecae* II^2 2492.1–31. Lease of land by deme Aexone, with provision for *dikê blabês* for attempted breach of contract. (345/4)

I. **Kirchner**, ed., ***Inscriptiones Graecae*** II^2 fasc. 2 (ed. min. Berlin 1931: text with Latin notes); E. S. **Roberts**-E. A. **Gardner**, *An Introduction to Greek Epigraphy, Part II: The Inscriptions of Attica* (Cambridge 1905) no. 129 (text and commentary); D. **Whitehead**, *The Demes of Attica* (Princeton 1986) 152–58.

In the terms of the lease below, the purpose of the vine-dresser (line 17) is "apparently to ensure that the vines shall be in good order for the next lessee" (Roberts-Gardner); the "produce of Demeter" (line 19) is grain (cf. headnote under **241** Ar. *Wasps* 1389–1408); the treasurers, demarch, and council hall (lines 21–23) are all those of the deme Aexone. With the boundary-markers (*horoi*) mentioned in line 23 compare those used to mark *apotimêmata* (see §**5.3.2**); on the war-tax (*eisphora*, lines 24–25), which could be levied by "the city" (i.e., the Athenian state), see p. 26 (and cf., e.g., **254** Dem. 39.1, 5, 7–18). Hecatombaeon (line 6), the first month of the Athenian year, corresponds roughly to July (see p. 7); Hebe (line 22) was the goddess of youth.

On the following terms the demesmen of Aexone have leased the [plot of land called] Phelleis to Autocles son of Auteas and Auteas son of Autocles for a term of forty years for 152 drachmas per year, with the provision that they may both plant [on it] and [use it] in any other manner they wish. They are to pay the rent during the month of Hecatombaeon, and if they do not pay, the demesmen of Aexone shall have the right to [seize] security [*enechyrasian*] both from the crops produced from the plot and from all the other property of the one who does not pay. It shall not be permitted to the demesmen of Aexone either to sell or to lease [the plot] to anyone else until the aforementioned forty years expire. If enemy forces bar access or destroy anything, the demesmen of Aexone shall have the right to half of what is produced on the plot. When the aforementioned forty years expire, the lessees shall hand over half the plot uncultivated, as well as any and all trees located on the plot; the demesmen of Aexone may send in a vine-dresser during the final five years [of the term of lease]. The term of the lease of the produce of Demeter begins in the archonship of Eubulus [345/4]; that of the produce of trees, in the archonship of the man following Eubulus. The treasurers serving during the term of Demosthenes as demarch shall inscribe the lease on stone pillars and shall place one in the sanctuary of Hebe, inside [the temple], and the other in the council hall; and they shall place boundary-markers [*horous*] on the plot no less than three feet high, two [markers] on each side [of the land]. If any [25] war-tax [*eisphora*] on the plot becomes due to the city, the demesmen of Aexone shall pay it; if the lessees pay it, it shall be counted toward the rent. No one shall be permitted to remove the earth that arises as a result of digging except onto the plot itself. If a person makes a motion or puts a motion to the vote in contravention of this [30] contract [*synthêkas*] before the aforementioned forty years expire, he shall be liable to the lessees for the damage [*blabês*].

259. [Demosthenes] 48 *Against Olympiodorus* (selections). *Dikê blabês* for financial loss arising from breach of contract. (ca. 341)

See **236** with references and headnote. In these passages, Callistratus explains the grounds for his *dikê blabês* against Olympiodorus and anticipates arguments that he expects Olympiodorus to employ in his defense. On "visible property" (**259a**: §§9, 12) see **185** Andoc. 1.117–21. Note that the torture of the slave Moschion described here was performed in the first instance (§16) by private agreement between Callistratus and Olympiodorus, and in the second instance (§18) on the sole initiative of Olympiodorus; in neither case was the torture employed in order to provide testimony usable in court (see p. 24, and contrast the descriptions of challenges to evidentiary torture at, e.g., **246** Isoc. 17.2–9, 11–16; **256d** Dem. 37.39–44).

a. [Dem.] 48.9–10, 12–18.

After that, we wrote up a contract [*synthêkas*] between ourselves concerning everything, and we swore weighty oaths to each other that we would divide the existing visible property [*phanera onta*] in good and just fashion, and that neither would take a single thing more than the other out of the property that Comon had left behind, and that we would investigate everything else jointly, and that we would act in consultation with one another as to whatever was necessary at any given time. [10] You see, men of the jury, we suspected that some other people too would come forward to lodge claims to Comon's estate—for example, my brother by the same father but not the same mother, who was abroad—and if in fact someone else wished to lodge a claim, we could not prevent it, since the laws command that any willing person may lodge a claim. So, foreseeing all this, we wrote up the contract and swore oaths so that neither of us might have the power either intentionally [*hekonti*] or unintentionally [*akonti*] to do anything at all on his own, but rather so that we might do everything in joint consultation with each other.

. . .

[12] After we swore the oaths to each other and the contract had been deposited with Androcleides, I made a division [of Comon's estate] into two parts, men of the jury. One part consisted of the house in which Comon himself had lived and the slaves who wove sackcloth, and the other part consisted of another house and the slaves who ground drugs. Whatever money Comon had left in cash [*phaneron*] at Heracleides' bank had just about all been spent on his burial and the other customary rites and the construction of the monument. [13] So I made the division into these two parts, and I gave my adversary Olympiodorus here the choice of which part he wanted to take, and he chose the drug-grinders and the little house, while I took the sackcloth-weavers and the other house. . . .

[14] In the part belonging to my adversary Olympiodorus here was one of the drug-grinders, whom Comon had thought to be particularly loyal to him; the man's name is Moschion. This slave pretty much knew all of Comon's other affairs, and in particular the location of the money that was inside Comon's house. [15] And as a matter of fact, without the knowledge of Comon, who was rather elderly and trusted him, this slave, Moschion, had secretly stolen the money. First he stole from Comon 1,000 drachmas that were located somewhere apart from the rest of the money; then he stole another 70 minae. . . .

[16] Not long, men of the jury, after we divided the parts, a certain suspicion and feeling about this man arose, and as a result of this suspicion I and my adversary Olympiodorus here decided to torture the man. And the man, men of the jury, denounced himself on his own, before being tortured, stating that he had stolen 1,000 drachmas from Comon. He said that he still had as much of it as had not been spent—he did not, however, say a word about the larger amount of money at that time—[17] and he paid back some 600 drachmas or so. Of this money, which the man paid back, . . . I took half and my adversary Olympiodorus here took half. [18] Afterwards, though, not much later, . . . Olympiodorus bound the man and tortured him on his own, by himself. . . . And, men of the jury, under constraint of torture on the rack, the man confessed that he had also taken the 70 minae, having stolen them from Comon, and he paid back that entire sum of money to my adversary Olympiodorus here.

b. [Dem.] 48.37–38.

A huge number of people have heard [Olympiodorus] say, in some cases, that he didn't receive the money from the man at all; and when that is proven false, he replies that he does have the money, but it came from his own slave, and he will give me no share of either the money or any of the other property that

Comon left behind. [38] And whenever one of his friends and mine asks why he will not give me my due, when he swore that he would make an equal division and the contract is still to this day on deposit, he claims that I am in breach of the contract and he has suffered terribly at my hands, and he claims that I consistently spoke and acted in opposition to him.

260. [Demosthenes] 33 *Against Apaturius* 19–20, 22, 32–33. *Dikê emporikê ?blabês* for debt. (*post* 342)

Schäfer, *Demosthenes* 4.297–300; **Blass**, *AB* 3.1.572–76; L. **Gernet**, *Démosthène: Plaidoyers civils, Tome I, Discours XXVII–XXXVIII* (Paris 1954: text, French translation, and notes); S. **Isager**-M. H. **Hansen**, *Aspects of Athenian Society in the Fourth Century B.C.: A Historical Introduction to and Commentary on the Paragraphe-speeches and the Speech Against Dionysodorus in the Corpus Demosthenicum (XXXII–XXXVIII and LVI)* (Odense 1975); **Usher**, *GO* 252–53; D. M. **MacDowell**, *Demosthenes, Speeches 27–38* (Austin 2004: translation with introduction and notes); ***idem***, *DO* 275–79.

Apaturius and Parmenon, two men from Byzantium who engaged in maritime commerce at Athens and elsewhere, had exchanged blows in an argument over a debt; they initiated cross-claims against each other but then dropped them, deciding to settle the affair by private arbitration (on which see p. 35). A contract governing the arbitration was drawn up but then disappeared; this led to a dispute among the litigants and arbitrators over its contents. Apaturius then filed a new lawsuit against the (unnamed) speaker; since both men were involved in maritime commerce and the fracas had occurred in the Peiraeus, the Athenian port of trade, Apaturius brought the lawsuit as a *dikê emporikê* (mercantile lawsuit: see chapter 10). The speaker responded by bringing a *paragraphê* on the grounds that Apaturius' lawsuit was illegal since no written contract existed (a written contract may have been required in *dikai emporikai*: see **326** Dem. 32.1) and since release and discharge from all contractual liability had occurred (see **324** [Dem.] 33.1–3, 23), and in this *paragraphê* he delivered [Demosthenes] 33. Apaturius' lawsuit against the speaker was probably a *dikê emporikê blabês*, a lawsuit for damage prosecuted under the rules of the *dikai emporikai*: as the speaker explains here, Apaturius alleged that the arbitration decision rendered against Parmenon by Aristocles was valid and that the speaker, as Parmenon's surety, was liable for the fine of 20 minae levied by Aristocles.

So at that point the arbitration agreement came undone, since the contract [*synthêkôn*] had disappeared and the arbitrators were quarreling. In their attempt to write another contract, they disagreed about it: my adversary demanded

Aristocles, while Parmenon demanded the same three men who had had the power of arbitration in the beginning. Then, since no other contract got written and the original one had disappeared, the man who had made the contract disappear reached such a level of shamelessness that he said he would render the arbitration decision all by himself! But Parmenon summoned witnesses and ordered Aristocles not to render a decision against him without the other arbitrators in violation of the contract. . . .

[20] After that, a terrible disaster befell Parmenon, men of the jury. He was living in Ophryneion, on account of his banishment from his home, when the earthquake in the region of the Chersonese occurred; his house collapsed, and his wife and children were killed. When he learned of the disaster, he left here and sailed back. And Aristocles, although the man had solemnly prohibited him in front of witnesses from rendering a decision against him without the other arbitrators, once the man had gone abroad on account of the disaster, decided the arbitration against him by default [*erêmên*].

. . .

[22] Now, since Apaturius has reached such a level of shamelessness that he is prosecuting me, bringing the charge that I undertook to pay any penalty that might be adjudged against Parmenon, and he claims that I was listed in the contract as surety, . . . first I will furnish you with witnesses to the fact that it was not I but Archippus of the deme Myrrhinus who stood surety for Parmenon, and then I will endeavor also to make my defense on the basis of argumentative proofs, men of the jury.

. . .

[32] Consider this, men of the jury: if in the present case my adversary Apaturius here were prosecuting not me but Parmenon, attempting to exact the 20 minae and relying upon Aristocles' verdict, . . . [33] . . . is there any one of you . . . who would decide that the arbitration that was decided in such an illegal manner should be valid?

261. Demosthenes 32 *Against Zenothemis* 25–28. ?*Dikê emporikê blabês* for withholding property and theft of contract document. (?ca. 340)

See especially A. C. **Cosman**, *Demosthenes' Rede tegen Zenothemis (Oratie XXXII)* (Leiden 1939: text and Dutch commentary); L. **Pearson**, *Demosthenes: Six Private Speeches* (Norman, OK 1972: text and commentary); **Gernet**, *Démosthène: Plaidoyers civils I* (text, French translation, and notes); **Isager-Hansen**, *Paragraphe-speeches*; **MacDowell**, *Demosthenes 27–38* (translation with introduction and notes); ***idem***, *DO* 272–75; also **Schäfer**, *Demosthenes* 4.292–96; **Blass**, *AB* 3.1.492–98; **Usher**, *GO* 251–52.

Demon, who delivered this speech (and who was related to its author Demosthenes: this Demon is probably the grandson of Demosthenes' uncle Demon who appears in **87** Dem. 27.4–5, and hence Demosthenes' first cousin once removed), lent funds to Protus to purchase and convey a cargo of grain from Syracuse (in Sicily) to Athens. Protus bought the grain and secured transport for it and himself aboard a ship owned and captained by Hegestratus, a citizen of Massalia (modern Marseilles, France). Hegestratus and his accomplice Zenothemis (also a citizen of Massalia) then fraudulently contracted loans in Syracuse on the security of the grain, claiming that they owned it. The loan contracts specified that Hegestratus and Zenothemis were liable to repay the money only if the ship reached its destination safely (on maritime loans see chapter 10); the two men then conspired to sink the ship so that they would not have to repay their creditors. But the plot was foiled, Hegestratus drowned, and after putting in at Cephallenia (an island off the west coast of the Greek mainland) for repairs, the ship continued on to Peiraeus, the Athenian port of trade.

There the ownership of the cargo of grain was disputed between Protus and Zenothemis; Zenothemis contended that the grain had been purchased by Hegestratus, who had then taken out a loan from him with the grain as collateral. Protus took possession of the grain, actively denying Zenothemis' claim. In response, Zenothemis brought a lawsuit against Protus. Protus, observing that the price of grain at Athens had fallen (§25) and he would have to take a loss if he maintained possession of the grain and sold it (since the debt he owed Demon was greater than the value of the grain: §§25–26), absconded from Athens, losing the lawsuit by default. Demon now assumed possession of the grain, and Zenothemis filed a new lawsuit against Demon. Owing to the litigants' status as merchants, Zenothemis filed the lawsuit as a *dikê emporikê* (mercantile lawsuit: see chapter 10); it was probably a *dikê emporikê exoulês* (for ejectment: see **§7.4.2**, and cf. **256c** Dem. 37.35–36). In order to block Zenothemis' prosecution, Demon brought a *paragraphê* (counter-indictment: p. 14) asserting that Zenothemis' lawsuit was illegal due to the absence of a written contract (see headnote under **260** [Dem.] 33.19–20, 22, 32–33). In this *paragraphê* Demon delivered Demosthenes 32.

In the following passage, Demon discusses the lawsuit that Zenothemis brought against Protus, which most scholars identify as a *dikê emporikê blabês* (cf. **260** [Dem.] 33.19–20, 22, 32–33). On the basis of Demon's narrative, it appears that Zenothemis claimed to have suffered intentional damage at Protus' hands, alleging in his written statement of the charge (*enklêma*, §27: cf., e.g., **264** D. H. *Din.* 3) that Protus not only had deprived him of the disputed grain but also, while still aboard the ship, had behaved recklessly and had stolen and tampered with relevant documents (§27, presumably including a written loan contract between Hegestratus and Zenothemis naming the latter as lender and specifying the grain as collateral). With Protus losing the lawsuit by default (§26), Zenothemis was awarded monetary compensation ("you have received justice," §28: on the hypothesis above, this will have amounted to double damages), but he did not collect, since Protus had fled Athens: according to Demon, the deal struck between Protus and Zenothemis (§§25–27) permitted Protus to avoid paying the judgment to Zenothemis on condition that he not testify against Zenothemis in support of Demon. Protus insisted on losing the lawsuit by default rather than in person (§27) because, if Zenothemis reneged on their deal, as a defaulting litigant Protus was permitted, provided that he could present a valid excuse for his absence, to file for a reopening of the case (according to Pollux, *Onomasticon* 8.61, the time limit for doing so was two months).

As long as Protus expected the grain to make a profit upon its arrival, he clung to it and preferred to make a profit for himself and repay us what we were due, rather than joining in league with our adversaries, making them partners in the gain, and doing us wrong. But when he arrived here and was dealing with these matters, grain dropped in price, and he immediately got a different idea. [26] At the same time . . . we who had made the loan were angry and bitter at him, since the loss on the grain was falling on us and we blamed him for having brought us a sycophant instead of money. As a result . . . , he inclined toward our adversaries, and he agreed to lose by default [*erêmên*] the lawsuit that my adversary had filed against him during the time when they had not yet reached their agreement. [27] If, you see, Zenothemis had let Protus off, he straightaway would have been exposed as maliciously prosecuting [*sykophantôn*] us. Protus, for his part, would not agree to be present [in court] when he lost the lawsuit; that way, if they did for him what they had agreed upon—, and if they didn't, he could file for a new hearing of the lawsuit he had lost by default.

But what does this matter? If Protus did what Zenothemis has written in the charge [*enklêma*], it seems to me that Protus deserved not just to lose a lawsuit but to be put to death. For if, in time of danger during a storm, he was drinking so much wine that his condition approximated insanity, what doesn't he deserve to suffer—or if he was stealing documents or secretly opening them? [28] Well, you will decide on your own among yourselves whatever the truth of these matters is. [To Zenothemis:] But don't you bring any part of that lawsuit into your lawsuit against me. If Protus has done you any wrong in word or deed, you have received justice, it seems; none of us hindered you or is interceding now.

262. Hypereides 3 *Against Athenogenes* 5–11, 18, 21–22. *Dikê blabês* for financial loss arising from contractual fraud; law on liability for slave. (330–324)

See especially D. **Whitehead**, *Hypereides: The Forensic Speeches* (Oxford 2000: translation and commentary); D. D. **Phillips**, "Hypereides 3 and the Athenian Law of Contracts," *TAPA* 139 (2009) 89–122; also **Blass**, *AB* 3.2.81–90; G. **Colin**, *Hypéride: Discours* (Paris 1946: text, French translation, and notes); **Usher**, *GO* 331–32; I. **Worthington**-C. **Cooper**-E. M. **Harris**, *Dinarchus, Hyperides, and Lycurgus* (Austin 2001: translation with introduction and notes).

This speech was delivered by an Athenian citizen, probably named Epicrates, in his prosecution of the metic Athenogenes; most scholars identify the procedure as a *dikê blabês* (note especially the phrase "those plotting against [*epibouleuontes*] the property of others," §21; cf., e.g., **264** D. H. *Din.* 3; **256b** Dem. 37.22–26, 28–33). Epicrates accuses Athenogenes of defrauding him in the formation of a contract of sale whereby Epicrates purchased from Athenogenes, for the price of 40 mn., three slaves (Midas and his two sons, in one of whom Epicrates had an erotic interest; hence his reference to "those in love," §21) and the perfumery they managed. Epicrates seeks to void the contract on the grounds that Athenogenes failed to disclose the full amount of debt incumbent on the perfumery. In the following passages, Epicrates discusses the formation of the contract, Athenogenes' deception as to the relevant debts, and a law on liability for losses caused by slaves (cf. **248** [Dem.] 53.19–20; **249d** Dem. 55.31–32, 34; **256e** Dem. 37.45, 47, 50–51). On "purchase and sale" (*ônê kai prasis*, §§5, 7; i.e., outright sale; for the phrase cf. Herodotus 1.153.2; Aristotle, *Nicomachean Ethics* 1131a3) see chapter 10; Nicon (§8) was listed in the contract as Epicrates' surety. "Joint loans" (*eranoi*, §11) were interest-free loans made to friends by groups of contributors ("joint lenders," §7).

[Antigona] brought us together, me and Athenogenes, and she reconciled us and bade us do well by one another in the future. I, for my part, said I would do so, and my adversary Athenogenes here said in response that I should be grateful to Antigona for what had happened. "And now," he said, "for her sake, I shall immediately demonstrate to you how much good I will do you. You," he said, "will pay the money for the freedom of Midas and his sons, and I will sell them to you by purchase and sale [*ônêi kai prasei*]. . . . [6] . . . Now, as for however much money they owe—the price of some perfume, owed to Pancalus and Procles, and if one of the customers has deposited money at the perfumery, whatever that comes to—these [debts]," he said, "you shall assume; they're very small, and there is merchandise in the workshop that is worth much more than these [debts]. . . ."

[7] And here, it seems, men of the jury, was the plot [*epiboulê*] and the great fabrication. If, you see, I paid the money for their freedom, I would lose only what I paid my adversary and would suffer nothing terrible; but if I bought them by purchase and sale, having agreed with him to assume the debts in the belief that they were of no value, due to my lack of foreknowledge, he would later sic his creditors and joint lenders [*plêrôtas tôn eranôn*] on me, having caught me in an agreement. And that's exactly what he did. [8] When he made this proposal and I agreed to it, he immediately took the written document from his lap and read it out. This was a contract [*synthêkai*] with me; I listened as it was read out, but I was in a hurry to take care of the business I had come on, and he sealed the contract immediately, in the same house, so that no one with his wits about him could hear the contents, having written in Nicon of the deme Cephisia along with me. [9] Then we went to the perfumery and deposited the document with Lysicles of the deme Leuconoeon, and I paid the 40 minae and made the purchase. After that happened, the creditors who had debts at Midas' shop and the joint lenders came and talked to me, and within three months all the debts had become evident, such that they amounted to . . . about five talents.

[10] When I realized the trouble I was in, at that point I collected my friends and family and we read the copy of the contract. In it the name of Pancalus and Polycles was written explicitly, along with the fact that prices of perfumes were owing; these prices were small, and they could say that the perfume in the workshop was of the same value as the money. But the majority of the debts, and the biggest ones, were listed not by names but as an addendum, as though they were nothing: "and whatever Midas owes to anyone else." [11] And among the joint loans, one was listed, which had three payments remaining; this was written under the name of Dicaeocrates. But as for the rest, on the basis of which Midas had received everything, and which were recently incurred, [Athenogenes] did not list these in the contract but concealed them.

. . .

[18] [To Athenogenes:] So, then, you are standing on the contract that you and your courtesan got sealed by catching me in a trap, and concerning which I am now prosecuting you for conspiracy [*bouleuseôs*]?

. . .

[21] If you, because of your lack of knowledge, did not inform me in advance of all the debts, and I made the contract in the belief that the debts I heard of from you were the only ones, which of us is the right person to pay them: the one who made the purchase later or the one who has long since possessed all the money that was lent? I think it's you. If we disagree about this, let our arbitrator be the law that was established not by those in love or those plotting

against [*epibouleuontes*] the property of others, but by the greatest of democrats, Solon. [22] He, knowing that many sales take place in the city, established a law . . . providing that whatever losses [*zêmias*] and expenses [*analômata*] slaves cause shall be discharged by the master for whom the slaves are working [*ton despotên par' hôi an ergasôntai hoi oiketai*].

263. [Demosthenes] 56 *Against Dionysodorus* (selections). *Dikê emporikê ?blabês* for financial loss arising from intentional breach of contract; contract specifying double damages for intentional breach. (323–322)

See especially F. A. **Paley**-J. E. **Sandys**, *Demosthenes: Select Private Orations* 1[3] (Cambridge 1898: text and commentary); C. **Carey**-R. A. **Reid**, *Demosthenes: Selected Private Speeches* (Cambridge 1985: text and commentary); **Bers**, *Demosthenes 50–59* (translation with introduction and notes); **MacDowell**, *DO* 284–87; also **Schäfer**, *Demosthenes* 4.307–14; **Blass**, *AB* 3.1.582–88; **Gernet**, *Démosthène: Plaidoyers civils III* (text, French translation, and notes); **Usher**, *GO* 256–57.

This speech was delivered by Darius in his prosecution of Dionysodorus by a *dikê emporikê*, presumably *blabês* (cf. **260** [Dem.] 33.19–20, 22, 32–33; **261** Dem. 32.25–28) for intentional damage; neither the prosecutor nor the defendant was an Athenian citizen. With the maritime loan described here compare the headnote under **261** Dem. 32.25–28, and see chapter 10. For the *epôbelia* (**263a**, at §4) cf. **244** Isoc. 18.1–8, 10–13, 33, 63; Darius faces imprisonment if he is fined the *epôbelia* but cannot pay it (see chapter 10 on the special rules obtaining in *dikai emporikai*). Metageitnion (§5) corresponds roughly to August (see p. 7). *Epitimia* (**263c**, at §44; singular *epitimion*, "fine [levied] in addition [to the repayment specified if the contract is obeyed]") refers to the penal clause in the contract specifying double damages for intentional breach (discussed also at §§20, 38); in the clauses of the contract read out by the court clerk at §§36 and 38, the ellipses in the translation correspond to ellipses in the text.

a. [Dem.] 56.3–6.

Dionysodorus . . . has reached such a level of audacity that, having borrowed 3,000 drachmas from us on the security of his ship on terms that he sail the ship back to Athens, and although we were supposed to recover the money during last year's sailing season, he brought the ship to port at Rhodes and there unloaded the cargo and sold it in violation of the contract [*syngraphên*] and your laws, and then dispatched the ship from Rhodes to Egypt and from there back to Rhodes, and to this day he has neither paid back the money to us, his lenders in Athens, nor produced [*kathistêsin*] his security [*enechyron*] in plain sight [*eis to emphanes*], [4] but instead for more than a year now he has been profiting off our property and keeping in his possession the loan and the business and the ship that was pledged as security to us, and despite all this he has come before you, obviously intending to get us fined the *epôbelia* and put in the prison, in addition to depriving us of our money. . . .

[5] Men of Athens, my adversary Dionysodorus here and his partner Parmeniscus approached us last year during the month of Metageitnion and said that they wanted to take out a loan on the security of their ship on terms that they sail to Egypt, and from Egypt to Rhodes or to Athens, after coming to agreement as to the interest [that would accrue] on the voyage to either of the aforementioned ports of trade. [6] When we replied, men of the jury, that we would not lend for a voyage to any port of trade other than Athens, they accordingly agreed to sail here, and on these agreed-upon terms they borrowed from us, on the security of the ship, 3,000 drachmas for a round-trip voyage, and they wrote up a contract concerning these matters. Now, Pamphilus here was listed as lender in the contract; I was his outside partner in the loan.

b. [Dem.] 56.19–21.

Now, then, you have heard what Dionysodorus has done, men of the jury, and I think you have been amazed for a while now hearing about his audacity and what he relies upon in having come here. How is it not audacious for a person to borrow money from the Athenians' port of trade [20] and to write up a contract [*syngraphên*] explicitly specifying the terms that he must sail the ship back to your port of trade, and that if he does not, he must pay back double the money, and then for him to fail to have returned the ship to the Peiraeus and to refuse to pay back the money to his lenders, after he unloaded and sold the grain at Rhodes, and after doing these things nonetheless to have the audacity to look you in your faces?

[21] Now listen to what he says in response to this. He claims that the ship was wrecked on the voyage from Egypt, and for that reason he was forced both to put in at Rhodes and to unload the grain there.

c. [Dem.] 56.31–32, 34–36, 38, 42–46.

It remains for me to explain this to you—and my adversary relies upon the same issue when he claims that the contract [*syngraphên*] commands the repayment of the loan if the ship returns safely. [32] We too assert that this should be the case. [To Dionysodorus:] And I would be happy to hear from you yourself whether you are talking about the ship as having been destroyed or as having returned safely.

. . .

[34] Consider, men of Athens, whether it is we who are making use of the rights provided by the contract, or our adversaries, who have sailed not to the agreed-upon port of trade but to Rhodes and Egypt, and who, although the ship returned safely and has not been destroyed, think they should get a release from the interest, when they have broken the contract. . . . [35] What is happening is most unprecedented of all: they are offering to pay us back the principal of the loan on the grounds that the ship has returned safely, but they think they should deprive us of the interest on the grounds that it has been destroyed! And yet the contract does not say one thing about the interest and another about the principal of the loan; [36] rather, the rights are the same concerning both, and the right of recovery is the same. [To the court clerk:] Please read the contract again.

CONTRACT. . . . from Athens to Egypt and from Egypt to Athens.

. . . Read the rest.

CONTRACT. If the ship returns safely to Peiraeus . . .

. . .

[38] Now, Dionysodorus claims that he is not guilty of wrongdoing for this very reason: he does not have to repay all the interest, since the ship did not sail back to the Peiraeus. But what does the contract say? Not, by Zeus, what you say, Dionysodorus; rather, if you do not either pay back the loan with the interest or surrender the securities in plain sight [*emphanê*] and unencumbered [*anepapha*], or if you do anything else in violation of the contract, it commands you to pay back double the money. [To the court clerk:] And please read that very part of the contract.

CONTRACT. And if . . . they do not surrender the securities in plain sight and unencumbered, or if they do anything in violation of the contract, let them repay double the money.

. . .

[42] Who, men of the jury, is more responsible for the ship's not having returned safely to the Peiraeus: we, who lent explicitly for a voyage to Egypt and [back] to Athens, or our adversary and his partner, who borrowed under this agreement, on terms that they sail back to Athens, and then sailed the ship into port at Rhodes? And it is obvious on many grounds that they did this intentionally [*hekontes*] and not out of necessity. [43] You see, if what happened really was unintentional [*akousion*] and the ship was wrecked, after that, when they had repaired the ship, they obviously would not have leased it out for voyages to other ports of trade but would have sent it back to you, thereby rectifying the unintentional misfortune. As it is, though, not only have they failed to rectify anything but, on top of their original offenses, they have committed much greater ones in addition and have come to contest the lawsuit with an attitude of mockery, assuming that it will be their prerogative, if you convict them, to repay only the principal and the interest. [44] Do not, men of Athens, permit

this to people such as these, nor allow them . . . , if they are unable to deceive you, to repay the simple amount owed; instead, punish them with the additional fines [*epitimiois*] provided in the contract. . . .

[45] So, then, the rights in this matter are brief [in their description] and easy to remember. We lent my adversary Dionysodorus here and his partner 3,000 drachmas for a voyage from Athens to Egypt and from Egypt [back] to Athens. We have not received the money or the interest; on the contrary, they have been possessing and using our property for over a year. To this day they have not returned the ship to your port of trade or surrendered it to us in plain sight, and the contract commands that if they do not surrender the ship in plain sight, they shall pay back double the money, and the recovery is permitted either from one or from both of them. [46] . . . My adversaries admit that they borrowed money and have not repaid it, but they contend that they do not have to pay the actual interest stated in the contract but only the interest [for the duration of the voyage] to Rhodes; they neither included this in the contract nor persuaded us [to agree to it].

264. Dionysius of Halicarnassus, *On Deinarchus* 3. *Dikê blabês* for intentional damage over lost property; written statement of charge (*enklêma*). (date of composition late 1st c. B.C.-early 1st c. A.D.; Deinarchus' *Against Proxenus* delivered 292–291 B.C.)

See references and headnote under **225**; also G. **Shoemaker**, "Dionysius of Halicarnassus, *On Dinarchus*," *GRBS* 12 (1971) 393–409 (translation with introduction and notes); **MacDowell**, *LCA* 151–52 (translation and commentary); M. **Nouhaud**-L. **Dors-Méary**, *Dinarque: Discours* (Paris 1990: text, French translation, and notes). Here Dionysius describes, and quotes the charge statement (*enklêma*: cf., e.g., **253** Dem. 36.2–4, 12, 18–20, at §20) from, a *dikê blabês* brought by Deinarchus against Proxenus. That Deinarchus charged Proxenus with intentional damage is apparent (1) from the fact that the penal assessment (*timêma*: cf., e.g., **257a** Dem. 38.2) of 2 tal. is roughly double the claimed loss (285 staters + 20 minae ≈ 7,700 dr.: see p. 4, and for the stater see **205** Lys. 19.39–40); and (2) from the specification "(by) plotting against" (*epibouleusas*: cf., e.g., **256b** Dem. 37.22–26, 28–33). "The king" is Demetrius I Poliorcetes of Macedon; in addition to Deinarchus' *Against Proxenus* (now fragmentary: see **Nouhaud-Dors-Méary**, *Dinarque*, fragmentary speech IX; N. C. **Conomis**, *Dinarchi orationes cum fragmentis* [Leipzig 1975], fragmentary speech XLVIII [text]), Dionysius cites the *Atthis* (*Attic History*) of Philochorus (ca. 340–260 B.C.: see F. **Jacoby**, *Die Fragmente der griechischen Historiker* [Leiden 1957-], no. 328).

When the king agreed that [Deinarchus] could return with the other exiles, he arrived in Athens and came to stay with one of his friends, Proxenus; there he lost his gold, being by now an old man with weak eyesight. Since Proxenus was negligent regarding the search, he filed a lawsuit [*dikên*] against Proxenus over the money; he filed in person, having never before come to court. That is the biography of the man; each of the aforementioned facts is set forth on the basis of the *Histories* of Philochorus and what Deinarchus wrote about himself in his speech *Against Proxenus*, which was delivered after his exile and has appended to it the following document: "Deinarchus son of Sostratus of Corinth against Proxenus, with whom I live, for damage [*blabês*], [penalty assessed at] 2 talents. Proxenus caused me damage [*eblapse*], having received me into his house in the country when, after being exiled from Athens, I returned from Chalcis, as to 285 gold staters, which I brought from Chalcis with Proxenus' knowledge and in possession of which I came into his house, and as to silver worth no less than 20 minae, by plotting against [*epibouleusas*] the aforementioned property."

265. *Lexica Segueriana* (selections). "Statutory" and "non-statutory" damage. (*Lexeis Rhêtorikai* compiled ?9th c. A.D.; *Synagôgê* compiled 8th or 9th c. A.D.)

I. **Bekker**, *Anecdota Graeca*, vol. 1: *Lexica Segueriana* (Berlin 1814: text); I. C. **Cunningham**, *Synagoge: ΣΥΝΑΓΩΓΗ ΛΕΞΕΩΝ ΧΡΗΣΙΜΩΝ* (Berlin 2003: text with introduction).

The *Lexica Segueriana* are a group of Byzantine lexica that includes, among others, the *Lexeis Rhêtorikai* (*Rhetorical Terms*) and the *Synagôgê Lexeôn Chrêsimôn* (*Collection of Useful Terms*). Below are the entries from the *Lexeis Rhêtorikai* under *enthesmos blabê* ("statutory damage") and from the *Synagôgê* under *athesmos blabê* ("non-statutory damage"). How much evidence (if any) these citations provide with regard to the *dikê blabês* is a matter of scholarly debate; some see in **265a** a reference to cases such as Demosthenes 55, where there seems to have been a penalty fixed by law (**249c** Dem. 55.23–25), as opposed to the majority of *dikai blabês*, which were assessable (*timêtoi*) and are perhaps the referent in **265b**.

a. *Lex. Seg.* (*Lex. Rhet.*) s.v. *enthesmos blabê*.

Enthesmos blabê [statutory damage]: that [damage] which is defined in the laws.

b. *Lex. Seg.* (*Synagôgê*) s.v. *athesmos blabê*.

Athesmos blabê [non-statutory damage]: There were some instances of damage [*blabai*] called "non-statutory" [*athesmoi*], concerning which there was no law established. The same was also called a "non-statutory lawsuit" [*athesmos dikê*].

CHAPTER 9

Theft

Handbooks: J. H. **Lipsius**, *Das attische Recht und Rechtsverfahren* (Leipzig 1905–15) 399–401, 438–43; A. R. W. **Harrison**, *The Law of Athens* (Oxford 1968–71) 1.206–7, 234–35; 2.15, 78, 81–82, 177, 221–32; D. M. **MacDowell**, *The Law in Classical Athens* (Ithaca, NY 1978) 147–49; S. C. **Todd**, *The Shape of Athenian Law* (Oxford 1993) 79–81, 117–19, 139–40, 283–84, 307–12; R. **Parker**, "Law and Religion," in *The Cambridge Companion to Ancient Greek Law*, ed. M. Gagarin-D. Cohen (Cambridge 2005) 61–81, esp. 63–65. **Studies:** K. **Latte**, "Beiträge zum griechischen Strafrecht," *Hermes* 66 (1931) 30–48, 129–58; L. **Gernet**, "Note sur la notion de délit privé en droit grec," in *Droits de l'antiquité et sociologie juridique: Mélanges Henri Lévy-Bruhl* (Paris 1959) 393–405; M. H. **Hansen**, Eisangelia: *The Sovereignty of the People's Court in Athens in the Fourth Century B.C. and the Impeachment of Generals and Politicians* (Odense 1975), esp. 28, 32, 45–46, 119; ***idem,*** Apagoge, Endeixis *and* Ephegesis *against* Kakourgoi, Atimoi *and* Pheugontes (Odense 1976), esp. 36–53; S. **Bianchetti**, "Osservazioni sulla ΓΡΑΦΗ ΙΕΡΟΣΥΛΙΑΣ e sulla ΓΡΑΦΗ ΚΛΟΠΗΣ ΙΕΡΩΝ ΧΡΗΜΑΤΩΝ," *Studi e Ricerche* (Istituto di Storia, Facoltà di Lettere e Filosofia, Università degli Studi di Firenze) 2 (Florence 1983) 55–61; D. **Cohen**, *Theft in Athenian Law* (Munich 1983), with review by D. M. **MacDowell**, *CR* n.s. 34 (1984) 229–31; T. **Saunders**, "Plato and the Athenian Law of Theft," in P. Cartledge-P. Millett-S. Todd, eds., *Nomos: Essays in Athenian Law, Politics and Society* (Cambridge 1990) 63–82; I. **Moneti**, "La 'γραφὴ κλοπῆς' nel diritto attico," *Civiltà Classica e Cristiana* 12 (1991) 7–10; E. M. **Harris**, "'In the Act' or 'Red-Handed'? Apagoge to the Eleven and Furtum Manifestum," in *Symposion 1993: Vorträge zur griechischen und hellenistischen Rechtsgeschichte*, ed. G. Thür (Köln 1994) 169–84; G. **Thür**, "Sachverfolgung und Diebstahl in den griechischen Poleis (Dem. 32, Lys. 23, IC IV 72 I, IPArk 32 u. 17)," in *Symposion 1999*, ed. G. Thür and F. J. Fernández Nieto (Köln 2003) 57–96.

Thefts can be categorized in various ways, depending, for example, on what and how a person steals. Accordingly, Athenian sources employ a variety of terms, often with legal significance, to describe theft and theft-related offenses (see especially **280**, **283**). The general term, *klopê* ("theft"), has a corresponding verb *kleptein* ("to steal") and agent noun *kleptês* ("thief"). The manner of theft may be described by verbs including *hyphairein* ("to steal, to remove secretly"), which denotes clandestine theft; *harpazein* ("to snatch, to rob"), which denotes forcible theft (in our terms, robbery); *aphairein* ("to take away, to deprive," by force or otherwise); and *aposterein* ("to deprive, to withhold, to rob, to embezzle"), which is regularly used of the wrongful appropriation of entrusted property (in our terms, embezzlement). The noun *toichôrychia* ("wall-digging"; verb *toichôrychein*, agent noun *toichôrychos*) refers to the act of digging through a house wall (with the presumed intent to steal or to commit another offense) and thus constitutes, in our terms, a form of burglary or breaking and entering. Special categories based (in part) on the object of theft included clothes-snatching (*lôpodysia*; verb *lôpodytein*, agent noun *lôpodytês*), purse-cutting (verb *ballantiotomein*, agent noun *ballantiotomos*), and temple-robbery (*hierosylia*; verb *hierosylein*, agent noun *hierosylos*). The verbal phrase *pherein kai agein*, "to carry [*scil.* portable property] and lead (away) [*scil.* slaves and livestock]," commonly used of the plundering of enemy territory in war, also appears in the context of non-wartime theft (**2** *IG* I[3] 104, at lines 37–38; **3g** Dem. 23.60).

The earliest surviving Athenian laws that deal with theft are Draco's provisions permitting the self-help killing of a highway robber, presumably if done in self-defense (**3f** Dem. 23.53), and of a person caught in the act of robbing the killer, if done in immediate self-defense (**2** *IG* I[3] 104, at lines 37–38; **3g** Dem. 23.60). These were among the Draconian homicide laws that remained in force after Solon's recension (**6b** [Arist.] *Ath. Pol.* 7.1; **266**). For the existence and contents of Draco's laws on theft per se, which were annulled by Solon, we have only meager sources (**266**, **284**). Plutarch's implication that Draco punished all thefts with death (**266**) reflects Classical and later Athenian common opinion (**26b** Lyc. 1.64–65) but receives explicit support only from other late sources. The core of Athenian theft law in the age of the orators was of Archaic or early Classical origin, and some of it probably was the work of Solon, as Athenian sources assume (e.g., **267b**, **284**; cf. **268**). In the fifth and fourth centuries, a variety of procedures existed for the redress of theft and related offenses, and the applicability of a given procedure—including, in some instances, permissible self-help—depended upon a complex set of circumstances that included the value of the stolen property, the ownership of the property (private, public, or sacred), the location of the theft, whether the thief was apprehended in the act, whether the thief used violence against a person, whether the thief broke into a house, and whether the theft occurred by day or at night.

For theft of private property, the default procedure was the *dikê klopês* (private lawsuit for theft: **282, 288, 289**). This lawsuit lay against any theft of private property—with the possible exception of embezzlement, which seems to have been regularly prosecuted by the *dikê blabês* (see chapter 8)—and was available against the actual thief and the accessory to theft, including the receiver of stolen property (**281**; cf. **298**). A person who suspected another of possessing stolen property was permitted by law to search the suspect's house (the technical term for which was the verb *phôran*); the searcher was not allowed to wear an outer garment, lest he plant the alleged object of his search or remove anything from the premises (**272, 286**). Obstructing the search was a punishable act (**267b**; cf. **286**) and may have made the obstructor liable as an accessory. Finding the object of the search would have provided strong evidence, but was not a necessary precondition, for a *dikê klopês*. Originally heard by the *(h)êliaia* (p. 3; **3b** Dem. 23.28), in the time of the orators the *dikê klopês* was subject to compulsory public arbitration (p. 36; **288**) and came to trial in a *dikastêrion* (p. 26); conviction resulted in a mandatory penalty of double (in some cases perhaps tenfold) damages and a discretionary penalty of five (in some cases perhaps ten) days' confinement in the stocks (**267b, 284, 289**). The lawsuit was assessable (*timêtos*: p. 40) in that the penalty was based on an assessment of the value of the stolen property. A person who accused another of forcible theft could alternatively prosecute by a *dikê biaiôn* (for acts of violence: **61** Harpo. s.v. *biaiôn*; **294**). Both the *dikê klopês* and the *dikê biaiôn* were available only to the victim (p. 29). A *graphê klopês*, posited by one source (**288**) as another alternative to the *dikê klopês*, is elsewhere attested only in connection with the theft of public or sacred property and may have been restricted to use against magistrates accused at their *euthynai* (see below).

A thief caught in the act (*ep' autophôrôi*, etymologically "in the very act of theft": **292, 293**; cf. **283, 284, 300, 301**, and for the application of the term to other offenses see, e.g., **14** Lys. 13.85–87; **57a** Aeschin. 1.91), whether the stolen property was private, public, or sacred, was liable to other remedies, depending on the circumstances of the offense. The most frequently mentioned of these remedies is *apagôgê* (summary arrest: p. 30). Under this procedure, any adult male citizen who apprehended in the act an offender belonging to certain categories could arrest the offender and take him to the Eleven. If the offender confessed, he was immediately executed; if he denied guilt, he was imprisoned pending trial in a *dikastêrion* (**57a** Aeschin. 1.91; **302b**). At that trial, the mandatory sentence for a convicted defendant was death, while a prosecutor who received less than one-fifth of the jury's votes was fined 1,000 drachmas. *Apagôgê* was available against a thief (**283, 284, 288, 289, 290, 292, 293, 302b**; cf. **303**) if he stole property worth over 50 drachmas during the daytime, if he stole anything at night (the captor of a nighttime thief, moreover, was permitted to chase and kill or wound him: observe the contrast with the immediate self-defense requirement in **2** *IG* I[3] 104, **3g** Dem. 23.60), or if he stole private property, or public property worth over 10 drachmas, from specified public places (**289**; cf. **303**). *Apagôgê* was also available against *lôpodytai* ("clothes-snatchers": **267a**, **274**, **283**, **302b**), *ballantiotomoi* (cutpurses: **283**), and *toichôrychoi* ("wall-diggers": **280**, **283**, **290**). The relevant discussions in Demosthenes' *Against Androtion* (**288**) and *Against Timocrates* (**289**) suggest that *ephêgêsis* and *endeixis* (p. 30; cf. **299**, **302b**), likewise available to any adult male citizen, could substitute for (or supplement) *apagôgê* in all the aforementioned cases.

Magistrates, who were entrusted *ex officio* with public and/or sacred property, were subject to special procedures that punished the theft (here especially including, but not limited to, embezzlement) of such property. At a magistrate's end-of-term review (*euthynai*: **289**, **299**, **301**, **302a**; cf. **271**, **273**, **277**, **295**, **297**), a person could prefer a charge that the magistrate had stolen property belonging to the state or to the gods. The *thesmothetai* (p. 2; **273**, **302a**) reviewed the charge; if they decided it merited prosecution, this was conducted by special prosecutors before a *dikastêrion*. If the magistrate was convicted, he was sentenced to pay tenfold damages. We have some evidence (**297**, **299**, **301**, **302a**) that the relevant procedures were called the *graphê* (with *klopês* understood or stated) *dêmosiôn chrêmatôn* (for theft of public property) and the *graphê* (again with *klopês* understood or stated) *hierôn chrêmatôn* (for theft of sacred property). A magistrate who was still in office, and possibly anyone else as well, could be prosecuted for stealing public or sacred property (among other offenses) by *eisangelia* (impeachment: **277**, **281**, **295**; on this type of *eisangelia* generally see chapter 12).

Under Athenian law, *hierosylia* (**266**, **270**, **273**, **275**, **276**, **278**, **283**, **285**, **287–289**, **291**, **296**, **300**; cf. **269**) constituted a special substantive category of theft (it could equally be treated as a special type of impiety: see **269** and chapter 11). The standard translation, used here, is "temple-robbery," but this implies an exactitude that does not correspond to our evidence for the offense. *Hierosylia* required the theft (not necessarily robbery) of sacred property (of some if not all types); the theft did not have to occur specifically from a temple but may have had to occur from a sacred location. It was the subject of a dedicated *graphê hierosylias*, which is named as such only by a late source (Pollux, *Onomasticon* 8.40), but given the absence by definition of an individual human victim, the report is credible and widely accepted. The *graphê hierosylias* could be brought by any adult male citizen (as regularly in public lawsuits: p. 30) and was tried in a *dikastêrion* (**276**, **278**, **285**, **287**); the penalty may have been fixed at death, confiscation of property, and denial of burial in Attica (**266**, **285**, **287**, **288**; cf., however, **276**, which may indicate that the *graphê hierosylias* was an assessable lawsuit). If they were caught in the act, *hierosyloi* were also liable to *apagôgê* (or *endeixis* or *ephêgêsis*), which carried a mandatory death sentence upon confession or conviction (see above; **283**, **300**; cf. **269**). Slaves who informed upon temple-robbers and other religious offenders—including their masters—were rewarded with freedom if their information resulted in a conviction (**278**; **329c** Lys. 7.16–17, 19, 22, 25–26 with additional references in headnote). Owing to the significant substantive overlap between *hierosylia* and the "theft of sacred property" (note especially **287**) that could give rise to a *graphê (klopês) hierôn chrêmatôn* or to *eisangelia*, it can be difficult to identify which procedure was used in a given instance (see **270**, **278**, **285**).

See also **2** *IG* I[3] 104, at lines 37–38; **3f** Dem. 23.53; **3g** Dem. 23.60; **8a** Ant. 5.9; **26b** Lyc. 1.64–65; **42** Dem. 54 (selections); **57a** Aeschin. 1.91; **61** Harpo. s.v. *biaiôn*; **160** Dem. 24.103, 107; **170** Andoc. 1.73–79; **329** Lys. 7 (selections); **345** *IG* I[3] 78; **351** *IG* II[2] 1177; **356** *IG* II[2] 1362; **375** Xen. *Hell.* 1.7.1–16, 20–26, 34–35; **381** Dem. 24.127; **391d** Hyp. 5 col. 24; **391j** Din. 1.60; **391l** Din. 1.77.

266. Plutarch, *Solon* 17.1–3. ?Draconian penalties for theft, temple-robbery (*hierosylia*), and other offenses. (date of composition late 1st-early 2nd c.A.D.; Draco's legislation dated 621/0 B.C.; Solon's legislation dated 594/3 B.C.)

See references and headnote under **1d**. Here Plutarch records the common opinion among later Athenians that Solon had abolished the bulk of Draco's laws (cf. **6b** [Arist.] *Ath. Pol.* 7.1) due to their severity. Demades was a fourth-century Athenian orator and politician. That Draco punished all thefts with death, as Plutarch implies here, is seconded by other late sources (e.g., Aulus Gellius 11.18.3, composed in the second century A.D.; for a similar opinion, which does not name Draco, cf. **26b** Lyc. 1.64–65). In later Archaic and Classical law, under some circumstances thieves could be put to death, either as a self-help measure or as a legal penalty, regardless of the value of the stolen property: see **57a** Aeschin. 1.91; **283** Xen. *Mem.* 1.2.62; **284** Xen. *Oec.* 14.4–7; **289** Dem. 24.104–5, 112–15, 120–21, 129, 146; **290** [Dem.] 35.47; **293** Dem. 45.80–81; **302b** [Arist.] *Ath. Pol.* 52.1; and cf. **268** schol. Ar. *Knights* 658.

First, then, [Solon] annulled all Draco's laws except those on homicide, due to their harshness and the severity of their penalties. [17.2] For the sole penalty prescribed for practically all offenders was death, and so men convicted of idleness [*argias*] were put to death, and men who stole [*klepsantas*] vegetables or fruit received the same punishment as temple-robbers [*hierosylois*] and killers. [17.3] For this reason Demades later gained repute for saying that Draco had written his laws in blood, not in ink.

267. Lysias 10 / *Against Theomnestus* (selections). (date of speech 384/3; laws ascribed to Solon, 594/3)

See references and headnote under **15**. The first passage below attests that *lôpodytai* (clothes-snatchers: cf. **274** Ar. *Birds* 493–98) were subject to *apagôgê* to the Eleven: cf. **57a** Aeschin. 1.91; **283** Xen. *Mem.* 1.2.62; **302b** [Arist.] *Ath. Pol.* 52.1. In the second passage, the speaker quotes and interprets clauses of one or more laws that he attributes to Solon; their language marks them as Archaic, even if they are not actually the work of Solon. That the first clause (binding in the stocks) addresses a convicted thief is suggested by comparison with **289** Dem. 24.104–5, 112–15, 120–21, 129, 146, at §§105, 114, 146 (note, however, that there the duration of confinement is five rather than ten days); on the *(h)êliaia* see **3b** Dem. 23.28. The third clause (blocking the door) explicitly deals with theft and targets a person who obstructs the apprehension of a thief inside a house (cf. **286** Isae. 6.39–42, at §40). Owing to its context, the second clause (giving security and absconding from justice) presumably relates to a thief who has been accused (and perhaps caught in the act) but not yet tried.

a. Lys. 10.10. *Apagôgê* (summary arrest) of *lôpodytês* ("clothes-snatcher").

Well, then, if you were one of the Eleven, you wouldn't accept it if a person arrested [*apagoi*] someone, claiming that he had had his cloak stripped away or his tunic stripped off; instead you would let [the accused] off in the same manner, because he was not called a clothes-snatcher [*lôpodytês*].

b. Lys. 10.15–17 (*leges* + commentary). Solonian laws on theft.

[To the court clerk:] Please read out these laws of Solon, the old ones.

[16] LAW. He shall be bound in the stocks [*podokakkêi*] for ten days by the foot, if the *hêliaia* imposes this as an additional punishment [*prostimêsêi*].

These "stocks," Theomnestus, are what is now called "being bound in the wood [*xylôi*]." . . .

[17] LAW. He shall give security after taking an oath [*epiorkêsanta*] by Apollo. If he is afraid of judgment, he shall run [*draskazein*].

This word "taking an oath" means "swearing an oath" [*omosanta*], and "to run" is what we now call "running away" [*apodidraskein*].

[LAW.] Whoever blocks [*apillei*] the door while the thief [*kleptou*] is inside.

This word "to block" is taken as meaning "to bar" [*apoklêiein*]. . . .

268. Scholion to Aristophanes, *Knights* 658 (= *Suda* s.v. *bolitou dikên*). "*Dikê bolitou*" and Solon's law of theft. (scholion of unknown Byzantine date; *Suda* composed late 10th c. A.D.; Aristophanes' *Knights* produced 425/4 B.C.; legislation of Solon dated 594/3 B.C.)

For the scholia to Aristophanes see references under **82**; for the *Suda* see references and headnote under **49**. The *Suda* entry is identical with the scholion from "that applies" on. The Greek word *boliton* was used both literally ("cattle dung") and figuratively (in the line of the *Knights* to which the scholion refers, the Sausage-Seller employs a double entendre in reference to a debate before the Council of 500 involving a proposed sacrifice of cattle: "When I realized I was being beaten by his bullshit [*bolitois*]"), a fact that may have escaped the scholiast and/or the compiler of the *Suda*, whose comment on Solon (unless it is to be taken as tongue-in-cheek) seems to result from a purely literal interpretation. For the punishment of petty theft in Archaic and Classical law cf. **266** Plut. *Solon* 17.1–3 with additional references in headnote.

There is also a proverb, "a lawsuit for bullshit" [*bolitou dikê*], that applies to people who undergo trials for trivial matters: Solon's law punishes even those who steal [*hyphelomenous*] cattle dung [*boliton*].

269. Cicero, *On Divination* 1.54. Temple-robbery. (date of composition 44 B.C.; Sophocles b. 490s B.C., d. 406/5 B.C.)

W. A. **Falconer**, *Cicero*: De Senectute, De Amicitia, De Divinatione (Cambridge, MA 1938: text and translation); A. S. **Pease**, *M. Tulli Ciceronis* De Divinatione (Darmstadt 1963: text and commentary); D. **Wardle**, *Cicero* On Divination: De Divinatione, *Book 1* (Oxford 2006: translation and commentary).

This anecdote from the treatise *On Divination* by the Roman orator and politician Cicero presents a textbook case of temple-robbery (*hierosylia*), which, owing to the involvement of the Council of the Areopagus, appears to have been treated under the category of impiety (*asebeia*: see chapter 11). Notably, however, another version of the story, in the anonymous ancient *Life of Sophocles* (§12), differs as to most of the important details (the stolen object was a gold crown; it was taken from the Acropolis, with no specific location named; it was found in an abandoned house, with no mention of the apprehension of the thief; Sophocles informed the Assembly, not the Areopagus).

To the philosophers let us add a most learned man, and a divine poet at that, Sophocles. After a heavy gold bowl had been stolen from the temple of Heracles, he saw in a dream the god himself saying who had done it. The first and second times, he ignored it. But when he had the same dream repeatedly, he went up to the Areopagus and reported the matter. The Areopagites ordered that the man named by Sophocles be arrested, and the man, under questioning, confessed and returned the bowl. From that deed the sanctuary in question is called that of Heracles the Denouncer.

270. Philochorus, *FGrHist* 328 F 121. Pheidias' theft of sacred property. (date of trial 438/7; Philochorus ca. 340–260; scholion to Aristophanes of unknown Byzantine date)

F. **Jacoby**, *Die Fragmente der griechischen Historiker* (Leiden 1957–) no. 328, fr. 121 (text: part IIIB pp. 134–35; commentary: part IIIb [Supplement] vol. 1 pp. 484–96, vol. 2 pp. 391–401).

At Aristophanes, *Peace* 605–6, Hermes says, "Pheidias started it first by doing evil deeds. Then Pericles, fearing lest he share in Pheidias' fate," issued the Megarian decree that led to the outbreak of the Peloponnesian War in 431. The following quotations, one direct and one indirect, from the *Atthis* of Philochorus (see headnote under **264** D. H. *Din.* 3), come from the scholiast to *Peace* 605. The chryselephantine (gold and ivory) statue of Athena Parthenos (the Virgin) executed by Pheidias was the cult statue in "the great temple" (i.e., the Parthenon on the Athenian Acropolis, part of Pericles' public building program); "the scales" in the first quotation belonged to the snakes mentioned in the second. For variant versions of the story of Pheidias, including the alleged complicity of Pericles, see Diodorus 12.39 (which states that an investigation led to the Assembly's ordering the arrest of Pheidias and that a prosecution of Pericles for *hierosylia* was initiated); Plutarch, *Pericles* 31.2–5 (also mentioning proceedings before the Assembly, and adding the highly suspect detail that Pheidias died in prison in Athens). For Pericles' later trial and conviction for theft of public property see **271** (Pericles' trial and conviction for theft of public property).

Philochorus, under the archonship of Theodorus [438/7], says this: "And the gold statue of Athena, with a weight in gold of 44 talents, was placed in the great temple under the supervision of Pericles, Pheidias being the sculptor. And Pheidias the sculptor was found to have fraudulently reckoned the cost of the ivory for the scales and was convicted; it is said that he fled to Elis and contracted to make the statue of Zeus at Olympia and, after he completed that, was put to death by the Eleans."

. . .

Pheidias, as Philochorus says, in the archonship of Theodorus, after constructing the statue of Athena, stole [*hypheileto*] the gold from the snakes of the chryselephantine Athena, for which he was convicted and sentenced to exile; he went to Elis, contracted from the Eleans to make the statue of Olympian Zeus, and was convicted by them of peculation [*nosphisamenos*] and executed.

271. Pericles' trial and conviction for theft of public property. (date of trial 430)

For Thucydides see references and headnote under **1b**. For Plato's *Gorgias*, one of the philosopher's Socratic dialogues, see W. R. M. **Lamb**, *Plato*: Lysis, Symposium, Gorgias (Cambridge, MA 1925: text and translation); E. R. **Dodds**, *Plato*: Gorgias (Oxford 1959: text and commentary). For Plutarch see the headnote under **1d**; for his *Life of Pericles* see P. A. **Stadter**, *Plutarch's* Pericles (Chapel Hill 1989: text and commentary); R. **Waterfield**, *Plutarch: Greek Lives* (Oxford 1998: translation with introduction and notes by P. A. Stadter).

The following passages discuss the prosecution, conviction, and sentencing of Pericles for theft of public property in 430. Plutarch appears to associate the events narrated in *Pericles* 32.1–4 with an earlier trial connected with the Pheidias affair of 438/7 (see **270** Philochorus, *FGrHist* 328 F 121 with headnote), but probably he has his chronology confused and these details belong to Pericles' trial of 430, which is discussed at *Pericles* 35.4–5 (and for which Plutarch has clearly used Thucydides among his sources). Among Plutarch's named sources, Idomeneus (ca. 325–270: Jacoby, *FGrHist* no. 338) was a historian and biographer from Lampsacus in northern Asia Minor; on Theophrastus (b. 372–370, d. 288–286) see headnote under **216** D. L. 3.41–43 and **312** Theophr. *Laws* fr. 21.1 Szegedy-Maszak; Heracleides Ponticus (4th c. B.C.) was a philosopher of the Platonic school. On impiety (*asebeia*: **271c**, §32.1) see chapter 11, and on the case of Anaxagoras see **344** (Anaxagoras and the sun); on *eisangelia* (impeachment, §32.2) see chapter 12; on the *prytaneis* (§32.3) see p. 6 and the headnote under **332** Dem. 21 (selections). "The altar" (§32.3) was that of Athena on the Acropolis; on charges of theft, bribery, or wrongdoing brought against a magistrate (§32.4) cf. **302a** [Arist.] *Ath. Pol.* 48.4–5, 54.2.

a. Thucydides 2.65.3–4. (composed 430-ca. 400)

And in fact it was not until they penalized [Pericles] with a monetary fine [*ezêmiôsan chrêmasin*] that everyone stopped being angry at him. [4] Not much later, though, as a crowd is wont to do, they again elected him general and entrusted all affairs to him. . . .

b. Plato, *Gorgias* 516a. (composed early 4th c. B.C.)

SOCRATES. . . . at the end of Pericles' life they convicted him of theft [*klopên*], and they nearly sentenced [*etimêsan*] him to death, obviously on the grounds that he was a scoundrel.

c. Plutarch, *Pericles* 32.1–4, 35.4–5. (composed late 1st-early 2nd c. A.D.)

Around this time Aspasia was on trial in a lawsuit [*dikên*] for impiety [*asebeias*] . . . , [32.2] and Diopeithes composed a decree providing for the impeachment [*eisangellesthai*] of those who did not acknowledge the divine or who taught doctrines about things in the sky; he was attempting to place suspicion on Pericles through Anaxagoras. [32.3] The Assembly received and welcomed the accusations, and so on the motion of Dracontides a decree was passed mandating that the accounts of the money be rendered by Pericles to the *prytaneis*, and that the jurors [*dikastai*] carry their votes from the altar and give judgment on the Acropolis. [32.4] Hagnon removed the last clause from the decree and proposed that the lawsuit [*dikên*] be judged in a court of 1,500 jurors [*dikastais*], whether it was for theft [*klopês*] and bribery [*dôrôn*] or for wrongdoing [*adikiou*] that someone wished to name the prosecution.

. . .

[35.4] And yet Pericles did not allay the [Athenians'] anger or win them over until they got their votes against him in their hands and, having become his masters, removed him from his generalship and penalized him with a monetary fine [*zêmiôsai chrêmasin*], which those who record the least amount give as 15 talents and those who record the greatest amount give as fifty. [35.5] Listed in the lawsuit [*dikêi*] as prosecutor was, as Idomeneus says, Cleon, but as Theophrastus says, Simmias; and Heracleides Ponticus has stated that it was Lacrateides.

272. Aristophanes, *Clouds* 497–99 and scholion. Search for stolen property. (original version of *Clouds* 424/3, partially revised *ante* 416; scholion of unknown Byzantine date)

See references and headnotes under **52** (for Aristophanes' *Clouds*) and **82** (for the scholion). In the passage from the *Clouds*, Socrates and Strepsiades are about to enter Socrates' school, and Strepsiades expresses his confusion as to Socrates' instruction to take off his cloak ("Have I done something wrong?" indicates that he expects a beating). The scholion explains the practice of removing at least the outer garment (not necessarily all clothing) in conducting a search for stolen property (cf. **286** Isae. 6.39–42).

a. Ar. *Clouds* 497–99.

SOCRATES. Come now, lay down your cloak.
STREPSIADES. Have I done something wrong?
SOCRATES. No; it's customary to go in unclothed [*gymnous*].
STREPSIADES. But I'm not going in to search for stolen property [*phôrasôn*].

b. Scholion to Ar. *Clouds* 499.

"But not to search for stolen property": the custom was that those going into a person's house to conduct a search go in unclothed, so that they could not hide anything under their cloaks without being noticed or, out of enmity, secretly deposit the object of the search without being noticed and so cause the person to be punished.

273. Aristophanes, *Wasps* 836–47, 893–900, 931–35, 952–66. Comedic mock trial for theft of public property by magistrate. (423/2)

See references and headnote under **183**. Here Bdelycleon stages a trial for Philocleon to judge as sole juror. The prosecutor, Dog (*Kyôn*), and the defendant (and fellow dog), Labes ("Grabber"; i.e., of cheese), represent (and have the same demotics as) the politicians Cleon and Laches respectively; the scene satirizes Cleon's allegation that Laches stole public funds while serving as a general in Sicily during the years 427–425 (hence the "Sicilian cheese," and the Cheese-Grater as "treasurer"). Since the lawsuit comes to trial before a (mock) *dikastêrion*, we are probably to presume that evidence was found against the defendant in the initial stages of his *euthynai*: cf. **302a** [Arist.] *Ath. Pol.* 48.4–5, 54.2 (note that Bdelycleon, who introduces the lawsuit, is cast as *thesmothetês*). For the penal assessment (*timêma*: cf., e.g., **257a** Dem. 38.2; **264** D. H. *Din.* 3) of a collar, proposed by the prosecutor in the indictment document, cf. **237** Xen. *Hell.* 2.4.41; **238** Plut. *Solon* 23.7–8, 24.3. Hestia, the goddess of the hearth, customarily received the first honors in prayer and sacrifice; hence "starting with Hestia" means "starting at the beginning," and "Hestia's pigpen" designates the pigpen in the courtyard of Philocleon's house. "He doesn't know how to play the lyre" (a standard part of the education of upper-class Athenian males) means "he is unrefined." (At the end of the trial, Labes wins acquittal because Bdelycleon tricks Philocleon into casting his vote into the wrong urn, on which cf. **234** [Dem.] 43.5–16, at §10).

BDELYCLEON. Tell me, what's going on?

XANTHIAS. Didn't you see? Labes, the dog, just darted past into the kitchen, snatched [*harpasas*] a loaf of Sicilian cheese, and ate it up!

BDELYCLEON. Well, then, that's the first offense I have to introduce before my father. You be there and prosecute.

XANTHIAS. Not me, by Zeus; but the other dog says he'll prosecute if someone introduces the indictment [*graphên*].

BDELYCLEON. Go on, then, bring them both here.

XANTHIAS. Will do.

BDELYCLEON. What's this here?

PHILOCLEON. Hestia's pigpen.

BDELYCLEON. You've committed temple-robbery [*hierosylêsas*] to bring it?

PHILOCLEON. No; it's so I can start with Hestia and crush somebody. Now hurry up and introduce the case; I've got my eye on assessing a penalty [*timan*].

. . .

[893] PHILOCLEON. Who's this defendant? Oh, how he's going to be convicted!

BDELYCLEON. Just listen to the indictment [*graphês*]. "Dog [*Kyôn*] of the deme Cydathenaeon has indicted [*egrapsato*] Labes of the deme Aexone for committing an offense by eating up all the Sicilian cheese by himself. Penalty [*timêma*]: a fig-wood collar."

PHILOCLEON. No; a dog's death, once he's convicted.

BDELYCLEON. And here's the defendant Labes.

PHILOCLEON. The wretch. And what a thieving [*klepton*] look he has!

. . .

[931] PHILOCLEON. Hooray! So many villainies he's accused him of! A thieving thing of a man. [To the Rooster:] Don't you think so too, rooster? [To the audience:] By Zeus, he's winking yes. [To Bdelycleon:] *Thesmothetês*! [To the audience:] Where is he? I need him to give me a chamberpot.

. . .

[952] BDELYCLEON. . . . For he's good, and he chases the wolves away.

PHILOCLEON. No; he's a thief [*kleptês*] and a conspirator [*synômotês*].

BDELYCLEON. By Zeus, no; he's the best dog alive today, able to stand guard over a lot of sheep.

PHILOCLEON. What's the use, if he eats up the cheese?

BDELYCLEON. What's the use? He fights for you, guards the door, and is excellent in other respects. If he stole [*hypheileto*], forgive him; he doesn't know how to play the lyre.

PHILOCLEON. I wish he hadn't learned his letters either, so that he couldn't be a malefactor [*kakourgôn*] when he wrote up his account for us.

BDELYCLEON. My good man, listen to my witnesses. [To the Cheese-Grater:] Come up, Cheese-Grater, and speak loudly: you were his treasurer. Answer this clearly: did you not grate for the soldiers what you received? [To Philocleon:] He says he did.

PHILOCLEON. He does, by Zeus, but he's lying.

274. Aristophanes, *Birds* 493–98. Act constituting *lôpodysia* ("clothes-snatching"). (414)

See references and headnote under **184**. Here Euelpides describes his falling victim to a *lôpodytês* ("clothes-snatcher": cf. **57a** Aeschin. 1.91; **267a** Lys. 10.10; **283** Xen. *Mem.* 1.2.62; **302b** [Arist.] *Ath. Pol.* 52.1). The referent in "because of him" and "he crowed" is a rooster. Halimus is the name of a deme; "the wall" is the city wall of Athens. On the *dekatê* (tenth-day naming ceremony) see the introduction to chapter 6.

EUELPIDES. . . . Poor pitiful me, I lost a cloak of Phrygian wool because of him. One time I'd been invited to a child's tenth-day ceremony [*dekatên*] and was having a drink in the city, and I'd just fallen asleep, and before the others had their dinner, he crowed. I thought it was dawn, so I started off for Halimus, and I'd just stuck my head outside the wall when a clothes-snatcher [*lôpodytês*] hit me in the back with a club. I fell down and was about to cry out, but he'd already carried off my cloak.

275. Isocrates 18 *Against Callimachus* 57. Temple-robbery. (*post* 404/3)

See references and headnotes under **10** and **244**. Here the speaker cites the case of one Philurgus as a paradigmatic instance of temple-robbery. Compare the generalizing statement at Isocrates 15.14: "My adversary, who himself is delivering composed remarks, has spoken more about my compositions than about all the other matters, thus doing something like a person prosecuting another for temple-robbery [*hierosylias*] when he himself manifestly has the gods' property in his own hands." A gold Gorgon's head was the blazon on the shield held by the statue of Athena in the Parthenon (cf. **270** Philochorus, *FGrHist* 328 F 121).

And having committed such serious offenses, he is going to try to say that we are lying. For him to do that is like Phrynondas criticizing someone for villainy, or Philurgus, who stole [*hyphelomenos*] the Gorgon's head, claiming that other people are temple-robbers [*hierosylous*].

276. Isocrates 20 *Against Lochites* 6. Penalties for theft and temple-robbery. (*post* 404/3)

See references and headnote under **36**. The speaker here manifestly engages in rhetorical exaggeration: the death penalty was not available in all cases of theft (and, judging from this passage, may not have been automatic for temple-robbery), and even when available, it was not always sought or imposed (see, e.g., **288** Dem. 22.25–27, 69–73; **289** Dem. 24.104–5, 112–15, 120–21, 129, 146). Unless the reference to *hierosylia* applies only to *apagôgê* and related procedures, the generalizing "you," referring to the jury (p. 27), suggests that the *graphê hierosylias* was tried before a *dikastêrion*.

And I see that when you convict a person of temple-robbery [*hierosylian*] or theft [*klopên*], you do not conduct your penal assessment [*timêsin*] according to the amount the offenders take; instead, you sentence all of them alike to death, believing it just that those who undertake the same deeds be punished with the same penalties.

277. Lysias 30 *Against Nicomachus* 21, 23–25. Theft of public property. (399)

See especially S. C. **Todd**, "Lysias against Nikomachos: The Fate of the Expert in Athenian Law," in *Greek Law in Its Political Setting: Justifications Not Justice*, ed. L. Foxhall-A. D. E. Lewis (Oxford 1996) 101–31; M. J. **Edwards**, *Lysias: Five Speeches: Speeches 1, 12, 19, 22, 30* (London 1999: text and commentary); S. C. **Todd**, *Lysias* (Austin 2000: translation with introduction and notes); also F. **Blass**, *Die attische Beredsamkeit* (Leipzig 1887–98) 1.463–70; R. C. **Jebb**, *The Attic Orators from Antiphon to Isaeus*[2] (London

1893) 1.218–21; S. **Usher**, *Greek Oratory: Tradition and Originality* (Oxford 1999) 74–76.

Nicomachus was one of the Recorders (of the Laws) (*anagrapheis* [*tôn nomôn*]) whose duty was to (re)publish the corpus of Athenian laws following the democratic restoration of 410 and again after the democratic restoration of 403 (pp. 12, 13; cf. **2** *IG* I³ 104, at lines 5–8; **12a** Andoc. 1.83–84). In 399, he was prosecuted, either at his *euthynai* (p. 32; cf. **302a** [Arist.] *Ath. Pol.* 48.4–5, 54.2; **299** [Dem.] 58.14–15; **301** Aeschin. 3.10; **289** Dem. 24.104–5, 112–15, 120–21, 129, 146; **273** Ar. *Wasps* 836–47, 893–900, 931–35, 952–66) or by *eisangelia* (impeachment: see chapter 12 and cf. **281** Lys. 29.1–2, 11), for misconduct in office. "Temple-robber" (*hierosylos*, §21) is here used metaphorically: the speaker alleges (§§19–20) that Nicomachus' including novel sacrifices in his recording of the sacred laws has prevented the performance of traditional sacrifices, since expenditures that should have gone to the latter went to the former.

And then this temple-robber [*hierosylos*] runs around saying that he has inscribed what is pious rather than what is cheap; and if this does not please you, he bids you erase it, and by that he thinks he will persuade you that he has committed no wrongdoing. But this is the man who in two years has already spent twelve talents more than he was supposed to. . . .

. . .

[23] Those who wish to steal [*kleptein*] public property are paying attention to how Nicomachus is going to fare at trial. . . .

. . .

[24] . . . Who has done the city less good or more wrong? [25] This man became recorder [*anagrapheus*] of both profane and sacred matters, and he has committed offenses against both. Remember that you have in the past put many citizens to death for theft [*klopêi*] of property. And yet those men caused you harm only for the time being, while my adversaries, by taking bribes for inscribing the laws, inflict losses upon the city for all time.

278. Lysias 5 *For Callias* 1, 5. Trial for temple-robbery before jury-court (*dikastêrion*); *mênysis* (informing) by slaves. (403–380)

See especially S. C. **Todd**, *A Commentary on Lysias, Speeches 1–11* (Oxford 2007: text, translation, and commentary); also **Blass**, *AB* 1.587–90; **Jebb**, *AO* 1.283–84; **Usher**, *GO* 113; **Todd**, *Lysias* (translation with introduction and notes).

The full manuscript title of this speech, which in this case is likely to be accurate, is *Defense Speech for Callias On a Charge of Temple-Robbery* (*hierosylias*). The speech, which was delivered by a *synêgoros* (advocate: p. 28) for the metic defendant Callias, survives in a truncated form that does not contain the substantive details of the charge. "Men of the jury" translates *ô andres dikastai*, which indicates a regular jury-court (*dikastêrion*: p. 26). The legal action cannot be precisely identified; it may have been a *graphê hierosylias*, a jury-trial resulting from an *apagôgê* or related procedure, or possibly an *eisangelia*. "For . . . a capital offense" translates *peri . . . tou sômatos*, on which phrase see **70** Lys. 9.5–12, 15–16. For *mênysis* by slaves concerning religious offenses, with the prospect of freedom if their information resulted in a conviction, cf. **329c** Lys. 7.16–17, 19, 22, 25–26 with additional references in headnote.

If it were for anything other than a capital offense that Callias was on trial, men of the jury, what has been said by the others would suffice for me.

. . .

[5] I think it is fitting to consider this trial not as the personal issue of these men but as a public issue for everyone in the city. These are not the only people who have slaves; everyone else does too, and those slaves, looking to the fortune of these men, will no longer consider what good service they might do their masters to become free, but instead what false information [*mênysantes*] they might give about them. . . .

279. Lysias 27 *Against Epicrates* 3–4, 6–7. Theft of public property; receiving bribes. (395–387/6)

Blass, *AB* 1.452–56; **Jebb**, *AO* 1.217–18; L. **Gernet**-M. **Bizos**, *Lysias: Discours*, 2 vols. (Paris 1989: text with French translation and notes); **Usher**, *GO* 98–99; **Todd**, *Lysias* (translation with introduction and notes).

This speech was delivered by a prosecutor of Epicrates in a lawsuit that cannot be identified but (on the basis of §7) appears to have been an *agôn timêtos* (assessable lawsuit: p. 40) in which the prosecution sought the death penalty. Here the speaker alleges that Epicrates and/or his associates have been convicted of receiving bribes and have stolen public property. The daggers surrounding "Onomasas" indicate that the text is corrupt at this point: Onomasas is not a likely Greek name.

And yet what hope of salvation should one have when whether the city is preserved or not depends on money, and these men, appointed by you as guardians, the punishers of offenders, steal [*kleptôsi*] the money and take bribes? This isn't the first time they have been seen offending: they have already previously been convicted of receiving bribes [*dôrôn*]. [4] And the charge I have to bring against you is that for the same offense you convicted †Onomasas† but acquitted my adversary, although the same man prosecuted all of them and the same witnesses testified against them, and these . . . were the very people who conducted the business of the money and the bribes with them. . . . [6] But now it is safe for them to steal [*kleptein*] your property. If they escape detection, they will have it to use without fear, and if they are seen, either they buy off the danger with a fraction of [the profits of] their offenses or they are put on trial and get acquitted because of their power. . . . [7] . . . But if you convict them and sentence [*timêsête*] them to death, by one and the same vote you will make others behave better than they do now and you will have exacted punishment from my adversaries.

280. Aristophanes, *Wealth* 366–74, 563–66. Types of theft. (388)

See references and headnote under **52**. In these passages, the characters mention and distinguish between various types of theft, including theft by stealth, theft by violence (robbery), embezzlement, and the related offense of *toichôrychia* ("wall-digging"; i.e., breaking and entering, burglary). On escaping detection as a thief and/or wall-digger, cf. **57a** Aeschin. 1.91; **283** Xen. *Mem.* 1.2.62; **292** Isae. 4.28–29; **293** Dem. 45.80–81.

CHREMYLUS. Man, you've got the black bile, by heaven.

BLEPSIDEMUS. Even his gaze won't stay in the same place; it's plain on his face that he has committed some villainy.

CHREMYLUS. I know what you're croaking about. You think I've stolen [*keklophotos*] something, and you're looking to take your share.

BLEPSIDEMUS. I'm looking to take my share? Of what?

CHREMYLUS. It's not like that, though; it's something else.

BLEPSIDEMUS. What, you didn't steal, but you robbed [*hêrpakas*]?

CHREMYLUS. You're delusional.

BLEPSIDEMUS. Well, certainly you didn't embezzle [*apesterêkas*] from someone?

CHREMYLUS. Absolutely not.

. . .

[563] POVERTY. Now, then, I will proceed on the topic of self-control, and I will explain to you that circumspection abides with me, while hubris belongs to Wealth.

CHREMYLUS. So, then, stealing [*kleptein*] and digging through walls [*tous toichous dioryttein*] is very circumspect!

BLEPSIDEMUS. By Zeus, yes: given that one has to escape detection, how is that not circumspect?

281. Lysias 29 *Against Philocrates* 1–2, 11. Liability of accessory to theft; receiving stolen property; receiving bribes. (ca. 388)

Blass, *AB* 1.452–63; **Jebb**, *AO* 1.215–17, 235–36; W. **Wait**, *Lysias: Ten Selected Orations* (New York 1898: text and commentary); **Gernet-Bizos**, *Lysias* (text with French translation and notes); **Usher**, *GO* 99–101; **Todd**, *Lysias* (translation with introduction and notes).

Lysias 29 was delivered in a prosecution of Philocrates by the *apographê* procedure (for confiscation of property owed to the state: see **302b** [Arist.] *Ath. Pol.* 52.1, and cf. **285** *SEG* 12.100.1–16). The speaker accuses Philocrates of retaining in his possession and failing to surrender money owed to the state by Ergocles, who has been convicted of stealing public property and receiving bribes and has been executed. The procedure used against Ergocles was probably *eisangelia* (impeachment: see chapter 12 and cf. **277** Lys. 30.21, 23–25) before the Assembly; Lysias wrote a prosecution speech for that trial as well (Lysias 28). Here the speaker, drawing an analogy with theft of private property, argues that Philocrates should be liable to capital punishment as an accessory to Ergocles' theft of public property (on the phrase *peri tou sômatos* cf. **278** Lys. 5.1, 5 and see **70** Lys. 9.5–12, 15–16).

This trial, men of the jury, has been more vacant than I expected: there were a lot of people who made threats and who claimed that they would prosecute Philocrates, and now none of them is to be seen. And that, it seems to me, is an indication second to none that the action for confiscation [*apographês*] is in fact truthful, for unless he had a lot of Ergocles' money, he wouldn't be able to get rid of his prosecutors so easily. [2] As for me, men of the jury, I think you all know that the reason you condemned Ergocles to death was that he managed the city's affairs poorly and thereby acquired an estate worth more than thirty talents. None of that money has come to light in the city. . . .

. . .

[11] I think, men of the jury, that he should not just be on trial for money but should be at risk for capital punishment [*peri tou sômatos*] as well. You see, it would be a terrible thing if those who are complicit with thieves [*kleptais*] with regard to property lost by private individuals should be liable to the same penalties [as the thieves], but my adversary, who is complicit with Ergocles' theft of city property and receipt of bribes for managing your affairs, should not meet with the same punishment [as Ergocles]. . . .

282. Plato, *Protagoras* 321c-322a. Mythical *dikê klopês*. (composed early 4th c. B.C.)

J. A. **Towle**, *Plato*: Protagoras (Boston 1892: text and commentary); J. **Adam**-A. M. **Adam**, *Platonis* Protagoras (Cambridge 1893: text and commentary); N. **Denyer**, *Plato*: Protagoras (Cambridge 2008: text and commentary); C. C. W. **Taylor**, *Plato*: Protagoras (Oxford 2009: translation with introduction and notes).

In this passage from Plato's *Protagoras*, Socrates recounts a speech given by the sophist Protagoras about the Greek myth wherein Prometheus gave mortals the gift of fire in violation of the commandment of Zeus, king of the gods. For other versions of the myth, see Hesiod, *Works and Days* 42–105, *Theogony* 507–616 (including Prometheus' brother Epimetheus, who accepted the gift of Pandora against Prometheus' advice); Aeschylus, *Prometheus Bound*. For his transgression, Prometheus was chained to a column (Hesiod, *Theogony* 521–25) or to the face of a cliff (Aeschylus, *Prometheus Bound* 15) and had his liver gouged out by an eagle every day (to regenerate nightly, according to Hesiod) or every other day (to regenerate on the off days, according to a fragment of Aeschylus' *Prometheus Loosed* [fr. 193 Nauck = fr. 324 Mette] preserved in translation by Cicero, *Tusculan Disputations* 2.23–25). Under Athenian law, no such punishment existed (for logistical if no other reasons), but Prometheus would have been liable to a *dikê klopês*, as Protagoras characterizes it; note his comment that Prometheus was not detected in the act.

"So Prometheus, at a loss as to what means of preservation he could devise for mankind, stole [*kleptei*] from Hephaestus and Athena their knowledge of their crafts, fire and all, . . . and gave it to mankind in the following way. . . . There was no longer time for Prometheus to enter the citadel, the dwelling of Zeus—and besides, Zeus' defenses were fearsome—but without being detected he entered the house of Athena and Hephaestus, which they held in common and in which the two of them practiced their crafts, and he stole [*klepsas*] Hephaestus' craft of the forge and the other crafts that belonged to Athena and gave them to mankind. From this an easy means of livelihood resulted for mankind, but later, as the story goes, a lawsuit for theft [*klopês dikê*] pursued Prometheus, thanks to Epimetheus."

283. Xenophon, *Memorabilia* 1.2.62. Death penalty for offenders caught in the act. (early 4th c. B.C.)

See references and headnote under **53**. Here Xenophon is arguing that Socrates, who did not commit any of the acts named below, did not merit the death penalty. With this list compare **57a** Aeschin. 1.91; **302b** [Arist.] *Ath. Pol.* 52.1; also Plato, *Republic* 575a (listing all the offenses below), 344b (temple-robbers, kidnappers, wall-diggers, embezzlers [*aposterêtai*], and thieves), 552d (thieves, cutpurses, and temple-robbers, all called *kakourgoi*); *Gorgias* 508d-e (purse-cutting, theft, kidnapping, and wall-digging); Demosthenes 4.47 (death penalty for kidnappers and clothes-snatchers, both called *kakourgoi*).

According to the laws, if a person is detected while stealing [*kleptôn*], clothes-snatching [*lôpodytôn*], purse-cutting [*ballantiotomôn*], wall-digging [*toichôrychôn*], kidnapping [*andrapodizomenos*], or temple-robbing [*hierosylôn*], the penalty is death.

284. Xenophon, *Oeconomicus* 14.4–7. Laws of Draco and Solon on theft. (first half of 4th c. B.C.)

S. **Pomeroy**, *Xenophon,* Oeconomicus: *A Social and Historical Commentary* (Oxford 1994: text, translation, and commentary).

In this passage from Xenophon's *Oeconomicus*, a treatise on household management, Ischomachus gives advice on the proper training of slaves. The "royal laws" are those of the kings of Persia. On theft laws ascribed to Draco cf. **266** Plut. *Solon* 17.1–3; since Solon abrogated all Draco's laws save those dealing with homicide (**266**; **6b** [Arist.] *Ath. Pol.* 7.1), the laws of Draco referred to here may have permitted the self-help killing of a thief (cf. **2** *IG* I^3 104, at lines 37–38; **3f** Dem. 23.53; **3g** Dem. 23.60; and for self-help remedies against theft ascribed to Solon, see **288** Dem. 22.25–27, 69–73; **289** Dem. 24.104–5, 112–15, 120–21, 129, 146). "Bound" (§14.5) may refer to the arrest and/or to the imprisonment of a thief under the *apagôgê* procedure (cf. **289**; **292** Isae. 4.28–29; **293** Dem. 45.80–81; **302b** [Arist.] *Ath. Pol.* 52.1).

"However," he said, "taking also some provisions from Draco's laws and some from Solon's, I try to guide my slaves to justice. These men too, you see," he said, "seem to me to have enacted many of their laws with the goal of teaching justice of this sort. [14.5] For it is written that those who undertake [to steal] are to be punished for their thefts, and bound, if a person is caught while committing the act [*poiôn*], and put to death. . . . [14.6] So, by applying some of these provisions and by citing other provisions from the royal laws, I try to make my slaves just with regard to the matters they manage. [14.7] You see, those laws serve only as punishments for offenders, but the royal laws not only punish the unjust but also help the just. . . ."

285. *Supplementum Epigraphicum Graecum* 12.100.1–16. Confiscation of property of person convicted *in absentia* of temple-robbery. (367/6)

M. **Crosby**-J. **Young**, "Greek Inscriptions," *Hesperia* 10 (1941) 14–30 (text, translation, and commentary); A. G. **Woodhead**, ed., *Supplementum Epigraphicum Graecum*, vol. 12, no. 100 (Leiden 1955: text); P. J. **Rhodes**-R. **Osborne**, *Greek Historical Inscriptions 404–323 BC* (Oxford 2003), no. 36 (text, translation, and commentary).

This inscription records transactions carried out by the *pôlêtai* (see headnote under **2** *IG* I^3 104) of the year 367/6. For the Athenian calendar see p. 7; on confiscation (*apographê*) cf., e.g., **281** Lys. 29.1–2, 11. That Theosebes absconded before trial suggests that he was prosecuted by a *graphê hierosylias* rather than by *apagôgê*; in the latter case he would have been imprisoned pending trial.

Pôlêtai in the archonship of Polyzelus [367/6].

Polyeuctus of the deme Lamptrae, Deinias of the deme Erchia, Theaeus of the deme Paeania, Theotimus of the deme Phrearrhioe, Aristogenes of the deme Iphistiadae, Glaucon of the deme Laciadae, Cephisocles of the deme Peiraeus, and Nicocles of the deme Anaphlystus, for whom Execestus of the deme Cothocidae was secretary, sold the following, having received it from the Eleven, Phaeax of the deme Aphidna and his colleagues in office. On the tenth of Munychion, Theomnestus son of Deisitheus of the deme Ionidae registered [*apegrapsen*] as public property a house in the deme Alopece belonging to Theosebes son of Theophilus of the deme Xypete, which is bounded on the north by the road leading to the Daedaleion and the Daedaleion and on the south by [the property of] Philippus of the deme Agryle, since Theosebes had been convicted of temple-robbery [*hierosylias*] and had not undergone trial, for the value [of the house] over and above the amount pledged as security [*hypokeitai*] to Smicythus of the deme Teithras, 150 drachmas. Summons-witness[es] [*klêtêr*]: Diogeiton of the deme Alopece, Philoetius of the deme Ionidae.

286. Isaeus 6 *On the Estate of Philoctemon* 39–42. Attempted search for stolen property. (365–363)

See references and headnotes under **144** and **211**. Here the speaker describes the machinations of his adversaries following the death of Euctemon. In §§41–42 "these men" are Chaerestratus and his supporters. On search for stolen property cf. **272** Ar. *Clouds* 497–99 and scholion; with "they barred [*apeklêisan*] the door" (§40) cf. **267b** Lys. 10.15–17.

. . . when Euctemon too died, they reached such a level of audacity that, while he lay dead in the house, they kept the slaves under guard, so that no one could report [the death] to his daughters or his wife or any of his family; and along with the woman, they removed the property from inside [the house] to the contiguous house, which one of my adversaries, Antidorus there, had rented and was living in. [40] And even when Euctemon's daughters and wife came, having heard the news from others, even then they would not allow them to come in; they barred [*apeklêisan*] the door, claiming that the women had no right to bury Euctemon. They were able to get in only with difficulty, around sunset. [41] When they went in, they found that Euctemon was lying dead in the house for the second day now, as the slaves said, and that everything had been removed from the house by my adversaries. So the women . . . occupied themselves with the deceased, and these men immediately displayed the condition of things inside the house to those who had accompanied them, and they first asked the slaves, in the presence of my adversaries, where the property had been taken. [42] When they said that my adversaries had removed it to the house next door, and these men immediately demanded to conduct a search for stolen property [*phôran*] in accordance with the law and demanded the surrender of the slaves who had removed the property, my adversaries refused to do anything just.

287. Xenophon, *Hellenica* 1.7.22. Law, with procedure and penalty, on temple-robbery and treason. (*Hellenica* published *post* 362; date of event described 406/5)

> See references and headnote under **237**; also P. **Krentz**, *Xenophon*: Hellenika *I–II.3.10* (Warminster 1989: text, translation, and commentary). At *Hellenica* 1.7.16–33, Xenophon recounts the speech delivered by Euryptolemus concerning the Athenian generals who were held responsible for the loss of shipwrecked sailors following the Battle of Arginusae (406/5: **375** Xen. *Hell.* 1.7.1–16, 20–26, 34–35). Euryptolemus argues that the procedure being used to try the generals is improper and unconstitutional, and suggests alternatives. Temple-robbery and treason (see chapter 12) are also juxtaposed at Xenophon, *Apology* 25 (along with other capital offenses); Plato, *Republic* 442e-443a (along with embezzlement, theft, and other offenses); Antiphon 5.10; Demosthenes 23.26; cf. also Lysias 28.11 (treason, theft of public property, and receiving bribes).

"Or, if you wish, try them in accordance with this law, which applies to temple-robbers [*hierosylois*] and traitors [*prodotais*], and which states that if a person either betrays the city or steals [*kleptêi*] sacred property [*ta hiera*], he shall be tried in a jury-court [*dikastêriôi*], and if he is convicted, he shall not be buried in Attica, and his property shall be confiscated."

288. Demosthenes 22 *Against Androtion* 25–27, 69–73. *Apagôgê*, *ephêgêsis*, *graphê klopês*, and *dikê klopês* as remedies for theft; temple-robbery; impiety (*asebeia*). (355/4)

See references and headnote under **63**. In these passages, the speaker lists remedies for theft (§§25–27) and alleges that Androtion's actions have rendered him liable for theft, temple-robbery, and impiety (*asebeia*: see chapter 11) (§§69–73). On the summary arrest (*apagôgê*) of a thief cf. **57a** Aeschin. 1.91; **289** Dem. 24.104–5, 112–15, 120–21, 129, 146; **292** Isae. 4.28–29; **293** Dem. 45.80–81; **302b** [Arist.] *Ath. Pol.* 52.1; 1,000 dr. was the amount of the fine levied upon the prosecutor in an *apagôgê* or a *graphê* (and in other public lawsuits) who received less than one-fifth of the jurors' votes (p. 33). On *ephêgêsis* see p. 30; on the *graphê klopês* see the introduction to this chapter. For the *dikê klopês* cf. **276** Isoc. 20.6; **281** Lys. 29.1–2, 11; **282** Pl. *Protagoras* 321c-322a; **289** Dem. 24.104–5, 112–15, 120–21, 129, 146; "an arbitrator" in this case refers to a public arbitrator (p. 36). Despite the speaker's attribution, it is unlikely that all these procedures originated with Solon (for the citation of Solon as default legislator see p. 4). The procession mentioned in §69 occurred at the festival of Athena known as the Panathenaea (cf. **254** Dem. 39.1, 5, 7–18; **331** [Arist.] *Ath. Pol.* 60.2–3); on the war-tax (*eisphora*) see p. 26 and cf., e.g., **254** Dem. 39.1, 5, 7–18. For the grouping of temple-robbery, impiety, theft, and "all the most terrible offenses" compare the very similar language at Demosthenes 24.177.

And in fact you must understand that Solon, who established these laws and the majority of the rest, . . . allowed those who were willing to exact punishment from wrongdoers not just in one way for each individual offense, but in many ways. . . . [26] He thought that no one should be deprived of obtaining justice in the manner in which each was able. How, then, would this happen? If by means of his laws he were to grant many ways to go after wrongdoers, as, for example, for theft [*klopês*]. You are strong and confident in yourself: arrest [*apage*] [the thief]; the risk is 1,000 drachmas. You are weaker: lead [*ephêgou*] the magistrates to him; they will do it. You fear even that: bring an indictment [*graphou*]. [27] You lack confidence in yourself and, being a working man, would not be able to pay 1,000 drachmas: bring a lawsuit [*dikazou*] for theft [*klopês*] before an arbitrator, and you will risk nothing.

. . .

[69] . . . What do you want me to mention? How he repaired the vessels carried in the procession, and his destruction of the crowns, or his fine fashioning of the bowls? Well, for these very actions, even if he had not done the city any other wrong, he clearly deserves to die three times, not just once, since he is

guilty of temple-robbery [*hierosyliai*] and impiety [*asebeiai*] and theft [*klopêi*] and all the most terrible offenses. [70] Now, I will pass over the majority of what he said in his attempt to deceive you; but he claimed that the crowns' leaves were falling off and were rotten due to age—as though they were from violets or roses rather than gold—and so persuaded you to melt them down. Then he added a clause stating that the public slave should be present at payments of the war-tax [*eisphorais*] . . . ; but in the case of the crowns that he broke to pieces, he did not add this same just clause but instead himself became politician, goldsmith, treasurer, and clerk of accounts. [71] [To Androtion:] And yet if you demanded that we entrust to you everything that you do for the city, you would not be detected [*ephôrô*] as a thief [*kleptês*] so easily. As it is, though, you established, as is right, that in the case of payments of the war-tax the city trust not you but its own slaves. But when you conduct some other business and meddle with sacred property, some of which was not even dedicated in our lifetime, and you manifestly have not written in the same protection as for payments of the war-tax, isn't it obvious why you did so? I think it is. [72] [To the jury:] . . . I think you all see, written at the bottom of the stands below the crowns, "The allies [have crowned] the people [*ton dêmon*] for manly virtue and justice," or "The allies [have dedicated this crown] to Athena as a prize for valor," or, in the case of individual cities, "So-and-so [have crowned] the people, having been saved by the people"; for example, "The Euboeans, having been liberated, have crowned the people," or again, "Conon [dedicated this crown] from the sea battle against the Spartans." Such, you see, were the inscriptions on the crowns. [73] So, then, these inscriptions, which brought you much admiration and honor, have disappeared now that the crowns have been destroyed.

289. Demosthenes 24 *Against Timocrates* 104–5, 112–15, 120–21, 129, 146. Laws, procedures, and penalties for theft: *euthynai*, *apagôgê*, theft from public places, *dikê klopês*, *endeixis*, temple-robbery, theft of public and sacred property; treason (*prodosia*); subversion of the people (*katalysis tou dêmou*). (353/2)

See **160** with references and headnote. In these passages, the speaker discusses a wide variety of legal remedies for various kinds of theft. The hooked brackets {} surrounding the text of the alleged theft law in §105 signify that the text is spurious: it does not give a full and accurate statement of the provisions read out by the court clerk at this point. However, the laws that were read out did include clauses on the binding of a thief, in the form of an "additional punishment" imposed by the (*h*)*êliaia* (see **267b** Lys. 10.15–17) upon conviction in a *dikê klopês* (cf. §§114–15 and **160** Dem. 24.103, 107, which treats confinement in the stocks as mandatory for all such convicted thieves who were not sentenced to death), and possibly also in the form of imprisonment supervised by the Eleven in the case of *apagôgê* and/or *ephêgêsis* (cf. §146). The interpolator has in all probability used genuine laws as his sources: cf. **267b** Lys. 10.15–17 (note, however, that the duration of confinement in the stocks is there given as ten days). Many scholars reject the authenticity of the tenfold penalty in the case where the victim does not recover his property; cf. §§114–15, where only double damages and confinement are mentioned. (On maltreatment of parents see **§6.4.1**; on *astrateia*, failure to serve on a military campaign, see **387** Lyc. 1 [selections] with additional references in headnote.) On theft of public and sacred property by magistrates (§§111–12, 120–21, 129), cf. **271** Thuc. 2.65.3–4, Pl. *Gorgias* 516a, Plut. *Pericles* 32.1–4, 35.4–5; **273** Ar. *Wasps* 836–47, 893–900, 931–35, 952–66; **277** Lys. 30.21, 23–25; **279** Lys. 27.3–4, 6–7; **295** Aeschin. 1.110–13; **297** Dem. 19.293–94; **299** [Dem.] 58.14–15; **301** Aeschin. 3.10; **302a** [Arist.] *Ath. Pol.* 48.4–5, 54.2. For the *agoranomoi* (Market Commissioners) see **241** Ar. *Wasps* 1389–1408; for the *astynomoi* (City Magistrates) see **65** [Arist.] *Ath. Pol.* 50.1–2; "deme dicasts" is an alternate title for the Forty (p. 14; cf. **302a**). On *apagôgê* for theft (§113; cf. §146) cf. **288** Dem. 22.25–27, 69–73 with additional references in headnote. The Lyceum, Academy, and Cynosarges (§114; cf. **197** Harpo. s.v. *notheia*) were gymnasia, public sites for athletic and intellectual training. That the list of public places given in §114 (cf. **303** Hyp. 5 col. 26) is not complete may be indicated by Aristotle, *Problems* 952a17–20: "Why is it that if a person steals [*klepsêi*] from a public bath or a wrestling-ground or the agora or another such place, he is penalized with death, but if a person steals from a house, he pays twice the value of what he stole?" On the *dikê klopês* (§114) cf. **288** with additional references in headnote. "Daric" (§129) is a synonym for "stater" (see **205** Lys. 19.39–40). In §146, on *endeixis* (denunciation) see p. 30 and cf. **299** [Dem.] 58.14–15; **302b** [Arist.] *Ath. Pol.* 52.1, and for other offenses, e.g., **8a** Ant. 5.9; on treason and subversion see chapter 12.

LAWS ON THEFT [*klopês*], MALTREATMENT OF PARENTS [*kakôseôs goneôn*], AND FAILURE TO SERVE ON A MILITARY CAMPAIGN [*astrateias*]. [105] {Whatever a person loses, if he gets it back, the punishment shall be double, and if he does not, tenfold, on top of the additional punishments [*epaitiois*]. He shall be bound in the stocks [*podokakkêi*] by the foot for five days and as many nights, if the *hêliaia* imposes this as an additional punishment [*prostimêsêi*]. Whoever wishes may propose additional punishment [*prostimasthai*] when the penal assessment [*timêmatos*] is being determined. . . .}

. . .

[111] . . . but when Androtion had to pay back the money that he had long

ago stolen [*hyphêirêto*] from the city—some of it sacred, some profane—then [Timocrates] proposed his law in order to deprive you of the double penalty in profane matters and the tenfold penalty in sacred matters. . . . [112] It seems to me that he deserves to suffer any penalty you could name: he thinks that if a person who has been Market Commissioner [*agoranomos*] or City Magistrate [*astynomos*] or deme dicast is convicted of theft [*klopês*] at his review [*euthynais*], . . . the tenfold penalty should apply to that man . . . ; but if men have been chosen as ambassadors by the Assembly—men who are wealthy—and have stolen [*hypheilonto*] a lot of money, some of it sacred and some profane, and have had it in their possession for a long time, he has devised for them a very precise way to suffer none of what either the laws or the decrees ordain.

[113] And yet Solon, men of the jury, . . . enacted a law providing that if a person stole [*kleptoi*] more than 50 drachmas by day, there should be summary arrest [*apagôgên*] to the Eleven, and if a person stole [*kleptoi*] anything at all at night, it should be permitted to chase and kill or wound him, or to arrest [*apagagein*] him and take him to the Eleven, if one so chose; and that anyone convicted of the offenses for which these summary arrests are permitted should not be allowed to appoint sureties and pay restitution for his thefts, but the penalty should be death. [114] Also, if a person stole [*hypheloito*] a cloak or a little oil-flask or any other thing, however cheap, from the Lyceum or from the Academy or from Cynosarges, or if he stole a piece of equipment from the gymnasia or from the harbors, over the value of 10 drachmas, for these too Solon legislated that the penalty was to be death. And if a person was convicted in a private lawsuit for theft [*idian dikên klopês*], he was to pay double the value assessed [*timêthen*], and the jury-court [*dikastêriôi*] was to be permitted to inflict upon the thief, on top of the monetary fine, the additional penalty [*prostimêsai*] of bondage [*desmon*] for five days and the same number of nights, so that all might see him bound. You just heard these laws [read out] a little earlier. [115] Solon believed that the man who committed shameful acts should not escape with only paying back what he stole [*hypheileto*] . . . but should pay it back double and, by suffering bondage in addition to this penal assessment, should live the rest of his life from then on in shame.

. . .

[120] Nor can [Timocrates] say that those on whose behalf he devised his law are not both thieves [*kleptai*] and temple-robbers [*hierosyloi*]: they have robbed [*sesylêkotes*] sacred property—the goddess' tithes and the other gods' two-percent offerings—and keep it themselves instead of paying it back; and they have stolen [*keklophotes*] the profane property that was coming to you. Their temple-robbery differs from the rest in that they never brought the money to the Acropolis at all, although they were supposed to. [121] As I see it, . . . this hubris and arrogance has not come upon Androtion by accident but has

been sent by the goddess, in order that . . . my adversaries destroy themselves by litigating against each other and pay back the money tenfold in accordance with the laws, or else be imprisoned.

. . .

[129] . . . And then, when [Glaucetes] was treasurer on the Acropolis, did he not steal [*hyphêirêmenos*] from the Acropolis the city's prizes for valor, which it took from the barbarians—the silver-footed throne and Mardonius' sword that weighed 300 darics?

. . .

[146] . . . You see, men of the jury, you would not be permitted to assess as a penalty [*timan*] "whatever [a convicted defendant] must suffer or pay" (since bondage [*desmos*] falls within "suffering"; it would not, then, be possible to assess a penalty of bondage), nor, for offenses for which denunciation [*endeixis*] or summary arrest [*apagôgê*] is available, would the additional clause have been written in the laws, "Let the Eleven bind in the stocks the man who is denounced or arrested," unless it were permitted to imprison people other than those who assemble with the purpose of treason [*prodosiai*] against the city or subversion of the people [*katalysei tou dêmou*], or who purchase tax contracts and fail to pay.

290. [Demosthenes] 35 *Against Lacritus* 47. *Toichôrychoi* and thieves as *kakourgoi.* (355–338)

See references and headnote under **171**. Here the speaker classifies wall-diggers (*toichôrychoi*) and thieves (*kleptai*) as *kakourgoi* (malefactors) liable to *apagôgê* to the Eleven and a death sentence upon conviction. Cf. **57a** Aeschin. 1.91; **283** Xen. *Mem.* 1.2.62; **288** Dem. 22.25–27, 69–73 with additional references in headnote. On mercantile contracts see chapter 10.

Well, then, where should one get justice concerning mercantile contracts, men of the jury? With what magistracy, or within what time? With the Eleven? But they bring to court wall-diggers [*toichôrychous*] and thieves [*kleptas*] and the other malefactors [*kakourgous*] who face the death penalty.

291. Aristotle, *Rhetoric* 1373b38–1374a5, 1374a15–16. Theft and temple-robbery. (?350s-322)

See references and headnote under **47**. In this part of the *Rhetoric*, Aristotle is advocating the stricter definition of legal offenses (on the characteristic lack of such definition in Athenian law see p. 28 and cf., e.g., **35** Dem. 21.47). Aristotle's implication that *hierosylia* (temple-robbery) necessarily involved sacred property ("the property of a god") presumably reflects actual legal practice, whether or not such language appeared in a law. On battery and hubris see chapter 2; on seduction see chapter 3.

But seeing that people often admit having committed an act but do not admit either the title [of the act] or what the title concerns—for example, [they admit] "taking" [*labein*] but not "stealing" [*klepsai*], or "striking first" [*pataxai proteron*] but not "committing hubris" [*hybrisai*], or "having intercourse" but not "seducing" [*moicheusai*], or "stealing" [*klepsai*] but not "committing temple-robbery" [*hierosylêsai*] (since [the stolen object] is not the property of a god). . . . Nor, if a person took [*elaben*] secretly, did he in all cases steal [*eklepsen*], but only if he did so for the purpose of damage [*blabêi*] [to another] and appropriation for himself.

292. Isaeus 4 *On the Estate of Nicostratus* 28–29. *Apagôgê* of thief caught in the act (*ep' autophôrôi*); role of Eleven; denunciation of *kakourgos* to Council of 500. (?ca. 350)

See references and headnote under **199**. Here the speaker describes the previous career of Chariades. For the *apagôgê* of a thief caught in the act cf. **288** Dem. 22.25–27, 69–73 with additional references in headnote; on *kakourgoi* (malefactors) cf., e.g., **290** [Dem.] 35.47 with additional references in headnote.

You see, my adversary, when he was here in town, first got arrested [*apêchthê*] in the act [*ep' autophôrôi*] as a thief [*kleptês*] and taken to the prison. That time he was released, along with some others, by the Eleven, all of whom you publicly condemned to death. When he was again denounced [*apographeis*] to the Council as a malefactor [*kakourgôn*], he slipped away and left rather than responding [to the charge]; [29] for seventeen years after that he did not return to Athens, until Nicostratus died.

293. Demosthenes 45 *I Against Stephanus* 80–81. *Apagôgê* of thief caught in the act (*ep' autophôrôi*). (?349)

See references and headnote under **56**. Here Apollodorus accuses Phormion of embezzling a significant portion of Pasion's estate. Whether Apollodorus' hypothetical question about forcing a man arrested in the act as a thief (on which cf. **288** Dem. 22.25–27, 69–73 with additional references in headnote) to carry the property in question back to its original location (where, presumably, the owner of the property might confirm or deny having entrusted it to the accused) reflects actual practice or is mere rhetoric cannot be determined. "You were a barbarian when you were bought" refers to Phormion's servile origins.

[To Phormion:] Then you, who commit acts of this sort and who personally have produced such powerful testimonies to your own hubris, have the gall to examine someone else's life? By day you're prudent, but at night you do things for which the punishment is death. . . . [To the jury:] If he were just, he would have managed his master's affairs and would now be a working man. As it is, though, having been established as *kyrios* of property so great in amount that he could escape detection in stealing [*klepsas*] as much of it as he now has, he thinks that he does not owe these things but possesses them as his patrimony! [81] [To Phormion:] And yet, by the gods, if I arrested [*apêgon*] you as a thief [*kleptên*], since I had caught you in the act [*ep' autophôrôi*], and I put on your back the property you were holding (if somehow that was possible), and if I then demanded, if you denied that you had gotten this property by stealing it [*hyphêirêmenos*], that you return it to where you got it from, to whom would you return it? For, you see, your father didn't bequeath it to you, you didn't find it, and you didn't get it from somewhere else before coming to us: you were a barbarian when you were bought. So, then, you, who ought to be publicly put to death for what you have done . . . , brought a counter-indictment [*paregrapsô*] stating that the lawsuit [*dikên*] for the property we named in our charge was inadmissible?

294. Demosthenes 21 *Against Meidias* 44–45. Forcible theft and the *dikê biaiôn*. (347/6)

See references and headnote under **22**. Harpocration (**61** Harpo. s.v. *biaiôn*) is presumably correct in relating the law(s) on forcible theft mentioned here to the *dikê biaiôn* (for acts of violence).

And again, why is it that if a willing person takes from another willing person one or two or ten talents and deprives him of it, he has no business with the city, but if a person takes something of very little value but takes it away by force [*biai*], the laws command that he be punished in addition with a fine payable to the public treasury of the same amount payable to the individual [victim]? [45] Because the lawgiver believed that all things a person does by force are public offenses. . . .

295. Aeschines 1 *Against Timarchus* 110–13. Theft of public (?and of sacred) property. (346/5)

See references and headnote under **57**; also **Hansen**, Eisangelia 119. Here Aeschines alleges that Timarchus has twice stolen public property. In the first instance (§§110–12), the property in question may technically have been sacred, since Timarchus is said to have colluded with the "treasurer of the property of the goddess" (i.e., Athena: cf., e.g., **169** [Dem.] 43.58; **170** Andoc. 1.73–79). "Topknot" (the name of a hairstyle) was the nickname of Hegesippus, a political ally of Aeschines' arch-enemy Demosthenes. "The Council" is the Council of 500, which in its first vote here described used olive leaves, and in the second used its regular "ballot" (either pebbles or the bronze disks used in other lawcourts). The fact that these events occurred during (not at the end of) Timarchus' term on the Council, together with the reference to a jury-court (*dikastêrion*) envisioned in the case of a conviction, indicates that the procedure was *eisangelia* (impeachment: see chapter 12). By law, at the end of each year, the Assembly held a vote whether to bestow upon the outgoing Council the collective "gift" of a gold crown (Demosthenes 22.5, 8). With regard to Timarchus' other previous theft (§113), of which he was convicted, "the laws" adduced by Aeschines are those governing *apagôgê* (cf. **57a** Aeschin. 1.91; **267a** Lys. 10.10; **288** Dem. 22.25–27, 69–73 with additional references in headnote; **300** Libanius, hyp. [Dem.] 25.1–2), whereas his description reveals that Timarchus was tried not by *apagôgê* but by an assessable lawsuit (*agôn timêtos*: p. 40), which is presumably to be identified as that available against a magistrate who has submitted to *euthynai* and is accused of stealing public property (cf. **277** Lys. 30.21, 23–25 with additional references in headnote).

During the same archonship when my adversary was a member of the Council, Hegesander, Topknot's brother, was treasurer of the property of the goddess, and they jointly and in a very comradely manner stole [*eklepton*] from the city 1,000 drachmas. A man of good standing, Pamphilus of the deme Acherdus, realized what was going on. After clashing with my adversary over something and getting angry, he stood up during a meeting of the Assembly and said, "Men of Athens, a man and wife are jointly stealing 1,000 drachmas from you." [111] You wondered what "man and wife" and what he was talking about. After a short pause, he said, "You don't know what I'm talking about? The man is Hegesander there—now, at any rate; he used to be Leodamas' wife—and the wife is Timarchus here. How the money is being stolen, I will tell you." After that he then went through the matter very knowledgeably and clearly. After he explained this, he said, "So what is it, men of Athens, that I advise you to do? If the Council convicts this person here of wrongdoing, votes by leaves to expel him, and hands him over to a jury-court [*dikastêriôi*], give them their gift. But if the Council doesn't punish him, don't give it to them but instead on that day bear it in mind against them." [112] After that, when the Council returned to the Council Hall, it voted by leaves to expel him but then readmitted him by ballot. And because it did not hand him over to a jury-court or expel him from the Council Hall—it pains me to say, but I must say it—it did not receive its gift. . . .

[113] . . . And who among you does not know that [Timarchus] was notoriously exposed as a thief [*kleptês*]? You see, he was dispatched by you as inspector of the mercenaries at Eretria; of the inspectors he alone admitted that he had taken money and did not make his defense on the issue but straightaway started begging you about his penal assessment [*timêmatos*], admitting that he was guilty. You punished [*etimêsate*] those who denied [their guilt] with a talent each, but him with 30 minae. But the laws command that, among thieves [*kleptôn*], those who admit guilt are to be punished with death, while those who deny it are to be put on trial.

296. Demosthenes 57 *Against Eubulides* 63–65. Temple-robbery; attempted burglary. (ca. 345/4)

See references and headnote under **76**. In this passage, Euxitheus accuses his adversaries of committing temple-robbery and attempting to burgle his house. On the office of demarch see **174** [Dem.] 43.57–58; for rents on sacred precincts cf. **169** [Dem.] 43.58. "The oath" is presumably that sworn by Euxitheus' demesmen at the *diapsêphisis* where he was expelled from the deme.

Now, if I must speak about my demarchy, for which certain people are angry at me because during it I became the object of quarrels by exacting debts from many of them, who owed rents on sacred precincts, as well as other public property that they had plundered, I would like you to listen, although perhaps you will assume that these matters are off the topic [*exô tou pragmatos*]. This, too, you see, I can demonstrate as proof that they formed a conspiracy: they erased from the oath the phrase "I shall vote in accordance with my best judgment and for the sake of neither gratitude nor enmity." [64] That became evident, as did the fact that, by committing temple-robbery [*hierosylêsantes*] of the arms . . . that I had dedicated to Athena, and by obliterating the decree that my demesmen had voted for me, my adversaries, who had had public debts exacted by me, were conspiring against me. . . . [65] Here's the most terrible thing of all, which they certainly couldn't say that I concocted. The disaster had just struck me when immediately, as though I were already an exile and a ruined man, some of my adversaries came against my little house in the country at night and tried to pillage what was inside; that's how much they despised you and the laws.

297. Demosthenes 19 *On the False Embassy* 293–94. Theft of public property; *graphê hierôn chrêmatôn* for theft of sacred property. (343)

See especially D. M. **MacDowell**, *Demosthenes:* On the False Embassy *(Oration 19)* (Oxford 2000: text, translation, and commentary); also A. **Schäfer**, *Demosthenes und seine Zeit* (Leipzig 1858–87) 2.382–417; **Blass**, *AB* 3.1.350–67; **Usher**, *GO* 234–37; H. **Yunis**, *Demosthenes, Speeches 18 and 19* (Austin 2005: translation with introduction and notes); D. M. **MacDowell**, *Demosthenes the Orator* (Oxford 2009) 333–42.

Demosthenes delivered this speech in his prosecution of Aeschines for misconduct as an Athenian ambassador to Philip II (see headnote under **24**). Moerocles was evidently accused of embezzling public property (note the parallels drawn with theft of public property in Elis and Megara); on mining concessions farmed out by the Athenian state cf., e.g., **256** Dem. 37 (selections). With the *graphê hierôn chrêmatôn* attested here against Cephisophon (about whose case no further details are known) compare the hypothetical *graphê hierôn* (*scil. chrêmatôn*) *klopês* ("for theft of sacred property"), with a proposed penalty of 2 tal., at Antiphon 2 α 6–9, β 9. The designation *ep' autophôrôi* has no legal significance here, since the context is not *apagôgê*; Demosthenes uses the phrase for the rhetorical purpose of emphasizing the flagrancy of the alleged offenses (cf. **301** Aeschin. 3.10).

[To Eubulus:] Why in the world is it that you accused Moerocles of taking a cut of twenty drachmas from each of the men who purchased mining concessions, and you prosecuted Cephisophon by an indictment for [theft of] sacred property [*graphên hierôn chrêmatôn*] for depositing seven minae at the bank three days late, but as for those who are in possession, confess, and are exposed in the act [*ep' autophôrôi*] as having committed these acts in order to destroy our allies, you don't accuse these men but actually bid us acquit them? [294] And that these are in fact terrible allegations requiring considerable caution and vigilance, while the charges of which you accused those men are a joke, [To the jury:] you will see from the following. Were there some men in Elis who were stealing [*kleptontes*] public property? Very probably. So, did any of them participate in the subversion of the people that just now occurred there? Not one. . . . In Megara, don't you think there is someone who is a thief [*kleptên*] and is secretly taking his cut of public property? Absolutely. And has any of them come to light as responsible for the events that have just now happened there? Not one.

298. [Demosthenes] 59 *Against Neaera* 45–46. Receiving stolen property. (date of speech 343–339; date of event ca. 370)

See references and headnote under **21**. In this passage, Apollodorus describes the private arbitration (see p. 35, and cf., e.g., **244** Isoc. 18.1–8, 10–13, 33, 63) of a dispute between Phrynion and Stephanus over Stephanus' assertion of Neaera's status as a free woman and Neaera's leaving Phrynion to cohabit with Stephanus. On "taking away to freedom" (*aphairesis eis eleutherian*), the subject of a dedicated *dikê*, see the introduction to chapter 8. *Kyria* is the feminine form of *kyrios*, on which term see the introduction to chapter 5; as a metic, Neaera still required a male citizen patron (*prostatês*: p. 23). For "clothes and gold jewelry," the standard phrase for a woman's personal property, cf., e.g., **103** Isae. 2.7–9; **118** Isae. 8.7–8.

So, then, when Phrynion filed a lawsuit [*dikên*] against [Stephanus], alleging that he had taken this woman Neaera away from him to freedom and that he had received the property that she had taken when she left his house, their friends brought them together and convinced them to submit the matter to arbitration by themselves. Satyrus of the deme Alopece, Lacedaemonius' brother, sat as arbitrator for Phrynion, and Saurias of the deme Lamptrae for my adversary Stephanus here. They selected in addition to themselves as joint arbitrator Diogeiton of the deme Acharnae. [46] So they assembled in the temple, heard what had happened from both parties and from the woman herself, and declared their judgment, and these two abided by it; namely, that the woman should be free and should be *kyria* of herself, but as for the property that Neaera had taken when she left Phrynion's house, apart from the clothes and gold jewelry and female slaves that had been bought for the woman personally, everything was to be returned to Phrynion.

299. [Demosthenes] 58 *Against Theocrines* 14–15. *Euthynai* and conviction of magistrate for theft of sacred property; law on *endeixis* (denunciation) for public or sacred debt. (ca. 340)

See references and headnote under **77**. The speaker here alleges that Theocrines has not paid the fine of 700 dr. levied when he was convicted of theft at his *euthynai* (cf. **277** Lys. 30.21, 23–25 with additional references in headnote) and is therefore liable to *endeixis* (p. 30; cf. **289** Dem. 24.104–5, 112–15, 120–21, 129, 146 with additional references in headnote) as owing a sacred debt. On the Eponymous Heroes, and for debts owed on sacred precincts, see **169** [Dem.] 43.58; **296** Dem. 57.63–65. For the bar on state debtors' prosecuting *graphai* (indictments), which was an element of their *atimia* (disfranchisement), see **170** Andoc. 1.73–79.

These, then, are two of the laws that he has broken—this man, who indicts [*graphomenos*] others for illegal proposals [*paranomôn*]. And the third is the law that commands that any willing citizen may conduct denunciations [*endeixeis*] in similar fashion against those who owe money to the public treasury and against anyone who owes money to Athena or any of the other gods or Eponymous Heroes. This is what my adversary will be proven to have done: he owes and has not repaid 700 drachmas, which he was sentenced to pay at his review [*euthynais*], to the Eponymous Hero of his own tribe. [To the court clerk:] Please read this part of this law.

LAW.

[15] Stop. [To Theocrines:] You there, do you hear what it says? "Or any of the Eponymous Heroes."

. . .

My adversary, men of the jury, would probably have consideration for few men . . . , given that, in the presence of his tribesmen, he felt neither fear nor shame: for one thing, he managed their common property in such a way that they convicted him of theft [*klopên*], and for another, although he is a debtor and knows full well that the laws prevent him from prosecuting indictments [*graphesthai graphas*] until he pays up, he violates them and thinks that while other debtors should have no share in public affairs, he himself is more powerful than the laws.

300. Libanius, hypothesis to [Demosthenes] 25 *1 Against Aristogeiton* 1–2. *Apagôgê* to Council of 500 of suspected temple-robber caught in the act; *graphê paranomôn*. (date of composition 4th c. A.D.; date of event described 332/1 B.C.)

See especially H. **Weil**, *Les plaidoyers politiques de Démosthène*, ser. 2 (Paris 1886: text and French commentary for [Dem.] 25 and hypothesis); J. H. **Vince**, *Demosthenes III: Against Meidias, Androtion, Aristocrates, Timocrates, Aristogeiton: XXI–XXVI* (Cambridge, MA 1935: text and translation of [Dem.] 25); G. **Mathieu**, *Démosthène: Plaidoyers politiques, Tome IV:* Sur la couronne, Contre Aristogiton I *et* II (Paris 1947: text, French translation, and notes for [Dem.] 25 and hypothesis); M. H. **Hansen**, Apagoge, Endeixis *and* Ephegesis *against* Kakourgoi, Atimoi *and* Pheugontes (Odense 1976) 30–35, 139–40; I. **Worthington**, *A Historical Commentary on Dinarchus* (Ann Arbor 1992) 298–99; **MacDowell**, *DO* 298–313; also **Schäfer**, *Demosthenes* 4.113–29; **Blass**, *AB* 3.1.408–18.

This extract from Libanius' hypothesis (introduction: see headnote under **253**) to [Demosthenes] 25 *1 Against Aristogeiton* is the fullest account we have of the incident described. Comparison with the other references, [Dem.] 25.87 and Deinarchus 2.12, indicates that the priestess in question served the cult of the goddess Artemis at Brauron (in eastern Attica) and was related to Hierocles. Reference to the *prytaneis* (p. 6; cf. **271c** Plut. *Pericles* 32.1–4, 35.4–5) shows that the *apagôgê* was lodged first with the Council of 500 (cf. **292** Isae. 4.28–29) and then brought before the Assembly. On *apagôgê* for temple-robbery cf. **269** Cic. *On Divination* 1.54; **283** Xen. *Mem.* 1.2.62; on the *graphê paranomôn* (for illegal proposals) see p. 14.

Pythangelus and Scaphon, seeing Hierocles carrying sacred clothing, on which there were inscriptions in gold identifying the dedicators, arrested [*apagousi*] him and took him to the *prytaneis* as a temple-robber [*hierosylon*], and the next day the *prytaneis* brought him before the Assembly. Hierocles asserted that he had been sent by the priestess to take the clothing, in order to convey it to the sacred hunt. Thereupon Aristogeiton proposed a decree that in the first place had not been subject to deliberation by the Council and in the second place was most fearsome: it ordered that if Hierocles admitted removing the clothing, he should be put to death immediately, and if he denied it, he should be put on trial. [2] The result of this would have been that if he admitted the truth, he would have been executed straightaway, while if he denied it, he would have suffered the same thing a short time later. Phanostratus, the father of the endangered Hierocles, indicted this decree as illegal [*grapsamenos paranomôn*], with Demosthenes joining him in the prosecution. He secured a conviction for an illegal proposal, and the jury-court [*dikastêrion*] fined Aristogeiton five talents.

301. Aeschines 3 *Against Ctesiphon* 10. *Euthynai* and theft of public property by magistrate. (330)

See references and headnote under **27**. Since the procedure being described is not *apagôgê* but *euthynai* (cf. **277** Lys. 30.21, 23–25 with additional references in headnote), the use of the phrase *ep' autophôrôi* is purely rhetorical (cf. **297** Dem. 19.293–94).

For very many magistrates under review [*hypeuthynôn*] who were exposed in the act [*ep' autophôrôi*] as thieves [*kleptai*] of public property [*tôn dêmosiôn chrêmatôn*] were escaping with acquittals from the jury-courts [*dikastêriôn*], and reasonably so: the jurors, I assume, were ashamed that the same man in the same city should be seen some short time ago announced at the games as being awarded a gold crown by the people for virtue and justice, but the same man a little later should leave the jury-court having been convicted of theft [*klopês*] at his review [*euthynas*].

302. [Aristotle], *Constitution of the Athenians* (*Ath. Pol.*) (selections). (332–322)

See references and headnote under **1c**. The first pair of passages below (**302a**) discusses the *euthynai* (review of conduct in office) that Athenian magistrates underwent at the end of their terms (p. 32; cf. **277** Lys. 30.21, 23–25 with additional references in headnote). The deme dicasts (§48.5) are identical with the Forty (cf. **289** Dem. 24.104–5, 112–15, 120–21, 129, 146); on the role of the *thesmothetai* cf. **273** Ar. *Wasps* 836–47, 893–900, 931–35, 952–66. The "advocates" (*synêgoroi*) in §54.2 are special prosecutors, not (as usually) a litigant's supporting speakers (p. 28; cf. **371** [Plut.] *Lives of the Ten Orators* 833d-834b). On bribery see chapter 12 and cf. **271c** Plut. *Pericles* 32.1–4, 35.4–5; **279** Lys. 27.3–4, 6–7; **281** Lys. 29.1–2, 11. "Wrongdoing" (*adikiou*) in the clause "they penalize him for wrongdoing" is here the technical name of a charge. For the tenfold fine for theft of public property cf. **381** Dem. 24.127; for the division of the year into prytanies see p. 6. The final passage (**302b**) discusses the duties of the Eleven. On *apagôgê* cf. **288** Dem. 22.25–27, 69–73 with additional references in headnote; on *endeixis* cf. **289** Dem. 24.104–5, 112–15, 120–21, 129, 146; **299** [Dem.] 58.14–15; on *apographê* (confiscation) cf. **281** Lys. 29.1–2, 11; **285** *SEG* 12.100.1–16; **319** *SEG* 12.100.16–21, 23–25, 30–39; [Aristotle], *Constitution of the Athenians* (*Ath. Pol.*) 47.2–5. For the *pôlêtai* cf. **2** *IG* I[3] 104. The participle "summarily arrested" (*apagomenous*) grammatically refers only to "thieves," but other sources (**267a** Lys. 10.10; **283** Xen. *Mem.* 1.2.62) demonstrate that *apagôgê* applied also to kidnappers and clothes-snatchers.

a. *Ath. Pol.* 48.4–5, 54.2. *Euthynai* (magistrate's end-of-term review): theft of public property, receiving bribes, and fiscal "wrongdoing" (*adikion*) by magistrate.

They also allot examiners [*euthynous*], one from each tribe, and two assistants [*paredrous*] for each examiner. . . . And if a person wishes to submit a charge for review [*euthynan*], whether private or public, against anyone who has rendered his accounts for review [*euthynas*] in the jury-court [*dikastêriôi*], within three days of the day when he rendered his accounts for review, he writes on a whitened tablet his name, that of the defendant, and whatever offense he charges, adds in writing whatever penal assessment [*timêma*] he decides upon, and gives it to the examiner. [48.5] The examiner takes this and reads it. If he finds against [the accused], he hands over private charges to the deme dicasts who introduce lawsuits for the relevant tribe; public charges he reports in writing to the *thesmothetai*. If the *thesmothetai* admit the charge for review, they introduce it again to the jury-court, and whatever the jurors decide is binding.

. . .

[54.2] They also allot ten auditors [*logistas*] and ten advocates [*synêgorous*] for them, to whom all those who have held office must submit an account. These are the only ones who conduct an audit for magistrates subject to review and who introduce the review [*euthynas*] to the jury-court [*dikastêrion*]. If they prove that a person is a thief [*kleptont'*], the jurors convict him of theft [*klopên*] and the amount determined [to have been stolen] is paid back tenfold. If they demonstrate that a person has taken bribes and the jurors convict him, they penalize him for bribery [*dôrôn*], and this too is paid back tenfold. If they convict him of wrongdoing, they penalize him for wrongdoing [*adikiou*]. This is paid back in the simple amount if a person pays before the ninth prytany; otherwise, it is doubled. The tenfold penalty, though, is not doubled.

b. *Ath. Pol.* 52.1. Duties of the Eleven: *apagôgê*, *apographê*, and *endeixis*.

[The Athenians] appoint the Eleven by lot as well. They are to oversee those in the prison, and as for summarily arrested [*apagomenous*] thieves [*kleptas*] and kidnappers [*andrapodistas*] and clothes-snatchers [*lôpodytas*], if they confess, they are to punish them with death; but if they dispute the matter, they are to bring them to the jury-court [*dikastêrion*], and if they are acquitted, they are to let them go, but if not, then they are to put them to death. They are also to bring to the jury-court plots of land and houses that are registered for confiscation [*apographomena*], and to hand over to the *pôlêtai* those that are found to be public property. They are also to introduce denunciations [*endeixeis*]: the Eleven introduce these too, but the *thesmothetai* also introduce some denunciations.

303. Hypereides 5 *Against Demosthenes* col. 26. Theft of public and/or sacred property; theft from Academy. (324/3)

See especially D. **Whitehead**, *Hypereides: The Forensic Speeches* (Oxford 2000: translation and commentary); D. D. **Phillips**, *Athenian Political Oratory: 16 Key Speeches* (New York and London 2004: translation with introduction and notes); also **Blass**, *AB* 3.2.72–76; G. **Colin**, *Hypéride: Discours* (Paris 1946: text, French translation, and notes); **Usher**, *GO* 337–38; I. **Worthington**, *Greek Orators II: Dinarchus and Hyperides* (Warminster 1999: text, translation, and commentary); I. **Worthington**-C. **Cooper**-E. M.

Harris, *Dinarchus, Hyperides, and Lycurgus* (Austin 2001: translation with introduction and notes).

Hypereides delivered this speech in the prosecution of Demosthenes over the Harpalus affair (see the headnote under **67** Din. 1.23, and **391** [*Apophasis* against Demosthenes and others for receiving bribes in the Harpalus affair]). Owing to the fragmentary nature of the papyrus on which it is preserved, Hypereides 5 is customarily cited by columns of the papyrus rather than by editorial sections. The theoric allotment of 5 dr. per year was a payment by the state treasury (from the designated "theoric fund") that financed the attendance of religious festivals by poor Athenians; hence Conon's misappropriation could be viewed as theft of public and/or of sacred property. "These men" refers to Demosthenes and his fellow defendants (exactly who prosecuted Conon is unknown); the legal action employed against Conon is not identified but was evidently assessable (*timêtos*: p. 40). On theft from the Academy (and other public places) cf. **289** Dem. 24.104–5, 112–15, 120–21, 129, 146, at §114; the lacuna at the end of the passage prevents our knowing what happened to Aristomachus.

Because Conon of the deme Paeania took the theoric allotment for his son, who was abroad, for the sake of five drachmas, and despite throwing himself on your mercy, he was fined a talent in the jury-court [*dikastêriôi*], with these men as his prosecutors. And because Aristomachus, after becoming president of the Academy, moved a spade from the wrestling-ground to his own garden, which was nearby, and used it and. . . .

CHAPTER 10

Contracts and Commerce

Handbooks: J. H. **Lipsius**, *Das attische Recht und Rechtsverfahren* (Leipzig 1905–15) 674–773; A. R. W. **Harrison**, *The Law of Athens* (Oxford 1968–71) 1.244–48, 253–304, 316–17; D. M. **MacDowell**, *The Law in Classical Athens* (Ithaca, NY 1978) 133–47, 155–59, 220–34; S. C. **Todd**, *The Shape of Athenian Law* (Oxford 1993) 59, 232–57, 262–68, 316–25, 334–40; A. **Maffi**, "Family and Property Law," and E. E. **Cohen**, "Commercial Law," in *The Cambridge Companion to Ancient Greek Law*, ed. M. Gagarin-D. Cohen (Cambridge 2005) 254–66, 290–302. **Studies:** L. **Gernet**, "Sur les actions commerciales en droit athénien," *REG* 51 (1938) 1–44 (repr. in ***idem,*** *Droit et société dans la Grèce ancienne* [Paris 1955] 173–200); F. **Pringsheim**, *The Greek Law of Sale* (Weimar 1950); L. **Gernet**, "Le droit de la vente et la notion du contrat en Grèce: d'après M. Pringsheim," *Revue historique de droit français et étranger* 29 (1951) 560–84 (repr. in ***idem,*** *Droit et société dans la Grèce ancienne* [Paris 1955] 201–24); M. I. **Finley**, "Some Problems of Greek Law: A Consideration of Pringsheim on Sale," *Seminar* 9 (1951) 72–91; J. V. A. **Fine**, *Horoi: Studies in Mortgage, Real Security and Land Tenure in Ancient Athens* (Baltimore 1951); H. J. **Wolff**, "Die Grundlagen des griechischen Vertragsrechts," *ZSS* 74 (1957) 26–72; E. E. **Cohen**, *Ancient Athenian Maritime Courts* (Princeton 1973); S. **Isager**-M. H. **Hansen**, *Aspects of Athenian Society in the Fourth Century B.C.: A Historical Introduction to and Commentary on the Paragraphe-speeches and the Speech Against Dionysodorus in the Corpus Demosthenicum (XXXII–XXXVIII and LVI)* (Odense 1975); M. H. **Hansen**, "Two Notes on the Athenian *Dikai Emporikai*," in *Symposion 1979: Vorträge zur griechischen und hellenistischen Rechtsgeschichte*, ed. P. Dimakis (Köln 1983) 167–75; M. I. **Finley**, *Studies in Land and Credit in Ancient Athens, 500–200 B.C.: The* Horos *Inscriptions*, repr. with a new introduction by P. Millett (New Brunswick, NJ 1985 [original edition New Brunswick, NJ 1952]); E. M. **Harris**, "When Is a Sale Not a Sale?: The Riddle of Athenian

Terminology for Real Security Revisited," *CQ* 38 (1988) 351–81 (repr. with addenda in ***idem***, *Democracy and the Rule of Law in Classical Athens* [Cambridge 2006] 163–206); P. **Millett**, "Sale, Credit and Exchange in Athenian Law and Society," in *Nomos: Essays in Athenian Law, Politics, and Society*, ed. P. Cartledge-P. Millett-S. C. Todd (Cambridge 1990) 167–94; P. **Millett**, *Lending and Borrowing in Ancient Athens* (Cambridge 1991); E. M. **Harris**, "*Apotimema*: Athenian Terminology for Real Security in Leases and Dowry Arrangements," *CQ* 43 (1993) 73–95 (repr. with addenda in ***idem***, *Democracy and the Rule of Law in Classical Athens* [Cambridge 2006] 207–39); D. C. **Mirhady**, "Contracts in Athens," in *Law, Rhetoric, and Comedy in Classical Athens: Essays in Honour of Douglas M. MacDowell*, ed. D. L. Cairns-R. A. Knox (Swansea 2004) 51–63; E. M. **Harris**, "Law and Economy in Classical Athens: [Demosthenes] *Against Dionysodorus*," in ***idem***, *Democracy and the Rule of Law in Classical Athens* (Cambridge 2006) 143–62; E. **Carawan**, "The Athenian Law of Agreement," *GRBS* 46 (2006) 339–74; A. **Lanni**, *Law and Justice in the Courts of Classical Athens* (Cambridge 2006) 149–74; D. D. **Phillips**, "Hypereides 3 and the Athenian Law of Contracts," *TAPA* 139 (2009) 89–122.

In his *Nicomachean Ethics* (1131a2–9), composed between 335 and 322, the philosopher Aristotle lists as examples of "voluntary obligations"—that is, contracts—sale and purchase (*prasis ônê*), loan for consumption (*daneismos*: typically loan of money), pledge (*engyê*), loan for use (*chrêsis*), deposit (*parakatathêkê*), and hire (*misthôsis*). This list includes most, but not all (the exception is partnership, *koinônia*), of the chief types of contract employed in Classical Athens. The present chapter addresses contracts in general (**§10.1**: **304–308**) and contracts of sale and of loan for consumption, the best-attested types of contract in our sources, in specific (**§§10.2–10.5**: **309–328**); the final section (**§10.5**: **322–328**) addresses laws concerning imports and exports and the allied and specially-regulated categories of maritime loans and the *dikai emporikai* (mercantile lawsuits).

For material concerning other types of contract see the following examples. On pledge, including marital pledge and suretyship: **320**; chapter 5 *passim*; **260** [Dem.] 33.19–20, 22, 32–33. On loan for use: **262** Hyp. 3.5–11, 18, 21–22. On deposit: **242** Isoc. 21.2–3; **246** Isoc. 17.2–9, 11–16; **247** [Dem.] 52.3–10, 12–15. On hire, including lease of real property: **321d**; **65** [Arist.] *Ath. Pol.* 50.1–2; **66** Hyp. 4.3; **116** Harpo. (selections); **117** Pollux, *Onomasticon* (selections); **§6.3**; **248** [Dem.] 53.19–20; **253** Dem. 36.2–4, 12, 18–20; **258** *IG* II^2 2492.1–31; **262** Hyp. 3.5–11, 18, 21–22. On partnership: **236** [Dem.] 48.22–32; **259** [Dem.] 48 (selections). The specific difference between loan for consumption and loan for use is that upon the expiry of the loan, loan for consumption entails the return of property of equivalent value (if *A* lends *B* 1,000 dr., *B* must return to *A* 1,000 dr. plus any accrued interest, but *B* is not expected, much less required, to return the exact coins that *A* lent him), while loan for use entails return of the exact property lent (if *A* lends *B* a mule, *B* must return the same mule to *A*). Loan for use differs from hire in that hire involves the receipt of compensation (rent) by the lender, while loan for use does not.

The Athenian law of contracts in general (**§10.1**: **304–308**) was enshrined in a statute, probably of Archaic date and quite possibly the work of Solon (**304**), that recognized as binding "whatever one person agrees with another." Although the language of a contract (*synthêkê*, plural *synthêkai* used of a single contract or of multiple contracts, corresponding verb *syntithesthai*; similarly *symbolaion*, plural *symbolaia*, corresponding verb *symballein*; *synallagma*, plural *synallagmata*, corresponding verb *synallattein*; cf. *homologia* "agreement," plural *homologiai*, corresponding verb *homologein* "to agree") might assert its paramount validity as against any contradictory law or decree (**307**, **323a**), the latitude of the right to contract was limited in some areas. Solon prohibited the contracting of loans on the security of the person (**313**) and outlawed the export of agricultural produce other than olive oil (**322**), which will have invalidated contracts formed for this purpose; the same principle was expressly applied to contracts concluded in violation of the law prohibiting Athenian residents from extending maritime loans on ships that were not transporting grain to Athens (**323c**). With the possible exception of the *dikai emporikai* (**326**), Athenian law did not regulate the form of a contract, which could be written (e.g., **308**, **321f**, **323a**) or oral (?**305**, **316**). The composition, sealing, and deposit of a written instrument of contract (**308**; **259a** [Dem.] 48.9–10, 12–18; **262** Hyp. 3.5–11, 18, 21–22), and witnesses to the contract's formation and/or contents (e.g., **323a**), were frequently employed as precautionary measures with an eye to proving the existence and contents of a contract in the case of a dispute (**308**), but in most—if not all—cases these elements were not legally required.

The few attested Athenian laws on sale (**§10.2**: **309–312**) were directed primarily at the protection of the retail consumer. There existed a blanket prohibition on lying in the agora, and the seller of a slave had to inform the buyer of any illness the slave suffered from, or else the sale was subject to rescission at the buyer's discretion (**309**). The Athenian reliance on imported grain and desire to keep its cost reasonable resulted in specific legislation in this area, including caps on the bulk purchase of grain (**310**) and on grain price markups (**310**, **311**). Sales of real property required the filing of public notice, in order to protect third parties with claims on the property, and may also have required a

1 percent down payment by the buyer, which will have advertised and secured the sale (**312**). The (very numerous) instances of sale in our sources are overwhelmingly sales for cash paid in full (e.g., **262** Hyp. 3.5–11, 18, 21–22), such that the existence and function of sale on credit in Classical Athens are topics of vigorous scholarly debate. A buyer's deposit or down payment (*arrhabôn*: **175** Isae. 8.21–24, at §23; cf. **312**, **319**, **321g**) is rarely mentioned, but this may be a function of the fact that litigants who were wealthy enough to hire a logographer (or who were logographers themselves) were more likely to be able to pay full purchase prices instantly than were persons of more modest means.

Loan (**§10.3**: **313–318**), like sale, was not heavily regulated. Solon prohibited lending on the security of the borrower's person (**313**), but lenders by law might charge any rate of interest they wished (**314**); a normal interest rate in the fourth century was 1 drachma per mina per month (= 1 percent monthly = 12 percent annually: **46** [Arist.] *Ath. Pol.* 52.2; **167** Dem. 27.9–11, at §9; **256a** Dem. 37.4–8, at §§4–5). A special type of loan was the *eranos*, an interest-free loan granted by a group of contributors (**316**; **46** [Arist.] *Ath. Pol.* 52.2; **262** Hyp. 3.5–11, 18, 21–22). Security for a loan could be either personal or real. In personal security (suretyship) a third party stands surety for the borrower, assuming responsibility for the debt in case of default (e.g., **320**). Real security involves the pledging of property belonging to the borrower as security for his debt; in the event of default, the borrower cedes ownership of the security to the lender (**§§10.3–10.4** *passim*, especially **320**). The pledged property might remain in the borrower's possession (as usually with real property: **316**; cf. **321f**) or might be transferred to that of the lender (as usually with movable property: **317**, **318**). The great majority of loans mentioned in the orators were for large amounts of money—again, this is a function of the economic status of the logographers and their clients—and were accordingly secured against property of significant value, chiefly real property and/or slaves (e.g., **316**; **167** Dem. 27.9–11), although other types of property might be pledged as well (**315**, **317**, **318**, **320**).

It is a matter of scholarly debate whether Athenian real security was substitutive or collateral in nature. Under a substitutive arrangement, default results in the surrender of the security to the creditor, whatever the relation of the value of the security to that of the debt; under a collateral arrangement, the defaulting debtor has a right to retain the excess value of the security over the debt. Evidence for both types of security exists: for substitutive security see, for example, **315**, **318**; for collateral security see, for example, **319**, **321a**.

Security for loans and other transactions might be raised by means of the transaction called *prasis epi lysei* ("sale on condition of release," **§10.4**: **319–321**;

plural *praseis epi lysei*), whereby a debtor "sold" property (or a partial interest in it) to his creditor on terms that the creditor release the debtor from the "sale," and restore to him unencumbered title to the property, upon the discharge of the debt; if the debtor defaulted, he surrendered his right to recover the property, of which the creditor gained full ownership. The object of the *prasis epi lysei*—in most cases real property or a partial interest therein (**319**; **321b-e**, **g**; **256** Dem. 37 [selections]), although other things too might be "sold on condition of release" (**320**, **321e**; **256** Dem. 37 [selections])—appears normally, but not always, to have remained in the possession of the "seller" (see especially **319**, **321f**). Despite its nomenclature, therefore, a *prasis epi lysei* is in many instances simply a secured loan: the price of the "sale" is the amount of the loan, the property "sold" functions as security for the loan, and the "seller" and "purchaser" are the borrower and lender respectively (e.g., **319**, **320**). In other cases, *prasis epi lysei* functions as a pledge of security for a dowry (**321a**, **321c**; see chapter 5) or for the lease on an orphan's estate (**321d**; see chapter 6), and we have at least one possible example (**321g**, if the "buyer" by *prasis epi lysei* is also the outright seller) of the object of a *prasis epi lysei* securing the outstanding purchase price of its own outright sale. When real property was encumbered by a loan, a *prasis epi lysei*, or another transaction, it was customary for the creditor(s) to place upon it one or more boundary-markers, called *horoi* (singular *horos*) (**321**; **112** [Boundary-markers (*horoi*) designating real property pledged as security (*apotimêmata*) for dowries]; for the pre-Solonian *horoi* see **313**), which advertised the encumbrance and thereby protected the interests of both the existing creditor(s) and prospective creditors or purchasers.

On the various terms for securities and secured transactions and the relationship between them, see especially the works of **Harris** cited above; for older interpretations see especially the works of **Finley**, **Fine**, and **Harrison** cited above. The chief terms, besides *prasis epi lysei* (the corresponding verbal phrase is *pipraskein epi lysei* "to sell on condition of release," from which the qualifying *epi lysei* is sometimes omitted), are (1) the verb *daneizein* "to lend" (typically money: e.g., **316**, **320**) and its corresponding nouns *daneion* and *daneisma* "loan" (e.g., **317**); (2) the noun *hypothêkê* "(item pledged as) security" (e.g., **323a**)—whence English "hypothec," "hypothecate," "hypothecation"—and the related verbs *hypotithenai* "to pledge as security" (e.g., **315**, **317**; cf. the corresponding simplex noun *thesis* "pledging" in **318**) and its quasi-passive *hypokeisthai* "to be pledged as security" (e.g., **319**, **321a**; note in particular the hybrid *hypokeisthai epi lysei* "to be pledged as security on condition of release" in **321h**); (3) the noun *enechyron* "(movable item pledged as) security" (**317**, **320**); (4) the noun *engyê* "pledge" and related words (e.g., **320**; see the introduction to chapter 5, and note also *engyêtês* "surety" in **320**); (5) the noun *apotimêma* "valuated security" and related words (see especially **116a** Harpo. s.v. *apotimêtai* etc.).

Regulations on imports, exports, and maritime commerce (**§10.5**: **322–328**) were motivated primarily by the aforementioned need to ensure a constant and affordable supply of grain in Attica; this concern is evident already in the law of Solon that prohibited the export of agricultural produce other than olive oil (**322**). In addition, by the fourth century, Athenian residents were prohibited by law from transporting grain to a destination other than Athens (with a possible penalty of death: **328**) and from extending maritime loans (see below) on any ship that was not transporting grain to Athens (**323c**); and whenever a merchantman docked at Peiraeus, the Athenian port of trade (*emporion*: e.g., **320**, **323c**, **324**), two-thirds of its grain cargo had to be taken to the city of Athens (**327**). Violation of these laws was subject to *phasis* (declaration: **323c**, **325**) before the Overseers of the Port of Trade (*epimelêtai tou emporiou*: **323c**, **325**, **327**).

At some point between 355 and 342, a major reform was enacted concerning the handling of lawsuits connected with interstate commerce: this was the creation by statute of a new class of regular, monthly *dikai emporikai* (mercantile lawsuits; singular *dikê emporikê*: **323**, **324**, **326**, **328**; **260** [Dem.] 33.19–20, 22, 32–33; **261** Dem. 32.25–28; **263** [Dem.] 56 [selections]). Its purview embraced all offenses that involved merchants and ship-captains and that occurred in, or during or concerning a voyage to or from, the Athenian port of trade (*emporion*) at Peiraeus (**324**, **326**, **328**; cf. the reference to *emporikoi nomoi*, "mercantile laws," in **171** [Dem.] 35.3–4). In a *dikê emporikê*, moreover, identical substantive and procedural rights applied to Athenian citizens, metics, and non-resident foreigners, and possibly even to slaves (see especially **323b**). Although we have, for example, an instance of a *dikê emporikê* initiated over a battery (*aikeia*: see chapter 2) committed by one man involved in maritime commerce against another in the port of trade (see the headnote under **260** [Dem.] 33.19–20, 22, 32–33), the majority of attested *dikai emporikai* concern loan contracts for maritime transport, and thus would be classified as *dikai emporikai blabês* (for damage: see chapter 8). These maritime loans (**323**, **328**; **263** [Dem.] 56 [selections]) were regularly secured on the ship and/or its cargo (hence the occasional application of the common-law term "bottomry loan," in which "bottom" refers to the ship's keel), with the loss thereof canceling the borrower's liability (e.g., **328**, but compare **323a**); owing to the inherent hazards of sea travel, including shipwreck and piracy, maritime loans tended to carry higher interest rates than other loans (e.g., 22.5–30 percent in **323a**). In cases where a contractual violation was alleged, a written instrument of contract may have been required in order to bring a *dikê emporikê* (**326**). Filing of *dikai emporikai* took place monthly from Boedromion to Munychion (see p. 7); the supervising magistrates were the *thesmothetai*, trial was held in a *dikastêrion*, and convicted defendants who were sentenced to pay a fine were subject to imprisonment until they paid it (**324**), while the prosecutor who failed to garner one-fifth of the jurors' votes—possibly, any unsuccessful prosecutor—had to pay the *epô-*

belia (a fine of one-sixth the sum at issue) and could likewise be imprisoned pending its payment (**263a** [Dem.] 56.3–6). *Paragraphê* (counter-indictment) was available against a *dikê emporikê* initiated in violation of the statutory terms of application (**323b**, **324**, **326**, **328**), and if an *epôbelia* was levied (upon either the prosecutor or the defendant: **244** Isoc. 18.1–8, 10–13, 33, 63, at §3) as the result of such a *paragraphê*, the party that owed the *epôbelia* was subject to imprisonment pending its payment (**323b**). In addition, the malicious prosecutor of a merchant or ship-captain was liable to *endeixis* and/or *apagôgê* (**325**).

The terminal dates for the creation of the monthly *dikai emporikai* (355 and 342) are, respectively, the earliest possible year of composition of Xenophon's *On Revenues*, which recommends that measures be taken to encourage the just and speedy trial of lawsuits involving merchants so that they are not unnecessarily detained from sailing (3.3), and the year when Hegesippus delivered his oration *On Halonnesus* ([Demosthenes] 7), which contains the earliest extant reference to the monthly *dikai emporikai* (§12). Between the mid-fifth century and the advent of the monthly *dikai emporikai*, lawsuits over interstate commercial activity appear commonly to have come under the supervision of the *nautodikai* (Judges of Sailors: **126** Harpo. s.v. *nautodikai*) or the *xenodikai* (Judges of Foreigners); for the limited evidence see, e.g., Lysias 17; D. **Lewis**, ed., ***Inscriptiones Graecae*** I[3] fasc. 1 (Berlin and New York 1981) no. 41, lines 90–92; I. **Kirchner**, ed., ***Inscriptiones Graecae*** II[2] pt. 1 fasc. 1 (ed. min. Berlin 1913) no. 46, line 11; no. 144, fr. a side A line 8. (The term *dikai emporikai* is attested as referring to this earlier system as well: **332h** Dem. 21.175–76, 178–80, with D. M. **MacDowell**, *Demosthenes:* Against Meidias *[Oration 21]* [Oxford 1990] 393–94.)

See also chapters 5–8 *passim*.

10.1. Contracts in General

See also **115** Dem. 30–31 (selections); **206** Isae. 10.9–10.

304. General law of contract. (date of law ?6th c.)

The following passages all cite a law that featured the phrase "whatever one person agrees with another shall be binding." That the law applied to contracts in general is indicated not only by its phrasing but also by the fact that litigants cite it with regard to different types of contracts, including sale (**304b**), loan (**304d**), partnership ([Demosthenes] 48.54), and others. Some sources represent this as the entirety of the law ("unlimited" variant: **304a**, **304b**), while others add language specifying the presence of witnesses ("witnessed" variant: **304c**, against which cf. **305** Lys. fr. 151 Carey, lines 246–55; **306** Isoc. 17.2) or that the contractants be "willing" ("volitional" variant: **304d**). There is no scholarly consensus as to which of these variants (or possible combinations thereof) represents the full text of the law, or as to the date of the law; although some scholars advocate a date as late as the end of the fifth century, the simplicity of the law rather suggests a sixth-century (perhaps Solonian) origin.

a. [Demosthenes] 47 *Against Euergus and Mnesibulus* 77. General law of contract (unlimited variant). (date of speech *post* 358/7)

See references and headnote under **17**. The debt in question, for which the speaker contends that Theophemus granted him an extension in payment, is the fine levied upon the speaker as a result of his conviction in a *dikê aikeias* (see **41b** [Dem.] 47.64).

But, to prove that I was not overdue in paying [Theophemus], [To the court clerk:] please read the deposition and the law that commands that whatever one person agrees with another shall be binding, in consequence of which I clearly was no longer overdue in paying him.

b. Hypereides 3 *Against Athenogenes* 13. General law of contract (unlimited variant, with alleged understood justice requirement). (date of speech 330–324)

See references and headnote under **262**. Epicrates here anticipates that Athenogenes will base his defense on the general law of contract (unlimited variant) and counters with the assertion that that law validates only "just" agreements. In support of his point, however, Epicrates does not quote the general law of contract but instead adduces other laws (**309** Hyp. 3.14–15; **83** [Dem.] 46.18, cited at §16; **201** [Dem.] 46.14, cited at §17) as proof by analogy. It is therefore evident that the general contract law contained no language specifying that the terms of a contract be "just" (cf. **236** [Dem.] 48.22–32; **259** [Dem.] 48 [selections]: Callistratus prosecutes Olympiodorus for breaching a contract that his own description shows to have violated Solon's law of intestate succession; nowhere in that speech does Callistratus anticipate that Olympiodorus will argue that the contract's illegality affects its validity).

Now, Athenogenes is going to say to you very soon that the law states that whatever one person agrees with another shall be binding. As to just agreements, yes, my good man; but as to those that are not just, on the contrary, the law forbids them to be binding.

c. [Demosthenes] 42 *Against Phaenippus* 12. General law of contract (witnessed variant). (date of speech 330–323)

See **122** with references and headnote. Here the speaker describes an abortive attempt to settle his dispute with Phaenippus.

Believing that it was the duty of a reasonable and easygoing citizen not to proceed immediately and headlong into court, I was persuaded . . . to agree to conduct the meeting about the settlement on the eighth day before the end of the month of Boedromion, and to conduct the inventory of the property on the sixth day before the end of the month. After obtaining both these requests from me, Phaenippus did not appear on either day; instead, he has come before you in violation of two laws instead of one: first, the law that commands that a person submit an inventory of his property within three days from the day he swears the oath, and second, the law that commands that whatever agreements people make with each other in the presence of witnesses shall be binding.

d. [Demosthenes] 56 *Against Dionysodorus* 2. General law of contract (volitional variant). (date of speech 323–322)

See references and headnote under **263**. "Lending on risk" refers to the practice of extending maritime loans (see **263** [Dem.] 56 [selections] and **§10.5**). For the volitional variant of the general contract law cf. Plato, *Symposium* 196c1–2: "everyone willingly renders all service to Eros, and the laws, the kings of the city, state that whatever one willing person agrees with another willing person is just"; [Demosthenes] 48.54.

Whatever, then, do we trust in, and what do we receive as security, when we lend on risk? We trust in you, men of the jury, and in your laws, which command that whatever one willing person agrees with another shall be binding.

305. Lysias fr. 151 Carey, lines 246–55. Unwitnessed (?oral) contract of loan. (403–380)

L. **Gernet**-M. **Bizos**, *Lysias: Discours* (2 vols., Paris 1989: text with French translation and notes), fr. XXXIX; S. C. **Todd**, *Lysias* (Austin 2000: translation with notes), fr. 8; C. **Carey**, *Lysiae orationes cum fragmentis* (Oxford 2007: text with Latin commentary), fr. 151 (cf. fr. 252).

In this fragmentary speech, conventionally titled *Against Theomnestus* and possibly delivered in a *dikê blabês* (see chapter 8), the speaker demands repayment of a loan of 30 mn. that he made to Theomnestus so that Theomnestus might avoid defaulting on a fine owed to Theozotides. The speaker explicitly describes the loan as having occurred without witnesses, and as he considered Theomnestus a friend and no written document is mentioned in the surviving parts of the speech, the contract may well have been oral.

. . . since he was a close friend, I gave Theomnestus 30 minae, because he had to pay a judgment to Theozotides before the sun set; otherwise, he would be overdue in payment. Having given it to him without witnesses, as was reasonable, I am being deprived of it and am thus forced to litigate.

306. Isocrates 17 *Trapeziticus* 2. Unwitnessed contracts. (393–391)

See references and headnote under **246**. Contracts with bankers would have comprised mostly deposits (such as the one alleged by the speaker: **246** Isoc. 17.2–9, 11–16) and loans (e.g., **317** [Dem.] 49.48–49, 51–52).

You see, contracts [*symbolaia*] with people who manage banks occur without witnesses, and those who are wronged are compelled to face risks against the sort of people who have a lot of friends, handle a lot of money, and are considered trustworthy on account of their profession.

307. [Demosthenes] 35 *Against Lacritus* 39. Assertion of paramount authority of contract. (355–338)

See references and headnote under **171**. Here the speaker gives his interpretation of a contractual clause (**323a** [Dem.] 35.10–13, at §13) that states, "Concerning these matters nothing else shall have greater authority than the contract." For similar language asserting the paramount authority of a contract cf. [Demosthenes] 56.26 "nor is anything more authoritative for us than the contract."

The contract [*syngraphê*] allows nothing to be more authoritative than its written contents, nor does it allow a law or decree or anything else whatsoever to be brought to bear against the contract.

308. [Demosthenes] 33 *Against Apaturius* 36. Sealing and deposit of written contract. (*post* 342)

See references and headnote under **260**. For specific instances of written contracts' being sealed and/or deposited with third parties, see (e.g.) **259a** [Dem.] 48.9–10, 12–18; **262** Hyp. 3.5–11, 18, 21–22. Copies of the contract were also generally kept by the contractants themselves (e.g., **262** Hyp. 3.5–11, 18, 21–22). For the use of the same procedures to safeguard a written will cf., e.g., **212** Lys. 32.5, 7; **218** Isae. 6.29–32.

. . . all men, when making a contract with each other, seal it and deposit it with people they trust, for this purpose: so that if they dispute something, they may revisit the document and from that conduct their scrutiny of the point at issue.

10.2. Sale

See also **175** Isae. 8.21–24; **250** Dem. 41.7–9, 11–12; **256** Dem. 37 (selections); **257** Dem. 38 (selections); **262** Hyp. 3.5–11, 18, 21–22; **316** [Dem.] 53.6–13; **319** *SEG* 12.100.16–21, 23–25, 30–39; **320** [Dem.] 33.6–12; **321g** Finley, *SLC* no. 12A.

309. Hypereides 3 *Against Athenogenes* 14–15. Law prohibiting lying in the agora; law mandating disclosure of illness in slave for sale. (date of speech 330–324; date of laws probably Archaic)

See references and headnote under **262**. For the prohibition on lying in the agora (p. 17) cf. Demosthenes 20.9; Harpocration s.v. *kata tên agoran apseudein*, which quotes this passage and adds, "The law apparently dealt with goods for sale: Theophrastus in his treatise *On Laws* [see **312** Theophr. *Laws* fr. 21.1 Szegedy-Maszak] says that it was the duty of the *agoranomoi* [**311** [Arist.] *Ath. Pol.* 51.1–3 with additional references in headnote] to oversee two things; namely, the maintenance of good order in the agora and the prevention of lying not only by sellers but by buyers as well."

So, then, one law commands that people not tell lies in the agora. . . . [15] And next after that, there is another law concerning contracts people make by agreement with one another, which provides that when a person is selling a slave, he must disclose any illness the slave has, or else return [*anagôgê*] of the slave is permitted.

310. Lysias 22 *Against the Grain Dealers* 5–6, 8. Laws on purchase and sale of grain. (date of speech ?386; date of laws unknown)

See especially C. D. **Adams**, *Lysias: Selected Speeches* (New York 1905, repr. Norman, OK 1970: text and commentary); R. **Seager**, "Lysias Against the Corndealers," *Historia* 15 (1966) 172–84; T. **Figueira**, "*Sitopolai* and *Sitophylakes* in Lysias' "Against the Graindealers:" Governmental Intervention in the Athenian Economy," *Phoenix* 40 (1986) 149–71; M. J. **Edwards**, *Lysias: Five Speeches (Speeches 1, 12, 19, 22, 30)* (London 1999: text and commentary); S. C. **Todd**, *Lysias* (Austin 2000: translation with introduction and notes); also F. **Blass**, *Die attische Beredsamkeit* (Leipzig 1887–98) 1.470–75; R. C. **Jebb**, *The Attic Orators from Antiphon to Isaeus*[2] (London 1893) 1.221–23; S. **Usher**, *Greek Oratory: Tradition and Originality* (Oxford 1999) 101–2.

The speaker of Lysias 22 prosecutes a group of metic grain dealers for violating legislation designed to prevent artificial inflation of grain prices. The lawsuit is being tried before a *dikastêrion* (§6; p. 26) following a preliminary hearing before the Council of 500 (of which the speaker is a member); the procedure has thus been identified as either *eisangelia* (see chapter 12) or *apagôgê* (p. 30). The first law mentioned below (§§5–6) permitted the purchase of no more than 50 "baskets" of grain and prescribed death as the penalty for violation; it is probable but not certain that "basket" (*phormos*) is here a synonym for "medimnus" (see **206** Isae. 10.9–10). There is scholarly debate as to whether the verbs *sympriasthai* and *synôneisthai* mean "buy up" (as they are translated here) or "buy together" (with other people; in the present case, with the rest of the defendants), and accordingly whether the law targeted stockpiling of grain or cartelizing among grain dealers. This may, however, be a distinction without a difference: by setting a cap on the bulk purchase of grain, whether the purchaser was an individual or a group, the law would have served to deter both activities. The same concern for consumer protection is demonstrated in the second law (§8), which permitted a retail markup of no more than one obol per drachma (i.e., one-sixth: p. 4) of the wholesale price. "The magistrates" are presumably to be identified as the *sitophylakes* (Grain Guardians: **311** [Arist.] *Ath. Pol.* 51.1–3).

[To a defendant:] So, do you deserve anything other than death if you have done in violation of the laws anything for which death is the penalty? [Defendant's response:] "I do not." [To the same defendant:] Then answer me: do you admit having bought up [*sympriasthai*] more than fifty baskets [*phormôn*] of grain, which the law ordains is permitted? [Defendant's response:] "I bought it up, because the magistrates ordered me to."

[6] Well, men of the jury, if he demonstrates that there is a law that commands grain dealers to buy up [*synôneisthai*] grain if the magistrates so order, acquit them; otherwise, it is right that you convict them. For we have provided you with the law that forbids anyone in the city to buy up [*synôneisthai*] more than fifty baskets of grain.

. . .

[8] When my adversaries tried to put the blame on them, we summoned the magistrates and questioned them. The others said that they knew nothing of the matter, but Anytus said that the previous winter, when grain was expensive because my adversaries were outbidding each other and fighting among themselves, he had advised them to stop being contentious, believing that it benefited you, who buy from them, for them to purchase it as cheaply as possible, since they had to sell it for only an obol more.

311. [Aristotle], *Constitution of the Athenians* (*Ath. Pol.*) 51.1–3. Duties of the *agoranomoi*, *metronomoi*, and *sitophylakes*. (332–322)

> See references and headnote under **1c**. On the *agoranomoi* (Market Commissioners) cf. headnote under **309** Hyp. 3.14–15; **241** Ar. *Wasps* 1389–1408; on standard Athenian weights and measures see pp. 3–4 and (e.g.) **206** Isae. 10.9–10. The word translated "bread-sellers" (*artopôlai*) is feminine, indicating that this occupation was generally held by women (cf. **241**). With the (here unspecified) limits on price markup for barley meal and loaves of bread in §51.3 cf. **310** Lys. 22.5–6, 8.

Ten Market Commissioners [*agoranomoi*] are also appointed by lot, five for Peiraeus and five for the city. These are assigned by the laws to oversee all goods for sale so that they are sold pure and unadulterated. [51.2] Ten Commissioners of Measures [*metronomoi*] are also appointed by lot, five for the city and five for Peiraeus; these oversee all measures and weights so that sellers use honest ones. [51.3] There used to be ten Grain Guardians [*sitophylakes*] appointed by lot, five for Peiraeus and five for the city, but now there are twenty for the city and fifteen for Peiraeus. These see to it, first, that the unground grain in the agora is for sale at a fair price, and second, that the millers sell their barley meal on the basis of the price of barley and that the bread-sellers sell their loaves on the basis of the price of wheat and at whatever weight the Grain Guardians assign (the law commands them to assign it).

312. Theophrastus, *On Laws* fr. 21.1 Szegedy-Maszak. Law(s) on sale of real property. (date of composition ?322–307; date of laws unknown)

A. **Szegedy-Maszak**, *The* Nomoi *of Theophrastus* (New York 1981: text, translation, and commentary).

In this part of his now-fragmentary treatise *On Laws*, the Peripatetic philosopher Theophrastus (see **216** D. L. 3.41–43) discusses regulations on the sale of real property in various Greek states. Owing to the ambiguity in Theophrastus' phrasing and the lack of supporting or contradictory evidence on the issue, we cannot securely conclude whether "as at Athens" refers only to registration with the magistrate (generally presumed to be the eponymous archon) or also to the 1 percent buyer's deposit. The phrase translated "by means of the payment" (Greek *tôi telei*) may alternatively mean "to the (aforementioned) official."

Some [lawgivers] mandate the filing of public notice with the magistrate no less than sixty days in advance, as at Athens, and that the buyer deposit one percent of the price, so that anyone who wishes may dispute [the sale] and lodge a protest, and so that he who has made a rightful purchase may be manifest [as such] by means of the payment.

10.3. Loan

See also **46** [Arist.] *Ath. Pol.* 52.2; **167** Dem. 27.9–11; **168** [Dem.] 49.1–2, 42–43, 69; **250** Dem. 41.7–9, 11–12; **251** [Dem.] 49.17–20; **256** Dem. 37 (selections); **262** Hyp. 3.5–11, 18, 21–22; **305** Lys. fr. 151 Carey, lines 246–55; **319** *SEG* 12.100.16–21, 23–25, 30–39; **320** [Dem.] 33.6–12; **321a** Finley, *SLC* no. 146; **321f** Finley, *SLC* no. 1; **321h** Finley, *SLC* nos. 80A, 81A.

313. Solon's *seisachtheia*. (594/3)

See references and headnotes under **1c** and **1d**; also E. M. **Harris**, "Did Solon Abolish Debt-Bondage?," *CQ* 52 (2002) 415–30, reprinted with addenda in ***idem***, *Democracy and the Rule of Law in Classical Athens* (Cambridge 2006) 249–69. For **313a** see also M. L. **West**, *Iambi et elegi Graeci ante Alexandrum cantati*[2] (2 vols., Oxford 1989–92: text).

According to the sources that follow, before the reforms of Solon (594/3: **6b** [Arist.] *Ath. Pol.* 7.1), Athenians commonly contracted loans on the security of their land and/or their persons. Presumably, despite the *Ath. Pol.*'s statement (**313b**) that "loans for all people were on the security of their persons until Solon," this was frequently a two-stage process. Given the choice between pledging his land and his person—along with those of his wife and/or children—as security, a man would naturally choose the former. If he defaulted, he might remain on the land—which would be marked by *horoi* (boundary-markers: **313a**) advertising that the plot was encumbered—on condition that he pay one-sixth of its produce to his creditor (hence the designation of the debtor as *hektêmoros*, "sixth-parter"; plural *hektêmoroi*) as rent—or interest—until the loan was repaid. The sharecropping status of the *hektêmoroi* will have tended to become permanent (and hereditary), since a person who cannot pay off a debt from the total produce of his land is even less likely to do so from five-sixths of it. The *hektêmoros*' security for this new arrangement with his creditor (and the security proffered by other borrowers with no other suitable property) consisted in the persons of himself and/or his family. In the case of default, the pledged persons were liable to enslavement by the creditor, who might keep them or sell them to others; if the *hektêmoros* himself was enslaved, he thereby lost the right to reclaim his land, which his creditor would now own unencumbered.

By his reform known as the *seisachtheia* (Shaking-Off of Burdens), Solon cancelled all existing debts, thereby restoring to the *hektêmoroi* unencumbered ownership of the lands they had pledged; at least some of those who had been enslaved for debt were freed (by what means, especially in the case of those who had been sold abroad [**313a**], we do not know), and Solon enacted a law that thenceforth prohibited loans on the security of the person. In the Classical period, and perhaps earlier, there was at least one potential exception to this rule: a prisoner of war who had been ransomed from the enemy became by law the property of his ransomer if he failed to reimburse the ransom (**316** [Dem.] 53.6–13, at §11); thus the payment of ransom by a third party, whether arranged formally as a loan or not, could be made on the security of the prisoner's person.

a. Solon fr. 36.1–15 West (= [Aristotle], *Constitution of the Athenians* [*Ath. Pol.*] 12.4) (composed 594/3-ca. 560)

In this fragment (possibly a complete poem), preserved by quotation in the *Ath. Pol.*, Solon describes his liberation of the land and people of Attica. For the use of *horoi* in the fourth century (and later), see **321** (Boundary-markers [*horoi*] designating encumbrances on real property, including *prasis epi lysei*); **112** (Boundary-markers [*horoi*] designating real property pledged as security [*apotimêmata*] for dowries).

Which of the things for which I brought the people together did I stop before accomplishing? To this black Earth, the supreme mother of the Olympian gods, could testify best in the court of Time: I removed from her the boundary-markers [*horous*] that had been fixed in many places, and she who was before a slave is now free. And I brought back to Athens, their god-founded ancestral land, many who had been sold [as slaves], some unjustly and others justly, and also those who had fled under dire necessity, who no longer spoke the Attic tongue, so far and wide had they wandered. And I set free those who were suffering shameful slavery right here, trembling at the temperaments of their masters.

b. [Aristotle], *Constitution of the Athenians* (*Ath. Pol.*) 2.1–2, 6.1. (composed 332–322)

In the following extracts, the author of the *Ath. Pol.* describes the debt crisis that plagued Attica in the decades leading up to Solon's archonship (§2.1–2) and the *seisachtheia* that Solon enacted to remedy it (§6.1). "After this" (§2.1) refers to the purification of Athens by Epimenides of Crete (**1c** [Arist.] *Ath. Pol.* 1), which the author places before the legislation of Draco (621/0: **6a** [Arist.] *Ath. Pol.* 4.1).

After this, it came about that the nobles and the masses engaged in civil strife for a long time. [2.2] For their constitution was oligarchic in all other respects, and in particular the poor were slaves to the rich, both themselves and their children and their wives. They were called "dependents" [*pelatai*] and "sixth-parters" [*hektêmoroi*], since they worked the fields of the rich at that rent. All the land was in the hands of a few, and if [the *hektêmoroi*] did not pay their rent, they became subject to seizure, both themselves and their children. And loans for all people were on the security of their persons until Solon; he became the first champion of the people.

. . .

[6.1] Having become master of affairs, Solon freed the people both for the present and for the future by prohibiting lending on the security of the person; he also established laws and made a cancellation of debts, both private and public, which they call the "Shaking-Off of Burdens" [*seisachtheian*], since they shook the weight off themselves.

c. Plutarch, *Solon* 13.4–5, 15.2. (composed late 1st-early 2nd c. A.D.)

Plutarch's account of the *hektêmoroi* and the *seisachtheia* clearly relies, at least in part, on that of the *Ath. Pol.* (**313b**); significantly, however, Plutarch clarifies that the *hektêmoroi* paid one-sixth of their produce as rent (the ambiguous language of the *Ath. Pol.* might be taken to mean either that they paid one-sixth or that they retained one-sixth, paying five-sixths). With Plutarch's comment regarding the selling of children into slavery (§13.5) compare the law ascribed to Solon that permitted a man to sell his unmarried daughter (or sister) if he caught her having had sex with a man (**50** Plut. *Solon* 23.1–2).

For the entire people was in debt to the rich. Either they farmed the land, paying them one-sixth of the produce and hence being called "sixth-parters" [*hektêmorioi*] and "hired laborers" [*thêtes*], or, by assuming debts on the security of their persons, they were subject to seizure by their creditors, some of them being enslaved in Attica and others sold abroad. [13.5] Many were even forced to sell their own children—since no law prohibited it—and to flee the city because of the harshness of their creditors.

. . .

[15.2] . . . Now, as to recent writers' statements that the Athenians politely gloss over the offensiveness of their practices by covering them up with pleasant and humane names . . . , this was, it seems, a contrivance of Solon first: he named his cancellation of debts the "Shaking-Off of Burdens" [*seisachtheian*]. This he made his first act of government, prescribing that existing debts were to be annulled and that for the future no one was to lend on the security of the person.

314. Lysias 10 / *Against Theomnestus* 18 (*lex* + commentary). Law permitting rate of interest at lender's discretion. (date of speech 384/3; law ascribed to Solon, 594/3)

See references and headnote under **15**. This passage appears amid a series of laws cited for their anachronistic language (for the others see **51** Lys. 10.18–19; **267b** Lys. 10.15–17; as in those cases, so too here the use of vocabulary that required interpretation to be comprehensible to an average fourth-century Athenian indicates that the law was very old, even if not, as the speaker posits, Solonian). Note that this law (or, more probably, fragment of a law) accords with, and establishes specifically with regard to the rate of interest on loans, the principle stated in the general law of contract (**304** [General law of contract]) that "whatever one person agrees with another shall be binding." Since Athens did not mint coins before the middle of the sixth century (p. 4), if the law was written by Solon, *argyrion* (literally "silver," metaphorically "money": cf. Latin *argentum*, whence French *argent*) referred originally to weighed but not coined silver.

[LAW:] The money [*argyrion*] shall be placed [*stasimon*] at whatever rate the lender wishes.

[To Theomnestus:] This word "placed," my good man, does not mean placing on a balance but exacting as much interest as one wishes.

315. Lysias 19 *On the Property of Aristophanes* 25–26. Rejected offer of loan, including duration of loan, interest, and bowl as security. (387/6)

See references and headnote under **108**. On the trierarchy see p. 25 and cf., e.g., **254** Dem. 39.1, 5, 7–18; "the Great King" is the king of Persia, in this case Artaxerxes II (r. 405/4–359/8). For the pledging of a bowl as security cf. **250** Dem. 41.7–9, 11–12.

Demus son of Pyrilampes, when he was serving as trierarch and destined for Cyprus, asked me to approach Aristophanes, saying that he had received as a token from the Great King a gold bowl, and that he would give it as security [*hypothêsei*] to Aristophanes if he received 16 minae for it, in order that he might have the money to spend on his trierarchy; when he arrived at Cyprus, he said, he would redeem [the bowl] by paying 20 minae. . . . [26] Aristophanes, though, despite hearing this from Demus and despite my request, and although he would take the gold bowl and receive 4 minae as interest, said that it was not possible. He swore that he had even borrowed from other sources [to pay] for the mercenaries; otherwise, he said, he would have been the happiest of men to take that token immediately and do us the favor we were asking.

316. [Demosthenes] 53 *Against Nicostratus* 6–13. Gifts and loans, including *eranos* (joint loan); oral and written contracts of loan; law(s) on (loan for) ransom; real and other property as security for loans. (*post* 368/7)

See references and headnote under **40**. Here Apollodorus describes the series of transactions performed in order to secure the freedom of Nicostratus, his former friend and present adversary. On *eranoi* (interest-free "joint loans") cf. **262** Hyp. 3.5–11, 18, 21–22; in this case Apollodorus ends up financing the entire 26 mn. ransom by himself (1,000 dr. at §§8–9, given as a gift, plus 16 mn. at §13, given as a loan) on the promise that Nicostratus will repay the loan ("redeem my property," §12: i.e., pay off the debts for which the property has been pledged and restore the property to Apollodorus unencumbered) by contracting new loans from the other (putative) contributors to the *eranos*. In §10, Arethusius refuses to allow Nicostratus

> to sell or pledge the plot of land in question because Nicostratus has already pledged it (or part of its value: cf. **321a** Finley, *SLC* no. 146; **321b** Finley, *SLC* no. 41) as security for a loan from Arethusius.

During my time abroad, three slaves ran away from my adversary's place in the country. . . . While in pursuit, he was caught by a trireme, brought to land at Aegina, and there sold. When I sailed home . . . , Deinon, my adversary's brother, approached me, telling me of my adversary's misfortune. . . . [7] Hearing this, and sharing his grief at my adversary's bad luck, I immediately sent Deinon . . . to get him, giving him 300 drachmas as traveling money. My adversary returned, came to me, and . . . asked me to help him . . . : crying, and saying that he had been ransomed for 26 minae, he urged me to contribute something toward his ransom. [8] . . . I told him in reply that . . . I would help him, and that I was releasing to him the 300 drachmas that I had given his brother . . . and would contribute 1,000 drachmas as a joint loan [*eranon*] toward his ransom. [9] And I didn't just promise this with words and fail to carry it through with actions: . . . I brought to Theocles, who was at that time engaged in banking, cups and a gold crown . . . and instructed him to give my adversary 1,000 drachmas; I gave him this money as a gift, and I admit that I gave it.

[10] But a few days later, he approached me, crying, and said that the foreigners who had lent [*daneisantes*] the ransom were demanding the rest of the money from him, and that it was in the contract [*syngraphais*] that he had to repay them within thirty days or owe double, and that no one was willing to purchase [*priasthai*] or receive as security [*thesthai*] the plot of land in my neighborhood, since his brother Arethusius . . . was not allowing anyone either to purchase it or to receive it as security, on the grounds that money was owed to him with it as security. [11] "You, then," he said, "must provide me with the remainder of the money before the thirty days expire, so that the thousand drachmas I have paid are not lost and I myself do not become subject to seizure. Once I collect the joint loan, after I get rid of the foreigners, I will pay you back whatever you lend me. You know," he said, "that in fact the laws command that a ransomed person shall be the property of the one who ransoms him from the enemy, if he does not repay the ransom." [12] . . . I told him in reply, . . . " . . . I will lend [*kichrêmi*] you whatever you wish out of my property; you can pledge as much of it as you need as security for the remaining money, use the money without interest for a year, and repay the foreigners. Once you have collected the joint loan, redeem my property, as you yourself promise."

[13] He heard this, thanked me, and urged me to act as quickly as possible. . . . So I pledged my apartment house for 16 minae to Arcesas of the deme Pambotadae . . . , who lent me the money at an interest rate of eight obols per mina per month. But once [Nicostratus] got the money, so far from demon-

strating any gratitude to me for the good treatment he had received, he immediately began plotting against me. . . .

317. [Demosthenes] 49 *Against Timotheus* 48–49, 51–52. Copper as security for loan. (362)

See references and headnote under **168**, and for the loan discussed here cf. **251** [Dem.] 49.17–20. Note that while Timotheus' specific claim that the admiral borrowed the disputed money on the security of a quantity of copper is rejected as fictitious, Apollodorus details the procedure that would normally have accompanied the pledging of copper and describes the receipt of portable items as security for loans by his father, the banker Pasion (cf., e.g., **92** Dem. 45.27–28, 30; **167** Dem. 27.9–11), as a regular occurrence. On the evidentiary torture of slaves see p. 24.

Now, concerning the thousand drachmas that [Timotheus] borrowed from Antiphanes in Calaureia . . . and that he paid to Philippus the ship-captain here [in Athens] after receiving it from my father, he claims that the Boeotian admiral borrowed it and gave my father copper as security [*hypotheinai*] for the money. [49] But I will give you weighty proof that he is not telling the truth. . . . [51] Well, he says, [the admiral] gave copper as security. How much copper, and from where? . . . And who were the men who brought the copper to my father? Hired men or slaves? And which of our slaves received it? [52] For if slaves brought it, he should have handed them over [for torture], and if it was hired men, he should have demanded [for torture] the slave of ours who received and weighed the copper; obviously neither the person taking the copper in pledge would receive it, nor would the person pledging it hand it over, without weighing it. Nor, again, would my father himself be the one to carry the copper or to weigh it; he had slaves who received the securities [*enechyra*] for loans [*daneismatôn*].

318. [Lysias] 8 *Against the Members of an Association* 10. Horse as security for loan. (date unknown)

See especially S. C. **Todd**, *A Commentary on Lysias, Speeches 1–11* (Oxford 2007: text, translation, and commentary); also **Blass**, *AB* 1.640–44; **Jebb**, *AO* 1.300–1; A. **Müller**, *Oratio quae inter Lysiacas fertur octava: Κατηγορία πρὸς τοὺς συνουσιαστὰς κακολογιῶν* (Münster 1926: text with Latin translation and commentary); **Usher**, *GO* 114–15; **Todd**, *Lysias* (translation with introduction and notes).

[Lysias] 8 purports to be a speech delivered to an association (of unknown type) by a man who is resigning his membership. This passage concerns a loan of 12 mn. that the speaker extended to Polycles on the security of a horse, which was placed in the speaker's possession pending repayment; Hegemachus and the association as a group ("you") appear to have played some intermediary role in arranging the loan. Return of the horse would have served as notice of the speaker's intent to call in the loan; the use of the verb "to return" (*anagein*) has led some scholars to conclude that the transaction was formally a *prasis epi lysei* (see **§10.4**, and cf. the use of the related noun *anagôgê* "return" in the context of outright sale at **309** Hyp. 3.14–15). While the speech may postdate the fourth century, the developments described below neatly illustrate the complications that might be encountered by a lender who accepted security that was liable to sudden severe depreciation (for which very reason maritime lenders charged relatively high interest rates: see the introduction to this chapter and **§10.5**); whether the death of the horse cancelled Polycles' debt (compare the common provision in maritime loan contracts absolving the borrower of the duty to repay if the ship is lost) is a matter of debate among modern scholars, just as it was for the interested parties.

. . . first of all, after I had conducted through you the whole business with Hegemachus regarding the pledging [*theseôs*] of the horse, when the horse got sick and I wanted to return [*anagein*] it, Diodorus here tried to dissuade me, saying that Polycles would raise no dispute about the twelve minae but would repay it. That's what he said then, but after the death of the horse he ended up taking his place as my opponent in litigation along with these men, saying that it was not right for me to recover the money.

10.4. *Prasis epi lysei* (Sale on Condition of Release)

See also **256** Dem. 37 (selections); **285** *SEG* 12.100.1–16; **318** [Lys.] 8.10.

319. *Supplementum Epigraphicum Graecum* 12.100.16–21, 23–25, 30–39. Loan on security of and *praseis epi lysei* of house. (367/6)

See **285** with references and headnote. As we see here and in **285** *SEG* 12.100.1–16, in the proceedings surrounding its confiscation, Theosebes' house was found to have multiple encumbrances due to previous transactions. These include (1) a loan of 150 dr. by Smicythus (lines 38–39; cf. **285** *SEG* 12.100.1–16, at lines 14–15), for which the house is "pledged as security" (*hypokeitai, ibid.*; cf. **321a** Finley, *SLC* no. 146; **321f** Finley, *SLC* no. 1); (2) a transaction that is described simply as a sale but is shown by the context to have been a *prasis epi lysei* (the "purchasers" are not asserting ownership of the house but merely claiming a debt secured on it, and see below on the comparison with the price of the house upon outright sale; for a similar reference to *prasis epi lysei* as sale without the qualification "on condition of release" see **320** [Dem.] 33.6–12) for 100 dr. to Cichonides and the members of his phratry (see the introduction to chapter 6) (lines 16–21); and (3) a *prasis epi lysei*, described as such, for 24 dr. to Aeschines and the members of his religious brotherhood (lines 30–35).

This inscription provides especially valuable evidence for the concepts of and relationship between loan, sale, and *prasis epi lysei*. Despite the variation in transactional terms and a coincidental difference in procedure (Theomnestus recognized Smicythus' claim in bringing the action for confiscation, while the other claims were asserted and upheld at the resulting lawsuit: see [Aristotle], *Constitution of the Athenians* [*Ath. Pol.*] 47.2–3; **302b** [Arist.] *Ath. Pol.* 52.1), there is no difference in substance (apart from the amounts claimed) among the creditors' rights of recovery against the house. Moreover, the simultaneous existence of multiple encumbrances on the house (cf. **321a** Finley, *SLC* no. 146; **321b** Finley, *SLC* no. 41), and their confirmation as valid by the jury in the confiscation lawsuit and by the *pôlêtai*, demonstrate that the house served as collateral rather than substitutive security (see the introduction to this chapter), and comparison between the prices of the two *praseis epi lysei* (100 dr. and 24 dr.) and the 575 dr. that Lysanias pays to purchase the house outright (lines 35–39) indicates that the *praseis epi lysei* must have been regarded by the participants as in essence loans secured on the partial value of the house rather than sales. The outright sale is itself a secured transaction, with the down payment (cf. **312** Theophr. *Laws* fr. 21.1 Szegedy-Maszak; **175** Isae. 8.21–24) presumably subject to forfeiture in the event of nonpayment of the remainder (the price of a confiscated house was paid in annual installments over five years: [Aristotle], *Constitution of the Athenians* [*Ath. Pol.*] 47.3).

Cichonides son of Diogeiton of the deme Gargettus and the association of members of the phratry Medontidae brought a claim against the confiscated property that 100 drachmas were owed to him and the phratry members on the house in the deme Alopece that Theomnestus of the deme Ionidae registered as the property of Theosebes of the deme Xypete . . . , [23] "since Theophilus of the deme Xypete, the father of Theosebes, sold [*apodomenou*] this house to me and the phratry members." It was decided that the debt was owed.

. . .

Aeschines of the deme Melite and the association of members of the religious brotherhood [*orgeônôn*] brought a claim against the confiscated property that 24 drachmas were owed to them on the house that Theomnestus of the deme Ionidae registered, "since we bought [*priamenôn*] this house from Theophilus for this sum of money on condition of release [*epi lysei*]." It was decided that the debt was owed.

Purchaser: Lysanias son of Palathion of the deme Laciadae, 575 drachmas. Of this, the city has the initial payment of one-fifth, the sales tax, and the auctioneer's fee, and Smicythus of the deme Teithras has the 150 drachmas.

320. [Demosthenes] 33 *Against Apaturius* 6–12. Loans on security of and *prasis epi lysei* of ship and slaves; personal security (suretyship) and real security. (*post* 342)

See references and headnote under **260**. Described below is a series of transactions involving a ship and its crew of slaves owned (at the outset) by Apaturius. (1) Apaturius has contracted a loan of 40 mn. (from an unspecified party) on the security of the ship (and the slaves?) and is on the verge of defaulting and losing the security (§6). (2) To keep from defaulting, Apaturius contracts two fresh loans: (a) from Parmenon (the "foreigner" and "exile" in §§10–12: see **260** [Dem.] 33.19–20, 22, 32–33, at §20) for 10 mn., and (b) from Heracleides' bank for 30 mn. with the speaker as surety (§§6–7). (3) Following a disagreement between Apaturius and Parmenon, the speaker becomes Apaturius' sole creditor by "purchasing" the ship and the slaves for 40 mn. by *prasis epi lysei* (§§7–8; observe, however, that in §12 the speaker describes the transaction as a loan) and paying off Apaturius' original debt. (4) After Apaturius attempts to abscond with the ship and slaves (§9), the speaker takes possession of the ship and proffers first the ship (for the use of the term *enechyron* for movable securities cf. **317** [Dem.] 49.48–49, 51–52) and then the slaves as security for his debt to the bank (§10), thereby substituting real for personal security (see the introduction to this chapter). (5) Finally, the ship (with the slaves?) is sold outright for 40 mn. (to an unspecified party), the proceeds are used to repay the bank and Parmenon, and the speaker and Apaturius make mutual quitclaims (§12; for the quitclaim formula "release and discharge" cf. **324** [Dem.] 33.1–3, 23).

My adversary and Parmenon approached me in the port of trade [*emporiôi*] and discussed money. My adversary here owed 40 minae on the security of his ship, and his creditors were pressuring him with their demands and were going to take possession of the ship, having seized it because he was overdue in payment. Since he was in distress, Parmenon agreed to give him 10 minae, and my adversary asked me to contribute 30 minae. . . . [7] Anyway, I didn't have any available money, but since I was friends with Heracleides the banker, I persuaded him to lend [*daneisai*] the money with me as surety [*engyêtên*]. But by the time the 30 minae had been procured, Parmenon had clashed with my adversary over something; and yet, since he had agreed to provide him with 10 minae and had already give him three minae of this sum, he was compelled on account of the money he had already lent to give him the rest. [8] For this reason he didn't want to make the contract [*symbolaion*] himself but urged me to see to it that his interests would be as secure as possible. I then took the seven minae from Parmenon, made a substitute agreement [*anthomologêsamenos*] with my adversary as to the three minae that my adversary had already received from Parmenon, and made a purchase [*ônên*] of the ship and the slaves until such time as he repaid the 10 minae that he had received through me and the 30 minae for which he had made me his surety with the banker. . . .

[9] In this manner my adversary Apaturius here got rid of his creditors. But not much later, after the bank went bankrupt and Heracleides at first was in hiding, my adversary here plotted to send the slaves out of Athens and sail the ship out of the harbor. This was the source of my first quarrel with him. You see, Parmenon found out, seized the slaves as they were being taken away, and prevented him from taking the ship out; he then sent for me and told me what was happening. [10] When I heard, . . . I considered how I might be released from my pledge [*engyês*] with the bank and how the foreigner might not lose what he had lent to my adversary through me. I placed guards on the ship and explained the matter to the bank's sureties, and I handed over the security [*enechyron*], telling them that the foreigner had [an interest of] 10 minae in the ship. After doing that, I pledged [*katêngyêsa*] the slaves, so that if any deficit arose, the shortfall could be recovered from the slaves. [11] . . . But Apaturius criticized me . . . and asked if it wasn't enough for me to get myself released from my pledge with the bank, but I was pledging the ship and the slaves for Parmenon's money as well, and making an enemy of him for the sake of an exile. [12] I said that I would neglect a man who had placed his trust in me all the less inasmuch as, when he was an exile and down on his luck, he was being wronged by Apaturius. After doing all I could and reaching a state of total enmity with my adversary, I just barely exacted the money, since the ship was sold for 40 minae, the exact amount of the pledge [*thesis*]. Once the 30 minae had been repaid to the bank and the 10 minae to Parmenon, in the presence of numerous witnesses we cancelled the contract [*syngraphas*] in accordance with which the money had been lent [*edaneisthê*], and we released and discharged each other from our obligations, so that he had no further business with me, nor I with him.

321. Boundary-markers (*horoi*) designating encumbrances on real property, including *prasis epi lysei.*

See **112** (Boundary-markers [*horoi*] designating real property pledged as security [*apotimêmata*] for dowries) with headnote and references; the *horoi* are numbered as in M. I. **Finley**, *Studies in Land and Credit in Ancient Athens, 500–200 B.C.: The* Horos *Inscriptions* (repr. with introduction by P. Millett, New Brunswick, NJ 1985). The following inscriptions, along with those given in **112**, illustrate the variety of transactions recorded on the preserved Attic *horoi* (on the use of *horoi* in the Classical period cf. **114** Dem. 41.5–7, 10; **115** Dem. 30–31 [selections]; **144** Isae. 6.35–37; **214** Dem. 41.16). On dotal security (**321a, 321c**) see **§5.3.2**; on security for the estate of an orphan (**321d**) see the introduction to chapter 6 and **144** Isae. 6.35–37. For multiple encumbrances on the same property (**321a, 321b**) cf. **319** *SEG* 12.100.16–21, 23–25, 30–39.

a. Finley, *SLC* no. 146. Land pledged as security for dowry and for loans. (ca. 360s)

I. **Kirchner**, ed., ***Inscriptiones Graecae*** II[2] (ed. min. Berlin 1913–40: text with Latin notes) no. 2670; **Fine**, *Horoi* 12, 45, 92, 141; **Finley**, *SLC* no. 146 and pp. 44–52; J. K. **Davies**, *Athenian Propertied Families 600–300 B.C.* (Oxford 1971) nos. 3716, 9238.

For "the excess value" (literally, "however much more [than the talent pledged as security for the dowry the designated property] is worth") cf. Demosthenes 31.6; 37.12. The Lycomidae were a clan (*genos*: see **1** [Trial and punishment of the Alcmaeonids for the killing of Cylon's partisans]; **136** Isae. 7.13–17, 27–28, 30), some of whose members belonged to the deme Phlya (which in turn belonged to the tribe Cecropis).

Boundary [*horos*] of plot of land, [security] for the dowry of Hippocleia daughter of Demochares of the deme Leuconoeon, 1 talent; the excess value [*hosôi pleionos axion*] [5] is pledged as security [*hypokeitai*] to the members of the tribe Cecropis, the Lycomidae, and the demesmen of Phlya.

b. Finley, *SLC* no. 41. Multiple *praseis epi lysei* of land. (?ca. 350)

IG II[2] 2723; **Fine,** *Horoi* 45, 154–56; **Finley,** *SLC* no. 41; S. D. **Lambert,** *The Phratries of Attica*[2] (Ann Arbor 1998) 78–79, 349–50 (text, translation, and commentary).

"The phratry members with [name]" designates a group composed of members of the same phratry (see the introduction to chapter 6) and led by the named person, not the phratry as a whole; the Glaucidae and Epicleidae are probably clans (*genê*).

Boundary [*horos*] of plot of land sold on condition of release [*pepramenou epi lysei*] to Cephisodorus of the deme Leuconoeon, 1,500 drachmas; and to the phratry members with Eratostratus of the deme Anaphlystus, 200 drachmas; and to the Glaucidae, 600 drachmas; and to the Epicleidae, 150 drachmas; and to the phratry members with Nicon of the deme Anaphlystus, 100 drachmas.

c. Finley, *SLC* no. 49. *Prasis epi lysei* of land securing dowry. (?4th or 3rd c. B.C.)

IG II^2 2681; **Fine**, *Horoi* 162–63; **Finley**, *SLC* no. 49 and pp. 44–52.

While this inscription does not identify the actual participants in the transaction (Euthydice's husband and her *kyrios* in the natal line), most likely the former is the "seller" of the land to the latter, who receives it as security for the dowry (see chapter 5): if the dowry becomes subject to restitution and is not repaid, the *kyrios* in the natal line may distrain upon the land; in all other cases, he releases it to the husband.

Boundary [*horos*] of plot of land sold on condition of release [*pepramenou epi lysei*] to Euthydice for her dowry, 1,050 drachmas.

d. Finley, *SLC* no. 57. *Prasis epi lysei* of land securing estate of orphan. (?4th or 3rd c. B.C.)

IG II^2 2658; **Fine**, *Horoi* 161–62; **Finley**, *SLC* no. 57 and pp. 38–44.

This *horos* marked the land "sold" by the lessee of the estate of Callistratus' orphaned son. When the latter reaches his majority, he will have the right to distrain upon the land (or, perhaps, the specified part of its value: cf. **321a**) if the lessee fails to hand over his estate in proper form; otherwise, he must release the land to the lessee. The symbol translated "1 . . . ," after which the inscription breaks off, is the Greek letter eta, which stood for 100 dr.; this indicates that the price of the *prasis epi lysei* was at least 100 dr. (exactly 100 dr. if no further numeric symbols followed the eta) but less than 500 dr. (if the amount were 500 dr. or greater, the initial symbol would not be eta).

Boundary [*horos*] of plot of land sold on condition of release [*pepramenou epi lysei*] to the son of Callistratus, 1[00 + *x* drachmas]. . . .

e. Finley, *SLC* no. 88. *Prasis epi lysei* of mine workshop and slaves. (?4th or 3rd c. B.C.)

IG II² 2747; **Fine**, *Horoi* 46; **Finley**, *SLC* no. 88.

This *horos* was discovered among the ruins of an ancient mine located in the deme of Thoricus in southeastern Attica. For *prasis epi lysei* of a mining workshop and the attached slaves cf. **256** Dem. 37 (selections). The salutation "God(s)" appears commonly at the head of inscriptions of various types (cf. **356** *IG* II² 1362) but rarely among the Attic *horoi.*

Gods. Boundary [*horos*] of workshop and slaves [5] sold on condition of release [*pepramenôn epi lysei*] to Pheidon of the deme Aexone, 1 talent.

f. Finley, *SLC* no. 1. Land and house pledged as security for loan; written contract specifying creditor's right of occupation. (?4th or 3rd c. B.C.)

IG II² 2758; **Fine**, *Horoi* 49, 69–71; **Finley**, *SLC* no. 1.

The rarity in the *horoi* of the stipulation that the creditor "has possession and control" (*echein kai kratein*) of the pledged property until the loan is repaid (cf. **Finley**, *SLC* no. 2A; Demosthenes 37.10) may well indicate that usually the debtor retained possession.

Boundary [*horos*] of plot of land and house pledged as security [*hypokeimenôn*], 800 drachmas, such that the creditor [*themenon*] has possession and control [*echein kai kratein*] in accordance with [5] the contract [*synthêkas*] on deposit with Deinias of the deme Euonymon.

g. Finley, *SLC* no. 12A. *Prasis epi lysei* of land, house, and gardens as security for partial value of land. (?4th or 3rd c. B.C.)

Finley, *SLC* no. 12A and pp. xiv-xviii.

In this instance an unnamed purchaser has bought (by outright sale) a plot of land with house and gardens; unable to pay the entire purchase price, he has "sold on condition of release"—here clearly equivalent to "pledged as security"—the land, house, and gardens for 3,000 dr., the outstanding balance of the outright purchase price, to Philinus, who is either the outright seller or a third party. Cf. **Finley**, *SLC* no. 3.

Boundary [*horos*] of plot of land, house, and gardens sold on condition of release [*pepramenôn epi lysei*] to Philinus of the deme Halae for the price owed for half the plot of land, 3,000 drachmas.

h. Finley, *SLC* nos. 80A, 81A. House "pledged as security on condition of release." (?late 5th-3rd c. B.C.)

B. D. **Meritt**, "Greek Inscriptions," *Hesperia* 32 (1963) 1–56, no. 53; **Finley**, *SLC* nos. 80A, 81A and pp. xii-xiv; **Harris**, "When Is A Sale Not A Sale?" 174–75.

This *horos* records two successive transactions in which a house was pledged as security to the same creditor. A Callias of Euonymon (I. **Kirchner**, *Prosopographia Attica* [Berlin 1901] no. 7864) was a treasurer of the Delian League (*Hellênotamias*: see **2** *IG* I^3 104) in 410/09 (D. **Lewis**, ed., ***Inscriptiones Graecae*** vol. 1 ed. 3 fasc. 1 [Berlin and New York 1981], no. 375, lines 26–27 = R. **Meiggs**-D. **Lewis**, *A Selection of Greek Historical Inscriptions to the End of the Fifth Century B.C.* [rev. ed. Oxford 1988], no. 84, lines 26–27), but the identification with this Callias is far from certain, since Callias is a very common Athenian name. The phrase "pledged as security on condition of release" is redundant (items pledged as security are by definition subject to release upon the discharge of the debt) and apparently arose from the conflation of the more usual "pledged as security" (e.g., **321a**, **321f**) and "sold on condition of release" (e.g., **321b-e**, **g**); this serves as a strong indication that the distinction between hypothecation and *prasis epi lysei* was terminological rather than substantive (cf. especially **320** [Dem.] 33.6–12, **321g**).

Boundary [*horos*] of house pledged as security on condition of release [*hypokeimenês epi lysei*] to Callias of the deme Euonymon, 100 drachmas.

Boundary [*horos*] of house pledged as security on condition of release [*hypokeimenês epi lysei*] to Callias of the deme Euonymon.

10.5. Imports, Exports, Maritime Loans, and the *Dikai emporikai* (Mercantile Lawsuits)

See also **46** [Arist.] *Ath. Pol.* 52.2; **79** [Arist.] *Ath. Pol.* 59.5; **167** Dem. 27.9–11; **171** [Dem.] 35.3–4; **260** [Dem.] 33.19–20, 22, 32–33; **261** Dem. 32.25–28; **263** [Dem.] 56 (selections); **290** [Dem.] 35.47; **304d** [Dem.] 56.2; **332h** Dem. 21.175–76, 178–80.

322. Plutarch, *Solon* 24.1–2. Solon's law banning export of agricultural products other than olive oil. (date of composition late 1st-early 2nd c. A.D.; date of law 594/3 B.C.)

See references and headnote under **1d**. Plutarch's citation of a specific axon (cf. **2** *IG* I[3] 104; **138** Harpo. s.v. *hoti hoi poiêtoi* etc.; **222** *POxy* 221 col. 14 lines 9–16) serves as a strong indicator that this law is the genuine work of Solon.

Among natural products, [Solon] permitted the distribution to foreigners of olive oil alone; he prohibited the export of the rest, and he commanded the archon to lay curses upon the exporters or else pay 100 drachmas to the public treasury himself. [24.2] The first axon is the one that contains this law.

323. [Demosthenes] 35 *Against Lacritus* (selections). (355–338)

See **171** with references and headnote. **323a** translates the text of the maritime loan contract between the lenders Androcles (the speaker of this oration) and Nausicrates of Carystus (on Euboea) and the borrowers Artemon and Apollodorus (not the son of Pasion: see, e.g., **317** [Dem.] 49.48–49, 51–52 with additional references in headnote) of Phaselis (in Asia Minor). Mende and Scione were located on the western prong of the Chalcidice; on (Cimmerian) Bosporus see **246** Isoc. 17.2–9, 11–16; the Borysthenes (modern Dnieper) River debouches into the Black Sea from the north; Hieron was on the eastern side of the Thracian Bosporus, which connects the Propontis (Sea of Marmara) and the Black Sea. References to the star Arcturus and the Dog Star (Sirius) are to their heliacal risings, in mid-September (after which sailing became more perilous) and late July, respectively. With the safe-return provisions in §§12–13 cf. **328** [Dem.] 34.3–7, 33, 36–37, 42, at §33. Jettison of cargo was a standard means of increasing a ship's speed or stability in an emergency; "any payment . . . to enemies" refers to ransom from hostile forces. "Rights of seizure" might be unilaterally asserted by one state for its own residents against residents of another state with which it had hostile relations (cf. [Dem.] 35.26; Demosthenes 51.13; Harpocration s.v. *sylas*; Demosthenes 24 hyp. 2 §1). For the clause asserting the paramount authority of the contract cf. **307** [Dem.] 35.39. In **323b**, note that the *epôbelia* applied to the losing litigant in any *paragraphê* who received less than 20 percent of the jurors' votes (**244** Isoc. 18.1–8, 10–13, 33, 63, at §3, states simply that the losing litigant was fined the *epôbelia*, and accordingly the share of votes garnered by the loser may have been irrelevant); if the *paragraphê* was brought in response to a *dikê emporikê*, the loser was imprisoned pending payment of the *epôbelia* (cf. **263a** [Dem.] 56.3–6). For the prohibitions stated in **323c** cf. **328** [Dem.] 34.3–7, 33, 36–37, 42, at §37; Lycurgus 1.27. On *kyrioi* see the introduction to chapter 5; on *phasis* (declaration) cf. **325** [Dem.] 58.5–6, 8, 10–12; **151** Harpo. s.v. *phasis*; on *apographê* (registration for confiscation) cf. **281** Lys. 29.1–2, 11; **285** *SEG* 12.100.1–16 with **319** *SEG* 12.100.16–21, 23–25, 30–39; **302b** [Arist.] *Ath. Pol.* 52.1. For the Overseers (*scil.* of the Port of Trade) see **327** [Arist.] *Ath. Pol.* 51.4 with additional references in headnote.

a. [Dem.] 35.10–13. Maritime loan contract.

Androcles of the deme Sphettus and Nausicrates of Carystus have lent to Artemon and Apollodorus of Phaselis 3,000 drachmas in cash for a voyage from Athens to Mende or Scione, and from there to Bosporus, and, if they wish, on the left side [of the Black Sea] as far as the Borysthenes, and back to Athens, at the rate of 225 drachmas per thousand (but if they sail out of the Black Sea for Hieron after [the rising of] Arcturus, at the rate of 300 per thousand), on the security of 3,000 Mendaean jars of wine, which shall be conveyed from Mende or Scione on the twenty-oared ship that Hyblesius captains. [11] They pledge this as security, not owing on it any money to anyone else, nor shall they take out additional loans on it. And they shall bring back to Athens in the same ship all the merchandise received from the Black Sea in exchange for the cargo. If the merchandise returns safely to Athens, the borrowers shall repay to the lenders the accruing money in accordance with the contract within twenty days from the day they return to Athens, in full, excepting any jettison that the passengers conduct by joint vote, as well as any payment they make to enemies, but in full as to everything else. And they shall provide to the lenders the security [*hypothêkên*] intact and unencumbered for them to control until they repay the accruing money in accordance with the contract. [12] If they do not make repayment in the agreed-upon time, the lenders shall have the power to pledge [the security] or to sell it at the prevailing price. And if there is any shortfall in the money that is supposed to accrue to the lenders in accordance with the contract, the lenders—each of the lenders by himself or both together—shall have the right to exact it from Artemon and Apollodorus, and from all their property on both land and sea, wherever it may be, just as if they had lost a lawsuit and were overdue in payment. [13] And if they do not enter the Black Sea, after waiting in the Hellespont for ten days after [the rising of] the Dog Star, they shall unload [their cargo] wherever there are no rights of seizure against Athenians, and from there they shall sail back to Athens and repay the interest written in the contract for the previous year. If the ship in which the merchandise is conveyed suffers irreparable damage but the security is salvaged, that which remains shall be the joint property of the lenders. Concerning these matters nothing else shall have greater authority than the contract. Witnesses:

Phormion of the deme Peiraeus, Cephisodotus of Boeotia, Heliodorus of the deme Pithus.

b. [Dem.] 35.45–46. Applicability of the mercantile laws; imprisonment pending payment of *epôbelia* issued in *paragraphê* against *dikê emporikê.*

And if one of us were the defendant in a lawsuit prosecuted by my adversary and had the audacity to bring a counter-indictment [*paragraphên*] on the grounds that the lawsuit was inadmissible, I am well aware that my adversary would be indignant and complain to you, saying that he was suffering terrible treatment and violation of the law if someone did not vote that his lawsuit [*dikên*] was admissible, it being a mercantile lawsuit [*emporikên*]. So, then, Lacritus, you think this is your right; why will it not be mine? Haven't the same laws and the same rights been written for all of us with regard to mercantile lawsuits? [46] . . . Well, what are you proposing, Lacritus? That it shouldn't be enough for us to be deprived of the money we lent you, but we should also be handed over to the prison by you for owing the additional penalty as well, if we don't pay it.

c. [Dem.] 35.50–51 (*lex* + commentary). Law(s) prohibiting Athenian residents from transporting grain to destination other than Athens and from extending maritime loan on ship not transporting grain to Attic port of trade.

For you know, men of the jury, how harsh the law is if any Athenian conveys grain to any place other than Athens or lends money for a voyage to any port of trade other than that of the Athenians; you know the sort of penalties there are for these things, how severe and terrible they are. [51] [To the court clerk:] Better yet, read them the actual law, so that they may understand more precisely.

LAW. And no Athenian or metic residing in Athens, and no person of whom the aforementioned are *kyrioi,* shall be permitted to lend money on any ship that is not going to bring grain to Athens. . . . If a person lends in violation of these provisions, the declaration [*phasin*] and registration [*apographên*] of the money shall occur before the Overseers [*epimelêtas*], in the same manner as has been stated with regard to the ship and the grain. No lawsuit shall be available to him regarding any money that he has lent for a voyage to any place other than Athens, and no magistrate shall introduce a lawsuit regarding such matters.

324. [Demosthenes] 33 *Against Apaturius* 1–3, 23. *Dikê emporikê:*

qualifying conditions, jurisdiction, penalties, and scheduling; *paragraphê* against *dikê emporikê*. (*post* 342)

See references and headnote under **260**. The translation of §23 follows the unanimous manuscript tradition; some editors and commentators transpose the names of the months (on the Athenian calendar see p. 7). In the former case *dikai emporikai* will have been held during the colder two-thirds of the year, when commercial voyages were relatively infrequent (note, e.g., Andocides 1.137: "What greater danger is there for men than to sail the sea in the winter season?"); in the latter case they will have been held during the warmer half of the year, which would have infringed upon commerce insofar as litigants had to remain in Athens for lawsuits instead of plying their trade. For the jurisdiction of the *thesmothetai* over *dikai emporikai* (§1) cf. **79** [Arist.] *Ath. Pol.* 59.5; [Demosthenes] 34.45; for imprisonment pending the payment of a fine levied in a *dikê emporikê* (*ibid.*) cf. **323b** [Dem.] 35.45–46. For "release and discharge" (§3) cf. **320** [Dem.] 33.6–12. On the class of "monthly lawsuits" (*dikai emmênoi*, §23) cf. **46** [Arist.] *Ath. Pol.* 52.2.

For merchants, men of the jury, and for ship-captains, the law commands that there be lawsuits [*dikas*] before the *thesmothetai* if they suffer any wrongdoing in the port of trade [*emporiôi*] or while they are sailing from there to somewhere else or from somewhere else to there, and upon offenders it has imposed the additional penalty of imprisonment until they pay whatever fine has been adjudged against them, so that no one may wrong any merchant on a whim. [2] But for those who are brought to trial over contracts that do not exist, the law has granted them the right to resort to counter-indictment [*paragraphên*], so that no one may be prosecuted maliciously [*sykophantêtai*] but that these lawsuits may be available only to those merchants and ship-captains who are truly being wronged. In fact, many previous defendants in mercantile lawsuits [*emporikais*] have brought counter-indictments in accordance with this very law, and have come before you and exposed their prosecutors as bringing unjust charges and prosecuting maliciously on the pretext of being merchants. [3] . . . Since Apaturius is bringing false charges against me and is prosecuting in violation of the laws, and since there has been release and discharge from all contracts that existed between me and him, and since I have no other contract with him, either maritime or on land, I have brought a counter-indictment against his lawsuit on the grounds that it is inadmissible according to these laws.

LAWS.

. . .

[23] . . . but the filings of the lawsuits for merchants are monthly [*emmênoi*]

from Boedromion to Munychion, so that they may obtain justice immediately and sail away.

325. [Demosthenes] 58 *Against Theocrines* 5–6, 8, 10–12. *Phasis* for illegal maritime mercantile activity; laws addressing sycophancy, including law providing for *endeixis* and *apagôgê* against malicious prosecutor of merchant or ship-captain. (ca. 340)

> See references and headnote under **77**. The *phasis* (declaration) described here was brought by Theocrines against Micon in accordance with the law attested at **323c** [Dem.] 35.50–51. For the fine of 1,000 dr. for nonprosecution of an initiated public lawsuit or for receiving less than 20 percent of the jurors' votes in the prosecution of a public lawsuit cf., e.g., **34** Aeschin. 2.93; **35** Dem. 21.47; **152** [Arist.] *Ath. Pol.* 56.6–7; **288** Dem. 22.25–27, 69–73. On *endeixis* (denunciation) cf., e.g., **289** Dem. 24.104–5, 112–15, 120–21, 129, 146 with additional references in headnote; on *apagôgê* (summary arrest) cf., e.g., **288** with additional references in headnote. For the *epimelêtai tou emporiou* (Overseers of the Port of Trade) cf. **327** [Arist.] *Ath. Pol.* 51.4 with additional references in headnote.

First, then, [the court clerk] will read to you the law concerning those who make declarations [*phainontôn*] and do not prosecute but instead come to terms in violation of the laws . . . ; then he will read the actual declaration [*phasin*] that my adversary made against Micon. [To the court clerk:] Read.

LAW.

[6] This law, men of the jury, explicitly states to those who choose to bring indictments [*graphesthai graphas*] or make declarations or do any of the other things listed in this law the conditions on which each of these things must be done. These conditions are, just as you heard from the law itself, that if a person prosecutes but does not receive one-fifth of the votes, he shall pay 1,000 drachmas, and if he does not prosecute, Theocrines, he shall pay another thousand, in order that no one may prosecute maliciously [*sykophantêi*]. . . . I therefore assert that, in regard to the present denunciation [*endeixin*], Theocrines is liable because he made a declaration against Micon of the deme Cholleidae and then did not prosecute him but instead took money and sold the matter.

. . .

[8] Men of the jury, my adversary here submitted this declaration [*phasin*], having summoned Micon, and the secretary of the Overseers of the Port of Trade [*tôn tou emporiou epimelêtôn*], Euthyphemus, received it. The declaration lay on display for a long time in front of their meeting-place, until my adversary took money and allowed it to be struck from the list when the mag-

istrates called him to the preliminary hearing [*anakrisin*].

. . .

[10] So, then, men of the jury, you have heard those who should know best testify that Theocrines brought a declaration against [*ephêne*] Micon's ship, and that the declaration lay on display for a long time, and that when he was called to the preliminary hearing he did not respond and did not prosecute. Now, that he is liable not only to the [fine of] 1,000 drachmas but also to summary arrest [*apagôgêi*] and all the other things that this law commands the person who maliciously prosecutes [*sykophantounta*] merchants and ship-captains to suffer, you will easily learn from the law itself. [11] You see, the man who made the law, wishing neither that those merchants who do wrong should go unpunished nor that the rest of them should have problems, simply prohibited people of this sort from bringing declarations unless someone was confident that he could demonstrate in your court that the matters concerning which he was making his declaration had occurred. If, however, a malicious prosecutor acted in violation of these provisions, he was to be liable to denunciation [*endeixin*] and summary arrest. [To the court clerk:] Better yet, read the law itself; it will give much clearer instruction than I can.

LAW.

[12] You hear from the law, men of the jury, what it commands the malicious prosecutor [*sykophantên*] to suffer. So, then, if Micon committed any of the acts that Theocrines stated in his declaration that he committed, and Theocrines let the matter drop and reconciled with the man, then Theocrines does all of you wrong and rightly owes the thousand drachmas. If, on the other hand, Micon rightfully sailed where he was supposed to . . . , and Theocrines has brought a declaration and made a summons, then Theocrines is maliciously prosecuting ship-captains and has violated not only the previous law but the one that was just read out. . . .

326. Demosthenes 32 *Against Zenothemis* 1. Qualifying conditions for *dikê emporikê* and for *paragraphê* against *dikê emporikê*. (?ca. 340)

See references and headnote under **261**. It is a matter of scholarly debate whether "for contracts concerning voyages to and from Athens" and "for matters regarding which there are written contracts" are joint or separate and sufficient conditions; that is, whether both must be met or either alone may suffice in order for a *dikê emporikê* to lie.

The laws command, men of the jury, that there be lawsuits [*dikas*] available to ship-captains and merchants for contracts [*symbolaiôn*] concerning voyages to and from Athens and for matters regarding which there are written contracts [*syngraphai*], but that if a person litigates in violation of these provisions, the lawsuit shall be inadmissible.

327. [Aristotle], *Constitution of the Athenians (Ath. Pol.)* 51.4. Duties of the *epimelêtai tou emporiou* (Overseers of the Port of Trade); requirement that two-thirds of grain cargo arriving at Attic port of trade be conveyed to city of Athens. (332–322)

See references and headnote under **1c**. This passage follows immediately upon **311** [Arist.] *Ath. Pol.* 51.1–3. For the *epimelêtai tou emporiou* cf. **323c** [Dem.] 35.50–51; **325** [Dem.] 58.5–6, 8, 10–12. The word translated "city" (*asty*) refers to the city of Athens proper, as distinct from the rest of Attica.

[The Athenians] appoint by lot ten Overseers of the Port of Trade [*emporiou . . . epimelêtas*]. These are assigned to oversee the trading stations and to compel merchants to convey to the city two-thirds of the grain that is brought by sea to the port of trade for grain.

328. [Demosthenes] 34 *Against Phormion* 3–7, 33, 36–37, 42. Qualifying conditions for *dikê emporikê* and for *paragraphê* against *dikê emporikê*; maritime loan contract; law prohibiting transport of grain by Athenian resident to destination other than Attic port of trade. (327/6)

See especially F. A. **Paley**-J. E. **Sandys**, *Demosthenes: Select Private Orations* 1^3 (Cambridge 1898: text and commentary); S. **Isager**-M. H. **Hansen**, *Aspects of Athenian Society in the Fourth Century B.C.: A Historical Introduction to and Commentary on the Paragraphe-speeches and the Speech Against Dionysodorus in the Corpus Demosthenicum (XXXII–XXXVIII and LVI)* (Odense 1975); D. M. **MacDowell**, *Demosthenes, Speeches 27–38* (Austin 2004: translation with introduction and notes); ***idem,*** *Demosthenes the Orator* (Oxford 2009) 279–84; also A. **Schäfer**, *Demosthenes und seine Zeit* (Leipzig 1858–87) 4.300–6; **Blass**, *AB* 3.1.576–82; F. C. **Doherty**, *Three Private Speeches of Demosthenes* (Oxford 1927: text and commentary); L. **Gernet**, *Démosthène: Plaidoyers civils, Tome I, Discours XXVII–XXXVIII* (Paris 1954: text, French translation, and notes); **Usher**, *GO* 255.

This dispute concerns a maritime loan of 20 mn. (= 2,000 dr.: p. 4) made by the speaker Chrysippus to his adversary Phormion (a different man from the Phormion in Demosthenes 36: **148** Dem. 36.20, 22) on terms that Phormion repay him 2,600 dr. upon returning to Athens (§23). Chrysippus filed a *dikê emporikê* to recover his money, but Phormion interposed a *paragraphê*, and at the trial of that *paragraphê* Chrysippus delivered this speech. With the (standard) clause in the maritime loan contract mandating repayment only if the ship returns safely (§33) cf. **323a** [Dem.] 35.10–13. On "direct trial" (*euthydikia*, §4) cf., e.g., **229** Isae. 6.3–4, 43–44, 52; here the meaning is that the defendant must answer the original lawsuit instead of interposing a *paragraphê*. Paerisades (§36) was king of Cimmerian Bosporus (see **246** Isoc. 17.2–9, 11–16, and cf. **323a** [Dem.] 35.10–13); Acanthus (*ibid.*) was a city in the Chalcidice. With the law discussed in §37, in which "the most extreme penalties" presumably refers to death, cf. **323c** [Dem.] 35.50–51; Lycurgus 1.27.

Now, as to the counter-indictment [*paragraphês*], my argument is brief. Even my adversaries, you see, do not categorically deny that a contract was made in your port of trade [*emporiôi*]; instead, they claim that no contract with them exists anymore, since they have done nothing outside the terms written in the contract. [4] But the laws, in accordance with which you sit as jurors, do not say that. Rather, with regard to contracts that have not been made at all, either in Athens or for the Athenian port of trade, the laws have granted the right to bring a counter-indictment [*paragraphesthai*]; but if a person admits that a contract was made but contends that he has done everything that was agreed on, the laws command that he come to court for direct trial [*euthydikian*] and defend himself, not prosecute his prosecutor. . . . [5] Consider, men of Athens, what is admitted by my adversaries themselves and what is disputed. . . . They admit that they borrowed the money and made a contract for the loan, but they claim that they repaid the money in gold to Lampis, Dion's slave, in Bosporus. We, however, will show not only that he did not repay it but that he could not have repaid it. . . .

[6] Men of Athens, I lent my adversary Phormion here 20 minae for a round-trip voyage to the Black Sea on the security of twice that sum, and I deposited a contract with Cittus the banker. But, although the contract mandated that he put on board the ship cargo worth 4,000 drachmas, he did the most amazing thing of all: straightaway, in the Peiraeus, without our knowledge, he took out additional loans of 4,500 drachmas from Theodorus the Phoenician and 1,000 from the ship-captain, Lampis. [7] And although he had to purchase in Athens cargo worth 115 minae if he was going to do for all his lenders what was written in the contracts, he purchased cargo worth only 5,500 drachmas, including the provisions; but he owed 75 minae. This, then, was the beginning of his wrongdoing, men of Athens: he neither provided the security nor put the merchandise on board the ship, although the contract mandated that it was compulsory to put it on board. [To the court clerk:] Please take the contract.

CONTRACT.

. . .

[33] He says that the contract orders him to repay the money if the ship returns safely. [To Phormion:] Right, and it also orders you to put the merchandise on board the ship or else pay 5,000 drachmas.

. . .

[36] . . . When Paerisades made a proclamation in Bosporus that if anyone wished to convey grain to Athens, to the Attic port of trade, he could export the grain tax-free, Lampis, who was in Bosporus, obtained permission to export grain and the tax exemption in the name of the city; then he filled a large ship with grain, conveyed it to Acanthus, and disposed of it there. . . . [37] And he did this, men of the jury, although he lives in Athens, and his wife and children are here, and the laws have set down the most extreme penalties for anyone living in Athens who conveys grain to any place other than the Attic port of trade. . . . And to prove that I am telling the truth, [To the court clerk:] please take the deposition and the law.

DEPOSITION. LAW.

. . .

[42] . . . But as to the fact that the lawsuit is admissible, the law itself testifies: it commands that mercantile lawsuits [*dikas . . . emporikas*] be available for contracts made in Athens or for the Athenian port of trade, and not only those made in Athens but all those that are made for the purpose of a sea-voyage to Athens. [To the court clerk:] Please take the laws.

LAWS.

CHAPTER 11

Impiety

Handbooks: J. H. **Lipsius**, *Das attische Recht und Rechtsverfahren* (Leipzig 1905–15) 62, 143, 358–68; A. R. W. **Harrison**, *The Law of Athens* (Oxford 1968–71) 2.59–64, 218–21; D. M. **MacDowell**, *The Law in Classical Athens* (Ithaca, NY 1978) 135, 192–202; S. C. **Todd**, *The Shape of Athenian Law* (Oxford 1993) 307–15; R. **Parker**, "Law and Religion," in *The Cambridge Companion to Ancient Greek Law,* ed. M. Gagarin-D. Cohen (Cambridge 2005) 61–81. **Studies:** K. **Latte**, *Heiliges Recht: Untersuchungen zur Geschichte der sakralen Rechtsformen in Griechenland* (Tübingen 1920); J. H. **Oliver**, *The Athenian Expounders of the Sacred and Ancestral Law* (Baltimore 1950); A. W. **Gomme**-A. **Andrewes**-K. J. **Dover**, *A Historical Commentary on Thucydides* (Oxford 1945–81) 4.264–88; D. M. **MacDowell**, *Andokides*: On the Mysteries (Oxford 1962); K. J. **Dover**, "The Freedom of the Intellectual in Greek Society," *Talanta* 7 (1975/76) 24–54; M. **Ostwald**, *From Popular Sovereignty to the Sovereignty of Law: Law, Society, and Politics in Fifth-Century Athens* (Berkeley and Los Angeles 1986), esp. 161–69, 191–98, 274–77, 328–33, 528–50; I. F. **Stone**, *The Trial of Socrates* (Boston 1988); R. W. **Wallace**, *The Areopagos Council, to 307 B.C.* (Baltimore 1989) 106–12, 204–5; T. C. **Brickhouse**-N. D. **Smith**, *Socrates on Trial* (Princeton 1989); D. M. **MacDowell**, *Demosthenes*: Against Meidias *(Oration 21)* (Oxford 1990); D. **Cohen**, *Law, Sexuality, and Society: The Enforcement of Morals in Classical Athens* (Cambridge 1991) 203–17; R. **Garland**, *Introducing New Gods: The Politics of Athenian Religion* (Ithaca, NY 1992); R. **Parker**, *Athenian Religion: A History* (Oxford 1996) 199–217; W. D. **Furley**, *Andokides and the Herms: A Study of Crisis in Fifth-Century Athenian Religion* (London 1996); L.-L. **O'Sullivan**, "Athenian Impiety Trials in the Late Fourth Century B.C.," *CQ* n.s. 47 (1997) 136–52; T. C. **Brickhouse**-N. D. **Smith**, eds., *The Trial and Execution of Socrates: Sources and Controversies* (Oxford 2002); S. C. **Todd**, "Revisiting the Herms and the Mysteries," and E. **Carawan**, "Andocides' Defence and

MacDowell's Solution," in *Law, Rhetoric, and Comedy in Classical Athens: Essays in Honour of Douglas M. MacDowell*, ed. D. L. Cairns-R. A. Knox (Swansea 2004) 87–102, 103–112; R. **Parker**, "What Are Sacred Laws?," in *The Law and the Courts in Ancient Greece*, ed. E. M. Harris-L. Rubinstein (London 2004) 57–70; S. C. **Todd**, *A Commentary on Lysias, Speeches 1–11* (Oxford 2007); R. **Waterfield**, *Why Socrates Died* (New York 2009).

While no legal definition of impiety (*asebeia*) survives, and quite possibly none existed (p. 28; compare, for example, the undefined offense of hubris: **35** Dem. 21.47), the wide variety of attested prosecutions for impiety demonstrates that any act that could be construed as violating a rule (including, before 403/2 [**338h**], a rule not stated in writing) affecting sacred matters—whether a law or decree of the Athenian state or a part thereof (e.g., **329**, **332**, **345**, **351**) or an ancestral religious custom that came under the purview of the *Exêgêtai* ("Interpreters" of the sacred law: e.g., **337b**, **338i**) or another authority (e.g., **356**)—might be categorized as impiety. This chapter treats offenses of impiety apart from the special category of *hierosylia* (temple-robbery), on which see chapter 9.

The dedicated and general legal remedy for impiety was the *graphê asebeias* (indictment for impiety: **339**, **340**, **342**, **349**, **355**; ?**329**, ?**337c**, ?**348**, ?**352**, ?**354**). This action was filed with the *basileus* and tried in a *dikastêrion*; it was an assessable lawsuit (*agôn timêtos*: p. 40) without penal limit, and accordingly prosecutors might propose any penalty up to and including death. (On the possible exceptions to these rules in cases involving sacred olive trees, see the next paragraph.) Other attested remedies for impiety, some of which lay only under certain defined circumstances, were *eisangelia* (impeachment: **333**, **334**, **335**, **337**, **338**, **345**; ?**353**, ?**356**; cf. chapter 12); *phasis* (declaration) before the *basileus* (**349b**; ?**329**, ?**352**); *probolê* (presentation: **332**, **333**); *endeixis* (denunciation: **337**, **338**); *apagôgê* (summary arrest: **349b**), which under normal circumstances was perhaps limited to *hierosylia* (see the introduction to chapter 9 and, e.g., **283** Xen. *Mem.* 1.2.62; **289** Dem. 24.104–5, 112–15, 120–21, 129, 146; **300** Libanius, hyp. [Dem.] 25.1–2) but was explicitly sanctioned by decree against the fugitive Diagoras of Melos (**337d**, **346b**); a lawsuit (?*dikê*) before the Eumolpidae (**349b**); and possibly *apophasis* (report) by the Areopagus (?**357**; cf. chapter 12).

An Athenian foundation myth held that Athena, by her gift of an olive tree on the Acropolis, had defeated Poseidon (who offered salt water) to become patron deity of the city. Throughout Attica, there were olive trees that were believed to be descended from Athena's original tree, and therefore sacred. Customarily, a sacred olive tree (*moria*; the general word for olive tree is *ela(i)a*) was surrounded by a fence (*sêkos*) that served to advertise its status;

whether the word *sêkos* came by extension to be applied to the tree it enclosed is a matter of continuing scholarly debate. Special legislation protected sacred olive trees and their products (**§11.1**: **329–331**), and the enforcement of these laws fell under the purview of the Council of the Areopagus. It was illegal to remove a sacred olive tree or (if in **329** *sêkos* refers solely to the fence, which is disputed) to remove the fence surrounding a sacred olive tree so as to conceal its status. A plausible reconstruction of the history of the relevant procedure, based on the varying testimony of the sources, is that originally the penalty for such violations was death (perhaps with confiscation of property) (**331**), but by the 390s, the penalty was reduced to exile and confiscation of property (**329**), and by the 330s or 320s, trials were no longer held (**331**). According to Lysias 7, the defendant's speech from the sole surviving attested lawsuit for removal of an olive tree/*sêkos* (**329**), there was no time limit (*prothesmia*: p. 34) for prosecution. Most scholars identify this lawsuit as a *graphê asebeias*, but the defendant stands trial before the Areopagus (as opposed to a *dikastêrion*) and envisages a fixed penalty of exile and confiscation of his property (as opposed to the assessable penalty elsewhere attested for the *graphê asebeias*); if the identification of the procedure is correct, cases relating to sacred olive trees will have had a special Areopagite jury and a fixed penalty. Owing to the importance of the olive to the Athenian economy (see the introduction to chapter 10 and **322** Plut. *Solon* 24.1–2), even olive trees that were not sacred were subject to strict legal control, with stated exceptions for sacral use (**330**).

At some point in the late fifth or early fourth century, the procedure called *probolê* (presentation) was introduced as a remedy for violations occurring at specified religious festivals (**§11.2**: **332–333**). The original law on *probolê* governed the festival of the Dionysia; its provisions were subsequently extended to other festivals (**332b**). Any willing adult male, Athenian or foreign (**332h**), might accuse a person of "wrongdoing concerning the festival" (*adikein peri tên heortên*: **332a**, **332b**, **332d**, **332h**) and bring the first phase of a *probolê* before the Assembly. This preliminary hearing culminated in a vote by the Assembly either in favor of the accuser (*katacheirotonia*, "[vote of] condemnation": **332a**, **332h**, **332i**, **332j**) or in favor of the accused (*apocheirotonia*, "[vote of] acquittal"; e.g., Demosthenes 21.214). The Assembly's vote was neither binding as to further action nor (other than formally) punitive (see especially **332j**); following the hearing before the Assembly, and regardless of its vote, an accuser who so wished could bring the *probolê* to trial in a *dikastêrion*. This lawsuit fell under the supervision of the *thesmothetai* (**333**; **44a** Dem. 21.31–33) and was assessable without penal limit (**332c**, **332d**, **332g**, **332h**), with the proviso that any fine imposed was payable to the state, not to the prosecutor (**332d**); some scholars see in several passages (**332c**, **332g**) evidence that in a *probolê*, in contrast to other assessable lawsuits, the jury was not bound to sentence a convicted defendant in accordance with the proposal of the prosecution or defense but had full penal discretion.

The most (in)famous incidents of impiety in Athenian history were the scandals of the herms and the Mysteries of the year 415 (**§11.3: 334–338**). On the night of June 6/7, during the preparations for an Athenian invasion of Sicily, the vast majority of herms (rectangular blocks with the head of the god Hermes on top and an erect phallus front and center) suffered mutilation. The resulting investigation also uncovered that the Eleusinian Mysteries, secret rites in honor of the goddesses Demeter and Persephone that were celebrated annually at the town of Eleusis in western Attica and required the initiation of participants, had been profaned by performances in private homes. This investigation and the following proceedings relied heavily on statements by informers, including foreigners, slaves, and women; informing (*mênysis*; plural *mênyseis*) by slaves about religious offenses normally resulted in the slaves' being set free if their statements proved accurate (**329c**; **278** Lys. 5.1, 5). The procedure employed against the accused was *eisangelia* (**335**, **338e**; see chapter 12); most of those convicted were sentenced to death (some *in absentia*, as they had fled to avoid arrest) and had their property confiscated. Andocides, one of those implicated in the scandals and accordingly arrested and imprisoned pending judgment, turned informer and was released; soon after his release, a decree authored by Isotimides (see especially **338g**) mandated that any person who had committed and confessed to an act of impiety was to be barred from the agora and sanctuaries. (Also in, or shortly before, 415/4, Diagoras of Melos had a bounty put on his head for profaning the Mysteries [**337d**, **344a**, **346**]: the exact relationship between this event and the scandals of 415 is unknown. For another, earlier violation of the Mysteries see **343**.) Some fifteen years later, in 400 or 399, Andocides was prosecuted by *endeixis* for violating the Isotimides decree, tried in a *dikastêrion* by a jury of men who had been initiated in the Mysteries, and acquitted (**337**, **338**).

In 399, either shortly before or shortly after the *endeixis* of Andocides (depending upon its date), the philosopher Socrates underwent the most famous trial in the annals of Athens (**§11.4: 339–342**). Socrates was tried by *graphê asebeias* on charges of "not acknowledging the gods whom the city [of Athens] acknowledges and . . . introducing other, novel divinities" and "corrupting the young" (see especially **342**). The accusation of failure to acknowledge the (traditional) gods (the verb *nomizein*, in this context usually translated here "acknowledge," denotes both believing in and paying proper worship to the gods) had a precursor in the decree of Diopeithes (**271c** Plut. *Pericles* 32.1–4, 35.4–5), passed probably in the 430s (but presumably no longer valid after 403/2:

see **338h**), which provided for *eisangelia* against "those who did not acknowledge the divine or who taught doctrines about things in the sky" and specifically targeted the philosopher Anaxagoras (**344**). Introducing novel divinities was likewise a standard manifestation of impiety (cf. **353e**); in Socrates' case the charge appears to have stemmed from his claim that a personal divinity (*daimonion*) occasionally told him not to do things (**340e**). "Corrupting the young" was not the name of an offense under Athenian law but rather a thinly-veiled reference to Socrates' having taught Critias, leader of the extremist faction of the Thirty Tyrants (p. 12; Aeschines 1.173). Socrates' *graphê asebeias* was an assessable lawsuit without penal limit; he was convicted, sentenced to death, and executed by self-administered hemlock (**340**, **341**, **342**).

Other attested cases of impiety (**§11.5**: **343–357**) further demonstrate both the range of potentially impious acts and the variety of procedures available to redress them (although the procedure in any given case frequently defies secure identification, and many of the sources on these cases are sufficiently late to warrant caution). These cases include profanation of the Eleusinian Mysteries, both intentional (**346**, **350b**) and unintentional (**343**); failure to acknowledge the gods (**344**, **347**); illicit astronomy (**344**); violation of a decree on honors paid to Demeter, Persephone, and various other gods, redressable by *eisangelia* (**345**); battery upon the Athenian superintendents of the sanctuary of Apollo on Delos, probably prosecuted by *graphê asebeias* (**348**); associating with a parricide (in a case where the defendant was the brother of the alleged victim and the uncle of the alleged killer), prosecuted by *graphê asebeias* (**349a**); introducing novel divinities and/or assembling illicit religious groups (**350a**, **351**, **353**); improper conduct of religious rites (**351**, **352**); removal of items from sanctuaries (**345**, **351**, **356**); sorcery (**350b**, **354a**); composition and performance of apparently impious poems, prosecuted by *graphê asebeias* (**355**); and verbal disrespect toward the cult statue of Athena in the Parthenon, possibly resulting in *apophasis* by the Areopagus (**357**).

See also **1** (Trial and punishment of the Alcmaeonids for the killing of Cylon's partisans); **17** [Dem.] 47.67–73; **269** Cic. *On Divination* 1.54; **270** Philochorus, *FGrHist* 328 F 121; **271** (Pericles' trial and conviction for theft of public property); **275** Isoc. 18.57; **276** Isoc. 20.6; **278** Lys. 5.1, 5; **285** *SEG* 12.100.1–16; **287** Xen. *Hell.* 1.7.22; **288** Dem. 22.25–27, 69–73; **289** Dem. 24.104–5, 112–15, 120–21, 129, 146; **291** Arist. *Rhet.* 1373b38–1374a5, 1374a15–16; **296** Dem. 57.63–65; **297** Dem. 19.293–94; **299** [Dem.] 58.14–15; **300** Libanius, hyp. [Dem.] 25.1–2; **365** Lyc. 1.117–18; **375** Xen. *Hell.* 1.7.1–16, 20–26, 34–35; **387f** Lyc. 1.147.

11.1. Sacred Olive Trees

329. Lysias 7 *On the* Sêkos (selections). (*post* 397/6)

See especially S. C. **Todd**, *A Commentary on Lysias, Speeches 1–11* (Oxford 2007: text, translation, and commentary); also F. **Blass**, *Die attische Beredsamkeit* (Leipzig 1887–98) 1.590–96; R. C. **Jebb**, *The Attic Orators from Antiphon to Isaeus*[2] (London 1893) 1.284–88; L. **Gernet**-M. **Bizos**, *Lysias* (2 vols., Paris 1989: text with French translation and notes); C. **Carey**, *Lysias: Selected Speeches* (Cambridge 1989: text and commentary); S. **Usher**, *Greek Oratory: Tradition and Originality* (Oxford 1999) 88–91; S. C. **Todd**, *Lysias* (Austin 2000: translation with introduction and notes).

The speaker of Lysias 7 is on trial before the Council of the Areopagus (**329a**, **329c**, **329d**) for removing, at least a year previously (**329b**), a *sêkos* (for the meaning of this and other terms relating to sacred olive trees see the introduction to this chapter) from a farm he owns. The procedure is usually identified as a *graphê asebeias* but may have been a *phasis* (declaration) before the *basileus* (cf. **349b** Dem. 22.27). The prosecutor is named Nicomachus, and the penalty in the case of conviction is exile and confiscation of property (**329a**, **329c**; contrast **331** [Arist.] *Ath. Pol.* 60.2–3, and note that elsewhere the *graphê asebeias* is attested as an assessable lawsuit: **340f** Pl. *Ap.* 36a5-b5, 36e1–37a1, 38b1–9, and perhaps **354b** Plut. *Dem.* 14.6). The defendant's statement as to the lack of risk faced by Nicomachus (**329d**) may indicate that Nicomachus did not face the 1,000-drachma fine, standard in most public lawsuits (and attested elsewhere for the *graphê asebeias*: **340f** Pl. *Ap.* 36a5-b5, 36e1–37a1, 38b1–9), for receiving less than one-fifth of the jurors' votes. The outcome of the trial is unknown. On the collection of sacred olives (**329a**) cf. **331** [Arist.] *Ath. Pol.* 60.2–3. On *mênysis* (informing) by slaves (**329c**, §§16–17) cf. **278** Lys. 5.1, 5; **334** Thuc. 6.27–29, 53, 60–61; **337e** Lys. 6.21–24; **338** Andoc. 1 (selections); **354a** [Dem.] 25.79–80. On the *prothesmia* (statute of limitations: **329c**, §17) see p. 34 and cf., e.g., **150** Dem. 38.3–4, 14–15, 17, 23. On *ephêgêsis*, which may be referred to in §22 (**329c**), see p. 30 and cf., e.g., **288** Dem. 22.25–27, 69–73. For the phrase *peri tou sômatos* (**329c**, §26) see **70** Lys. 9.5–12, 15–16. In §37 (**329d**) "they" are the defendant's slaves: the defendant has tendered to Nicomachus a challenge to torture them (p. 24), but Nicomachus has refused.

a. Lys. 7.1–3. Jurisdiction, charge, and penalty.

Previously, councillors, I used to think that a person who so wished could, by leading a quiet life, avoid being involved in lawsuits and troubles; but now I have so unexpectedly fallen victim to accusations and depraved sycophants. . . . [2] And this trial is difficult for me because I was at first indicted for removing an olive tree [*elaian*] from the ground, and they approached and made inquiries of the men who had purchased the right to collect the fruits of the sacred olive trees [*moriôn*]; but since they were unable by that means to discover that I had done anything wrong, they now claim that I have removed a *sêkos*. . . . [3] And as for the accusations that my adversary has plotted against me before coming here, I must hear them at the same time as you who will pass judgment on the matter, and I must stand trial at the risk of both my country and my property.

b. Lys. 7.11. Date of alleged offense.

The prosecutor claims that a *sêkos* was cut out [*ekkekophthai*] by me in the archonship of Suniades [397/6]. . . .

c. Lys. 7.16–17, 19, 22, 25–26. *Mênysis* (informing) by slaves; *prothesmia* (statute of limitations); details of alleged offense; ?*ephêgêsis*; jurisdiction of and oversight by Areopagus and *epignômones* (inspectors); penalties.

And how would I not have been the most miserable of all men if, for the rest of my life, I was going to have my servants not as my slaves but as my masters, since they had knowledge of a deed of this kind? Even if they committed the most grievous offenses against me, I could exact no punishment from them, since I would have been well aware that it was in their power both to punish me and, by informing [*mênysasin*], themselves to become free. [17] Moreover . . . , how would I have dared, when so many people had leased [the plot of land] and all of them knew about it, to remove the *sêkos* for the sake of a small profit, when there was no statute of limitations [*prothesmias*] for the danger, and so it was in the interest of all those who worked the plot of land alike for the *sêkos* to be preserved, so that if anyone made an accusation against them, they could refer the blame to the person they passed the land on to?

. . .

[19] . . . [Nicomachus] claims that I stood by, my slaves cut out the roots, and the ox-driver loaded up the wood and took it away.

. . .

[22] [To Nicomachus:] And yet if, at the time when you claim to have seen me removing the sacred olive tree [*morian*], you had brought in [*epêgages*] the nine archons, or else some members of the Areopagus, you would have needed no other witnesses: that way the very men who were going to pass judgment on the matter would have known you were telling the truth.

. . .

[25] . . . [To the jury:] Moreover, I shall provide you yourselves as witnesses to these things. You conduct oversight each month and dispatch inspectors [*epignômonas*] each year, and none of these has ever punished me for working the land around the sacred olive trees [*morias*]. [26] Now, obviously I would not consider small penalties [*zêmias*] so significant while considering risks concerning my person [*peri tou sômatos*] so insignificant. . . .

d. Lys. 7.37–38. Jurisdiction; risk to prosecutor.

You see, if they said about me what my adversary wanted them to say, I would have had no defense, and if they did not agree with him, he would have been liable to no penalty. . . . [38] You must bear in mind, councillors, whom you should believe more—those for whom many men have testified or the one for whom no one has dared testify—and whether it is more likely that my adversary is lying at no risk or that I committed such a deed at such considerable risk. . . .

330. [Demosthenes] 43 *Against Macartatus* 71 (*lex*). Law on olive trees. (date of speech ?ca. 345; date of law 508/7 or later)

See references and headnote under **4**. "Public or demotic" means of the entire Athenian people or of a deme, respectively; the reference to demes indicates that the law cannot antedate the reforms of Cleisthenes (p. 6). "The goddess" is Athena (cf., e.g., **169** [Dem.] 43.58). On *prytaneia* (court fees) cf., e.g., **244** Isoc. 18.1–8, 10–13, 33, 63. For the *praktores* ("Exactors") cf. **170** Andoc. 1.73–79. The angled brackets (< >) enclose an editorial supplement to the text.

If a person digs out an olive tree [*elaan*] at Athens, unless for a sacred rite of the Athenians, public or demotic, or for his own use, of up to two olive trees per year, or for necessary use for a decedent, he shall owe 100 drachmas to the public treasury for each olive tree, and one-tenth of this shall be the property of the goddess. And he shall also owe to the individual who prosecutes him 100 drachmas for each olive tree. Lawsuits [*dikas*] concerning these things shall be before the archons for those cases which each of them judges. The prosecutor shall deposit the court fees [*prytaneia*] for his own side. When any person is convicted, the archons before whom the lawsuit takes place shall submit in writing to the Exactors [*praktorsin*] the amount due to the public treasury, and to the Treasurers of the Property of the Goddess <the amount due to the goddess>. If they do not submit it in writing, they themselves shall owe it.

331. [Aristotle], *Constitution of the Athenians* (*Ath. Pol.*) 60.2–3. Regulations on sacred olive trees and their oil. (332–322)

See references and headnote under **1c**. Here the author describes the collection and distribution of oil from the sacred olive trees, with reference to past practice (cf. **329** Lys. 7 [selections]). "The archon" is the eponymous archon (p. 2), who along with his fellow archons "ascended to the Areopagus" at the end of his year in office (p. 2). The *kotylê* (pl. *kotylai*), as a measure of liquid capacity, was equal to approximately 8.6 fl. oz. (256 ml.). For the *athlothetai* (Commissioners of the Games) and the Panathenaea, cf. **254** Dem. 39.1, 5, 7–18.

The olive oil is collected from the sacred olive trees [*moriôn*]; the archon exacts it from the possessors of the plots of land on which the sacred olive trees are located, 1½ *kotylai* from each trunk. Previously the city used to sell [the contract for collecting] the crop, and if a person dug out or cut down a sacred olive tree, the Council of the Areopagus held the trial, and if it convicted someone, it punished him with death. But since the possessor of the plot of land has been paying the olive oil, the law continues to exist, but the trial has been done away with. The city receives the olive oil on the basis of the piece of landed property, not from the trunks. [60.3] The archon, then, collects the oil that comes due in his year of office and hands it over to the treasurers on the Acropolis, and he is not permitted to ascend to the Areopagus until he hands all of it over to the treasurers. The treasurers keep it on the Acropolis the rest of the time, and at the Panathenaea they distribute it to the Commissioners of the Games; the Commissioners of the Games distribute it to the winning contestants. The prizes are, for winners of the musical competition, silver and gold; for winners of the competition in manliness, shields; and for winners of the athletic competition and the horse race, olive oil.

11.2. *Probolê* (Presentation)

See also **44** Dem. 21 (selections); **255** Dem. 21 (selections).

332. Demosthenes 21 *Against Meidias* (selections). (347/6)

See references and headnote under **22**. (The debate over whether this speech was ever delivered at trial centers around Aeschines 3.52: "and then there's this, the matter of Meidias and the punches [Demosthenes] took in the orchestra while he was serving as chorus-producer, and how he sold for 30 minae . . . the Assembly's condemnation [*katacheirotonian*] that it voted against Meidias in the Theater of Dionysus"; the 30 mn. may refer to a bribe to avert trial, or to the *timêma* Demosthenes proposed at trial.) On the *chorêgia* (**332a**) see p. 25 and cf., e.g., **254** Dem. 39.1, 5, 7–18. In **332b**, for the *prytaneis* (§8) see p. 6 and cf., e.g., **271c** Plut. *Pericles* 32.1–4, 35.4–5; in the early fourth century, allotted *proedroi* ("presiders": §9) replaced the *prytaneis* as the presiding officials for meetings of the Council of 500 and the Assembly. The Pandia, Lenaea, and Thargelia were all religious festivals: the Pandia occurred soon after the City Dionysia in the month of Elaphebolion (on the Dionysia cf., e.g., **139** Lys. 32.8–10, 19–24; for the Athenian calendar see p. 7), the Lenaea in Gamelion, and the Thargelia in Thargelion. "The archon" (§9) is the eponymous archon. On debt and security (§10) see chapter 10; "the other offenders" (*ibid.*) are those specified in the first law (§8). Note that "those who use violence" (§11) are not mentioned in either law, and that the law in §8 (and, by inference, that in §10) was enacted at some time after the incident described in **332f** (which occurred sometime before 406). In **332c**, "these acts" are the specific acts of wrongdoing imputed to Meidias by Demosthenes: see **332a**; **255a** Dem. 21.16–17, 25. "Whatever you think is just," addressed to the jury, has (along with **332g**) indicated to some commentators that the penal assessment in a *probolê*, besides being unlimited (cf. **332d**; for the formula "whatever he must suffer or pay" cf., e.g., **340f** Pl. *Ap.* 36a5-b5, 36e1–37a1, 38b1–9; **35** Dem. 21.47), was (unlike in other assessable [*timêtoi*] lawsuits: p. 40) at the jury's sole discretion, the proposals by the prosecution and defense notwithstanding. In **332d**, note that financial gain for a successful prosecutor was possible in a "private lawsuit" for damage (*dikê blabês*: see chapter 8), but not in a *graphê hybreôs* (see chapter 2, especially **44b** Dem. 21.45). In **332e**, note that the unreal condition "even if one convicted him of impiety [*asebeian*]" indicates that Meidias is not formally charged with *asebeia* (but rather with "wrongdoing concerning the festival": **332a**, **332b**, **332h**); for specific characterization of Meidias' acts as constituting impiety cf. especially Dem. 21.199, 226. In §56, "take a seat" refers to exclusion from the chorus. On the confrontation between Alcibiades and Taureas (**332f**) cf. [Andocides] 4.20–21, according to which Taureas attempted legally (contrast **332e**) to expel a foreign member of Alcibiades' boys' chorus; Plutarch, *Alcibiades* 16.4–5. In **332h**, note that prosecution of a *probolê* by Menippus of Caria indicates that the procedure was available to non-citizens. "The man" in §176 is Menippus; on mercantile lawsuits (*dikai emporikai*) see chapter 10. The date of the event described in §178 is 363/2, the archonship of Charicleides. **332j**: the scholion to this passage (no. 716 Dilts) states: "This [Aristophon], while a tax [or 'tribute'] collector, kept in his own possession the tithes of the goddess [i.e., Athena], from which [revenue] crowns were supposed to be made and dedicated to the goddess of the Athenians. He was prosecuted by Eubulus, but before the introduction [of the case (?to the jury-court)], he dedicated the crowns, and the presentation [*probolê*] ceased."

a. Dem. 21.1–2. Procedure and charge; preliminary hearing before Assembly resulting in *katacheirotonia*; trial in *dikastêrion*.

. . . I have brought this presentation [*proubalomên*] against Meidias for wrongdoing concerning the festival [*adikein peri tên heortên*] not only because I received blows at his hands at the Dionysia, but also because I suffered many other acts of violence throughout my entire tenure as chorus-producer [*chorêgian*]. [2] After . . . the Assembly . . . condemned [*katecheirotonêsen*] him, many people approached me, men of the jury [*ô andres dikastai*]—many of you who are now in the jury-court [*dikastêriôi*] and many other citizens—and demanded and urged that I prosecute this man and hand him over to you. . . .

b. Dem. 21.8–11 (*leges* + commentary). Laws on *probolê*.

First [the court clerk] will read to you the law in accordance with which presentations [*probolai*] are available. . . .

LAW. The *prytaneis* shall hold a meeting of the Assembly in the Theater of Dionysus on the day after the Pandia. At this meeting, business shall first be conducted concerning sacred matters, and then they shall hand over the presentations [*probolas*] that have taken place regarding the procession or the competitions at the Dionysia and have not been paid in full.

[9] This, men of Athens, is the law in accordance with which presentations [*probolai*] take place. It states, as you heard, that a meeting of the Assembly is to be held in the Theater of Dionysus after the Pandia, and at this meeting, after the *proedroi* conduct the business provided by the archon, they shall also conduct business concerning any wrongdoing or illegality by anyone concerning the festival. . . .

[10] I also want [the court clerk] to read you the next law. . . .

LAW. Euegorus made the motion. Whenever there is taking place the procession for Dionysus in Peiraeus and the comedies and tragedies, or the procession and tragedies and comedies at the Lenaea, or the procession for the Dionysia in the city and the [chorus of] boys and the revel and the comedies and tragedies, and at the procession and competition of the Thargelia, it shall not be permitted to seize securities [*enechyrasai*] or take anything else from another—even from overdue debtors—during the aforementioned days. If a person violates any of these provisions, he shall be liable to prosecution by his victim, and presentations [*probolai*] against him for his offense shall take place at the meeting of the Assembly in the Theater of Dionysus, just as has been specified concerning the other offenders.

[11] Consider, men of the jury, that while in the first law presentation [*probolês*] is available against those who do wrong concerning the festival, in this law you created presentations [*probolas*] also against those who exact money from overdue debtors or who seize anything else from someone or use violence.

c. Dem. 21.21. Penal assessment in *probolê.*

So, for all these acts together, make a single penal assessment [*timêma*], whatever you think is just.

d. Dem. 21.25, 28. Unlimited penal assessment in *probolê*, with no financial gain for prosecutor.

Now, the first thing that he is obviously going to say . . . is that if I really had suffered the things I claim, I should have filed private lawsuits [*dikas idias*] against him: a lawsuit for damage [*blabês*], for the destruction of the clothes and the gold crowns and all the spiteful abuse concerning the chorus, and a lawsuit for hubris [*hybreôs*], for the hubris I claim to have suffered to my person; but, by Zeus, he will say, I should certainly not try him publicly [*dêmosiai*] and threaten him with a penal assessment [*timêma*] of whatever he must suffer or pay.

. . .

[28] . . . but let him show that he did not commit the acts of which I have accused him, or that he did commit those acts but is not guilty of wrongdoing concerning the festival: this is the subject of the presentation I have brought [*proubalomên*] against him, and concerning this you will presently cast your votes. Given that I have forsaken the gain possible in private lawsuits, have left his punishment to the city, and have chosen this lawsuit from which I can derive no profit, that would reasonably bring me favor, and certainly not harm, from you.

e. Dem. 21.51, 55–56. *Probolê* and impiety (*asebeia*); law on inquiry into citizen status of choristers.

If, men of Athens, I had not been chorus-producer [*chorêgos*] when I suffered these things at Meidias' hands, one could have convicted him only of hubris [*hybrin*] for what he did; but as things are, it seems to me, even if one convicted him of impiety [*asebeian*], he would be doing what is fitting.

. . .

[55] . . . When, then, a person commits hubris [*hybrizonta*] against any of these choristers or chorus-producers in pursuit of enmity, and does so during the actual competition and in the sanctuary of the god, what else will we say of him than that he commits impiety [*asebein*]?

[56] And you know, as a matter of fact, that although you want no foreigner to compete, you have not permitted any chorus-producer simply to issue a summons and investigate choristers; rather, if he does summon one, you have ordered him to pay 50 drachmas, and if he commands one to take a seat, 1,000 drachmas. Why? So that when a person has been crowned and is serving the god, on that day no one may summon him, treat him with spite, or commit hubris against him for malicious purposes.

f. Dem. 21.147. Alcibiades and Taureas; date of law cited at Dem. 21.8 (**332b**).

And yet what hubris did Alcibiades commit that was as serious as that for which my adversary now stands exposed? He struck Taureas, who was serving as chorus-producer, on the jaw. Be that as it may, but he did that to a chorus-producer when he was himself a chorus-producer, and he was not yet in violation of this law, since it had not yet been established.

g. Dem. 21.151–52. Procedure, including trial in *dikastêrion* and penal assessment.

. . . some of those who associate with [Meidias] have approached me, men of the jury, recommending that I get rid of this lawsuit and let it drop, and when they could not persuade me, . . . they had recourse to this argument: "He has already been convicted and condemned; what do you expect the jury-court [*dikastêrion*] to assess as his penalty [*timêsein*]? . . ." [152] Well, for my part, in the first place, I don't presume that you will do anything ignoble, nor do I suppose that you will assess upon him any penalty less than a price sufficient to make him stop his hubris: that is, best of all, death; otherwise, deprivation of all his property.

h. Dem. 21.175–76, 178–80. Previous instances of *probolê*.

Furthermore, men of Athens, I want to mention to you those men whom in the past you have convicted following the Assembly's vote of condemnation [*katacheirotonêsantos*] for wrongdoing concerning the festival. . . . First, then—to mention first the conviction that occurred most recently—the Assembly condemned [*katecheirotonêsen*] Euandrus of Thespiae for wrongdoing concerning the Mysteries; the one who brought the presentation [*probalomenou*] against him was Menippus, some person from Caria. The law about the Mysteries is the same as this one about the Dionysia; that one was enacted after this one. [176] For what act, then, men of Athens, did you condemn Euandrus? Listen to this. He had convicted Menippus in a mercantile lawsuit [*dikên emporikên*], and, having been unable to catch him earlier (as he said), he seized him when he was in town at the Mysteries. You condemned [*katecheirotonêsate*] him for this reason . . . , and when he entered the jury-court [*dikastêrion*], you wanted to punish him with death. But since the man who brought the presentation [*probalomenou*] had been persuaded [otherwise], you both compelled Euandrus to dismiss in its entirety the lawsuit that he had previously won—it was for two talents—and sentenced him in addition [*prosetimêsate*] to pay the damages [*blabas*] that the man reckoned as having befallen him in his dealings with you, while he remained [in Athens] as a result of the vote of condemnation [*katacheirotoniai*].

. . .

[178] You once decided that another man was guilty of wrongdoing concerning the Dionysia, and you condemned [*katecheirotonêsate*] him, while he was serving as assistant [*paredreuontos*] to his son who was archon, because he laid hold of someone who was taking a seat, in the process of barring him from the theater. This was the father of . . . Charicleides the former archon. [179] . . . However, he did not come to the jury-court [*dikastêrion*] but died beforehand.

[180] Yet another man whom the entire Assembly condemned [*katecheirotonêsen*] for wrongdoing concerning the festival, and whom you sentenced to death when he came to court, was Ctesicles, because he had taken part in the procession holding a whip, and with this, while drunk, he had struck some enemy of his.

i. Dem. 21.206. Procedure: witnesses and *katacheirotonia* at preliminary hearing of *probolê* by Assembly.

Moreover, men of Athens, Eubulus was present and sitting in the theater when the Assembly condemned [*katecheirotonêse*] Meidias, and although he was called upon by name, and Meidias here begged and pleaded, as you know, he did not stand up. And yet, if he believed that the presentation [*probolên*] had taken place when Meidias had done no wrong, at that time, obviously, being his friend, he should have spoken in support of him and helped him. . . .

j. Dem. 21.217–18. *Katacheirotonia* by Assembly; case of Aristophon.

The Assembly heard what my adversary had done. So what did it do? It condemned [*katacheirotonêsas*] him and handed him over to you. [218] . . . if you punish him, you will be deemed to be prudent and honorable gentlemen and haters of the wicked, while if you acquit him, you will be deemed to have been overcome by some other concern. For [Meidias] is on trial not as the result of a political motive, nor is it like the case of Aristophon, who returned the crowns and put an end to the presentation [*probolên*]. . . .

333. [Aristotle], *Constitution of the Athenians* (*Ath. Pol.*) 59.2. Jurisdiction of *thesmothetai* over *eisangelia*, *probolê*, and other procedures. (332–322)

See references and headnote under **1c**. For the role of the *thesmothetai* in *probolai* cf. **44a** Dem. 21.31–33, and for the duties of the *thesmothetai* generally cf., e.g., **60** [Arist.] *Ath. Pol.* 59.3; **79** [Arist.] *Ath. Pol.* 59.5. On *eisangelia* (impeachment) for impiety see **335** Plut. *Alcib.* 22.4–5 with additional references in headnote, and on *eisangelia* generally see chapter 12; on the *graphê paranomôn* and the *graphê nomon mê epitêdeion theinai* see p. 14.

These also introduce the impeachments [*eisangelias*] that people bring before the Assembly, as well as all votes of condemnation [*katacheirotonias*] and presentations [*probolas*], and also indictments [*graphas*] for illegal proposals [*paranomôn*] and for enacting an unsuitable law [*nomon mê epitêdeion theinai*]. . . .

11.3. The Scandals of the Herms and the Mysteries (415) and the Trial of Andocides (400 or 399)

See also **185** Andoc. 1.117–21.

334. Thucydides 6.27–29, 53, 60–61. The mutilation of the herms and the profanation of the Mysteries. (date of composition 415-ca. 400; date of events 415)

See references and headnote under **1b**. Below is Thucydides' description of the religious scandals of 415 and their immediate results. The probable date of Thucydides' death is ca. 400, and he may well have composed these passages before Andocides' trial of 400 or 399. The mutilation of the herms occurred on the night of June 6/7, 415, and the Sicilian expedition sailed later in June. That the genitalia of the herms as well as their faces (6.27.1) were vandalized is evident from Aristophanes, *Lysistrata* 1093–94, where the chorus warns the ithyphallic Athenians and Spartans: "If you're prudent, you'll take your cloaks; make sure none of the Hermocopids ["herm-choppers"] sees you [without them]." On *mênysis* (informing) cf. **329c** Lys. 7.16–17, 19, 22, 25–26; **337e** Lys. 6.21–24; **338** Andoc. 1 (selections); **354a** [Dem.] 25.79–80. "There" (6.53.1) is Catana, Sicily, whence Alcibiades was recalled in late summer 415. The "tyranny of Peisistratus and his sons" (6.53.3) ended in 511/0 with the expulsion of Peisistratus' younger son, Hippias; on the assassination of the elder son, Hipparchus, by a group led by Harmodius and Aristogeiton (514) see **78** Hyp. 2.3. On the *dikê erêmê* (lawsuit decided by default: 6.61.7) see p. 37 and cf., e.g., **335** Plut. *Alcib.* 22.4–5; **249a** Dem. 55.1–5; **249d** Dem. 55.31–32, 34; **261** Dem. 32.25–28.

During this time, of all the stone herms in the city of Athens (according to local custom, their construction is rectangular, and there are many of them in both private doorways and those of temples), on a single night the great majority had their faces mutilated. [27.2] No one knew who the perpetrators were; they were sought after with large rewards offered by the state, and the Athenians in addition decreed that if anyone knew about any other act of impiety [*asebêma*] that had occurred, anyone who so wished, whether citizen, foreigner, or slave, could inform [*mênyein*] with immunity [*adeôs*]. [27.3] They took the matter very seriously, since it appeared to be an omen for the expedition and to have occurred in furtherance of a conspiracy to commit revolution and subversion of the people.

[28.1] Information was then given [*mênyetai*] by some metics and slaves, not about the herms, but about some previous mutilations of other statues by young men in drunken jest, and also about the performance of the Mysteries in private houses in a spirit of hubris; they accused Alcibiades of this. [28.2] Seizing upon these accusations, those who were most irritated at Alcibiades because he was an obstacle to their enjoying secure leadership of the people . . . magnified them and proclaimed that the [profanation of the] Mysteries and the mutilation of the herms had occurred with the goal of subverting the people. . . .

[29.1] Alcibiades wanted to defend himself against the informers' statements [*mênymata*] on the spot and was prepared to stand trial before sailing out as to whether he had done any of these things . . . , and he was prepared, if he had done any of them, to pay the penalty, and if he was acquitted, to continue his command. . . . [29.3] But his enemies, fearing that he would have the army on his side if he stood trial now, and that the people would go soft on him . . . , endeavored to prevent this and argued vehemently against it, sending in other speakers who proposed that he sail now and not delay the departure, and that he return and stand trial within a stated number of days; they wanted him to return under summons and stand trial on the basis of a more serious accusation, which they would more easily provide in his absence. And it was decided that Alcibiades should sail.

. . .

[53.1] There they found that the ship *Salaminia* had come from Athens for Alcibiades, to order him to sail home to defend himself against the charges made by the city, and also for some other soldiers who had been informed against [*memênymenôn*] along with him for committing impiety [*asebountôn*] concerning the Mysteries, and some [who had been informed against for committing impiety] concerning the herms as well. [53.2] For the Athenians, after the expedition set sail, were conducting no less diligently their investigation of what had transpired in the matter of the Mysteries and in the matter of the herms. They did not scrutinize their informers [*mênytas*] but accepted everything in their state of suspicion, and thanks to the trust they put in worthless individuals, they arrested and imprisoned very good citizens. . . . [53.3] Since the people knew from hearsay that the tyranny of Peisistratus and his sons had been harsh in the end, and moreover had been brought down not by themselves and Harmodius but by the Spartans, they were constantly afraid and took everything with an attitude of suspicion.

. . .

[60.1] The Athenian people . . . was at this time harsh and suspicious toward those who had incurred the blame for the [profanation of the] Mysteries; they thought it had all been done in furtherance of an oligarchic and tyrannical plot. [60.2] Because of their anger at such a thing, many noteworthy men were already in the prison, and there seemed to be no end of it: every day they were increasing in savagery and arresting still more people. At this point one of the imprisoned men, who was deemed to be most culpable, was convinced by one of his fellow prisoners to inform [*mênysai*], whether truthfully or not—guesses are made on both sides, but no one, either at the time or later, can speak with certainty about who perpetrated the deed. [60.3] He spoke to him and persuaded him that even if he had not done it, he should procure immunity [*adeian*] for himself and thereby save himself and give the city respite from its current state of suspicion; his safety, he said, was more secure if he confessed [*homologêsanti*] with immunity than if he denied guilt and went through a trial. [60.4] So he informed against himself and others in the matter of the herms, and the Athenian people . . . immediately released the informer [*mênytên*], and with him all the others whom he had not denounced; as for the accused, they held trials, and they executed all those who had been arrested and sentenced to death those who had fled, publicly offering money to anyone who killed them. [60.5] In this it was not clear whether the sufferers had been punished unjustly, but nonetheless the rest of the city for the time being manifestly benefited.

[61.1] Alcibiades' enemies . . . kept accusing him, and the Athenians were in a foul mood towards him; now that they thought they had the clear truth about the herms, it seemed to them all the more that the matter of the Mysteries, for which he was blamed, had occurred at his instigation and with the same motive of conspiracy against the people. . . . [61.4] . . . And so, wishing to bring him to trial and execute him, they sent the ship *Salaminia* to Sicily to get him and others who had been informed against. [61.5] The instruction had been given to order him to follow the *Salaminia* home to make his defense, but not to arrest him: they were taking care not to cause a disturbance for their own troops in Sicily and for the enemy. . . . [61.6] Alcibiades, on his own ship and with his fellow accused, set sail with the *Salaminia* from Sicily as though on course for Athens; when they reached Thurii, they stopped following, disembarked from the ship, and got themselves out of sight, fearing to sail home for trial in the face of the prejudice against them. [61.7] For a while the men of the *Salaminia* searched for Alcibiades and those with him, but since they were nowhere to be seen, they went sailing away. Alcibiades, now a fugitive, soon thereafter crossed from Thurii to the Peloponnese on a ship; the Athenians convicted him and those with him by default [*erêmêi dikêi*] and sentenced them to death.

335. Plutarch, *Alcibiades* 22.4–5. *Eisangelia* (impeachment) of Alcibiades. (date of composition late 1st-early 2nd c.A.D.; date of event 415 B.C.)

See references and headnote under **98b**. Here Plutarch relates the impeachment (*eisangelia:* for the use of this procedure against impiety cf. **338** Andoc. 1 (selections); **345** *IG* I³ 78; **353** (Trial of Phryne); on *eisangelia* generally see **333** [Arist.] *Ath. Pol.* 59.2 and chapter 12) of Alcibiades for profanation of the Mysteries in 415. The hierophant, from the *genos* (clan) Eumolpidae, and the torch-bearer, from the *genos* Ceryces, were the chief priests in charge of the Mysteries; "herald" was the title of another official. On the hierophant cf. **337g** Lys. 6.54; **345** *IG* I³ 78; **352** [Dem.] 59.116; **355b** D. L. 5.5–6; on the torch-bearer cf. **345** *IG* I³ 78. *Epoptai* were higher-ranking initiates of the Mysteries (see, e.g., Harpocration s.vv. *anepopteutos*, *epôpteukotôn*). The Two Goddesses are Demeter and Persephone, the honorands of the Mysteries (cf. **338d** Andoc. 1.31–33; **345** *IG* I³ 78); for the *dikê erêmê* cf. **334** Thuc. 6.27–29, 53, 60–61, at 6.61.7.

The impeachment [*eisangelian*] that they put on record is as follows: "Thessalus son of Cimon of the deme Laciadae has impeached [*eisêngeilen*] Alcibiades son of Cleinias of the deme Scambonidae for committing wrongdoing concerning the Two Goddesses, by imitating the Mysteries and showing them to his companions in his own house, wearing a robe of the sort that the hierophant wears when he shows the sacred things, and by naming himself hierophant, Pulytion torch-bearer, and Theodorus of the deme Phegaea herald, and by calling his other companions initiates and *epoptai*, in violation of the lawful practices and rules established by the Eumolpidae and Ceryces and the priests of Eleusis." [22.5] They convicted him by default [*erêmên*] and confiscated his property, and in addition they also decreed that all priests and priestesses curse him; of these, they say, Theano, daughter of Menon of the deme Agryle, was the only one to object to the decree, saying that she had become a priestess to pray, not to curse.

336. Selections from the Attic Stelai. Sales of property confiscated from persons convicted in the scandals of 415. (414–413)

E. L. **Hicks**-G. F. **Hill**, *Greek Historical Inscriptions*, rev. ed. (Oxford 1901), no. 72 (includes text of and commentary on **336a**, lines 20–49, and **336b**); D. **Lewis**, ed., ***Inscriptiones Graecae*** vol. 1 ed. 3 fasc. 1 (Berlin and New York 1981), nos. 421 (**336a**), 430 (**336b**) (text with Latin notes; see also nos. 422–429); C. W. **Fornara**, *Archaic Times to the End of the Peloponnesian War*[2] (Cambridge 1983), no. 147D (includes translation with notes of **336a**); R. **Meiggs**-D. **Lewis**, *A Selection of Greek Historical Inscriptions to the End of the Fifth Century B.C.*, rev. ed. (Oxford 1988), no. 79 (includes text of and commentary on **336a**).

The conventionally-named (from Pollux, *Onomasticon* 10.97) "Attic Stelai (pillars)" record the sales, presumably superintended by the *pôlêtai* (see **2** *IG* I³ 104, **302b** [Arist.] *Ath. Pol.* 52.1; cf. **345** *IG* I³ 78), of property confiscated from those found guilty of mutilating the herms and/or profaning the Mysteries in 415. Where three columns appear, the first records the tax exacted on the sale, the second records the sale price, and the third records the item sold (apart from one personal name—Pistus: **336a**, line 28—slaves are here designated by place of origin and sex). In **336a**, ellipses in the translation correspond to lacunae in the inscription; "85 dr. + *x*" (line 49) represents a figure with a lacuna in the middle; the amount was no less than 85 dr. 1 ob. and no more than 87 dr. 1 ob. In **336b**, on the Athenian calendar and the division of the year into prytanies (line 5) see pp. 6–7. "Concerning both" (line 13) means that the named individual(s) were convicted of impiety concerning both the Mysteries and the herms: cf., e.g., *IG* I³ 422.226–27 "for impiety [*asebeiai*] concerning the Mysteries"; *IG* I³ 527.1 "Of those who committed impiety [*asebêsantôn*] concerning the Mysteries." The Olatians (line 7) were a Thracian people.

a. *IG* I³ 421.12–49.

Of Alcibiades son of Cleinias of the deme Scambonidae, the following furnishings were sold:

. . .	. . .	. . .
. . .	. . .	bronze pot
. . .	. . .	bronze pot
. . .	. . .	bronze pot
. . .	. . .	bronze . . .

. . .

3 ob.	18 dr.	crop at Thria
3 ob.	20 dr.	crop at Athmonon

Total including taxes: 4,723 drachmas 5 obols.
Of Polystratus son of Diodorus of the deme Ancyle:

2 dr. 1 ob.	202 dr.	Pistus
1 dr.	42 dr.	crop at Ancyle

Total including taxes: 247 drachmas 1 obol.
Of Cephisodorus the metic living in Peiraeus:

2 dr.	165 dr.	Thracian female
1 dr. 3 ob.	135 dr.	Thracian female
2 dr.	170 dr.	Thracian male
2 dr. 3 ob.	240 dr.	Syrian male
1 dr. 3 ob.	105 dr.	Carian male
2 dr.	161 dr.	Illyrian male
2 dr. 3 ob.	220 dr.	Thracian female
1 dr. 3 ob.	115 dr.	Thracian male
1 dr. 3 ob.	144 dr.	Scythian male
1 dr. 3 ob.	121 dr.	Illyrian male
2 dr.	153 dr.	Colchian male
2 dr.	174 dr.	Carian boy
1 dr.	72 dr.	Carian child
3 dr. 1 ob.	301 dr.	Syrian male
2 dr.	151 dr.	Melitt . . .
1 dr.	85 dr. + *x*	Lydian female

. . .

b. *IG* I^3 430.5–20.

The following were sold in the seventh prytany, that of the tribe Erechtheis:
On Gamelion 7, of Axiochus son of Alcibiades of the deme Scambonidae:

2 dr.	195 dr.	Olatian man

On Gamelion 22, of Axiochus son of Alcibiades of the deme Scambonidae:

1 dr. 3 ob.	130 dr.	Messenian man

On Gamelion 25, of Adeimantus son of Leucolophides of the deme Scambonidae:

1 dr.	50 dr.	crop reaped from the land in Ophryneion

Sum total: 379 drachmas 3 obols.

Of those [convicted] concerning both: on Gamelion 25, of Euphiletus son of Timotheus of the deme Cydathenaeon:

1 dr. 3 ob.	105 dr.	house in the deme Semachidae
1 dr. 3 ob.	105 dr.	plot of land in the deme Gargettus
2 dr. 3 ob.	205 dr.	plot of land in the deme Myrrhinutta with garden and house
3 ob.	10 dr.	plot of land in the deme Aphidna

Sum total: 431 drachmas.

Total of both together: 810 drachmas 3 obols.

337. Lysias 6 *Against Andocides* (selections). (400 or 399)

See references and headnote under **30**. Andocides was among those arrested and imprisoned in 415 for the mutilation of the herms and the profanation of the Mysteries; on condition of immunity, he turned informer and was released (**337b**, **337e**, **337f**; **334** Thuc. 6.27–29, 53, 60–61, esp. 6.60.2–5; **338e** Andoc. 1.34, 36–37, 43–45, **338f** Andoc. 1.51, 61–62). Soon after Andocides' release, a decree authored by Isotimides barred from the Athenian agora and sanctuaries (thereby imposing *atimia* upon: cf. **170** Andoc. 1.73–79) anyone who had committed and confessed to an act of impiety (see especially **338g** Andoc. 1.71–72; also **337b**, **337e**, **337f**; **338a** Andoc. 1.10, **338d** Andoc. 1.31–33). Andocides left Athens and spent most of the next dozen years in exile, returning in 403. Upon his return, he initiated a lawsuit against Archippus for mutilating a herm (**337c**). In 400 or 399, Andocides was prosecuted by *endeixis* (see p. 31 and cf., e.g., **289** Dem. 24.104–5, 112–15, 120–21, 129, 146 with additional references in headnote) for attending, in violation of the Isotimides decree, the most recent annual celebration of the Eleusinian Mysteries (**337f**; **338a** Andoc. 1.10, **338d** Andoc. 1.31–33, **338g** Andoc. 1.71–72, **338i** Andoc. 1.110–12, 115–16); the prosecution also alleged that during or after the festival Andocides had illegally placed a suppliant-branch in the Eleusinion (temple of Demeter and Persephone) in Athens (**338i** Andoc. 1.110–12, 115–16; cf. **337a**). The prosecutor of record was Cephisius; this speech was delivered at trial by one of his *synêgoroi* (p. 28), Meletus, Epichares, and Agyrrhius. The trial was heard in a *dikastêrion* (p. 26) by a jury of men who had been initiated in the Mysteries (**338d** Andoc. 1.31–33). Andocides delivered in his own defense his oration *On the Mysteries* (see **338** Andoc. 1 [selections]) and won acquittal; the penalty sought by the prosecution (and probably mandatory in this case, although not in all *endeixeis* against persons who violated the terms of their *atimia*: pp. 31, 42) was death (**338d** Andoc. 1.31–33).

337a: For the phrase "do wrong or commit impiety concerning the sacred things" cf. **332** Dem. 21 (selections). On the *Exêgêtai* (Interpreters: **337b**, ?**337g**), who were drawn from the *genos* (clan) Eumolpidae, cf. **338i** Andoc. 1.110–12, 115–16; **339b** Pl. *Euthyphr.* 4c3-d5; **345** *IG* I³ 78. **337b**: On "unwritten laws" see the introduction to this chapter, and for Pericles cf., e.g., **270** Philochorus, *FGrHist* 328 F 121; **271** (Pericles' trial and conviction for theft of public property). The ellipsis in §9 between "the sanctuaries" and "even now" corresponds to a lacuna in the text. **337c**: The lawsuit (*dikê* is here presumably used in the general sense: see p. 29 and cf. **339a** Pl. *Euthyphr.* 2a1–6, **355b** D. L. 5.5–6) against Archippus will have been either a *graphê asebeias* or a *phasis* before the *basileus* (**349b** Dem. 22.27). "His own" is ambiguous but probably refers to Andocides rather than Archippus. **337d**: On Diagoras of Melos cf. **344a** Joseph. *Ap.* 2.265–67; **346** (Diagoras and the Mysteries). For summary arrest (*apagôgê*) see, e.g., **288** Dem. 22.25–27, 69–73 with additional references in headnote. For "not acknowledging the gods" cf. **340** Pl. *Ap.* (selections); **342** D. L. 2.40. **337e**: The duration of Andocides' imprisonment is a matter of scholarly debate, since Andocides in his *On the Mysteries* gives the impression that he was in prison for only a brief time. With the prohibitions in **337e** and **337f** compare those imposed on killers (see especially **18** Dem. 20.157–58). **337g**: On the hierophant see **335** Plut. *Alcib.* 22.4–5 with additional references in headnote; this office and that of *Exêgêtês* (Interpreter) were both privileges of the Eumolpidae, and so Diocles may have given his advice in the latter capacity. This passage (and likewise **337b**: Pericles died in 429) provides an excellent example of Athenian speakers' habit of using "you" to refer not only to the present audience but to any manifestation of the *dêmos* [p. 27]: in all probability Diocles' advice preceded Andocides' trial by over thirty years.

a. Lys. 6.4. Oversight of Mysteries by *basileus*.

Tell me, if Andocides now gets off unpunished from this lawsuit thanks to you, comes forward for allotment to be one of the nine archons, and is allotted as *basileus*, what else will happen than that, on your behalf and in accordance with ancestral custom, he will conduct the sacrifices and make the prayers, some at the Eleusinion here and others at the sanctuary at Eleusis, and will oversee the festival during the Mysteries so that no one may do wrong or commit impiety concerning the sacred things [*adikêi mêde asebêi peri ta hiera*]?

b. Lys. 6.9–10. Isotimides decree; "unwritten laws" and the *Exêgêtai* (Interpreters).

And [Andocides] has reached such a level of audacity that he even talks about the law, saying that the law that is established about him has been annulled and that he may now enter the agora and the sanctuaries . . . even now in the Council Hall [*bouleutêriôi*] of the Athenians. [10] And yet they say that Pericles once recommended to you, concerning those who commit impiety [*asebountôn*], that in their case you make use of not only the written laws but also the unwritten laws, in accordance with which the Eumolpidae issue their interpretations [*exêgountai*], and which no one ever has gained the authority to annul or dared to oppose; people do not even know who established them. . .

c. Lys. 6.11–12. Lawsuit for impiety against Archippus.

But Andocides has so scorned the gods . . . that before he had been in the city for ten days, he issued a summons for a lawsuit for impiety [*dikên asebeias*] before the *basileus*, and . . . filed it, claiming that Archippus was guilty of impiety [*asebein*] with regard to his own ancestral herm. [12] Archippus contended in response that the herm was in fact sound and whole and had suffered none of the things the other herms had; nonetheless, so that he would not be involved in troubles at the hands of my adversary, such as he is, he gave him money and got rid of the matter.

d. Lys. 6.17–19. Diagoras of Melos.

This is how much more impious [*asebesteros*] my adversary has been than was Diagoras of Melos: Diagoras committed impiety [*êsebei*] with words, concerning other people's sanctuaries and festivals; this man has done so with deeds, concerning those in his own city. . . . [18] And do not set free those offenders whom you have in your possession while seeking to catch those in flight by proclaiming that you will give a talent of silver to the man who summarily arrests [*apagonti*] or kills them. . . . [19] And [Andocides] has demonstrated to the Greeks too that he does not acknowledge the gods [*theous ou nomizei*].

e. Lys. 6.21–24. Imprisonment and release of Andocides; Isotimides decree.

After Andocides committed the offense, he was brought into the jury-court [*dikastêrion*] by design and imprisoned himself, by assessing upon himself [*timêsamenos*] a penalty of imprisonment if he did not hand over the slave; [22] he was well aware that he would not be able to hand over the slave, since on account of Andocides and his offenses the slave had died so that he could not turn informer [*mênytês*]. . . . [23] As a result of this penal assessment [*timêmatos*], he had been imprisoned for close to a year, and while imprisoned he informed [*emênyse*] against his own relatives and friends, with immunity [*adeias*] having been granted to him if he were deemed to have informed truthfully. . . . [24] After that, after he had killed the people he said he considered most important, he was deemed to have informed truthfully and was released; and you decreed in addition [*prosepsêphisasthe*] that he be barred from the agora and the sanctuaries, so that even if he were wronged by his enemies he could not exact punishment.

f. Lys. 6.51–52. Details of Andocides' alleged offenses, including violation of Isotimides decree.

My adversary put on a robe and, imitating the sacred rites, displayed them to the uninitiated and spoke the forbidden words with his voice; and as for the gods . . . , he mutilated them. For these reasons priestesses and priests stood facing west and cursed him and shook their scarlet cloaks, in accordance with the old ancient custom. And my adversary admitted that he did it. [52] Moreover, he transgressed the law that you enacted, which ordained that he be barred from the sacred things as an offender: violating all these provisions, he has come into our city, sacrificed at the altars where he was not permitted, attended the sacred rites concerning which he had committed impiety [*êsebêsen*], entered the Eleusinion, and washed his hands with the holy water.

g. Lys. 6.54. Lawsuit for impiety (unspecified procedure, with trial in *dikastêrion*); advice given ?by *Exêgêtês* (Interpreter).

I also want to tell you what my grandfather, Diocles son of the hierophant Zacorus, advised you when you were deliberating what should be done with a Megarian man who had committed impiety [*êsebêkoti*]. While others were calling for his immediate execution without trial, he recommended trying him, for the sake of the populace, so that other people would listen and watch and be more prudent; and for the gods' sake he recommended that each man come from his home and enter the jury-court [*dikastêrion*] having decided in his own mind what a man who committed impiety [*asebounta*] deserved to suffer.

338. Andocides 1 *On the Mysteries* (selections). (400 or 399)

See references and headnote under **12** and headnote under **337**. The passages given here include descriptions of the statements by informers concerning the Mysteries (**338b**, **338c**, **338e**) and the herms (**338e**) and of Andocides' imprisonment, informing, and release (**338e**, **338f**), all in 415; and material relating to the *endeixis* of Andocides in 400 or 399 (**338a**, **338d**, **338g**, **338h**, **338i**). The principal points of Andocides' defense are that he did not commit or confess to impiety in 415 (**338a**, **338d**); that the Isotimides decree therefore does not apply to him and in any event is no longer valid (**338g**, **338h**); and that he did not place a suppliant-branch in the Eleusinion, as his prosecutors allege (**338i**).

On the *prytaneis* (**338b**, **338i**) see p. 6 and, e.g., **332b** Dem. 21.8–11. "The Council" is the Council of 500. On sureties (**338b**, **338e**) see chapter 10; on the *graphê paranomôn* see p. 14 and cf. **333** [Arist.] *Ath. Pol.* 59.2. On *eisangelia* (impeachment: **338c**, **338e**) see **335** Plut. *Alcib.* 22.4–5 with additional references in headnote. **338d**: For the penalty imposed upon prosecutors by *endeixis* and other public procedures who received less than 20 percent of the jurors' votes see, e.g., **288** Dem. 22.25–27, 69–73; on forms of *atimia* (disfranchisement) see especially **170** Andoc. 1.73–79. **338c**: The "investigators" (*zêtêtai*) were a special board appointed in 415 to investigate the scandals that had come to light; "the decree of the archonship of Scamandrius" (an unknown year preceding 480/79) prohibited torturing Athenian citizens; the "wheel" was an instrument of torture. For confinement in the stocks cf. **267b** Lys. 10.15–17; **289** Dem. 24.104–5, 112–15, 120–21, 129, 146. **338f**: On Cynosarges see **289** Dem. 24.104–5, 112–15, 120–21, 129, 146; the Phorbanteion was a sanctuary. **338h**: Andocides cites these laws to prove that the Isotimides decree is now invalid. The first series of laws, among other provisions, established for the first time in Athens the rule of statutory construction that laws (*nomoi*) trump decrees (*psêphismata*) (p. 13). In the first clause of the final law, the use of the past tense "occurred" indicates that the reference is to judgments and arbitrations conducted before passage of the law; "while [the city] was under democratic government" excludes judgments and arbitrations conducted during the regime of the Thirty Tyrants (p. 12). The second clause of the final law immunizes Athenians from prosecution for acts committed before 403/2, and specifically under the Thirty. See further **170** Andoc. 1.73–79; **11** [Arist.] *Ath. Pol.* 39.5–6; **12** Andoc. 1 (selections). **338i**: Andocides' ascription to Solon of the law mentioned in §111 is presumably false (or generalizing: p. 4), since the Council of 500 was instituted by Cleisthenes (p. 6). With the ceremonial robe worn by Callias (§112) cf. **335** Plut. *Alcib.* 22.4–5; **337f** Lys. 6.51–52; on the Ceryces (and the Eumolpidae, who alone were eligible to be *Exêgêtai*) see **335** Plut. *Alcib.* 22.4–5 and **337** Lys. 6 (selections) with additional references in headnotes. Eucles (§115) is "the herald" (§112).

a. Andoc. 1.10. *Endeixis* and charge against Andocides.

As I previously told you, gentlemen, I will make my defense on all points, starting from the beginning: first, with regard to the actual charge from which this denunciation [*endeixis*] arose and on account of which I have been put on trial here, that in the matter of the Mysteries no impiety was committed [*êsebêtai*] by me, nor was there any informing [*memênytai*] or confession [*hômologêtai*], nor do I know whether those who informed to you about these matters did so falsely or truthfully. . . .

b. Andoc. 1.11–13, 15–17, 20. *Mênyseis* regarding profanation of Mysteries.

There was a meeting of the Assembly for the generals destined for Sicily, Nicias, Lamachus, and Alcibiades, . . . and Pythonicus stood up in the Assembly and said, " . . . I shall demonstrate to you that Alcibiades the general is guilty of performing the Mysteries in a [private] house along with others, and if you vote immunity [*adeian*] for the person I propose, a servant of one of the men present here, although he is uninitiated, will relate the Mysteries to you. . . ." [12] Although Alcibiades raised many objections and denied it, the *prytaneis* decided to remove the uninitiated and to go get themselves the young man whom Pythonicus proposed. They left and brought back a servant of Alcibiades; Andromachus was his name. After they voted him immunity, he said that the Mysteries had taken place in the house of Pulytion; Alcibiades, Nicides, and Meletus were the ones who performed them, and others were present with them and watched what went on, and even slaves were present: himself, his brother, Hicesius the flute-player, and Meletus' slave. [13] Andromachus was the first to inform [*emênyse*] regarding these things, and he listed these men, of whom Polystratus was arrested and put to death, while the others fled into exile, and you condemned them to death.

. . .

[15] Then a second [act of] informing [*mênysis*] occurred. Teucrus was a metic here who had left and slipped away to Megara. From there he sent word to the Council that if they gave him immunity, he would inform concerning the Mysteries, being a participant, and would inform on the others who performed them along with him, as well as informing regarding what he knew about the mutilation of the herms. The Council, which had full power to do so, voted

him immunity, and people went to Megara to get him. He was brought back, obtained immunity, and listed the men [who had performed the Mysteries] with him. These men fled into exile in consequence of Teucrus' informing. . . .

[16] A third [act of] informing occurred. The wife of Alcmeonides, who had also been the wife of Damon (Agariste was her name), herself informed that Alcibiades, Axiochus, and Adeimantus performed the Mysteries in the house of Charmides next to the Olympieion; these men all fled upon this [act of] informing.

[17] One more [act of] informing occurred. Lydus, the slave of Pherecles of the deme Themacus, informed that the Mysteries took place in the house of his master Pherecles in Themacus. He listed the other participants and stated that my father was present but sleeping. . . . Speusippus, who was a member of the Council, handed the men over to a jury-court [*dikastêriôi*]. My father then posted sureties [*engyêtas*] and indicted [*egrapsato*] Speusippus for an illegal proposal [*paranomôn*]; the trial took place before a jury of six thousand Athenians, and out of that many jurors [*dikastôn*] Speusippus did not even receive two hundred votes.

. . .

[20] . . . For the law was as follows: if a person informed [*mênyseie*] truthfully, he was to have immunity [*adeian*], but if he informed falsely, he was to be put to death.

c. Andoc. 1.27–28. Rewards for informers.

After the [acts of] informing [*mênyseis*] took place, there was a dispute about the informers' rewards [*mênytrôn*]—according to the decree of Cleonymus the amount was 1,000 drachmas, but according to that of Peisander it was 10,000—among the aforementioned informers, and Pythonicus, who claimed he had been the first to bring an impeachment [*eisangeilai*], and Androcles, on behalf of the Council. [28] The Assembly decided that those who had been initiated should, in the jury-court [*dikastêriôi*] of the *thesmothetai*, hear the statements that each informer had given and decide between the disputants [*diadikasai*]. They voted Andromachus first and Teucrus second, and at the Panathenaic contest Andromachus received 10,000 drachmas and Teucrus one thousand.

d. Andoc. 1.31–33. Composition of jury and risks to prosecutor and to defendant at Andocides' *endeixis*.

And I am reminding you of what happened—you, who will cast your vote about me after you swore weighty oaths, calling down the most grievous curses upon yourselves and your children, that you would render a just vote about me, and who in addition have been initiated and have seen the sacred rites of the Two Goddesses, in order that you may punish those who commit impiety [*asebountas*] and acquit those who do no wrong. [32] . . . If I have committed any impiety, made any confession, or informed against anyone—or anyone else has informed on me—put me to death; I seek no leniency. [33] If, however, I have committed no offense and I demonstrate this clearly to you, I ask that you make it manifest to all the Greeks that I have been put on trial here unjustly. If, you see, the man who denounced [*endeixas*] me, my adversary Cephisius here, fails to receive one-fifth of your votes and gets disfranchised [*atimôthêi*], he is not permitted to enter the sanctuary of the Two Goddesses, or he will be put to death.

e. Andoc. 1.34, 36–37, 43–45. *Mênysis* regarding mutilation of herms and profanation of Mysteries; *eisangelia* initiated by Diocleides before Council of 500; arrests of Andocides and others.

When Teucrus came from Megara, having obtained immunity, he informed [*mênyei*] as to what he knew concerning the Mysteries and concerning those who had mutilated the dedications, and he listed eighteen men. After these men were listed, some of them fled into exile, and others were arrested and put to death in consequence of Teucrus' informing [*mênysin*].

. . .

[36] After that happened, Peisander and Charicles, who were among the investigators [*zêtêtôn*], . . . said that the acts that had taken place were not the acts of a few men but were aimed at the subversion of the people, and that it was necessary to investigate further. . . . [37] Encouraged, then, by the city's troubles, Diocleides brought an impeachment [*eisangellei*] to the Council, stating that he knew who had mutilated the herms and that they numbered around three hundred.

. . .

[43] His impeachment [*eisangelia*], gentlemen, was of that sort; and he listed the names of the men he claimed he had recognized, forty-two of them: first Mantitheus and Apsephion, who were members of the Council and sitting in [the Council Hall], and then the rest. Peisander stood up and said that they should void the decree of the archonship of Scamandrius and put the listed men on the wheel. . . . The Council shouted out that it was a good proposal. [44] Upon hearing this, Mantitheus and Apsephion sat down as suppliants at the hearth, begging not to be tortured but instead to post sureties [*exengyêthentes*] and be put on trial. Having barely secured this request, once they posted their

sureties [*engyêtas*], they mounted their horses and left, deserting to the enemy and leaving behind their sureties, who were by necessity liable to the same penalties as those for whom they had stood surety. [45] The Council then went out in secret and arrested us and confined us in the stocks.

f. Andoc. 1.51, 61–62. *Mênysis* by Andocides.

When Charmides said this, gentlemen, and the others entreated me, each one of them begging me, I thought to myself, " . . . should I stand by and watch my own relatives being unjustly put to death, not only being executed themselves but having their property confiscated, and on top of that being inscribed on pillars as offenders against the gods, when they are responsible for none of what happened . . . , or should I tell the Athenians what I heard from Euphiletus, the very man who did it?"

. . .

[61] For these reasons I told the Council that I knew who had done it, and I laid out the facts: Euphiletus introduced the plan while we were drinking, I objected, and at that time it did not happen, thanks to me. Later, though, while I was at Cynosarges riding a pony I had, I took a fall, broke my collarbone, had my head cut open, and was taken home carried on a litter. [62] Euphiletus, after learning of my condition, told the others that I had been persuaded to do it with them and had agreed to take part in the deed with him and mutilate the herm by the Phorbanteion. He said this and deceived them; that is why the herm that you all see, the one by my ancestral house, which the tribe Aegeis dedicated, is the only herm in Athens that was not mutilated, since I was the one who was supposed to do it, as Euphiletus told them.

g. Andoc. 1.71–72. The *endeixis* of Andocides and the Isotimides decree.

My adversary Cephisius here denounced [*enedeixe*] me in accordance with the existing law, but he is conducting his prosecution in accordance with a decree issued in the past on the proposal of Isotimides, which has no relation to me. Isotimides proposed that those who had committed impiety [*asebêsantas*] and confessed [*homologêsantas*] be barred from the sacred things. But I have done neither: no impiety was committed, and no confession was made. [72] Moreover, I shall also demonstrate to you that this decree has been annulled and is invalid.

h. Andoc. 1.87 (*leges*). Laws prohibiting use of unwritten law, granting laws primacy over decrees, and prohibiting (with proviso) enactment of law applying to individual; law confirming previous judgments and arbitrations conducted under democracy and mandating application of laws from 403/2 on. (date of laws 403/2)

LAWS. The magistrates shall not employ an unwritten law in any case whatsoever. No decree, either of the Council or of the Assembly, shall have greater authority than a law. Nor shall it be permitted to establish a law that applies to a man unless the same law applies to all Athenians, unless the decision is made by 6,000 voting by secret ballot.

. . .

LAW. All judgments and arbitrations that occurred in the city while it was under democratic government shall be valid; but the laws shall be employed from the archonship of Eucleides [403/2] on.

i. Andoc. 1.110–12, 115–16. Allegations regarding and laws concerning placement of suppliant-branch.

In their prosecution they also talked about the suppliant-branch, saying that I placed it in the Eleusinion, and that there is an ancestral law providing that anyone who places a suppliant-branch during the Mysteries shall be put to death. And they are so audacious that they . . . are actually conducting a prosecution of me for committing the offense that they themselves concocted. [111] You see, when we returned from Eleusis and the denunciation [*endeixis*] had taken place, the *basileus* came forward to report the events of the rite at Eleusis, as is custom. The *prytaneis* said they would bring him before the Council and instructed him to summon me and Cephisius to be present at the Eleusinion. (The Council was going to hold its session there in accordance with the law of Solon that commands the holding of a session in the Eleusinion the day after the Mysteries.)

[112] We presented ourselves according to our instructions. And when the Council was full, Callias son of Hipponicus, wearing the robe, stood up and said that there was a suppliant-branch lying upon the altar, and he showed it to them. Then the herald made a proclamation asking who had placed the suppliant-branch, and no one responded. We were standing there, and my adversary saw us. . . .

. . .

[115] When Eucles told the Council that no one had responded, Callias again stood up and said that there was an ancestral law that if a person placed

a suppliant-branch in the Eleusinion, he should be put to death without trial, and that his father Hipponicus had once issued an interpretation [*exêgêsato*] of this to the Athenians, and that he had heard that I had placed the suppliant-branch. At that point this man Cephalus here jumped up and said, [116] "Callias, you most unholy of all men, in the first place, you are issuing an interpretation [*exêgêi*] when you are one of the Ceryces and it is not sanctioned for you to issue interpretations; in the second place, you talk about an ancestral law, while the pillar next to which you are standing commands the payment of 1,000 drachmas if a person places a suppliant-branch in the Eleusinion."

11.4. The Trial of Socrates (399)

339. Plato, *Euthyphro* (selections). (composed early 4th c.)

J. **Burnet**, *Plato*: Euthyphro, Apology of Socrates, *and* Crito (Oxford 1924: text and commentary); H. **Tredennick**-H. **Tarrant**, *Plato: The Last Days of Socrates (*Euthyphro, Apology, Crito, Phaedo*)* (rev. ed. London 1993: translation with introduction and notes).

The dramatic date of this dialogue between Socrates and Euthyphro is 399, after the filing but before the trial of the *graphê asebeias* against Socrates. **339a** and **339c** identify the lawsuit as a *graphê asebeias* (cf. **340** Pl. *Ap.* [selections]; **342** D. L. 2.40) filed before the *basileus* (cf. Hypereides 4.6), whose office was located in the Royal Stoa (cf. **2** *IG* I[3] 104); in his response to Euthyphro's question in **339a**, Socrates plays upon the distinction between the general and specific uses of the word *dikê* "lawsuit" (see **337c** Lys. 6.11–12 with additional references in headnote). On the Lyceum (**339a**) see **289** Dem. 24.104–5, 112–15, 120–21, 129, 146. For consultation of the *Exêgêtai* regarding a homicide (**339b**) cf. **17** [Dem.] 47.67–73; on the *Exêgêtai* generally see **337** Lys. 6 (selections) with additional references in headnote.

a. Pl. *Euthyphro* 2a1–6. Procedure and jurisdiction.

EUTHYPHRO. What novel thing has happened, Socrates, that you've left your haunts at the Lyceum and are now spending time here around the Royal Stoa? Surely you don't have a lawsuit [*dikên*] before the *basileus* as I do.

SOCRATES. Athenians don't call it a [private] "lawsuit" [*dikên*], Euthyphro, but an "indictment" [*graphên*].

b. Pl. *Euthyphro* 4c3-d5. Function of *Exêgêtai* (Interpreters).

EUTHYPHRO. You see, the dead man was a day-laborer of mine, and when we were farming on Naxos, he worked there for us. In a fit of drunken violence, he got angry at one of our slaves and slaughtered him. So my father bound his feet and hands, threw him into a ditch, and sent a man here [to Athens] to inquire of the Interpreter [*exêgêtou*] what he should do. During this time, he ignored and neglected the prisoner on the grounds that he was a killer and it was no matter even if he died—which is exactly what happened to him: he died of hunger, cold, and his bonds before the messenger arrived from the Interpreter.

c. Pl. *Euthyphro* 5c4–8. Procedure.

SOCRATES. I too . . . desire to become your student, knowing that . . . my adversary Meletus . . . has observed me so keenly and easily that he has indicted me for impiety [*asebeias egrapsato*].

340. Plato, *Apology of Socrates* (selections). (composed early 4th c.)

L. **Dyer**-T. D. **Seymour**, *Plato*: Apology of Socrates *and* Crito, *with Extracts from the* Phaedo *and* Symposium *and from Xenophon's* Memorabilia (Boston 1908: text and commentary); **Burnet**, *Plato:* Euthyphro, Apology of Socrates, *and* Crito (text and commentary); **Tredennick-Tarrant**, *Plato: The Last Days of Socrates* (translation with introduction and notes).

Plato's *Apology of Socrates* comprises Plato's versions of three speeches delivered by Socrates at his trial in 399: the first is Socrates' main trial speech, arguing for his innocence (from which are taken **340a-e**); the second is the speech delivered by Socrates in the penalty phase of the trial following his conviction (from which is taken **340f**); and the third is an address by Socrates following his sentencing. The trial occurred in a *dikastêrion* (**340a**, **340c**); the prosecutor of record was Meletus, and his *synêgoroi* (p. 28) were Anytus and Lycon (**340c**, **340e**, **340f**; cf. **339c** Pl. *Euthyphr.* 5c4–8; **342** D. L. 2.40). The *graphê asebeias* ("corrupting the young," although it appears as a separate charge in **342** D. L. 2.40 [cf. **340b**, **340c**], is not attested as a named offense in Athenian law) was an *agôn timêtos* (assessable lawsuit: p. 40) without penal limit (**340f**); accordingly, in the written statement of the charges (variously referred to as an *antômosia* [**340b**; **342** D. L. 2.40; cf. **231** Isae. 5.6–7, 9, 12–18; **232** Isae. 3.3–7], *enklêma* [**340b**; cf. the introduction to chapter 8 and **253** Dem. 36.2–4, 12, 18–20; **256b** Dem. 37.22–26, 28–33; **261** Dem. 32.25–28; **264** D. H. *Din.* 3], *graphê* [**340c**, **340e**; see p. 30 and cf. **273** Ar. *Wasps* 836–47, 893–900, 931–35, 952–66], or *antigraphê* [**340d**]), Meletus proposed a penalty of death (**342** D. L. 2.40; **340b**, **340c**, **340d**, **340e**, **340f**), and after his conviction Socrates made a counter-proposal (**340f**). The jury voted in favor of Meletus' proposal (on the margins of the conviction and sentencing votes see below), and Socrates was accordingly sentenced to death by hemlock (see **341** Pl. *Phaedo* [selections]).

340c: On Anaxagoras cf. **344** (Anaxagoras and the sun). **340e**: "You the people" refers to the Assembly. For the role of Socrates' *daimonion* in the charges against him cf. Xenophon, *Memorabilia* 1.1.2. **340f**: Scholars tend to assume that the total number of jurors was 501; on this assumption, Socrates' comment about a hypothetical thirty-vote swing would mean that the vote for conviction would have been 280–221. Diogenes Laertius 2.41, however, states that the votes for conviction outnumbered those for acquittal by 281. He adds (2.42) that the margin of the sentencing vote was 80 more jurors in favor of the prosecution than in the conviction vote. For "what[ever one must] suffer or pay," the penal formula for an assessable lawsuit without penal limit, cf., e.g., **332d** Dem. 21.25, 28; **35** Dem. 21.47. For maintenance in the Prytaneion cf. **163** [Dem.] 58.30–32; on suretyship and securities cf., e.g., **338e** Andoc. 1.34, 36–37, 43–45, and see chapter 10. For the thousand-drachma penalty incurred by the prosecutor of a *graphê asebeias* who received less than one-fifth of the jurors' votes, cf. **349** Dem. 22 (selections); Demosthenes 57.8; Diogenes Laertius 5.37 (but note **329d** Lys. 7.37–38, which may indicate that in that case no such sanction existed); for the 1,000 dr. penalty for malicious prosecution of other public procedures see, e.g., **288** Dem. 22.25–27, 69–73; **338** Andoc. 1 (selections).

a. Pl. *Apology* 17d2–3. Jurisdiction.

This is the first time I have appeared before a jury-court [*dikastêrion*], although I am seventy years old. . . .

b. Pl. *Apology* 24b7-c2. Written statement of charges and oath by prosecution.

> . . . let's take my adversaries' affidavit [*antômosian*]. It goes something like this: "Socrates," it says, "commits an offense by corrupting the young and by not acknowledging the gods whom the city acknowledges, but rather other, novel divinities [*daimonia*]." The charge [*enklêma*] is something like that; let's examine each element of this charge individually.

c. Pl. *Apology* 26b2-d9. "Corrupting the young" and Socrates' belief in gods.

But tell us anyway: how do you claim that I corrupt the young, Meletus? Or is it obvious that, according to the indictment [*graphên*] that you filed [*egrapsô*], I do so by teaching them not to acknowledge the gods whom the city acknowledges, but instead other, novel divinities? Isn't that what you say I corrupt them by teaching?

[Meletus' response:] "Absolutely right, I say that."

. . . I cannot understand whether you are claiming that I teach the belief that there are some gods—and that I myself in fact believe that gods exist and am not entirely an atheist and am not guilty of wrongdoing in that way—but that these gods, though, are not those the city acknowledges but others, and that is what you are charging me with: that it is other gods; or you are asserting that I do not acknowledge gods at all myself and that I teach this to others.

[Meletus' response:] "That's what I'm saying: that you don't acknowledge gods at all."

Meletus, you very strange man, what makes you say that? So in fact I don't believe that either the sun or the moon is a god, as the rest of mankind does?

[Meletus' response:] "No, by Zeus, men of the jury [*ô andres dikastai*], since he says the sun is a rock and the moon is [made of] earth."

Do you think you're prosecuting Anaxagoras, my dear Meletus? Do you have such contempt for these jurors, and do you think they're so illiterate, that they don't know that the books of Anaxagoras of Clazomenae are full of such statements?

d. Pl. *Apology* 27c5–8. Written statement of charges and oath by prosecution.

[To Meletus:] So, then, you say that I acknowledge and teach about divinities [*daimonia*]—whether novel or old, I at least acknowledge divinities, according to your statement, and you even swore to that in your indictment [*antigraphêi*].

e. Pl. *Apology* 31c4-d4. Socrates' *daimonion* and the written statement of charges.

It might well seem strange that I go around giving this advice privately and make a busybody of myself, but publicly I do not venture to present myself before you the people and give advice to the city. The reason for this is what you have often and in many places heard me talking about; namely, that something godly and divine [*daimonion*] comes to me: this is the very thing that Meletus mocks in the indictment [*graphêi*] that he filed [*egrapsato*]. I have had this since I was a boy: a voice comes to me, and when it does, it always dissuades me from what I am about to do; it never encourages me.

f. Pl. *Apology* 36a5-b5, 36e1–37a1, 38b1–9. Verdict and margin of votes; *timêsis* (penal proposal by prosecution) and *antitimêsis* (penal proposal by defense).

. . . as it turns out, apparently, if only thirty votes had fallen differently, I would have won acquittal. Anyway, as it seems to me, even so I have won acquittal from Meletus—and not only won acquittal, but this is obvious to everyone: if Anytus and Lycon had not appeared to prosecute me, Meletus would in fact have been fined 1,000 drachmas for failing to receive one-fifth of your votes.

So, then, the man proposes a penalty [*timatai*] of death for me. All right; what counter-proposal shall I make [*antitimêsomai*] to you, men of Athens? . . . What do I deserve to suffer or pay. . . ?

. . .

[36e1] So, if I should propose a penalty according to my just deserts, this is the penalty I propose: maintenance [*sitêseôs*] in the Prytaneion.

. . .

[38b1] Now, if I had money, I would have proposed a penalty of as much money as I had a chance of paying . . . ; but as it is, since I have no money, that's not possible, unless you are actually willing to assess a penalty of as much money as I would be able to pay. I could probably pay you about a mina of silver, so I propose that amount.

Men of Athens, Plato here and Crito and Critobulus and Apollodorus are urging me to propose a penalty of 30 minae, with themselves standing surety [*engyasthai*]. So I propose that amount, and these worthy men will be your sureties [*engyêtai*] for the money.

341. Plato, *Phaedo* (selections). (composed early 4th c.)

Dyer-Seymour, *Plato:* Apology of Socrates *and* Crito (text and commentary); J. **Burnet**, *Plato's* Phaedo (Oxford 1911: text and commentary); **Tredennick-Tarrant**, *Plato: The Last Days of Socrates* (translation with introduction and notes); C. J. **Rowe**, *Plato*: Phaedo (Cambridge 1993: text and commentary).

Plato's *Phaedo* describes Socrates' imprisonment pending his execution (the delay in carrying out the sentence is explained in **341a**) and culminates with an account of his death by hemlock (**341b**). **341a**: Theseus was the mythical Athenian king who slew the Minotaur (the half-bull, half-human illegitimate son of the wife of Minos, king of Crete) and thereby liberated Athens from the necessity of sending, every nine years, seven young men and seven young women to feed the monster (Plutarch, *Theseus* 15–23). The stern of the ship sent to Delos was crowned with a wreath of laurel, the tree sacred to Apollo. According to Xenophon, *Memorabilia* 4.8.2, Socrates spent thirty days in jail. **341b**: On execution by hemlock see p. 41 and cf. **14** Lys. 13.85–87. "The magistrates" (116c4) are the Eleven (116b8); Asclepius was the god of healing.

a. Pl. *Phaedo* 58a6-c5. Law regarding sacred embassy to Delos and consequent delay of Socrates' execution.

PHAEDO. A chance occurrence happened to him, Echecrates: by chance, the day before his trial, the stern of the ship that the Athenians send to Delos was crowned.

ECHECRATES. What's that?

PHAEDO. It's the ship, as the Athenians say, in which Theseus once traveled to Crete with the famous "twice seven" and saved both them and himself. At the time, it is said, the Athenians made a vow to Apollo that if they returned safely, every year they would send a sacred embassy to Delos, which embassy, from that time to this day, they still send to the god annually. Now, when they begin the sacred embassy, they have a law that during this time they must keep the city ritually pure and must not publicly execute anyone until the ship has made it to Delos and back to Athens. This sometimes takes a long time, when it happens that the winds take them off course. The beginning of the sacred embassy is when the priest of Apollo crowns the stern of the ship; this chanced to happen . . . the day before the trial. That's why Socrates spent a long time in the prison between his trial and his death.

b. Pl. *Phaedo* 116b7-c4, 116c8-d2, 117a4-b2, 117b6-c5, 117e4–118a8. Administration of hemlock.

PHAEDO. [Socrates] came and sat down, having bathed, and then conversed a little. Then the attendant of the Eleven arrived, stood next to him, and said, "Socrates, I will not presume in your case what I presume of others; namely, that they get angry and curse me when I order them to drink the drug under compulsion by the magistrates. . . . [116c8] So now, since you know what I have come to announce, farewell, and try to bear what you must as lightly as you can." Shedding a tear, he turned around and left.

. . .

[117a4] And Crito . . . nodded to his slave, who was standing nearby. The slave left and, after spending quite some time, returned with the man who was going to give the drug, which he was carrying ground up in a cup. Socrates caught sight of the man and said, "All right, my good man, you're the expert in these matters; what am I supposed to do?"

"All you do," he said, "is drink it and walk around until you feel a weight in your legs, then lie down. That way the drug will work by itself." And he held the cup out to Socrates.

. . . [117b6] "What do you say," said Socrates, "about this drink, as far as pouring a libation to someone? Is it permitted or not?"

"Socrates," the man said, "we grind only as much as we think is adequate to drink."

"I understand," said Socrates. . . . And . . . he held his breath and very unsqueamishly and easily drank it all down.

. . .

[117e4] He walked around, and when he said his legs were getting heavy, he lay down on his back—since that was what the man told him to do—and this man, the one who had given the drug, kept hold of him, and after some time inspected his feet and legs, then pushed hard on his foot and asked if he felt it, and Socrates said no. Then he did the same with his calves, and moving upward, showed us that Socrates was growing cold and stiff. He kept hold of him and said that when it reached his heart, he would go.

At this point the area around his abdomen, roughly speaking, was getting cold, and . . . he said—and this in fact was the last thing he uttered—"Crito," he said, "we owe a rooster to Asclepius; pay it, and don't neglect it."

342. Diogenes Laertius 2.40. Written statement of charges. (composed 2nd-3rd c. A.D.)

See references and headnote under **155**. Here Diogenes quotes verbatim the charge statement filed against Socrates by Meletus (cf. the paraphrases of this document at **340b** Pl. *Ap.* 24b7-c2; Xenophon, *Memorabilia* 1.1.1). On "corrupting the young" see the headnote under **340**. Favorinus was a prolific author of the first half of the second century A.D.; the Metroon, located in the agora, served as the public records office of Athens from the fourth century B.C. onward (p. 17).

The affidavit [*antômosia*] for the lawsuit [*dikês*] had this form—for it is on display to this day, states Favorinus, in the Metroon—"Meletus son of Meletus of the deme Pithus has filed [*egrapsato*] and sworn to [*antômosato*] the following charges against Socrates son of Sophroniscus of the deme Alopece: Socrates commits an offense by not acknowledging the gods whom the city acknowledges and by introducing other, novel divinities; he also commits an offense by corrupting the young. Penalty [*timêma*]: death."

11.5. Other Cases

See also **1** (Trial and punishment of the Alcmaeonids for the killing of Cylon's partisans); **269** Cic. *On Divination* 1.54; **270** Philochorus, *FGrHist* 328 F 121; **271** (Pericles' trial and conviction for theft of public property); **275** Isoc. 18.57; **276** Isoc. 20.6; **278** Lys. 5.1, 5; **285** *SEG* 12.100.1–16; **288** Dem. 22.25–27, 69–73; **289** Dem. 24.104–5, 112–15, 120–21, 129, 146; **296** Dem. 57.63–65; **297** Dem. 19.293–94; **299** [Dem.] 58.14–15; **300** Libanius, hyp. [Dem.] 25.1–2; **337c** Lys. 6.11–12; **337d** Lys. 6.17–19; **337g** Lys. 6.54; **340c** Pl. *Ap.* 26b2-d9; **365** Lyc. 1.117–18; **375** Xen. *Hell.* 1.7.1–16, 20–26, 34–35; **387f** Lyc. 1.147.

343. Aeschylus and the Mysteries. (499–458)

In one or more of his plays, the tragedian Aeschylus unwittingly divulged rites of the Eleusinian Mysteries. Aeschylus' first and last plays in Athens were produced in 499 and 458 respectively. See M. **Librán Moreno**, "El proceso por impiedad de Esquilo," *Habis* 35 (2004) 39–56.

a. Aristotle, *Nicomachean Ethics* 1111a8–10. (335–322)

J. A. **Stewart**, *Notes on the* Nicomachean Ethics *of Aristotle* (2 vols., Oxford 1892: commentary); J. **Burnet**, *The* Ethics *of Aristotle* (London 1900: text and commentary); W. D. **Ross**, ed., *The Works of Aristotle*, vol. 9 (Oxford 1925: translation); H. H. **Joachim**, *Aristotle:* The Nicomachean Ethics, ed. D. A. Rees (Oxford 1951: commentary).

In this passage of his *Nicomachean Ethics*, a treatise on human morality and the quest for the Good, Aristotle is discussing intentional and unintentional acts; he cites the case of Aeschylus as an example of the effect of ignorance on volition.

Or a person might be ignorant of what he is doing, as when people say that something escaped them unawares, or that they did not know that it was forbidden, as Aeschylus said about the Mysteries. . . .

b. Clement of Alexandria, *Stromateis* 2.60.1–3. (late 2nd-early 3rd c. A.D.)

J. **Ferguson**, *Clement of Alexandria,* Stromateis, *Books 1–3* (Washington 1991: translation with introduction and notes).

This passage of the *Stromateis* (*Miscellanies*) of the early Christian author Clement of Alexandria (b. ca. A.D. 150, d. A.D. 211–216) clearly draws in part upon Aristotle (**343a**); Aeschylus' lack of initiation in the Mysteries and consequent unfamiliarity with their content will have meant that his impiety was unintentional.

Now, that which is unintentional is not judged. . . . [60.2] For either a person was ignorant of himself . . . [60.3] or he was ignorant of the thing that he was doing, as with Aeschylus: he pronounced the Mysteries upon the stage, was put on trial at the Areopagus, and won acquittal by proving that he had not been initiated. . . .

c. Aelian, *Varia Historia* 5.19. (late 2nd-early 3rd c. A.D.)

N. G. **Wilson**, *Aelian:* Historical Miscellany (Cambridge, MA 1997: text and translation).

Below is the version of Aeschylus' trial given in the *Varia Historia* (*Miscellaneous History*) of Aelian (b. A.D. 165–170, d. A.D. 230–235). The naval battle of Salamis (480) was a signal victory by the Hellenic League over the Persians. Stoning was not a standard method of execution in the time of the orators and is very rarely attested in general (see **1d** Plut. *Solon* 12.1–9; **366** [Killing of Lycides/Cyrsilus]). The word *dikastai* might suggest a regular jury-court (*dikastêrion*), but the anecdote immediately preceding this one (5.18) involves a trial before the Areopagus.

Aeschylus the tragedian was tried for impiety [*asebeias*] because of a play. The Athenians were ready to stone him, but his younger brother Ameinias threw aside his cloak and showed his forearm, which was missing a hand. Ameinias had lost his hand while winning highest distinction at Salamis; he was the first Athenian to win the prize of valor. When the jurors [*dikastai*] saw what the man had gone through, they remembered his deeds and acquitted Aeschylus.

344. Anaxagoras and the sun. (?437/6 B.C.)

While the details of his case are debated among (and even within: **344b**) the sources, it is clear that the philosopher Anaxagoras of Clazomenae ran afoul of the Athenians for his assertion that the sun was not a god but a "red-hot mass of stone." See also **340c** Pl. *Ap.* 26b2-d9; **271c** Plut. *Pericles* 32.1–4, 35.4–5; Xenophon, *Memorabilia* 4.7.7; Plutarch, *Nicias* 23.3; *Moralia* 169f (*On Superstition* 10); Diodorus 12.39.2; Lucian, *Timon* 10; J. **Mansfeld**, "The Chronology of Anaxagoras' Athenian Period and the Date of His Trial," *Mnemosyne* 32 (1979) 39–69; L. **Woodbury**, "Anaxagoras and Athens," *Phoenix* 35 (1981) 295–315.

a. Josephus, *Against Apion* 2.265–67. Anaxagoras and others accused of impiety. (*post* A.D. 94)

H. St. J. **Thackeray**, *Josephus:* The Life, Against Apion (Cambridge, MA 1926: text and translation).

Josephus' *Against Apion*, a treatise in defense of Judaism, culminates with a comparison of Greek and Mosaic law. In this passage, he discusses famous cases of impiety from Classical Athens. On Diagoras cf. **337d** Lys. 6.17–19; **346** (Diagoras and the Mysteries); on Protagoras, **347** (Protagoras and the gods); on Ninus, **350** (Trial of Ninus).

Anaxagoras was from Clazomenae, but because the Athenians thought the sun was a god and he said it was a red-hot mass of stone, they came within a few votes of condemning him to death. [266] They announced a reward of a talent for Diagoras of Melos, for anyone who killed him, because he was said to mock their Mysteries. Protagoras, if he had not been so quick to flee, would have been arrested and put to death, since he was deemed to have written something that did not agree with the Athenians concerning the gods. [267] And why should we be amazed that they were so disposed toward such trustworthy men when they did not even spare women? For they executed Ninus the priestess because someone accused her of initiating people into the mysteries of foreign gods: this was prohibited by law in Athens, and the penalty for those who introduced a foreign god was defined as death.

b. Diogenes Laertius 2.12–14. Varying accounts of the trial of Anaxagoras and its aftermath. (2nd-3rd c. A.D.)

See references and headnote under **155**. Sotion of Alexandria wrote his *Succession of the Philosophers* probably in the first quarter of the second century B.C.; Satyrus, Hermippus of Smyrna, and Hieronymus of Rhodes were active in the third century B.C. "Thucydides" is Thucydides son of Melesias, not the historian (son of Olorus); "medism" means collaboration with Persia.

Concerning his trial various things are said. Sotion states in his *Succession of the Philosophers* that he was prosecuted by Cleon for impiety [*asebeias*] because he said that the sun was a red-hot mass of stone; Pericles, his student, spoke in his defense, and he was fined five talents and exiled. Satyrus in his *Lives* states that the lawsuit was brought to trial by Thucydides because he was a political opponent of Pericles, that the charge was not just impiety but medism too, and that Anaxagoras was sentenced to death *in absentia.* [13] . . . Hermippus in his *Lives* states that he was confined in the prison pending his execution; Pericles came before the Assembly and asked whether they had any charge to bring against himself in regard to his life, and when they said they had none, he said, "Well, I am his student, so do not be stirred up by false accusations and put the man to death, but listen to me and let him go." So they let him go, but Anaxagoras could not bear the hubris and so committed suicide. [14] Hieronymus, in the second book of his *Random Recollections,* states that Pericles brought him to the jury-court [*dikastêrion*] wasting away and emaciated by disease, and so he was acquitted due more to pity than to judgment of the case.

345. *Inscriptiones Graecae* I^3 78 (*decretum*). Decree on offering of first-fruits to Demeter and Persephone and other sacred matters. (?ca. 422)

I. **de Prott**-L. **Ziehen**, *Leges Graecorum sacrae* (Leipzig 1896–1906), no. 4 (text and Latin commentary); M. N. **Tod**, *Greek Historical Inscriptions* (Oxford 1946–48, repr. with addenda Chicago 1985), no. 74 (text and commentary); F. **Sokolowski**, *Lois sacrées des cités grecques* (Paris 1969), no. 5 (text and French commentary); ***IG*** I^3 no. 78 (text with Latin notes); **Fornara**, *Archaic Times to the End of the Peloponnesian War*, no. 140 (translation with notes); **Meiggs-Lewis**, *Greek Historical Inscriptions*, no. 73 (text and commentary).

This inscribed decree comprises two parts: the original draft motion (lines 1–46) and the rider proposed by Lampon (lines 47–61). The "Council" (line 2 and throughout) is the Council of 500; "the people" (line 2 and elsewhere) is the Assembly; on prytanies (line 2) see p. 6. For the medimnus (lines 5ff.) see **206** Isae. 10.9–10; a *hekteus* is one-sixth of a medimnus. "The allies" (lines 14ff.) are the members of the Delian League/Athenian Empire (cf. **30** Lys. 6.15). For the hierophant and torch-bearer (lines 24–25) see **335** Plut. *Alcib.* 22.4–5 with additional references in headnote. On the Eumolpid *Exêgêtai* (lines 36–37) see **337** Lys. 6 (selections) with additional references in headnote. In lines 38–39, Triptolemus and Eubulus are names of gods, "the god" is Hades, and "the goddess" is Persephone. Lampon (line 47) was a seer and *Exêgêtês* (Eupolis, fr. 319 Kassel-Austin; Plutarch, *Pericles*

6.2; scholion to Aristophanes, *Clouds* 332). For the *pôlêtai* (line 51) cf. **336** (Selections from the Attic Stelai) with additional references in headnote; the *kôlakretai* (lines 51–52) were magistrates who disbursed public funds. "The new archon shall intercalate the month of Hecatombaeon" (lines 53–54): whoever is appointed eponymous archon for the next year is to interpose a second month of Hecatombaeon between Hecatombaeon and Metageitnion; since the Athenian calendar was lunar (p. 7), intercalation of months was occasionally necessary in order to keep the months of the year consistent with the seasons. The Pelargicon (lines 55–57) was an area below the Acropolis; with the prohibition on removing stones or earth cf. **351** *IG* II^{2} 1177; **356** *IG* II^{2} 1362. For *eisangelia* (impeachment) see **335** Plut. *Alcib.* 22.4–5 with additional references in headnote.

Timoteles of the deme Acharnae was secretary. Resolved by the Council and the people; the tribe Cecropis held the prytany, Timoteles was secretary, Cycneas presided; the Compilers [*xyngrapheis*] drafted the motion as follows. The Athenians shall give the first-fruits of the crop to the Two Goddesses according to ancestral custom and the oracular response from Delphi: from each hundred medimni of barley, no less than a *hekteus*; and from each hundred medimni of wheat, no less than one-half *hekteus*; if a person produces more crop than this, or less, he shall give first-fruits according to the same calculation. The demarchs shall collect it in their demes and shall hand it over to the Sacral Commissioners [*hieropoiois*] of Eleusis at Eleusis. Three granaries shall be constructed at Eleusis according to ancestral custom, wherever the Sacral Commissioners and the architect decide is appropriate, from the money of the Two Goddesses. There they shall place any crop they receive from the demarchs; and the allies shall also give first-fruits in accordance with the same rules. The [allied] cities shall select collectors of the crop in accordance with however they decide the crop will best be collected, and once it is collected, they shall send it to Athens; those who bring it shall hand it over to the Sacral Commissioners of Eleusis at Eleusis. If they do not receive it within five days after the announcement, when the people from the city from which the crop comes are handing it over, the Sacral Commissioners shall be fined 1,000 drachmas each. They shall receive [the crop] from the demarchs in accordance with the same rules. The Council shall select heralds and send them to the cities to report what has now been decreed by the people; this shall occur for now as soon as possible, and in the future whenever the Council decides. The hierophant and the torch-bearer shall bid the Greeks, at the Mysteries, to give first-fruits of their crop according to ancestral custom and the oracular response from Delphi. They shall inscribe on a board the amount of the crop received from the demarchs, deme by deme, and that received from the cities, city by city, and they shall place [the boards] in the Eleusinion at Eleusis and in the Council Hall. [30] The Council shall make announcement also to all the other Greek cities, wherever it decides it is possible, telling them the rules by which the Athenians and their allies are giving first-fruits, not ordering them but bidding them to give first-fruits, if they wish, according to ancestral custom and the oracular response from Delphi. The Sacral Commissioners shall receive [35] [the crop] from these cities as well, if a person brings it, according to the same rules. They shall sacrifice from the [proceeds of the] sacrificial flour in accordance with whatever interpretation the Eumolpidae issue [*exêgôntai*]; from the [proceeds of the] barley and the wheat a sacrifice of three animals, beginning with a bull, with gilded horns, to each of the Two Goddesses; and to Triptolemus, to the god and the goddess, and to Eubulus, a perfect sacrificial animal each; and [40] to Athena a bull with gilded horns. The Sacral Commissioners shall sell the remaining barley and wheat and along with the Council shall make dedications to the Two Goddesses, doing whatever the people of Athens decides, and shall place an inscription on the dedications stating that they have been dedicated from the first-fruits of the crop and by whoever among the Greeks gives first-fruits. For those who do the aforementioned things, [45] let there be many good things and good and abundant crops, provided that they do not wrong the Athenians or the city of the Athenians or the Two Goddesses.

[47] Lampon made the motion: Let the rest be as [stated in] the draft motion on the first-fruits of the crop for the Two Goddesses. But the secretary of the Council shall inscribe the draft motion and this decree on two stone pillars [50] and shall place one at Eleusis in the sanctuary and the other on the Acropolis. The *pôlêtai* shall let out the contract for the two pillars, and the *kôlakretai* shall provide the funds. They shall inscribe on the two pillars the aforementioned measures concerning the first-fruits of the crop for the Two Goddesses, and the new archon shall intercalate the month of Hecatombaeon. The *basileus* shall delimit the sanctuaries in the [55] Pelargicon, and in the future altars shall not be established in the Pelargicon without the consent of the Council and the people; nor shall stones be cut from the Pelargicon, nor shall earth or stones be removed. If a person violates any of these provisions, he shall pay 500 drachmas, and the *basileus* shall bring an impeachment [*eisangelletô*] before the Council. Concerning the first-fruits of olive oil, [60] Lampon shall draft a motion and present it to the Council during the ninth prytany, and the Council shall, under mandate, bring it before the people.

346. Diagoras and the Mysteries. (?415/4)

Cf. **337d** Lys. 6.17–19; **344a** Joseph. *Ap.* 2.265–67; Diodorus 13.6.7, who dates the proclamation to 415/4 (it may have been slightly earlier but definitely occurred before the production of Aristophanes' *Birds* in 414); Aristophanes, *Frogs* 318–320 with scholion to line 320, which specifies that the work of Craterus cited in **346b** was his *Collection of Decrees* (see **126** Harpo. s.v. *nautodikai*) and adds that the Athenians encouraged the city-states of the Peloponnese to cooperate in the hunt for Diagoras. See L. **Woodbury**, "The Date and Atheism of Diagoras of Melos," *Phoenix* 19 (1965) 178–211.

a. Aristophanes, *Birds* 1072–74. (414)

See references and headnote under **184**.

CHORUS. And on this very day public proclamation has been made that if any of you kills Diagoras of Melos, he shall receive a talent. . . .

b. Scholia to Aristophanes, *Birds* 1073. (unknown Byzantine date)

See references under **82**. Melos was captured by the Athenians in 416/5 (Thucydides 5.84–116). Melanthius was active in the second half of the fourth and/or the first half of the third century.

This man, after the capture of Melos, lived at Athens and disparaged the Mysteries, so as to turn many away from the rite. So the Athenians issued this proclamation against him and inscribed it on a bronze pillar, as Melanthius states in his *On the Mysteries*.

Other version: [Aristophanes] has taken this from the decree. For [the Athenians] proclaimed that the person who killed him would receive a talent, and the person who brought him back would receive two talents. This proclamation was made because of his impiety [*asebes*]: he described the Mysteries in detail to everyone, making them common and insignificant, and dissuading those who wished to be initiated, as Craterus relates. His banishment by proclamation occurred right around the capture of Melos. . . . Melanthius in his *On the Mysteries* provides a transcript of the bronze pillar on which they made the proclamation against him. . . . On it was inscribed this: "If a person kills Diagoras of Melos, he shall receive a talent of silver; if a person brings him back alive, he shall receive two."

347. Protagoras and the gods. (Protagoras d. ?410s B.C.)

Cf. **344a** Joseph. *Ap.* 2.265–67; Cicero, *On the Nature of the Gods* 1.63; Plutarch, *Nicias* 23.3. While the philosopher Protagoras of Abdera's profession of agnosticism is securely attested, the historicity of the trial discussed in these later sources is rejected by some scholars on the basis of Plato, *Meno* 91e3–9, where Socrates states that Protagoras, for his entire career and after his death, has enjoyed an uninterrupted good reputation. See D. **Lenfant**, "Protagoras et son procès d'impiété: peut-on soutenir une thèse et son contraire?," *Ktema* 27 (2002) 135–54.

a. Sextus Empiricus, *Against the Professors* 9.56–57. (?late 2nd c. A.D.)

R. G. **Bury**, *Sextus Empiricus*, 4 vols. (Cambridge, MA 1933–49: text and translation).

The treatise *Against the Professors* by the philosopher and physician Sextus Empiricus attacks the proponents of various schools of philosophy and other disciplines. "Ran into misfortune at sea" is clarified by Athenaeus, *Deipnosophistae* 611b, who states that Protagoras died in a shipwreck. Timon of Phlius was a philosopher and author of the third century B.C.; "Socrates' cold draught" is hemlock (**341b** Pl. *Phaedo* 116b7-c4, 116c8-d2, 117a4-b2, 117b6-c5, 117e4–118a8).

. . . and Protagoras, who in one place wrote expressly, "Concerning gods, I am able to say neither whether they exist nor of what sort they are, since the obstacles hindering me are many." For this reason the Athenians voted to condemn him to death, but he escaped, ran into misfortune at sea, and died. [57] Timon of Phlius recounts this story in the second book of his *Satires*, where he relates the following: " . . . he strove for flight, lest he descend to Hades by drinking Socrates' cold draught."

b. Diogenes Laertius 9.51–52, 54. (2nd-3rd c. A.D.)

See references and headnote under **155**. The opening reference is to the beginning of Protagoras' treatise *On Gods*. On the oligarchy of the Four Hundred (411/10) see p. 11 and cf., e.g., **170** Andoc. 1.73–79.

Elsewhere he began in this way: "Concerning gods, I cannot know either that they exist or that they do not exist, since the obstacles to knowing are many: the uncertainty, and the fact that a man's life is short." [52] Because of this beginning of his treatise, he was exiled by the Athenians, and they burned his books in the agora, having collected them by command of a herald from each person who possessed them.

. . .

[54] . . . Pythodorus son of Polyzelus, one of the Four Hundred, prosecuted him; Aristotle, however, states that it was Euathlus.

c. Philostratus, *Lives of the Sophists* 1.10. (A.D. 229–238)

W. C. **Wright**, *Philostratus and Eunapius: The Lives of the Sophists* (Cambridge, MA 1921: text and translation).

Philostratus' *Lives of the Sophists* includes discussion of a number of philosophers and rhetoricians from the fifth century B.C. to the early third century A.D. "This" is Protagoras' assertion of agnosticism (**347a**, **347b**); "a vote . . . taken against him" would refer to a decree.

Because of this, he was driven out of every land by the Athenians: according to some, after he was tried, but as others think, because a vote was taken against him without his being tried.

348. *Inscriptiones Graecae* II² 1635.134–40. Conviction and sentencing of Delians for impiety. (376/5)

I. **Kirchner**, ed., ***Inscriptiones Graecae*** vol. 2 ed. 2 minor (Berlin 1913–40), no. 1635, lines 134–40 (text with Latin notes); **Tod**, *Greek Historical Inscriptions*, no. 125, lines 134–40 (text and commentary); P. J. **Rhodes**-R. **Osborne**, *Greek Historical Inscriptions 404–323 B.C.* (Oxford 2003) no. 28, B(a) lines 24–30 (text, translation, and commentary).

The island of Delos and its famous sanctuary of Apollo were at this time controlled by Athens, and the sanctuary was superintended by a board of Athenians called the Amphictyons. This extract comes from an inscription that records the activities of the Amphictyons from 377/6 to 374/3. It is probable that the procedure employed against the Delians named below was the *graphê asebeias* and that their trial (or trials, if the cases of one or more defendants were severed) occurred in Athens.

The following Delians were convicted of impiety [*asebeias*] during the archonship of Charisander at Athens [376/5] and of Galaeus on Delos, [and sentenced to] the penalty [*timêma*] written below and also [to] perpetual exile [*aeiphygia*], because they brought the Amphictyons out of the temple of Delian Apollo and beat them: Epigenes son of Polycrates, 10,000 drachmas; Pyrrhaethus son of Antigonus, 10,000 drachmas; Patrocles son of Episthenes, 10,000 drachmas; [name and amount erased]; Aristophon son of Leucippus, 10,000 drachmas; Antiphon son of Tynnon, 10,000 drachmas; Odoeteles son of Antigonus, 10,000 drachmas; Telephanes son of Polyarces, 10,000 drachmas.

349. Demosthenes 22 *Against Androtion* (selections). (355/4)

See references and headnote under **63**; also, for **349a**, D. D. **Phillips**, *Avengers of Blood: Homicide in Athenian Law and Custom from Draco to Demosthenes* (Stuttgart 2008) 105–9. **349a**: Compare the description of the same trial in Demosthenes 24.7–8, where the same speaker, Diodorus, implies that he himself, rather than his uncle, was the defendant, and states that Androtion was fined 1,000 drachmas for receiving less than 20 percent of the jury's votes (the standard penalty for malicious prosecution in *graphai* and other public procedures: cf., e.g., **340f** Pl. *Ap.* 36a5-b5, 36e1–37a1, 38b1–9). On the pollution (*miasma*) that might be communicated by a killer to those who "associat[ed] in the same place" with him, cf. **8c** Ant. 5.82–83; Antiphon 5.11. **349b**: For the context see **288** Dem. 22.25–27, 69–73. For *apagôgê* (summary arrest) cf., e.g., **288** Dem. 22.25–27, 69–73 with additional references in headnote; for *phasis* (declaration) cf. **151** Harpo. s.v. *phasis*, and for possible cases of *phasis* for impiety see **329** Lys. 7 (selections); **337c** Lys. 6.11–12; **352** [Dem.] 59.116. Lawsuits (titled *dikai*, if, as is probable, Demosthenes here uses the verb *dikazesthai* in the strict sense: see p. 29) before the Eumolpidae (see **335** Plut. *Alcib.* 22.4–5 and **337** Lys. 6 [selections] with additional references in headnotes) are not otherwise attested; probably they were available only for offenses against the Eleusinian Mysteries (note especially **337b** Lys. 6.9–10; **338i** Andoc. 1.110–12, 115–16; **345** *IG* I^3 78), and the penal competence of the court is unknown.

a. Dem. 22.2–3. *Graphê asebeias* for associating with parricide.

For after bringing an accusation against me . . . that I had killed my own father, and after concocting an indictment for impiety [*graphên asebeias*]—not against me but against my uncle, stating in the indictment that he was guilty of impiety [*asebein*] by associating in the same place with me, who had allegedly committed the act—he brought the lawsuit to trial. . . . [3] But I pled my case in your court and was acquitted, not by a small margin but such that my adversary failed to receive one-fifth of the votes. . . .

b. Dem. 22.27. Remedies for *asebeia*: *apagôgê*; *graphê asebeias*; ?*dikê* before Eumolpidae; *phasis* before *basileus*.

For impiety [*asebeias*], in the same way [as for theft], one may employ summary arrest [*apagein*], bring an indictment [*graphesthai*], bring a lawsuit [*dikazesthai*] before the Eumolpidae, or bring a declaration [*phainein*] before the *basileus*.

350. Trial of Ninus. (*ante* ca. 349/8)

That one Menecles prosecuted and convicted Ninus before ca. 349/8 is securely attested by Demosthenes 39.2; cf. [Demosthenes] 40.9 and Dionysius of Halicarnassus, *On Deinarchus* 11, which calls Ninus a priestess. Whether the scholiast (**350b**, scholion 495a) is correct in stating that Ninus is the "[other] priestess" in **350a** is a matter of debate.

a. Demosthenes 19 *On the False Embassy* 281. (343)

See references and headnote under **297**. The son of Atrometus and Glaucothea is the defendant Aeschines. For "assembling [illicit] religious groups" cf. **351** *IG* II² 1177; **353e** Anon. Seg. *Rhet.* p. 455.6–11 Spengel.

. . . but having gotten hold of the son of Atrometus the schoolteacher and Glaucothea, who assembles the religious groups for which another priestess has been put to death, . . . are you going to acquit him?

b. Scholia to Dem. 19.281. (unknown Byzantine date)

M. R. **Dilts**, *Scholia Demosthenica*, 2 vols. (Leipzig 1983–86), nos. 495a, 495b (text).

These scholia are explanations of the phrase "for which another priestess has been put to death" (**350a**). Note that the two scholia give different reasons for the execution of the priestess, and that Ninus is named only in the first.

[495a] For the drugs for which another priestess was put to death. He is talking about the woman called Ninus. Menecles prosecuted her for making love-potions for the young.

[495b] They put the priestess to death because they believed that these initiation rites were from the beginning a mockery and an act of hubris against the real Mysteries; after that, since the god declared by an oracle that they should allow them to take place, they permitted Aeschines' mother to conduct initiations.

351. *Inscriptiones Graecae* II² 1177 (*decretum*). Decree of the deme Peiraeus governing the Thesmophorion. (mid-4th c.)

de Prott-Ziehen, *Leges Graecorum sacrae*, no. 33 (text and Latin commentary); ***IG*** II² no. 1177 (text with Latin notes); **Sokolowski**, *Lois sacrées*, no. 36 (text and French commentary).

The Thesmophorion was a sanctuary of Demeter located in Peiraeus; the Thesmophoria, a festival for Demeter from which men were excluded, occurred in the month of Pyanopsion (for the Athenian calendar see p. 7). The Plerosia (or Proerosia), Calamaea, and Scira (or Scirophoria) were likewise religious festivals; the last named was celebrated in the month of Scirophorion. For "assembling [here including (otherwise) licit?] religious groups" cf. **350a** Dem. 19.281; **353e** Anon. Seg. *Rhet.* p. 455.6–11 Spengel. On the removal of items from sanctuaries cf. **345** *IG* I^{3} 78; **356** *IG* II^{2} 1362.

The demarch . . . who is in office at any given time, along with the priestess, shall oversee the Thesmophorion, in order that no one manumits slaves or assembles religious groups, and that no sanctuaries are established, and that people do not perform purifications or approach the altars or the shrine, without permission of the priestess, except during the festival of the Thesmophoria or at the Plerosia or at the Calamaea or the Scira or any other day when the women assemble according to ancestral custom. It shall stand as decreed by the demesmen of Peiraeus that if a person does any of the aforementioned things in violation of the aforementioned provisions, the demarch shall impose a fine and bring [the matter] to the jury-court [*dikastêrion*], employing the laws that are established concerning these matters. Concerning the gathering of wood from the sanctuaries: if a person gathers wood, the ancient laws that are established concerning these matters shall be authoritative. The Boundary Commissioners, along with the demarch, shall inscribe this decree and place it next to the way up to the Thesmophorion.

352. [Demosthenes] 59 *Against Neaera* 116. Trial of Archias for impiety. (date of speech 343–339)

See references and headnote under **21**. The procedure used against Archias was probably *graphê asebeias* or *phasis* before the *basileus* (**349b** Dem. 22.27); the festival of the Haloa (celebrated in the month of Poseideon), during which he committed his offense, is not listed among those governed by *probolê* (**332** Dem. 21 [selections]). On the hierophant see **335** Plut. *Alcib.* 22.4–5 with additional references in headnote.

It is worth remembering this too, men of Athens, that when Archias the former hierophant was exposed in the jury-court [*dikastêriôi*] as guilty of impiety [*asebein*] for conducting the sacrifices in violation of ancestral custom, you punished him; among the accusations brought against him was that he had sacrificed for Sinope the courtesan, at the Haloa, on the hearth in the courtyard at Eleusis, a sacrificial victim that she had brought, although it was not lawful to sacrifice victims on that day and the sacrifice was not his duty but that of the priestess.

353. Trial of Phryne. (?340s-330s)

I. G. **Baiter**-H. **Sauppe**, *Oratores Attici*, vol. 2 (Zürich 1850) pp. 301–3 (Hypereides, *For Phryne*: fragmentary speech LVIII, fragments 202–210: text with Latin commentary); C. **Jensen**, *Hyperidis orationes sex cum ceterarum fragmentis* (Leipzig 1917) xxv-xxxi (pseudo-Plutarchan life of Hypereides: text and Latin notes); 143–45 (Hypereides, *For Phryne*: fragmentary speech LX, fragments 171–180: text with Latin notes); I. **Worthington**-C. **Cooper**-E. M. **Harris**, *Dinarchus, Hyperides, and Lycurgus* (Austin 2001) pp. 147–48 (Hypereides, *For Phryne*: fragmentary speech 60, fragments 171, 172, 173, 179: translation with introduction and notes); C. **Cooper**, "Hyperides and the Trial of Phryne," *Phoenix* 49 (1995) 303–18.

The famous courtesan Phryne was put on trial for impiety, prosecuted by Euthias (**353d**, **353f**; Harpocration s.v. *Euthias*) and defended by Hypereides, who secured her acquittal (although the veracity of the anecdote about her being disrobed before the court [**353a**, **353c**] has been questioned). Hypereides' celebrated speech *For Phryne*, now lost except for fragments and testimonia, appears still to have been extant at the date of composition of all the passages below. That the procedure used against Phryne was *eisangelia* (see **335** Plut. *Alcib.* 22.4–5 with additional references in headnote, and chapter 12), which at the time of her trial was tried in a *dikastêrion* (cf. **353a**, **353c**) and featured a standard (if not statutory) death penalty (cf. **353c**, **353f**), is strongly suggested by **353d** (cf. **385a** Hyp. 1 fr. 3 Jensen; **373** Hyp. 4.7–8).

a. [Plutarch], *Lives of the Ten Orators* 849e. (1st or 2nd c. A.D.)

Hypereides fr. 202 Baiter-Sauppe; fr. 171 and pp. xxix–xxx Jensen; H. N. **Fowler**, *Plutarch's* Moralia, vol. 10 (Cambridge, MA 1936: text and translation).

The *Lives of the Ten Orators* ascribed to Plutarch and included in manuscripts of his *Moralia* are in fact the product of another author contemporary with Plutarch; they include much valuable information about the lives and careers of the canonical Attic orators.

And in fact, when Phryne the courtesan was on trial for impiety [*asebein*], [Hypereides] came under examination along with her; he himself makes this clear in the beginning of his speech. And when she was about to be convicted, he brought her into the midst [of the court], tore off her clothing, and displayed the woman's breasts; the jurors [*dikastôn*] were distracted by the sight of her beauty, and she was acquitted.

b. Harpocration s.v. *Isodaitês*. (Harpocration *fl.* 2nd c. A.D.)

Hypereides fr. 208 Baiter-Sauppe; fr. 177 Jensen; for Harpocration see references and headnote under **28**. Performing rites for Isodaites presumably served as part of the accusation of impiety against Phryne: cf. **353e**.

Isodaites: Hypereides in his *For Phryne*. A foreign divinity for whom common and not very respectable women performed rites.

c. Athenaeus, *Deipnosophistae* 590e. (ca. A.D. 200)

Hypereides fr. 209 Baiter-Sauppe; fr. 178 Jensen; for Athenaeus see references and headnote under **127**. The description of Phryne as "the expoundress and temple-attendant of Aphrodite" may rely on nothing other than her occupation, which was clearly connected with the goddess of erotic love. The (alleged) decree that resulted from Phryne's trial may well be apocryphal.

Hypereides, when he was speaking in support of Phryne, and he was accomplishing nothing with his speech and the jurors [*dikastai*] were expected to convict, brought her into the open, tore off her garments, and bared her breasts. He then brought to bear the rhetoric of pity characteristic of perorations, drawing upon her appearance, and he caused the jurors to feel superstitious fear and to indulge their pity and not to put to death the expoundress and temple-attendant of Aphrodite. She was acquitted, and after that a decree was composed stating that no one speaking on behalf of another might engage in appeals to pity, and that no male or female defendant might be in view while they were on trial.

d. Alciphron, *Letters* 1.32. (2nd or 3rd c. A.D.)

Baiter-Sauppe, p. 301; Hypereides fr. 179 Jensen; fr. 179 Worthington-Cooper-Harris; A. R. **Benner**-F. H. **Fobes**, *The Letters of Alciphron, Aelian and Philostratus* (Cambridge, MA 1949: text and translation).

Alciphron's *Letters* are fictional epistles to and from fourth-century B.C. Athenians. *Letters* 1.30 (from the courtesan Bacchis to Hypereides), 1.31 (from Bacchis to Phryne), and 1.32 (from Bacchis to the courtesan Myrrhine) all refer to Phryne's trial. In this letter Bacchis threatens Myrrhine with the fate of Phryne, whom Euthias first frequented as a client and then prosecuted.

May you never find a better lover, . . . but may Euthias, whom you now treat so well, live with you for the rest of your life. . . . Ask for something from him, and you will find yourself either having set fire to the dockyards or subverting the laws.

e. Anonymus Seguerianus, *Rhetoric* p. 455 Spengel, lines 6–11. (3rd c. A.D.)

Baiter-Sauppe, p. 302; L. **Spengel**, *Rhetores Graeci*, vol. 1 (Leipzig 1853: text).

This passage from a treatise on rhetoric by an anonymous third-century A.D. author (designated Anonymus Seguerianus by modern scholars) uses the accusations against Phryne (a favorite case in later ancient rhetorical education) as a hypothesis for the composition of a rhetorical exercise in the form of a prosecution speech against her. On the Lyceum see **289** Dem. 24.104–5, 112–15, 120–21, 129, 146 and cf. **339a** Pl. *Euthyphr.* 2a1–6. For the introduction of novel divinities cf. **340** Pl. *Ap.* (selections); **342** D. L. 2.40; for "assembl[ing] illegal religious groups" cf. **350a** Dem. 19.281; **351** *IG* II² 1177.

For example, Phryne is on trial for impiety [*asebeias*], since she has held a revel in the Lyceum, introduced a novel god, and assembled religious groups of men and women. So, then, "I have demonstrated to you that Phryne is impious [*asebê*], that she shamelessly held a revel, that she is the introducer of a novel god, and that she assembled illegal religious groups of men and women."

f. Syrianus, *Commentaries on Hermogenes* vol. 2 p. 31 Rabe, lines 14–25. (5th c. A.D.)

Hypereides fr. 203 Baiter-Sauppe; fr. 172 Jensen; fr. 172 Worthington-Cooper-Harris; H. **Rabe**, *Syriani in Hermogenem commentaria* (2 vols., Leipzig 1892–93: text).

This passage from Syrianus' fifth-century A.D. *Commentary on Hermogenes'* Art of Rhetoric (second century A.D.) includes a direct quotation from Hypereides' *For Phryne*.

And Hypereides again in his *For Phryne,* when the equation existed that he and Euthias had both had relations with Phryne . . . , came up with a difference and escaped the equation by stating: "For it is not the same thing for one man to seek by all means her preservation, and the other her destruction."

354. Trial of Theoris. (*ante* ca. 325)

While the earliest source for this case (**354a**) does not identify a procedure, and the sources are not consistent in their details, the prosecution of Theoris was probably a *graphê asebeias*: note the *mênysis* in **354a** (cf., e.g., **329c** Lys. 7.16–17, 19, 22, 25–26), the mention of penal assessment in **354b** (cf. **340f** Pl. *Ap.* 36a5-b5, 36e1–37a1, 38b1–9), and the description of Theoris' offense as impiety in **354c**. See D. **Collins**, "Theoris of Lemnos and the Criminalization of Magic in Fourth-Century Athens," *CQ* n.s. 51 (2001) 477–93.

a. [Demosthenes] 25 *1 Against Aristogeiton* 79–80. (?325 or 324)

See references under **300**. [Demosthenes] 25 and 26 (*1* and *2 Against Aristogeiton* respectively) were delivered by men prosecuting Aristogeiton by *endeixis* for speaking before the Assembly and prosecuting lawsuits while a state debtor (see **170** Andoc. 1.73–79; **172** Dem. 24.200–1). "This man here" is Aristogeiton's brother Eunomus.

This man here—I will say nothing of the rest, but the things for which you put to death that foul woman Theoris, the Lemnian, the sorceress [*pharmakida*], her and her entire family [*genos*]—[80] these things, the drugs and the incantations, he got from Theoris' slave woman, the one who informed [*emênysen*] against Theoris at that time; and by the very same woman this sorcerer [*baskanos*] has procreated, and he is playing superstitious tricks and deceiving people and claiming that he heals epileptics. . . .

b. Plutarch, *Demosthenes* 14.6. (late 1st-early 2nd c. A.D.)

On Plutarch see headnote under **1d**; on his *Life of Demosthenes* see H. A. **Holden**, *Plutarch's* Life of Demosthenes (Cambridge 1893: text and commentary); I. **Scott-Kilvert**, *Plutarch: The Age of Alexander*, with introduction by G. T. Griffith (London 1973: translation).

[Demosthenes] also prosecuted the priestess Theoris for committing numerous misdeeds, including, in particular, teaching her slaves to deceive; he proposed a penalty [*timêsamenos*] of death and got her executed.

c. Harpocration s.v. *Theôris*. (Harpocration *fl.* 2nd c. A.D.)

See references and headnote under **28**; also F. **Jacoby**, *Die Fragmente der griechischen Historiker* (Leiden 1957–), no. 328 fr. 60; on Philochorus see **264** D. H. *Din.* 3; **270** Philochorus, *FGrHist* 328 F 121.

Theoris: Demosthenes, in his speech *Against Aristogeiton*, if genuine. Theoris was a seer, and she was tried for impiety [*asebeias*] and put to death, as Philochorus also says in his sixth book.

355. Aristotle and Hermias. (323 or 322 B.C.)

Hermias was tyrant of the city of Atarneus (located on the north central coast of Asia Minor) in the mid-fourth century; he was executed by the Persian king Artaxerxes III Ochus in 341. On Aristotle's flight from Athens, motivated by the filing against him of the *graphê asebeias* described here, cf. Aelian, *Varia Historia* 3.36.

a. Athenaeus, *Deipnosophistae* 696a-d. (ca. A.D. 200)

See references and headnote under **127**. The song quoted by Democritus (another version is given by Diogenes Laertius [5.7–8]: cf. **355b**) is Aristotle fr. 675 Rose (V. **Rose**, *Aristotelis qui ferebantur librorum fragmenta* [Leipzig 1886: text]); "the sons of Leda" are Castor and Pollux.

. . . Democritus said, "However, the song written by the most learned Aristotle and dedicated to Hermias of Atarneus is not a paean, as was stated by the man who brought the indictment [*graphên*] for impiety [*asebeias*] against the philosopher—Demophilus, who had been suborned by Eurymedon . . . —on the grounds that Aristotle was committing impiety, and in particular, singing every day in the banquet-rooms a paean dedicated to Hermias. That the song has none of the appearance of a paean . . . I shall make clear to you from its actual wording:

"'O Virtue, most toilsome to the race of mortals, finest target in life, for your form, O virgin, death and suffering terrible unceasing troubles are a doom sought after throughout Greece: such immortal reward do you place in the mind, better than gold and [noble] parentage and languid-eyed sleep. For your sake Heracles son of Zeus and the sons of Leda endured many toils, hunting after your power with their deeds. Out of yearning for you Achilles and Ajax entered the house of Hades. For the sake of your beloved form too the nursling of Atarneus has forsaken the rays of the sun. And so for his deeds the Muses shall extol him as an immortal subject of song—the daughters of Memory, who extol the majesty of Zeus the Protector of Hospitality and the honor of steadfast friendship.'"

b. Diogenes Laertius 5.5–6. (2nd-3rd c. A.D.)

See references and headnote under **155**. On the hierophant see **335** Plut. *Alcib.* 22.4–5 with additional references in headnote; on Favorinus see **342** D. L. 2.40. The "hymn dedicated to . . . Hermias" is the song quoted in **355a** (Diogenes gives his version at 5.7–8); the epigram quoted here is Aristotle fr. 674 Rose. For the general use of *dikê* "lawsuit" cf. **337c** Lys. 6.11–12 with additional references in headnote.

Aristotle, then, came to Athens, and after leading his school for thirteen years, he slipped away to Chalcis, since Eurymedon the hierophant—or Demophilus, as Favorinus states in his *Miscellaneous History*—had indicted [*grapsamenou*] him in a lawsuit [*dikên*] for impiety [*asebeias*] because he had written the hymn dedicated to the aforementioned Hermias, [6] and furthermore an epigram inscribed on [the base of] his statue in Delphi, as follows: "This man the king of the bow-carrying Persians killed unrighteously, in violation of the holy law of the gods—not openly, by overcoming him with the spear in bloody battle, but by using the trust of a treacherous man."

356. *Inscriptiones Graecae* II^{2} 1362. Regulations for sanctuary of Apollo Erithaseus. (late 4th c.)

de Prott-Ziehen, *Leges Graecorum sacrae*, no. 34 (text and Latin commentary); ***IG*** II^{2} no. 1362 (text with Latin notes); **Sokolowski**, *Lois sacrées*, no. 37 (text and French commentary).

For the salutation "Gods" cf. **321e** Finley, *SLC* no. 88; Erithaseus is an Attic cult title of the god Apollo. The precise identification of the various items specified in lines 6–7 ("timber" through "fallen leaves") is disputed among scholars, but it is clear that the intent of the provisions is to forbid any taking of any tree or part thereof, living or dead, from the sanctuary (for removal of items from sanctuaries cf. **345** *IG* I^{3} 78; **351** *IG* II^{2} 1177). "The Council" is the Council of 500.

Gods. The priest of Apollo Erithaseus makes proclamation and prohibition on behalf of himself, his demesmen, and the Athenian people [5] that no one shall cut wood from the sanctuary of Apollo or carry timber, logs, branches, or fallen leaves from the sanctuary. If a person is caught cutting or carrying any of the forbidden things from the sanctuary, if it is a slave who has been caught, he shall be whipped [10] fifty blows, and the priest shall hand over him and the name of his master to the *basileus* and the Council in accordance with the decree of the Council and people of Athens; if it is a free person, the priest,

[15] along with the demarch, shall fine him 50 drachmas and shall hand over his name to the *basileus* and the Council in accordance with the decree of the Council and people of Athens.

357. Diogenes Laertius 2.116. Banishment of Stilpon. (date of composition 2nd-3rd c. A.D.; Stilpon d. late 4th-early 3rd c. B.C.)

See references and headnote under **155**. Stilpon was a philosopher from Megara; for "the Athena of Pheidias" see **270** Philochorus, *FGrHist* 328 F 121. If Diogenes' information is accurate, this may be a case of Areopagite *apophasis*, on which see chapter 12.

They say that Stilpon propounded an argument of this sort concerning the Athena of Pheidias: "Is Athena daughter of Zeus a god?" And when someone said "Yes," Stilpon said, "But this Athena is not Zeus' but Pheidias'." And when that was agreed to, he said, "Well, then, she is not a god." Even when he was summoned to the Areopagus for this, he did not deny it but asserted that his examination had reached the correct conclusion, since she was not a god but a goddess; gods were the male ones. All the same, the Areopagites ordered him to leave the city immediately.

CHAPTER 12

Treason, Subversion, Bribery, and *Apatê tou dêmou* (Deceiving the People)

Handbooks: J. H. **Lipsius**, *Das attische Recht und Rechtsverfahren* (Leipzig 1905–15) 176–219, 374–83, 399–404; A. R. W. **Harrison**, *The Law of Athens* (Oxford 1968–71) 2.13–15, 28–31, 50–64, 81–82, 86–87, 105, 154 n. 4, 160, 228; D. M. **MacDowell**, *The Law in Classical Athens* (Ithaca, NY 1978) 175–91; S. C. **Todd**, *The Shape of Athenian Law* (Oxford 1993) 82, 106, 112–15, 121, 140–43, 160, 302–7. **Studies:** R. J. **Bonner**-G. **Smith**, *The Administration of Justice from Homer to Aristotle* (Chicago 1930–38) 1.294–309; M. **Ostwald**, "The Athenian Legislation against Tyranny and Subversion," *TAPA* 86 (1955) 103–28; P. J. **Rhodes**, *The Athenian Boule* (Oxford 1972); M. H. **Hansen**, Eisangelia: *The Sovereignty of the People's Court in Athens in the Fourth Century B.C. and the Impeachment of Generals and Politicians* (Odense 1975); P. J. **Rhodes**, "ΕΙΣΑΓΓΕΛΙΑ in Athens," *JHS* 99 (1979) 103–14; M. H. **Hansen**, "Eisangelia in Athens: A Reply," *JHS* 100 (1980) 89–95; M. **Gagarin**, "The Thesmothetai and the Earliest Athenian Tyranny Law," *TAPA* 111 (1981) 71–77; J. T. **Roberts**, *Accountability in Athenian Government* (Madison 1982); D. M. **MacDowell**, "Athenian Laws about Bribery," *RIDA* ser. 3 vol. 30 (1983) 57–78; E. M. **Carawan**, "*Apophasis* and *Eisangelia*: The Rôle of the Areopagus in Athenian Political Trials," *GRBS* 26 (1985) 115–40; M. **Ostwald**, *From Popular Sovereignty to the Sovereignty of Law: Law, Society and Politics in Fifth-Century Athens* (Berkeley and Los Angeles 1986); E. M. **Carawan**, "*Eisangelia* and *Euthyna*: the Trials of Miltiades, Themistocles, and Cimon," *GRBS* 28 (1987) 167–208; R. W. **Wallace**, *The Areopagos Council, to 307 B.C.* (Baltimore 1989); I. **Worthington**, *A Historical Commentary on Dinarchus: Rhetoric and Conspiracy in Later Fourth-Century Athens* (Ann Arbor 1992); E. M. **Carawan**, "Tyranny and Outlawry: *Athenaion Politeia* 16.10," in *Nomodeiktes: Greek Studies in Honor of Martin Ostwald*, ed. R. M. Rosen-

J. Farrell (Ann Arbor 1993) 305–19; D. D. **Phillips**, "Why Was Lycophron Prosecuted by *Eisangelia*?," *GRBS* 46 (2006) 375–94; A. **Queyrel Bottineau**, *Prodosia: la notion et l'acte de trahison dans l'Athènes du Ve siècle. Recherche sur la construction de l'identité athénienne* (Bordeaux 2011).

Major offenses against the Athenian state were divisible into four principal and mutually permeable substantive categories: treason, military or civil (**362**, **365**, **367**, **369**, **370**, **371**, **373**, **375**, **377**, **381**, **383**, **385a**, **387**, **390**, **391h**, **391k**, **392b**, **392c**; cf. **366**, **368**, **391i**, **391l**); subversion of the constitution and the government (**359**, **362**, **372**, **373**, **374**, **384**, **385**, **387f**, **392b**, **392c**; cf. **391i**), including tyranny, actual, attempted, or conspired (**358**, **360**, **363**, **372**, **384**); the giving and receipt of bribes (**361**, **373**, **374**, **388**, **390**, **391**, **392c**; cf. **368**); and—under the democracy, if not earlier—*apatê tou dêmou* ("deceiving the people" in assembly) (**364**, **375**, **376**, **379**, **382**, **386**, **390**, **392b**, **392c**; cf. **373**, and for the analogous offenses of deceiving the Council of 500 or a court of law see **379**, **382**).

As was typical in Athens, there existed a variety of laws and procedures to redress these offenses. For the period before the establishment of the Cleisthenic democracy in 508/7, we have evidence for laws on and/or lawsuits for tyranny (**358**, **360**: punishable by personal and hereditary outlawry; cf. **1** [Trial and punishment of the Alcmaeonids for the killing of Cylon's partisans]), subversion (**359**: a precursor to *eisangelia* if not already known by that name, judged by the Council of the Areopagus; cf. **392b**), and possibly deception (**379**, **382**).

In the fourth century, if not already in the fifth (for certain or possible cases see **363**, **364**, **365**, **367**, **370**, **371**, **375**), the dominant procedure used to redress major offenses against the state was *eisangelia* (usually rendered in English as "impeachment"; compare the U.S. Constitution, Article II, Section 4: "The President, Vice President and all civil Officers of the United States, shall be removed from Office on Impeachment for, and Conviction of, Treason, Bribery, or other high Crimes and Misdemeanors"). The latest Classical impeachment statute (*nomos eisangeltikos*: **373**), enacted probably between 410 and 404, specified as grounds for *eisangelia* acts including subversion (actual, attempted, or conspired: see **385** with **59** Hyp. 1.12; cf. **392b**, **392c**); military (and presumably civil: cf. **385a**) treason (see **377**, **378**, **387**, **390**, **391h**, and possibly **375**; cf. **392b**, **392c**); and proposals to the Assembly made against Athenian interests under the influence of bribery (see **390**; cf. **376**: *eisangelia* for *apatê tou dêmou*, with no mention of bribery, and **392b**). *Eisangelia* was a public lawsuit (*dikê dêmosia*: p. 29): any willing and qualified Athenian citizen might initiate the procedure by bringing a written statement (the word *eisangelia* is used of this impeachment document [e.g., **385b**, **390a**, **390b**] as well as of the procedure) either before the Council of 500 (**371**, **377**, **378**, **380**, ?**375**; cf. **392a**, **392b**) or before the Assembly (**385b**, **387**, **390**, ?**364**, ?**365**, ?**367**, ?**370**; cf. **392a**).

If it accepted the impeachment, the Council or Assembly decided either to try the lawsuit itself (trial by Council: **378**; trial by Assembly: ?**364**, ?**365**, ?**367**, ?**370**) or to refer the lawsuit to a *dikastêrion* (referral by Council: **371**, **378**, **380**, ?**377**; cf. **392b**; referral by Assembly: **385**, **387**, **390**; cf. **373**); in a trial before the Council, since the Council could not impose a penalty exceeding 500 drachmas, if it convicted the defendant and found that more severe punishment was warranted, it referred the case to the Assembly (?**375**) or to a *dikastêrion* (**378**). Trial by *eisangelia* took place under the terms of an *ad hoc* decree of the Council and Assembly (**371**, **385**, **387**, **390**, ?**370**, ?**375**). An author of the decree normally served as the prosecutor of record (**385**, **387**, **390**), although the decree might specify special public prosecutors (called *synêgoroi*: **371**); the use of advocates (*synêgoroi* in its more frequent sense: p. 28) by both prosecution (**385**) and defense (**385**, **387e**, **390**) was common. The decree might mandate the imprisonment of the defendant pending trial (**380**, ?**375**; cf. **362**, **377**) and might specify the penalty to be imposed in the case of a conviction (**371**, ?**370**, ?**375**); the standard, but probably not statutory, penalty was death, denial of burial in Attica, and confiscation of property (**371**, **385c**, **387**, **390**; cf. ?**367**; for cases in which this penalty was not imposed see **378**, **271** [Pericles' trial and conviction for theft of public property], ?**364**, and cf. **392b**, according to which *eisangelia*, at least when tried before a *dikastêrion*, was an *agôn timêtos* [assessable lawsuit: p. 40] without penal limit).

Until very near the end of the Classical period, *eisangelia* differed from most other public lawsuits in that prosecutors who received less than 20 percent of the trial jury's votes were not penalized 1,000 drachmas for sycophancy (**392b** with **59** Hyp. 1.12); this penalty was extended to *eisangelia* at some point between 333 and 330 (**389**; cf. **392a**), presumably in response to growing complaints about the use of the impeachment procedure against defendants accused of acts such as seduction (**385** with **59** Hyp. 1.12), abandoning Attica in wartime (**387e**), overcharging for prostitutes, fraudulent deme registration, and making a false report to the Assembly of a dream experienced in the Temple of Amphiaraus at Oropus (**390**). It is probably the accounts of such marginal cases as these that impelled some later authors (**392**) to assert that *eisangelia* lay not just against the offenses specified in the *nomos eisangeltikos* (**373**) but also against novel and/or unwritten offenses (i.e., those not addressed by any statute). This assertion is likely false (note, e.g., that the impeachments of Lycophron for seduction [**385**], of Leocrates for abandoning Attica [**387**], and of Euxenippus for falsely reporting his dream [**390**] were prosecuted under the subversion, treason, and proposal clauses of the *nomos eisangeltikos* respectively), but the issue remains a topic of debate among modern scholars.

Other legislation and procedures targeting one or more major offenses against the state included a law on bribery, specifying a penalty of personal and hereditary outlawry (**361**); a decree of 413 or soon thereafter providing for *apagôgê* against persons who defected to the Spartan garrison at Deceleia and then returned to Athens (**369**); the decree of Demophantus on subversion and tyranny, which accompanied the restoration of democracy in 410 (**372**); a law providing for prosecution by *graphê* for offenses including conspiracy, bribery, and subversion (**374**; on the *graphê dôrôn*, for bribery, see also **388**; **302a** [Arist.] *Ath. Pol.* 48.4–5, 54.2; **391d**, **391j**); the decree of Cannonus on trial procedure and punishment for offenses against the state (**375**, at 1.7.20–21, 34); a law on temple-robbery and treason (**375**, at 1.7.22; cf. **371**, at 833f); a prescriptive curse (**382**) and one or more laws providing the death penalty for *apatê tou dêmou* (**379**); a law or decree instituting *probolê* for *apatê tou dêmou*, passed soon after the trial of the Arginusae generals in 405 (**375**, at 1.7.35; **386**); the law of Eucrates on tyranny and subversion, with particular attention to the Council of the Areopagus, passed in 337/6 (**384**); and *apophasis* ("report" by the Council of the Areopagus: **383**, **391**), a procedure created by a decree of Demosthenes ca. 344/3 (**391k**) and employed most famously against Demosthenes and other leading politicians in connection with the Harpalus affair of 324/3 (**391**).

See also **1** (Trial and punishment of the Alcmaeonids for the killing of Cylon's partisans); **59** Hyp. 1.12; **60** [Arist.] *Ath. Pol.* 59.3; **66** Hyp. 4.3; **99** Lys. 14.28; **170** Andoc. 1.73–79; **224** [Arist.] *Ath. Pol.* 43.4; **254** Dem. 39.1, 5, 7–18; **277** Lys. 30.21, 23–25; **279** Lys. 27.3–4, 6–7; **281** Lys. 29.1–2, 11; **287** Xen. *Hell.* 1.7.22; **289** Dem. 24.104–5, 112–15, 120–21, 129, 146; **302a** [Arist.] *Ath. Pol.* 48.4–5, 54.2; **310** Lys. 22.5–6, 8; **333** [Arist.] *Ath. Pol.* 59.2; **334** Thuc. 6.27–29, 53, 60–61; **335** Plut. *Alcib.* 22.4–5; **336** (Selections from the Attic Stelai); **338c** Andoc. 1.27–28; **338e** Andoc. 1.34, 36–37, 43–45; **344b** D. L. 2.12–14; **345** *IG* I^3 78; **353** (Trial of Phryne); **357** D. L. 2.116.

358. Plutarch, *Solon* 19.4. Solon's amnesty law (*lex* + commentary). (date of composition late 1st-early 2nd c.A.D.; date of law 594/3 B.C.)

See references and headnote under **1d**. Citation by axon (cf., e.g., **2** *IG* I^3 104; **322** Plut. *Solon* 24.1–2) and order of laws on the axon, and the reference to Solon's archon year (594/3), are strong indicators of the authenticity of the quoted law. For the roles of the Areopagus, *ephetai*, Prytaneion, and kings in the law of homicide see chapter 1, especially **2** *IG* I^3 104; **3a** Dem. 23.22; **20** Dem. 23.65–80; **25** [Arist.] *Ath. Pol.* 57.2–4. On outlawry as the original meaning of *atimia* see p. 41 and cf., e.g., **360** [Arist.] *Ath. Pol.* 16.10; **361** Dem. 21.113; **368** Dem. 9.41–45; **371** [Plut.] *Lives of the Ten Orators* 833d-834b; **384** *SEG* 12.87. "Slaughters" is generally taken as referring to mass killings occurring during civil strife (cf. **1** [Trial and punishment of the Alcmaeonids for the killing of Cylon's partisans]; **170** Andoc. 1.73–79). Most scholars who accept the authenticity of the law believe that the Areopagus held jurisdiction over cases of (attempted) tyranny before Solon (cf. **359** [Arist.] *Ath. Pol.* 8.4); since the only known case is the Cylonian conspiracy, the default assumption is that those who had been outlawed for tyranny were surviving supporters of Cylon.

Solon's thirteenth axon contains the eighth law, written verbatim as follows: "All outlaws [*atimôn*] who were outlawed before the archonship of Solon shall have their rights restored, except those who were in exile issued by the Areopagus or by the *ephetai* or the Prytaneion, having been judged guilty by the kings, for homicide [*phonôi*], slaughters [*sphagaisin*], or tyranny, at the time when this law [*thesmos*] was promulgated."

359. [Aristotle], *Constitution of the Athenians (Ath. Pol.)* 8.4. Law of Solon on *eisangelia*. (date of composition 332–322; law ascribed to Solon, 594/3)

See references and headnote under **1c**. Solon's law on *eisangelia* presumably did not include language about "subversion of the people," which is characteristic of the later democracy (e.g., **373** Hyp. 4.7–8; **374** [Dem.] 46.26; **384** *SEG* 12.87). The anachronism will have arisen from the subversion clause in the impeachment law current in the fourth century (**373** Hyp. 4.7–8) and the widely-held but inaccurate fourth-century belief that Solon had founded the Athenian democracy (e.g., **262** Hyp. 3.5–11, 18, 21–22, at §21; [Arist.] *Ath. Pol.* 9.1).

. . . and in particular, [the Council of the Areopagus] judged those who conspired to subvert the people [*epi katalysei tou dêmou*], Solon having established a law of impeachment [*eisangelias*] concerning them.

360. [Aristotle], *Constitution of the Athenians (Ath. Pol.)* 16.10 (*lex* + commentary). Law on tyranny. (date of composition 332–322; law described as in force 561/0–528/7)

See references and headnote under **1c**. "Those times" are those of the tyrannies of Peisistratus (561/0–528/7: see p. 4); the law is therefore probably Solonian and is sometimes equated with Solon's *eisangelia* law (**359** [Arist.] *Ath. Pol.* 8.4). On outlawry for tyranny as "ancestral custom" cf. **358** Plut. *Solon* 19.4; the switch from the plural "any persons" to the singular "a person . . .

he" corresponds to the language of the text. The author's characterization of the law as "mild" indicates that he either misinterpreted *atimon* (taking it to mean "disfranchised," as commonly in the fourth century: p. 41) or considered outlawry (see **358** Plut. *Solon* 19.4 with additional references in headnote) more lenient than execution by the state, which was provided or permitted under, for example, the fourth-century *eisangelia* law (**373** Hyp. 4.7–8; cf. **387b** Lyc. 1.8, 89).

Moreover, the Athenians' laws concerning tyrants were mild during those times, especially the one that had most to do with the establishment of tyranny. This was their law: "The following is a law and ancestral custom of the Athenians: if any persons engage in uprising with the goal of tyranny or a person cooperates in the establishment of a tyranny, he shall be outlawed [*atimon*], both himself and his descendants."

361. Demosthenes 21 *Against Meidias* 113 (*lex*). Law on bribery. (date of speech 347/6; date of law ?508/7-early 5th c.)

See references and headnote under **22**. That the offender's property is described as *atimos* (cf. **3h** Dem. 23.62, and see **358** Plut. *Solon* 19.4 with additional references in headnote) rather than subject to confiscation (as in, e.g., **371** [Plut.] *Lives of the Ten Orators* 833d-834b; **372** Andoc. 1.96–98; **375** Xen. *Hell.* 1.7.1–16, 20–26, 34–35; **384** *SEG* 12.87) indicates the relative antiquity of the law; a putative upper limit is furnished by the phrase "to the detriment of the people," which is unlikely to predate the establishment of the Cleisthenic democracy (p. 5; see **359** [Arist.] *Ath. Pol.* 8.4 with additional references in headnote).

If any Athenian takes from anyone, or himself gives to another, or corrupts any persons by making promises, to the detriment of the people or the private detriment of any citizen, by any way or means whatsoever, he shall be outlawed [*atimos*], as shall his children and his property.

362. Demosthenes 24 *Against Timocrates* 144–45 (*iusiurandum* + commentary). Clause of bouleutic oath restricting power to imprison, with exceptions including cases of treason and subversion. (date of speech 353/2; date of oath 501/0–412)

See references and headnote under **160**. The quotation comes from the oath sworn by the Council of 500 annually since 501/0 ([Aristotle], *Constitution of the Athenians* 22.2) but modified on subsequent occasions. Some form of the provision on sureties is attested at Antiphon 5.17, delivered between 427 and 412; "of the same class" refers to the Solonian income classes (p. 3). On imprisonment by the Council of 500 cf. **380** Dem. 24.63.

And to speak about that law . . . in which is written, "I shall not imprison any Athenian who appoints three sureties of the same class [as himself], except if a person has been caught assembling with the aim of betraying [*prodosiai*] the city or subverting the people [*katalysei tou dêmou*], or has purchased [the contract to collect] a tax or stood surety [for the purchaser] or is a tax-collector and does not pay," listen to me about this too. [145] . . . This law . . . applies not to those who have been tried and pled their cases but to those who have not been tried; its purpose is that they not be forced to plead their cases worse, or even be completely unprepared, because they have been imprisoned.

363. Herodotus 6.104.2. Trial of Miltiades for tyranny. (date of composition 440s-420s; date of event 493–491)

See references and headnote under **1a**. Around 516, Hippias and Hipparchus, the sons of Peisistratus (p. 5; cf. **360** [Arist.] *Ath. Pol.* 16.10), dispatched Miltiades to assume control of the Thracian Chersonese (modern Gallipoli, the peninsula on the European side of the Hellespont), which had been previously governed by his brother and his uncle. Miltiades supported the Ionian Greeks in their revolt against Persia (499–494) and fled to Athens after the revolt ended in failure. As one of Athens' ten generals in 490/89, Miltiades played a signal role in the victory over the Persians at the Battle of Marathon (August 490).

. . . as soon as . . . [Miltiades] arrived in his own country and thought he was now in safety, straightaway his enemies intercepted him, haled him before a jury-court [*dikastêrion*], and prosecuted him for tyranny in the Chersonese. But he escaped them as well and was thus appointed general of the Athenians, elected by the people.

364. Herodotus 6.136. Trial of Miltiades for deceiving the people (*apatê tou dêmou*). (date of composition 440s-420s; date of event 489)

See references and headnote under **1a**, and **363** with headnote. Following the Battle of Marathon, Miltiades convinced the Assembly to grant him command of seventy ships; without specifying the target of his expedition, he promised that he would make the Athenians rich. The result was an unsuccessful siege of the island of Paros in which Miltiades suffered a wound to the thigh. With 6.136.3 contrast Plato, *Gorgias* 516d9-e2: the Assembly "voted to cast Miltiades . . . into the pit [see **369** Lyc. 1.120–21 with additional references in headnote], and if it were not for the *prytanis* [presiding officer: see **332** Dem. 21 (selections) with headnote], he would have been cast in." On false promises to the Assembly cf. **376** [Dem.] 49.66–67; **379** Dem. 20.100, 135; **386** [Arist.] *Ath. Pol.* 43.5.

After Miltiades returned from Paros, the Athenians discussed him constantly, especially Xanthippus son of Ariphron, who brought Miltiades before the Assembly on a death-penalty charge and prosecuted him for his deception [*apatês*] of the Athenians. [136.2] Miltiades, although present, did not speak in his own defense (he was unable, since his thigh was septic), but, as he lay in view on a couch, his family and friends spoke for him, mentioning at length the battle that had taken place at Marathon and the capture of Lemnos. . . . [136.3] The Assembly came over to his side to the extent of absolving him from the death penalty but fined him 50 talents for his offense. After this, Miltiades died, his thigh having gone gangrenous and septic, and his son Cimon paid the fifty talents.

365. Lycurgus 1 *Against Leocrates* 117–18. Trial of Hipparchus son of Charmus for treason. (date of speech 330; date of event 482–480)

See references and headnote under **26**. In 488/7 Hipparchus son of Charmus became the first Athenian to be ostracized (p. 8); as a relative of the Peisistratids (probably the maternal grandson of Hippias and named after Hippias' brother), he was suspected of collaboration with the Persians, whose landing at Marathon (see headnote under **363** Hdt. 6.104.2) had been directed by Hippias. At some point between 482 and 480, the Athenians recalled all ostracized men (see [Aristotle], *Constitution of the Athenians* 22.8 and the Themistocles decree [R. **Meiggs**-D. **Lewis**, *A Selection of Greek Historical Inscriptions to the End of the Fifth Century B.C.* (rev. ed. Oxford 1988), no. 23 (text and commentary) = C. W. **Fornara**, *Archaic Times to the End of the Peloponnesian War*[2] (Cambridge 1985), no. 55 (translation with notes), lines 44–47]); Hipparchus disobeyed the summons and was accordingly tried *in absentia.*

When Hipparchus son of Charmus did not await his trial for treason [*prodosias*] in the Assembly but let the trial go against him by default [*erêmon*], they sentenced him to death. Since they could not hold his person hostage for his offense, they took down his statue from the Acropolis, melted it down, and made a pillar, and they decreed that [the names of] offenders against the gods and traitors [*prodotas*] be inscribed upon it. Hipparchus himself is inscribed on that pillar, as are the other traitors too. [118] [To the court clerk:] Please take first the decree by which Hipparchus' statue was taken down from the Acropolis, then the inscription on the base of the pillar, along with the [names of the] traitors who were later added in writing on that pillar, and read them, clerk.

366. Killing of Lycides/Cyrsilus. (date of event 479)

The following passages are generally taken as referring to a single incident, despite their discrepancies with regard to such important facts as the name of the councillor (presumably a member of the Council of 500) whose proposal to forward peace terms from the Persian commander Mardonius to the Assembly led to his death, the chronology (Herodotus, who places the event in 479, is to be preferred to Demosthenes, who places it in 480), and whether the killing was a spontaneous stoning or an execution carried out by decree.

a. Herodotus 9.4–5. (date of composition 440s-420s)

R. W. **Macan**, *Herodotus: The Seventh, Eighth, and Ninth Books*, 2 vols. in 3 (London 1908: text and commentary); W. W. **How**-J. **Wells**, *A Commentary on Herodotus*, 2 vols. (ed. corr. Oxford 1928); R. B. **Strassler**, ed., *The Landmark Herodotus* (New York 2007: translation with introduction and notes).

See headnote under **1a**.

When Mardonius arrived in Athens, he sent to Salamis Murychides, a man from the Hellespont, bearing the same proposals that Alexander of Macedon had conveyed to the Athenians. . . . [5.1] [Murychides] came to the Council and reported the proposals from Mardonius. One of the councillors, Lycides, moved a resolution, stating that he thought it better to accept the proposal that Murychides brought to them and bring it before the Assembly. [5.2] He declared this resolution—whether because he had in fact received money from Mardonius or because it was his opinion—and on the spot the Athenians became indignant, both those from the Council and those outside, when they heard, and they surrounded Lycides and stoned him to death. . . . [5.3] A clamor arose on Salamis over Lycides, and the Athenians' women found out what was happening. They passed and received the word, woman to woman, and they came to Lycides' house at their own bidding and stoned to death his wife and his children.

b. Lycurgus 1 *Against Leocrates* 122. (date of composition 330)

See references and headnote under **26**.

It is also worthwhile to hear the decree that was passed concerning the man who was put to death on Salamis. The Council removed its crowns and killed this man with its own hands because he attempted by words alone to betray [*prodidonai*] the city.

c. Demosthenes 18 *On the Crown* 204. (date of composition 330)

See references and headnote under **80**.

. . . who could fail to admire the virtue of those men? So that they would not have to do as they were ordered, they dared to embark on their triremes and abandon their country and their city, having elected as general Themistocles, who gave them this advice, and having stoned to death Cyrsilus, the man who declared his opinion that they should obey the commands laid upon them—and not just him: your women stoned his wife to death too.

367. Banishment of Themistocles for treason. (date of event ca. 471/0 B.C.)

Themistocles, who had served with great distinction as an Athenian commander and strategist during the Second Persian War, especially at the Battle of Salamis (cf. **343c** Aelian, *VH* 5.19; **366c** Dem. 18.204), was ostracized in the late 470s. Following his ostracism, the Spartans accused him of medism (collaboration with Persia: cf. **344b** D. L. 2.12–14) in connection with Pausanias, the Spartan former commander in the Hellespontine region. Themistocles was never apprehended and eventually made his way to Persia, where Artaxerxes I (r. 465–424) appointed him governor of the region centered at Magnesia on the Maeander. Cf. **392c** *Lex. Cantab.* s.v. *eisangelia*, and see also (*inter alia*) Plato, *Gorgias* 516d8–9; Diodorus 11.54–55; Aelian, *Varia Historia* 10.17; Suda s.vv. *Themistoklês*, *Themistokleous paides.*

a. Thucydides 1.135.2–136.1, 138.6. (date of composition 431-ca. 400 B.C.)

See references and headnote under **1b**. For the denial of burial in Attica to a traitor cf. **387** Lyc. 1 (selections); **391** (*Apophasis* against Demosthenes and others for receiving bribes in the Harpalus affair).

As for the medism of Pausanias, the Spartans sent ambassadors to the Athenians and accused Themistocles as well, on the basis of their discoveries from the scrutiny concerning Pausanias, and they demanded that Themistocles receive the same punishment. [135.3] The Athenians consented, and since he had been ostracized and was living in Argos but making habitual visits to the rest of the Peloponnese as well, they sent along with the Spartans, who were eager to join the pursuit, men who had been told to arrest him wherever they found him. [136.1] Themistocles, however, learned of this in advance and fled from the Peloponnese. . . .

. . .

[138.6] His relatives say that his bones were brought home at his bidding and were buried in Attica without the Athenians' knowledge: it was not permitted to bury him [there], since he was in exile for treason [*prodosiai*].

b. Idomeneus, *FGrHist* 338 F 1 (= scholion to Aristophanes, *Wasps* 947). (date of composition ca. 300-ca. 270 B.C.)

F. **Jacoby**, *Die Fragmente der griechischen Historiker* (Leiden 1957-), no. 338, fr. 1 (text: part IIIB p. 190; commentary: part IIIb vol. 1 pp. 85–86, vol. 2 p. 59); A. **Angeli**, "I frammenti di Idomeneo di Lampsaco," *Cronache Ercolanesi* 11 (1981) 41–101 (text and Italian translation).

This fragment comes from the second book of Idomeneus of Lampsacus' treatise *On Demagogues*. If the sentence of exile included Themistocles' descendants, it was revoked (or ignored) as to them in time for his son Cleophantus to return to Athens (Plato, *Meno* 93d1-e4); compare the "perpetual exile" of the Alcmaeonids (**1** [Trial and punishment of the Alcmaeonids for the killing of Cylon's partisans]).

The Athenians condemned [Themistocles] and his descendants to perpetual exile [*aeiphygian*] for his betrayal [*prodidontos*] of Greece, and his property was confiscated.

c. Plutarch, *Themistocles* 23.1, 4, 6; 25.3. (date of composition late 1st-early 2nd c. A.D.)

F. J. **Frost**, *Plutarch's Themistocles: A Historical Commentary*, rev. ed. (Chicago 1998); R. **Waterfield**, *Plutarch: Greek Lives* (Oxford 1998: translation with introduction and notes by P. A. Stadter).

On Plutarch see the headnote under **1d**. The wording in §23.1 might imply a *graphê prodosias*, but Craterus, presumably on the basis of a surviving decree (see **126** Harpo. s.v. *nautodikai*), identified the action as an *eisangelia* (**392c** *Lex. Cantab.* s.v. *eisangelia*); Plutarch may therefore be using the verb *graphein* "to indict" in its general sense (p. 30; cf., e.g., **392a** Harpo. s.v. *eisangelia* with **161** Isae. 11.6, 31, 35). "Before the Greeks" (§23.6): cf. Diodorus 11.55.4–5, where the prospective venue is "the common council of the Greeks"; that is, of the Hellenic League, the association of city-states formed in 481 to resist the imminent Persian invasion (cf. the headnote under **343c** Aelian, *VH* 5.19). This detail is rejected by many scholars but cannot be conclusively dismissed, since Themistocles was never brought to trial. §25.3: Theopompus of Chios (?378/7-*post* 320) was the author of numerous works; his (now fragmentary) historical treatise the *Philippica* is Plutarch's source for the figure of 100 tal. On Theophrastus see **312** Theophr. *Laws* fr. 21.1 Szegedy-Maszak.

When Themistocles had been expelled from the city and was living in Argos, what had transpired concerning Pausanias gave his enemies means to attack him. The man who indicted [*grapsamenos*] him for treason [*prodosias*] was Leobotes son of Alcmaeon of the deme Agryle; the Spartans joined in the accusation as well. . . . [23.4] Thus, after Pausanias was put to death, some letters and documents concerning these matters were uncovered and placed Themistocles under suspicion. The Spartans were clamoring against him, and those of his fellow citizens who envied him brought accusations; he was not present but defended himself by letters. . . . [23.6] . . . the Assembly, persuaded by his accusers, sent men who were told to arrest him and bring him back to be tried before the Greeks.

. . .

[25.3] Much of his property was smuggled out thanks to his friends and made its way by ship to Asia; as for what was discovered and collected into the public treasury, Theopompus states that it amounted to 100 talents, and Theophrastus, 80 talents. . . .

368. Demosthenes 9 *3 Philippic* 41–45 (*decretum* + commentary). Decree outlawing Arthmius of Zeleia and his descendants. (date of speech 341; date of event 460s–450s)

See references and headnote under **5**. The first sentence contrasts the corruption of contemporary Athenian politicians with past practice. "The Medes" means the Persian Empire (see headnote under **367** [Banishment of Themistocles for treason]), with which the Delian League ("the Athenian people and its allies": see p. 11 and cf., e.g., **345** *IG* I³ 78) was at war; Greek authors commonly refer to monarchs' subjects as their slaves. "*Atimia* in the ordinary sense" in the fourth century was disfranchisement (p. 41; cf. especially **170** Andoc. 1.73–79); hence Demosthenes explains that in the Arthmius decree the term *atimos* means that Arthmius and his descendants may be killed with impunity (cf. **372** Andoc. 1.96–98, and see **358** Plut. *Solon* 19.4 with additional references in headnote). See also Demosthenes 19.270–72; Aeschines 3.258; Deinarchus 2.24–25; Plutarch, *Themistocles* 6.4; Aelius Aristeides 2.287 with scholion (**Fornara**, *Archaic Times to the End of the Peloponnesian War* no. 69); R. **Meiggs**, *The Athenian Empire* (ed. corr. Oxford 1975) 508–12.

That the opposite was the case in earlier times I will demonstrate not in my own words but by reciting a document of your ancestors, which they inscribed on a bronze pillar and set up on the Acropolis. . . . [42] It states, "Arthmius son of Pythonax of Zeleia shall be an outlaw [*atimos*] and public enemy of the Athenian people and its allies, himself and his descendants." Then the reason that this happened is written: "because he brought the gold from the Medes to the Peloponnese." . . . [43] . . . Because a man from Zeleia, Arthmius, a slave of the Persian king (Zeleia is in Asia), in the service of his master brought gold to the Peloponnese—not to Athens—they inscribed him and his descendants as enemies of themselves and their allies, and as outlaws [*atimous*]. [44] Now, this was not what one would call *atimia* in the ordinary sense; what was it to a Zeleite if he was not to share in the common rights of Athenians? That, however, is not what it means. Rather, the meaning is as it is written in the homicide laws, concerning persons in whose cases no homicide trial is granted, but whose killing is sanctioned: "and let him die an outlaw [*atimos*]." What this means is that the killer of one of these persons is free of pollution. [45] They, then, thought that the safety of all the Greeks was their concern: they would not have cared if a person bought and corrupted people in the Peloponnese unless this were their understanding. . . .

369. Lycurgus I *Against Leocrates* 120–21. Decree providing for *apagôgê* (summary arrest) and execution of persons who returned to Athens following defection to Spartans at Deceleia. (date of speech 330; date of decree 413 or slightly later)

See references and headnote under **26**. The Spartan seizure of Deceleia (in northern Attica) in 413 opened the final phase of the Peloponnesian War (p. 11). Defectors to Deceleia included over 20,000 Athenian slaves (Thucydides 7.27) and most of the leaders of the oligarchy of the Four Hundred (p. 11) after its fall in 411 (Thucydides 8.98; see further **370** Lyc. 1.112–15). On *apagôgê* see p. 30 and cf., e.g., **57a** Aeschin. 1.91; **288** Dem. 22.25–27, 69–73 with additional references in headnotes. Being thrown into the "pit" (*orygma* or *barathron*) was a form of execution apparently used (in the Classical period, at least) only on persons who committed major offenses against the state (cf. **375** Xen. *Hell.* 1.7.1–16, 20–26, 34–35; **391k** Din. 1.61–63; Pl. *Gorgias* 516d9-e2, in headnote under **364** Hdt. 6.136).

[To the court clerk:] Please take the other decree as well, the one concerning those who defected to Deceleia when the people was under siege by the Spartans. . . .

DECREE.

[121] Listen, gentlemen, to this decree too, by which the Assembly condemned those who had defected to Deceleia during the war and decreed that if any of them came back and was caught, any willing Athenian was to arrest him [*apagagein*] and take him to the *thesmothetai*, and the *thesmothetai*, upon receiving him, were to hand him over to the man in charge of the pit.

370. Lycurgus 1 *Against Leocrates* 112–15. *Post mortem* trial of Phrynichus for treason. (date of speech 330; date of events 411/10)

See references and headnote under **26**. Phrynichus was a leader of the oligarchy of the Four Hundred (p. 11), which was deposed shortly after his assassination; Apollodorus and Thrasybulus were metics from Megara and Calydon respectively. Cf. D. **Lewis**, ed., ***Inscriptiones Graecae,*** vol. 1 ed. 3 fasc. 1 (Berlin and New York 1981), no. 102 = **Meiggs-Lewis**, *Greek Historical Inscriptions* no. 85 (text and commentary) = **Fornara**, *Archaic Times to the End of the Peloponnesian War* no. 155 (translation with notes), a decree and two riders of 410/09 that grant citizenship to Thrasybulus, confer benefits upon his fellow conspirators, and provide for the trial and punishment of those guilty of bribery in connection with the decree; Thucydides 8.92–93, 98; Lysias 13.71–72; Plutarch, *Alcibiades* 25 (which mentions Phrynichus' *post mortem* trial and conviction); **371** [Plut.] *Lives of the Ten Orators* 833d-834b; Craterus, *FGrHist* 342 F 17 (= scholion to Aristophanes, *Lysistrata* 313). With regard to Aristarchus and Alexicles, Lycurgus has at least telescoped events, if not invented them outright. Aristarchus survived the fall of the Four Hundred, betrayed Oenoe (on the border between Attica and Boeotia) to the Boeotians, and was put on trial at some point between 411/10 and the Battle of Arginusae in 406 (Thucydides, *loc. cit.*; Xenophon, *Hellenica* 1.7.28; cf. **375** Xen. *Hell.* 1.7.1–16, 20–26, 34–35). Alexicles was arrested in the wake of Phrynichus' killing but released after a very brief time in detention; he then defected to the Spartans at Deceleia (Thucydides, *loc. cit.*), for which act he would have been liable to execution if captured (cf. **369** Lyc. 1.120–21).

After Phrynichus was slaughtered at night near the spring in the osiers by Apollodorus and Thrasybulus, when they were arrested and placed in the prison by Phrynichus' friends, the Assembly, upon learning what had happened, brought out the men who had been detained, conducted questioning under torture, held a hearing of the matter, and in its investigation found that Phrynichus was guilty of betraying [*prodidonta*] the city and that his killers had been detained unjustly. [113] And the Assembly, on the motion of Critias, decreed that the corpse [of Phrynichus] should stand trial for treason [*prodosias*] and that if it was decided that one who was a traitor [*prodotês*] had been buried in the country, his bones should be dug up and cast over the borders of Attica. . . . [114] They also decreed that any persons who spoke in defense of the deceased should, if the deceased were convicted, be themselves also liable to the same penalties. . . . [115] . . . They then dug up the bones of the traitor and cast them over the borders of Attica, and executed those who had spoken in his defense, Aristarchus and Alexicles, and did not permit them to be buried in the country either. . . .

371. [Plutarch], *Lives of the Ten Orators* 833d-834b (*decretum* + commentary). *Eisangelia* of Archeptolemus, Onomacles, and Antiphon for treason. (date of composition 1st or 2nd c. A.D.; date of event 411/10 B.C.)

L. **Gernet**, *Antiphon: Discours* (Paris 1923: text with French translation and notes); H. N. **Fowler**, *Plutarch's* Moralia, vol. 10 (Cambridge, MA 1936: text and translation).

See headnote under **353a**. Archeptolemus, Onomacles, and Antiphon (the orator), as well as Andron, the author of the decree providing for their impeachment, were members of the oligarchy of the Four Hundred (p. 11; cf. **369** Lyc. 1.120–21; **370** Lyc. 1.112–15); on Antiphon's role in the oligarchy cf. Thucydides 8.68. Caecilius' (see **223** Harpo. s.v. *exoulês*) source was Craterus (Harpocration s.v. *Andrôn*; on Craterus see **126** Harpo. s.v. *nautodikai* and cf. **392c** *Lex. Cantab.* s.v. *eisangelia*). "The Council" is the Council of 500. On the division of the year into prytanies see p. 6; with the accusation of passage through Deceleia cf. **369** Lyc. 1.120–21; on the Eleven see p. 31 and cf., e.g., **375** Xen. *Hell.* 1.7.1–16, 20–26, 34–35; **380** Dem. 24.63; on the *thesmothetai* see p. 2 and cf., e.g., **369** Lyc. 1.120–21; **374** [Dem.] 46.26; **380** Dem. 24.63. The term *synêgoroi* (advocates) in 833f refers, as the context shows, not to private persons appearing in support of a litigant but to special public prosecutors (cf. **302a** [Arist.] *Ath. Pol.* 48.4–5, 54.2; **391h** Din. 1.48, 50–52). For "the law . . . . concerning traitors" (833f) cf. **375** Xen. *Hell.* 1.7.1–16, 20–26, 34–35, at 1.7.22. That Onomacles appears in the impeachment decree but not in the sentence indicates that he absconded before trial. In the sentence, *atimon* and *atimos* may mean "outlawed" (see **358** Plut. *Solon* 19.4 with additional references in headnote) rather than merely "disfranchised"; on confiscation of property see the headnote under **361** Dem. 21.113 ("the goddess" [834a] is Athena: cf. **372** Andoc. 1.96–98 with additional references in headnote). For "the decrees concerning Phrynichus" cf. **370** Lyc. 1.112–15 with additional references in headnote.

Especially praised are [Antiphon's] speech *Concerning Herodes*, his speech *Against Erasistratus Concerning the Peacocks*, his speech *Concerning the Impeachment* [*eisangelias*], which he wrote in his own defense. . . .

The decree passed in the archonship of Theopompus [411/10], when the Four [833e] Hundred were deposed, by which it was resolved that Antiphon should stand trial, is provided by Caecilius: "Resolved by the Council on the twenty-first day of the prytany; Demonicus of the deme Alopece was secretary, Philostratus of the deme Pallene presided, Andron made the motion. Concerning the men whom the generals report for serving as ambassadors to Sparta to the detriment of the city of Athens and the army, sailing upon an enemy [833f] ship, and traveling by land through Deceleia: Archeptolemus, Onomacles, and Antiphon shall be arrested and handed over to the jury-court [*dikastêrion*] to face punishment. The generals, along with up to ten members of the Council decided upon and selected by the generals, shall hand them over, so that their trial occurs with them present. The *thesmothetai* shall summon them tomorrow and, when the summonses have been delivered, shall introduce to the jury-court the lawsuit for treason [*prodosias*], to be prosecuted by the chosen advocates [*synêgorous*], the generals, and others, if someone so wishes. Anyone whom the jury-court convicts shall be dealt with in accordance with the law that has been established concerning traitors [*prodontôn*]."

[834a] Under this resolution is written the sentence. "Found guilty of treason [*prodosias*]: Archeptolemus son of Hippodamus of the deme Agryle, present; Antiphon son of Sophilus of the deme Rhamnus, present. The sentence passed upon them was that they be handed over to the Eleven, that their property be confiscated and one-tenth belong to the goddess, and that their houses be razed and boundary-markers [*horous*] placed upon the sites of the houses with the inscription 'Property of Archeptolemus and Antiphon, the traitors [*prodotain*].' Their demarchs shall register [834b] their property for confiscation, and it shall not be permitted to bury Archeptolemus and Antiphon in Athens or any land that the Athenians control. Archeptolemus, Antiphon, and their descendants,

both illegitimate and legitimate, shall be disfranchised [*atimon*], and if a person adopts any of the descendants of Archeptolemus or Antiphon, the adopter shall be disfranchised [*atimos*]. These provisions shall be inscribed on a bronze pillar, and this shall be placed in the same location where the decrees concerning Phrynichus are set up."

372. Andocides 1 *On the Mysteries* 96–98 (*decretum*). Decree of Demophantus on subversion of the democracy and tyranny. (date of speech 400 or 399; date of decree 410)

> See references and headnote under **12**. "The Council" is the Council of 500; "the people" refers to the Assembly; on the division of the year into prytanies see p. 6. "When the Council of 500 was selected by lot . . . first secretary": the decree went into effect at the beginning of the civil year 410/09, following the deposition of the Four Hundred and of the Five Thousand and the restoration of democracy (p. 12). "He shall be a public enemy of the Athenians and shall be killed with impunity": cf. **368** Dem. 9.41–45, and see **358** Plut. *Solon* 19.4 with additional references in headnote. "The goddess" is Athena (cf., e.g., **371** [Plut.] *Lives of the Ten Orators* 833d–834b; **375** Xen. *Hell.* 1.7.1–16, 20–26, 34–35; **384** *SEG* 12.87). The angled brackets < > enclose an editorial supplement to the text. On Harmodius and Aristogeiton see **78** Hyp. 2.3; **334** Thuc. 6.27–29, 53, 60–61. "In camp": the oligarchic plot that led to the installation of the Four Hundred (p. 11; cf. **369** Lyc. 1.120–21; **370** Lyc. 1.112–15; **371** [Plut.] *Lives of the Ten Orators* 833d–834b) began in the Athenian military camp on Samos (Thucydides 8.47–848). "The Dionysia" is here the Greater (City) Dionysia (see, e.g., **139** Lys. 32.8–10, 19–24; **332** Dem. 21 [selections]). On the Demophantus decree cf. Lycurgus 1.124–27; Demosthenes 20.159.

Resolved by the Council and the people; the tribe Aeantis held the prytany, Cleigenes was secretary, Boethus presided. Demophantus drafted the following motion. The starting date of this decree is when the Council of 500 was selected by lot, for whom Cleigenes was the first secretary.

If a person subverts the democracy at Athens or holds any office after the democracy has been subverted, he shall be a public enemy of the Athenians and shall be killed with impunity; his property shall be confiscated, and one-tenth shall belong to the goddess. The person who kills one who has committed these acts and the person who counsels the killing shall be pure of guilt and pollution. [97] All Athenians shall swear over perfect sacrifices by tribes and by demes to kill one who has committed these acts. The oath shall be as follows: "I shall kill <by word and by deed, by vote and> with my own hand, if I am able, anyone who subverts the democracy at Athens, and anyone who, after the democracy has been subverted, thenceforth holds any office, and anyone who engages in uprising to become tyrant or cooperates in establishing a tyrant. And if someone else kills him, I shall consider that person to be pure of guilt before gods and divinities, since he has killed a public enemy of the Athenians; and I shall sell all the possessions of the dead man and give half to the killer, and I shall not withhold anything. [98] And if a person is killed while killing or attempting to kill one of the aforementioned, I shall do well by him and his children, just as I do Harmodius and Aristogeiton and their descendants. All oaths that have been sworn at Athens or in camp or anywhere else in opposition to the people of Athens, I annul and disown." All Athenians shall swear this over perfect sacrifices as their lawful oath before the Dionysia, and they shall pray that he who keeps his oath enjoy many benefits and that he who breaks his oath be destroyed, himself and his kin.

373. Hypereides 4 *For Euxenippus* 7–8 (*lex* + commentary). Law on impeachment (*nomos eisangeltikos*). (date of speech 330–324; date of law ?410–404)

See **66** with references and headnote. Here Hypereides quotes and comments upon the final version of the Classical impeachment law, which most probably was enacted under the democracy between the oligarchy of the Four Hundred and that of the Thirty (although some scholars have advocated a date as late as the mid-fourth century). The quotation cannot be complete, since it lacks provisions on procedure (presumably beginning "any willing Athenian shall bring an impeachment" and continuing with clauses specifying the roles of the Council of 500, the Assembly, the *thesmothetai* [**380** Dem. 24.63], and the jury-court) and penalty. The final quoted phrase, "taking money," may have been followed by "and gifts from those acting in opposition to the people (of Athens)": cf. **390** Hyp. 4 (selections). For *skêpsis* ("excuse") cf. **19b** Dem. 54.27–28; for *hypômosia* ("postponement") cf. **75** Dem. 21.79, 81, 83–84, 88.

For what offenses, then, do you believe impeachments [*eisangelias*] should occur? You have already written this in detail in the law, so that no one could fail to know. "If a person," it states, "subverts the people of Athens [*ton dêmon ton Athênaiôn katalyêi*]"—and reasonably so, men of the jury: such an accusation admits of no excuse [*skêpsin*] or postponement [*hypômosian*] but must come before the jury-court [*dikastêriôi*] as quickly as possible—[8] "or assembles at any place for the purpose of subverting the people [*epi katalysei tou dêmou*] or assembles a faction, or if a person betrays [*prodôi*] a city or ships or an army on land or sea, or, as a politician, does not propose what is best for the people of

Athens, taking money." You wrote the first parts of the law to apply against all citizens (since those offenses could be committed by all) but the last part of the law to apply only against politicians, who have the power to compose decrees.

374. [Demosthenes] 46 *2 Against Stephanus* 26 (*lex*). Law on conspiracy, bribery, subversion, and paid advocacy. (date of speech ?349; date of law ?late 5th c.)

See references and headnote under **83**. This law prescribed the death penalty at least for judicial and legislative bribery (Isocrates 8.50; Aeschines 1.86–88) and presumably for the other specified offenses as well. The meaning of the opening condition ("If a person commits conspiracy, or bribes . . .") is disputed: either the verb *synistêtai* ("conspires, commits conspiracy") is used absolutely, as it is translated here, or it is to be construed loosely with what follows ("If a person commits conspiracy/conspires [to bribe] or [actually] bribes . . ."). On the *(h)êliaia* see, e.g., **3b** Dem. 23.28; **35** Dem. 21.47; **96** [Dem.] 43.75; on *synêgoroi* (advocates) see p. 28; on private and public lawsuits see p. 29. For the jurisdiction of the *thesmothetai* in the *graphê dôrôn* cf. **302a** [Arist.] *Ath. Pol.* 48.4–5, 54.2.

If a person commits conspiracy, or bribes [*syndekazêi*] the *hêliaia* or any of the jury-courts [*dikastêriôn*] in Athens or the Council, giving or receiving money for the purpose of bribery [*dôrodokiai*], or assembles a faction for the purpose of subverting the people [*epi katalysei tou dêmou*], or as an advocate [*synêgoros*] takes money for lawsuits [*dikais*], private [*idiais*] or public [*dêmosiais*], the indictments [*graphas*] for these offenses shall be before the *thesmothetai.*

375. Xenophon, *Hellenica* 1.7.1–16, 20–26, 34–35. Trial (?*eisangelia*) of the Arginusae generals; decree of Cannonus; *probolê* (presentation) for deceiving the people (*apatê tou dêmou*). (date of publication *post* 362; date of trial 405)

See references and headnotes under **237** and **287**; on the trial of the generals and its aftermath cf. Diodorus Siculus 13.101.1–103.2 and see also P. **Cloché**, "L'affaire des Arginuses (406 avant J.-C.)," *Revue historique* 130 (1919) 5–68; A. **Andrewes**, "The Arginousai Trial," *Phoenix* 28 (1974) 112–22; B. M. **Lavelle**, "*Adikia*, The Decree of Kannonos and the Trial of the Generals," *Classica et Mediaevalia* 39 (1988) 19–41.

Following their victory at the battle of the Arginusae islands (located between Lesbos and the Asia Minor coast) in 406/5, the eight Athenian commanding generals were recalled; the six who answered the summons were put on trial—probably by *eisangelia*, although the identification is not certain—for failing to rescue shipwrecked sailors, convicted, and executed. Whether this trial was constitutional remains a subject of scholarly debate. Erasinides (1.7.2) may have been prosecuted by a *graphê* (*klopês*) *dêmosiôn chrêmatôn* for his misappropriation of public funds (see chapter 9). "The Council" (1.7.3 and *passim*) is the Council of 500. On the office of trierarch (1.7.5) see p. 25 and cf., e.g., **254** Dem. 39.1, 5, 7–18. The Apaturia festival (1.7.8) occurred annually in the month of Pyanopsion (cf. **131a** Dem. 39.2–4, **128** *IG* II[2] 1237.9–125; for the Athenian calendar see p. 7). 1.7.10: On the Eleven see p. 31 and, e.g., **371** [Plut.] *Lives of the Ten Orators* 833d–834b; **380** Dem. 24.63; for confiscation of property and tithing to "the goddess" (i.e., Athena) see the headnote under **361** Dem. 21.113, and **372** Andoc. 1.96–98 with additional references in headnote. On the *graphê paranomôn* (1.7.12) see p. 14 and cf., e.g., **333** [Arist.] *Ath. Pol.* 59.2; **390a** Hyp. 4.1–3, 14–20, 30–31, 39, at §§15–18. 1.7.14–15: On the *prytaneis* see p. 6 and **332b** Dem. 21.8–11; Socrates is the philosopher. For the decree of Cannonus (1.7.20–21, 34), of uncertain date, cf. Aristophanes, *Ecclesiazusae* 1089–90 with the scholion to line 1089, which states that the decree ordained that "a man on trial by *eisangelia* must make his defense while bound on each side" (i.e., presumably, by each hand separately). On death by precipitation ("being cast into the pit," 1.7.20) see **369** Lyc. 1.120–21 with additional references in headnote. 1.7.22: cf. **371** [Plut.] *Lives of the Ten Orators* 833d–834b, at 833f, and see chapter 9, especially **287** Xen. *Hell.* 1.7.22. 1.7.35: On *probolê* for deceiving the people cf. **386** [Arist.] *Ath. Pol.* 43.5; Cleophon was tried (probably by *graphê lipotaxiou*: see the headnote under **387** Lyc. 1 [selections]) and executed in 404 (cf. Lysias 13.12; 30.12–14).

The Athenians at home deposed these generals with the exception of Conon. . . . [2] Of the generals who had fought in the naval battle, Protomachus and Aristogenes did not return to Athens. Of the six who did sail home—Pericles, Diomedon, Lysias, Aristocrates, Thrasyllus, and Erasinides—Archedemus . . . inflicted a fine upon Erasinides and prosecuted him in a jury-court [*dikastêriôi*], claiming that Erasinides was in possession of money from the Hellespont that belonged to the people; he also prosecuted him concerning his generalship. The jury-court decided to imprison Erasinides. [3] After that, the generals described in detail in the Council the naval battle and the severity of the storm. Timocrates then proposed that the other generals also be imprisoned and handed over to the Assembly, so the Council imprisoned them.

[4] Then a meeting of the Assembly took place, at which other people, and in particular Theramenes, denounced the generals as deserving to undergo a hearing for failing to recover the shipwrecked men. To prove that the generals attached blame to no one else, Theramenes displayed as evidence a letter that

the generals had sent to the Council and the Assembly blaming nothing other than the storm. [5] Each of the generals then briefly defended himself (since they were not given the opportunity for a speech in accordance with the law); they described the events in detail, stating that they themselves were sailing in pursuit of the enemy and had assigned the retrieval of the shipwrecked men to those of the trierarchs who were capable men and had previously served as generals; namely, Theramenes, Thrasybulus, and others of that sort. [6] If it was necessary to blame people, they said, they had no one else to blame for the retrieval than those to whom it had been assigned. "And just because they are accusing us," they said, "we will not lie and claim that they are to blame; it was, rather, the severity of the storm that prevented the retrieval." As witnesses to these things they provided the helmsmen and many others of their fellow sailors. With such arguments they began to persuade the Assembly, [7] and many private citizens stood up and volunteered to stand surety, but it was decided that the matter be postponed to another Assembly meeting (since at that point it was late and they would not be able to see the [vote by] hands) and that the Council deliberate beforehand and bring in a proposal as to how the men were to be tried.

[8] After that the Apaturia occurred. . . . So Theramenes and his supporters suborned many people to wear black cloaks and have themselves shaved to the scalp during this festival, so that they would arrive at the Assembly pretending that they were relatives of the men who had been lost; and they persuaded Callixenus to prosecute the generals in the Council. [9] From there they held a meeting of the Assembly, to which the Council brought in its resolution, proposed by Callixenus, as follows: "Since they have heard at the previous Assembly meeting both those who accuse the generals and the generals' defense, the Athenians shall all vote by tribes. Two urns shall be placed for each tribe, and a herald shall proclaim for each tribe that whoever finds the generals guilty of an offense for not having retrieved the victors in the naval battle shall cast his vote into the first urn, and whoever finds them not guilty shall cast his vote into the second urn. [10] If they are found guilty, they shall be sentenced to death and handed over to the Eleven; their property shall be confiscated, and one-tenth shall belong to the goddess."

[11] Someone then came before the Assembly claiming that he had made it to safety atop a barrel of barley and that the dying men had enjoined him, if he made it to safety, to report to the Assembly that the generals had failed to recover those who had been the bravest for their country. [12] Euryptolemus son of Peisianax and some others issued a summons against Callixenus, stating that he had composed an illegal proposal [*paranoma*]. Some in the Assembly praised this, but the majority shouted that it was a terrible thing for a person to forbid the Assembly to do whatever it wished. [13] When, following this,

Lyciscus proposed that those men too be tried by the same vote as the generals unless they revoked their summons, the mob shouted again in approval, and they were forced to revoke their summonses. [14] When some of the *prytaneis* then refused to put the matter to the vote in violation of the law, Callixenus stood up again and made the same accusations against them, and the Assembly shouted for the summons of those who were refusing. [15] The *prytaneis* in their fright all agreed to put it to the vote, except for Socrates son of Sophroniscus: he refused to do anything but conduct all matters in accordance with the law. [16] Then Euryptolemus stood up and gave the following speech in defense of the generals.

. . .

[20] "You all know, men of Athens, that the decree of Cannonus is most severe: it commands that if a person commits an offense against the people of Athens, he shall defend himself in bonds in the Assembly, and if he is convicted of an offense, he shall die by being cast into the pit, and his property shall be confiscated and one-tenth shall belong to the goddess. [21] I urge you to try the generals in accordance with this decree. . . . [22] Or, if you wish, try them in accordance with this law, which applies to temple-robbers [*hierosylois*] and traitors [*prodotais*], and which states that if a person either betrays [*prodidôi*] the city or steals [*kleptêi*] sacred property [*ta hiera*], he shall be tried in a jury-court [*dikastêriôi*], and if he is convicted, he shall not be buried in Attica, and his property shall be confiscated. [23] By whichever of these laws you wish, men of Athens, let these men be tried, each one individually and with the day divided into three parts: one in which you are to assemble and vote whether they are deemed guilty of an offense or not, another in which the prosecution is made, and another in which the defense is made. [24] If this happens, the guilty will meet with the most severe punishment, and the innocent will be set free by you, Athenians, and will not be unjustly destroyed. [25] And you will behave piously, remain true to your oath, and judge in accordance with the law, rather than fighting on the side of the Spartans by destroying these men, who took seventy ships from the Spartans and defeated them, without trial, in violation of the law.

[26] "What are you so afraid of that you are acting in such great haste? Is it that you may not kill or free whomever you wish if you judge according to the law, but this is not the case if you judge in violation of the law, as Callixenus persuaded the Council to propose to the Assembly, by a single vote? . . ."

. . .

[34] After making this speech, Euryptolemus drafted a resolution that the men be tried in accordance with the decree of Cannonus, each separately. The resolution of the Council was to try them all by a single vote. In the voting between these proposals, at first the Assembly decided for that of Euryptolemus, but when Menecles made an objection under oath and the vote took place

again, they decided for that of the Council. After that they voted to convict the generals who had fought in the naval battle, all eight, and the six who were present were put to death. [35] Not long afterward the Athenians regretted this, and they voted that there should be presentations [*probolas*] against any persons who had deceived the people, that these persons should post sureties until they were tried, and that Callixenus should be among them. Four other men had presentations brought against them and were placed in confinement by their sureties. Later, though, after some civil strife arose, in which Cleophon was put to death, they ran away before trial; Callixenus returned when the men of the Peiraeus returned to the city, but he was hated by all and died of starvation.

376. [Demosthenes] 49 *Against Timotheus* 66–67. *Eisangelia* for deceiving the people (*apatê tou dêmou*). (date of speech 362)

See references and headnote under **168**. On the *graphê xenias* (for fraudulent claims to Athenian citizenship) see **94** [Dem.] 59 (selections) and **§6.1**; on false promises to the people (i.e., the Assembly) cf. **364** Hdt. 6.136; **379** Dem. 20.100, 135; **386** [Arist.] *Ath. Pol.* 43.5.

You know that my adversary swore an oath in the Assembly, calling down destruction upon himself and dedicating his property to the gods if he did not indict [*grapsaito*] Iphicrates for being a foreigner [*xenias*]. Having made this oath and promise in the Assembly, a short time later, for his own benefit, he gave his daughter in marriage to Iphicrates' son. [67] So, given that he felt no shame at making a promise to you and deceiving you, although there are laws providing that if a person makes a promise to the people and deceives them, there shall be impeachment [*eisangelian*] concerning him. . . .

377. Demosthenes 51 *On the Trierarchic Crown* 8–9. *Eisangelia* of trierarchs for treason and desertion. (date of speech 360/59; date of event 361/0)

See especially L. **Gernet**, *Démosthène: Plaidoyers civils, Tome III, Discours XLIX–LVI* (Paris 1959: text with French introduction, translation and notes); V. **Bers**, *Demosthenes, Speeches 50–59* (Austin 2003: translation with introduction and notes); D. M. **MacDowell**, *Demosthenes the Orator* (Oxford 2009) 133–36; also A. **Schäfer**, *Demosthenes und seine Zeit* (Leipzig 1858–87) 4.152–58; F. **Blass**, *Die attische Beredsamkeit* (Leipzig 1887–98) 3.1.242–49; S. **Usher**, *Greek Oratory: Tradition and Originality* (Oxford 1999) 189–91.

Demosthenes delivered this speech before the Council of 500 in a dispute over the award of a crown to the trierarch (see p. 25 and, e.g., **375** Xen.

Hell. 1.7.1–16, 20–26, 34–35, at 1.7.5) of 360/59 who prepared his ship and crew first. "The naval battle against Alexander," tyrant of Pherae in Thessaly, occurred at Peparethos (an island east of the northern extremity of Euboea) in 361/0; the general Leosthenes was also tried (and convicted) by *eisangelia* following the battle (Diodorus 15.95.1–3; **390a** Hyp. 4.1–3, 14–20, 30–31, 39, at §1). For desertion as treason cf. **387** Lyc. 1 (selections).

When you were defeated in the naval battle against Alexander, believing that those trierarchs who had leased out their trierarchies were most responsible for what had happened, you handed them over to the prison, having passed a vote of condemnation against them for betraying [*prodedôkenai*] their ships and leaving their post [*leloipenai tên taxin*]. [9] Aristophon was the prosecutor, and you judged them; and if the anger you felt were not more moderate than their wickedness, nothing would have prevented them from being put to death.

378. [Demosthenes] 47 *Against Euergus and Mnesibulus* 41–43. *Eisangelia* for failure to return naval equipment; 500-drachma limit on penalty imposed by Council of 500. (date of speech *post* 358/7; date of event 357/6)

See references and headnote under **17**. The speaker, a trierarch (see p. 25 and, e.g., **375** Xen. *Hell.* 1.7.1–16, 20–26, 34–35, at 1.7.5; **377** Dem. 51.8–9) of 357/6, had been assigned to recover outstanding trireme equipment from Theophemus, who had served as trierarch the previous year. Under the authority of a law and several decrees that permitted recovery of the equipment or seizure of its cash equivalent, the speaker went to Theophemus' home and ordered Theophemus to satisfy his debt. When Theophemus refused, the speaker attempted to distrain upon some of Theophemus' property to serve as security for the debt (see chapter 10 and, on public debts, **§7.1.2**); Theophemus prevented the distraint and struck the speaker.

"The Council" is the Council of 500; Theophemus' acts will have qualified for *eisangelia* as constituting betrayal of ships and/or subversion ("hindering the expedition," §42; cf. **373** Hyp. 4.7–8). On the *prytaneis* see p. 6 and, e.g., **332b** Dem. 21.8–11; **375** Xen. *Hell.* 1.7.1–16, 20–26, 34–35; on the oversight of the Athenian navy by the Council of 500 cf., e.g., **377** Dem. 51.8–9; [Aristotle], *Constitution of the Athenians* (*Ath. Pol.*) 46. The inscribed records of the Superintendents of the Dockyards (*epimelêtai tôn neôriôn*: cf. **173** *IG* II^2 1631.429–41) for 356/5 (*Inscriptiones Graecae* II^2 1612) list Theophemus and another man as having returned hull-braces, a sail, and anchors owed on the trireme *Euphyês* (lines 313–16).

After I was deprived of the securities by Theophemus and beaten up, I went to the Council, displayed the [marks of the] blows, and told them what I had suffered and that it had happened while I was recovering the equipment for the city. The Council, angry at what I had suffered, seeing my condition, and believing that the victim of hubris was not me but itself and the people, which had issued the decree, and the law that compelled recovery of the equipment, [42] ordered me to bring an impeachment [*eisangellein*] and the *prytaneis* to give him advance notice for a trial in two days for committing an offense in hindering the expedition by refusing to return the equipment, withholding the securities, and beating up me, the one who was conducting the recovery and serving the city.

Theophemus' trial then took place in the Council in accordance with the impeachment [*eisangelian*] that I had brought. Each of us was given opportunity to speak; then the councillors voted by secret ballot, and he was convicted in the Council Hall and found guilty of an offense. [43] When the Council was in the process of voting whether to hand him over to a jury-court [*dikastêriôi*] or fine him the 500 drachmas that was the limit of its authority under the law, my adversaries all begged and pleaded and . . . offered to pay back the inventory of the equipment straightaway in the Council and said they would entrust the matter of the blows to any Athenian I proposed, so I agreed that Theophemus would be fined 25 drachmas.

379. Demosthenes 20 *Against Leptines* 100, 135. Law(s) on deceiving the people (*apatê tou dêmou*), council, or lawcourt. (date of speech 355/4)

> See references and headnote under **18**. On false promises to the people (i.e., the Assembly) cf. **364** Hdt. 6.136; **376** [Dem.] 49.66–67; **386** [Arist.] *Ath. Pol.* 43.5; for the triad of people, council, and lawcourt cf. **382** Dem. 23.97.

You have, of course, a law providing that if a person makes a promise to the people or a council or a lawcourt and deceives it, he shall suffer the extreme sanction.

. . .

[135] . . . You have an ancient law . . . providing that if a person makes a promise to the people and deceives them, he shall stand trial, and if convicted, he shall be sentenced to death.

380. Demosthenes 24 *Against Timocrates* 63 (*lex*). Law of Timocrates on procedure in *eisangelia* initiated before the Council of 500. (date of speech 353/2)

See references and headnote under **160**, and cf. **362** Dem. 24.144–45. The authenticity of this law is debated among scholars; if genuine, it was proposed by Timocrates and passed after approval by the Lawgivers (p. 13; **12a** Andoc. 1.83–84) before the delivery of Demosthenes 24. On the division of the year into prytanies see p. 6 and cf., e.g., **336b** *IG* I[3] 430.5–20; for "the secretary serving by prytany" cf. **372** Andoc. 1.96–98; **384** *SEG* 12.87, at lines 1–5. For "the law on impeachment" at this time see **373** Hyp. 4.7–8. On the role of the Eleven as superintendents of the prison cf., e.g., **341b** Pl. *Phaedo* 116b7-c4, 116c8-d2, 117a4-b2, 117b6-c5, 117e4–118a8; on the *(h)êliaia* see p. 3 and, e.g., **374** [Dem.] 46.26 with additional references in headnote. For "whatever . . . he deserves to suffer or pay," the formula denoting an *agôn timêtos* (p. 40) without penal limit, cf., e.g., **35** Dem. 21.47; **340f** Pl. *Ap.* 36a5-b5, 36e1–37a1, 38b1–9.

Timocrates made the motion. With regard to all those Athenians who, in accordance with an impeachment [*eisangelian*] proceeding from the Council, either are now in the prison or may be put there in the future, if the judgment against them has not been handed over to the *thesmothetai* by the secretary serving by prytany in accordance with the law on impeachment [*ton eisangeltikon nomon*], let it be resolved by the Lawgivers that the Eleven shall bring them before the jury-court [*dikastêrion*] within thirty days after the date on which they have received [the judgment], unless some public business prevents it; otherwise, at the first opportunity. Any willing Athenian to whom it is permitted shall prosecute. If a person is convicted, the *hêliaia* shall punish him with whatever it decides he deserves to suffer or pay. If he is punished with a fine, he shall be imprisoned until he pays whatever fine he has been condemned to pay.

381. Demosthenes 24 *Against Timocrates* 127. Fine for treason; tenfold fine for theft of public property. (date of speech 353/2)

See references and headnote under **160**. The man described in this passage is named (§126) as Melanopus; the term "delegate" refers to his representing Athens either at a peace conference held at Sparta in 371/70 (Xenophon, *Hellenica* 6.3.2) or in the congress of the Second Athenian Confederacy (p. 14). For the tenfold fine for theft of public property cf. **302a** [Arist.] *Ath. Pol.* 48.4–5, 54.2.

But if, being the son of a worthy father, he was a scoundrel and a thief, and he was convicted of treason [*prodosias*] and paid a fine of three talents, and after he served as a delegate, the jury-court [*dikastêrion*] convicted him of theft [*klopên*] and he paid a tenfold fine . . . , shouldn't he be in prison all the more . . . ?

382. Demosthenes 23 *Against Aristocrates* 97. Curse for deceiving the people (*apatê tou dêmou*), council, or *hêliaia*. (352/1)

> See references and headnote under **3**. Depending on the antiquity of this curse, which was specified by law and recited at meetings of the Council of 500 as well as the Assembly (cf. Demosthenes 18.282, 19.70–71; Deinarchus 1.47; and the parody at Aristophanes, *Thesmophoriazusae* 331–51), its clause on deceiving "a council" may originally have referred to the Council of the Areopagus. On the *(h)êliaia* see p. 3 and, e.g., **374** [Dem.] 46.26 with additional references in headnote. With the terms of the curse cf. **379** Dem. 20.100, 135, at §100.

That is why at every meeting of the Assembly the herald pronounces a curse . . . against any person who by speaking deceives a council or the people or the *hêliaia*.

383. Demosthenes 18 *On the Crown* 132–33. *Apophasis* for conspiracy to commit treason. (date of speech 330; date of event *post* 346/5)

> See references and headnote under **80**. Antiphon (not the orator, who was executed in 411/10: **371** [Plut.] *Lives of the Ten Orators* 833d-834b) was struck from the citizen rolls during the revision of 346/5 (see the headnote under **76** Dem. 57.30). "Philip" is Philip II of Macedon. "This sorcerer" (§132) and "this fine orator here" (§133) refer to Demosthenes' adversary Aeschines.

Who among you does not know of that Antiphon who was rejected from the list of citizens and who came back to the city after promising to Philip that he would burn the dockyards? When I caught him hiding in Peiraeus and brought him to the Assembly, this sorcerer shouted and screamed that in a democracy what I was doing was terrible—committing hubris against unfortunate citizens and intruding into houses without a decree—and thus got him released. [133] And if the Council of the Areopagus had not learned of the matter, seen that your mistake had happened at the wrong time, conducted a new investigation of the man, arrested him, and brought him back before you, a person of that sort would have been snatched away from you; he would have slipped away from punishment and been escorted out [of Attica] by this fine orator here. As it happened, though, you tortured and executed him. . . .

384. *Supplementum Epigraphicum Graecum* 12.87 (*lex*). Law of Eucrates on tyranny, subversion of democracy, and the Council of the Areopagus. (337/6)

See especially P. J. **Rhodes**-R. **Osborne**, *Greek Historical Inscriptions 404–323 BC* (Oxford 2003), no. 79 (text, translation, and commentary); also A. G. **Woodhead**, ed., *Supplementum Epigraphicum Graecum*, vol. 12, no. 87 (Leiden 1955: text); P. **Harding**, *From the End of the Peloponnesian War to the Battle of Ipsus* (Cambridge 1985), no. 101 (translation with notes).

In the preamble (lines 1–5, translated as the first paragraph below), for prytanies see p. 6 and cf., e.g., **380** Dem. 24.63; the *proedroi* ("presiders") are probably the presiding members of the board of Lawgivers (see below) rather than those of the Council of 500 and the Assembly (**332b** Dem. 21.8–11). The law follows (lines 5–29, translated as the second paragraph below). For the Lawgivers (lines 6–7) see **12a** Andoc. 1.83–84 and cf. **380** Dem. 24.63. With the provision for the lawful and pollution-free killing of an offender (lines 10–11) cf. **368** Dem. 9.41–45; **372** Andoc. 1.96–98. For personal and hereditary *atimia* (in the sense of full "outlawry": see **358** Plut. *Solon* 19.4 with additional references in headnote), confiscation of property, and tithing to the goddess Athena (lines 20–22) see the headnote under **361** Dem. 21.113, and **372** Andoc. 1.96–98 with additional references in headnote.

In the archonship of Phrynichus [337/6], in the ninth prytany, that of the tribe Leontis, for which Chaerestratus son of Ameinias of the deme Acharnae was secretary: of the presiders [*proedrôn*], Menestratus of the deme Aexone put the motion to the vote; Eucrates son of Aristotimus of the deme Peiraeus made the motion.

With good fortune for the people of Athens. Let it be resolved by the Lawgivers: If a person engages in uprising against the people with the goal of tyranny or cooperates in the establishment of a tyranny or subverts the people of Athens or the democracy at Athens, anyone who kills one who has committed any of these acts shall be pure of guilt. No councillor of the Council of the Areopagus shall be permitted, if the people or the democracy at Athens has been subverted, to go up to the Areopagus or sit together in session or deliberate about any matter. If, after the people or the democracy has been subverted at Athens, any councillor of the Areopagus goes up to the Areopagus or sits together in session or deliberates about anything, he shall be outlawed [*atimos*], both himself and his descendants; and his property shall be confiscated, and one-tenth shall belong to the goddess. The secretary of the Council shall inscribe this law on two stone pillars and shall place one at the [25] entrance to the Areopagus where you enter the Council Hall and the other in the Assembly; for the inscription of the pillars the treasurer of the people shall pay 20 drachmas from the people's expense funds for decrees.

385. Hypereides 1 *For Lycophron* (selections). *Eisangelia* for seduction. (333–330)

See **59** with references and headnote. From this lawsuit, in addition to Hypereides 1, written for delivery by the defendant Lycophron, there are surviving fragments of a defense speech delivered by an advocate (*synêgoros*: p. 28) of Lycophron (B. P. **Grenfell**-A. S. **Hunt**, *The Oxyrhynchus Papyri*, vol. 13 [London 1919], no. 1607; G. **Colin**, *Hypéride: Discours* [Paris 1946: text with French introduction, translation, and notes]; M. **Marzi**-P. **Leone**-E. **Malcovati**, *Oratori attici minori*, vol. 1 [Turin 1977: text with Italian introduction, translation, and notes]; I. **Worthington**-C. **Cooper**-E. M. **Harris**, *Dinarchus, Hyperides, and Lycurgus* [Austin 2001: translation with introduction and notes]) and of two prosecution speeches written by Lycurgus (Lycurgus, fragmentary speeches X–XI Conomis, fragmentary speech(es) IX Durrbach [F. **Durrbach**, *Lycurgue*: Contre Léocrate, *Fragments* (Paris 1932: text with French translation and notes)]; fragmentary speeches XI–XII Marzi-Leone-Malcovati; fragments 10–11 Worthington-Cooper-Harris).

With the partial and fragmentary list of offenses subject to *eisangelia* given in **385a** compare the (incomplete) text of the impeachment law in force at the time of Lycophron's trial (**373** Hyp. 4.7–8); Lycophron's accusers alleged that he was liable under its subversion clause (**59** Hyp. 1.12; cf. Lycurgus fr. X–XI.2 Conomis). The impeachment document mentioned in **385b** was composed by Ariston, the prosecutor of record (Hyp. 1 fr. 4 Jensen). For the penalties faced by Lycophron (**385c**) cf. **367a** Thuc. 1.135.2–136.1, 138.6; **387** Lyc. 1 (selections); **391** (*Apophasis* against Demosthenes and others for receiving bribes in the Harpalus affair).

a. Hyp. 1 fr. 3 Jensen. Offenses subject to *eisangelia*.

. . . or betrayal [*prodosian*] of dockyards or arson of government buildings or seizure of a citadel . . .

b. Hyp. 1.3. Initiation of *eisangelia* in Assembly; details of charge.

It is worthwhile, men of the jury, to examine the matter from another angle as well; namely, from the first accusations they made straightaway in the Assembly. My family sent me a letter describing the impeachment [*eisangelian*] and the accusations they made against me in the Assembly when they handed in the impeachment; among these accusations it was written that Lycurgus states, claiming to have heard it from the family, that I was in attendance when Charippus was marrying the woman, and that I urged her not to have relations with Charippus but to guard herself carefully.

c. Hyp. 1.20. Penalty.

. . . I am on trial and risking not only death . . . but being cast over the border and not even being buried in my homeland after I die.

386. [Aristotle], *Constitution of the Athenians (Ath. Pol.)* 43.5. *Probolê* (presentation) for deceiving the people (*apatê tou dêmou*) and for sycophancy. (332–322)

See references and headnote under **1c**. In this passage, the author continues his discussion of the duties of the tribal delegation of the Council of 500 that holds the prytany (see p. 6 and cf., e.g., **380** Dem. 24.63; **384** *SEG* 12.87); for the context see **224** [Arist.] *Ath. Pol.* 43.4. For *probolê* for *apatê tou dêmou* cf. **375** Xen. *Hell.* 1.7.1–16, 20–26, 34–35, at §35; for other types of *probolê* see the introduction to chapter 11 and **§11.2**. On false promises to the people (i.e., the Assembly) cf. **364** Hdt. 6.136; **376** [Dem.] 49.66–67; **379** Dem. 20.100, 135; on sycophants see p. 33.

In the sixth prytany, in addition to the aforementioned matters, they also . . . admit presentations [*probolas*] against sycophants, Athenians and metics, up to three of each, and against any person who has made a promise to the people but not performed.

387. Lycurgus 1 *Against Leocrates* (selections). *Eisangelia* of Leocrates for treason. (330)

See references and headnote under **26**. The *eisangelia* of Leocrates was initiated in the Assembly (§19) and then referred for trial to a *dikastêrion*, where Leocrates won acquittal by a margin of one vote (Aeschines 3.252: either a tie vote or one more vote for the defense than for the prosecution). **387a**: For the impeachment law in force at the time of Leocrates' trial see **373** Hyp. 4.7–8. **387b**: Whether the death penalty was actually mandated by statute for persons convicted by *eisangelia* is a matter of scholarly debate: for the death penalty, aggravated by denial of burial in Attica, cf., e.g., **367a** Thuc. 1.135.2–

136.1, 138.6; **385c** Hyp. 1.20; and, by way of analogy, **391** (*Apophasis* against Demosthenes and others for receiving bribes in the Harpalus affair); but note *contra* **378** [Dem.] 47.41–43; **271** (Pericles' trial and conviction for theft of public property); and (if the procedure was *eisangelia*) **364** Hdt. 6.136. See also **392b** Pollux, *Onomasticon* 8.51–53, which describes *eisangelia* using the penal formula ("whatever [the convicted defendant] deserved to suffer or pay") for an *agôn timêtos* (p. 40) without penal limit. **387c**: On the Battle of Chaeroneia, fought in 338, see p. 15. The promontory of Acte lay adjacent to the harbor at Peiraeus. **387c-d**: For the treatment of desertion as treason cf. **377** Dem. 51.8–9. **387d**: "You yourselves" indicates that Autolycus (a member of the Council of the Areopagus: [Plutarch], *Lives of the Ten Orators* 843d-e) was tried in a *dikastêrion*; the procedure was probably *eisangelia*, and Lycurgus was the prosecutor ([Plutarch], *ibid.*; Lycurgus, fragmentary speech III Conomis). **387e**: On *synêgoroi* (advocates) see p. 28 and cf., e.g., **374** [Dem.] 46.26. For the Athenian evacuations to Salamis in 480 and 479 see **366** (Killing of Lycides/Cyrsilus); Xerxes was king of Persia during the Second Persian War (p. 9). **387f**: On impiety see chapter 11; on maltreatment of parents see **§6.4**. Desertion and avoidance of military service were the subjects of dedicated legal actions, the *graphê lipotaxiou* and *graphê astrateias* respectively, each carrying a penalty of *atimia* (**170** Andoc. 1.73–79; Demosthenes 15.32; [Demosthenes] 59.27; Aeschines 3.175–76).

a. Lyc. 1.1–2, 5. Prosecution under treason clause of *nomos eisangeltikos.*

For I pray to Athena and the other gods and heroes . . . that if it is with justice that I have impeached [*eisêngelka*] and am prosecuting Leocrates for having betrayed [*prodont'*] their temples, seats, and shrines, and their honors specified in the laws and their sacrifices handed down by your ancestors, [2] they make me on this day a worthy prosecutor of Leocrates' offenses. . . .

. . .

[5] And I, Athenians, have brought this impeachment [*eisangelian*] in the knowledge that Leocrates fled the dangers to his country, abandoned his own fellow citizens, has betrayed [*prodedôkota*] your entire military force, and is liable to all the written charges.

b. Lyc. 1.8, 89. Penalty of death and denial of burial in Attica.

The most severe and extreme of penalties, death, is the punishment compelled by the laws but is insufficient for Leocrates' offenses.

. . .

[89] But Leocrates . . . alone among all would fittingly be cast out of the land, which he abandoned to the enemy when he left: it is not right that the same land cover those who excel in virtue and the worst of all mankind.

c. Lyc. 1.16–18, 21. Details of charge.

After the battle at Chaeroneia took place, . . . the Assembly decreed that the children and women be brought inside the walls from the fields, and that the generals assign the Athenians and the others residing in Athens to guard duties however they saw fit. [17] But Leocrates paid no heed to this: he packed up the possessions he had with the help of his slaves and brought them onto his skiff—his ship was already lying off shore near Acte—and around evening he, along with his courtesan Eirenis, . . . sailed to the ship and departed in flight. . . . [18] When he landed and arrived at Rhodes, . . . he reported that when he left the city itself had been captured and the Peiraeus was under siege. . . .

. . .

[21] After that, gentlemen, when time passed, ships from Athens were arriving at Rhodes, and it was evident that nothing terrible had happened to the city, he became afraid, set sail again, from Rhodes, and arrived at Megara; he then lived in Megara for more than five years. . . .

d. Lyc. 1.52–53. Reactions at Athens to the Battle of Chaeroneia.

The Council of the Areopagus . . . arrested and executed those who at that time fled their country and abandoned it to the enemy. . . . [53] . . . you yourselves convicted Autolycus, who had personally remained during the danger but was accused of removing his sons and wife to safety, and you punished him. . . . Moreover, the Assembly . . . decreed that those who fled the danger to their country were to be liable for treason [*prodosiai*], believing them worthy of the most extreme punishment.

e. Lyc. 1.55, 59, 68. Elements of Leocrates' defense.

So, then, gentlemen, it is evident that Leocrates is liable to all the charges stated in the impeachment. I hear, though, that he will try to deceive you by saying that he sailed out as a merchant and left Athens for Rhodes on that business.

. . .

[59] [Leocrates] will probably . . . arrive at the argument, which some of his advocates [*synêgorôn*] have recommended to him, that he is not liable to the charge of treason [*prodosiai*], since he was not in charge of dockyards or gates or military encampments or anything else at all belonging to the city.

. . .

[68] And I am especially angry, gentlemen, when I hear one of those with my adversary saying that it is not an act of betrayal [*prodidonai*] if a person left the city, since in fact your ancestors once left the city behind, when they were at war with Xerxes, and crossed over to Salamis.

f. Lyc. 1.147. Treason, subversion of the people, and other offenses.

And I believe, gentlemen, that on this day you are casting a single vote concerning all the most serious and terrible offenses, for all of which, you can see, Leocrates is liable: treason [*prodosias*], because by abandoning the city to the enemy he made it subject to them; subversion of the people [*dêmou . . . katalyseôs*], because he did not remain to face the danger to our freedom; impiety [*asebeias*], because, as far as lay in him, he was responsible for the ravaging of our sacred precincts and the razing of our temples; maltreatment of parents [*tokeôn . . . kakôseôs*], by causing their monuments to disappear and depriving them of their customary rites; and desertion [*lipotaxiou*] and avoiding military service [*astrateias*], by not providing his person to the generals for assignment.

388. Aeschines 3 *Against Ctesiphon* 232. *Graphê dôrôn.* (330)

See references and headnote under **27**. Cf. **302a** [Arist.] *Ath. Pol.* 48.4–5, 54.2 (tenfold penalty for bribery levied upon conviction in *dikastêrion* following *euthynai*); see also Deinarchus 2.17. For *atimia* consequent upon failure to pay a public debt cf. §**7.1.2**.

And, strangest of all, in the very same jury-courts [*dikastêriois*] where you disfranchise [*atimoute*] people convicted in indictments [*graphas*] for bribery [*dôrôn*], are you going to crown the man who you yourselves know conducts his political life for pay?

389. Demosthenes 18 *On the Crown* 250. Penalty for malicious prosecution by *eisangelia*. (330)

See references and headnote under **80**. "Their fraction of the votes" is the 20 percent of the jurors' votes that a prosecutor had to garner in order to avoid being fined 1,000 drachmas for sycophancy (malicious prosecution: p. 33). Although the impeachments to which Demosthenes refers occurred in 338 or soon thereafter, Lycophron's statement in **59** Hyp. 1.12 that the *eisangelia* against him was brought "without risk" to his prosecutors indicates that the thousand-drachma penalty for sycophancy did not yet obtain at the date of his trial. That penalty, common in other public lawsuits (cf., e.g., **288** Dem.

22.25–27, 69–73), was applied to *eisangelia* after the delivery of Hypereides 1 (between 333 and 330) but before the delivery of Demosthenes 18 (330); in the present passage, Demosthenes retrojects current practice onto his earlier impeachments.

So, when I was being impeached [*eisêngellomên*] and you acquitted me and did not give my prosecutors their fraction of the votes. . . .

390. Hypereides 4 *For Euxenippus* (selections). (date of speech 330–324)

See **66** and **373** with references and headnotes.

a. Hyp. 4.1–3, 14–20, 30–31, 39. *Eisangeliai* of Euxenippus and others.

§1: Philon of Anaea (a city on the coast of Asia Minor opposite Samos) is unknown; for Leosthenes see **377** Dem. 51.8–9 with headnote. Timomachus commanded the Athenian fleet at Thasos (in the northern Aegean) in 361/60 and was impeached for treason; Theotimus served as general in 361/60 or 360/59, when Sestos (a city in the Thracian Chersonese) dissolved its alliance with Athens; Callistratus, who was acquitted in an *eisangelia* in 366/5, was evidently impeached again and convicted *in absentia* (§2). With the reasons given in §1 for the impeachments of these men compare the terms of the *eisangelia* law current in the fourth century (**373** Hyp. 4.7–8), to which Hypereides refers in §3. §3: On the case(s) of Diognides and Antidorus see **66** Hyp. 4.3; Agasicles was impeached for enrolling himself in a deme and thereby usurping the status of an Athenian citizen (see **§6.1**). §§14ff.: Amphiaraus (§16) is "the god" (§15, in the phrase "he had misrepresented the god"; note, however, that later in §15, in the phrase "you should have sent to Delphi to learn the truth from the god," "the god" is Apollo, whose oracle at Delphi was a major Panhellenic religious site) in whose temple (§14) Euxenippus and two others were assigned to spend the night so as to receive divine guidance, and to report to the Assembly accordingly, as to the disposition of territory in Oropus (a city on the border between Attica and Boeotia) that had been assigned to the Athenian tribes Acamantis and Hippothoontis. §§15–18: Polyeuctus was convicted in a *graphê paranomôn* (see p. 14 and, e.g., **333** [Arist.] *Ath. Pol.* 59.2; **375** Xen. *Hell.* 1.7.1–16, 20–26, 34–35). §18: For the penalty faced by Euxenippus cf. **387** Lyc. 1 (selections) with additional references in headnote. §19: Olympias was the mother of Alexander the Great, the reigning king of Macedon; the statue of Hygieia (goddess of health) in question was in Athens. §31: The *antigraphê* ("writ in response") is here the written statement made by the defendant in reply to the prosecution's impeachment document (contrast **340d** Pl. *Ap.* 27c5–8). §39 identifies the clause of the *eisangelia* law (**373** Hyp. 4.7–8) under which Euxenippus is being impeached; for the phrase "taking money and gifts from those acting in opposition to the people of Athens" see **390b** Hyp. 4.28–30 with headnote.

Well, for my part, men of the jury, as I was just saying to those sitting next to me, I am surprised that you are not already sick of impeachments [*eisangeliai*] of this kind. In the past those who were impeached [*eisêngellonto*] in your court were Timomachus and Leosthenes and Callistratus and Philon of Anaea and Theotimus who lost Sestos and others of that sort. Some of these were accused of betraying ships, others of betraying cities belonging to the Athenians, and one because, as a politician, he proposed what was not best for the people. [2] Of these five men, not one awaited his trial: they departed in flight from the city, as did many others under impeachment; it was rare to see a person on trial by impeachment, having obeyed his summons to the jury-court [*dikastêrion*]. That is how serious and notorious the offenses were for which impeachments occurred back then. [3] Now, though, what is going on in the city is utterly ridiculous. Diognides and Antidorus the metic are impeached for hiring out female flute-players for more than the law ordains; Agasicles from Peiraeus, because he was enrolled among the demesmen of Halimus; and Euxenippus, on account of the dreams he says he had. Obviously, not one of these accusations has any connection to the law on impeachment [*tôi eisangeltikôi nomôi*].

. . .

[14] [To Polyeuctus:] ". . . the things he has done are terrible and deserving of death," as you state in your prosecution. [To the jury:] Now consider this, men of the jury, examining each matter individually. The Assembly assigned Euxenippus, along with two others, to incubate in the temple, and this man states that in his sleep he had a dream, which he reported to the Assembly. . . . [15] [To Polyeuctus:] But if, as you now say, you believed he had misrepresented the god and made a false report to the Assembly to ingratiate himself to certain people, you should not have composed a decree in response to the dream; rather, . . . you should have sent to Delphi to learn the truth from the god. You, however, . . . composed a decree on your own authority against two tribes that not only was completely unjust but also contradicted itself; that is why you were convicted for an illegal proposal [*paranomôn*], not because of Euxenippus.

[16] Let's examine the matter in the following way. The tribes, in groups of two, divided up the mountains in Oropus according to the Assembly's grant. Acamantis and Hippothoontis were allotted the mountain in question. You

proposed that these tribes give the mountain back to Amphiaraus, along with the value of what they had sold, on the grounds that the Boundary Commissioners, the Fifty, had previously reserved it for the god and marked it off, and so the two tribes were in possession of the mountain improperly. [17] A little later in the same decree you propose that the other eight tribes provide the difference and pay it to these two tribes, so that they are not at a disadvantage. . . .

[18] When these provisions were examined in the jury-court [*dikastêriôi*], they were found to have been composed incorrectly, and the jurors convicted you. So, if you had been acquitted in the indictment [*graphên*], this man would not have misrepresented the god, but since you got convicted, Euxenippus has to be destroyed? And you . . . were fined 25 drachmas, but the man who incubated in the temple by the Assembly's command must not even be buried in Attica?

[19] "Yes," you say, "because he did a terrible thing in the matter of the bowl, allowing Olympias to dedicate it at the statue of Hygieia." . . . [20] . . . here, however, you express hatred of Olympias in order to destroy Euxenippus, and you claim that he is a toady of her and the Macedonians.

. . .

[30] . . . But as for the things you claim Euxenippus proposed that were not best for the people, you had nothing to write in your impeachment; you are prosecuting a private citizen as though he were a politician. [31] And after saying a few things about the writ in response [*antigraphês*], you have come bringing other slanderous allegations against him, claiming that he tried to give his daughter in marriage to Philocles and undertook Demotion's arbitration, and making other accusations of that sort. . . .

. . .

[39] [To the jury:] Polyeuctus, you see, has impeached [Euxenippus] for proposing what was not best for the people of Athens, taking money and gifts from those acting in opposition to the people of Athens. . . . As it is, though, he claims that it is Athenians from whom Euxenippus has taken the gifts.

b. Hyp. 4.28–30. *Eisangelia* of Philocrates and other previous lawsuits prosecuted by Hypereides.

The prosecution of Aristophon mentioned here is probably to be identified with a *graphê paranomôn* (cf. **390a** Hyp. 4.1–3, 14–20, 30–31, 39, at §§15–18, with headnote) of 363/2 (cf. Hypereides, fragmentary speech VIII Jensen). Diopeithes was a prominent politician of the 340s; no details of his trial survive. Philocrates was impeached, and convicted and sentenced to death *in absentia*, in 343 for treasonous conduct in negotiating the treaty between Athens and Macedon (then ruled by Philip II) that had been concluded in

346 (p. 15). The terms of Hypereides' impeachment against Philocrates and of Polyeuctus' impeachment against Euxenippus (**390a** Hyp. 4.1–3, 14–20, 30–31, 39, at §39) may indicate that "and gifts from those acting in opposition to the people (of Athens)" followed "taking money" in the final preserved clause of the fourth-century impeachment law (**373** Hyp. 4.7–8).

Whom, then, have I prosecuted and brought to trial? Aristophon of the deme Azenia, who has become a very powerful man in the state; he was acquitted in this jury-court [*dikastêriôi*] by two votes. [29] Diopeithes of the deme Sphettus, who was considered to be the most formidable man in the city. Philocrates of the deme Hagnus, who conducted his political life with the greatest audacity and insolence. I impeached him for the services he had performed for Philip against the city and convicted him in the jury-court, and I composed the impeachment in just form and as the law commands, stating that "as a politician, he proposed what was not best for the people of Athens, taking money and gifts from those acting in opposition to the people." [30] And I was not content to hand in the impeachment just like that, but I added in writing below, "He made the following proposal that was not best for the people, having taken money," and then I wrote his decree underneath; and again, "He made the following proposal that was not best for the people, having taken money," and I appended the decree. I wrote this five or six times, since I believed it necessary to make the trial and prosecution just.

391. *Apophasis* against Demosthenes and others for receiving bribes in the Harpalus affair. (324/3)

For Hypereides 5 (**391a-e**) see references and headnote under **303**; for Deinarchus 1 (**391f-l**) see references and headnote under **67**. Among the references at the head of this chapter, on *apophasis* and the Harpalus affair see especially E. M. **Carawan**, "*Apophasis* and *Eisangelia*: The Rôle of the Areopagus in Athenian Political Trials," *GRBS* 26 (1985) 115–40; R. W. **Wallace**, *The Areopagos Council, to 307 B.C.* (Baltimore 1989).

A decree composed by Demosthenes and passed ca. 344/3 (**391k**) created a legal procedure called *apophasis* (report; plural *apophaseis*), under which the Council of the Areopagus was empowered, either on its own initiative or by decree of the Assembly (**391h**), to investigate and report to the Assembly offenses threatening the security of the state, and which thus targeted essentially the same offenses as did *eisangelia*. The best-attested instance of *apophasis* occurred in 324/3, following the appearance in Athens of Harpalus, the fugitive treasurer of Alexander the Great. The Athenians deposited the 700 talents (see p. 4) that Harpalus had brought with him on the Acropolis for safekeeping; shortly thereafter, Harpalus fled Athens, and an inventory of the funds discovered only 350 talents remaining (Hypereides 5 coll. 9–10). Empowered by a decree authored by Demosthenes early in 324/3 (**391a**, **391k**; cf. **391e**, **391h**), the Council of the Areopagus investigated the matter for six months and then issued its report, which accused Demosthenes and other leading politicians of receiving bribes from Harpalus (**391b**, **391c**, **391e**, **391g**, **391h**). Special prosecutors (**391e**, **391h**), ten in number (Deinarchus 2.6), were chosen to prosecute the defendants in a *dikastêrion* (**391a**, **391e**, **391h**) manned by a jury of 1,500 (Deinarchus 1.107). One of the special prosecutors was Hypereides, whose speech against Demosthenes (Hypereides 5) survives in substantial (but not complete) form; the logographer Deinarchus composed speeches delivered by another prosecutor against Demosthenes (Deinarchus 1), Aristogeiton (Deinarchus 2), Philocles (Deinarchus 3), and others. Demosthenes, the first defendant to stand trial, was convicted. Although both the decree of Demosthenes that initiated the *apophasis* (**391k**) and the trial prosecutors (**391f**) demanded the death penalty (aggravated by denial of burial in Attica: **391l**; cf. **367a** Thuc. 1.135.2–136.1, 138.6; **385c** Hyp. 1.20; **387** Lyc. 1 [selections]), and alternative penalties for receiving bribes included a fine of ten times the amount of the bribe (**391d**, **391j**), Demosthenes was sentenced to a fine of 50 talents (two and a half times the amount of the bribe for which he was convicted: **391a**); imprisoned pending payment, he managed to escape (Plutarch, *Demosthenes* 26.2).

a. Hypereides 5 *Against Demosthenes* col. 2. Accusation against Demosthenes; decree authored by Demosthenes initiating *apophasis* by Areopagus against Demosthenes and others; trial in *dikastêrion*.

Consider the matter, men of the jury [*ô andres dikastai*], as follows. [To Demosthenes:] The Assembly accused you, Demosthenes, of having taken twenty talents to the detriment of the constitution and the laws. You denied having taken it, and you composed a challenge in the form of a decree and brought it before the Assembly, entrusting the matters you were accused of to the Council of the Areopagus. . . .

b. Hypereides 5 *Against Demosthenes* col. 6. *Apophaseis* submitted in writing by Areopagus.

The Council has drafted all these reports [*apophaseis*] concerning Harpalus' money in similar form and has drafted the same reports against all [the accused]; it has not added to any report why it was reporting [*apophainei*] each man but simply wrote in summary form how much gold each man took, and that he should therefore owe that amount.

c. Hypereides 5 *Against Demosthenes* col. 7. Areopagus' finding against Demosthenes.

I believe, though, that your condemnation by the Council . . . is sufficient proof to the jurors [*dikastais*] that you took the gold. . . .

d. Hypereides 5 *Against Demosthenes* col. 24. Penalties for *adikion* (fiscal "wrongdoing" by magistrate) and for receiving bribes.

> Cf. **302a** [Arist.] *Ath. Pol.* 48.4–5, 54.2; **391j** Din. 1.60 with additional references in headnote.

Now, the laws order those who commit [ordinary] wrongdoing [*adikousin*] to pay a simple fine but those who take bribes [*dôrodokousin*] to pay a tenfold fine. . . .

e. Hypereides 5 *Against Demosthenes* col. 38. Special prosecutors chosen by Assembly; *apophasis* by Areopagus; trial in *dikastêrion*.

. . . [the Assembly] ordered us, the chosen prosecutors, to prosecute and expose in the jury-court [*dikastêriôi*] those who had received the money and taken bribes [*dôrodokêsantôn*] against the interests of their country. It assigned the reporting [*apophênai*] of the recipients to the Council of the Areopagus, which identified these men to the Assembly.

f. Deinarchus 1 *Against Demosthenes* 18. Penalty sought by prosecution.

Men of Athens, will you not put this foul person to death. . . ?

g. Deinarchus 1 *Against Demosthenes* 45. Investigation and reports by Areopagus.

Or do you think that the Council of the Areopagus, which on account of Demosthenes and Demades and Cephisophon conducted an investigation for six months, has made its reports [*apophaseis*] to you unjustly?

h. Deinarchus 1 *Against Demosthenes* 48, 50–52. *Apophasis*, preliminary condemnation by Areopagus, and trial in *dikastêrion*; special prosecutors; *apophasis* by decision of Areopagus or decree of Assembly; *eisangelia* tried in *dikastêrion* before jury of 2,500.

With the application of the verb *synêgorein* (to act as *synêgoros*, advocate) to a special public prosecutor cf. **371** [Plut.] *Lives of the Ten Orators* 833d-834b (for the more common meaning of the term see p. 28 and, e.g., **374** [Dem.] 46.26; **387e** Lyc. 1.55, 59, 68). The defendant in the *eisangelia* discussed in §52 is identified later (§53) as a member of the Council of the Areopagus named Pistias; Pythocles was an Athenian politician.

. . . [Demosthenes] is going to have the audacity to say (as I hear) that the Council once condemned [*kategnô*] me, and that I am doing the strangest of all things (as he claims): on a previous occasion, in opposition to the Council's report [*apophasei*], I defended myself at trial, but now I am acting as the Council's advocate [*synêgorôn*] and his prosecutor in the matter of the report that has taken place.

. . .

[50] Gentlemen, the Council of the Areopagus must conduct all its reports in one of two ways. What are these? Either it must make the decision itself or it must conduct the investigation upon an order given to it by the Assembly. Apart from these, there is no way by which it may act. [To Demosthenes:] So, then, . . . if you claim that the Council conducted its investigation and made its report concerning me upon the Assembly's order, [51] show the decree, and show who were my prosecutors when the report took place, just as both things have happened now: there is a decree by which the Council conducted its investigation, and there are prosecutors voted by the Assembly, from whom the jurors [*dikastai*] are now learning about the offenses. . . . If, however, you claim that the Council reported me by its own decision, provide the Areopagites as your witnesses, just as I will provide them to prove that I was not reported. [52] Moreover, I impeached [*eisangeilas*] the man who misrepresented me and the Council . . . as a scoundrel and a traitor [*prodotên*], exposed him in a court of 2,500 citizens as having sold himself to Pythocles and committed these acts against me, and with the help of those who served as jurors [*dikasantôn*] on that occasion, I got my revenge.

i. Deinarchus 1 *Against Demosthenes* 54–58. Procedure in and previous instances of *apophasis*.

§54: Despite the speaker's reference to the 20 percent of jurors' votes that prosecutors in most public lawsuits had to receive in order to avoid penalties for sycophancy (cf., e.g., **389** Dem. 18.250 with additional references in headnote), no such penalty appears to have obtained in *apophasis.* §55: "Offenses it has been ordered to investigate by you" refers to *apophaseis* initiated by decree of the Assembly (such as the case mentioned in §58); "offenses that have occurred among its own members" will frequently have given rise to *apophaseis* initiated by the Areopagus on its own authority (such as, apparently, those listed in §56; for the two categories of *apophasis* cf. **391h** Din. 1.48, 50–52). §56: For the five-drachma payment see **303** Hyp. 5 col. 26. §58: The Athenian exiles at Megara were suspected of conspiring to subvert the Athenian democracy (§94).

. . . and is the slander that is going to be spoken by my adversary against the Council going to prevail over the truth? He will say that the Council has reported [*apopephanken*] for offenses against the people many men who were acquitted when they came to the jury-court [*dikastêrion*], and that in some cases the Council has failed to receive one-fifth of the votes. But you will all easily realize how this happens. [55] The Council, gentlemen, investigates offenses it has been ordered to investigate by you and offenses that have occurred among its own members—not in the way that you . . . are occasionally accustomed to judge, assigning more weight to pardon than to justice; rather, it simply reports anyone who is liable for the offenses under investigation, and anyone who has committed any offense at all against ancestral practices. . . . [56] That is why it fined and reported to you one of its own members, who deprived the ferryman of his fare; in another instance, it reported to you the man who saw fit to take the five-drachma payment in the name of one who was not present; it also in the same manner fined and expelled the man who had the audacity to sell the portion of meat granted to [members of] the Areopagus in violation of regulations. [57] You tried these men and acquitted them. . . . [58] When the Assembly ordered the Council to investigate Polyeuctus of the deme Cydantidae, to see whether he was going to Megara with the exiles, and after investigation to report to you, it reported that he was. You chose prosecutors in accordance with the law, he came before the jury-court [*dikastêrion*], and you acquitted him, although Polyeuctus admitted that he was going to Megara to see Nicophanes, since Nicophanes was married to his mother. He seemed to you to be doing nothing strange or terrible in conversing with his mother's husband, who had met with misfortune, and assisting him, to the extent that he was able, when he had been deprived of his country.

j. Deinarchus 1 *Against Demosthenes* 60. Penalties for fiscal malversation and for receiving bribes.

Cf. **302a** [Arist.] *Ath. Pol.* 48.4–5, 54.2; **374** [Dem.] 46.26; **388** Aeschin. 3.232; **391d** Hyp. 5 col. 24.

The laws command the payment of double damages for other offenses relating to accounting for money, but for those who take bribes [*dôrodokountôn*] they have established only two penalties: either death . . . or a penalty for bribery [*dôrôn*] of ten times the original amount received. . . .

k. Deinarchus 1 *Against Demosthenes* 61–63. Decree of Demosthenes (324/3) initiating *apophasis* against himself and others, with stipulated penalty of death; decree of Demosthenes creating *apophasis* procedure (ca. 344/3); previous instances of *apophasis*.

The first decree of Demosthenes mentioned here (§61) is that which authorized the *apophasis* of Demosthenes and others in connection with the Harpalus affair (324/3); the second (§62) is that which created the *apophasis* procedure (ca. 344/3). For "the man in charge of the pit" see **369** Lyc. 1.120–21 with additional references in headnote; on Harmodius see **78** Hyp. 2.3; on Antiphon cf. **383** Dem. 18.132–33. Charinus had been convicted of treason and exiled by ca. 340 ([Demosthenes] 58.38).

[To Demosthenes:] But you alone of all who have ever been reported [*apopephasmenôn*] demanded of your own volition that these men be your judges and investigators; you wrote the decree against yourself and made the Assembly witness to the agreement, setting for yourself a penalty of death if the Council reported you as having received any of the money that was brought to the country by Harpalus. [62] And in fact you, Demosthenes, previously proposed that in the cases of all these men, and the rest of the Athenians too, the Council of the Areopagus should have the authority to punish anyone who offended against the laws, using the ancestral laws. . . . And in accordance with your decree two citizens are dead, father and son, who were handed over to the man in charge of the pit; [63] one of the descendants of Harmodius was imprisoned by your order; these men, persuaded by the report [*apophasei*] of the Council, tortured Antiphon and put him to death; and you expelled Charinus from the city for treason [*prodosiai*] in accordance with the reports and punishments of the Council.

l. Deinarchus 1 *Against Demosthenes* 77. Prosecution's proposed penalty of death and denial of burial in Attica.

Cf. **391f** Din. 1.18; **391k** Din. 1.61–63. *Ep' autophôrôi* ("in the act") has here purely rhetorical force (cf. **297** Dem. 19.293–94; **301** Aeschin. 3.10), since the procedure is *apophasis*, not *apagôgê* or a related action; for the relevance of the term *ep' autophôrôi* in *apagôgê* and related procedures for theft and related offenses see chapter 9, especially the references to *apagôgê* in the headnote under **288** Dem. 22.25–27, 69–73.

. . . you must . . . put to death this man who has been caught in the act [*ep' autophôrôi*] as a thief and a traitor [*prodotên*] . . . and cast him over the borders of the city. . . .

392. Lexicographers' definitions of *eisangelia*.

The debate among the ancient lexicographers over whether, in the time of the Attic orators, *eisangelia* applied not only to the offenses specified in the impeachment law (**373** Hyp. 4.7–8) but also to novel and/or unwritten offenses (i.e., those not specified in any law) continues among modern scholars (see the introduction to this chapter).

a. Harpocration s.v. *eisangelia*. (Harpocration *fl.* 2nd c. A.D.)

See references and headnote under **28**. "The Council" is the Council of 500. On the various types of and remedies for maltreatment (*kakôsis*) see **§6.4**, for the relevant passages of Isaeus' *On the Estate of Hagnias* see **161** Isae. 11.6, 31, 35.

Impeachment [*eisangelia*] is the name of a public lawsuit [*dêmosias . . . dikês*], and there are three types of impeachments. One is for public offenses that are most serious and do not admit of delay, and for offenses for which no magistracy has been appointed and no laws are established for the magistrates in accordance with which they are to introduce the lawsuit; rather, the first presentation occurs before the Council or the Assembly. For these offenses very severe penalties are imposed upon the defendant if he is convicted, while the prosecutor, if he does not get a conviction, is not punished, except if he does not receive one-fifth of the votes: in that case he pays 1,000 drachmas; formerly, though, these men too were punished more severely. A second type of impeachment is mentioned for acts of maltreatment [*kakôsesin*]; these impeachments come before the archon and involve no penalty for the prosecutor even if he does not receive one-fifth of the votes. Another type of impeachment is against arbitrators: if a person was wronged by an arbitrator, he could impeach [*eisangellein*] him before the jurors [*dikastas*], and if convicted, [the arbitrator] was disfranchised. Isaeus, though, [in his speech] *On the Estate of Hagnias*, called the same thing an "impeachment" [*eisangelian*] and an "indictment" [*graphên*].

b. Pollux, *Onomasticon* 8.51–53. (late 2nd c. A.D.)

See references and headnote under **117**; also A. **Szegedy-Maszak**, *The* Nomoi *of Theophrastus* (New York 1981), fragment 4(b) (partial text, translation, and commentary). The ellipses in §51 correspond to lacunae in the text; for the material omitted from §53 (marked by an ellipsis) see **165** Pollux, *Onomasticon* 8.53 = Dem. fr. 7 Baiter-Sauppe. "The law on impeachment" (§51) is presumably **373** Hyp. 4.7–8; "the Council" is the Council of 500. §52: "Whatever [the convicted defendant] deserve[s] to suffer or pay" was the penal formula for an *agôn timêtos* (p. 40) without penal limit: cf., e.g., **35** Dem. 21.47; **332d** Dem. 21.25, 28; **340f** Pl. *Ap.* 36a5-b5, 36e1–37a1, 38b1–9; and see the headnote under **387** Lyc. 1 (selections). On Theophrastus' *On Laws* see **312** Theophr. *Laws* fr. 21.1 Szegedy-Maszak with headnote; for the reference to Hypereides see **59** Hyp. 1.12. §53: Demetrius of Phaleron studied under Theophrastus; during his tenure as Macedonian-appointed governor of Athens (318/7–307), he wrote a number of laws.

Impeachment [*eisangelia*] was prescribed for unwritten public offenses. Under the law on impeachment [*ton nomon ton eisangeltikon*] . . . (statements are made on both sides), which was established . . . concerning things for which no laws existed; and if a person, whether a magistrate or a politician, was caught doing wrong, impeachment to the Council was granted against him. If he was found guilty of moderate offenses, the Council inflicted a fine; [52] if the offenses were more serious, it handed him over to a jury-court [*dikastêriôi*], and the penalty was whatever he deserved to suffer or pay. Impeachments also occurred against politicians who subverted the people, did not propose what was best for the people, went off to the enemy without having been sent, or betrayed a fort, army, or ships, as Theophrastus states in his first book *On Laws*. Hypereides in his speech *For Lycophron* states that the man who brought the impeachment and did not get a conviction was not subject to a fine. [53] Theophrastus, however, states that those who prosecuted other public lawsuits [*graphas*] were fined 1,000 drachmas if they did not receive one-fifth of the votes, and were disfranchised in addition, but those who brought impeachments were not disfranchised but were fined the thousand drachmas; it is probable that this provision was added later because of people who brought impeachments lightly. . . . Under Solon, 1,000 [jurors] judged impeachments; under [Demetrius] of Phaleron, 500 more in addition.

c. *Lexicon Cantabrigiense* s.v. *eisangelia.* (*Lexicon* of unknown Byzantine date)

E. O. **Houtsma**, *Lexicon rhetoricum Cantabrigiense* (Leiden 1870, repr. in K. **Latte**-H. **Erbse**, *Lexica Graeca minora*, Hildesheim 1965: text with Latin notes); F. **Jacoby**, *Die Fragmente der griechischen Historiker* (Leiden 1957–), no. 328, fr. 199 (text: part IIIB p. 154; commentary: part IIIb [Supplement] vol. 1 pp. 564–65, vol. 2 pp. 452–54); **Szegedy-Maszak**, Nomoi, fragment 2 (partial text, translation, and commentary).

See headnote under **81**. On Caecilius see **223** Harpo. s.v. *exoulês* with headnote; on Theophrastus and Demetrius of Phaleron see **392b** Pollux, *Onomasticon* 8.51–53 with headnote; on Craterus see **126** Harpo. s.v. *nautodikai* and cf. the headnote under **371** [Plut.] *Lives of the Ten Orators* 833d-834b. For the impeachment of Themistocles see **367** (Banishment of Themistocles for treason); on Philochorus see the headnote under **264** D. H. *Din.* 3 and cf. **270** Philochorus, *FGrHist* 328 F 121. The text as we have it is clearly problematic and likely corrupt in one or more places. The clause "Sometimes they would bring impeachments denouncing people who were being prosecuted maliciously" may alternatively refer (in a confused manner) not to *eisangeliai* brought by sycophants against their victims but to (supposed) *eisangeliai* against sycophants: note the juxtaposition of **224** [Arist.] *Ath. Pol.* 43.4, which mentions *eisangelia*, and **386** [Arist.] *Ath. Pol.* 43.5, on *probolê* for sycophancy (*eisangelia* and *probolê* are also mentioned together in **333** [Arist.] *Ath. Pol.* 59.2; note the juxtaposition with **60** [Arist.] *Ath. Pol.* 59.3, which mentions the *graphê sykophantias*); Isocrates 15.314 lists the remedies for sycophancy as "*graphai* before the *thesmothetai* [**60** [Arist.] *Ath. Pol.* 59.3], *eisangeliai* before the Council, and *probolai* in the Assembly").

Impeachment [*eisangelia*] [lay] against novel and unwritten offenses. That, at any rate, is the opinion of Caecilius. Theophrastus, however, states in his fourth book *On Laws* that it occurred if a politician subverted the people or did not advise what was best, taking money, or if a person betrayed a place, ships, or a land army, or if a person went over to the enemy, resided with them, served in the military with them, or took bribes. The impeachment of Themistocles, which according to Craterus was brought by Leobotes son of Alcmaeon of the deme Agryle, accords with what Theophrastus says. Some of the orators, though, were accustomed to call even offenses that were not serious by the name "impeachment." Sometimes they would bring impeachments denouncing people who were being prosecuted maliciously; as Philochorus [states], with 1,000 [jurors] in session, but as Demetrius of Phaleron [states], with 1,500. Caecilius gave this definition: "Impeachment is what the laws have granted submission of concerning novel offenses."

Bibliography

Adam, J., and A. M. Adam. 1893. *Platonis* Protagoras. Cambridge.

Adams, C. D. 1905. *Lysias: Selected Speeches.* New York, repr. Norman, OK 1970.

Adler, A. 1928–38. *Suidae lexicon.* Leipzig.

Andrewes, A. 1974. "The Arginousai Trial." *Phoenix* 28: 112–22.

Angeli, A. 1981. "I frammenti di Idomeneo di Lampsaco." *Cronache Ercolanesi* 11: 41–101.

Apostolakis, K. E. 2009. *[Δημοσθένους]* Πρὸς Φαίνιππον περὶ ἀντιδόσεως. Athens.

Arnaoutoglou, I. 1998. *Ancient Greek Laws: A Sourcebook.* London and New York.

Arnott, W. G. 1979–97. *Menander*, 2 vols. Cambridge, MA.

Aujac, G., et al. 1978–. *Denys d'Halicarnasse: Opuscules rhétoriques*, 5 vols. Paris.

Bain, D. M. 1983. *Menander:* Samia. Warminster.

Baiter, J. G., and H. Sauppe. 1850. *Oratores Attici*, vol. 2. Zürich.

Bearzot, C. 1997. *Lisia e la tradizione su Teramene.* Milan.

Beauchet, L. 1897. *Histoire du droit privé de la république athénienne.* Paris.

Bekker, I. 1814. *Anecdota Graeca*, vol. 1: *Lexica Segueriana.* Berlin.

Benner, A. R., and F. H. Fobes. 1949. *The Letters of Alciphron, Aelian and Philostratus.* Cambridge, MA.

Bers, V. 2003. *Demosthenes, Speeches 50–59.* Austin.

Bethe, E. 1910–31. *Lexicographi Graeci*, vol. IX: *Pollucis Onomasticon*, 2 vols. Stuttgart.

Bianchetti, S. 1983. "Osservazioni sulla ΓΡΑΦΗ ΙΕΡΟΣΥΛΙΑΣ e sulla ΓΡΑΦΗ ΚΛΟΠΗΣ ΙΕΡΩΝ ΧΡΗΜΑΤΩΝ." *Studi e Ricerche* (Istituto di Storia, Facoltà di Lettere e Filosofia, Università degli Studi di Firenze) 2.55–61. Florence.

Blass, F. 1887–98. *Die attische Beredsamkeit.* Leipzig.

Blok, J. H. 2009. "Pericles' Citizenship Law: A New Perspective." *Historia* 58: 141–70.

Blok, J. H., and A. P. M. H. Lardinois, eds. 2006. *Solon of Athens: New Historical and Philological Approaches.* Leiden.

Boardman, J., et al. 1988. *The Cambridge Ancient History*, vol. 4 ed. 2: *Persia, Greece and the Western Mediterranean* c. *525–479 B.C.* Cambridge.

Boardman, J., and N. G. L. Hammond, eds. 1982. *The Cambridge Ancient History*, vol. 3 pt. 3 ed. 2: *The Expansion of the Greek World, Eighth to Sixth Centuries B.C.* Cambridge.

Boegehold, A. L. 1995. *The Athenian Agora*, vol. XXVIII: *The Lawcourts at Athens: Sites, Buildings, Equipment, Procedure, and Testimonia.* Princeton.

Bonner, R. J., and G. Smith. 1930–38. *The Administration of Justice from Homer to Aristotle.* Chicago.

Brickhouse, T. C., and N. D. Smith. 1989. *Socrates on Trial*. Princeton.

Brickhouse, T. C., and N. D. Smith, eds. 2002. *The Trial and Execution of Socrates: Sources and Controversies*. Oxford.

Burnet, J. 1900. *The* Ethics *of Aristotle*. London.

Burnet, J. 1911. *Plato's* Phaedo. Oxford.

Burnet, J. 1924. *Plato:* Euthyphro, Apology of Socrates, *and* Crito. Oxford.

Bury, J. B., and R. Meiggs. 1975. *A History of Greece to the Death of Alexander the Great.*[4] New York.

Bury, R. G. 1933–49. *Sextus Empiricus*, 4 vols. Cambridge, MA.

Caillemer, E. 1879. *Le droit de succession légitime à Athènes*. Paris.

Cairns, D. L., and R. A. Knox, eds. 2004. *Law, Rhetoric, and Comedy in Classical Athens: Essays in Honour of Douglas M. MacDowell.* Swansea.

Cantarella, E. 1976. *Studi sull'omicidio in diritto greco e romano*. Milan.

Cantarella, E. 1997. "Filiazione e cittadinanza ad Atene." In *Symposion 1995*, edited by G. Thür and J. Vélissaropoulos-Karakostas, 97–111. Köln.

Cantarella, E. 2005. "Gender, Sexuality, and Law." In *The Cambridge Companion to Ancient Greek Law*, edited by M. Gagarin and D. Cohen, 236–53. Cambridge.

Capps, E. 1910. *Four Plays of Menander*: The Hero, Epitrepontes, Periceiromene, *and* Samia. Boston.

Carawan, E. 1998. *Rhetoric and the Law of Draco*. Oxford.

Carawan, E. 2004. "Andocides' Defence and MacDowell's Solution." In *Law, Rhetoric, and Comedy in Classical Athens: Essays in Honour of Douglas M. MacDowell*, edited by D. L. Cairns and R. A. Knox, 103–12. Swansea.

Carawan, E. 2006. "The Athenian Law of Agreement." *GRBS* 46: 339–74.

Carawan, E. 2008. "Pericles the Younger and the Citizenship Law." *CJ* 103: 383–406.

Carawan, E. M. 1985. "*Apophasis* and *Eisangelia*: The Rôle of the Areopagus in Athenian Political Trials." *GRBS* 26: 115–40.

Carawan, E. M. 1987. "*Eisangelia* and *Euthyna*: the Trials of Miltiades, Themistocles, and Cimon." *GRBS* 28: 167–208.

Carawan, E. M. 1993. "Tyranny and Outlawry: *Athenaion Politeia* 16.10." In *Nomodeiktes: Greek Studies in Honor of Martin Ostwald*, edited by R. M. Rosen and J. Farrell, 305–19. Ann Arbor.

Carey, C. 1989. *Lysias: Selected Speeches*. Cambridge.

Carey, C. 1992. *Greek Orators VI: Apollodorus*: Against Neaira: *[Demosthenes] 59*. Warminster.

Carey, C. 1995. "Rape and Adultery in Athenian Law." *CQ* 45: 407–17.

Carey, C. 2000. *Aeschines*. Austin.

Carey, C. 2007. *Lysiae orationes cum fragmentis*. Oxford.

Carey, C. 2012. *Trials from Classical Athens*[2]. London and New York.

Carey, C., and R. A. Reid. 1985. *Demosthenes: Selected Private Speeches*. Cambridge.

Cartledge, P., P. Millett, and S. Todd, eds. 1990. *Nomos: Essays in Athenian Law, Politics and Society*. Cambridge.

Chambers, M. 1994. *Aristoteles*: ΑΘΗΝΑΙΩΝ ΠΟΛΙΤΕΙΑ, corrected edition. Stuttgart and Leipzig.

Clavaud, R. 1987. *Démosthène: Lettres et fragments*. Paris.

Cloché, P. 1919. "L'affaire des Arginuses (406 avant J.-C.)." *Revue historique* 130: 5–68.

Cohen, D. 1983. *Theft in Athenian Law*. Munich.

Cohen, D. 1991. *Law, Sexuality, and Society: The Enforcement of Morals in Classical Athens*. Cambridge.
Cohen, D. 1995. *Law, Violence and Community in Classical Athens*. Cambridge.
Cohen, E. E. 1973. *Ancient Athenian Maritime Courts*. Princeton.
Cohen, E. E. 2000. "Whoring under Contract: The Legal Context of Prostitution in Fourth-Century Athens." In *Law and Social Status in Classical Athens*, edited by V. Hunter and J. Edmondson, 113–47. Oxford.
Cohen, E. E. 2005. "Commercial Law." In *The Cambridge Companion to Ancient Greek Law*, edited by M. Gagarin and D. Cohen, 290–302. Cambridge.
Cohen, E. E. 2006. "Free and Unfree Sexual Work: An Economic Analysis of Athenian Prostitution." In *Prostitutes and Courtesans in the Ancient World*, edited by C. A. Faraone and L. K. McClure, 95–124. Madison.
Cohn-Haft, L. 1995. "Divorce in Classical Athens." *JHS* 115: 1–14.
Cole, S. G. 1984. "Greek Sanctions against Sexual Assault." *CP* 79: 97–113.
Colin, G. 1946. *Hypéride: Discours*. Paris.
Collins, D. 2001. "Theoris of Lemnos and the Criminalization of Magic in Fourth-Century Athens." *CQ* n.s. 51: 477–93.
Conomis, N. C. 1970. *Lycurgi oratio in Leocratem cum ceterarum Lycurgi orationum fragmentis*. Leipzig.
Conomis, N. C. 1975. *Dinarchi orationes cum fragmentis*. Leipzig.
Cooper, C. 1995. "Hyperides and the Trial of Phryne." *Phoenix* 49: 303–18.
Cope, E. M., and J. E. Sandys. 1877. *The* Rhetoric *of Aristotle*, 3 vols. Cambridge.
Cosman, A. C. 1939. *Demosthenes' Rede tegen Zenothemis (Oratie XXXII)*. Leiden.
Crosby, M., and J. Young. 1941. "Greek Inscriptions." *Hesperia* 10: 14–30.
Csapo, E., and W. J. Slater. 1995. *The Context of Ancient Drama*. Ann Arbor.
Cudjoe, R. V. 2005. "The Purpose of the 'Epidikasia' for an 'Epikleros' in Classical Athens." *Dike* 8: 55–88.
Cudjoe, R. V. 2010. *The Social and Legal Position of Widows and Orphans in Classical Athens*. Athens.
Cunningham, I. C. 2003. *Synagoge: ΣΥΝΑΓΩΓΗ ΛΕΞΕΩΝ ΧΡΗΣΙΜΩΝ*. Berlin.
Dalmeyda, G. 1930. *Andocide: Discours*. Paris.
Davies, J. K. 1971. *Athenian Propertied Families 600–300 B.C.* Oxford.
de Prott, I., and L. Ziehen. 1896–1906. *Leges Graecorum sacrae*. Leipzig.
Denyer, N. 2008. *Plato:* Protagoras. Cambridge.
Dilts, M. R. 1983–86. *Scholia Demosthenica*, 2 vols. Leipzig.
Dilts, M. R. 1992. *Scholia in Aeschinem*. Stuttgart.
Dilts, M. R. 1997. *Aeschinis orationes*. Stuttgart and Leipzig.
Dilts, M. R. 2002–9. *Demosthenis orationes*, 4 vols. Oxford.
Dimakis, P., ed. 1983. *Symposion 1979: Vorträge zur griechischen und hellenistischen Rechtsgeschichte*. Köln.
Dindorf, G. 1846–51. *Demosthenes*, 9 vols. Oxford.
Dindorf, G. 1853. *Harpocrationis lexicon in decem oratores Atticos*. Reprint, Athens 2004.
Dodds, E. R. 1959. *Plato*: Gorgias. Oxford.
Doherty, F. C. 1927. *Three Private Speeches of Demosthenes*. Oxford.
Dorjahn, A. P. 1946. *Political Forgiveness in Old Athens: The Amnesty of 403 B.C.* Evanston, IL.
Dover, K. J. 1968. *Aristophanes*: Clouds. Oxford.

Dover, K. J. 1968. *Lysias and the* Corpus Lysiacum. Berkeley and Los Angeles.
Dover, K. J. 1975/76. "The Freedom of the Intellectual in Greek Society." *Talanta* 7: 24–54.
Dover, K. J. 1989. *Greek Homosexuality.*[2] Cambridge, MA.
Dover, K. J. 1994. *Greek Popular Morality in the Time of Plato and Aristotle*, corrected edition. Indianapolis.
Dübner, F. 1842. *Scholia Graeca in Aristophanem.* Paris.
Dunbar, N. 1995. *Aristophanes*: Birds. Oxford.
Durrbach, F. 1932. *Lycurgue*: Contre Léocrate, *Fragments.* Paris.
Dyer, L., and T. D. Seymour. 1908. *Plato*: Apology of Socrates *and* Crito, *with Extracts from the* Phaedo *and* Symposium *and from Xenophon's* Memorabilia. Boston.
Edwards, M. 1995. *Greek Orators IV: Andocides.* Warminster.
Edwards, M. 2007. *Isaeus.* Austin.
Edwards, M., and S. Usher. 1985. *Greek Orators 1: Antiphon and Lysias.* Warminster.
Edwards, M. J. 1999. *Lysias: Five Speeches: Speeches 1, 12, 19, 22, 30.* London.
Engels, J. 2008. *Lykurg: Rede gegen Leokrates.* Darmstadt.
Falconer, W. A. 1938. *Cicero*: De Senectute, De Amicitia, De Divinatione. Cambridge, MA.
Faraguna, M. 1992. *Atene nell' età di Alessandro.* Rome.
Faraone, C. A., and L. K. McClure, eds. 2006. *Prostitutes and Courtesans in the Ancient World.* Madison.
Ferguson, J. 1991. *Clement of Alexandria*, Stromateis, *Books 1–3.* Washington.
Figueira, T. 1986. "*Sitopolai* and *Sitophylakes* in Lysias' 'Against the Graindealers:' Governmental Intervention in the Athenian Economy." *Phoenix* 40: 149–71.
Fine, J. V. A. 1951. *Horoi: Studies in Mortgage, Real Security and Land Tenure in Ancient Athens.* Baltimore.
Fine, J. V. A. 1983. *The Ancient Greeks: A Critical History.* Cambridge, MA.
Finley, M. I. 1951. "Some Problems of Greek Law: A Consideration of Pringsheim on Sale." *Seminar* 9: 72–91.
Finley, M. I. 1985. *Studies in Land and Credit in Ancient Athens, 500–200 B.C.: The* Horos *Inscriptions.* Reprinted with a new introduction by P. Millett. New Brunswick, NJ. Original edition New Brunswick, NJ, 1952.
Fisher, N. 2001. *Aeschines*: Against Timarchos. Oxford.
Fisher, N. R. E. 1990. "The Law of *hubris* in Athens." In *Nomos: Essays in Athenian Law, Politics and Society*, edited by P. Cartledge, P. Millett, and S. Todd, 123–38. Cambridge.
Fisher, N. R. E. 1992. *Hybris.* Warminster.
Flacelière, R., and E. Chambry. 1964. *Plutarque: Vies, Tome III.* Paris.
Fornara, C. W. 1983. *Archaic Times to the End of the Peloponnesian War*[2]. Cambridge.
Fowler, H. N. 1936. *Plutarch's* Moralia, vol. 10. Cambridge, MA.
Foxhall, L. 1989. "Household, Gender and Property in Classical Athens." *CQ* 39: 22–44.
Frohberger, H. 1882. *Ausgewählte Reden des Lysias.* Leipzig.
Frost, F. J. 1998. *Plutarch's Themistocles: A Historical Commentary.* Revised edition. Chicago.
Furley, W. D. 1996. *Andokides and the Herms: A Study of Crisis in Fifth-Century Athenian Religion.* London.
Gagarin, M. 1978. "Self-Defense in Athenian Homicide Law." *GRBS* 19: 111–20.
Gagarin, M. 1979. "The Athenian Law Against Hybris." In *Arktouros: Hellenic Studies Presented to Bernard M. Knox*, edited by G. W. Bowersock, W. Burkert, and M. C. J. Putnam, 229–36. Berlin.

Gagarin, M. 1979. "The Prosecution of Homicide in Athens." *GRBS* 20: 301–23.

Gagarin, M. 1981. "The Thesmothetai and the Earliest Athenian Tyranny Law." *TAPA* 111: 71–77.

Gagarin, M. 1981. *Drakon and Early Athenian Homicide Law.* New Haven, CT.

Gagarin, M. 1989. *The Murder of Herodes.* Frankfurt am Main.

Gagarin, M. 1997. *Antiphon: The Speeches.* Cambridge.

Gagarin, M. 2008. *Writing Greek Law.* Cambridge.

Gagarin, M., ed. 2011. *Speeches from Athenian Law.* Austin.

Gagarin, M., and D. Cohen, eds. 2005. *The Cambridge Companion to Ancient Greek Law.* Cambridge.

Gagarin, M., and D. M. MacDowell. 1998. *Antiphon and Andocides.* Austin.

Gagliardi, L. 2002. "Per un'interpretazione della legge di Solone in materia successoria." *Dike* 5: 5–59.

Garland, R. 1992. *Introducing New Gods: The Politics of Athenian Religion.* Ithaca, NY.

Gernet, L. 1917. *Recherches sur le développement de la pensée juridique et morale en Grèce.* Reprint, Paris, 2001.

Gernet, L. 1921. "Sur l'épiclérat." *REG* 34: 337–79.

Gernet, L. 1923. *Antiphon: Discours.* Paris.

Gernet, L. 1938. "Sur les actions commerciales en droit athénien." *REG* 51: 1–44. Reprinted in L. Gernet, *Droit et société dans la Grèce ancienne*, 173–200. Paris, 1955.

Gernet, L. 1951. "Le droit de la vente et la notion du contrat en Grèce: d'après M. Pringsheim." *Revue historique de droit français et étranger* 29: 560–84. Reprinted in L. Gernet, *Droit et société dans la Grèce ancienne*, 201–24. Paris, 1955.

Gernet, L. 1954. *Démosthène: Plaidoyers civils, Tome I, Discours XXVII–XXXVIII.* Paris.

Gernet, L. 1955. *Droit et société dans la Grèce ancienne.* Paris.

Gernet, L. 1957. *Démosthène: Plaidoyers civils, Tome II, Discours XXXIX–XLVIII.* Paris.

Gernet, L. 1959. "Note sur la notion de délit privé en droit grec." In *Droits de l'antiquité et sociologie juridique: Mélanges Henri Lévy-Bruhl*, 393–405. Paris.

Gernet, L. 1959. *Démosthène: Plaidoyers civils, Tome III, Discours XLIX–LVI.* Paris.

Gernet, L. 1960. *Démosthène: Plaidoyers civils, Tome IV, Discours LVII–LIX.* Paris.

Gernet, L., and M. Bizos. 1989. *Lysias: Discours*, 2 vols. Paris.

Glazebrook, A. 2006. "The Bad Girls of Athens: The Image and Function of *Hetairai* in Judicial Oratory." In *Prostitutes and Courtesans in the Ancient World*, edited by C. A. Faraone and L. K. McClure, 125–38. Madison.

Glotz, G. 1904. *La solidarité de la famille dans le droit criminel en Grèce.* Paris.

Gomme, A. W., A. Andrewes, and K. J. Dover. 1945–81. *A Historical Commentary on Thucydides*, 5 vols. Oxford.

Gomme, A. W., and F. H. Sandbach. 1973. *Menander: A Commentary.* Oxford.

Goodwin, W. W. 1901. *Demosthenes:* On the Crown. Cambridge.

Goodwin, W. W. 1906. *Demosthenes:* Against Midias. Cambridge.

Grenfell, B. P., and A. S. Hunt. 1899. *The Oxyrhynchus Papyri, Part II.* London.

Grenfell, B. P., and A. S. Hunt. 1919. *The Oxyrhynchus Papyri*, vol. 13. London.

Hall, J. M. 2007. *A History of the Archaic Greek World ca. 1200–479 BCE.* Malden, MA.

Halliwell, S. 1991. "Comic Satire and Freedom of Speech in Classical Athens." *JHS* 111: 48–70.

Hansen, M. H. 1975. Eisangelia*: The Sovereignty of the People's Court in Athens in the Fourth Century B.C. and the Impeachment of Generals and Politicians.* Odense.

Hansen, M. H. 1976. Apagoge, Endeixis *and* Ephegesis *against* Kakourgoi, Atimoi *and* Pheugontes. Odense.

Hansen, M. H. 1980. "Eisangelia in Athens: A Reply." *JHS* 100: 89–95.
Hansen, M. H. 1981. "The Prosecution of Homicide in Athens." *GRBS* 22: 11–30.
Hansen, M. H. 1983. "*Graphe* or *dike traumatos*?" *GRBS* 24: 307–20.
Hansen, M. H. 1983. "Two Notes on the Athenian *Dikai Emporikai.*" In *Symposion 1979: Vorträge zur griechischen und hellenistischen Rechtsgeschichte*, edited by P. Dimakis, 167–75. Köln.
Hansen, M. H. 1987. *The Athenian Assembly in the Age of Demosthenes.* Oxford.
Hansen, M. H. 1991. *The Athenian Democracy in the Age of Demosthenes.* Oxford.
Harding, P. 1985. *From the End of the Peloponnesian War to the Battle of Ipsus.* Cambridge.
Harmon, A. M. 1936. *Lucian*, vol. 5. Cambridge, MA.
Harris, E. M. 1988. "When Is a Sale Not a Sale?: The Riddle of Athenian Terminology for Real Security Revisited." *CQ* 38: 351–81. Reprinted with addenda in E. M. Harris, *Democracy and the Rule of Law in Classical Athens*, 163–206. Cambridge, 2006.
Harris, E. M. 1990. "Did the Athenians Regard Seduction As a Worse Crime Than Rape?" *CQ* 40: 370–77. Reprinted with addenda in E. M. Harris, *Democracy and the Rule of Law in Classical Athens*, 283–95. Cambridge, 2006.
Harris, E. M. 1993. "*Apotimema*: Athenian Terminology for Real Security in Leases and Dowry Arrangements." *CQ* 43: 73–95. Reprinted with addenda in E. M. Harris, *Democracy and the Rule of Law in Classical Athens*, 207–39. Cambridge, 2006.
Harris, E. M. 1994. "'In the Act' or 'Red-Handed'? Apagoge to the Eleven and Furtum Manifestum." In *Symposion 1993: Vorträge zur griechischen und hellenistischen Rechtsgeschichte,* edited by G. Thür, 169–84. Köln. Reprinted with addenda in E. M. Harris, *Democracy and the Rule of Law in Classical Athens*, 373–90. Cambridge, 2006.
Harris, E. M. 1994. "Law and Oratory." In *Persuasion: Greek Rhetoric in Action*, edited by I. Worthington, 130–50. London and New York.
Harris, E. M. 1995. *Aeschines and Athenian Politics.* Oxford.
Harris, E. M. 2002. "Did Solon Abolish Debt-Bondage?" *CQ* 52: 415–30. Reprinted with addenda in E. M. Harris, *Democracy and the Rule of Law in Classical Athens*, 249–69. Cambridge, 2006.
Harris, E. M. 2006. "Law and Economy in Classical Athens: [Demosthenes] *Against Dionysodorus.*" In *Democracy and the Rule of Law in Classical Athens*, by E. M. Harris, 143–62. Cambridge.
Harris, E. M. 2006. *Democracy and the Rule of Law in Classical Athens: Essays on Law, Society, and Politics.* Cambridge.
Harris, E. M. 2008. *Demosthenes, Orations 20–22.* Austin.
Harris, E. M., and L. Rubinstein, eds. 2004. *The Law and the Courts in Ancient Greece.* London.
Harrison, A. R. W. 1968–71. *The Law of Athens.* Oxford. Reprint, Indianapolis, 1998.
Hedrick, C. W. 1990. *The Decrees of the Demotionidai.* Atlanta.
Heitsch, E. 1980. *Recht und Argumentation in Antiphons 6. Rede.* Mainz and Wiesbaden.
Hicks, E. L., and G. F. Hill. 1901. *Greek Historical Inscriptions*, revised edition. Oxford.
Hicks, R. D. 1958–59. *Diogenes Laertius: Lives of Eminent Philosophers*, 2 vols. Cambridge, MA.
Hignett, C. 1952. *A History of the Athenian Constitution to the End of the Fifth Century B.C.* Oxford.
Hillgruber, M. 1988. *Die zehnte Rede des Lysias.* Berlin.
Holden, H. A. 1893. *Plutarch's* Life of Demosthenes. Cambridge.

Hornblower, S. 2011. *The Greek World 479–323 BC.*[4] London and New York.
Hornblower, S., and A. Spawforth, eds. 1996. *The Oxford Classical Dictionary*[3]. Oxford.
Houtsma, E. O. 1870. *Lexicon rhetoricum Cantabrigiense.* Leiden. Reprinted in K. Latte and H. Erbse, *Lexica Graeca minora.* Hildesheim, 1965.
How, W. W., and J. Wells. 1928. *A Commentary on Herodotus*, 2 vols., corrected edition. Oxford.
Humbert, J., and L. Gernet. 1959. *Démosthène: Plaidoyers politiques, Tome II*: Contre Midias, Contre Aristocrate. Paris.
Humphreys, S. C. 1985. "Lycurgus of Butadae: An Athenian Aristocrat." In *The Craft of the Ancient Historian: Essays in Honor of Chester G. Starr*, edited by J. W. Eadie and J. Ober, 199–252. Lanham, MD.
Humphreys, S. C. 1986. "Kinship Patterns in the Athenian Courts." *GRBS* 27: 57–92.
Humphreys, S. C. 1991. "A Historical Approach to Drakon's Law on Homicide." In *Symposion 1990*, edited by M. Gagarin, 17–45. Köln.
IG, Inscriptiones Graecae. See Kirchner, I.; Lewis, D.
Ireland, S. 1995. *Menander*: The Bad-Tempered Man (ΔΥΣΚΟΛΟΣ). Warminster.
Isager, S., and M. H. Hansen. 1975. *Aspects of Athenian Society in the Fourth Century B.C.: A Historical Introduction to and Commentary on the Paragraphe-speeches and the Speech Against Dionysodorus in the Corpus Demosthenicum (XXXII–XXXVIII and LVI).* Odense.
Jacoby, F. 1957–. *Die Fragmente der griechischen Historiker.* Leiden.
Jebb, R. C. 1893. *The Attic Orators from Antiphon to Isaeus*[2]. London.
Jensen, C. 1917. *Hyperidis orationes sex cum ceterarum fragmentis.* Leipzig.
Joachim, H. H. 1951. *Aristotle:* The Nicomachean Ethics. Edited by D. A. Rees. Oxford.
Julien, J.-M. and H. L. de Péréra. 1902. *Eschine: Discours sur l'ambassade.* Paris.
Just, R. 1989. *Women in Athenian Law and Life.* London.
Kapparis, K. 1995. "When Were the Athenian Adultery Laws Introduced?" *RIDA* ser. 3 vol. 42: 97–122.
Kapparis, K. 1996. "Humiliating the Adulterer: The Law and the Practice in Classical Athens." *RIDA* ser. 3 vol. 43: 63–77.
Kapparis, K. A. 1999. *Apollodoros*: 'Against Neaira' *[D. 59].* Berlin.
Karabelias, E. 1990. "La succession *ab intestat* en droit attique." *JJP* 20: 55–74.
Karabelias, E. 2002. *L'épiclérat attique.* Athens.
Karnezis, J. E. 1976. "The Law of *Engye* in Demosthenes XLVI. 18, 20, 22." *Apollinaris* 49: 278–85.
Keaney, J. J. 1991. *Harpocration*: Lexeis *of the Ten Orators.* Amsterdam.
Kenyon, F. G. 1906. *Hyperidis orationes et fragmenta.* Oxford.
Kirchner, I. 1901. *Prosopographia Attica.* Berlin.
Kirchner, I., ed. 1913–40. *Inscriptiones Graecae*, vol. 2 ed. 2 min. Berlin.
Koerte, A., and A. Thierfelder. 1959. *Menandri quae supersunt*, vol. 2. Leipzig.
Koster, W. J. W., et al. *Scholia in Aristophanem*, fasc. IB, edited by N. G. Wilson, *Scholia in Aristophanis Acharnenses.* Groningen, 1975.
Kremmydas, C. 2012. *Commentary on Demosthenes* Against Leptines *with Introduction, Text, and Translation.* Oxford.
Krentz, P. 1982. *The Thirty at Athens.* Ithaca, NY.
Krentz, P. 1989. *Xenophon:* Hellenika *I–II.3.10.* Warminster.
Krentz, P. 1995. *Xenophon:* Hellenika *II.3.11–IV.2.8.* Warminster.
Lacey, W. K. 1968. *The Family in Classical Greece.* Ithaca, NY.

Lamb, W. R. M. 1925. *Plato:* Lysis, Symposium, Gorgias. Cambridge, MA.

Lambert, S. D. 1998. *The Phratries of Attica.*[2] Ann Arbor.

Lanni, A. 2006. *Law and Justice in the Courts of Classical Athens.* Cambridge.

Lape, S. 2002–3. "Solon and the Institution of the 'Democratic' Family Form." *CJ* 98: 117–39.

Lape, S. 2006. "The Psychology of Prostitution in Aeschines' Speech against Timarchus." In *Prostitutes and Courtesans in the Ancient World*, edited by C. A. Faraone and L. K. McClure, 139–60. Madison.

Latte, K. 1920. *Heiliges Recht: Untersuchungen zur Geschichte der sakralen Rechtsformen in Griechenland.* Tübingen.

Latte, K. 1931. "Beiträge zum griechischen Strafrecht." *Hermes* 66: 30–48, 129–58.

Latte, K., and H. Erbse. 1965. *Lexica Graeca minora.* Hildesheim.

Lavelle, B. M. 1988. "*Adikia*, The Decree of Kannonos and the Trial of the Generals." *Classica et Mediaevalia* 39: 19–41.

Lenfant, D. 2002. "Protagoras et son procès d'impiété: peut-on soutenir une thèse et son contraire?" *Ktema* 27: 135–54.

Lewis, D., ed. 1981. *Inscriptiones Graecae*, vol. 1 ed. 3 fasc. 1. Berlin and New York.

Lewis, D. M., et al. 1992. *The Cambridge Ancient History*, vol. 5, ed. 2: *The Fifth Century B.C.* Cambridge.

Lewis, D. M., et al. 1994. *The Cambridge Ancient History*, vol. 6, ed. 2: *The Fourth Century B.C.* Cambridge.

Librán Moreno, M. 2004. "El proceso por impiedad de Esquilo." *Habis* 35: 39–56.

Liddell, H. G., and R. Scott. 1996. *A Greek-English Lexicon*, ed. 9. Revised by H. S. Jones with the assistance of R. MacKenzie, with revised supplement. Oxford.

Linforth, I. M. 1919. *Solon the Athenian.* Berkeley.

Lipsius, J. H. 1905–15. *Das attische Recht und Rechtsverfahren.* Leipzig. Reprinted Hildesheim, 1984.

Loening, T. C. 1987. *The Reconciliation Agreement of 403/402 B.C. in Athens: Its Content and Application.* Stuttgart.

Loomis, W. T. 1972. "The Nature of Premeditation in Athenian Homicide Law." *JHS* 92: 86–95.

Macan, R. W. 1895. *Herodotus: The Fourth, Fifth, and Sixth Books*, 2 vols. London.

Macan, R. W. 1908. *Herodotus: The Seventh, Eighth, and Ninth Books*, 2 vols. in 3. London.

MacDowell, D. M. 1962. *Andokides:* On the Mysteries. Oxford.

MacDowell, D. M. 1963. *Athenian Homicide Law in the Age of the Orators.* Manchester.

MacDowell, D. M. 1971. *Aristophanes:* Wasps. Oxford.

MacDowell, D. M. 1976. "Bastards as Athenian Citizens." *CQ* 26: 88–91.

MacDowell, D. M. 1978. *The Law in Classical Athens.* Ithaca, NY.

MacDowell, D. M. 1983. "Athenian Laws about Bribery." *RIDA* ser. 3 vol. 30: 57–78.

MacDowell, D. M. 1984. Review of D. Cohen, *Theft in Athenian Law* (Munich, 1983), *CR* n.s. 34: 229–31.

MacDowell, D. M. 1989. "The *Oikos* in Athenian Law." *CQ* 39: 10–21.

MacDowell, D. M. 1990. *Demosthenes:* Against Meidias *(Oration 21).* Oxford.

MacDowell, D. M. 1994. "The Case of the Rude Soldier (Lysias 9)." In *Symposion 1993*, edited by G. Thür, 153–64. Köln.

MacDowell, D. M. 1995. *Aristophanes and Athens.* Oxford.

MacDowell, D. M. 2000. "Athenian Laws about Homosexuality." *RIDA* ser. 3 vol. 47: 13–27.

MacDowell, D. M. 2000. *Demosthenes:* On the False Embassy *(Oration 19).* Oxford.
MacDowell, D. M. 2004. *Demosthenes, Speeches 27–38.* Austin.
MacDowell, D. M. 2009. *Demosthenes the Orator.* Oxford.
Maffi, A. 1989. "Matrimonio, concubinato, e filiazione illegittima nell'Atene degli oratori." In *Symposion 1985*, edited by G. Thür, 177–214. Köln.
Maffi, A. 2005. "Family and Property Law." In *The Cambridge Companion to Ancient Greek Law,* edited by M. Gagarin and D. Cohen, 254–66. Cambridge.
Mandilaras, B. G. 2003. *Isocrates: Opera omnia*, 3 vols. Munich and Leipzig.
Manfredini, M., and L. Piccirilli. 1977. *Plutarco:* La vita di Solone. Verona.
Mansfeld, J. 1979. "The Chronology of Anaxagoras' Athenian Period and the Date of His Trial." *Mnemosyne* 32: 39–69.
Marchant, E. C. 1959. *Xenophon:* Memorabilia *and* Oeconomicus. Cambridge, MA.
Marchant, E. C., and G. E. Underhill. 1906. *Xenophon:* Hellenica. Oxford.
Martin, V., and G. de Budé. 1928. *Eschine: Discours, Tome II.* Paris.
Martin, V., and G. de Budé. 1952. *Eschine: Discours, Tome I.* Paris.
Marzi, M., P. Leone, and E. Malcovati. 1977. *Oratori attici minori*, vol. 1. Turin.
Mathieu, G. 1946. *Démosthène: Plaidoyers politiques, Tome III:* Sur les forfaitures de l'ambassade. Paris.
Mathieu, G. 1947. *Démosthène: Plaidoyers politiques, Tome IV:* Sur la couronne, Contre Aristogiton I *et* II. Paris.
Mathieu, G., and E. Brémond. 1928. *Isocrate: Discours, Tome I.* Paris.
Meiggs, R. 1975. *The Athenian Empire*, corrected edition. Oxford.
Meiggs, R., and D. Lewis. 1988. *A Selection of Greek Historical Inscriptions to the End of the Fifth Century B.C.* Revised edition. Oxford.
Meritt, B. D. 1963. "Greek Inscriptions." *Hesperia* 32: 1–56.
Meyer-Laurin, H. 1965. *Gesetz und Billigkeit im attischen Prozess.* Weimar.
Miles, J. C. 1950. "The Attic Law of Intestate Succession (Demosthenes, *Contra Macart.* 51)." *Hermathena* 75: 69–77.
Miller, N. 1987. *Menander: Plays and Fragments.* London.
Millett, P. 1990. "Sale, Credit and Exchange in Athenian Law and Society." In *Nomos: Essays in Athenian Law, Politics, and Society*, edited by P. Cartledge, P. Millett, and S. C. Todd, 167–94. Cambridge.
Millett, P. 1991. *Lending and Borrowing in Ancient Athens.* Cambridge.
Mirhady, D., I. Arnaoutoglou, and M. J. Sundahl. NOMOI: Ancient Greek Law on the World Wide Web. http://www.sfu.ca/nomoi.
Mirhady, D. C. 2004. "Contracts in Athens." In *Law, Rhetoric, and Comedy in Classical Athens: Essays in Honour of Douglas M. MacDowell*, edited by D. L. Cairns and R. A. Knox, 51–63. Swansea.
Mirhady, D. C., and Y. L. Too. 2000. *Isocrates I.* Austin.
Modrzejewski, J. M. 1983. "La structure juridique du mariage grec." In *Symposion 1979*, edited by P. Dimakis, 37–71. Köln.
Mommsen, T., P. Krueger, and A. Watson, eds. 1985. *The Digest of Justinian*, 4 vols. Philadelphia.
Moneti, I. 1991. "La 'γραφὴ κλοπῆς' nel diritto attico." *Civiltà Classica e Cristiana* 12: 7–10.
Müller, A. 1926. *Oratio quae inter Lysiacas fertur octava: Κατηγορία πρὸς τοὺς συνουσιαστὰς κακολογιῶν.* Münster.
Mummenthey, H. 1971. *Zur Geschichte des Begriffs Βλάβη im attischen Recht.* Dr. jur. diss., Albert-Ludwigs-Universität Freiburg.

Murray, O. 1990. "The Solonian Law of *hubris*." In *Nomos: Essays in Athenian Law, Politics and Society*, edited by P. Cartledge, P. Millett, and S. Todd, 139–45. Cambridge.
Navarre, O., and P. Orsini. 1957. *Démosthène: Plaidoyers politiques, Tome I:* Contre Androtion, Contre la loi de Leptine, Contre Timocrate. Paris.
Nouhaud, M., and L. Dors-Méary. 1990. *Dinarque: Discours.* Paris.
Ogden, D. 1996. *Greek Bastardy in the Classical and Hellenistic Periods.* Oxford.
Ogden, D. 1997. "Rape, Adultery and the Protection of Bloodlines in Classical Athens." In *Rape in Antiquity*, edited by S. Deacy and K. F. Pierce, 25–41. London.
Oliver, J. H. 1950. *The Athenian Expounders of the Sacred and Ancestral Law.* Baltimore.
Olson, S. D. 2006–11. *Athenaeus:* The Learned Banqueters, 7 vols. Cambridge, MA.
Omitowoju, R. 2002. *Rape and the Politics of Consent in Classical Athens.* Cambridge.
Osborne, M. J. 1981–83. *Naturalization in Athens.* Brussels.
Osborne, R. 2009. *Greece in the Making, 1200–479 BC.*[2] London and New York.
Ostwald, M. 1955. "The Athenian Legislation against Tyranny and Subversion." *TAPA* 86: 103–28.
Ostwald, M. 1986. *From Popular Sovereignty to the Sovereignty of Law: Law, Society, and Politics in Fifth-Century Athens.* Berkeley and Los Angeles.
O'Sullivan, L.-L. 1997. "Athenian Impiety Trials in the Late Fourth Century B.C." *CQ* n.s. 47: 136–52.
Page, D. L. 1973. *Lyrica Graeca Selecta*, corrected edition. Oxford.
Paley, F. A., and J. E. Sandys. 1898. *Demosthenes: Select Private Orations* 1[3]. Cambridge.
Paoli, U. E. 1936. "L'ἀγχιστεία nel diritto successorio attico." *SDHI* 2: 77–119.
Parker, R. 1996. *Athenian Religion: A History.* Oxford.
Parker, R. 2004. "What Are Sacred Laws?" In *The Law and the Courts in Ancient Greece*, edited by E. M. Harris and L. Rubinstein, 57–70. London.
Parker, R. 2005. "Law and Religion." In *The Cambridge Companion to Ancient Greek Law*, edited by M. Gagarin and D. Cohen, 61–81. Cambridge.
Patterson, C. 1981. *Pericles' Citizenship Law of 451–50 B.C.* New York.
Patterson, C. 2005. "Athenian Citizenship Law." In *The Cambridge Companion to Ancient Greek Law*, edited by M. Gagarin and D. Cohen, 267–89. Cambridge.
Patterson, C. B. 1990. "Those Athenian Bastards." *ClAnt* 9: 40–73.
Patterson, C. B. 1998. *The Family in Greek History.* Cambridge, MA.
Pearson, L. 1972. *Demosthenes: Six Private Speeches.* Norman, OK.
Pease, A. S. 1963. *M. Tulli Ciceronis* De Divinatione. Darmstadt.
Petrie, A. 1922. *Lycurgus: The Speech Against Leocrates.* Cambridge.
Philippi, A. 1870. *Beiträge zu einer Geschichte des attischen Bürgerrechtes.* Berlin.
Phillips, D. D. 2004. *Athenian Political Oratory: 16 Key Speeches.* New York and London.
Phillips, D. D. 2006. "Why Was Lycophron Prosecuted by *Eisangelia*?" *GRBS* 46: 375–94.
Phillips, D. D. 2007. "*Trauma ek pronoias* in Athenian Law." *JHS* 127: 74–105.
Phillips, D. D. 2008. *Avengers of Blood: Homicide in Athenian Law and Custom from Draco to Demosthenes.* Stuttgart.
Phillips, D. D. 2009. "Hypereides 3 and the Athenian Law of Contracts." *TAPA* 139: 89–122.
Φιλολογική Ομάδα Κάκτου. 2004. *Πολυδεύκης· 'Ονομαστικόν*, 2 vols. Athens.
Pomeroy, S. 1994. *Xenophon,* Oeconomicus*: A Social and Historical Commentary.* Oxford.
Pomeroy, S. B. 1975. *Goddesses, Whores, Wives, and Slaves.* New York.
Pringsheim, F. 1950. *The Greek Law of Sale.* Weimar.

Queyrel Bottineau, A. 2011. *Prodosia: la notion et l'acte de trahison dans l'Athènes du Ve siècle. Recherche sur la construction de l'identité athénienne.* Bordeaux.
Rabe, H. 1892–93. *Syriani in Hermogenem commentaria*, 2 vols. Leipzig.
Rhodes, P. J. 1972. *The Athenian Boule.* Oxford.
Rhodes, P. J. 1978. "Bastards as Athenian Citizens." *CQ* 28: 89–92.
Rhodes, P. J. 1979. "ΕΙΣΑΓΓΕΛΙΑ in Athens." *JHS* 99: 103–14.
Rhodes, P. J. 1984. *Aristotle:* The Athenian Constitution. London.
Rhodes, P. J. 1993. *A Commentary on the Aristotelian* Athenaion Politeia. Revised edition. Oxford.
Rhodes, P. J. 2010. *A History of the Classical Greek World 478–323 BC*[2]. Malden, MA.
Rhodes, P. J., and R. Osborne. 2003. *Greek Historical Inscriptions 404–323 BC.* Oxford.
Richardson, R. B. 1889. *Aeschines:* Against Ctesiphon. Boston.
Riess, W. 2008. "Private Violence and State Control: The Prosecution of Homicide and Its Symbolic Meanings in Fourth-Century BC Athens." In *Sécurité collective et ordre public dans les sociétés anciennes*, edited by P. Ducrey and C. Brelaz, 49–101. Geneva.
Roberts, E. S., and E. A. Gardner. 1905. *An Introduction to Greek Epigraphy, Part II: The Inscriptions of Attica.* Cambridge.
Roberts, J. T. 1982. *Accountability in Athenian Government.* Madison.
Rose, V. 1886. *Aristotelis qui ferebantur librorum fragmenta.* Leipzig.
Rosivach, V. J. 1984. "*Aphairesis* and *Apoleipsis*: A Study of the Sources." *RIDA* ser. 3 vol. 31: 193–230.
Ross, W. D., ed. 1921. *The Works of Aristotle*, vol. 11. Oxford.
Ross, W. D., ed. 1925. *The Works of Aristotle*, vol. 9. Oxford.
Roussel, P. 1960. *Isée: Discours.* Paris.
Rowe, C. J. 1993. *Plato:* Phaedo. Cambridge.
Rubinstein, L. 1993. *Adoption in IV. Century Athens.* Copenhagen.
Ruschenbusch, E. 1960. "ΦΟΝΟΣ: Zum Recht Drakons und seiner Bedeutung für das Werden des athenischen Staates." *Historia* 9: 129–54.
Ruschenbusch, E. 1962. "ΔΙΑΤΙΘΕΣΘΑΙ ΤΑ ΕΑΥΤΟΥ. Ein Beitrag zum sogenannten Testamentsgesetz des Solon." *ZSS* 79: 307–11.
Ruschenbusch, E. 1965. "*Hybreos graphe*: ein Fremdkörper im athenischen Recht des 4. Jahrhunderts v. Chr." *ZSS* 82: 302–9.
Ruschenbusch, E. 1966. *ΣΟΛΩΝΟΣ ΝΟΜΟΙ: Die Fragmente des solonischen Gesetzeswerkes mit einer Text- und Überlieferungsgeschichte.* Wiesbaden.
Ruschenbusch, E. 1968. *Untersuchungen zur Geschichte des athenischen Strafrechts.* Köln.
Ruschenbusch, E. 2010. *Solon: Das Gesetzeswerk—Fragmente: Übersetzung und Kommentar.* Stuttgart.
Sandys, J. E. 1890. *The Speech of Demosthenes Against the Law of Leptines.* Cambridge.
Sandys, J. E. 1912. *Aristotle's* Constitution of Athens[2]. London.
Sandys, J. E. 1962. *Demosthenes:* On the Peace, Second Philippic, On the Chersonesus *and* Third Philippic. Reprint, revised edition. London.
Sandys, J. E., and F. A. Paley. 1910. *Demosthenes: Select Private Orations* 2[4]. Cambridge.
Saunders, T. 1990. "Plato and the Athenian Law of Theft." In *Nomos: Essays in Athenian Law, Politics and Society*, edited by P. Cartledge, P. Millett, and S. Todd, 63–82. Cambridge.
Scafuro, A. C. 1997. *The Forensic Stage: Settling Disputes in Graeco-Roman New Comedy.* Cambridge.

Scafuro, A. C. 2011. *Demosthenes, Speeches 39–49*. Austin.
Schäfer, A. 1858–87. *Demosthenes und seine Zeit*. Leipzig.
Schaps, D. M. 1979. *Economic Rights of Women in Ancient Greece*. Edinburgh.
Schmitz, W. 1997. "Der nomos moicheias—Das athenische Gesetz über den Ehebruch." *ZSS* 114: 45–140.
Schulthess, O. 1886. *Vormundschaft nach attischem Recht*. Freiburg.
Scott-Kilvert, I. 1973. *Plutarch: The Age of Alexander*, with introduction by G. T. Griffith. London.
Seager, R. 1966. "Lysias Against the Corndealers." *Historia* 15: 172–84.
Sealey, R. 1976. *A History of the Greek City-States ca. 700–338 B.C.* Berkeley and Los Angeles.
Sealey, R. 1990. *Women and Law in Classical Greece*. Chapel Hill, NC.
Shoemaker, G. 1971. "Dionysius of Halicarnassus, *On Dinarchus*." *GRBS* 12: 393–409.
Shuckburgh, E. S. 1892. *Lysiae orationes XVI*. London.
Smith, J. R. 1903. *Xenophon:* Memorabilia. Boston.
Sokolowski, F. 1969. *Lois sacrées des cités grecques*. Paris.
Sommerstein, A. H. 1982. *Aristophanes:* Clouds. Warminster.
Sommerstein, A. H. 1987. *Aristophanes:* Birds. Wiltshire.
Sommerstein, A. H. 1996. *Aristophanes:* Wasps, corrected edition. Warminster.
Sommerstein, A. H. 2001. *Aristophanes:* Wealth. Warminster.
Sommerstein, A. H. 2004. "Comedy and the Unspeakable." In *Law, Rhetoric, and Comedy in Classical Athens: Essays in Honour of Douglas M. MacDowell*, edited by D. L. Cairns and R. A. Knox, 205–22. Swansea.
Spatharas, D. G. 2009. *'Ισοκράτης·* Κατὰ Λοχίτου. Athens.
Spengel, L. 1853. *Rhetores Graeci*, vol. 1. Leipzig.
Stadter, P. A. 1989. *Plutarch's* Pericles. Chapel Hill, NC.
Stewart, J. A. 1892. *Notes on the* Nicomachean Ethics *of Aristotle*, 2 vols. Oxford.
Stone, I. F. 1988. *The Trial of Socrates*. Boston.
Strassler, R. B., ed. 1996. *The Landmark Thucydides*. New York.
Strassler, R. B., ed. 2007. *The Landmark Herodotus*. Translated by A. L. Purvis. New York.
Strassler, R. B., ed. 2009. *The Landmark Xenophon's* Hellenika. Translated by J. Marincola. New York.
Stroud, R. 1979. *The Axones and Kyrbeis of Drakon and Solon*. Berkeley.
Stroud, R. S. 1968. *Drakon's Law on Homicide*. Berkeley.
Sundahl, M., D. Mirhady, and I. Arnaoutoglou. 2011. *A New Working Bibliography of Ancient Greek Law (7th–4th Centuries B.C.)*. Athens.
Szegedy-Maszak, A. 1981. *The* Nomoi *of Theophrastus*. New York.
Taylor, C. C. W. 2009. *Plato:* Protagoras. Oxford.
Thackeray, H. St. J. 1926. *Josephus:* The Life, Against Apion. Cambridge, MA.
Thalheim, T. 1897. "Βλάβης δίκη." In *Paulys Realencyclopädie der classichen Altertumswissenschaft*, vol. III, 1, coll. 552–54. Stuttgart.
Thalheim, T. 1903. *Isaei orationes cum deperditarum fragmentis*. Leipzig.
Thalheim, T. 1914. *Antiphontis orationes et fragmenta*. Leipzig.
Theodoridis, C. 1982–. *Photii Patriarchae lexicon*. Berlin.
Thompson, W. E. 1976. De Hagniae Hereditate: *An Athenian Inheritance Case*. Leiden.
Thür, G., ed. 1994. *Symposion 1993*. Köln.
Thür, G. 2003. "Sachverfolgung und Diebstahl in den griechischen Poleis (Dem. 32, Lys. 23, IC IV 72 I, IPArk 32 u. 17)." In *Symposion 1999*, edited by G. Thür and F. J. Fernández Nieto, 57–96. Köln.

Thür, G. 2005. "The Role of the Witness in Athenian Law." In *The Cambridge Companion to Ancient Greek Law*, edited by M. Gagarin and D. Cohen, 146–69. Cambridge.

Tod, M. N. 1946–48. *Greek Historical Inscriptions*. Oxford. Reprinted with addenda. Chicago, 1985.

Todd, S. C. 1993. *The Shape of Athenian Law*. Oxford.

Todd, S. C. 1996. "Lysias against Nikomachos: The Fate of the Expert in Athenian Law." In *Greek Law in Its Political Setting: Justifications Not Justice*, edited by L. Foxhall and A. D. E. Lewis, 101–31. Oxford.

Todd, S. C. 2000. *Lysias*. Austin.

Todd, S. C. 2004. "Revisiting the Herms and the Mysteries." In *Law, Rhetoric, and Comedy in Classical Athens: Essays in Honour of Douglas M. MacDowell*, edited by D. L. Cairns and R. A. Knox, 87–102. Swansea.

Todd, S. C. 2007. *A Commentary on Lysias, Speeches 1–11*. Oxford.

Towle, J. A. 1892. *Plato:* Protagoras. Boston.

Tredennick, H., and H. Tarrant. 1993. *Plato: The Last Days of Socrates* (Euthyphro, Apology, Crito, Phaedo). Revised edition. London.

Tredennick, H., and R. Waterfield. 1990. *Xenophon: Conversations of Socrates*. London.

Trevett, J. 1992. *Apollodoros the Son of Pasion*. Oxford.

Trevett, J. 2011. *Demosthenes, Speeches 1–17*. Austin.

Tulin, A. 1996. *Dike Phonou: The Right of Prosecution and Attic Homicide Procedure*. Stuttgart.

Usher, S. 1974–85. *Dionysius of Halicarnassus: The Critical Essays*, 2 vols. Cambridge, MA.

Usher, S. 1999. *Greek Oratory: Tradition and Originality*. Oxford.

van Effenterre, H., and F. Ruzé. 1994–95. *Nomima*. Rome.

Vince, J. H. 1935. *Demosthenes III: Against Meidias, Androtion, Aristocrates, Timocrates, Aristogeiton: XXI–XXVI*. Cambridge, MA.

Volonaki, E. 2000. "'Apagoge' in Homicide Cases." *Dike* 3: 147–76.

Wait, W. 1898. *Lysias: Ten Selected Orations*. New York.

Wallace, R. W. 1989. *The Areopagos Council, to 307 B.C.* Baltimore.

Wallace, R. W. 1994. "The Athenian Laws against Slander." In *Symposion 1993*, edited by G. Thür, 109–24. Köln.

Wallace, R. W. 1997. "On Not Legislating Sexual Conduct in Fourth-Century Athens." In *Symposion 1995*, edited by G. Thür and J. Vélissaropoulos-Karakostas, 151–66. Köln.

Wallace, R. W. 2005. "Law, Attic Comedy, and the Regulation of Comic Speech." In *The Cambridge Companion to Ancient Greek Law*, edited by M. Gagarin and D. Cohen, 357–73. Cambridge.

Wardle, D. 2006. *Cicero* On Divination: De Divinatione, *Book 1*. Oxford.

Waterfield, R. 1998. *Plutarch: Greek Lives*. With introduction and notes by P. A. Stadter. Oxford.

Waterfield, R. 2009. *Why Socrates Died*. New York.

Wayte, W. 1882. *Demosthenes:* Against Androtion *and* Against Timocrates. Cambridge.

Wehrli, F. 1969. *Die Schule des Aristoteles*, vol. 7. Basel.

Weil, H. 1886. *Les plaidoyers politiques de Démosthène*, ser. 2. Paris.

West, M. L. 1989–92. *Iambi et elegi Graeci ante Alexandrum cantati*[2], 2 vols. Oxford.

Wevers, R. F. 1969. *Isaeus: Chronology, Prosopography, and Social History*. The Hague.

Whitehead, D. 1986. *The Demes of Attica*. Princeton.

Whitehead, D. 2000. *Hypereides: The Forensic Speeches*. Oxford.

Wilson, N. G. 1997. *Aelian:* Historical Miscellany. Cambridge, MA.

Wolff, H. J. 1943. "The ΔΙΚΗ ΒΛΑΒΗΣ in Demosthenes, *Or.*, LV." *AJP* 64: 316–24.
Wolff, H. J. 1944. "Marriage Law and Family Organisation in Ancient Athens." *Traditio* 2: 43–95.
Wolff, H. J. 1957. "Die Grundlagen des griechischen Vertragsrechts." *ZSS* 74: 26–72.
Wolff, H. J. 1957. "Προίξ." In *Paulys Realencyclopädie der classischen Altertumswissenschaft*, vol. XXIII, 1, coll. 133–70. Stuttgart.
Wolff, H. J. 1966. *Die attische Paragraphe*. Weimar.
Wolpert, A. 2002. *Remembering Defeat: Civil War and Civic Memory in Ancient Athens*. Baltimore.
Wolpert, A., and K. Kapparis. 2011. *Legal Speeches of Democratic Athens: Sources for Athenian History*. Indianapolis.
Woodbury, L. 1965. "The Date and Atheism of Diagoras of Melos." *Phoenix* 19: 178–211.
Woodbury, L. 1981. "Anaxagoras and Athens." *Phoenix* 35: 295–315.
Woodhead, A. G., ed. 1955. *Supplementum Epigraphicum Graecum*, vol. 12. Leiden.
Worthington, I. 1992. *A Historical Commentary on Dinarchus: Rhetoric and Conspiracy in Later Fourth-Century Athens*. Ann Arbor.
Worthington, I. 1999. *Greek Orators II: Dinarchus and Hyperides*. Warminster.
Worthington, I., C. Cooper, and E. M. Harris. 2001. *Dinarchus, Hyperides, and Lycurgus*. Austin.
Wright, W. C. 1921. *Philostratus and Eunapius: The Lives of the Sophists*. Cambridge, MA.
Wyse, W. 1904. *The Speeches of Isaeus*. Cambridge.
Yunis, H. 2001. *Demosthenes:* On the Crown. Cambridge.
Yunis, H. 2005. "The Rhetoric of Law in Fourth-Century Athens." In *The Cambridge Companion to Ancient Greek Law*, edited by M. Gagarin and D. Cohen, 191–208. Cambridge.
Yunis, H. 2005. *Demosthenes, Speeches 18 and 19*. Austin.

Index Locorum

All references are to passage numbers.

AELIAN
Varia Historia
5.19: **343c**
AESCHINES
1 *Against Timarchus*
13–15: **64a**
19–20: **64b**
28–30, 32: **64c**
87: **64d**
91: **57a**
110–13: **295**
119: **64e**
158: **162**
183: **57b**
194: **64f**
2 *On the False Embassy*
87: **24**
93: **34**
3 *Against Ctesiphon*
10: **301**
21: **208**
232: **388**
244: **27**
ALCIPHRON
Letters
1.32: **353d**
ANDOCIDES
1 *On the Mysteries*
10: **338a**
11–13, 15–17, 20: **338b**
27–28: **338c**
31–33: **338d**
34, 36–37, 43–45: **338e**
51, 61–62: **338f**
71–72: **338g**
73–79: **170**
83–84: **12a**
87: **338h**
90–91: **12b**
94: **12c**
96–98: **372**
110–12, 115–16: **338i**
117–21: **185**
[4] *Against Alcibiades*
13–14: **98a**
ANONYMUS SEGUERIANUS
Rhetoric
p. 455 Spengel, lines 6–11: **353e**
ANTIPHON
1 *Against the Stepmother*
25: **7d**
26: **7b**
28: **7c**
28–30: **7a**
5 *On the Killing of Herodes*
9: **8a**
14: **8b**
82–83: **8c**
6 *On the Chorister*
9: **9a**

ANTIPHON (*continued*)
15–16, 19: **9b**
35–36: **9d**
42: **9c**
ARISTOPHANES
Birds
493–98: **274**
1072–74: **346a**
1641–70: **184**
Clouds
497–99: **272a**
1083–84: **52a**
1371–72: **93a**
Wasps
583–86: **183**
836–47, 893–900, 931–35, 952–66: **273**
1389–1408: **241**
Wealth
168: **52b**
366–74, 563–66: **280**
ARISTOTLE
[*Constitution of the Athenians* (*Athênaiôn Politeia*)]
1: **1c**
2.1–2, 6.1: **313b**
4.1: **6a**
7.1: **6b**
8.4: **359**
12.4: **313a**
16.10: **360**
26.4: **125**
35.2: **203**
39.5–6: **11**
42.1–2: **134**
43.4: **224**
43.5: **386**
48.4–5, 54.2: **302a**
50.1–2: **65**
51.1–3: **311**
51.4: **327**
52.1: **302b**
52.2: **46**
56.6–7: **152**
57.2–4: **25**
58.3: **200**
59.2: **333**
59.3: **60**
59.5: **79**
60.2–3: **331**
Nicomachean Ethics
1111a8–10: **343a**
Rhetoric
1373b38–1374a5, 1374a15–16: **291**
1378b14–30: **47a**
1402a1–3: **47b**
ATHENAEUS
Deipnosophistae
577b-c: **127c**
590e: **353c**
696a-d: **355a**

CICERO
On Divination
1.54: **269**
CLEMENT OF ALEXANDRIA
Stromateis
2.60.1–3: **343b**

DEINARCHUS
1 *Against Demosthenes*
18: **391f**
23: **67**
45: **391g**
48, 50–52: **391h**
54–58: **391i**
60: **391j**
61–63: **391k**
77: **391l**
DEMOSTHENES
9 *3 Philippic*
41–45: **368**
44: **5**
18 *On the Crown*
123: **80**
132–33: **383**
204: **366c**
250: **389**
19 *On the False Embassy*
281: **350a**
293–94: **297**
20 *Against Leptines*
100, 135: **379**
104: **72**
157–58: **18**
21 *Against Meidias*
1–2: **332a**

8–11: **332b**
16–17, 25: **255a**
21: **332c**
25, 28: **332d**
31–33: **44a**
35: **255b**
43: **22a, 255c**
44–45: **294**
45: **44b**
47: **35**
51, 55–56: **332e**
71, 75: **22b**
79, 81, 83–84, 88: **75**
113: **361**
147: **332f**
151–52: **332g**
175–76, 178–80: **332h**
206: **332i**
217–18: **332j**
22 *Against Androtion*
2–3: **349a**
21, 23–24: **63a**
25–27, 69–73: **288**
27: **349b**
30: **63b**
73: **63c**
23 *Against Aristocrates*
22: **3a**
28: **3b**
37: **3c**
44–45: **3d**
50: **43, 73, 240**
51: **3e**
53: **3f**
60: **3g**
62: **3h**
65–80: **20**
82: **3i**
97: **382**
24 *Against Timocrates*
63: **380**
103, 107: **160**
104–5, 112–15, 120–21, 129, 146: **289**
127: **381**
144–45: **362**
200–1: **172**
[25] *1 Against Aristogeiton*
79–80: **354a**
27 *1 Against Aphobus*
4–5: **87**
9–11: **167**
15–17: **119**
34, 40, 46, 49–50, 58, 60–61, 67: **145**
55: **91**
28 *2 Against Aphobus*
15–16: **146**
29 *3 Against Aphobus*
15–16: **252**
30–31: **147**
33: **120**
30 *1 Against Onetor*
7–11: **115a**
15–17: **102**
19–22: **115b**
31 *2 Against Onetor*
2–4: **115c**
11: **115d**
32 *Against Zenothemis*
1: **326**
25–28: **261**
[33] *Against Apaturius*
1–3, 23: **324**
6–12: **320**
19–20, 22, 32–33: **260**
36: **308**
[34] *Against Phormion*
3–7, 33, 36–37, 42: **328**
[35] *Against Lacritus*
3–4: **171**
10–13: **323a**
39: **307**
45–46: **323b**
47: **290**
50–51: **323c**
36 *For Phormion*
2–4, 12, 18–20: **253**
8–9, 11, 34: **179**
14: **207**
20, 22: **148**
37 *Against Pantaenetus*
4–8: **256a**
22–26, 28–33: **256b**
33: **45**
35–36: **256c**
39–44: **256d**
45–46: **164**

DEMOSTHENES (*continued*)
45, 47, 50–51: **256e**
59: **23**
38 *Against Nausimachus and Xenopeithes*
2: **257a**
3–4, 14–15, 17, 23: **150**
6–9: **257b**
39 *1 Against Boeotus*
1, 5, 7–18: **254**
2–4: **131a**
20–21: **131b**
35: **166**
39: **131c**
[40] *2 Against Boeotus*
6–7: **88**
10–11: **131d**
14: **121a**
19–20, 25: **111**
28: **131e**
49: **74**
50: **121b**
59: **121c**
41 *Against Spudias*
3–4: **101**
5–7, 10: **114**
7–9, 11–12: **250**
16: **214**
26–28: **109**
[42] *Against Phaenippus*
12: **304c**
27: **122**
[43] *Against Macartatus*
5–16: **234**
51: **176**
54: **181**
57: **4**
57–58: **174**
58: **169**
71: **330**
75: **96**
[44] *Against Leochares*
15–16: **230a**
17–19: **137a**
24–26, 32–34: **196**
41: **137b**
42–43: **230b**
45–50: **230c**
46–47: **137c**
57–59: **230d**
64: **221**
67–68: **209**
45 *1 Against Stephanus*
3–4: **56**
27–28, 30: **92**
37: **149**
80–81: **293**
[46] *2 Against Stephanus*
14: **201**
18: **83**
19–20: **182**
22–23: **227**
24: **210**
26: **374**
[47] *Against Euergus and Mnesibulus*
40: **41a**
41–43: **378**
56–57: **110**
64: **41b**
67–73: **17**
77: **304a**
[48] *Against Olympiodorus*
9–10, 12–18: **259a**
22–32: **236**
37–38: **259b**
[49] *Against Timotheus*
1–2, 42–43, 69: **168**
17–20: **251**
48–49, 51–52: **317**
66–67: **376**
51 *On the Trierarchic Crown*
8–9: **377**
[52] *Against Callippus*
3–10, 12–15: **247**
[53] *Against Nicostratus*
6–13: **316**
16: **40**
19–20: **248**
54 *Against Conon*
1: **42a**
8–9: **42b**
17–19: **33**
25: **19a**
27–28: **19b**
55 *Against Callicles*
1–5: **249a**

20–21: **249b**
23–25: **249c**
31–32, 34: **249d**
[56] *Against Dionysodorus*
2: **304d**
3–6: **263a**
19–21: **263b**
31–32, 34–36, 38, 42–46: **263c**
57 *Against Eubulides*
20–21: **95**
30: **76, 127a**
46: **132**
63–65: **296**
[58] *Against Theocrines*
5–6, 8, 10–12: **325**
14–15: **299**
30–32: **163**
40: 77
[59] *Against Neaera*
9–10: **21**
16–17: **94a**
45–46: **298**
51–53: **94b**
64–70: **58a**
87: **58b**
116: **352**
fr. 7 Baiter-Sauppe: **165**
DIGEST
10.1.13: **239**
DIOGENES LAERTIUS
1.55: **155**
2.12–14: **344b**
2.40: **342**
2.116: **357**
3.41–43: **216**
5.5–6: **355b**
5.11–16: **217**
9.51–52, 54: **347b**
DIONYSIUS OF HALICARNASSUS
Demosthenes
11: **38**
Isaeus
15.1: **225**
On Deinarchus
3: **264**

EUMELUS
FGrHist 77 F 2: **127b**
HARPOCRATION
aikias: **48**
apotimêtai etc.: **116a**
biaiôn: **61**
bouleuseôs: **28**
eisangelia: **392a**
enetimato: **116b**
epidikos etc.: **192**
exoulês: **223**
hoti hoi poiêtoi etc.: **138**
hypophonia: **29**
Isodaitês: **353b**
kakôseôs: **154**
karkinos: **243**
nautodikai: **126**
notheia: **197**
phasis: **151**
sitos: **123**
Theôris: **354c**
HERODOTUS
5.71: **1a**
6.104.2: **363**
6.130.2: **84**
6.136: **364**
9.4–5: **366a**
HYPEREIDES
1 *For Lycophron*
fr. 3 Jensen: **385a**
3: **385b**
12: **59**
20: **385c**
2 *Against Philippides*
3: **78**
3 *Against Athenogenes*
5–11, 18, 21–22: **262**
13: **304b**
14–15: **309**
4 *For Euxenippus*
1–3, 14–20, 30–31, 39: **390a**
3: **66**
7–8: **373**
28–30: **390b**
5 *Against Demosthenes*
col. 2: **391a**
col. 6: **391b**
col. 7: **391c**
col. 24: **391d**
col. 26: **303**

HYPEREIDES (*continued*)
col. 38: **391e**
fr. 100 Jensen: **81**

IDOMENEUS
FGrHist 338 F 1: **367b**
INSCRIPTIONS
Finley, *SLC*
1: **321f**
12A: **321g**
41: **321b**
49: **321c**
57: **321d**
80A, 81A: **321h**
88: **321e**
133: **112a**
134: **112b**
146: **321a**
Inscriptiones Graecae
I^3 78: **345**
I^3 104: **2**
I^3 421.12–49: **336a**
I^3 430.5–20: **336b**
II^2 1177: **351**
II^2 1237.9–125: **128**
II^2 1362: **356**
II^2 1631.429–41: **173**
II^2 1635.134–40: **348**
II^2 2492.1–31: **258**
II^2 2658: **321d**
II^2 2659: **112a**
II^2 2662: **112b**
II^2 2670: **321a**
II^2 2681: **321c**
II^2 2723: **321b**
II^2 2747: **321e**
II^2 2758: **321f**
Supplementum Epigraphicum Graecum
12.87: **384**
12.100.1–16: **285**
12.100.16–21, 23–25, 30–39: **319**
ISAEUS
1 *On the Estate of Cleonymus*
14–15: **219a**
18–19: **219b**
24–25: **219c**
43: **219d**
2 *On the Estate of Menecles*
7–9: **103**
13–17, 19: **135**
3 *On the Estate of Pyrrhus*
2: **90**
3–7: **232**
8–10: **97**
28–29: **107**
35–37: **113**
40–50, 57–60, 62: **228**
64: **186a**
67–69: **204**
70: **85**
72–74: **186b**
75–76: **129**
77–78: **100**
4 *On the Estate of Nicostratus*
9: **199**
13: **215**
24–25: **235**
28–29: **292**
5 *On the Estate of Dicaeogenes*
6–7, 9, 12–18: **231**
10–11: **141**
6 *On the Estate of Philoctemon*
3–4, 43–44, 52: **229**
5–7: **211**
25, 28, 63: **178**
29–32: **218**
35–37: **144**
39–42: **286**
46: **189**
7 *On the Estate of Apollodorus*
5–7: **195**
13–17, 27–28, 30: **136**
18–20: **190**
8 *On the Estate of Ciron*
7–8: **118**
14, 28–29: **86**
18–20: **130**
21–24: **175**
31, 33: **187**
32: **159**
34: **177**
40–41: **39**
41–42: **143**
9 *On the Estate of Astyphilus*
3: **220**
7–12: **213**

17–19: **16**
10 *On the Estate of Aristarchus*
4–5: **188**
9–10: **206**
11 *On the Estate of Hagnias*
1–5, 8–12, 17–18, 29–30: **194**
6, 31, 35: **161**
45–46: **233**
12 *For Euphiletus*
9: **133**
ISOCRATES
16 *On the Team of Horses*
1, 43–44, 46–47: **245**
17 *Trapeziticus*
2: **306**
2–9, 11–16: **246**
18 *Against Callimachus*
1–8, 10–13, 33, 63: **244**
52–54: **10**
57: **275**
20 *Against Lochites*
2: **36**
3: **69**
6: **276**
21 *Against Euthynus*
2–3: **242**

JOSEPHUS
Against Apion
2.265–67: **344a**

LEXICA SEGUERIANA
Lexeis Rhêtorikai
enthesmos blabê: **265a**
Synagôgê Lexeôn Chrêsimôn
athesmos blabê: **265b**
LEXICON CANTABRIGIENSE
eisangelia: **392c**
kakêgorias dikê: **81**
LIBANIUS
hypothesis to [Demosthenes] 25 *1 Against Aristogeiton*
1–2: **300**
LUCIAN
Eunuch
10: **62**
LYCURGUS
1 *Against Leocrates*
1–2, 5: **387a**
8, 89: **387b**
12–13: **26a**
16–18, 21: **387c**
52–53: **387d**
55, 59, 68: **387e**
64–65: **26b**
112–15: **370**
117–18: **365**
120–21: **369**
122: **366b**
147: **387f**
LYSIAS
1 *On the Killing of Eratosthenes*
24–33: **54**
30–31: **13a**
50: **13b**
3 *Against Simon*
1: **31a**
28: **31b**
38: **31c**
41–43: **31d**
4 *On an Intentional Wounding*
5–9: **32a**
10–11: **32b**
13: **32c**
5 *For Callias*
1, 5: **278**
6 *Against Andocides*
4: **337a**
9–10: **337b**
11–12: **337c**
15: **30**
17–19: **337d**
21–24: **337e**
51–52: **337f**
54: **337g**
7 *On the* Sêkos
1–3: **329a**
11: **329b**
16–17, 19, 22, 25–26: **329c**
37–38: **329d**
[8] *Against the Members of an Association*
10: **318**
9 *For the Soldier*
5–12, 15–16: **70**
10 *1 Against Theomnestus*

LYSIAS (*continued*)
1–2: **71a**
6–9: **71b**
10: **267a**
11: **15**
12: **71c**
15–17: **267b**
18: **314**
18–19: **51**
30: **71d**
12 *Against Eratosthenes*
21: **105a**
13 *Against Agoratus*
45: **105b**
66: **55**
85–87: **14**
91: **157**
14 *1 Against Alcibiades*
28: **99**
16 *For Mantitheus*
10: **105c**
19 *On the Property of Aristophanes*
8–9: **142**
14–15: **108a**
25–26: **315**
39–40: **205**
59: **108b**
22 *Against the Grain Dealers*
5–6, 8: **310**
27 *Against Epicrates*
3–4, 6–7: **279**
29 *Against Philocrates*
1–2, 11: **281**
30 *Against Nicomachus*
21, 23–25: **277**
32 *Against Diogeiton*
5, 7: **212**
6: **106**
8–10, 19–24: **139**
fr. 151 Carey (*Against Theomnestus*), lines 246–55: **305**
fr. 178 Carey *Against Isocrates*: **37**
fr. 206 Carey *Defense Speech Concerning the Dog*: **243**
fr. 279 Carey *Against Teisis*: **38**
fr. 428 Carey: **140**

MENANDER
Aspis
250–73: **191**
Dyscolus
841–44: **89b**
Periceiromene
1013–15: **89a**
Samia
726–29: **89c**
fr. 279 (328) Koerte-Thierfelder: **153**

OXYRHYNCHUS PAPYRI
221 col. 14 lines 9–16: **222**

PHILOCHORUS
FGrHist 328 F 121: **270**
PHILOSTRATUS
Lives of the Sophists
1.10: **347c**
PHOTIUS
Lexicon
hybris: **49**
sitou dikê: **124**
PLATO
Apology of Socrates
17d2–3: **340a**
24b7-c2: **340b**
26b2-d9: **340c**
27c5–8: **340d**
31c4-d4: **340e**
36a5-b5, 36e1–37a1, 38b1–9: **340f**
Euthyphro
2a1–6: **339a**
4c3-d5: **339b**
5c4–8: **339c**
Gorgias
516a: **271b**
Phaedo
58a6-c5: **341a**
116b7-c4, 116c8-d2, 117a4-b2, 117b6-c5, 117e4–118a8: **341b**
Protagoras
321c-322a: **282**
PLUTARCH
Alcibiades
8.4–6: **98b**
22.4–5: **335**
Demosthenes
14.6: **354b**

[*Lives of the Ten Orators*]
833d-834b: **371**
849e: **353a**
Pericles
32.1–4, 35.4–5: **271c**
Solon
12.1–9: **1d**
13.4–5, 15.2: **313c**
17.1–3: **266**
19.4: **358**
20.2–4: **180**
20.6: **104**
21.1–2: **68**
21.3–4: **202**
22.1, 4: **156**
23.1–2: **50**
23.7–8, 24.3: **238**
24.1–2: **322**
Themistocles
23.1, 4, 6; 25.3: **367c**
POLLUX
Onomasticon
3.33: **193**
3.35–36: **117a**
8.32: **226**
8.51–53: **392b**
8.53: **165**
8.142: **117b**

SCHOLIA TO AESCHINES
1.39: **127b**
SCHOLIA TO ARISTOPHANES
Acharnians 67: **82a**
Birds 1073: **346b**
Birds 1297: **82b**
Clouds 499: **272b**
Clouds 1371: **93b**
Knights 658: **268**
Wasps 947: **367b**
SCHOLIA TO DEMOSTHENES
19.281: **350b**
SEXTUS EMPIRICUS
Against the Professors
9.56–57: **347a**
SOLON
fr. 36.1–15 West: **313a**
SUDA
bolitou dikên: **268**
engeion: **140**
epiklêros: **198**
hybris: **37, 49**
sitou dikê: **124**
SYRIANUS
Commentaries on Hermogenes
vol. 2 p. 31 Rabe, lines 14–25: **353f**

THEOPHRASTUS
On Laws
fr. 21.1 Szegedy-Maszak: **312**
THUCYDIDES
1.126.3–12: **1b**
1.135.2–136.1, 138.6: **367a**
2.65.3–4: **271a**
6.27–29, 53, 60–61: **334**

XENOPHON
Hellenica
1.7.1–16, 20–26, 34–35: **375**
1.7.22: **287**
2.4.41: **237**
Memorabilia
1.2.62: **283**
2.1.5: **53**
2.2.13: **158**
Oeconomicus
14.4–7: **284**

General Index

References are to passage numbers, except where preceded by "p(p).," designating page number(s); "ch(s).," designating chapter number(s); or "§(§)," designating section(s) of a chapter.

agônes atimêtoi (non-assessable lawsuits). *See* lawsuits, assessable and non-assessable, defined

agônes timêtoi (assessable lawsuits). *See* lawsuits, assessable and non-assessable, defined

agora, p. 17, p. 19, p. 31, p. 36, p. 41, p. 42, **2**, **12**, **18**, **20**, **25**, **46**, p. 125, **76**, **145**, **160**, **170**, p. 288, **241**, **289**, p. 372, **309**, **311**, p. 410, **337**, **342**, **347b**

agoranomoi (Market Commissioners), p. 288, **241**, **289**, **309**, **311**

akôn, *akousios*, meanings of, pp. 45–46, pp. 287–88

amateurism, p. 26, p. 28

Amnesty of 403, p. 12, p. 14, p. 43, p. 47, **10**, **11**, **12**, **14**, **244**, **245**

anagrapheis (Recorders), p. 12, p. 13, **2**, **277**

anakrisis (preliminary hearing), pp. 34–35, p. 36, p. 38, **152**, p. 221, **232**, **236**, **325**

anchisteia, defined, pp. 217–19

animals, liability of and for, p. 46, **25**, **46**, p. 286, p. 287, **237**, **238**, **243**, **249**

antidosis (exchange), p. 26, **122**, **304c**

antigraphê, p. 34, p. 35, **340d**, **390a**

antitimêma (penal counter-assessment), p. 40, **340f**

antômosia (affidavit), p. 35, **231**, **232**, **340b**, **340d**, **342**

apagôgê (summary arrest), p. 28, pp. 30–31, p. 34, **11**, **12b**, **162**, **254**, **310**, **337d**, **346b**, p. 466, **369**; against *kakourgos* (malefactor), p. 31, p. 33, p. 40, p. 42, p. 47, **3b**, **8**, **12c**, **14**, **20**, **42**, p. 104, **54**, **57a**, **67**, pp. 334–35, **267**, **276**, **278**, **283**, **284**, **285**, **288**, **289**, **290**, **292**, **293**, **295**, **300**, **302b**, p. 408, **349b**, **391l**; against malicious prosecutor of merchant or ship-captain, p. 31, p. 376, **325**; against person caught in specified public area from which he has been banned, p. 31, p. 42, **20**; against person caught in violation of exile, p. 31, pp. 41–42, **369**; *ep' autophôrôi* (in the act), p. 31, p. 33, p. 47, **14**, **57a**, p. 334, **292**, **293**, **297**, **301**, **391l**; types of, pp. 30–31

aphairesis eis eleutherian (removal to freedom; i.e., assertion of the free status of an alleged slave), p. 288, **246**, **298**

aphanês ousia (invisible property), **185**, **225**

aphesis and *apallagê* (release and discharge). *See* pardon and quitclaim

apographê (registration [for confiscation]), p. 30, pp. 31–32, p. 43, **40**, **70**, **108**, **173**, **224**, **248**, **281**, **285**, **302b**, **319**, **323c**

apokêryxis (renunciation), **131**
apophasis (report), p. 13, p. 15, p. 16, p. 21, p. 26, p. 28, p. 30, p. 32, p. 33, **67**, **303**, p. 408, p. 411, **357**, p. 466, **383**, **391**
arbitration, arbitrators, p. 13, p. 14, p. 32, pp. 35–36, p. 37, **19b**, **58a**, p. 125, **71b**, **75**, **131d**, **133**, **145**, p. 288, **244**, **247**, **249**, **250**, **251**, **253**, **260**, p. 334, **288**, **298**, **338h**, **378**, **392a**; private and public, pp. 35–36
archein cheirôn adikôn, **2**, p. 86, **32**, **41a**, **43**, **47b**
archons, p. 2, p. 3, p. 6, p. 7, pp. 8–9, p. 26, p. 27, **1**, **3b**, **64b**, **329c**, **330**, **337a**; *basileus*, p. 2, p. 34, p. 45, p. 46, **2**, **9c**, **17**, **25**, **70**, **169**, **170**, **254**, p. 408, **329**, **337**, **338i**, **339**, **345**, **349b**, **352**, **356**; eponymous, p. ix, p. 2, p. 3, p. 5, p. 7, p. 33, **44a**, **45**, p. 140, **96**, **98**, **100**, **102**, **116a**, **124**, p. 177, p. 178, **136**, **144**, **151**, **152**, **162**, **163**, **164**, p. 221, **181**, **196**, **218**, **227**, **228**, **229**, **230b**, **231**, **234**, **236**, **254**, **312**, **322**, **331**, **332**, **345**, **392a**; polemarch, p. 2, p. 34, p. 219, p. 221, **200**, **227**, **246**; secretary of the *thesmothetai*, p. 6; *thesmothetai*, p. 2, p. 34, **3b**, p. 86, **35**, **36**, **43a**, **45**, p. 104, **56**, **58a**, **59**, **60**, p. 117, **63a**, p. 125, **79**, **94a**, **94b**, **170**, p. 288, **254**, p. 335, **273**, **302**, p. 375, **324**, p. 409, **333**, **338c**, **369**, **371**, **373**, **374**, **380**, **392c**
Areopagus, Council of, p. 2, p. 5, p. 8, p. 12, p. 15, p. 28, p. 32, p. 46, **3a**, **7**, **12**, **13a**, **15**, **18**, **19**, **20**, **25**, **26**, **28**, p. 86, **30**, **31**, **34**, **54**, **67**, **170**, **269**, p. 408, p. 409, p. 411, **329**, **331**, **343b**, **343c**, **357**, p. 464, p. 466, **358**, **359**, **382**, **383**, **384**, **387**, **391**
Arginusae, p. 12, **287**, p. 466, **370**, **375**
arrhabôn, **175**, p. 373
arson, **3a**, **25**, **353d**, **385a**
Assembly, p. 3, p. 5, p. 6, pp. 7–8, p. 9, p. 13, p. 15, p. 16, p. 18, p. 20, p. 22, p. 23, p. 24, p. 25, p. 26, p. 27, p. 28, p. 32, p. 34, p. 41, and *passim*
astynomoi (City Magistrates), **65**, **219a**, **289**
Athenian Empire. *See* Delian League/ Athenian Empire
athlothetai (Commissioners of the Games), **254**, **331**
atimia (outlawry/disfranchisement), p. 30, p. 33, pp. 41–42, p. 43, **3h**, **5**, **39**, **44a**, **57**, **58**, p. 118, **64c**, p. 125, **94**, p. 178, **145**, **155**, **157**, **158**, **160**, **169**, **170**, **172**, **245**, **252**, **256b**, **299**, **337**, **338**, p. 464, pp. 465–66, **358**, **360**, **361**, **368**, **371**, **384**, **387**, **388**, **392a**, **392b**; types of, pp. 41–42, **170**
Attic orators, canon of and evidentiary issues, pp. 18–23
axon, *axones*, p. vi, **2**, **3b**, **62**, **123**, **138**, **222**, **322**, **358**

basileus. *See* archons
burglary. See *toichôrychia*, *toichôrychos*

calendar, Athenian, p. 7
Chaeroneia, p. 15, p. 20, p. 21, **26**, **387**
citizens, citizenship, p. viii, p. ix, p. 2, p. 3, p. 6, p. 8, p. 11, p. 13, pp. 23–27, p. 30, pp. 32–33, p. 34, p. 36, p. 41, p. 42, p. 46, **2**, **3a**, **7**, **8**, **12**, **13**, **14**, **18**, **19**, **21**, **28**, p. 86, **36**, **40**, **44**, p. 103, p. 104, **56**, **58a**, **60**, p. 117, p. 118, **64d**, **67**, p. 125, **76**, chs. 5–7 *passim*, **242**, **245**, **254**, **256b**, p. 334, p. 335, **299**, p. 375, **332e**, **334**, **338**, p. 464, **361**, **370**, **373**, **376**, **383**, **390a**
claim. See *lêxis*; *epidikasia*
Cleisthenes of Athens, p. 3, pp. 5–8, p. 13, **1a**, **1d**, **78**, **125**, **169**, **174**, **330**, **338**
Cleisthenes of Sicyon, **84**, **125**
codification of laws, p. vi, p. 2, p. 3, p. 13, **1d**, p. 124
coinage, units of, p. 4
Compilers. See *syngrapheis*
constitution, Athenian, p. v, Introduction *passim*, **1c**, p. 464, **391a**. See also *graphê nomon mê epitêdeion theinai*; *graphê paranomôn*
Council of 500, p. 3, p. 5, pp. 6–7, p. 8, p. 12, p. 13, p. 17, p. 18, pp. 26–27, p. 28, p. 34, **2**, **12**, **14**, p. 118, **64**, p. 175, **134**, **170**, **173**, **224**, **244**, **254**, **268**, **292**, **295**, **300**, **310**, **332**, **338**, **345**, **356**, p. 464, **362**, **366**, **371**, **372**, **373**, **374**, **375**, **377**, **378**, **380**, **382**, **384**, **386**, **392a**, **392b**

de cuius, defined, p. 217
decrees, relation to laws, p. 4, pp. 13–14, **338h**
default, judgment by. See *dikê erêmê*
Delian League/Athenian Empire, p. 11, p. 25, **2**, **5**, **30**, **321h**, **345**, **368**
Delphinion, court at, p. 46, **13**, **20**, **25**, **170**
demarch, **174**, **258**, **296**, **345**, **351**, **356**, **371**
deme dicasts, p. 5, p. 11, p. 14, **289**, **302**. *See also* Forty, the
demes, p. 6 and *passim*
democracy, p. v, p. viii, p. 4, pp. 5–7, p. 12, p. 13, p. 16, p. 26, **1a**, **11**, p. 126, **78**, **125**, **203**, **242**, **338h**, ch. 12 *passim*, and *passim*
dêmos, meanings of, p. 5
deposition (*martyria*), generally, p. 22, pp. 38–39
diadikasia (adjudication), pp. 29–30, p. 34, p. 35, p. 38, p. 40, p. 43, **4**, **16**, **39**, **122**, **136**, **150**, **152**, **161**, pp. 220–21, **183**, **185**, **188**, **190**, **199**, **219**, **§7.4.4**, **§7.4.6**, **251**, **338c**. *See also epidikasia*
diamartyria (declaration on oath), p. 35, **137c**, p. 221, **178**, **192**, **226**, **§7.4.4**, **231**, **232**
dikai atimêtoi (non-assessable lawsuits). *See* lawsuits, assessable and non-assessable, defined
dikai dêmosiai (public lawsuits). *See* lawsuits, private and public
dikai emmênoi (monthly lawsuits), p. 34, **46**, **238**, p. 375, p. 376, **324**
dikai emporikai (mercantile lawsuits), p. vii, p. 15, p. 24, p. 29, p. 34, **79**, **171**, p. 288, **260**, **261**, **263**, pp. 371–72, pp. 375–76, **§10.5**, **332h**
dikai idiai (private lawsuits). *See* lawsuits, private and public
dikai metallikai (mining lawsuits), **23**, **79**, **164**, pp. 287–88, **256**
dikai timêtai (assessable lawsuits). *See* lawsuits, assessable and non-assessable, defined
dikastêrion (jury-court), pp. 8–9, p. 11, p. 14, p. 17, pp. 26–28, p. 31, p. 32, pp. 36–38, and *passim*; size of jury, generally, p. 26, p. 37
dikastês (juror), pp. 8–9, p. 26, and *passim*
dikê, *dikazein*, meanings of, p. xiii, p. 29, **339a**
dikê aikeias (for battery), p. x, p. 29, p. 40, **17**, **19**, ch. 2 *passim*, **228**, **255b**, **256b**, **260**, **291**, p. 375, **304a**
dikê aphaireseôs eis eleutherian (for removal to freedom; i.e., for assertion of the free status of an alleged slave), p. 288, **298**
dikê aphormês (for [repayment of] capital), **253**
dikê apostasiou (for deserting a patron), p. 23, **200**
dikê aprostasiou (for not having a patron), p. 23, **200**
dikê argyriou (for money due), **247**
dikê (?) *asebeias* (for impiety), p. 408, **349b**
dikê biaiôn (for acts of violence), p. 29, **45**, pp. 104–5, **51**, **54**, **61**, **154**, **256b**, p. 334, **294**
dikê blabês (for damage), pp. viii–ix, p. 29, p. 105, **51**, **74**, **101**, **150**, **168**, **236**, ch. 8 *passim*, p. 334, ch. 10 *passim*, **332d**
"*dikê bolitou*," **268**
dikê eis datêtôn hairesin (for the selection of distributors), **152**
dikê eis emphanôn katastasin (for production in plain sight), **152**, **218**, **225**
dikê eis epitropês katastasin (for the establishment of a guardianship), **152**
dikê engyês (for a pledge; i.e., to compel a surety to discharge his obligation), **231**
dikê epitropês (for [abuse of] a guardianship), p. 29, **87**, **106**, **115**, p. 178, **§6.3**, **152**, **257b**
dikê erêmê (lawsuit decided by default), p. 36, p. 37, **75**, **249**, **260**, **261**, **334**, **335**, **365**
dikê exoulês (for ejectment), p. 29, p. 43, **102**, **115**, p. 220, **170**, **§7.4.2**, **228**, **256**, **261**
dikê kakêgorias (for defamation), p. ix, p. 29, p. 43, **15**, **33**, **44a**, ch. 4 *passim*
dikê klopês (for theft), p. 29, **160**, ch. 9 *passim*
dikê lipomartyriou (for failure to appear as a witness), **251**

dikê parakatathêkês (for [recovery of] a deposit), **242**, **246**
dikê phonou (for homicide), p. vi, p. vii, p. viii, p. ix, p. x, p. 3, p. 8, p. 12, p. 24, p. 26, p. 28, p. 29, p. 34, p. 36, p. 37, p. 40, p. 42, p. 43, ch. 1 *passim*, p. 86, **33**, **43**, p. 103, **54**, **62**, **73**, **170**, p. 288, **240**, p. 333, **266**, **284**, **339**, **358**, **368**
dikê proikos (for a dowry), p. ix, p. 29, **46**, **74**, pp. 140–41, **97**, **100**, **119**, **121**
dikê pseudomartyriôn (for false witness), p. 29, p. 35, p. 39, p. 43, **17**, **56**, **85**, **103**, **135**, **137**, **144**, **147**, p. 221, **170**, **230**, **§7.4.5**, p. 287, **252**
dikê sitou (for maintenance), p. ix, p. 29, p. 141, **94b**, **97**, **100**, **119**, **120**, **123**, **124**, p. 177, **152**
diômosia, p. 37, p. 46, **7c**, **9**, **15**, **17**, **20**, **21**, **24**, p. 86, **31a**
documents, generally, p. 22, p. 36, p. 38
dokimasia (scrutiny): of boys, p. 32, **87**, p. 175, **134**, **137b**, **139**; of magistrates, p. 30, p. 32, **132**, **158**
dokimasia tôn rhêtorôn (scrutiny of public speakers), p. 32, **57**, p. 118, **64**, **295**
drachma. *See* coinage, units of; weight, units of
Draco, p. vi, pp. 2–4, p. 7, p. 13, ch. 1 *passim*, p. 103, **50**, **62**, p. 333, **266**, **284**, **313b**

eisangelia (impeachment), p. xi, p. 30, pp. 32–33, p. 411, **333**; against arbitrator, **392a**; for major offenses against the state, p. ix, p. 16, p. 20, p. 21, p. 28, p. 33, p. 34, **26**, p. 104, **59**, **66**, p. 178, **224**, pp. 335–36, **271**, **277**, **278**, **281**, **295**, **310**, p. 408, p. 410, **333**, **334**, **335**, **337**, **338c**, **338e**, **345**, **353**, ch. 12 *passim*; *kakôseôs epiklêrou* (for maltreatment of an *epiklêros*), p. 178, **152**, **154**, **§6.4.3**, **228**; *kakôseôs goneôn* (for maltreatment of parents), p. 178, **152**, **154**, **§6.4.1**; *kakôseôs oikou orphanikou* (for maltreatment of the estate of an orphan), p. 178, **152**; *kakôseôs orphanôn* (for maltreatment of orphans), p. 178, **152**, **154**, **§6.4.2**; types of, p. 32, **392a**
eisphora (war-tax), pp. 25–26, **122**, **145**, **254**, **258**, **288**
ek pronoias. See *pronoia*
Eleven, the, p. 28, p. 31, p. 34, p. 41, **11**, **12b**, **14**, p. 334, **267a**, **285**, **289**, **290**, **292**, **302b**, **341b**, **371**, **375**, **380**
endeixis (denunciation), p. 28, pp. 30–31, p. 34, **11**, **12b**, **170**, **254**, **299**, **302b**; against *kakourgos* (malefactor), p. 31, p. 42, p. 47, **8**, pp. 335–36, **289**, **302b**, p. 408; against malicious prosecutor of merchant or ship-captain, p. 31, p. 376, **325**; against person caught in specified public area from which he has been banned, p. 31, pp. 41–42, **12**, **30**, **77**, **185**, p. 410, **337**, **338**, **354a**; against person caught in violation of exile, p. 31, pp. 41–42, **3e**, **30**; types of, p. 31. See also *apagôgê*
enklêma (charge statement), p. 34, **48**, **147**, **150**, pp. 287–88, **245**, **253**, **256b**, **261**, **264**, **340b**
enktêsis gês kai oikias ([right of] acquisition of land and house), p. 176
ep' autophôrôi (in the act). See *apagôgê*
ephêgêsis ("conducting, leading to"), p. 28, pp. 30–31, p. 34, **329c**; against *kakourgos* (malefactor), p. 31, pp. 335–36, **288**, **289**; against malicious prosecutor of merchant or ship-captain, p. 31; against person caught in specified public area from which he has been banned, p. 31; against person caught in violation of exile, p. 31, p. 42; types of, pp. 30–31. See also *apagôgê*
ephetai, p. 46, **2**, **3c**, **4**, **10**, **21**, **25**, **170**, **358**
epidikasia (claim, adjudication, award), p. 138, p. 175, **152**, pp. 220–21, **185**, **186b**, **188**, **201**, **204**, **§§7.4.3–7.4.6**. See also *diadikasia*
epiklêros, p. vii, p. 29, p. 32, p. 33, p. 34, p. 43, **45**, p. 140, **83**, **96**, **104**, p. 175, p. 178, **150**, **152**, **154**, **§6.4.3**, ch. 7 *passim*, **256b**; defined, pp. 217–18
episkêpsis (denunciation), p. 221, **§7.4.5**
epôbelia, p. 14, p. 33, **41b**, **145**, **244**, **263**, pp. 375–76, **323b**
eponymous archon. *See* archons

eranos (joint loan), **46**, **262**, p. 373, **316**
Eupatrids, p. 2, p. 8
euthydikia, p. 221, **190**, **229**, **328**
euthynai (review), p. 28, p. 30, p. 32, **11**, **12b**, **70**, p. 220, **170**, **208**, p. 334, p. 335, **273**, **277**, **289**, **295**, **299**, **301**, **302a**, **388**
evidence: for Athenian law, generally, pp. v–vii, p. ix, p. x, p. xi, pp. 17–23; in Athenian law, generally, p. 23, p. 24, p. 35, p. 36, pp. 38–40
Exactors (*praktores*), **70**, **170**, **330**
Exêgêtai (Interpreters), p. 28, **17**, p. 408, **337**, **338**, **339**, **345**
exômosia (oath of denial), p. 38, **16**, **251**, **252**

filing. See *lêxis*
Five Thousand, the, pp. 11–12, **372**
Forty, the, p. 14, p. 34, p. 36, p. 37, p. 86, **45**, **46**, p. 125, **75**, **79**, p. 288, **289**, **302**
Four Hundred, the, p. 11, p. 18, **170**, **347b**, **369**, **370**, **371**, **372**, **373**

genos (clan), **1**, **136**, **321a**, **321b**, **335**, **337**
gnêsios, defined, p. 175
graphê, *graphein*, meanings of, p. xi, p. 4, p. 30, p. 34
graphê adikiou (for [fiscal] wrongdoing), **302a**, **391d**
graphê adikôs heirchthênai hôs moichon (for having been unjustly detained as a seducer), p. 30, p. 104, **58a**
graphê agraphiou (for failure to register a state debtor), **60**
graphê anaumachiou (for failure to serve in the navy), **170**
graphê argias (for idleness), **266**
graphê asebeias (for impiety), p. 30, p. 34, **269**, **271c**, **288**, ch. 11 *passim*, **387f**
graphê astrateias (for avoiding military service), p. 30, **99**, **170**, **254**, **289**, **387f**
graphê bouleuseôs (for conspiracy; i.e., for fraudulently keeping on the register of state debtors a man who has discharged his debt), **60**
graphê deilias (for cowardice), **170**
graphê dêmosiôn chrêmatôn (for [theft of] public property). *See graphê klopês*
graphê dôrôn (for bribery), p. 30, **60**, **170**, **271c**, **279**, **302a**, p. 466, **374**, **388**, **391d**, **391j**
graphê dôroxenias (for bribery in a *graphê xenias*), **60**
graphê hetairêseôs (for prostitution), p. 30, **50**, **51**, **§3.2**
graphê hierôn chrêmatôn (for [theft of] sacred property). See *graphê klopês*
graphê hierosylias (for temple-robbery), p. 30, ch. 9 *passim*. See also *hierosylia*
graphê hybreôs (for hubris), p. ix, p. 30, p. 33, p. 40, **§2.2** *passim*, pp. 104–5, **56**, **59**, p. 117, **64a**, **67**, **255b**, **256b**, **291**, **332d**, **332e**
graphê klopês (for theft), p. 30, **170**, p. 334, p. 335, **288**, **297**, **299**, **301**, **302a**, **375**, **381**
graphê lipotaxiou (for desertion), p. 30, **99**, **170**, **254**, **375**, **387f**
graphê moicheias (for seduction), p. 30, p. 33, **§3.1**, **291**
graphê nomon mê epitêdeion theinai (for enacting an unsuitable law), p. 14, p. 30, **160**, **333**
graphê paranoias (for insanity; i.e., for squandering an estate due to insanity), **152**
graphê paranomôn (for illegal proposals), p. 14, p. 30, **3**, **20**, **27**, **63**, **78**, **160**, **299**, **300**, **333**, **338**, **375**, **390a**, **390b**
graphê proagôgeias (for pandering), p. 30, **50**, **51**, **57**, **§3.2**
graphê prodosias (for treason), **367c**
graphê pseudengraphês (for false registration of a state debtor), **60**
graphê pseudoklêteias (for false witness to a summons), **60**, **170**
graphê sykophantias (for sycophancy), **60**, **392c**
graphê traumatos ek pronoias (for intentional wounding), p. viii, p. ix, p. x, p. 8, p. 26, p. 30, p. 36, p. 37, p. 42, **3a**, **20**, **25**, pp. 85–86, **§2.1**
graphê xenias (for being a foreigner; i.e., for falsely posing as a citizen), p. 30, p. 42, **21**, **58**, **60**, **94**, p. 176, **197**, **376**

Harmodius and Aristogeiton, p. 126, **78, 334, 372, 391k**
hekôn, *hekousios*, meanings of, pp. 45–46, pp. 287–88
hektêmoros (sixth-parter), **313**
(*h*)*êliaia*, p. 3, p. 8, pp. 26–27, **3b**, p. 86, **35, 96**, p. 334, **267, 289, 374, 380, 382**
Hellenic League, pp. 9–10, **343c, 367c**
hemlock, p. 41, **14**, p. 411, **340, 341b, 347a**
hierosylia (temple-robbery), *hierosylos* (temple-robber), p. x, p. 30, **26b**, p. 333, pp. 335–36, **266, 269, 270, 273, 275, 276, 277, 278, 283, 285, 287, 288, 289, 291, 296, 300**, p. 408, **375**
Hippias and Hipparchus (sons of Peisistratus), p. 5, p. 9, **78, 334, 363, 365**
horoi (boundary-markers), **112, 114, 115c, 144, 214, 258**, p. 374, **313, 321, 371**

inanimate objects, liability of and for, p. 46, **20, 25, 27**, p. 286, **238, 239, 249**
income classes, Solonian, p. 3, p. 218, **181, 362**
inter vivos, defined, p. 176
Introducers (*Eisagôgeis*), p. 34, p. 86, **45, 46**
invisible property. *See aphanês ousia*

juror. See *dikastês*
jury-court. *See dikastêrion*

kakourgos (malefactor). See *apagôgê*; *endeixis*; *ephêgêsis*
kidnapping, p. 31, **67, 283, 302b**
kyrios, p. 23, p. 24, p. 29, p. 43, p. 117, **64a**, pp. 138–41, **83, §5.1.2, 94b, 101, 102, 105, 113, 115, 122**, pp. 177–78, **136, 141, 146, 148, 176, 180, 182, 187, 191, 194, 196, 203, 217, 218, 227, 229, 230c, 232, 234, 253, 256b, 256e, 257b, 293, 298, 321c, 323c**

laws: form and content of, generally, p. vii, p. 28; interpretation of, p. viii, p. xi, p. 22, p. 28; relation to decrees, p. 4, pp. 13–14, **338h**; unwritten, p. 13, p. 408, **337b, 338h**
lawsuits: assessable and non-assessable, defined, p. 29, p. 37, pp. 40–41; private and public, p. 23, p. 24, p. 26, pp. 29–33, p. 34, p. 35, pp. 37–38, p. 42, p. 43, **42, 56, 161, 228, 374**
lêxis (filing, claim): for adjudication of estate or *epiklêros*, p. 221, **§7.4.3**, and ch. 7 *passim*; generally, pp. 34–35, p. 221, **254**, and *passim*
liturgies, generally, p. 23, pp. 25–26, p. 30, **139, 195, 254**
logographer, logography, p. 18, p. 19, p. 21, p. 28, p. 373, **391**
lôpodysia (clothes-snatching), *lôpodytês* (clothes-snatcher), p. 31, **8a, 42a, 57a**, p. 333, p. 335, **267a, 274, 283, 302b**

Marathon, p. 9, **363, 364, 365**
medism, p. 10, **344b, 367**
men, *passim*
metics, p. 19, p. 21, pp. 23–26, p. 30, p. 32, p. 34, p. 42, **25**, p. 118, **66**, p. 176, p. 219, p. 221, **199, 200, 217, 227, 262, 278, 298**, p. 375, **310, 323c, 334, 336a, 338b, 370, 386, 390a**
metronomoi (Commissioners of Measures), **311**
Metroon, p. 17, **342**
mina. *See* coinage, units of; weight, units of
mining lawsuits. See *dikai metallikai*
misthôsis oikou (lease of estate), p. 178, **139, 144, 145, 146, 150, 152**, p. 374, **321d**
Mysteries, Eleusinian, p. 19, **12, 30, 67, 185**, p. 410, p. 411, **332h, §11.3, 343, 344a, 345, 346, 349, 350b**

naturalization, p. 110, p. 176, **157, 199, 370**
nautodikai (Judges of Sailors), **126**, p. 376
nomos (law), defined, p. 13
nomothetai (Lawgivers), p. 13, **12a, 380, 384**
notheia (bequest to illegitimate child), p. 219, **184, 197, 198**
nothos, defined, p. 175
noxal liability, p. 287, p. 288, **237, 238, 243, 248, 249, 256, 262**

oath: evidentiary, sworn by woman, p. 23, **131a, 131d, 133**; heliastic, pp. 26–27, p. 39, **12b, 26a, 161, 375**. See also *antômosia*; *diamartyria*; *diômosia*; *exômosia*

obol. *See* coinage, units of; weight, units of
oikos, defined, p. 138
orphans, p. vi, p. 32, p. 34, **96**, **116a**, **123**, pp. 177–78, **139**, **140**, **141**, **144**, **150**, **151**, **152**, **154**, **§6.4.2**, **192**, p. 374, **321**. See also *epiklêros*
ostracism, pp. 7–8, **98a**, **365**, **367**
Overseers of the Port of Trade (*epimelêtai tou emporiou*), p. 375, **323c**, **325**, **327**

Palladion, court at, p. 46, **7**, **9**, **10**, **17**, **19**, **20**, **21**, **24**, **25**, **28**
paragraphê (counter-indictment), p. 14, p. 35, p. 40, **23**, **75**, **148**, **150**, **171**, **225**, **244**, **256**, **260**, **261**, **293**, p. 376, **323**, **324**, **326**, **328**
pardon and quitclaim, generally, p. 43
Peisistratus, pp. 4–5, p. 11, **334**, **360**, **363**
Peloponnesian War, pp. 11–12, p. 14, p. 15, p. 19, p. 26, **1b**, **127**, **170**, **270**, **369**, **370**, **371**, **375**
penalties, generally, p. 29, p. 31, p. 32, p. 33, p. 35, p. 37, pp. 40–43
per stirpes, defined, p. 217
Pericles, p. 8, p. 11, p. 23, pp. 27–28, **1b**, p. 139, **94**, pp. 175–76, p. 177, **125**, **126**, **127**, **134**, **270**, **271**, **337b**, **344**
Persian Wars, pp. 9–10, **1a**, **170**, **365**, **366**, **367**, **387**
phanera ousia (visible property), **185**, **218**, **246**, **257b**, **259a**
phasis (declaration), p. 30, pp. 31–32, p. 43, **11**, p. 178, **150**, **151**, **244**, **254**, p. 375, **323c**, **325**, p. 408, **329**, **337**, **349**, **352**
Philocrates, Peace of, p. 15, p. 20, **390b**
phratry, defined, p. 175
Phreatto, court at, p. 46, **20**, **25**
phylobasileis (tribe-kings), p. 46, **2**, **25**
piracy, p. 31, **247**, p. 375
poisoning, **3a**, **7**, **25**
polemarch. *See* archons
pôlêtai (Sellers), **2**, **173**, **285**, **302b**, **319**, **336**, **345**
praktores. *See* Exactors
prison, imprisonment, p. 16, p. 20, p. 31, p. 42, **11**, **20**, **35**, **160**, **214**, **263**, p. 334, **267b**, **284**, **285**, **289**, **292**, **302b**, p. 375, p. 376, **323b**, **324**, p. 410, **334**, **337**, **338**, **341**, **344**, p. 465, **362**, **370**, **375**, **377**, **380**, **381**, **391k**
probolê (presentation), p. 30, p. 32, **333**; for *apatê tou dêmou* (deceiving the people), p. 32, p. 466, **375**, **386**; for sycophancy, p. 32, **386**, **392c**; for violations at specified religious festivals, p. 32, **44**, **255**, p. 408, pp. 409–10, **§11.2**; types of, p. 32
procedure, procedural law, p. v, pp. vii-ix, p. xi, Introduction §2, and *passim*; flexibility and variety, p. viii, p. 33, **36**, p. 103, pp. 104–5, p. 116, p. 333, **288**, **289**, p. 411, **349b**, p. 464
prodikasia (preliminary hearing in *dikê phonou*), p. 34, p. 45, **9c**
proedroi (presiders), p. 7, **332b**, **384**
pronoia (intent), p. x, pp. 45–46, **2**, **3a**, **3d**, **9b**, **22a**, **25**, pp. 85–86, **31**, **32**, **240**
prostatês (patron), p. 23, **200**, **298**
prothesmia (statute or clause of limitations), p. 34, **150**, **228**, **234**, p. 409, **329c**
Prytaneion, court at, p. 46, **20**, **25**, **27**, **170**, **358**
prytany, *prytaneis*, defined, pp. 6–7
psêphisma (decree), defined, p. 13

radishing, p. 104, **52a**
real property, right to own. See *enktêsis gês kai oikias*
Recorders. See *anagrapheis*
release and discharge. *See* pardon and quitclaim
relevance, rules of, pp. 26–27, pp. 39–40, **9a**, **26a**, **296**
Revolution of 404. *See* Thirty Tyrants
Revolution of 411, p. 11. *See also* Four Hundred, the; Five Thousand, the
rhêtôr (public speaker, politician), p. 8, p. 32, **57**, p. 118, **64**, **373**, **390**, **392b**, **392c**

Salamis, p. 10, **1d**, **343c**, **366a**, **366b**, **367**, **387e**
sanctuaries, leases of, **169**, **296**, **299**
Second Athenian Confederacy, pp. 14–15, p. 25, **381**
seisachtheia (Shaking-Off of Burdens), p. 3, p. 42, **313**

self-defense, **2**, **3g**, **22b**, **32b**, **43**, p. 333, p. 335. See also *archein cheirôn adikôn*
self-help, p. 104, **50**, **52**, p. 333, **266**, **284**; general importance of, pp. 28–29
sitophylakes (Grain Guardians), **310**, **311**
slaughters (*sphagai*), slaughterers (*sphageis*), **170**, **358**
slaves, slavery, p. 3, pp. 23–24, p. 29, p. 42, and *passim*; evidentiary torture of, p. 24, **19b**, **32b**, **41a**, **86**, **246**, **256d**, **317**, **329d**
Solon, p. vi, p. ix, pp. 2–4, p. 8, p. 12, p. 13, pp. 21–22, p. 30, p. 42, p. 45, **1d**, **3a**, **6b**, **12a**, **35**, p. 103, p. 104, **50**, **51**, **57b**, **62**, p. 117, **63b**, **64f**, p. 124, p. 125, **68**, **72**, p. 138, **83**, **96**, **104**, **123**, p. 175, p. 176, **134**, **135**, **138**, **155**, **156**, **160**, pp. 217–20, **176**, **180**, **181**, **182**, **184**, **193**, **201**, **202**, **203**, **204**, **206**, **209**, **210**, **222**, **227**, p. 286, **237**, **238**, **239**, **240**, **243**, **249**, **262**, p. 333, **266**, **267**, **268**, **284**, **288**, **289**, pp. 372–73, p. 375, **304**, **313**, **314**, **322**, **338i**, **358**, **359**, **360**, **392b**; general ascription of laws to, p. 4, p. 22, **3**, **288**, **338i**
sphagai, *sphageis*. *See* slaughters
stocks, confinement in, p. 42, **160**, p. 334, **267b**, **289**, **338e**
stoning, **1d**, **343c**, **366**
substance, substantive law, p. v, pp. vii–xi, p. 28, pp. 335–36, p. 375, **319**, **321h**, p. 464, and *passim*
summons, generally, p. 34
Superintendents of the Dockyards (*epimelêtai tôn neôriôn*), **173**, **378**
sycophancy, sycophant: defined, p. 28, p. 32, p. 33; penalties for, p. 33, **20**, **34**, **35**, **41b**, **63a**, p. 178, **145**, **152**, **164**, **228**, p. 334, **288**, pp. 375–76, **325**, **329**, **340**, **349**, p. 465, **386**, **389**, **391i**, **392a**, **392b**, **392c**. *See also epôbelia*; *graphê sykophantias*; *probolê*
synêgoros (advocate): normal sense, defined, pp. 28–29, p. 40; used of special public prosecutor, **302**, p. 465, **371**, **391**
syngrapheis (Compilers), p. 12, p. 13, **345**

ta aporrhêta ("the forbidden words"), ch. 4 *passim*
talent. *See* coinage, units of; weight, units of
temple-robbery. See *hierosylia*, *hierosylos*
Themistocles, pp. 9–10, **365**, **366c**, **367**, **392c**
thesmos, p. 13, **3h**, **12a**, **358**
thesmothetai. *See* archons
Thirty Tyrants, pp. 12–13, p. 19, p. 47, **11**, **12**, **14**, **105**, p. 219, **203**, **237**, **242**, **244**, p. 411, **338**, **373**
timêma (penal assessment), p. 40, **145**, **147**, pp. 287–88, **244**, **245**, **257a**, **264**, **273**, **289**, **295**, **302a**, **332**, **337e**, **340f**, **342**, **354b**. *See also antitimêma*
toichôrychia (wall-digging), *toichôrychos* (wall-digger), p. 333, p. 335, **280**, **283**, **290**
Treasurers of the Goddess and of the Other Gods, **70**, **170**
tribes, p. 6 and *passim*
trierarch, trierarchy, p. 25, **46**, **56**, **139**, **173**, **195**, **231**, **254**, **315**, **375**, **377**, **378**
trireme, defined, p. 25, **173**
tyranny, tyrant, pp. 2–3, pp. 4–5, p. 7, p. 9, p. 27, **1**, **20**, **78**, **84**, **125**, **170**, **184**, **334**, **355**, p. 464, p. 466, **358**, **360**, **363**, **372**, **384**. *See also* Thirty Tyrants

visible property. See *phanera ousia*
vocabulary, Athenian legal, generally, p. viii

water-clock (*klepsydra*), pp. 37–38, **154**, **234**
weight, units of, p. 4
widows, p. vi, p. 34, p. 139, **96**, **121**, **122**, **123**, **152**, **187**
witnesses, generally, p. 22, p. 23, p. 24, p. 29, p. 36, p. 37, pp. 38–39, p. 40, p. 43
women, *passim*; rights and status of, generally, pp. 23–24, **21**, p. 117, p. 138, **164**, p. 220, **206**, **207**

xenodikai (Judges of Foreigners), p. 376

zoning, p. 286, **238**, **239**, **249**

CPSIA information can be obtained
at www.ICGtesting.com
Printed in the USA
LVHW05s0951220618
581570LV00007B/27/P

9 780472 035915